SOUTH-EAST ASIA
A political profile

For Fiona, Cailan and Alexandra

SOUTH-EAST ASIA
A political profile

SECOND EDITION

DAMIEN KINGSBURY

OXFORD

UNIVERSITY PRESS

OXFORD
UNIVERSITY PRESS

253 Normanby Road, South Melbourne, Victoria 3205, Australia

Oxford University Press is a department of the University of Oxford.
It furthers the University's objective of excellence in research, scholarship,
and education by publishing worldwide in

Oxford New York

Auckland Cape Town Dar es Salaam Hong Kong Karachi
Kuala Lumpur Madrid Melbourne Mexico City Nairobi
New Delhi Shanghai Taipei Toronto

With offices in

Argentina Austria Brazil Chile Czech Republic France Greece
Guatemala Hungary Italy Japan Poland Portugal Singapore
South Korea Switzerland Thailand Turkey Ukraine Vietnam

OXFORD is a trade mark of Oxford University Press
in the UK and in certain other countries

National Library of Australia
Cataloguing-in-Publication data:

Kingsbury, Damien.
    South East Asia : a political profile

    2nd ed.
    Bibliography.
    Includes index.
    ISBN 0 19 551757 1.

    1. Asia, Southeastern — Politics and government — 1945– .
    2. Asia, southeastern — Politics and government. I. Title.
    II. Title : Southeast Asia.

320.959

Typeset by OUPANZS
Printed through Bookpac Production Services, Singapore

CONTENTS

LIST OF MAPS

LIST OF ABBREVIATIONS

ABRI	Angkatan Bersenjata Republik Indonesia (Republic of Indonesia Armed Forces)
ADB	Asian Development Bank
AETIVP	Australia East Timor International Volunteer Program
AFP	Armed Forces of the Philippines
AFPFL	Anti-Fascist People's Freedom League (Burma)
AHWA	Governing council of Indonesian Mujahidin Council (also Guomindang and Cambodia)
APEC	Asia Pacific Economic Cooperation
ARF	ASEAN Regional Forum
ARMM	Autonomous Region in Muslim Mindanao (Philippines)
ARVN	Army of the Republic of Viet Nam (South Vietnamese Army)
ASDT	Timorese Social Democratic Association
ASEAN	Association of South-East Asian Nations
ASG	Abu Sayyaf Group, originally known as the Mujahideen Commando Freedom Fighters (MCFF) and also referred to as the Islamic Movement (Philippines)
BCP	Burmese Communist Party
BIA	Burma Independence Army
BII	Bank Internasional Indonesia
BIN	Badan Intelijen Negara (State Intelligence Agency) (Indonesia)
BLO	Bangsamoro Liberation Organisation (Philippines)
BN	National Front coalition (Malaysia)
BRTT	People's Front of East Timor
BS	Socialist Front (Singapore)
BSPP	Burma Socialist Programme Party
CDI	Center for Defence Information (USA)
CGDK	Coalition Government of Democratic Kampuchea

CIA	Central Intelligence Agency
CNRM	Council of National Maubere Resistance (East Timor)
CNRT	National Council for Timorese Resistance
CPB	Communist Party of Burma
CPD-RDTL	Committee for the Popular Defence of the Democratic Republic of East Timor
CPP	Cambodian People's Party
CPP	Communist Party of the Philippines
CPV	Communist Party of Vietnam
DAP	Democratic Action Party (Malaysia)
DMZ	Demilitarised Zone
DPD	Regional Representatives Council (Indonesia)
DPR	Indonesia's Legislative Assembly
DPRD	Regional People's Representative Council (Indonesia)
DRV	Democratic Republic of Vietnam (North Vietnam)
EU	European Union
FDI	Foreign Direct Investment
F-FDTL	Falintil-East Timor Defence Force
FKAWI	Sunni Communication Forum (Indonesia)
FPDK	Forum for Peace, Democracy and Justice (East Timor)
FUNCINPEC	National United Front for a Neutral, Peaceful, Cooperative and Independent Cambodia
GAM	Free Aceh Movement (Indonesia)
GATT	General Agreement on Tariffs and Trade
GDP	gross domestic product
GMIP	Pattani Islamic Holy Struggle Organisation (Thailand)
GPII	Indonesian Muslim Youth Movement
GRCs	Group Representational Constituencies (Singapore)
HDI	Human Development Index
ICG	International Crisis Group
ICMI	Indonesian Association of Muslim Intellectuals
ICP	Indochinese Communist Party (Vietnam, Laos
IMF	International Monetary Fund
InterFET	International Force in East Timor
ISA	Internal Security Act (Malaysia)
JI	Jema'ah Islamiyah (Islamic Community)
KIA/O	Kachin Independence Army/Organisation
KMM	Malaysian Militant Community
KMT	Kuomingtang (Chinese Nationalist Army;
KNIL	Royal Netherlands Indies Army
KNLP	Kayan New Land Party (Burma)
KNU	Karen National Union (Burma)
KOTA	Sons of the Mountain Worriers (East Timor)

KPM	Koninklijke Paketvert Maatschappij (Dutch owned shipping company) (Indonesia)
KPU	National Electoral Commission (Indonesia)
LJ	Islam Holy Struggle Troops (Indonesia)
LM	Radical wing of MMI (Indonesia)
LPNLA	Lao People's National Liberation Army
LPRP	Lao People's Revolutionary Party
MCA	Malaysian Chinese Association
MCP	Malayan Communist Party
MDU	Malayan Democratic Union
MIC	Malaysian Indian Congress
MILF	Moro Islamic Liberation Front (Philippines)
MIRG	Moro Islamist Reformist Group (Philippines)
MMI	Indonesian Mujahidin Council
MNLF	Moro National Liberation Front (Philippines)
MPAJA	Malayan People's Anti-Japanese Army
MPR	People's Consultative Assembly (Indonesia)
MRLA	Malayan Races Liberation Army
MTA	Mong Tai Army (Burma)
NAM	Non-Aligned Movement
NCP	Nanyang Communist Party (Singapore)
NDF	National Democratic Front (Philippines)
NEP	New Economic Policy (Malaysia)
NII	Indonesian Islamic State
NLD	National League for Democracy (Burma)
NLF	National Liberation Front (South Vietnam)
NPA	New People's Army (Philippines)
NTUC	National Trade Union Congress (Singapore)
NU	Awakening of Religious Scholars (Indonesia)
NUFK	National United Front of Kampuchea (Cambodia)
NUFPA	National Union Front for Political Affairs (East Timor)
NUP	National Union Party (Burma)
NVA	North Vietnam Army
OCAJNSA	Overseas Chinese Anti-Japanese National Salvation Association (Malaysia)
OPM	Organisasi Papua Merdeka (Free Papua Organisation)
OSS	Office of Strategic Services (USA)
PAN	Partai Amanat Nasional (National Mandate Party)
PAP	People's Action Party (Malaysia)
PAS	Malaysian Islamic Party
PBB	Partai Bulan Bintang (Moon Star Party) (Indonesia)
PBR	Partai Bintang Reformasi (Reform Star Party) (Indonesia)
PBS	United Sabah Party (Malaysia)

PCGG	Presidential Commission on Good Government (Philippines)
PD	Democratic Party (East Timor)
PDC	Christian Democratic Party of Timor
PDI	Democratic Party of Indonesia
PDM	Maubere Democratic Party
PDS	Prosperous Peace Party (Indonesia)
PKB	National Awakening Party (Indonesia)
PKI	Indonesian Communist Party
PKP	Communist Party of the Philippines
PKS	Reinvented Partai Keadila (Indonesia)
PL	Liberal Party (East Timor)
PNI	Indonesian Nationalist Party
PNT	Timorese Nationalist Party
PPI	Pasukan Perjuangan Integrasi (Integration Struggle Troops) (East Timor)
PPP	Purchasing Parity Power
PPP	United Development Party (Indonesia)
PPT	People's Party of Timor
PRRI	Pemerintah Revolusionar Republik Indonesia (Revolutionary Government of the Republic of Indonesia)
PSD	Social Democrat Party of East Timor
PSI	Socialist Party (Indonesia)
PST	Socialist Party of Timor
PTT	Timor Labor Party
PULO	Pattini United Liberation Organisation (Thailand)
RAM	Reform the Armed Forces Movement, later the Revolutionary Alliance Movement (Philippines)
RCs	Residents' Committees (Singapore)
RLG	Royal Lao Government
RUSI	Republic of the United States of Indonesia
SDP	Singapore Democratic Party
SEA	South-East Asia
SEATO	South-East Asian Treaty Organisation
SLORC	State Law and Order Restoration Council (Burma)
SNC	Supreme National Council (Cambodia)
SPDC	State Peace and Development Council (Burma)
SRP	Sam Rainsy Party
TNI	Tentara Nasional Indonesia (Indonesian National Military)
UBCV	United Buddhist Church of Vietnam
UDC	Christian Democratic Union of Timor
UDT	Timor Democratic Union

UMEHC	Union of Myanmar Economic Holdings Company (Burma)
UMNO	United Malays National Organisation
UN	United Nations
UNAMET	United Nations Assistance Mission to East Timor
UNDP	United Nations Development Program
UNMISET	United Nations Mission in Support of East Timor
UNTAC	UN Transitional Authority in Cambodia
UNTAET	United Nations Transitional Authority in East Timor
USA	United States of America
UWSA	United Wa State Army (Burma)
VAT	value added tax
VC	Viet Cong
VNQDD	Nationalist Party (Vietnam)
VOC	Dutch East India Company
VPA	Vietnam People's Army (also North Vietnamese Army, or NVA)
VRYL	Vietnam Revolutionary Youth League
WTO	World Trade Organization
WWI	First World War
WWII	Second World War
ZOPFAN	Zone of Peace, Freedom and Neutrality (ASEAN agreement)

PREFACE TO THE
SECOND EDITION

Writing a book on a subject as broad as the politics of South-East Asia raises a number of questions, one of which must be how one geographically defines the region and why such a definition must be adopted. Accepting that the borders of the region's states are products of the colonial experience, the limits of South-East Asia is very much a post-colonial product. In reality, the influences of the regions that abut South-East Asia meld with it, begging the question of where one starts and the other finishes. India and China have both been significant influences on South-East Asia and the borders between them have, in different ways, been quite porous. Similarly, the way that the eastern part of the South-East Asian archipelago blends with the western Pacific, geographically and culturally, begs questions about the drawing of boundaries on maps. Yet the postcolonial world does exist and its states are also recognised as existing, even if we are to accept that the shape of contemporary states is not absolute for all time.

Any book on the region immediately calls into question its method of organisation. The two most obvious methods are to present chapters that each focus on separate countries or to present chapters that focus on themes that run through the region. Both methods have much to recommend them and have been employed by others. Both methods also have limitations and have been argued against in various reviews. The first edition of this book tried to strike a middle ground by including thematic and country chapters. Needless to say, critics on either side thought it should have been constructed either wholly one way or the other. Happily, however, this was not a major complaint in reviews and readers, by and large, seemed to think the approach taken worked sufficiently well. For this reason, the structure of this second edition closely follows that of the first.

It is worth noting here that the thematic chapters are intended to raise issues that generally apply to the whole region and, in most cases, can also be applied more broadly. However, they are not absolute and do reflect particular perspectives and preoccupations. In particular, the offer of some political definitions, while commonly accepted (if political dictionaries and the like are any guide), are not singular. There has been some effort here to note the ambiguity or plurality of meanings, but short of writing a book on this subject, it is impossible to fully consider or explain the range of possible interpretations. As with the term 'democracy', it should be reasonably clear that there is no single definition. Those definitions that are offered are intended as much to explain how they are used within this book as they are to provide a basis of further discussion and much more than they are suggested as final.

Again, similarly, in trying to conceptualise the region, there can be said to be some distinction between mainland and archipelagic South-East Asia. The two, of course, share many common historical and cultural features, but there are also some differences: in the way that states were historically organised, in the extent of external influences and in the impact of colonialism. For the purposes of trying to present a book that is more manageable—or less daunting—for the reader, this was agreed to constitute one method of organising the chapters. As a result of these factors, the second edition follows the style of the first in that it is comprised of three sections.

One review also expressed some dismay at the use of a fictional character to start the book, which led to serious contemplation about the removal or total rewriting of this section. However, as a characterisation of the realities of life in much of South-East Asia, others felt this scene was not an inaccurate portrait and it appears to remain valid. The drift from the countryside to the cities continues and it may be that some further edition will place the protagonist, or his family, in an urban setting (although, if it does, it will probably be one marked by relative poverty). But at this stage, most people in the region still live in villages and small towns and still survive from an association with agriculture. For these people, change still continues at a slow, sometimes imperceptible, pace. So, for now, the protagonist stays, his feet still firmly in the mud of a rice field and the wider, changing world still removed from much of his immediate existence.

Much has happened in South-East Asia, of course, since the first edition was published. The process of democratisation that has, incompletely, developed in the region has led to a change in a number of public faces. Gone are Burma's Ne Win and Khin Nyunt, Thailand's Chavalit Yongchaiyudh, Malaysia's Mahatir Mohamad, Indonesia's Abdurrahman Wahid and Megawati Sukarnoputri, the Philippines' Joseph Estrada and Singapore's Go Chock Tong, while change has been less noticeable in Cambodia, Vietnam, Laos and Brunei. More importantly, though, for many states there has also been an evolution of political processes. This edition is intended to refresh the first, bringing events as up to date as possible and noting the evolution of political styles where they have happened, stasis where they have not and regression where that has occurred.

It has been suggested by some observers that democratisation and liberalism will be the end result for all political societies. Yet this optimism, which has characterised much of the post-Cold War era, incorporated not a little naivety and quite a bit of patronising hubris. This is not to suggest that democratisation or the political values the term normatively represents are not to be aspired to, but it is to suggest that, in the struggle between structure and agency—between political will and material circumstances and the interests they represent—there is much that materially constrains the realisation of such aspirations. In this, South-East Asia stands as a good example. Even where the process of democratisation is championed, it has rarely occurred in ways that would be more than superficially recognisable by most societies in the West. But it is a process and, if it is possible to borrow a folk tradition from one of the region's religions, there is no final political destination; it is the process that is ultimately the end in itself.

As with the first edition of this book, this edition is intended to shed some light on the circumstances and conditions that help shape these processes. If it does little more than spark an interest in such processes, then it will have been successful.

Damien Kingsbury
Melbourne
February 2005

ACKNOWLEDGMENTS

The first edition of this book was written while working at the Monash Asia Institute, Monash University. In particular, I would like to thank Professor John McKay for his friendship, guidance and support for this project and more generally. This second edition was written while working at Deakin University and would not have been possible without the granting of time away from campus to undertake necessary research. At Deakin, I would like to thank for their support Associate Professor Joe Remenyi, Dr Scott Burchilly, Dr Clinton Fernandes and Professor Joan Beaumont.

A book covering as wide a field as this relies greatly on the advice and critical comments of a number of readers. To that end, I would like to acknowledge the helpful comments and criticisms of Dr Laine Berman, Professor Arief Budiman, Dr Ian Chalmers, Dr Sue Downie, (the late) Dr Herb Feith, Professor Kevin Hewison, Emeritus Professor John Legge, Professor Mark McGillivray, Keryn O'Sullivan, Dr Garry Rodan, Kelvin Rowley, Professor Martin Stuart-Fox and Garry Woodard. Any text covering a field as broad as this is bound to make some errors of interpretation, or of fact, for which I apologise in advance. Such shortcomings are in no way attributable to those who have in different ways assisted with this project and are my responsibility alone.

Finally, I would like to again thank my wife, Fiona Delahunt, and my children, Alexandra and Cailan, for putting up with my time away undertaking research, and for providing such a loving and warm home to come back to.

INTRODUCTION

The fine, rich mud slid with familiar sensuality between his toes as Ni stooped to continue planting the rice seedlings in the carefully flooded field. It was an oft-repeated ritual, one that he had practised twice every year since he was a small boy, helping his parents. Ni's older brother and sister were there then, too, but they had long since left to work in the city, that magnificent, confusing, crowded, noisy, dirty place of impossibly tall buildings and too many motorscooters, cars and trucks and too much to buy; that place of so many unfamiliar faces. That was the way of it these days. Ni had considered leaving too, but his parents were getting old now: his father was well over fifty, an old man, and his mother could not do enough work to keep them both. His sense of respect and loyalty, shared to different degrees by all the children, held him close.

Then there was Ni's two younger sisters and the youngest child, another brother, who were still at school. There would have been seven, but one had died in infancy of a water-borne disease. By the time the clinic advised his parents about medicine, it was too late. Babies and young children had always died easily, though for a while subsidised medicine had improved the situation. But now treatment was more expensive as the clinic was no longer able to provide the subsidised medicine. The three younger children who had survived the lottery of childhood helped in the paddy or around the house in the half-day they each had off from school, but their help alone was not enough to support themselves and their parents.

There was also Ni's own family, living in a small, simple house close to his parents. His young wife helped at planting and harvesting time, as well as tending the fruit trees and chickens, selling their small surplus at the local market and looking after their own two small children. They would have no more because, despite the long-standing tradition of large families, the cost of education and the limited amount of land left meant that having children was becoming too expensive. Besides, the government encouraged smaller rather than larger families and offered a small amount of help to those families who limited themselves to just two children.

Ni's sister, Sri, the oldest of the six children, worked in a clothing factory. Sri's bus trips back to the village occurred less and less frequently, her days off were fewer and the overtime more, she had said; this overtime was usually unpaid. Doing it was the only way of keeping her job when so many others would willingly work the same hours for no more and possibly less. She had seemed unhappy when she returned, but then she had also seemed unhappy with village life.

Ni's older brother, Bang, returned even less often, just for special celebrations, saying that he had to work from early morning until well after dusk every day just to keep his streetside food stall running. Bang had married a young woman in the city and he too had his own family now. Bang was drifting further and further from the family and from the life of the village. He spoke disparagingly about the sameness and backwardness of the village, which Ni regarded more as the slow but constant rhythm of life.

There were problems, of course. Ni's own health was not always good, which sometimes made it hard to work. The quality of the water from the well, the only water readily available, was poorer than it once had been. Water collected from the roof during the wet season was good but did not last long and the water from the nearby river had not been drinkable for years due to the contamination caused by more and more people living on the riverbank and the processing factories upstream using it as a drain. There were regulations about this, he had been told, but they had never been enforced. The factory owners had money and paid the local officials a small amount to look the other way. It was always the same: if you had enough money, you could buy anything. If you had little or none, you were at the mercy of those who had plenty. Piped water was available in larger villages, but, as with a sealed road, it had not yet made it to Ni's town.

Even Ni's ownership of the family's land was in doubt. They had, for a long time, borrowed a small amount each year from a money lender in the next town, a man not well liked in the area, to pay for the grain to plant. The rice crops were bigger than in the old days, but the special, high-yielding grain had to be bought, along with fertilisers and pesticides. The increased size of the crops had tapered off, but money was more expensive to borrow and even the money lender had to pay more himself. His not being of local origin further prejudiced feelings against him.

Perhaps if the land was claimed as forfeit Ni could challenge the claim in court. But even the courts were open to financial persuasion and often interpreted the law very broadly. The police, who often adjudicated such matters in the first instance, were also not to be trusted. Sleek and well fed in their smart uniforms and sunglasses, they were quick to spot an offence and only a little slower in extracting some form of 'fine'.

There were many such problems, but the village chief was rarely interested in them, seeming more concerned with keeping the local government member happy. The local government representative lived and worked in the city and would only sometimes send someone to the villages and towns, usually every few years, around the time when Ni and his neighbours were told for whom to vote. There was more political competition now, but with sufficient inducements, villages still tended to vote for the same candidates. The village chief, the police, the local politician, though all seen sufficiently often to be familiar, had a smug air about them, as though they held the secret that granted them the privilege of demanding the deference and respect Ni held only for his father and mother. Once, he and some other villagers had protested over their high-handedness, but they were beaten and nothing had changed. There was much he wanted to see changed, but Ni recognised there was little hope of achieving this.

Still, in some ways it was not a bad life. Within the confines of clearly ordered, close social relations, the village was safe and familiar. Ni and his family rarely went hungry and he had his faith, which was comforting and shared by his fellow villagers. This helped make sense of the world. But for closer events, the small things of everyday life, there were also the local spirits who lived in the fields and the groves. One did not speak too openly about the spirits, but they were there nonetheless. Sometimes they could only be acknowledged through more officially sanctioned worship, but alongside the official religion they better explained the change of seasons, the wind, the rain.

It was hot in the field. By late morning the sun was high and the sky, bright blue, with puffs of cloud beginning to gather for what would be the late afternoon downpour. Even shaded by the long cloth of his shirt and wrap and under the wide brim of his woven conical hat, Ni's skin was darkened by the sun. This was the mark of a field worker, not the refined skin and lighter tones of someone who spent their time in the shade. After being bent double for some time, Ni stood upright for a moment, straightened his back and looked across the paddy to the cluster of houses and palms that made up the village. His gaze rested on the rusting iron and thatched roofs of the simple houses scattered around the rough, unsealed road.

Trying to understand his world and his life, the past held him, providing patterns and contexts, reassurance and familiarity, bonds and restrictions. The tension between the way things had always been done and how they could be tugged at him. He was confused, too, by a distant echo: he had heard of the government in the city talking about the way things had been and were still done, linking that with the bigger world in ways that failed to make sense to him. He thought they might have been talking about him, or people like him, but such talk seemed too disconnected for him to be sure. As with his need to finish the planting, the present held Ni with its immediate concerns and prosaic requirements. The future shimmered on the horizon, holding out faint hopes for a better material life blended with the satisfaction of seemingly impossible desires. Ni noted, with some wryness, that the somnolent cycle of the seasons seemed quick compared to the speed at which his life moved towards these nebulous aspirations.

...

The fictional character of Ni, presented above, could be from any of the countries of South-East Asia. While there are considerable differences between these countries in culture and politics, there are also many similarities. This is especially so at the village level, where most people in South-East Asia still live. The concerns of the people of such places are, if not exactly the same everywhere, then similar across this region. If the basics of village life are not so different, then neither is the dichotomy between this life and the process of development, exemplified by increasingly crowded industrial cities, materialism and, very often, self-serving political elites.

Of course, the approximately contemporary situation that each of these societies finds itself in as a transitional moment in the trajectory of history, varies from place to place. The circumstances of each manifests in both common and particular ways. To this end, this book attempts to canvass some of the general political issues affecting the countries of South-East Asia, noting differences and, where they exist, broad tendencies. It then considers each of the countries of the region in its own right. In this sense, while each of the countries can be identified in a formal sense, they all have intertwining histories that cannot be neglected. It also mentions, albeit fleetingly, some of the states of the region that no longer exist.

Indeed, the contemporary states of South-East Asia are all constructions, in one form or another, of the period of European colonialism. Had this colonialism not happened the political make-up of the region would undoubtedly be quite different. But it did happen and aspirations for independence by some groups within postcolonial states, along with historical memories of former imperial glories of others, have, in part, been relegated to the dust heap of history—at least for the time being. But, like culture, history is far from static and perhaps the political constructions we see now are but a fleeting moment when seen from a future historical perspective.

Like the region itself, the politics of South-East Asia is heterogenous, diffused and a product of local conditions, histories and influences. There are some parallels between political processes and attendant ideologies within the region and, at a very basic level, there are some universals, but anything more than a quick glance reveals local distinctions, the intricacy of which is indeed fine. As a result, no single analysis can hope to adequately cover the extent of the diversity, complexity and richness of the various political forces at work in this geographic region. However, it is possible to propose methods that could be useful as a point of departure when looking at particular political situations. It is also valuable to consider political situations not necessarily for how they are portrayed (although one could possibly consider why they are thus portrayed), but for what they actually mean in terms of the people they affect.

This book takes a longer-term view of political development, tracing the construction of the current states of the region to their precolonial and colonial past. It considers them insofar as they correspond to the idea of nation, how the states were conceived and the ways in which respective states manifest legitimacy or power. It also considers some of the recent major issues that have affected these states and how some of their institutions have responded to such issues. Any book trying to deal with South-East Asia at the moment cannot possibly hope to keep pace with the rate of change there and this book is no exception. Rather, it attempts to chart the trajectory for political development, to indicate the possible directions of the region's states.

METHODOLOGY

In terms of methodology and based at least on previous comments on my work, most readers, especially those from other disciplines, will probably consider this work to belong within the political science category. However, I do not believe that politics is or can be a science or, indeed, a discipline that is somehow removed from other disciplinary bases in the humanities. A quick glance will soon reveal a reasonable appreciation of history, without which nothing can be understood. All events exist within a historical context and are a product of preceding circumstances. I trust this is implicit in the text.

Those who look at politics from a political economy perspective tend to regard my work as being culturalist or institutionalist. From such a perspective, my work is seen more as political economy. To clarify, politics is based in the real, material world and responds to real, material interests and pressures. In this sense, its prime concerns are with economic matters, broadly defined; particular economic interests will, therefore, usually end up dominant in the political sphere. I regard this as a given. However, cultural elements also often reflect—or shape—the way interests are defined and decisions are taken. In this respect, culture can be seen to be that common world view shared by a bonded social group and that which is manifested in an acceptance of particular perspectives and the repetition of sets of practices. It may be, in some cases, that such perspectives and practices are a product of a long history of imposed social or political relations, which, in turn, reflect historical material interests. Further, in many respects, as states and their constituent components become more deeply entrenched, decisions are also taken by and reflect the interests of institutions. Such institutions are semi-permanent bodies or organisations themselves reflecting a coherence of values or concerns and can be seen to be represented by political offices (presidency, cabinet and so on), the judicial structure, the armed forces or civil groups, such as the media, trade unions, students and others. All of these contribute to the actuality of the political process, their respective contributions varying according to the prevailing circumstances. Similarly, the failure of institutions to act other than in their own narrowly defined interest is a key marker of political style and is, perhaps, the single most important contributor to state failure.

If there is one valid criticism in the way all of this is addressed in this book, it is that it tends to focus on the political activities of the elites. This, sadly, is true. In simple terms, the broad sweep of politics is most easily (and sometimes only) reflected in the affairs of the elites and is a consequence of decisions taken by them. Yet this should not be seen to imply a disregard for non-elite people. To quote American Politics Professor David Wurfel, an exemplar of a generation of scholars on South-East Asia for whom I have nothing but respect, 'If readers should find passages in this book characterised by cool calculations of power, they may be assured that my work is informed by continuing concern for the fate of the powerless' (1988: xiv). If this text, then, has an otherwise unstated agenda, it is one predicated on such a concern.

By definition, any book attempting to consider this region in some sort of totality will necessarily dip only lightly into various issues. Clearly, not just each country, but each period of each country's development and, indeed, contemporary issues within each country, are each deserving of a book in their own right. Specialist South-East Asian scholars will not learn much that is new to them here, although those who are less familiar with the region might gain some preliminary insights. As an introductory text, then, this book hopes to have raised at least some of the more salient points and offered some explanations for why things have been as they appeared. Perhaps, more than anything, after opening the door to at least some newcomers, these readers will invite themselves in to further explore in greater detail the vast richness of events, issues and ideas that contribute to the conception of the region the world knows as South-East Asia.

The structure of this book is intended to introduce readers to some of the key themes and issues in South-East Asia, then to consider each country in the region. It is hoped that this structure makes the subject clear, intelligible and accessible.

Thematic Issues | 1

1 | Constructing the Modern State

What constitutes nationhood, sometimes even statehood, in South-East Asia (SEA) is open to debate. Challenges come from within the state and, sometimes, outside the state, while questions of legitimacy regarding the institutions of the state are also often debated. To understand the contemporary states of SEA and the construction of national identities, it is necessary to consider how states were formed, what their claims are to national identity and the various styles of government that have been, in large part, predicated on methods of achieving power. This chapter will consider these issues and, in doing so, will then discuss the role of revolution in state development and national identity, including military-supported or derived governments whose origins continue to determine political parameters. Further, this chapter will note the style and forms of governments that have been peacefully inherited and how they have been modified to suit the requirements of various interest groups, such as elites and ethnic majorities. Finally, the adoption of modern state forms will be considered within the context of the adoption of Western ideas of statehood (the idea of the nation state), institutional development and the process of modernisation.

SOME POLITICAL DEFINITIONS

In any study of political matters, it is necessary to clarify some definitions. Those defined here are not absolute, but are intended as clarification for the use of terms in this text. Particularly in relation to distinctions within the broad political structure, I would like to offer a brief clarification of the conceptions of nation, state, state institutions, regime and government. In the first instance, 'nation' is intended here to mean a wider, politically bonded group identity or group of people who understand themselves to have common interests and world views, who usually share a common language and, most commonly, a contiguous or proximate territory. This may or may not comply with the 'state', which is the spatially defined organisational territory under a single political authority and which can (or can attempt to) claim for or compel the compliance of its citizens to its laws up to the extent of its sovereign boundaries.

The idea of 'state institution' implies the functional or institutional capacity or ability of the state and the means (legislative, institutional) by which it achieves (or attempts to achieve) desired outcomes. Within this text I refer to specific institutions by their formal names (for example, the armed forces). The idea of a 'regime', which is often used in the context of South-East Asian governments (for example, the Hun Sen regime), literally means the method or system of government (democratic, communist, authoritarian and so on), but is usually regarded as a pejorative term reserved for the party of government, tending to imply that it is an authoritarian government and, as such, a preexisting antithesis and so is not used here for that reason. The term 'government', which instead is used throughout this text, implies the political institution that makes and implements decisions for the citizens of the state. The term 'sovereignty' or 'sovereign' is used here to denote the political independence of a state or institution within a state to act fully within its organisationally defined area of authority. A sovereign power, therefore, does not share authority within

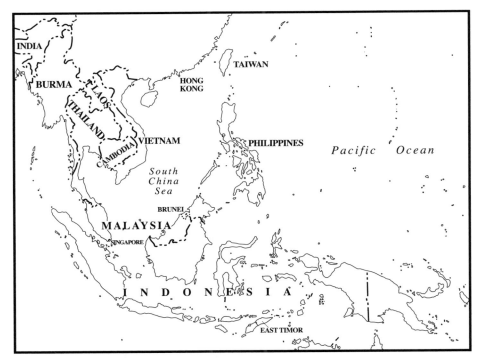

Map 1   South-East Asia

its defined area or will resist attempts to do so. This might apply to the sovereignty of the courts to decide legal matters (that is, to enjoy a separation of powers from the executive and legislature) or of the state to determine matters within its territorial boundaries.

The population of each state is usually defined as its 'citizens'. A citizen is a member of a state who is entitled to such political and civil rights that exist in the state and who owes an obligation of duty as defined by the state. Citizenship has been, since modern times, regarded as universal for all legal inhabitants of a state. However, in the past, citizenship was conferred on select members of the state and based on wealth, gender or status. Finally, the term 'ideology' requires some minor clarification as it has become an oft-abused term. An ideology is a basic or first-principle set of ideas through which an intellectual order is made of social and political experience. The original use of the term applied to the study of ideas, but in its more contemporary use, it has a distinctly political overtone.

CONCEPTIONS OF THE STATE

The state, as it is understood in the contemporary sense, refers to a specific and delineated area in which a government exercises, or claims to exercise, political and judicial control and claims a monopoly on the legitimate use of force. Of course, the state is not just its territory, however that may be defined. But the spatial quality of the state 'is integral to its functions and agencies' (Smith 1986: 235), that is, the area of the state defines the functional sovereign reach of its agencies. In the modern sense, this implies up to the limits of its borders, although in more traditional (precolonial or pre-Westphalian) societies this historical border area was far more ambiguous. This conception of the state is distinct from that of the nation, which, as noted, refers to a group of people who regard themselves in common, usually through language although sometimes through or with other cultural signifiers such as religion, for example, the Islamic *ummat*, or community.

Within a given territory, the state can be identified by the activities of its institutions. Such institutions include state bureaucracies, the armed forces, educational institutions, state industries, the judiciary and a police and penal system. It should be noted, however, that while these are typical institutions of the state, the size and role of the state at the beginning of the twenty-first century was under challenge from ideological influences, world bodies such as the International Monetary Fund (IMF) and the World Trade Organisation (WTO) and from an increasingly globalised economy. In particular, state industries and government bureaucratic services were being sold to private providers. The state, however, has generally retained legislative responsibility for these institutions.

GLOBAL CHALLENGES TO THE STATE

The question of the sovereignty of the state became increasingly open to debate in the late twentieth century as ideas of what constitutes state sovereignty began to be challenged (see Weber & Bierstaker 1996: 282; Hinsley 1978: 285–6; Camilleri 1994: 130–1; Camilleri & Falk 1992; Kearney 2001; Keohane 2002; Stiglitz 2003; Kingsbury 2004). For example, the role of the United Nations (UN) and some other international bodies, such as the IMF and the WTO, can and do use a degree of compulsion in requiring sovereign states to bend to their requirements. This capacity can, perhaps, be seen as a parallel to the capacities of the state itself, where the state can use compulsion in relation to its citizens, usually with their consent in principle, while the UN, for example, can use compulsion in relation to its members, also usually with their consent in principle. 'Consent in principle' implies that it is agreed that the rules consented to are to apply to all members in principle, but may be applied in a way that might have precluded consent in practice to specific members.

Further, a global trend towards the removal of restrictions to trade and the related growth of global capital has removed from many states their capacity to make independent economic decisions. The Thai, Indonesian and Malaysian governments noted this loss of economic sovereignty during the regional economic crisis of 1997–98. Yet the idea of the state continues to be adhered to as a viable means of geosocial organisation and, in many cases, as a reflection of national (or nationalist) aspiration.

While no contemporary states seriously challenge the idea of fixed and clearly defined borders, many do disagree about where those borders should be or, indeed, about whether existing states contain embryonic states. Examples of embryonic states included East Timor (now realised), Aceh and West Papua within Indonesia, the Karen and Kachin states of Burma, Bangsa Moro in the southern Philippines and so on (see Fowler & Bunck 1995: 1–62). Further, there have been disputes about the exact location of borders between, for example, Thailand and Laos, Thailand and Burma, Malaysia and the Philippines and between a number of states over seabed boundaries.

THE CONTEMPORARY STATE

There is also the question of the relationship between the government and the state. In principle, in the contemporary sense, the state has an existence independent of the government and, with its institutions, continues, while governments come and go. However, the distinction between the state and the government was historically less clear, especially in SEA. Prior to the colonial period, the strength or ability of a government or ruler created, maintained or expanded the state. With the loss of that government or ruler, the state was often prey to the interests of other states or collapsed due to a lack of internal cohesion.

A state within the contemporary political context, in SEA or elsewhere, can be determined as having a number of characteristics that define it as a state. As outlined by Morris (1998), the state and its institutions must have an enduring quality and, in particular, be able to survive changes of government or political leadership. In this sense, the state must also transcend the rulers and the ruled, while the institutions of the state must be able to continue, regardless of political change. These institutions must be differentiated from other, non-state institutions or agents and must, if the state is to function, be coordinated with each other. For example, the police and the judiciary must be coordinated in their support and application of the rule of law, while the executive and the military must act together to protect the sovereignty of the state. The state must, therefore, also correspond to a clearly defined territory so that its sovereignty is identifiable and its application specifically enforceable.

Within that territory, the agents of the state must have full and equally distributed authority. The territory of the state must be sovereign, in that the state can legitimately claim a monopoly on the use of force within its territory. Jurisdiction must extend to the full extent of the territory of the state. The legitimacy of the state and its right to claim a monopoly on the use of force (or compulsion) should, preferably, be consented to and must be adhered to by members of the state and in that the state is the ultimate authority (Morris 1998: 45–6; see also, Laski 1934: 21–4). This adherence should be in the form of an allegiance to the state that supersedes all other allegiances. To ensure this allegiance, the state should function to protect and promote the interests of its members. However, in some circumstances it can be claimed that the state does not do this, even though it still claims adherence to its right to the monopoly of force.

MODELS OF THE STATE

In the post-Second World War (post-WWII) period there has been a general acceptance in principle of the idea of a separation between the government and the state (Morris 1998: 21–2). However, the practice has, in some cases, been somewhat different. In part this has been a consequence of the role played by certain agents, especially armies, but also political parties or individuals, in the creation of the state. There has also been a tendency to draw on or re-invent precolonial traditions that characterise the state as being embodied within the army, the party or in the person of the political leader. The distinction between the army and the state in Burma, for example, is effectively non-existent, while the separation of the party and the state in Vietnam or Laos is similarly difficult to discern. In Indonesia under Sukarno (the Guided Democracy period) and Suharto and, to a lesser extent, in Singapore under Lee, the state has been reflected in the person of the president or the prime minister. In the cases of the state being reflected in the person of the leader, each state has shown itself to be greater and more permanent than the leader; however, in each case the independence of state functions, especially the judiciary and the electoral system, has been seriously compromised.

The idea of the state with clearly delineated borders is relatively new; it was only beginning to be formulated in Europe from the time of the Treaty of Westphalia in 1648 and only in the nation-state sense from the early nineteenth century. As an idea, it is still disputed in areas where the authority of the state is challenged by assertions of the nation. The most obvious examples of this outside SEA are the former USSR, Yugoslavia, Czechoslovakia, Iraq and, to a lesser extent, Belgium, Italy (Putnam 1993: ch. 2) and Canada. Within SEA, Indonesia, Burma, the Philippines, and Thailand all have had localised nationalist rebellions against the spatial–functionalist claims of the state. In spite of these protests against incorporation into established states, these rebellions are not opposed to the idea of the state as such and, indeed, are aimed at creating their own new states. As a borrowed, if useful, model then, the modern idea of the state is uniformly accepted by the governments and other political movements of SEA.

All of the current states of SEA, with the exception of Thailand, were colonies and even Thailand had its contemporary borders defined by colonial powers and was, in large part, economically colonised by the United Kingdom. Hence, the physical characteristics of the state were defined not so much by geography[1] or national cohesion, but by the methods and requirements of colonial powers. Further, and again with the exception of Thailand, all of these states had their traditional or indigenous models of political authority dismantled or emasculated, which required the establishment of new forms of state authority. Even in the case of Thailand, an approximation of the British model was adopted there after 1932.

There is no single idea of the state, although there are some general guides to what can constitute a state. In the most simple, anthropological sense, the state could simply be a shared agreement among a group of people about the rules under which they jointly live. It may, indeed, imply a form of government without a state (Krader 1976: ch. 2; see also, Gamble 1986; Crone 1986). This view of the state does not include more explicit, complex and formal agencies of government, which are the usual markers of state existence (Krader 1976: 13). Indeed, it probably bears closer relationship to the idea of culture, as a shared world view or set of values, or nation, which is a group of people so identifying themselves.

Another marker of the state is its internal integration, although this tends to apply more to modern (fixed boundary, postcolonial) states than to premodern (usually precolonial) states in which issues of integration were more ambiguous. Claims to state control in, for example, the Javanese Majapahit Empire of the fourteenth century, were far more rhetorical than they were actual. A further characteristic of the state is the degree to which it is established and, similarly, the degree to which it can operate independently of external agencies. This idea of the embeddedness of the state refers to the degree to which the state is able to implement its programs and policies within its given territory (Evans 1995).

Most, though not all, states are marked by a type of social contract, in which the ruler and the ruled agree to conditions of participation in the state.[2] This implies a type of *modus vivendi* connected with a sense of mutual consent (Plamenatz 1968: ch. 1) or mutual advantage (Rawls 1973: 4), but might in fact be a non-jural consideration, that is, being born into a particular state and with few or no realistic options for change or flight, participation in and effective acceptance of state rules might be a *fait accompli*. There are even some states that have been referred to as 'predatory', meaning that the state elites prey on their constituent populations (as discussed, for example, by Evans 1995: 12, 43–7).

Morris has noted in particular that strong (authoritarian) states have a greater tendency to engage in harmful behaviour towards their own citizens or others and that democratic states do not have a record of going to war with each other (Morris 1998: 14–19). The implication of this is that, where the power of the state is not in balance with a duty to its citizens, it can act contrary to their interests. Such a balance is most recognisably achieved through the agencies of the state being accountable to the government and the government in turn being accountable to the citizens. In SEA there are numerous examples of strong states and of states acting in ways that do not accord with the interests of their citizens.

THE CULTURAL AS POLITICAL

The intersection between culture and politics has been a contested field in the study of politics, with debate over the influence of one over the other, whether the two can be separated and whether such a focus is a distraction from the main game, which is the deployment of power as the embodiment of political practice. Politics is, in a functional sense, the practice of the attainment, exercise and maintenance of power. Yet, like all things, politics does not exist in a vacuum; rather, it reflects particular sets of historically and materially based circumstances, the variables of social relations and the capacities of individuals. Yet in SEA there has been a high degree of reductionism, with many of the governments of the region at one time or another claiming that their political forms reflect their prevailing cultures and cite this as a justification for behaviour that often fails to meet internationally accepted norms of practice. This raises the questions of the validity of cultural relativism, of the singularity of culture within a state framework and of the accuracy of these governments' representations of such cultures.

If culture is defined as a shared set of codes of behaviour or a world view common in its basic principles, there is necessarily social pressure to conform to such codes or principles. Without a degree of conformity, societies cannot function cohesively, nor would they be able to identify in common, that is, they would not form functioning societies. Equally, conformity to social codes is often undertaken, generally quite willingly, by the individual to ensure retention within a social framework. That is to say, social organisation identifies itself as contextually located and is, via its constituent members, conscious of its principle or system of continuation through defining the past to represent a continuum into the present and the future, of a particular world view or set of values. This continuum is manifested as 'tradition, combined with the needs of practical adjustment, [which] are the main elements guiding overall system reproduction' (Giddens 1987: 153–4). In this sense, the term 'culture' is here intended to define that aspect of social relations within a bonded group that refers to obligation, hierarchy and authority. It is not intended to refer to those qualities that reflect taste or preference, even though these might intersect with symbolic aspects of obligation, hierarchy and authority.

Conforming to particular codes of behaviour or ascribing to a version of events that locates the present as part of a social continuum helps to ensure a form of normative social cohesion. In cases where individuals or subgroups do not conform, which, by definition, represents a challenge to social cohesion, it is common for formal and informal sanctions to be placed upon them. Much depends on the types of challenges or threats facing the social collective and how much tolerance can be expressed before non-standard forms of behaviour become unacceptable. In SEA, social codes of behaviour are often defined under the auspices of non- or quasi-representative power-oriented institutions, authoritarian government being the most obvious example, but also including the military, police, capitalists, a non-reflexive bureaucracy, in some cases religious institutions and others. As a consequence, codes of acceptable behaviour may be interpreted or (re)defined to suit the needs of the powerful to preserve or enhance their authority. In assessing issues of social codification, one must consider who it is that acts as the keeper of social codes of behaviour; who has the authority to be the arbiter or the cultural police.

In regard to the resolution of conflict and the control of violence, social codification is usually enacted as law (the legal code) and is policed in a literal sense. Conflict in the physical sense and the control of, or capacity to employ, violence is normatively the sole preserve of the state. In this, the authority for social constraint is relinquished by citizens to the government on the understanding that government will employ such violence only for purposes that are sanctioned by formal codification; that it will normatively act dispassionately, consistently and equally on behalf of all citizens.

Beyond social conflict and violence, codes of behaviour take on more of a political than a legal tone. For instance, abusive language may imply the threat of violence and so be restricted, but critical language is merely offensive to certain sensibilities or seen as a challenge to a position, such as that of a dominant religion or the assertion of a particular idea or interest. Yet within SEA, the law can and does often rule on both under the one set of statutes, reflecting the imposition of legal preserves on behalf of particular groups or individuals. When this is challenged, it is usually justified on cultural grounds, even though limitations of critical speech, particularly of ideas or interests, are explicitly political. It may be that culture can influence political style or method and that contestation over elements of culture may be quite political, but at the point where such contestation exists, the issue is not about the validity or otherwise of the culture in question, it is about the use of power to determine the interpretation of culture. And if this, in turn, reflects particular traditions, they are necessarily political rather than cultural traditions. For example, deference may be imbued in a culture, but it reflects considerations that go to questions of power, even if internalised and naturalised, and not to questions of taste.

Conformity to social codes, then, occurs within a legal framework designed to ensure a society's physical security and to ensure its cultural security, as well as through non-legal, socially based (cultural) mechanisms. Throughout SEA, adherence to formal social codification is flexible, reflecting in part traditional forms of social sanction, but, more importantly in a contemporary context, allowing considerable flexibility for the achievement of politically influenced outcomes. In this way, where traditional cultural values or the law conform to the requirements of government, they are generally maintained or enforced. Where they do not, they are often reconfigured or disposed of and replaced by other, often malleable, codes, sometimes dressed up as tradition, sometimes not.[3]

IDEOLOGY

All political systems represent ideological assumptions, even when such an assumption is not explicit, that is to say, political leaders might claim to be pragmatic, to assert the good of the state or the nation above ideology or to represent not contemporary ideologies but traditional patterns of political behaviour, but in each case, they are usually representing ideas that derive from classical or neoclassical economic theory, from Leninist interpretations of Marxism, from nationalist ideologies or from resurrected feudal or prefeudal traditions. Such has often been the case in SEA, where political rhetoric, say, on land redistribution (the Philippines), free markets (Singapore), socialism (Vietnam), the role of the armed forces (Burma, Indonesia) or human rights, has not necessarily been matched by corresponding political practice.

As noted, ideology was originally the study of ideas, yet its more contemporary meaning has it as a coherent and largely internally consistent system of first principle ideas through which an intellectual order is made of social and political experience or a set of ideas that inform a particular political perspective. Ideologies that have received general recognition are specifically identified, with the names given to them intended to convey (if not always accurately) their core values and goals. Better known examples of ideologies include Marxism or communism, liberalism, capitalism and fascism, although religious beliefs such as Christianity and Islam (theocracy), ideas about the nation (nationalism) or the state (unitarianism, federalism) can also function as ideologies. As a consequence of the role of the military, in some instances, in both the liberation and hence the state-creation process, military thinking has also come to exhibit characteristics of an ideology. This is especially relevant in terms of the relationship between the state, its institutions and individual citizens and in terms of more broad conceptions of power, hierarchy and authority. The role of the military can be clearly seen in a number of SEA countries, including Burma, Thailand, Cambodia, Laos, Vietnam, Indonesia and the Philippines. In some places, the role of the military in political affairs has declined (Thailand, Cambodia, the Philippines and, it seems, Indonesia), in some increased (Burma) and in others simply changed (Vietnam, Laos). The lessening of military involvement in political affairs has usually been regarded as a sign of the political maturity of the state, a sign that the state is capable of assuming responsibility for its affairs (Dodd 1972: 50–4).

It is necessary to note that, while an ideology is usually understood as the expression of an idea, it is a logical error to ascribe to a political system a particular ideological label, regardless of the claims made on behalf of that system, if its practice does not comply. That is to say, a state that calls itself socialist but which practices free market capitalism is not socialist at all, but rather a single-party state, usually employing aspects of authoritarianism (for example, Vietnam). Similarly, claims to nationalism, which most often find themselves reflecting a romanticised, organicist idea, may reflect an aspiration but may not necessarily represent reality (for example, the 'Unitary State of the Republic of Indonesia'). To determine the ideology of a state, it is first necessary to consider the rules of operation of a state and how these are put into practice. Only then is it helpful to compare the reality of ideological practice with claims in ideological rhetoric.

In that there is commonly a gap between ideological rhetoric and lived political reality, the ideological assumptions that underpin each state might be claimed to be in the interests of most people, but may not be the most accurate representation of the interests or wishes of most of the people of such states. Such interests tend to be most accurately represented where there is a high degree of political accountability and, as such, rhetoric tends to be reflected, even if imperfectly, in reality. As a consequence, one must ask of the extent to which the political interests of state constituents—the citizens of the state—are represented or to what extent such constituents are satisfied that their interests are represented.

CITIZENS

Like the term 'ideology', the meaning of the term 'citizen' has changed somewhat from its original usage, when it referred to an inhabitant of a town. However, with the European revolutions, in particular that of France, the term and idea of citizen took on a more specifically political (if geographically dispersed) meaning. In this, the idea of the town dweller was bound up with the rights claimed under the new state. The modern term 'citizen', therefore, applies to the individual constituent members of the state and implies political rights and obligations, including the right to participation in state affairs, the protection of the state in external and internal affairs and from the state in certain instances, as well as a duty to the state. In this, the state is identified as the spatially and institutionally ordered manifestation of the public will, which is often bound up with the idea of 'nation' (to be discussed). However, while this is a fairly conventional idea of citizenship and within the context of the contemporary state could be said to apply as a first principle of statehood, in some political contexts in SEA it does not necessarily apply. States do not always offer their protection nor do they always regard citizens as having rights in relation to the state, while participation in state affairs can be quite circumscribed. However, duty to the state, including compliance with its laws, tends to be a given. Being a citizen also more generally, if in a more limited way, implies being a constituent member of a state, being subject to its laws, the rights under which might vary considerably, and being internationally recognised as such.

The idea of a citizen did not effectively apply in much of SEA until the post-WWII period, as a large proportion of its inhabitants were colonial subjects and not citizens as such. Prior to the colonial period, the conception upon which the state was based often granted little political status to those other than the ruling elites and their functionaries and constituent members of the state often had utility value similar to that of livestock or as manifestly lesser on a scale of human value. It was only with the establishment of the modern state, in particular with delineated borders and, at least theoretically, full and equal legal authority up to those borders, that citizenship became available and in principle applied to the people of SEA.

NATIONALISM

It has been suggested that nationalism is itself an ideology. The detailed form of this ideology varies from place to place, for example from the organicist (protofascist) origins of the Indonesian state to the Leninist model of the Vietnamese state. What they feature in common, however, is not just a desire for independent unity and, consequently, self-determination, but the creation of an idea of a common bonded identity (Connor 1994; Anderson 1991; Smith 1986: 231–5; Smith 2003: 198-200; Gellner 1983). Means of creating or attempting to create such a common identity are various, but usually revolve around a (sometimes manufactured) common history, an (often manufactured) common language and more broadly shared (or imposed) cultural values. Within this categorisation, it is necessary to distinguish between organic nationalism and artificial nationalism.

It can be suggested that all nationalisms are constructed in that they are a consequence of a systematic building of common understanding or identity around shared core ideas. However, this is perhaps less helpful than understanding whether the nationalism in question is the product of local, voluntary conditions, that is, organic, or whether it is a consequence of coercion (often external), that is, artificial. This is not to suggest that there is not a high degree of artificiality in many nationalisms; many of the states of Europe, for example, comprise non-core groups that have been obliged to share in the nationalist project. However, the ordering of state borders, which in Europe are usually claimed to be contiguous with nationalisms (hence the term 'nation state'), has usually been undertaken on a more or less voluntary basis. While there are exceptions, such as the Germanic speakers of northern Italy, there is a relatively high degree of cultural coherence within nations. By contrast, the states of SEA do not always correspond comfortably to assertions of nationalism, primarily because of the often arbitrary manner in which their borders were defined by external colonial powers and much less as a reflection of the will of local inhabitants or even, as in the case of Europe, an historical trade-off that allowed borders to occur along approximately national lines or along lines that corresponded to the political reach of core national groups. Importantly, though, within the SEA context, the bond born of fighting against a common colonialist enemy has been a key component in the construction of national identities. In this last sense, the common aspiration and struggle for liberation has helped forge a common identity through a common cause, often through shared common hardship and through the identification of the newly bonded group in opposition to its common enemy. As in the case of Europe, this common bonded identity, then, has been regarded as the basis for an assertion of legitimate control over the nation's territory (SarDesai 1997: chs 18, 24).

The idea of nationalism in SEA is also complicated by the fact that the modernist adoption (or imposition) of fixed borders clashed with the ebb and flow of traditional SEA polities, not to mention the drift of immigrants from one region to another. In the contemporary political world, the free flow of people is regarded as challenging state control of its borders, upsetting patterns of established land use and ownership and threatening loyalty to the state. Historically, however, such immigration was encouraged, as a means of strengthening the state in both economic and military terms. This had implications for precolonial state formation and how that has influenced contemporary states. But the ideas that derive from the precolonial period also inform—sometimes consciously, sometimes subconsciously—the way political leaders look at their own country and those around them.

With the establishment of European colonies in the region, colonisers sought to extend their authority either to or beyond the limits of the state as they found it, as a part of their empire creation. To that end, the Dutch included not just Java in their colony of the Dutch East Indies, but also islands that had only peripheral relations with Java, despite what has been claimed, albeit briefly, for the Majapahit Empire. Similarly, the United Kingdom incorporated not just the core state of Burma within the Irrawaddy Valley, which it acknowledged as Burma Proper, but also states that had a separate or conflicting history in relation to Burma, which they acknowledged, as the Frontier States. The French correctly assumed the connectedness of the three states of Vietnam, as they found them, as Cochin-China, Annam and Tonkin. However, it was only through the shallow establishment of a Vietnamese claim to suzerainty that they then annexed the Lao state of Luang Prabang, extended to incorporate the other Lao states of Vieng Chan (Vientiane) and Champassak. That Thailand also claimed suzerainty over these states little worried the French, although the Thai claim to southern Malay provinces has caused continuing conflict. Further, to compound this lack of acknowledgment for what political arrangements did and did not exist, the French then chose to delineate their newly acquired Lao territory along the Mekong River, with the exception of small northern and southern sections. The Mekong had traditionally been the main artery within the Lao nation and, earlier, within the Lao state of Lan Xang. This had little meaning for the French, but left a majority of ethnic Lao Loum in what was thereafter defined as Thailand rather than in Laos.

MANDALAS

Prior to colonialism, nowhere in SEA was there a state that had clearly delineated borders or which ruled with any permanent authority in all its outer regions. Almost by definition, the states that existed in precolonial SEA were in a constant state of expansion or retraction, with all authority located at what was often seen as an exemplary centre. In an idealised condition, it is from this centre that a monarch ruled, his authority radiating outwards. Acknowledged in practice but less so in rhetoric, that power receded the further it travelled. At or near the centre, authority was greatest; at the periphery, it was dispersed, often through local rulers of increasing independence (Tambiah 1976: 114; see also, McCloud 1995: 93–7) and increasingly doubtful loyalty, until it ceased to exist in practice. At this point the authority from another centre would begin to resonate. Where two centres of authority came into contact, other than through truces, suzerainty or rare marriages of convenience, conflict was almost inevitable. A state that could not maintain or continue to expand its authority was, by definition, in decline and, given the quasimagical or metaphysical qualities associated with power, once a loss of power was manifest, decline was usually inevitable. Without wishing to overstate the point, aspects of this model continued to be reflected in the postcolonial period, in particular in Suharto's rule of Indonesia, Hun Sen's rule of Cambodia and Ne Win's dominance of Burma.

A further elaboration of this idea is that, with the power of the state strengthening towards the centre, the highest source of authority within the state is the individual who resides at its centre, the monarch (or absolute ruler). Through patronage, as opposed to bureaucracy or feudal obligation, the monarch dispenses favour or otherwise, balancing competing forces within his sphere. In a practical sense, the monarch might also need to enter into arrangements with other powerful individuals or substates, diminishing the purity of this centralising model. However, there remains not only a parallel, but also a direct relationship between the central patrimonial system of monarchy and the notion of a centralised state. The centralisation of power and the distribution of patronage continue to be hallmarks of SEA political models, to varying degrees applying in each of the region's states.

This idea of state organisation has, generally, been referred to as a 'mandala', the Buddhist model of the universe in which all matter radiates from and revolves around an exemplary centre (Wolters 1999; Stuart-Fox 1997: 2–4; Moertono 1981: 71, n.b. 207; Wilson 1969: 7).[4] The idea of the mandala as a political model derives from India and has been used to describe the construction of the early Buddhist and Hindu states of SEA. However, a similar model for political authority applied to China and the states it directly influenced, including Korea, Vietnam and Japan, as well as its own western provinces.[5]

MANDALAS OR IMPERIA?

Oliver Wolters (1999) and Martin Stuart-Fox (1999, personal comm-unication) have suggested a distinction between the state as mandala and the state as an imperium. Vietnam, both authors suggest, was an imperium, based on two criteria. The first is that Vietnam, as a state originating in the Red River delta region, only ever expanded and hence did not exhibit the expansion and contraction of a classic mandala (Wolters 1999: 144). Further, they both claim that Vietnam had more clearly defined boundaries and that its authority was complete up to that clearly defined boundary. Wolters also claims that Vietnam enjoyed a hereditary form of government that reflected dynastic succession that was not in keeping with a mandalic rise and fall of individual rulers and that it retained a constant political focus on Hanoi (see 1999: 143–54).

In part, Stuart-Fox and Wolter's definitions are based on a distinction between the Indianised states of SEA and the Sinicised state of Vietnam. Vietnam certainly had a different historical experience as a consequence of

China's cultural and political influence and the form of Buddhism it enjoyed (and continues to enjoy) was the more inclusive and syncretic Mahayana version, also derived from China. The rest of the mainland, in particular, converted to the Theravada version of Buddhism, founded in Sri Lanka. However, this sets up a dichotomy in Buddhism that is, perhaps, overstated.

More importantly, though, its logic also suggests that the notion of a mandala was reflected in the way society organised itself rather than the mandala being conceived to describe that preexisting social construction. To this end, one need only look at the feudal states of Europe or the precolonial states of Africa and Latin America to find numerous other political forms that parallel the construction of a mandala, even though Hinduism and Buddhism of either main variety were completely unknown to them. By way of illustration, it has been suggested that the political forms that, until the period of colonisation, dominated much of Asia were in fact similar to those that dominated Europe until the end of the Middle Ages or later (Steadman 1969: 26–7). In this respect, these states reflected a particular stage of economic and related political development.[6]

An idea parallel to that of the mandala—that the universe revolved around the earth and that the state was centred on the court—was dominant in Europe until at least the mid seventeenth century. Weber discussed a similar idea in his model of patrimonial-prebendal states, in which the ruler dispensed with patronage and ensured loyalty from a central point (Weber 1958, 1968; see also, Bakker & Ferrazzi 1997). In that sense, as is often the case, the idea, in this case the mandala, reflected and rationalised a preexisting state of affairs or corresponding world view rather than helped to shape them.

By contrast, the idea of an imperium suggests immutability. Vietnam has enjoyed a series of capitals at or near the site of modern Hanoi, but has also had capitals at a number of other sites across the length of the state. Similarly, Vietnam experienced dynastic succession, but also saw dynasties fall and individual rulers last for short periods. Even the boundaries of the state, most clearly defined by the Annamite Cordillera, are physical rather than political. Where geography has allowed, there has been a lack of clarity over what did and did not constitute the territory of the Viets, especially in the highland areas of the northwest and in the expanding south. There were, at various times, different methods of delineating the boundary of the Vietnamese state, but these were often similar to those used elsewhere, such as language, architectural style and regional loyalty. Further, while the Vietnamese maintained a fairly clearly defined sense of national identity and expanded south at the expense of the Chams and later the Khmers, their efforts to do so were not without reversal. The state of Champa attacked and occupied much of Vietnam in 979 CE, while the Khmer empire of Angkor occupied territory claimed by Vietnam during the period 1112–50 CE (Smith 1964a: 598; Nguyen 1993; 29; Osborne 1997: 20, 26,

32). All of this, of course, does not include the tendency of the Vietnamese state to fragment and reform, which it has done several times since the end of China's main period of occupation in 938 CE. The ideas of the mandala and the imperium are, therefore, like Weber's types of power, idealised, with the reality being a variation of or a diluted or combined form of the models.

EMPIRES

Insofar as the above discussion can be applied as a model for precolonial SEA states, it can also be used for precolonial SEA empires (superstates). The empire is but an extension of central authority: in the traditional format, the greater the power of the central authority the greater its reach. Within a single linguistic or cultural group the reach of authority can be regarded as encompassing the state as a nation. Once the state uses force to encompass other linguistic or cultural groups—other nations of peoples—it becomes an empire. In precolonial times, empires encompassing diverse nations of peoples were not only common throughout Asia, but were also a logical, perhaps necessary, extension of the successful state. In the postcolonial period, empires in the classical sense are almost universally regarded as illegitimate. Colonialism does not have to be exercised by Europeans to be regarded as normatively undesirable.

Each of the contemporary regional states reflects attributes of empire (imperium), especially with the imposition of clearly defined borders and nominal judicial and administrative authority up to those borders, often in spite of some degree of national difference. Each also reflects attributes of a mandala, with practical political authority often not being fully implemented. Examples of such are found in the ethnic states of Burma, the minorities of Laos, the separatist aspirations within Indonesia and the warlordism of Cambodia, especially around Pailin, and parts of Thailand, Laos, Burma, Indonesia and the Philippines. The idea of the mandala, then, lives on in a practical sense, in the form of modern states, in how they sometimes arrange their internal structures of authority and, not surprisingly, in particular cases of interstate relations.

COLONIAL INFLUENCES

Having noted the above, most SEA states more closely represent the area of their former colonial boundaries than they do states based on single cultural or historical groups. In this sense, a number of dominant nations have come to exercise authority over often reluctant smaller nations, thus comprising some modern states effectively as empires. Javanese domination of Indonesia, Thai domination of T'ai[7] and non-T'ai minorities and Bhamese domination of Burma's minorities are but a few examples of states which, in historical terms, would have been considered empires.

While the idea of the nation state inspired much postcolonial political thinking, there are few states that are also single nations of peoples. Vietnam is, in its core areas, a relatively homogeneous nation state, as is Cambodia. But even these have exceptions of numerous indigenous minorities—Cambodia has around 200 000 or so Chams in its population of 11 million,[8] while Vietnam counts some fifty-three minority groups among its people—and other states are much more heterogeneous. This has led to a number of postcolonial states striving to manufacture a sense of national identity, for example, through a common language or what are claimed to be shared historical events. Indonesia is the outstanding example of attempted nation building, in that it has sought to bring together numerous diverse cultural groups with usually very separate histories into a unitarian state. The means of achieving this have been the use of Bahasa Indonesia, a common, if synthetic, language and a glorified common history, in this case under the Majapahit Empire and through the claimed unity of the anti-colonial struggle. Thailand also conducted an exercise in the construction of national identity in the latter part of the nineteenth and the early part of the twentieth centuries, as have most other states, with varying degrees of effort and success.

Further enhancing the composite form of a number of contemporary SEA states, several European colonies that later became states were either based on preexisting regional empires or regions of political dominance or were, in effect, empires in their own right. The borders of Burma were determined by the British, who had marginal regard for the significant ethnic minorities of the region. Malaysia comprises a number of earlier sultanates and modern Indonesia is a state based on the composite empire of the Dutch East Indies, reflecting Dutch colonial control in the archipelago.

Yet again, other ethnic and linguistic groups were divided by colonial boundaries, which have translated into modern states. Examples of this include the Lao of Thailand,[9] the ethnic T'ai (Shan, Wa and so on) of Burma, the Papuans of Indonesia and the somewhat arbitrary division between Sumatra and the Malay Peninsula. In the case of Thailand, its modern boundaries include the old Thai principality of Lan Na, based on Chiang Mai, which was not formally incorporated into the state until 1907 and which, until as late as 1930, remained outside Thailand's taxation system and retained its own currency. Similarly, the eastern border of Thailand was not defined until 1907, incorporating as it did a majority of the Lao people in the northeastern Korat Plateau, although there were to be short-lived readjustments during WWII under the auspices of imperial Japan. Similarly, although Vietnam's invasion of Cambodia in 1978 was in response to attacks by Khmer Rouge units across the border, its occupation until 1989 was perceived by many, including in Cambodia and Thailand, as a renewal of age-old Vietnamese imperial or expansionist ambitions.

Beyond this tendency towards expansion or retraction, SEA was and largely remains politically divided by its geography which, allowing for colonial reorganisation, is reflected in the borders of the region's contemporary states. By way of illustration, the rise of the Han, the preceding Ch'in and the unification of the Chinese empire drove numerous ethnic minorities from China's southern provinces into SEA, forcing them to follow the natural contours of the geography. The spread southwards of Annamites (Vietnamese) was channelled by the Annamite Chain of mountains, which divides Vietnam from Laos and, in part, from Cambodia. The various T'ai groups settled in geographically distinct regions; the various Lao in the region of the upper Mekong River, the Thai in the Menam Valley and the Shan in the Salwein Valley, while Tibeto–Burmans settled in the Irrawaddy Valley. The Mon–Khmer settled in the lower Mekong region of Cambodia (originally including the Mekong Delta) and across what is now southern Thailand and around the Irrawaddy Delta of Burma. Later cultural and political influences also followed the local geography, with Hinduism and later Buddhism spreading from India and Sri Lanka along coastal routes into SEA, while the more syncretic Mahayana Buddhism flowed into China and south into Vietnam.

EXPANSIONIST AMBITIONS

This process of settlement and influence was not without conflict. Earlier settlers were often displaced or absorbed, such as the Chams of central Vietnam by the Annamite community (a Cham community continues to exist in Vietnam, with a larger community living near Phnom Penh in Cambodia), the Mon by the Burmans and numerous ethnic minorities, not least of whom were SEA's original Austronesian aborigines, by numerically and militarily superior regional majorities. As late as 1828, Thailand resolved the problem of its rebellious Lao subjects by physically shifting tens of thousands of them from the eastern mountains and valleys of what was to become Laos into the northern part of the administratively more convenient Korat Plateau on the west side of the Mekong River. Although already a Lao region and once a part of the ancient Lao empire of Lan Xang, this relocation effectively divided the Lao between those under direct administration and those who owed suzerainty to Bangkok. The subsequent French occupation of the non-Thai region of old Lan Xang formalised this division.

In considerable part, the placement and displacement of peoples in turn reflected the rise and fall of regional powers and empires, which in turn reflected the aforementioned idea of expansion or contraction of political authority. This state of affairs was still dynamic when, in the sixteenth century, Europeans first began to encroach on the region, originally as traders, sometimes missionaries and then, simply as other powers in a wide-ranging field of political competition. But as European technology and political manipulation took effect in the form of colonies and protectorates, the border regions of Asia began to solidify, although not reaching their final colonial form until the early years of the twentieth century.

Yet there are still competing interests between the states of SEA and much of the political manoeuvring within and between states can be attributed to the solidification of a formerly fluid political environment. Border disputes have been prevalent between Thailand and Laos, Vietnam and Cambodia, Burma and China, the Philippines and Malaysia, Indonesia and Malaysia, Indonesia and the Netherlands (in West Papua) and, over the Spratly Islands, between China, Taiwan, Vietnam, the Philippines and Malaysia. The colonial anomaly of Portuguese Timor was absorbed into the postcolonial construction of the state that is Indonesia and while this made sense geographically it did not reflect the wishes of the great majority of East Timorese and again recalled the mandalic idea of imperial expansion.[10]

There also continues to be a tendency for some states to play an active role in the affairs of their neighbours, acting out in what were perceived to be areas of influence or what was once, in more practical terms, called suzerainty. China has been active in Cambodia and briefly in Vietnam and has been forging close links with Burma, Laos and Thailand. Vietnam has also engaged in neighbourly intrigues, influencing and, at times, contributing to events in Laos and Cambodia, as has Thailand. Indonesia has sought to influence affairs in Malaysia to the extent of opposing the state in its entirety. Perhaps states have always and will always seek to influence their neighbours, despite the non-interference principles of the Association of South East Asian Nations (ASEAN), which now comprises all the SEA states. Such influence can be interpreted as an effect of manifest destiny and continues to give strength to the idea of the mandala as a political model.

Within the states, often quite distinct ethnic groups can be amalgamated or brought together under a single political structure, usually under the tutelage of a dominant ethnic group that controls the administrative and military mechanisms. In Burma, for instance, there are significant minorities of Shan, Chin, Kachin, Kyah, Karen and others in their own regions as well as other absorbed minorities. In Indonesia, there is a continuing history of the assertion of a separate political identity and rebellion in the northern province of Aceh, once a separate sultanate, and in West Papua, as well as serious levels of disaffection elsewhere. East Timor, incorporated by force in 1976 (invaded in 1975), was separated from Indonesia in October 1999. There are separatist claims by Muslims in the southern Philippines and southern Thailand and there are disputes between majority lowland and upland Lao (such as the Hmong, Yao, Kha), including conflict with the government in Vieng Chan, in part over political control and in part over the production of opium. There also remains disaffection between mainstream Thai and Lao of northeast Thailand and with the minorities of the north and Muslims of the south, which, in the late 1960s and early to mid 1970s, spilled over into Marxist rebellion.

Faced with competing historical interests, conceptions of national or tribal identity and a requirement to forge a unified state that more or less complies with contemporary requirements to be self-administering, viable and independent, the postcolonial states of postwar SEA have drawn strongly on their respective local histories and political styles as well as many of the organising principles of government derived from the West. In this sense, as the states of SEA have sought to model themselves on the relatively recent European idea of a legally delineated territory, they have often also sought to implement political institutions that could correspond to administering that territory. This has become especially important to those states that have engaged in increasingly complex interstate relations, including trade and diplomacy, which, within the modern context, traditional political forms were unable to adequately provide for.

This political process does not then imply a particular ideology of government, but it does imply a government that, theoretically at least, exercises full sovereignty to the limits of its borders (Morris 1998: 21) and that acknowledges citizenship of the permanent residents within those borders, as well as having independence from external powers (Morris 1998: 174). In a formal sense, sovereignty is, or should be, absolute, inalienable and indivisible (Morris 1998: 178). Sovereignty can be limited where governments may be constitutionally deprived of certain juridical powers, for example, making state religion (Morris 1998: 205).

The idea of the state, then, is not immutable and especially not so in SEA. Localisms challenge existing states from within, while global tendencies challenge them from without. Even the simple management of states can present a challenge to their cohesion, while many states only partially fulfil the requirement regarded by Morris as standard for their legitimate claim to existence. Yet each state continues to assert itself, assuming in some senses an existence beyond that of the group or area it claims to represent. Here we see the morphing of the institutions of state with the state itself and the role and ideology of government as defining the style and scope of the state. In this, the states of SEA perhaps reflect older conceptions of statehood or more universalist ones. The idea of the state has been fulsomely adopted throughout the region, but, like other political forms, how it has been interpreted has been shaped by local desires, values, requirements and impositions. There was little guarantee that the states that existed at the end of the twentieth century, or even what was understood to be meant by the term 'state', would continue in some precise form indefinitely.

NOTES

1   Contemporary river boundaries are a European convention. Rivers were a means of travel within states in precolonial times.
2   The idea of a 'social contract' has been extensively discussed by Hobbes, Locke and Rousseau, among others, although rejected by Mill (1961: 552).
3   See Pemberton (1994) for a useful illustration of this point in relation to Indonesia.

4   In its original cosmic sense, the mandala was intended to be a metaphorical rather than literal interpretation of the universe. It reflected a desire for order and balance as much as it did a method of explanation. Further, particular models of mandalas, like other forms of cultural expression, also varied from one cultural environment to another and, while retaining the same basic characteristics, said as much about their makers as about the thing they were supposed to represent.

5   Stuart-Fox (1996: 5–6) suggests that within the SEA context, Vietnam was not a mandalic state, in that it had clearly defined borders. It was, he says, an imperium in the same manner as China. Vietnam did have more formally defined borders than other precolonial SEA states. However, its expansion southwards into what was Champa and into Cambodia and the poorly defined nature of its boundaries and suzerainty to its north-west suggest a similar pattern of authority to other SEA states. (Similarly, the extent of the authority of the Chinese imperium has waxed and waned according to internal circumstances and external forces.)

6   A related idea is that power is radiated in concentric circles, but with those circles alternating in favour and disfavour towards the centre. That is, my neighbour is by definition my enemy, hence his neighbour must be his enemy and is perforce my ally, although his neighbour in turn will again be my enemy (see Moertono 1981: 71 nb207; Steinberg 1971: 400).

7   The term 'T'ai' refers here to the linguistic family of T'ai speakers, including the Shan, Thai and Lao, as well as T'ai who are spread from Assam in India to north-west Vietnam and southern China.

8   The actual figure is not known as statistical records are incomplete. What is known is that a very large proportion—perhaps half—of the Cham population did not survive the Khmer Rouge period.

9   About 6 000 000 ethnic Lao live in Thailand, while only about 4 000 000 Lao live in Laos.

10   Further, the Indonesian government argued that, to allow East Timor independence would encourage separatism on the part of Indonesia's other provinces, reflecting the mandalic idea that a state—or empire—that is not expanding, or at least maintaining, is threatened with shrinkage.

2 | Authority and Legitimacy

This chapter will consider models of political legitimacy and their application in SEA, with particular reference to the nature of authority and its relationship to notions of legitimacy within the SEA context. Central to discussions of legitimacy are issues of how governments organise themselves and how they behave towards their constituent members, which is usually referred to under the rubric of civil and political rights.

REPRESENTATION AND PARTICIPATION

One way of understanding political processes is to ask whether people are satisfied with their lot and to then look at the conditions that offer that degree of satisfaction or otherwise. This could be seen as an indicator of whether a political system is working and, indeed, what type of political system it is and whose interests it primarily represents. In most cases, representation of interests is determined by levels of participation, which can be active or passive, or exclusion from the political process.

The positive version of political participation means having some constructive input into the political process to which a citizen of a state is subject. In the negative, this could mean being opposed to such political processes. Somewhere in between lies passive participation. Passive participation implies that citizens are not prepared to engage in the political process, but not to reject it, that they are sufficiently satisfied to disregard it and get on with other matters or that they see no practical value in actively opposing it, that is, the political process is, for all practical intentions, accepted. This does raise the issue of what could be termed 'political psychology'. It has been suggested that, in some circumstances, membership in a political process is not a question of will, but a fact of life. Members born into a political community are sometimes not asked if they are happy with the order of things, rather, they are expected to accept this order and comply with it (and it is at this point that culture blends with politics). In instances where there is dissonance between the desires of the individuals and the circumstances in which they find themselves and where they have little or no control over those circumstances, there is a tendency for individuals to try to reduce that dissonance by complying with their circumstances, that is, passive acceptance of a particular political situation does not necessarily reflect acceptance, but a recognition of the futility of rejection.

Within such a discussion, the question of lawful behaviour becomes implicit. It is a normative requirement that states act within the laws they themselves have framed through their institutions. It is also a normative requirement that those institutions that have framed the law have done so in an equitable and just manner, that they are broadly socially acceptable and reflect the values of the society to which they are intended to apply (Maravall & Przeworski 2003). If the state behaves in a way that corresponds to the law, it can be said in one sense to be legitimate (Morris 1998: 103). However, if the state does not behave in a way that corresponds to its own laws or if its laws are not broadly socially acceptable or they do not reflect the values of the society to which they are intended to apply, then the state could be said to be illegitimate. It may be claimed that social acceptability of the law is not the sole criterion for the legitimacy of the state and, clearly, there are complicating factors when agents of the state act outside the law. But if the state does not generally act lawfully or if the laws it acknowledges are arbitrary or predatory, the legitimacy of the state could come under fundamental challenge from within and without.

The issue of legitimacy and the rule of law can be further complicated by what is generally referred to as 'state failure', that is, where the state or its institutions are no longer capable of functioning or of functioning across the extent of the state's territory. State failure may result from civil conflict, excessive corruption or venality or an autoreferential (default) decrease in institutional capacity. In such cases, the capacity of the state to assert or to claim authority is diminished, its legitimacy recedes relative to its authority and its capacity to assert the rule of law as a principal institution of state is similarly eroded. It should be noted here that, where the rule of law erodes, this erosion will gain momentum once it passes the point where state capacity is seen to have fundamentally broken down, thus accelerating the pace of state decline and movement towards failed state status (see Fukuyama 2004 for discussion on state failure and rebuilding).

Beyond consensual lawful behaviour lies coercion. Coercion is a product of force or power and is perhaps the primary ingredient in any political process, especially in many of those found within SEA. Coercion is closely related to the abovementioned resolution of dissonance in that it implies a lack of choice on the part of the individual. In the case of accepting an unchangeable situation, an individual does not necessarily run into conflict. Coercion implies that the individual is behaving a particular way and that some greater power enjoins them to change that behaviour against their will, usually with the explicit or implicit threat of violence. In that the individual will usually seek to avoid such violence or through the use of violence against them or others understand that future violence is best avoided, they are, in effect, complying with circumstances over which they have little or no control.

The scale between passive acceptance and coercion is often ambiguous and is frequently misrepresented. It is often difficult to determine at what point coercion is no longer being used and what the lingering effects of coercion can be on individual behaviour. In that sense, it is unclear at what stage a threat, especially an implied threat, ceases to have force. It is even more difficult, given the process of resolving individual dissonance, to determine whether even relatively happy or satisfied passive acceptance can constitute endorsement of a regime of threat. This creates problems when political leaders claim that there is no objection to their rule based on its passive acceptance by others. We cannot know, for example, whether in other circumstances there might not be a more active rejection of that rule. Nor can we know the extent to which such passive acceptance has been the product of earlier intimidation or coercion. In this sense, an apparent lack of discontent with particular political rule does not necessarily imply support for it, as has so often been claimed by SEA political leaders. Rather, it is— or should be—beholden upon political leaders who make such claims to provide evidence to support their assertions. Of course, they cannot be compelled to provide such evidence and, as a consequence, they do not.

APPROACHES TO THE PRACTICE OF POWER

The single most crucial issue in regard to the exercise of power is that of legitimacy or the right to exercise power that, within an organisational context, is translated as authority (the other manifestation of power being force). Of the various formulations of legitimacy, the great social theorist Max Weber proposed that its foundations are based on three, usually interactive, sets of criteria. Qualifying his definitions of types of legitimacy, Weber noted that it was not necessarily correct to assume that every case of submissiveness to people in positions of power was primarily—or even at all—oriented to the belief that 'appropriate attitudes' and 'corresponding practical conduct [from the power holder] will ensue'. 'Loyalty,' he said, 'may be hypocritically simulated by individuals or by whole groups on purely economic grounds, or carried out in practice for reasons of material self-interest. Or people may submit from individual weakness and helplessness because there is no acceptable alternative' (Weber 1964: 326).

This qualification of legitimacy is important as, while authority might be exercised and might be held to be legitimate as a consequence of the acquiescence of its subjects, the motivation for acquiescence may be a product of inflexible circumstances. Therefore, what passes as political legitimacy might only be through lack of free subject choice. Otherwise, legitimacy can be understood to mean the rightful or appropriate rule or exercise of power based on a principle, such as consent, which is accepted by the ruler and the ruled. Such a relationship may imply force within particular, usually prescribed, circumstances, such as the enforcement of laws.

Of Weber's three types of ideal legitimate authority, rational–legal authority is based on the acceptance of 'the "legality" of patterns of normative rules and the right of those in authority under such rules to issue commands (legal authority)'. Traditional authority is based on 'an established belief in the sanctity of tradition and the legitimacy of the status of those exercising authority'. Charismatic authority is based on 'devotion to the specific and exceptional sanctity, heroism or exemplary character of an individual person and the normative patterns or order revealed or ordained by him' (Weber 1964: 328). The distinctions noted by Weber were proposed as ideal types and were, in part, intended to highlight the differences between types of authority. In this, they tended to exaggerate or purify most circumstances, which were and remain in reality considerably more blended and affected by other considerations.

Rational–legal authority presupposes the rational and consistent nature of the legal apparatus and the subject's compliance with it. However, the legal apparatus might not be rational—it might not necessarily act consistently or may be unduly influenced by a diminution of the separation of powers (of the judiciary and government in a parliamentary model or of the judiciary, executive and legislature in a republican model). Similarly, the subject's compliance might be rational only insofar as to not comply would invite an unwelcome response.

Legal authority can be regarded as rational if and to the extent that the rules on which it is based are

> [in] pursuit of the interests which are specified in the order governing the corporate group within the limits laid down by legal precepts and following principles which are capable of generalised formulation and are approved in the order governing the group, or at least not disapproved in it.

Further, the application of such laws or rules must be applied impersonally and consistently and they must be equally obeyed impersonally rather than as an obligation of obedience to an individual (Weber 1964: 330).

POWER AND GOVERNMENT IN SOUTH-EAST ASIA

A number of governments in SEA do not, in practice, recognise a separation of powers between the state and the judiciary. Rather, they encourage the law to be applied in ways that reflect political rather than legal concerns. This might be through customary law, which incorporates cultural values not formally codified into the legal process. Where the law is codified, it may still be repressive or operate within a flexible and highly interpretable framework and be quite open to political influence. In this latter case, it is where courts return verdicts or sentences that reflect the wishes of politicians rather than reflecting the balance of evidence or the seriousness of the crime. Further, an obligation of duty is owed to the state as a manifestation of legal authority, but in practice—and in some aspects in law—an obligation of duty is also owed to political leaders or other wielders of authority. Hence, the legality of patterns of rules and the right of those elevated to authority under such rules to issue commands might apply only in a qualified sense. This situation could have been said to apply to Indonesia under Suharto, Singapore under Lee, Thailand under Sarit, Burma under Ne Win and Cambodia under Pol Pot.

In this sense, it follows Weber's view that 'traditional' authority is open to a 'sanitisation' that renders what passes as traditional not so, but rather, a politically convenient cultural reconstruction. In traditional authority, loyalty is based on allegiance to a 'personal chief' (a political patron), where 'his administrative staff does not consist primarily of officials [public servants] but of personal retainers [clients]. Further, loyalty is not to the office of the 'chief' [the presidency and so on], but to the 'person of the chief [the individual concerned]' (Weber 1964: 341).

Where tradition has been reconstructed and sanitised, what constitutes traditional limitations on chiefly behaviour is equally reconstituted, while 'the obligations of obedience on the basis of personal loyalty [that] are essentially unlimited' is enhanced. In the case of administrative staff, senior officials may be appointed on the basis of their closeness or loyalty to the chief, as a consequence of patron–client relations, or personal retainers may be appointed to official positions. David Wright-Neville might have been specifically thinking about much of SEA when he said that such sanitised tradition tends to emerge in non-reflexive societies, usually after its rigorous reinterpretation by state-reflexive bodies. These 'traditions' are then disseminated in a non-critical manner through the state apparatus, including schools and universities and via a media industry that is often dominated by and usually beholden to the government. As a consequence, there is no way of knowing whether what passed as legitimacy actually reflected the views or aspirations of ordinary people or whether it just served elite interests (Wright-Neville 1993: 21–2).

Absolute traditional authority has always been a rare occurrence and in a period of competing interests spurred on by rapid technological and economic change, such as the late twentieth and early twenty-first centuries world, it was effectively non-existent. However, when a personal administrative staff or a staff of officials owe their positions to their chief, 'especially a military force under control of the chief, traditional authority tends to develop into "patrimonialism"', in which the patron personally looks after the interests of his clients and they are personally loyal to him.

Under such patrimonialism, citizens of the state are treated as subjects. Authority of the chief, which was previously regarded as exercised on behalf of such citizens, becomes personal authority that the chief appropriates in the same way as any other possession. The chief might choose to sell it, pledge it, or divide it.

The primary means of support for such patrimonial authority is an army or paramilitary police. Through these instruments of force, the chief may broaden the range of arbitrary power that can then become free of traditional restrictions and put the chief in a position to dispense patronage at the expense of the traditional limitations typical of patriarchal and gerontocratic structures (Weber 1964: 347). This is the point where the duty of care of the state, as embodied in the leader, can shift from the benign to the malign, where the state (or its leader) breaks the notion of reciprocity as a method of legitimacy and instead rules by fiat or will, limited only by that leader's personal understanding of the limits of power and not those that are consensually shared.

Among others, Suharto, Lee, Ne Win, Marcos and Sarit come to mind when considering this broadening of arbitrary power. Further, the tendency for authoritarian leaders—in particular Suharto and Marcos, but also others such as Sarit—to engage in corrupt practices, paralleled Weber's view of authoritarian rule that was organised partly by profit-making businesses, partly by fees (or corruption) and partly by taxes. With the economy dominated or influenced by such a ruling group, its growth is usually hampered by their personal ambitions and ability to influence its direction (Weber 1964: 355).

The orientation of charismatic authority towards the individual rather than the office or preexisting forms of authority has enabled the expectation of a duty of obedience to the individual, regardless of legal or traditional proscription. To fail in this personal commitment is to be regarded as delinquent in one's duty (Weber 1964: 360). However, charismatic authority is vulnerable to misfortunes that may be beyond the leader's actual control, but that are assumed to reflect on the control vested in him through his charismatic status—that his 'gift of grace' has deserted him (Weber 1964: 360). In cases of a challenge, the victor is implicitly in 'the right' (Weber 1964: 361).

Within the traditions of a number of SEA states, power had—and still often has—a quasimetaphysical (magical or religious) quality for many people, particularly those whose formal education remains limited. In this sense, power is still sometimes understood not as a system of social, economic and political relations, but as an independent quality that reflects the purity or holiness, in a normative ethical sense, of the individual. One of the better contemporary examples of this phenomenon is Megawati Sukarnoputri, who was the leader of the Indonesian Democratic Party struggle. Megawati was a classic case of representing little in a concrete sense, but standing for the only vaguely articulated aspirations of millions of Indonesian people. Megawati was perceived to stand not for particular policies but for change, even though she was a political conservative, for an end to authoritarianism, even though she was close to the top ranks of the army, and for democracy, even though her party did not encourage or reflect local level participation. But, as a symbol, up until the time that the reality of her position overwhelmed this mythical perception of purity, for very many Indonesians she could do no wrong. In this she embodied a publicly identified sense of purity. To a far lesser, but still valid extent, Suharto was similarly seen as pure by at least some of Indonesia's population, as perhaps too were some of the political leaders of the Philippines, especially Corazon Aquino. Having such qualities, diluted, modified or cynically reconstructed though they may have been in the contemporary context, leaders are perceived as representing not just the office, but also themselves, as leader. Many SEA political systems thus reflect a mix of forms of authority, as defined by Weber, with a notable continuation of charismatic and traditional models.

THE SUBTLETY OF POWER

While Weber's analysis of power can be seen, in broad terms, to apply to issues of power and authority in South-East Asia, it does not take into account the range of subtleties through which power can be manifested and how these can shape peoples' lives, values and actions. Professor Steven Lukes discussed the range of influences of power by proposing that power be defined as 'dimensional' (Lukes 1974). The first dimension of power, as discussed by Dahl (1971), focuses on behaviour in making decisions on issues over which there is an observable conflict of interests. This may be expressed as policy preferences and demonstrated through political participation (Lukes 1974: 15).

What Lukes called a 'two-dimensional' view of power, which was elaborated on by Bachrach and Baratz (1962: 947–52), incorporated not just active or overt uses of power, but also passive or covert uses of power. This could be said to parallel Weber's capacity for the exercise of power, in which a person or group creates or reinforces barriers to the public discussion of conflict, such as through media control, limits to free speech or other more subtle forms of control of communication (see Berman 1998, for discussion of this last point in relation to Java). This places much greater emphasis on exclusion or what Lukes calls 'non-decision making' (Lukes 1974: 18), that is, power is not just about acknowledging certain subjects being legitimate for discussion, but about the delegitimisation of certain subjects for discussion, for example, the political role of the armed forces or the removal of certain subjects from the public agenda, for example, the legitimacy of the king. This developed behaviouralist perspective is sometimes referred to as 'culturalism' (see, for example, Pye 1985[1]) or 'institutionalism' (see, for example, Liddle 1996), or 'political order' (Robison, in Higgott & Robison 1985: 295–6).

Lukes saw this type of analysis of power as still relying too heavily on observable conflict. This follows Weber, who stressed that power was the realisation of one's will, despite the resistance of others. Yet power may be exercised by shaping the thoughts and desires of another, to have them act in a required manner that may not be in their interests. Such thought control may take more mundane forms than Huxley's *Brave New World*, such as 'through the control of information, through the mass media and through the processes of socialisation' (Lukes 1974: 24).

Lukes suggested that, because grievances about a power structure may not be aired or be able to be uncovered, does not necessarily imply that the grievances do not exist. If a person or group does not have access to sets of ideas that inform them they may have a grievance, they continue to experience 'an undirected complaint arising out of everyday experience, a vague feeling of unease or sense of deprivation'. Further, power may be exercised by shaping understanding in such a way as to legitimise respective roles in the existing order of things, a legitimisation that comes about because individuals cannot see or imagine an alternative, because it is seen as natural and unchangeable or because it is valued as 'divinely ordained and beneficial'. The absence of grievance does not necessarily equal genuine consensus, as it deletes the possibility of false or manipulated consensus by 'definitional fiat'[2] (Lukes 1974: 24). Lukes' definition of power, then, closely accords with the concept of hegemony, as articulated by Antonio Gramsci. Hegemony in this sense implies the establishment and maintenance not only of political and economic control, but also of agreement by a subordinate social group or class with a dominant group or class that a prevailing state of affairs is desirable (Gramsci 1971: xii–xiv). Applied to SEA governments, it could be seen that what are regarded as social and political norms and the processes by which they are maintained, operate at conscious and unconscious levels. Further, they are reinforced overtly and covertly by existing power structures, which tends to act primarily in the interests of the power brokers who exercise them. Some governments can, therefore, be seen to act primarily in their own interests, that of their close associates and of the elite in general.

MARXIST AND RELATED APPROACHES

Lukes was also critical of the focus on a methodology in which power is about individuals realising their wills (Lukes 1974: 21). He argued that the power to control the political agenda and exclude potential issues could not be adequately analysed unless it is seen as a function of collective forces and social arrangements. This then leads to a more broadly Marxist or political-economy approach, such as that taken by Richard Robison. Robison summarised it as an 'analysis of the development of capitalist relations of production and the development of a class of capital accumulators'. He said that the state, in this case Indonesia, is crucial because of its strategic role in the process of capital accumulation and, consequently, class formation and conflict (Robison 1985: 298). This role of the state in capital accumulation has indeed been critical in many SEA states, where classes, in the conventional industrial sense, have begun to emerge. However, their emergence has been fitful and weak and class conflict in the traditional Marxist sense has been less important than other forms of communal rivalry, in which challenges for ownership of farming land and religious affiliation have been critical. In the case of capital accumulation, in some instances this has occurred not through conventional capitalist practices, but through economic systems that rely on patronage, corruption and cronyism.

In his 1985 analysis, Robison posited the other main analytical grouping as the 'dependency approach', which agrees with the idea that classes, in the conventional sense, 'were too weakly developed to constitute the basis of politics'. Instead, it was proposed that networks of patrons and clients provided a more substantial basis for political organisation (Robison, paraphrasing Mortimer, 1971: 298). While this was intended to apply to Indonesia under Suharto, the relationship between SEA governments and foreign capital is more complex than just the outflow of surplus implied by dependency analysis. A considerable surplus also accumulated to indigenous (comprador and nationalist) elites and there has been a considerable economic strengthening of the state and its infrastructure. Further, broad living standards have, in most cases, improved rather than declined, even if, in some cases, this has been marginal and even if longer-term trends have been reversed (seemingly temporarily).

ASIAN VALUES

Any discussion of political legitimacy in SEA must at least acknowledge the claim made by some of the region's political leaders to what has been called 'Asian values'. These Asian values are intended to cover a broad range of social relations, but have a particular application to politics as a consequence of their emphasis on hierarchy, order and obedience. Notable proponents of Asian values, or the cultural specificity of an Asian approach to politics, have included Singapore Prime Minister Lee Kuan Yew, Malaysia's Mahathir Mohamad, Indonesia's Suharto and, as Research and Technology Minister, later president, Habibie, Brunei's Sultan Hassanal Bolkiah and Burma's various political leaders. Interestingly, the leaders of Laos, Cambodia and Vietnam have usually appealed to either ideological dogma or the exigencies of running a state, while the political leadership of Thailand and the Philippines has rarely, in recent times, made such appeals the basis for their legitimacy. This, then, begs the question: What are Asian values?

In one sense, the whole notion of Asian values is nonsensical, if for no other reason than it implies a commonly held set of principles that apply across the region known as Asia. Yet the idea of Asia is itself problematic, being a European construction developed at a time when the unity of Otherness was defined by its geographical location, that of east of Europe. If Afghanistan is taken as the beginning of Asia, one would be hard pressed to find some cultural affinity between it and, say, Japan. Meanwhile, many Indians identify themselves as quite Asian, but at the same time as quite distinct from their Chinese counterparts.

If the definition is further narrowed to East Asia, there are distinct differences between societies as diverse as Japan and the Philippines, China and Indonesia, Korea and Laos and Taiwan and Brunei. Narrowing further to South-East Asia there are increasing areas of overlap between each of the states of the region, but there remain distinct areas of difference. The Thai and Lao, for example, can claim some broad cultural affinity although, beyond religion, the Bhamese of Burma and the Cambodians would have difficulty in making a similar claim. Vietnam, by comparison, is set aside, at once very much reflecting long-standing Chinese influence as well as the Vietnamese's own well-developed sense of cultural identity. In the archipelagic region, there is some commonality and mixing between the Proto and Deutero Malays,[3] as well as literally hundreds of linguistic and cultural groups. But, with the exception of some parts of Sumatra and the Malay Peninsula, it would be difficult to establish any significant claim to cultural commonality. This, of course, defines culture as belonging to states, which are administrative regions, rather than nations, which are social collectives. Yet among the states of the region are numerous national or ethnic distinctions: more than 300 in Indonesia, more than a dozen in Malaysia, almost seventy in Laos and more than fifty in Vietnam, with many more in Thailand, dozens in the Philippines, Burma, Cambodia and even in Brunei. Within these groups, perhaps only a small minority is numerically significant, but claims to cultural homogeneity in SEA exist only on very poorly supported evidence (Vervoorn 1998: ch. 4). Beyond ethnic distinction are others, such as status and class, which create further levels of identity and the value systems that inform such identity. In these myriad particularisms, some overarching Asian value system starts to look very poorly grounded.

The claim to Asian values, then, reflects less a common cultural framework of the people it is suggested to represent and more the values of a particular group of people who make such claims.[4] This is not to suggest that there is not some authentic cultural commonality between these political elites, rather, it is to suggest that the claim to cultural commonality is misidentified, probably quite intentionally, for overt political reasons. More accurately, if the political leaders of SEA and their supporters require a particular value system, they might be better and more accurately served by considering one of the political universal theorists, such as Machiavelli.[5]

Considering who has been making such claims, the one characteristic they have in common is their political leadership, usually acquired or maintained through means that are neither openly participatory nor genuinely representative. Singapore opposition leader Chee Soon Juan made this point and stated that many people in Asia do not subscribe to the Asian values idea (Chee 1998). Beyond this core group, there are its supporters, beneficiaries, hangers-on and a grab-bag of pro-authority sycophants. The intellectual coherence of an idea does not have to be particularly strong in order for it to exercise a powerful grip over the imaginations of some. Rather, it can achieve allegiance through its promise of stability and, supposedly as a consequence, security. However, as has been demonstrated in Burma, Cambodia and Indonesia (and elsewhere if one cares to look closely enough), authoritarian stability has been brittle and usually comes at a high, repressive price. If, then, we are to look for some cultural commonality in the claim to Asian values, it is connected to the attainment, maintenance and exercise of political power.

The models of government of modern Asia—or at least East Asia—have been identified by some commentators as having a common thread running through them, in part reflecting the economic development of many East Asian countries, but more reflecting a tendency towards authoritarian forms. This common thread has been identified by Segal (1990: 117–24), among others, as deriving from the (reconstructed) Confucian principle of respect for authority and a strong central government. Thus, the authoritarian tendencies of many East Asian governments have been claimed by some observers to be able to be explained by appealing to the ethical precepts of the dominant country of the region, China.

What is referred to as Confucianism is, indeed, an important cultural factor in a number of East Asian states, including Vietnam, North and South Korea and, of course, China. As a predominantly ethnic Chinese city state, it could also be said to apply to Singapore. However, any claim to Confucian political values having a more widespread application confronts the reality that a number of states in the region find their ethical inspiration elsewhere. Indeed, Confucius' *Analects* have been argued to not support the claims made for it by apologists for contemporary authoritarian governments (Leys 1997). Moreover, Confucius himself[6] formulated the *Analects* in response to the political turmoil of the Chou Dynasty in the period in which he lived (circa 551–479 BCE). Within the *Analects* can be found a prevailing humanist theme (Ping-chia 1965: 19–23; Schurmann & Schell 1977: 10–11, 48), which was noted by scholars of Enlightenment Europe, including Voltaire (1979: 78–95). Confucius has been regarded as a social reformer (as evidenced in his *Analects* 1995: iii) and in favour of dissent (Leys 1997), rather than as a supporter of an authoritarian status quo.

If Confucianism has been seen as endorsing authoritarianism, it is because, as a highly interpretable text, it was bent to the requirements of

China's absolutist monarchies (which, in a benevolent, enlightened form, it endorsed), in particular from the period of the Sung Dynasty (960–1279 BCE). It was from this time that Confucianism was reconstructed in neo-Confucian form in which 'conservative and nationalistic, it imposed narrow shackles on men's minds down to the nineteenth century' (Ping-chia 1965: 45). But even here there is confusion. The early Vietnamese nationalists wished to dispose of Confucianism, as identified by the traditional scholar class (Steinberg 1971: 305), while one of their leaders, Phan Boi Chau, was 'himself a Confucian revolutionary, more at home with Mencius than with Montesquieu', admiring the 'unhurried mythological "democracy" of Chinese sage-emperors, who acknowledged that their throne belonged to the people, not to themselves'. Chau's objection was to an 'ossified' Confucianism (Steinberg 1971: 306).

More appropriately, what should be considered in Asia's contemporary political philosophy is not some overarching Confucian contribution to its practice, but the degree to which political systems derive their style from conventional forms of authoritarianism, the basis of that authoritarianism, the degree to which traditional authoritarian models have been reinvented, and the extent to which current authoritarian models reflect recent or contemporary circumstances and sectional interests. Examples of all of these factors can be discerned in Brunei and Burma, in the late Sukarno and late Suharto periods of government in Indonesia and, to a lesser extent, in a number of other governments, including Cambodia under Prince Norodom Sihanouk, in postunification Vietnam, in Singapore and in Thailand. If traditional political models, or a re-invention and reconfiguration of such models, informs at least some of contemporary Asian political behaviour, so too has Western political thinking. Western ideologies have come to the states of SEA either through the free will of an influential national (or nationalist) group—sometimes a majority, sometimes not—or have been left behind as a legacy of colonial intervention.

THE EFFECTS OF COLONIAL LEGACY ON FORMS OF GOVERNMENT

In the case of colonial intervention, it has been suggested that, of the colonial powers, the United Kingdom tended to impart its political traditions but not its culture, while France and, to a lesser extent, the Netherlands imparted their culture, but not their political traditions (Scalapino 1989: 29–32). In the case of the free will of an influential national group, probably the most important institution that reflected British culture was, and is, its parliament. The history of British parliamentarianism dates to the thirteenth century[7] (Pirenne 1939: 421), while the ideas that inspired it are considerably older. Perhaps the major distinction between the colonial powers was that the United Kingdom occupied its colonies and protectorates in a way that preserved significant aspects of traditional political society, while France, in conjunction with compliant traditional rulers, tended to impose its own administrative structures on colonial populations. Technically, only Cochin China was directly administered, although all of Indochina was, in practical terms, directly ruled by France (Jumper & Normand 1969: 384).

Following the turmoil of WWII, France returned to Indochina to reassert its colonial authority, to restore its economic interests and, when conflict arose, to suppress linked nationalist and communist aspirations. The policy it adopted in the immediate postwar years differed little from that it had pursued as an imperial power. The Netherlands was also loath to release what was to become Indonesia as, 'Economically, the Netherlands was more dependent on its colony than any other Western colonial power in Asia' (Feith 1969: 193).

The United Kingdom gave up its colonial possessions in SEA in the postwar period in a somewhat more equitable manner. Weakened by WWI and then by WWII, the United Kingdom regarded the cutting of such colonial ties as inevitable and, in most cases, desirable. In Burma it chose to acknowledge rather than fight the Burma Independence Army, while in Malaya it supported political moderates, but launched a police action against communist guerrillas. By generally acceding to more moderate demands for independence, the United Kingdom was able to leave behind a number of institutional structures, including a political system and a more or less workable bureaucracy. Yet the political model system bequeathed by the United Kingdom did not survive unscathed.

It has been suggested that, as a non-indigenous political model, parliamentary democracy has been modified in line with local circumstances where it has been adopted in SEA, in particular reflecting the considerable authority and legitimacy that the first postcolonial governments derived from helping found the new state. While parliamentary politics has been more stable in Malaysia and Singapore, it has been so at the expense of its democratic component. Both states have had one governing party since independence. The Malaysian United Malay National Organisation has retained power through a coalition arrangement based on the country's three main, broad ethnic groups: Malays, Chinese and Indians. This domination of Malaysian politics by one party has resulted in an autocratic style of government with distinctly authoritarian overtones, including hobbling the judiciary and restrictions on freedom of expression. In Singapore, the dominant People's Action Party has subverted the political system by making it very difficult to stand against the government or, more importantly, to criticise it. An authoritarian state, Singapore retains the shell of parliamentarianism without the substance.

The parliamentary system can also be seen at work in Thailand, which has proven increasingly resilient, despite numerous coups, attempted coups and threatened coups. The pivotal aspect of Thai politics is, again, the legitimacy or otherwise lent to governments by the Thai king, who retains the position of head of state. Brunei retains a sultanate in which the king is not elected and appoints his own, non-elected cabinet, perhaps being able to do so because of the oil-based prosperity of the tiny nation's people and at least in part because of successful countermeasures against democratic reformers in the 1960s.

As a republic, the Philippines has a system similar to that of parliamentary democracy, though the president is elected separately from ordinary representatives and the executive is separate to the legislature. This model was derived from the USA, but was underscored by a landed economic elite derived from the nation's Spanish colonial past. This has led to disaffection culminating in rebellion and, from 1972 until 1986, the suspension of democratic participation under martial law. In the late 1980s there was a series of attempted coups against the government, but the government and the country's political processes survived intact.

As a consequence, at least in part, of the role of the military in independence movements, the armed forces have continued to play a dominant role in the affairs of Burma and Indonesia and, for different reasons, in Thailand, the Philippines, Laos and Vietnam. In the case of Burma, its early attempts at parliamentary rule were destabilised by the significant role of the army in political affairs and the separatist ambitions of its ethnic minorities. Conflict between ethnic minorities and the state in the late 1950s and again from the early 1960s onwards provided an opportunity for the army to be granted, and soon after to assume power, which it retains into the twenty-first century.

Although increasingly wearing a more civilian face, Indonesia, from 1958, was run with the backing of the army, its electoral process only superficially satisfying the form and certainly not the function of democracy. Indonesia initially adopted a parliamentary democratic system in which political, religious, geographic and ethnic distinctions were balanced. However, largely because of the pressing of claims by the central, Jakarta-based government, this mixture proved to be unstable and was eventually abandoned for Guided Democracy, introduced in the period from 1957–59. Under this strongly presidential system, Indonesian politics polarised into a split between the Indonesian Communist Party and the armed forces, resulting in a showdown in late 1965 and, as anti-communist purges, into 1966 and beyond.

The New Order government that developed in Indonesia between 1966 and 1999 was underpinned by the armed forces and, until 1999, allowed extremely limited political activity. Reflecting the rise of wealthy and/or militarily powerful individuals within a context dominated by Suharto, a political system in which patron–client relations are fundamental has been allowed or encouraged to develop.

France and the Netherlands, while perhaps even more weakened by the two world wars than was the United Kingdom, were reluctant to let go of their colonial possessions, in part for economic reasons, in part for reasons of national prestige. As a consequence, with the exception of Cambodia, the peoples of these colonies were obliged to fight for their independence and, as a result, neither inherited, nor generally desired, the political institutions of their former colonial masters.

In the case of Vietnam, Marxism–Leninism—generically referred to as communism—was not just a guiding ideology, but was also explicitly anti-colonialist and in favour of economic redistribution. Initially allied with other nationalist forces under the name of Viet Minh, the Leninist element of the ideology was a particularly useful organisational tool for a nationalist struggle (Salisbury 1971: xi; Steinberg 1971: 308). Indeed, the early nationalist movement, from 1927 the Viet Nam Quoc Dan Dang (VNQDD), which was closely modelled on the Chinese nationalist Guomindang, adopted a version of Leninist organisational structure, as did the non-communist, later anti-communist, Guomindang itself, while the socialist principles of economic redistribution and collective action were also popular with early Vietnamese nationalists, although the VNQDD neglected the issue of land redistribution. In large part, the VNQDD failed as a consequence of French repression in 1929 and an abortive uprising in 1930, in which it was effectively broken as a viable organisation. This left Vietnam's political stage to the communists, although they too were repressed in 1931. Drawing on a small proletarian base, the Vietnamese communists expanded their appeal in the late 1930s by claiming that 'poor people are proletarians' (Steinberg 1971: 312), thereby adopting the tactics of China's communists in bringing rural peasants to the revolutionary movement.

The Marxian element of the politically successful Vietnamese ideology also appealed to notions of revolutionary liberation. The war against France had, up to 1954, brutalised and hence radicalised many Vietnamese and, from the later 1950s until 1975, the war against the USA supported by the Republic of Vietnam in the south, further radicalised much of the population. Issues that pushed much of the population into supporting the communists included the corrupt and inefficient government in Saigon, the brutality of the Army of the Republic of Vietnam and its military allies, indiscriminate bombing campaigns, forced relocation and the widespread understanding that the war was not just—or even primarily—pro or anti-communist, but a continuation of the war of liberation against foreign powers. Marxism–Leninism might not have been universally endorsed, but various of its elements were popular and it was in so dominant a political position that, even from the early 1950s, there was little doubt that Vietnam, once independent, would become a communist state.

Similarly in Cambodia, granted independence in 1953, the quietly pro-Chinese and pro-North Vietnamese so-called neutralist policies of Prince

Norodom Sihanouk eventually brought down American wrath in the form of intensive, socially dislocating bombing. These bombings were directed against North Vietnamese military bases inside Cambodian territory and against the north to south supply routes, which entered Cambodian territory from the north. Unwilling to tolerate Sihanouk's unsupportive position on the conflict in Vietnam, the USA endorsed his overthrow in March 1970, having him replaced by the pro-USA Lon Nol. Already on the offensive, the Cambodian communists, the peasant-based Khmer Rouge, toppled Lon Nol in 1975 (Sagar 1991: 93–6).

The Khmer Rouge adopted a version of the then Chinese, peasant-based interpretation of communism and, supported by a largely illiterate peasant army, was unable to administer an urban-centred state. The Khmer Rouge policy of emptying the cities and establishing a rural society, complete with murderous prejudices against perceived urban elites, initiated a period of terror, famine and increasing paranoia. That paranoia spilled over into wrath against erstwhile military allies, Cambodia's historical enemies, the Vietnamese. In response to Khmer Rouge border attacks and a policy of violent discrimination against ethnic Vietnamese in Cambodia, Vietnam invaded Cambodia in late 1978, installing a puppet government under the leadership of Heng Samrin (Sagar 1991: 132–41). This event and the subsequent Chinese attack on Vietnam, indicated that historical animosities and competition for regional hegemony could be, and in this case were, more powerful political factors than strategic or ideological considerations.

With the communist victories in Vietnam and Cambodia in 1975, the intrigues of American-influenced Laotian politics, in which Right, neutral and Left factions had juggled for power since 1954, was also tipped in favour of the peasant-based communist Pathet Lao. The pro-Vietnamese Pathet Lao added another aspect to the regional political matrix, which had permutations for Laotian support of a pro-Chinese communist insurgency in northeast Thailand, although support was withdrawn and that wing of the Thai insurgency collapsed.

In each case, the states of SEA have drawn on a colonial legacy, the examples provided by the colonial powers, such as industrialisation, or other Western conceptions, such as parliamentary or republican democracy, or Marxism, for their models of legitimacy. In some cases these legacies have been retained in form but not in content, such as Malaysia and Singapore; in some cases they have been entirely abandoned, such as in Burma and, until 1999, in Indonesia. Indonesia subscribes to the republican model, although modifying it in ways that have suited particular interests portrayed by Javanese conceptions of authority and legitimacy. The Burmese state, though, only matches contemporary conceptions of legitimacy in that it retains some of the institutions of state that ordinarily imply a functioning government, such as a bureaucracy and a nominal legal system. The Burmese government itself could not be said to be legitimate in any meaningful sense of the term, nor does it generally correspond to ideas of government in a modern sense, even though it claims it does.

THE RULE OF LAW

Issues of legitimacy revolve mainly around maintaining socially desired codes of behaviour, usually understood as the application of the rule of law. Insofar as a degree of certainty about rules and responses is a requirement for legitimacy, consistency in the application of the rule of law is a key criterion for legitimacy (Morris 1998: 24, 105–11; Rawls 1991: 7). In each case, the political systems and processes adopted by the states of SEA reflected not just a range of styles and types, but indicated that, even within the respective categories, there was considerable scope for interpretation and reformulation to suit the needs and interests of prevailing political groups or organisations. In this respect, the frequent failure of the separation of powers between the executive and the judiciary did not just allow laws to be interpreted inconsistently, but allowed for the development of tyranny (see Morris 1998: 287), that is, the application of the rule of law was not applied consistently in practice and, in some cases, was not intended to be applied consistently even in principle. This has, then, begged the legitimacy of some governments or, indeed, some states.

In this sense, what is perhaps important is less the particular political model used by a contemporary state, but more whether it accurately reflects the freely expressed needs and desires of its citizens. To that end, theoretically, pluralist liberal democracy might not be regarded as an appropriate political model, while paternalistic authoritarianism or Marxist–Leninist centralism might, if expressed as the genuine wishes of its constituency. Alternatively, paternalistic authoritarianism or Marxist–Leninist centralism might not be regarded as necessary or desirable by the citizens of a given state, but because these political systems do not allow open expressions of meaningful dissent, it is difficult to know. Further, with the shift towards market economies in all previously Marxist–Leninist states, such as Vietnam, Laos and the now officially multiparty Cambodia, and the central control exercised over the economies of many effectively single-party, supposedly free capitalist states, such as Singapore, Malaysia and, until 1999, Indonesia, such definitions and the preconceptions they bring with them are becoming increasingly redundant. Where major problems with legitimacy of the state have arisen, it has often been reflected by the state taking on a life of its own, manifested as state interest, as separate from or above those citizens it represents.

Yet the state as the state cannot claim to have a legitimate interest in the preservation of particular laws. Laws that do exist owe their legitimacy to popular support, so it would, in principle, be analogous that those laws are not or should not be immune from popular rejection or change (Schauer 1982: 190).

The problem is that this applies in practice only if the government derives its legitimacy from free support. Implicit in the notion that law is not beyond popular change is the idea that government legitimately represents the interests of its people and that, among those interests, there is free expression in favour of such representation, which normatively finds its home in the state. Notions of justice, on the other hand, are not predicated on the legitimacy or otherwise of governments, but find their home in conceptions of natural rights.

To that end, the question of contemporary politics in Asia resides less with what label a political system has or is given and more with whether it is a participatory and hence representative state or whether it is an authoritarian and hence coercive state.

OPPOSITIONS

Political oppositions exist in SEA across the full spectrum of dissent from government. At one end, for example in the Philippines and Thailand, the opposition is formalised within the political process and is considered loyal. In some countries, at some times, the opposition has been fundamentally opposed to the existence of the government and, indeed, sometimes even the principles by which the state is constructed. These oppositions fall into two categories: those who wish to overthrow the state and rebuild its structure, for example, the New People's Army of the Philippines, the pre-1975 Lao People's Revolutionary Party and Cambodia's Khmer Rouge. Then, there are those who wish to secede from the state, for example, some ethnic states of Burma and some provinces of Indonesia, the southern Philippines and southern Thailand. In between, oppositions can and have existed within government factions, in extragovernmental state apparatuses, such as the armed forces, through trade unions, non-government organisations, religious groups and others.

Western assessments of political development in SEA usually derive from the normative premise of liberal democracy, although very few states in the region could be said to embrace a liberal democratic model. Indeed, the tendency has been to contest such a model. Malaysia and Singapore, for example, have become less rather than more democratic, although Indonesia was, from 2004, establishing more democratic credentials, in particular in relation to its direct elections for the presidency. Thailand and the Philippines were largely democratic at the time of writing, although Brunei, Burma, Laos and Vietnam were not, while Cambodia was only marginally so. Also important is the fact that very few of the oppositions that existed in the region embraced liberal democracy. Most were interested in re-ordering power structures or in creating political space within which they could exercise a greater degree of self-determination, but these aspirations were not always synonymous with participatory representative government.

In this sense, the Western notion of state-based democracy, perhaps only a passing historical moment in the West itself, has rarely been translated in SEA with much success. Indeed, there has been considerable debate, not from the political elites but from ordinary people about what democracy actually means within local contexts. Yet many people, in countries as diverse as Thailand, Cambodia, East Timor, Burma, the Philippines and Indonesia, have been enthusiastic about the voting process, for example, and have expressed a desire for politicians who are answerable to them.

CONSENSUS

One idea that did have some currency throughout SEA, especially among elites and mostly for its ability to avoid open conflict, was that of consensus. Consensus politics is essentially about reducing the greatest objections to arrive at a workable formula. The source of the consensus model in SEA is generally held to be the village or small social grouping, in which face-to-face contact is a regular occurrence and in which the maintenance of harmonious social relations is important. To this end, when a matter affecting the broader community was to be decided, it was not so much done by a majority who had the potential to seriously disadvantage the minority, but by reducing the objections of the minority to make the outcome more broadly acceptable. This, then, helped ensure social cohesion and mutual cooperation.

As a political system, however, consensus is taken out of its original context and is often decided by elites, who might not be representative of larger groups of people. While consensus in this circumstance retains its quality of removing major objections and making outcomes more broadly acceptable, it also has the distinct problem of not being directly answerable to individual voters, relying rather on the goodwill or good judgment of elites. It also tends to be favoured by such elites for its ability to ensure continuing elite control of political processes. A consensus candidate for the presidency, for example, would ultimately not be beholden to any group, but more amorphously to the nation, thereby opening up the possibility of the abuse of power and of corruption, both of which are common enough. Established in power, a consensus politician could then build a coterie of sycophants to ensure that consensus remained with them. This was most clearly seen during Suharto's tenure in office in Indonesia, but could also be applicable to Lee in Singapore and Mahathir in Malaysia.

RIGHTS AS CULTURALLY RELATIVE

Before proceeding with this discussion, the question of what constitutes a human right needs to be established. A human right, according to Ralph Pettman, 'is a general moral claim. It is the assertion of a just entitlement pertaining anywhere, any time … to the enjoyment of certain goods or the satisfaction of particular interests deemed fundamental in some way' (Pettman 1979: 76). As a general moral claim, the rights pertaining to being human are not contingent upon their cultural or political location. However, that human rights constitute a moral claim does represent a value judgment and, as such, necessarily reflects specifically located values. The question is: At what point can morality claim to have stepped beyond the particular into the universal? Pettman argues that there is a universal foundation to human rights, not only based on common humanity but also, as stated by UNESCO, 'globally shared norms' agreed to by 'transcultural consensus', including

> social solidarity, the sense of self, the value of life and the duty to protect the lost, sick and weak, the idea of the legitimacy of power and a duty to rebel when power's legitimacy is lost, the limitations to be placed upon the arbitrary exercise of power, the idea of juridical impartiality, the civil freedom to travel and to work elsewhere, the freedom to think and publicly criticise, tolerance of social rights, including to strike, work and so on, securing freedom by securing material wellbeing, the right to knowledge and learning, the right of a people to their identity and the universality of human enterprise or endeavour (UNESCO 1979: 80).

At various times and by various people, in particular by former Singapore's prime minister, Lee Kwan Yew, it has been widely claimed throughout SEA that the whole idea of human rights is ethnocentric, being as it is based on European values (and specific ones at that) and not reflecting South East Asia's own values and rich traditions. In one respect, this generalised assertion is correct. Notions of human rights, particularly civil and political rights, do derive from European tradition generally and the Enlightenment in particular. However, as has been equally widely pointed out, although notions of human rights can be traced back to ancient Greek and early Christian tradition, there are parallels in other traditions. Basic human needs such as freedom and dignity are implicit in some of the earliest written and oral codes. Hindu and Buddhist texts focus on the human condition, while notions of human virtue and compassion characterise early Confucianism, a quality neglected by Lee's claims to Confucianism as a basis for Asian values. Many local traditions throughout SEA include sanctions on the exercise of power, the reciprocal nature of political relations and often high degrees of local autonomy.

To illustrate how these more local traditions reflect similar sentiments towards issues of human rights, Burmese political leader Aung San Suu Kyi has drawn on the Theravada Buddhist tradition as a basis for a tolerant and lawful society, in her opposition to the military government, which itself draws on an equally strong martial tradition. Vietnamese monks have drawn on a similar, Mahayana Buddhist tradition, opposing both the authoritarianism of the government of the former Republic of South Vietnam as well as that of the later Socialist Republic of United Vietnam.

Indonesian Islamic intellectual Nurcholish Majid has argued for tolerance and mutual support based on Islamic principles, as did Indonesia's President Abdurrahman Wahid when he was leader of the Nahdlatul Ulama, before his rise to political power. Throughout the region, among ordinary people and many of their leaders, there is a recognition that some principles will always hold and that some common standards of behaviour are universally valid and applicable on the basis of common humanity and international law, not their ethnic specificity and local law. Further, governments that have argued against a universal concept of human rights, including those that have signed the relevant UN covenants, have invariably done so because it suits their immediate political interests.

Apart from culturally relativised reasons for rejecting the universality of notions of human rights, the Marxist–Leninist approach to the role of the individual in the state, based on that of Hegel and its cooption by quasi-Marxist states, such as Vietnam and Laos, is that notions of human rights are a liberal subterfuge. The general Marxist critique is that human rights are ineffective because a capitalist world order requires human rights abuses as a method of enforcing hegemony within a potentially dissenting framework. Such rights are held, in this argument, to be only genuinely possible within complete economic, political, social and cultural emancipation (Campbell 1983: 7). Perhaps there is some ground for this argument, but it does represent a utopian condition for the enjoyment of more prosaic human rights and, as such, tended to disqualify them from serious consideration.

A somewhat different critique of human rights derives from the organicist or protofascist model of the state, in which the citizen is regarded as an integral part of the state and without an independent political existence. This was the model first conceived of in the foundation of Indonesia and, in a practical sense, informs states such as Burma and, to some extent, Vietnam. To illustrate this position, the chief framer of Indonesia's 1945 constitution, Supomo, argued against a formal acknowledgment of human rights, saying, 'There is no need to guarantee the fundamental rights and liberties of the individual against the state, because the individual is an organic part of the state, with his own position and an obligation to help realise the state's greatness …' (Supomo, in Feith & Castles 1970: 191). In drafting the 1945 constitution, Supomo had himself 'envisaged a compromise between basic human rights and the right of the government to suppress them when necessary' (Vatikiotis 1993: 114).

This view of human rights was not, of course, monolithic. Anwar Nasution asserted that the relativisation of human rights via cultural difference

confuses what is, or what happens, with what is right. This kind of argument ignores the fact that in the struggle for Indonesian independence (since the beginning of the twentieth century and during the national revolution from 1945–49) as well as in the post independence period to the present, democratic tendencies have always existed alongside authoritarian ways of thinking (Nasution 1993).

It should be noted that within the assertion of Asian values, it has been said that there is a greater focus on the collective than the individual, that there is no tradition of explicit rights and that there is a social requirement for group members not to express dissenting opinions. This issue of cultural authenticity, then, raises concerns not so much about a broad notion of rights, but about what rights retain validity and how they might work vis-à-vis social obligations. All societies impose some sort of requirement upon their members to conform to social codes; the question of rights, in all cases, exists within this context.

This raises a number of subsequent issues, the first of which begs the question of whether cultures and hence the values they express are static or dynamic. The various cultures of SEA have been remarkably dynamic over the nineteenth, twentieth and the twenty-first centuries, no more so than in the last decades of the twentieth and the first years of the twenty-first. There is, then, a political tension between change and tradition, or between varying interpretations of tradition. However, change is not always easily or comfortably accepted, especially when it upsets established norms of behaviour, or contravenes established political practices. In this there is legitimacy in asking whether particular rights retain applicability and, if so, in what ways they could be accommodated to local conditions or sets of values. Alternatively, if such rights are claimed to be not applicable, there needs to be a fairly closely scrutinised case for such rejection, in particular for the participatory nature of that rejection.

Related to this issue is the source of such values that may impose them as a consequence of an unequal power structure. They may or may not be accepted or internalised, but it cannot be claimed that such values are natural or immutable. A further issue, noted elsewhere, is the status of the state in SEA and the legitimacy that it claims or is accorded as the manifestation of the will of its citizens. Assuming the legitimacy of the structure of the nation state, especially as currently conceived, the states of SEA have adopted a form of political organisation derived from the West in which there are certain organisational and structural arrangements. One of these is the identification of citizenship, which implies certain basic rights thereof, one of which is the right of dissent, including from culturalist interpretations of rights.

The question of human rights, including social and political rights, economic rights (see UNHCHR 1999) and so on, is therefore a site of significant political contest. There may be no absolute answer to this debate—although its protagonists usually argue strongly that there is—but it is very much at the core of social content or, more often, discontent and how that manifests itself in power relations within states.

AUTHORITY AND LEGITIMACY REVISITED

In some traditional political forms, to hold power, such as military power, was synonymous with holding political power and to hold political power was synonymous with legitimacy. To draw on the traditional Javanese model (which found parallels elsewhere), power included conventional notions of political power, legitimacy and charisma; it either existed or it did not and questions of legitimacy were not a part of the equation. At various times in the post-WWII period throughout SEA, political leaders have exercised a very similar style of political power, neither relying on public consent nor allowing their right to rule to be called into question. Political power has been concentrated largely, if not exclusively, in the hands of assertive individuals who have sometimes ruled almost as autocratically as their precolonial and colonial forebears.

This is not to suggest that the governments or political leaders of SEA are re-inventions of the past, even though in many instances they have clothed their rule in tradition or tradition modified to suit modern conditions. And it is further not to suggest that issues of legitimacy and the use of authority are not more open to question, in most cases, than they have ever been. In part, this has been a consequence of the globalisation of ideas, in particular normative ideas about political behaviour.

But in the symbols of state power, in the rationalisations for political styles and methods, in the patrimonial forms many political leaders employ and in their often repressive apparatus, authority is actively wielded. The question of legitimacy, on the other hand, often finds itself floating on a sea of hegemony and formal opposition to the articulation of alternative aspirations.

NOTES

1   It has been suggested by some that my views on the connection between culture and politics puts me in a similar position to Pye (1985). Our positions are, in fact, quite different. Pye tends to use culture as the explanation for political forms, while I see those aspects of culture reflecting authority and status as essentially political in the first place and often reinvented for the purposes of the maintenance of power.

2   Lukes' analysis was challenged by Clegg, who argued that it was surpassed, particularly by approaches under the general rubric 'post-structuralism' (Clegg 1989: 147, 150). However, Lukes' broadening of the power framework to incorporate the subtleties as well as the bluntness of power indicates a tolerance for ambiguity (a central post-structural theme) in the diffusion of power.

3   Proto-Malays are those first wave Malays, who may be distinguished from later, or second wave, Deutero-Malays by language, social organisation (including shifting rather than wet-rice agriculture) and other aspects of culture. The former tend to live in highland regions or in the more remote parts of the east, the latter in lowland or valley areas and predominantly in the west (see Fisher 1968: ch. 8).

4   To illustrate this point, while I believe that Pye (1985) overstates specific cultural inputs into political processes, he does identify the respective cultures of the region and their impact on politics as quite distinct.

5   Niccolo Machiavelli (1998), a sixteenth century writer and political theorist, proposed that the attainment, exercise and maintenance of political power was universal in scope and application.

6   His actual name was Master K'ung, or K'ung-fu-tzu, being Latinised in a Jesuit translation.

7   In 1297 Edward I formally acknowledged the right of parliament to vote on questions of taxation.

3 | Development

More than any other issue, that of development has been the overriding rhetorical concern of the governments of SEA. Development has been the point by which governments have attempted to legitimise their rule and policies[1] and it has been the goal of development that has acted as a major rationalisation for the employment of authoritarian methods of political control, as well as for democratic processes.

Any discussion of development begs the question of what exactly has been meant by the term. For much of the three decades or so after WWII, the term 'development' was almost exclusively defined as meaning growth in per capita gross domestic product (GDP). It was this ratio of how much money a country earned in a year from local production divided by its population that was viewed as the primary indicator of development. This formula, as the sole or primary indicator, is still adhered to by some more conservative development economists and some governments. It is worth noting that, once countries move away from low levels of per capita GDP, there is often a correlation between this formula and median standards of living. Indeed, some economists have noted that the higher the per capita GDP ratio, the smaller the relative discrepancies in income distribution, meaning that, not only is there more wealth, but also that the wealth is more evenly shared (McGillivray 1991). The factors that come in to play in income-sharing of overall wealth themselves require closer attention, as they are sometimes the result of long processes of political struggle as well as economic development, such as in developed Western countries. Further, some countries with growing per capita GDP reflect increasing disparities in income distribution.

COMPARATIVE DEVELOPMENT

In SEA, aspects of both situations have arisen. Singapore, for example, had in 2003 a relatively high level of per capita GDP by world standards, at around

US$24 000 per annum, but a purchasing parity power (PPP) at a level slightly lower than that. This also resulted in a relatively high median rate of income, although critics have noted that the purchasing parity power of lower-paid workers only enabled them to attain the most meagre of existences. Purchasing parity power is the purchasing power of a country's currency relative to a basket of goods and services that can be bought in another, denominated currency, usually American dollars. The purpose of the PPP system is that it shows not only how much people might have in a given currency (usually, American dollars) at a particular exchange rate, but, more importantly, also what can be purchased in each country with that particular income. For example, a kilo of rice might cost $2 in the USA, but significantly less in exchange-rate terms in the currency of another country. The PPP is intended to illustrate the capacity for material standard of living, rather than simple exchange rates presuming a commonality of prices of goods.

In contrast to Singapore, Indonesia, until the economic collapse starting in mid 1997, had relatively strong economic growth, a claimed per capita GDP of US$1100 per annum and, at a claimed US$2857, a significantly better PPP for basic commodities, but a poor rate of income distribution (on a scale of 162 countries, Singapore was ranked twenty-sixth in terms of income distribution, while Indonesia was ranked one hundred and second). That is, although the average purchasing power of an Indonesian person was close to US$3000 a year,[2] the vast majority of people earned much less than this. In part, the rate of income distribution in each of these countries reflected not so much the absolute level of income, but, to a considerable extent, the income distribution policies of their respective governments. While Singapore could be fairly accused of having an authoritarian government, at least initially it was one that saw benefit in raising the standard of living of most of its citizens by helping to ensure some degree of income distribution. Indonesia, on the other hand, throughout the period of the New Order government, retained a policy that kept ordinary incomes at artificially low levels to help ensure Indonesia's competitive advantage (low wage rates) and hence its attraction to foreign investment compared to other developing economies, such as that of the Philippines.

Perhaps more important, though, is the fact that the per capita GDP definition of development is inadequate in a broader sense and for this reason is not used alone by the UN Development Program (UNDP) indexes. If development is intended to refer only to material issues, then nutrition, literacy, health care, sanitation, education, housing, environmental degradation, fertility, infant mortality rates, average life expectancy and causes of death also need to be taken into consideration. This is generally referred to as the Human Development Index (HDI), with the formal HDI as used by the UNDP being quite complex.[3] More than this, though, ideas of development have increasingly begun to take into consideration non-material qualities, such as notions of human dignity, personal fulfilment, self-determination and access to political participation and representation. These somewhat more nebulous or less formally quantifiable areas are not yet fully accepted in SEA in debates about development, but increasingly there is disquiet about a purely material focus on what constitutes development. It is at the point in which such nebulous categories are manifested as politics that there is increasing movement towards widening the development index to consider aspects of human welfare as well as more conventional concerns, such as governance, transparency and accountability.

POLITICAL DEVELOPMENT

In development circles, which are dominated by economists and, to a lesser extent, geographers of one type or another, the notion of political development has only recently begun to be discussed, and then, usually in the instrumentalist terms of governance and institution building, not least in response to the recently assumed role of the USA as a state builder (for example, Afghanistan, Iraq). However, at one level, political development is the most fundamental aspect of development, if that term is understood in its wider sense. Michael Hutchcroft noted that, in the Philippines, political underdevelopment was—and no doubt remains—the prime cause of continuing economic underdevelopment (Hutchcroft 1998), as also discussed by Evans in relation to sub-Saharan Africa (Evans 1995) and, more recently, by Fukuyama (2004). Political development can be thought of as reflecting a process of change from archaic political forms, such as single-source (prebendal) patrimonialism or feudalism, through to oligarchic, authoritarian or oppressive political systems, the most extreme end of the scale being a parasitic or predatory type of government. A more developed or mature political system could be typified by being benign, inclusive and participatory, accurately reflecting the aspirations of most citizens. Interestingly, the emphasis on political development via institution building by more conservative thinkers such as Francis Fukuyama (2004) and Samuel Huntington (1968) has not adequately noted that successful institutions tend to correspond not just to a narrowly conceived democratisation, but also to the full range of social political values that could be categorised under the idea of advanced political development. Similarly, limited institutional existence or failure tends to correspond more closely with lower-order social political development. The idea that institutions can be constructed somewhat apart from or prior to their preexisting primary political context—that is, the rights and other political circumstances of constituent members of the state—delinks institutional development in ways that leave it immediately vulnerable to collapse. Without popular legitimacy, institutions are, or quickly become, meaningless. That is to say, for institutions to function properly, there needs to be checks and balances on them, in some cases as competing elements that nevertheless find an equilibrium between them (Smith 2003: 109). Overwhelmingly, this implies the need to have a vibrant civil society that can be said to include free and questioning media, an active intelligentsia, non-government organisations and trade unions and independent arbiters, such as ombudsmen. There is, of course, debate about the definitions that can be said to apply to political development and many more authoritarian governments try to argue that they represent a maturation of local politics more suited to local conditions. This implies an approximately normative model of government.

Often, discussion about normative models of government defaults to notions of democracy or democratisation. The problem with this default is that it very rarely spells out what is intended by the term 'democracy' (see Lijphart 1999) and whether other types of political systems cannot also fulfil the needs of citizens. Where it is spelt out, it is usually the minimalist democratic model, which assumes that unhindered voting for representatives constitutes the full democratic experience. It also assumes that a model of democracy as practised in the West, usually by the USA, is an ideal aspiration, not taking into account that there is no single Western democratic standard nor is the USA seen as an ideal political or social model by very many developing countries, with even Huntington noting that America's political 'modernisation' was 'strangely attenuated and incomplete' (1968: 98). Nor is such an approximate Western standard necessarily applicable to countries in which illiteracy is high, communication poor, patronage dominant and consensus preferred. However, it must be conceded that some governments' attempts to appropriate the word 'democracy' for what are clearly non-democratic systems of government tends to imply the need for some particular definitions for a meaningful use of the term. Similarly, illiteracy, poor communication, patronage and consensus need not preclude democratisation; the catch here is that the only way for a people to reject a particular political model in ways that can adequately reflect the genuine nature of such rejection, be it democracy or some other, is through a free and open decision-making process—that is, democracy.

For the purpose of this exercise, the term 'democracy' is taken to mean a form of rule in which citizens either act as the policy-making authority (direct democracy) or are represented by others to make policy on their behalf (representative democracy). In either case, as argued by Jan-Erik Lane and Svante Ersson, democracy is, or should be 'the political regime where the will of the people *ex ante* becomes the law of the country (legal order) *ex post* (2003: 2). The former tends only to exist in small or closed societies, while the latter is the more applicable model. The issue of participation might also be included in such a definition, allowing citizens opportunities to stand for election as representatives and to express their views outside the formal policy-making or representative-election process. In the case of representative democracy, which is exclusively the type practised at the state level, citizens must have the capacity to vote for candidates of their choice, without fear or hindrance and their vote must be weighted equally with all other votes. Attendant to this, citizens must have free access to all information about and from candidates and other sources of relevant information, the freedom to speak or otherwise communicate on issues they deem relevant and the freedom to assemble with others to discuss such matters, to form associations or to non-violently protest decisions or situations they regard as objectionable. In all of this, not only must these conditions exist, but also, negative conditions, such as fear of arrest, punishment, torture and so on in relation to these matters, must not be present. While these criteria are not especially controversial in democratic theory, they rarely exist in pristine form in fact in even the most democratic of countries (although they do largely exist in functional form in such countries). And the problem here arises that, even in such a system, there is the capacity for a majority—'50 per cent plus one'—to assert its will over the minority, which may preclude inclusive decision making and thus preclude models of democracy that are more complex than the simple majoritarian model (Lane & Ersson 2003: 3–9)

Finally, a strong argument has been put claiming that economic development precedes political development and that a strong government is a necessary precondition for the economic development of the state. There is some—though far from overwhelming—evidence to suggest that this proposition could be, at least partially, correct. Political stability is a preferred environment for investors to instability and policy consistency is preferred to a political environment in which policy can change from year to year, depending on the whims of the electorate or the influence of pressure groups.

Somewhat ironically, this argument is usually put forward by political conservatives, yet the idea of economic development providing the foundation of political development comes directly from the revolutionary Karl Marx. There have, however, been exceptions for and against democratisation reflecting economic development. Singapore, for example, has become less democratic, even though it has become more economically successful. On the other hand, the Philippines and Indonesia, relative to the Marcos and Suharto eras, have both become more democratic, despite both being very poor and dealing with continuing economic difficulties. Similarly, Cambodia and East Timor have engaged in a number of elections and continue to embed democracy, with varying degrees of success, despite not only very low levels of economic development, literacy and communication, but also, in each case, histories that would otherwise tend to militate against relatively open and contested political processes. So, while the argument of political development being built on economic development might have some validity as a general tendency, it is far from a rule of politics and other factors can also influence political outcomes.

FULL BELLIES

This idea of economic development before political development has been referred to as the 'Full Bellies Thesis': the idea that people need and want to have full bellies before considering other, more esoteric, issues such as political participation (Howard 1983). This was nowhere more clearly stated than at a major regional statement on human rights, the Bangkok Declaration of the World Conference on Human Rights (1993), that said civil and political rights, which are the preconditions for political development, were conditional on economic development. The declaration agreed to 'Underline the essential need to create favourable conditions for effective enjoyment of human rights at both the national and international levels'] (World Conference on Human Rights 1993: 3.2). Such 'favourable conditions' usually include limitations on political activity and censorship of the media. It has been suggested that such an approach is in keeping with the 'Asian' experience. Yet not all 'Asians' accepted such conditions:

> Two justifications for authoritarianism in Asian developing countries are … that Asian societies are authoritarian and paternalistic and so need governments that are also authoritarian and paternalistic; that Asia's hungry masses are too concerned with providing their families with food, clothing and shelter, to concern themselves with civil liberties and political freedom; that the Asian conception of freedom differs from that of the West; that, in short, Asians are not fit for democracy. Another is that developing countries must sacrifice freedom temporarily to achieve rapid economic development that their exploding populations and rising expectations demand; that, in short, government must be authoritarian to promote development. The first justification is racist nonsense. The second is a lie; authoritarianism is not needed for developing; it is needed to perpetuate the status quo. Development is not just providing people with adequate food, clothing and shelter; many prisons do as much (Diokno 1981).

Clarence Diaz, president of Third World Lawyers, concurred when he said at the Bangkok meeting:

> The notion that in order to get bread you have to sacrifice freedom doesn't hold true in the region. We've had a number of governments giving that as a rationale and in fact they've ended up providing their people—significant sections of their people—with neither bread nor freedom' (Diaz 1993).

More recently, key thinkers at institutions such as the World Bank have accepted the positive link between political and economic development (for example, Stiglitz 2002), while the World Bank itself has increasingly focused its concerns on issues of governance, accountability and transparency, which it recognises are most effectively achieved through an open political framework.

Also against the argument in favour of authoritarian government is the fact that a representative government is less prone to corruption (Lane & Errson 2003: 222) and is less likely to spend vast sums on an unproductive security force. Such a government is also more likely to offer soft political changes, rather than the more abrupt, often violent, changes that occur when an authoritarian leader is finally dumped and their usually tainted bureaucracy requires a fundamental overhaul. Further, the free flow of ideas in such a system is more likely to invigorate market development as opposed to a culture of silence in which original ideas are not encouraged, indeed, sometimes regarded as dangerous (see Howard 1983: 478; Donnelly 1984: 258; Goodin 1979, see also, Lane & Ersson 2003: 194). Finally, as Lane and Ersson note, while democracy is good for development, if not always in straightforward ways, it still represents 'a number of intrinsic values, which makes it preferable to non-democracy' (2003: 65).

But in SEA, as elsewhere, the rhetoric of governments continues to focus on per capita GDP or, more commonly, (economic) growth. This then returns to development in the more constrained, economic sense of the term and the approaches that have been taken to development in the postwar period.

THE ORIGINS OF DEVELOPMENT

Since they first began to be discussed by governments, world bodies and academics in the post-WWII period, notions of development have been far from static. In part, these ideas corresponded to conceptions of what development meant in a more broad sense. But they also in part reflected, and continue to reflect, the ideological paradigms of their respective periods. In this, the debates and discussions have been led by academics and social critics, referred to and sometimes acted upon by world bodies and, via policy, enacted or ignored by governments.

The growth of development as a major issue in world affairs began in the period after 1945 in direct response to the process of decolonisation, that is, the creation of new states and the attendant rhetoric of liberation implied an improvement in living standards, which were supposed to arrive as a consequence of the end of exploitative colonial relations. However, neither the process of decolonisation nor the improvements in standards of living were as easy to achieve as the rhetoric had implied.

While some colonising states agreed to the process of decolonisation relatively peacefully, others were quite reluctant to give up their lucrative possessions. In SEA, the Dutch fought a bitter campaign in what was to become Indonesia, while the French became involved in an even bloodier conflict in Indochina. The USA had already agreed to independence for the Philippines prior to the Japanese invasion and occupation, so the process was interrupted, although not unnecessarily delayed, by the colonial power. Burma, meanwhile, had, in effect, secured its own independence in cooperation with the Japanese, although it too had been moving in this direction prior to WWII. The actual agreement to grant independence was based more on resolving issues of internal representation—which, ultimately, failed in practice—than on whether such independence should be granted. In Malaysia, Singapore and Brunei, independence was more a matter of ensuring adequacy of domestic systems of representation and administration and defeating an indigenous communist insurgency than of any quibble over the ultimate desirability of independence. After choosing not to join Malaysia, Brunei was somewhat slower in achieving independence, although not because of the United Kingdom's reluctance to break its colonial bonds. Indeed, as a state that relied on the United Kingdom for military support, Brunei was reluctant to be granted full independence, even at as late a stage as 1984.

The process of decolonisation was a two-sided affair and was not simply a case of emergent or protostates claiming the right to self-determination. The reality of Japanese occupation had demonstrated that the European powers were not invincible in SEA—or elsewhere—and that there was nothing inherently superior about European rule. Further, the European powers were deeply damaged by the conflict at home and their economic resources, such as they remained, were more in demand for postwar reconstruction than they were for maintaining increasingly troublesome colonies. Following the general principles of self-determination and anti-imperialism enunciated by former president Woodrow Wilson, the USA, on the other hand, was determinedly in favour of decolonisation and, outside its own concerns with the Philippines, used its economic power, under the Marshall Plan for reconstruction, to pressure the European states. The break, in political relations at least, was inevitable. The two questions that were only partly answered were: What would be the shape and style of the new, postcolonial states? and to what extent would those states be economically viable?

MODELS OF DEVELOPMENT

The first, most clearly identifiable, model of development, which arose in the immediate postwar period and lasted more or less unchallenged in the non-communist world until the mid 1960s, was that of modernisation.[4] Modernisation, in this context, was intended to be the glue that held together the fragile new states that were emerging in the postwar period. With development, such states would be strong and cohesive and better able to build a national self-image around mutual prosperity. More importantly for new and often insecure governments, development through modernisation also acted as a method of legitimation (Hettne 1990: 29–31). Such modernisation was based on a particular view of the world, including the ideas that development and economic growth were identical, that economic growth was separate to other political considerations (Hettne 1990: 28) and that growth could be achieved by applying technological answers to development problems (McKay 1990: 55). Further, according to this model, all societies should pass through a series of technological stages, usually prompted by investment. At a certain point, this technologisation would become self-fulfilling, leading to take-off. The consequent economic growth then led to the modernisation of social, institutional and political forms, including the establishment of the primacy of the individual over the collective and the establishment of democratisation (Rostow 1991). This modernisation process would have the benefit not only of assisting the societies concerned but also, according to this theory, lessening ideological tension between states (the logic being that capitalism and democracy would become the dominant forms).

Needless to say, at the time this theory was being promoted, there did exist sharp ideological divisions in the world order. The Cold War between capitalist countries spearheaded by the USA and communist or centrally planned economy countries led by the Soviet Union, offered starkly contrasting models of modernisation and development (Cohen 1995; Leffler & Foner 1994). According to the Soviet model, largely adopted by China and later other allied countries, the economy could be planned and run from the centre and modernised and supplied according to central command. This view was a part of a wider understanding of the value of communism to newly emerging states, a significant part of which was also based on political liberation (Brewer 1980; Rhodes 1970). While some elements of a Marxist critique were useful for explaining the iniquities of feudalism, capitalism and colonial capitalism (Brown 1974), the organising principles of the Leninist interpretation of revolutionary Marxism were equally as useful as tools for organising nationalist, anti-colonial movements (see, for example, Lacouture 1969).

To this end, every state of SEA has had at some stage a revolutionary communist organisation that had the explicit goal of overthrowing the prevailing political order.[5] In those states that had the most oppressive colonial governments and that were least willing to depart quietly, Marxism–Leninism took strongest root. This was especially the case in Indochina, led by Vietnam, where the less left-leaning anti-colonial forces were routed by the French before they could adequately organise themselves and where the communist forces had battled the occupying Japanese during their own interregnum. Conversely, communist and leftist forces in Indonesia were targeted for special attention by the colonial Dutch forces, which left them in a state of relative disorganisation when Japan encouraged Indonesia's declaration of independence in 1945 (Hindley 1964: 18). Communist and leftist forces in the Philippines were poised to assert some degree of authority in the postwar period. However, American assistance in excluding them from the legitimate political process and then in crushing their consequent rebellion, reduced that challenge to the level of regional threat rather than a direct threat to the state (Wurfel 1964: 698–701).

MODERNISATION STUMBLES

By the mid 1960s, it was clear that, for many countries, the modernisation project of postcolonial growth was failing to deliver its promised development. Further, when and where development did occur there was sometimes disquiet about what were perceived to be assumptions about cultural identity implicit and often explicit in the idea of modernisation, in particular, the appeal of individualism and consumerism (Frank 1981). If the aspiration and achievement of the capitalist version of modernisation was proving to be problematic, the centrally planned economy version fared no better. In particular, 'The market incentives that imposed discipline on firm managers and encouraged producers to increase output were not always provided by the state' (Rapley 1997: 47). Similarly, the values that derived from centrally planned systems did not always fit easily with existing methods of production, while the application of the Leninist model of top-down political organisation and control, while suiting many political leaders, was often not favourably received by ordinary people.

Many countries, especially in Asia, Africa and Latin America, were also not willing or able to embark on a radical course of economic and political revolution. Simply, the task being proposed was, in many cases, too radical a leap from prevailing circumstances; even where it was seen as desirable, it was not always practical. Moving from a peasant-based agricultural society directly to industrialisation is a rare achievement and, in the two cases where it has been at least partially achieved—the former Soviet Union and China—it came with an enormously high cost in human life. In other cases, even where the goals were more modest, many newly emerging countries found that, while they had achieved political independence, their economies continued to be subjected to the often one-sided demands of former colonial trading partners or new countries that took the economic position of former colonial masters. All colonial powers in SEA continued to maintain significant investments in their former colonies long after independence had been achieved.[6] In this they were often later assisted or buttressed with investment by other industrialised or postcolonial states.

By the early 1960s, the decolonisation process was manifesting as revolutionary responses to unresolved postcolonial tensions. Burma, under a socialist military government, had opted out of the international process and, having achieved only a partial settlement to its decolonisation claims, Indochina was moving towards the Second Indochina War. Malaysia and Brunei were attempting to ward off threats from Indonesia, construed as neo-imperialism, while Indonesia itself continued a downward economic spiral, in part abetted by and in part producing polarised political positions and the notion of continuing revolution. In Indonesia, material tensions and competing visions for Indonesia's future resulted in the political and civil convulsion of 1965–66, which left the state firmly in the USA-led camp.

Thailand and the Philippines were economic beneficiaries of American strategic policy in the region. However, while Thailand developed economically, though not without political convulsions of its own, the Philippines slid into a Latin American-style leadership of corrupt power characterised by a weak state and a strong, predatory oligarchy.

Absorbed by its own critical events, the attention of the SEA states during the 1960s was inwardly focused. As a battleground by proxy for a larger ideological conflict, procapitalist governments were too directly supported by the USA to be critical of the capitalist model of modernisation. Indeed, for many of the region's elites the idea of emulating the USA, at least superficially, was extremely attractive. With the deepening of ideological division, the anti-capitalist or revolutionary leftist groups were in no mood—or position—to offer a more moderate critique of capitalism. However, outside the region, a number of developing countries that were not caught up in the throes of revolutionary processes or outright warfare were more ambiguous about fully accepting the supposed benefits of the international capitalist system. The experience in many developing states had been one of greater acceptance of international capitalism leading to the greater impoverishment of their people. The economies of many developing states were still linked to those of their former colonial masters, or neocolonial economic masters. Rather than wealth coming into these countries, the experience was more that it flowed out.

DEPENDENCY

This situation led to a new critique of development that came to be termed the 'dependency' theory. While the dependency critique came primarily from academics and intellectuals, such as Paul Baran (1957) and Andre Gunder Frank (1967) and was originally intended as an explanation for underdevelopment in Latin America, it was also accepted in varying degrees by some other governments. Dependency theory relied for its analytical foundation on a Marxian critique of relations between rich and poor countries, in which the latter were exploited by the former (Hettne 1990: 82–7).

Broadly, aspects of this dependency theory of development focused on the idea that development could not take place while developing countries were in the process of having their economies systematically exploited by developed countries. Indeed, based on this analysis, the Third World condition of these countries was a direct result of earlier economic exploitation. However, dependency theorists were not classical Marxists and their critique of relations between developed and developing countries took on a number of guises, including universal as opposed to particular analyses, external versus internal causal factors, sociopolitical versus economic causes, sectoral and regional analysis versus class analysis, absolute underdevelopment versus cyclical underdevelopment and voluntarist (actor-driven) versus determinist (material-driven) analyses (Hettne 1990: 89–90).

In practical, if simple, terms, especially from the mid 1970s, many countries, mostly those without a manufacturing base, were encouraged to export, usually primary commodities such as crops and minerals. However, the international economy was shifting orientation and these countries found the value of their exports falling on the world market. To counter this loss of revenue they produced and exported more, flooding the market and further lowering prices, a situation that led to the identification of an international economic centre, linked to but not reliant on an economic periphery. The centre was dominant, while the periphery was subservient. Further, some groups and individuals within these countries, including government officials, assumed the often lucrative role of middle men in exploiting their own countries' wealth. These were known as 'comprador elites'. Accordingly, the only hope for these countries to develop was to cut their links with developed countries.

These ideas manifested themselves in a number of forms, from total isolation, as practised by Burma throughout the 1960s and 1970s, to revolutionary activity[7] to the more common focus on creating industries that met local needs rather than importing expensive foreign goods. During the 1950s to the 1970s, the Philippines was a strong example of this policy, although there was, in this case, also the significant influence of President Marcos offering lucrative and protected industries to his associates. In the late 1990s, Malaysia and, to a lesser extent, Indonesia re-adopted variations on the dependency critique in their relations with international finance. In particular, after the economic downturn that began in mid 1997, Indonesia and Malaysia only partially accepted the free market economic remedies proposed by the International Monetary Fund (IMF). Malaysia in particular tightened financial regulations to slow the outflow of capital and to rebalance the exchange rate in mid 1998, while Indonesia moved to limit some of the conditions that impacted directly on ordinary people, including the provision of subsidies on essential commodities, in particular, oil products

As a critique of the failure of the modernisation project, dependency theory itself had two main failings. The first was that, given the right circumstances and incentives, developing countries could constructively engage in the process of modernisation through industrialisation and export-driven policies. John McKay and G. Missen noted that economic, though not necessarily political, development could come from a close alliance between large-scale capital and a participatory state (McKay 1991; Missen 1991). The second was that, where there continued to be failings of the modernising capitalist state, dependency theory's 'conception of the domestic bourgeoisie as parasitic and dependent on foreign capital was simplistic … time would show that many Third World capitalists were anything but parasitic, sluggish, or dependent' (Rapley 1997: 48, see also Randall & Theobald 1998: ch. 4).

NEOCLASSICAL ECONOMICS AND EXPORT ORIENTATION

The dominant model for economic development throughout SEA at the beginning of the twenty-first century was the export orientation model. In short, this model was based on a number of related premises, all of which linked into the international market and to the dominant economic paradigm of neoclassical economic theory and practice developed in the early 1980s. The first premise was that growth in exports, based on competitive advantage, would produce an inflow of foreign currency and would enhance economic growth more than could be achieved by domestic consumption. This so-called competitive advantage could, in theory, be anything from exploitation of particular natural resources to an uncanny ability in one particular economic area. In most cases, however, such competitive advantage has started and sometimes remained with low-cost production via low wages.

The second premise was founded on the general neoclassical economic theory that government was an only marginally necessary evil that should be limited in its functions and that markets would find their own natural equilibrium in a free or unregulated environment. Following on, if individuals or individual enterprises prospered, then the whole of society would prosper through a flow-on effect. Under this system, enterprises prospered or failed in their ability to meet market demand and, as such, the market was the greatest incentive for and determinant of efficient production. Under such a system, that which was not efficient lost its right to exist.

Further advantages of this were that industries that relied on state support to exist, which practice often engendered cronyism or corruption, were required to survive or otherwise on their own merits. Delinking business and government had the effect of limiting official cronyism and corruption, although it would be quite incorrect to suggest that such practices were ended by introducing free market principles. Indeed, the major limitations to such practices were through greater corporate regulatory processes and accountability.

DISADVANTAGES OF THE FREE MARKET

Disadvantages of the free market system included the fact that many industries that were only marginally competitive but which offered other benefits, such as high levels of employment and related social welfare, were challenged and often closed. While this begged the question of the purpose of industrial development, the logic of neoclassical economics was such that those who pondered too long the value of the system were left behind in the mad rush for competitiveness and profitability.

A related disadvantage of the neoclassical economic model was that it tended to reduce the whole of society to its ability to fit into or become a part of a globally efficient production machine. In particular, there was a focus on short-term profits—often at the expense of long-term investment—in education, social welfare and the environment. In a related sense, so-called free markets do not usually fully account for their production costs, especially in terms of disposal of waste, which was frequently inadequate, or use of infrastructure. Finally, even when this model worked, it tended to enlarge gaps between the rich, through capital accumulation, and the poor, through having to compete for a position in the workforce, in which their only bargaining position relied on the cost of their labour. In those societies that did create more wealth, as Mark McGillivray (1991) noted, the disparities between the rich and the poor tended to shrink rather than increase and overall standards of living rose, although Bleaney and Nishiyama (2002) argue that growth does not appear to affect inequality over time.

While growth might become available and, depending on distribution policies, could apply across whole societies, some sectors of society and, indeed, some whole societies, were left out of the process of economic growth, creating political tensions over the distribution of income and, in more humanitarian terms, simply causing high levels of seemingly unnecessary misery. One need only consider the specific examples of each SEA country to see where such neoclassical policies have been introduced and where some sections of society have been left behind. Illustrations of this included the rural populations of Thailand, notably in the northeast), the Philippines, Indonesia, Laos, Cambodia and Vietnam (Cowen & Shenton 1996: 433–7, UNDP 2004: *Indicators*). Industrial workers, especially women, were also left behind in Indonesia (Berman 1998: 160–213) and the Philippines. The labour pool[8] of unemployed and underemployed in all of these countries, but especially in those that have developed urban industrialisation, such as Indonesia and the Philippines, was to become their competitive advantage vis-à-vis higher cost economies. Further, where the free market could potentially work in favour of employees, especially through unionisation and collective bargaining, governments have tended to limit the rights of union organisation and collective bargaining. This is one of the clearer illustrations of how neoclassical economic theory was less a commitment to an absolute principle than it was an ideological position that could vary in practice according to the ability of prevailing circumstances to meet business needs.

A COMPETITIVE ADVANTAGE?

The premise that each country had a competitive advantage that it could exploit to secure a niche in the world market, could be in the production of a particular good, type of goods or service. Such a competitive advantage would be achieved by using the available resources to produce those goods or services at a lower cost than their competitors, hence securing the desired position in the world market. Available resources to assist such advantage could be the educational level of the constituent population, prior experience with particular types of production, access to cheap raw materials or, quite commonly, access to cheap labour.

In this last case, a country that did not have access to an educated workforce, prior experience or raw materials was obliged to reduce the cost of its labour in relative terms to make its products more competitive on the world market, either through reducing the value of its currency or reducing absolute wages. The problem with this was that, with so many countries only having potentially cheap labour as a competitive advantage, they tended to undercut each other to strengthen that advantage. This, in turn, meant that the real incomes relative to hours worked for many people did not rise, but rather, they shrank. The sweatshop culture that pervades Indonesia's textile and footwear manufacturing industry, for example, got worse rather than better as a consequence of the dramatic fall in the international value of the rupiah. Working hours went up and, already disinclined to pay the minimum wage, textile manufacturers trimmed wages further and increased hours.[9]

While low wages and other forms of competitive advantage assisted some countries in exporting into the world market, other countries frequently undercut them through cross-subsidisation programs. This was especially prevalent during the 1980s, when the EU and the USA subsidised agricultural exports that were then dumped on the world market, often below cost price. Without similar subsidies, even otherwise efficient agricultural producers could not compete without similarly slashing prices, which in turn cut income to farmers. The process of subsidisation has decreased since the late 1980s, in particular since the finalisation of the Uruguay Round of GATT—and the establishment of the World Trade Organization—which cut subsidies to agricultural products. But the world has still not managed to get to the stage of presenting a level playing field on which all competitors start without any advantage other than that based on their ability to produce efficiently.

More positively, however, a number of SEA states have managed to lift their export income quite significantly through the adoption of export-oriented economic planning. Singapore, Thailand and Malaysia are the strongest examples, while Indonesia also moved ahead until its economic collapse of the late 1990s, with Vietnam coming more slowly behind. Laos has too little infrastructure to actively participate in export-oriented industry, except at the level of selling unprocessed teak logs; Cambodia has been in a similar position, although with the added export of gems and a clothing manufacturing industry that relied heavily on onselling Chinese garments. Similarly, Burma has relied on logging, oil and gem exports for its legal income, while all three latter countries derive considerable income from the export of illicit drugs, illegally felled timber and other smuggling of various goods. As an oil producer and exporter, Brunei is in a fortunate position; while having virtually a single product for export, it is a product for which there is a great and seemingly inexhaustible demand, hence enabling the price to remain generally high.

FOREIGN INVESTMENT

It is taken as given by virtually all states throughout the world, with the exception of those very few that run a consistent budget surplus, that foreign investment is a necessary ingredient for economic growth. This is not to suggest that foreign investment alone can produce economic growth (it can, but that growth is shallow and vulnerable to collapse), but that the inflow of capital from external sources is a primary means of replacing domestic capital formation for investment in economic development.

In SEA, foreign investment has been eagerly sought by all governments, though by some more keenly than by others, and with, perhaps, the exception of Brunei. Such foreign investment has taken two broad forms, the first of which has been what is termed 'foreign direct investment' (FDI), which refers to foreign investment by private companies in wholly owned or joint ventures, is the primary means of foreign investment by business and is that which is most eagerly sought by regional governments. Foreign investment can also come from private loans to incountry financial institutions, which in turn disburse those funds on a commercial basis to private companies. A third major source of foreign income for the countries of SEA is by way of loans from development banks, such as the Asian Development Bank (see ADB 1999, 2004: *Policies*).

The major development banks are the World Bank, or its local variation, the ADB, and the IMF. The primary difference between the two is that the World Bank or ADB are primarily intended to provide long-term loans for infrastructure, major private projects and specific assistance and local development programs. The IMF operates more as a direct source of funds for government consolidated revenue or to assist in financing economic restructuring programs (IMF 1999: ch. 1, 2004: Article 1).

In order to meet eligibility criteria for such loans, recipient countries usually have to agree to conditions of repayment (see IMF 2000, 2004: *Conditionality*). Such conditions do not only include a timetable for repayment, but often also the adoption of economic policy prescriptions intended to ensure such repayment. From the early 1980s, such policy prescriptions imposed a small government-free market ideology, the assumption being that this would not only better guarantee the repayment of loans, but would also ensure the financial viability of the recipient government into the future. There has been considerable debate about the appropriateness of such policy prescriptions, particularly in regard to their impact on the poorest people of recipient countries (IMF 2000: 27, 2004), often in Latin America and, more obviously, in Africa. However, broadly speaking, these policies, IMF sponsored or otherwise, have appeared to work in SEA.[10]

INDOCHINA

The process of attracting foreign investment has not been easy here. The communist or former communist states of Vietnam, Laos and Cambodia have all sought foreign investment, but have either intentionally or unintentionally erected hurdles to that investment, not least through inefficient bureaucratic administration and, as in some other places, through high levels of corruption. A further issue for foreign investment has been governments' willingness to offer a floating currency, the rationale being that a floating currency will rest at a level designed to balance the flow of capital into and out of the country. A high-value currency will increase imports and send money out, a low-value currency will decrease imports, which become proportionately more expensive, and proportionately increase cheaper exports. In most cases, the desire is to increase exports in order to strengthen the local economy. Conversely, a fixed exchange rate may make exports more expensive, as fixed exchange rates generally, though not universally, tend to overvalue the currency they are designed to protect (although they can intentionally undervalue such currencies to promote export competitiveness).

Vietnam has generally been the most successful of these states in attracting foreign investment as a result of its stable, if authoritarian, government, relatively large and seemingly industrious population, natural resources, such as oil, and relatively low labour costs. However, Vietnam's slowness in adopting reform, especially of its exchange rate, saw a downturn in its FDI towards the end of the 1990s.

Cambodia, with its floating exchange rate, has also had success in attracting foreign investment, although much of that investment introduced to the country has, in fact, been a blind for importing goods made elsewhere, such as in China, and exporting them under Cambodia's preferential, low-tax trading arrangements. Laos, on the other hand, has had Vietnam's stability—and authoritarianism—and a floating exchange rate, but a debilitating lack of skills and infrastructure. Added to a small population base that has not exhibited much entrepreneurialism and the fact that it is far removed from most transhipment points, Laos has not been sought out by the international investment community as a desirable destination for funds.

INDONESIA

Indonesia has had one of the more interesting foreign investment policies of any SEA state, if only because it has varied from period to period depending on the economic circumstances of the domestic economy, divided by the level of official corruption operating at that particular time. The underlying tendency within Indonesia was for its governments to accept foreign investment only grudgingly, this position being predicated on a perceived sense or desirability of economic nationalism, although this situation had markedly shifted in the early twenty-first century. That is, the preference of most Indonesian economic decision makers has been to assert the country's economic independence where and when possible, which has positioned it against the free flow of foreign investment. In particular, although the New Order government under Suharto openly encouraged foreign investment in the late 1960s, government policy and practice became increasingly restrictive as the price of oil rapidly increased during the 1970s, encouraging what many Indonesians then believed to be the establishment of the country's effective economic independence (Winters 1996: ch. 3).

However, with the collapse of oil prices in the early to mid 1980s, government policy returned to a more open encouragement of foreign investment, especially in regard to dropping requirements for foreign investors to enter into joint investment arrangements. Such arrangements usually meant that the foreign investor was required to put up funds that would then be administered by domestic management. Needless to say, a number of foreign investors had their financial fingers burnt through such exercises. From the late 1980s onwards, though, foreign investment was allowed without joint partnership, which raised the problem of foreign companies reaping considerable profits at the expense of Indonesia's low-paid workers.

In this varying and, at times, unpredictable scenario has been Indonesia's now internationally appreciated penchant for official and unofficial corruption. It is now common knowledge that the Suharto period of government saw official corruption scale previously undreamed of heights, both through simple skimming from other ventures to the allocation of lucrative contracts with payments or shared ownership in often monopoly situations (Kingsbury 1998: ch. 11). For example, until the end of the New Order, almost any investment in Indonesia required the services of a consultant, so-called, often a Suharto family member or someone who had close links to Suharto. This consultant would, for a percentage of the total proposed investment, ensure that the investment was approved and went ahead unhindered. In reality, what this amounted to was a type of protection racket, whereby the potential investor could not be guaranteed an investment licence or other permits without first paying a bribe to a Suharto family member or crony. Indeed, there was often a guarantee: that the proposed investment would meet insurmountable hurdles if such payments were not made. Beyond this debilitating official corruption, large numbers of senior and middle management employed to oversee foreign- and often domestic-owned operations in Indonesia lined their own pockets through various means, including claiming wages bills for staff not actually employed and making up the difference with enforced, unpaid overtime and through entering into preferential purchasing and selling deals that ensured a financial kickback.

Foreign investors had only looked closely at Indonesia because, up until mid 1997, it offered what appeared to be a stable political and economic environment with low wage rates and low levels of labour unrest, which were due to tight government restrictions on labour organisation. Once it became apparent that Suharto's tenure was coming to a close, domestic investors rapidly took their money offshore, precipitating a meltdown of the economy and ensuring Suharto's political demise. This, then, turned Indonesia from a relatively secure if corruption-ridden investment climate into one that was dominated by economic collapse and political unrest. Most foreign investors simply wrote off their losses in Indonesia, refusing to tip more funds into the political and economic quagmire, while previously potential investors stayed well away from the wreckage of the Indonesian state. This situation was exacerbated by the move from centralised to subprovincial investment regulation, in which regional administrations determined an often inconsistent range of foreign investment procedures. A further impact of decentralisation was that corruption was also decentralised and, according to organisations such as Transparency International, had actually increased, which further deterred foreign investors. Added to real and perceived threats against foreigners from Islamist extremists, the period after 1998 was characterised by a foreign investment strike in Indonesia, which had the direct impact of capping economic growth.

MALAYSIA

Malaysia had a more consistent foreign investment policy and, indeed, much of its economic growth from the mid 1980s was predicated on high levels of offshore investment, often in platform assembly of knocked-down products manufactured in Japan, South Korea or Taiwan. While Malaysia had a significantly cleaner government than that of Indonesia, it was still prone to the letting of contracts to sources close to the ruling clique within the government. It also enforced the paying of lip service to the requirement that companies have a positive discrimination policy up to the highest levels of corporate administration, which resulted in ethnic Malays (*bumiputeras*) often being employed to satisfy government requirements, rather than to actually do a job (Crouch 1996: 181–9, 200–3; Milne & Mauzy 1999: 23). This meant that when the so-called Asian economic meltdown began in mid 1997, Malaysia was also vulnerable, although not so much so as Indonesia.

When Malaysia's notoriously irascible prime minister, Dr Mahathir Mohamad, castigated foreign investors generally, the West most of all and Jews in particular, he further alienated already wary foreign investment opinion (Skehan 1998b; Singh & Oorjitham 1998). Mahathir's emotional outbursts were taken as a sign of political unpredictability and a very clear unwillingness to play the foreign investment game according to internationally established rules.

In the end, in August 1998, Mahathir broke with the international investment community by limiting the convertibility of the Malaysian ringgit and the repatriation of investments or profits from Malaysia. In this, Mahathir was opposed by his deputy prime minister, finance minister and heir apparent, Anwar Ibrahim, who was promptly sacked and made the object of unrelated—and later dismissed—charges. Needless to say, the international financial community looked askance at Mahathir's manoeuvring and limited further investment, despite which Mahathir's bid to run contrary to global finance was successful. Malaysia's economy did not slide further and, after stabilising, began to improve into late 1999, prompting new foreign investment. If nothing else, this showed that there was more than one policy prescription for economic management.

SINGAPORE

Singapore was hit by the economic crisis of the late 1990s primarily as a consequence of its exposure through investment in Indonesia. While this affected sections of the Singaporean economy, it did not go to its heart.

From the mid 1960s, Singapore had built a robust economy by linking government investment in and support for business within a relatively free financial environment. At a time when, in economic terms, 'government' was almost synonymous with 'undesirable', Singapore continued to retain a high level of government involvement in its economy, in particular in industries linked to the government through official or quasi-official investment. By 2004, global economists and policy makers had taken note of the continuing success of Singapore—as well as in other countries with a high degree of corporate accountability—and had begun to champion the necessity of corporate governance and strong state institutions.

Like most countries that have one political party or leader in power for too long, Singapore had begun to exhibit some of the characteristics of a corrupt state, if nepotism and favouritism can be taken to imply corrupt practices (see, for example, *Singapore Business Times*, 22 May 1996). However, such corruption tended to occur primarily at the upper reaches of government, being quarantined from the larger sectors of the bureaucracy and workforce, and was small in scale relative to the size of the Singaporean economy as compared with, for example, Vietnam or Indonesia. In very large part, Singaporeans either did not know or did not want to know about such official abuse when, on the whole, the economic system worked well for them compared not only to their neighbours, but also to most other countries globally.

THAILAND

Thailand was perhaps the star of the miracle economies of SEA, managing to post growth rates in excess of 10 per cent a year for the decade to 1997 and thus becoming the world's fastest-growing economy. The Thai government had wholeheartedly adopted export-oriented industrial policies and provided several incentives for local and foreign investment in the Greater Bangkok region. The scale of development in this region was staggering, with the face of Bangkok being transformed from that of a large but pleasant urban centre to that of a megametropolis almost bursting at its seams.

The fate that befell Thailand in mid 1997, as discussed in the chapter on Thailand, was, in part, in response to the overenthusiasm for lending into what had become a stagnant economic environment, a lack of corporate regulation, corruption and, in part, the speculative boom and bust nature of capitalism. In simple terms, when world demand for Thai products slowed in the early to mid 1990s, investment and easy credit continued to flow into the country, with much of it being siphoned off into artificially high property prices, bad businesses and corrupt schemes. When the time came for these debts to begin to be repaid, the defaults began, with businesses and then financial institutions going to the wall (*Asiaweek* 1998b; Chalongphob 1998, Phongpaichit & Baker 1998, 2004). In turn, the value of the Thai currency, the baht, collapsed by around half, ensuring that remaining debts denominated in foreign currencies effectively doubled. A similar problem also hit Indonesia, although there it was much worse due to the vastly greater scale of corruption and the capital flight that had preceded the resignation of Suharto. In part, a flow-on effect, in part a response to similar issues in other regional countries, the economic crisis that had started in Thailand quickly spread throughout the region, affecting virtually all countries.

In Thailand's case, due in part to new economic measures aimed at cleaning up marginal financial practices and some corruption, the economy began to rebound by 1999 (see Gearing 2000). Capitalism's cycle appeared to be on the upswing again. This effect was slower to take place in other SEA countries, although it did appear as though it would occur. More importantly, the human cost of this economic collapse, in terms of the shattered lives of ordinary people who lost their livelihoods through no fault of their own, indicated that, as a system, SEA's boom capitalism was probably an immature approach to economic development.

THE PHILIPPINES

The Philippines had the highest level of per capita GDP of any country in SEA in the 1950s and considerable capacity for building on that, including relatively high literacy levels and the widespread use of English. Yet, within two decades, the Philippines was mired in corruption, poverty, economic turmoil and a dictatorial government.

If one were to seek out the primary ingredient in this descent into chaos—a chaos from which the Philippines has yet to fully recover—it would be the weakness of the state. In simple terms, the government has been too close to or too easily manipulated by the country's oligarchy, which, in turn, has raided the economy on a regular basis (see Hutchcroft 1998). Even in the post-Marcos period, social change was very slow in being achieved; economic change through land redistribution or the strengthening of regulations and institutional support was effectively non-existent and political change reflected a return to the cosy relationships between government and vested interests of the pre-Marcos period. Regardless of policy prescriptions implemented at a public level, little had changed in the Philippines from the 1950s other than the decrease in its support from the USA. With an elite steeped in the art of self-enrichment and the government essentially being hostage to that elite, notions of policy outside short-term elite interests were alien concepts.

THE BALANCE SHEET

Economic development in SEA has been mixed, with some countries making impressive strides towards modernisation and overall economic growth, while others have languished. The respective abilities of the countries of the region to link into the world economy have been determined, in part, by their state ideologies and support for capital accumulation in targeted industries, but more sustainably so by aspects such as adequate transparency, governance and other regulatory systems and issues such as political stability and corruption. In many cases, so-called development has been little more than elites further entrenching and enriching themselves at the expense of the people who have, historically, been excluded from or allowed only limited access to political and economic participation. In this sense, widespread economic development has not exclusively but most often reflected political development:

> The distribution of development's fruits typically reflects the pattern of political power, not the pattern of human need.
>
> All too often this happens because development efforts are simply hijacked, to their own material advantage, by proximate power-holders. In particular, intended beneficiaries at lower levels of power and income will suffer from the political process which Porter has labelled—simply if inelegantly—'the rip-off upward' (Porter 1986: 243, quoted in Goldsworthy 1988).

In the first few years of the twenty-first century, it could be suggested that the broad trajectory for economic and political development in SEA was looking up. Indeed, Fukuyama's thesis (1993) on the seeming inevitability of the success of free market capitalism and democracy incorporated the normative assumption that both were not only desirable, but also, inevitably, had some support. Yet the sometimes supposed structural linkages between free market capitalism and democratisation, as inferred by Fukuyama, was disproved by the economic success of Singapore and Malaysia, the cause of which Fukuyama (2004) came to acknowledge, while Indonesia and the Philippines embraced versions of democracy while retaining weak and corrupt capitalist economies. Other states, such as Thailand—again, have economic growth and democratisation or, like Laos and Burma, have little or none of either. It may be that democracy, however it is defined, is but a passing historical phase and that there is nothing inevitable about its application, although the aspirations of ordinary people, if manifested, tend to produce something like the generally understood idea of democracy. Similarly, free market capitalism, as Marx suggested, has shown itself to have inbuilt contradictions that could limit its existence, even if it has also shown itself to be remarkably resilient to seemingly temporary setbacks. If both can be taken to be a product of a particular historical and, perhaps, cultural environment, like civilisations before them, they too could collapse, wither away or, due to their broad environmental unsustainability, die from lack of clean air and water. But it would be a foolish person—or government—who predicated policy planning on such a potentially long-term assumption.

In the interim, governments and their critics, states and individuals, all compete with varying degrees of success for influence over or ownership of ideas that define social organisation. To date, there has been no proven correct answer to the questions this raises, nor, perhaps, can there be. In many senses, the competition between ideas on these and other questions—perhaps the only true subject for an absolutely free market—is the foundation stone of real development. It may also be that such reflection is difficult without first securing immediate material needs, but the assertion that one without the other can comprise anything deserving of the name 'development', is to sell short not just the idea, but also the people to whom it applies.

NOTES

1   To illustrate, former President Suharto referred to himself as 'the Father of Development'.

2   This is an official claim of income for 1993; like many other economic statistics from Indonesia under the New Order government, its accuracy is at best dubious.

3   The UNDP version of the HDI is now quite complex, having thirty-three categories with several subcategories in each.

4   There is some debate about whether the term 'modernisation' should apply to the postwar development process in its entirety. I have used 'modernisation' in its more limited context to differentiate it from other theories and practices of development.

5   It is worth noting that the largest communist organisation in SEA, the Communist Party of Indonesia (PKI), attempted to work within the government to achieve political change.

6   The major exception is North Vietnam.
7   Revolutionary models picked up by dependency theorists were usually Latin American based, although the various communist insurgencies of SEA could probably (though not explicitly) illustrate the same critiques of existing political and economic orders.
8   It is a common critique of free market capitalism that it requires a pool of labour, based on unemployment or underemployment, to draw on in order to keep down wages and hence production costs.
9   This observation is based on a discussion with NGOs working in that area.
10   Malaysia in particular and Indonesia to some extent have bucked the IMF's policy prescriptions, in the former case by rejecting them and the IMF entirely in 1998. Indonesia successfully bargained with the IMF for softer conditions for its own bailout package in 1999.

4 | Security Issues

Increasing attention has been focused—again—on the issue of security since the international preoccupation with Islamist terrorism. While this seems to be a recent phenomenon, security issues dominated the international sphere until the beginning of the 1990s and, for many of the world's peoples, they have not ceased to be of overriding concern. As importantly, the idea of security has been hijacked, to some extent, to refer to security from armed attack. Yet security equally refers to security from a predatory government and from lack of adequate nutrition or health care, categories that can probably be included under the (previously addressed) rubric of 'development'.

In more conventional security terms, the region of SEA sits at a geographic, cultural and political juncture between the two great regions of the earth—South Asia and North-East Asia, land masses which, between them, account for two-thirds of the world's population. Situated half in the Indochinese peninsula and half in the archipelago north of the Australasian continent, dominating the sea lanes between the Indian and Pacific Oceans, SEA has, since time immemorial, been regarded by other states as among the most strategically vital regions in the world. Historically, whoever controlled the Straits of Malacca between Sumatra and the Malay Peninsula was, by definition, a world power. The Malacca Strait is, arguably, the world's busiest waterway, through which travels around one-quarter of the world's oil, two-thirds of its liquid natural gas and up to one-third of all other trade (Ong 2003: 2).

In the nuclear age, whoever controls the Ombai-Wetar Straits (Timor Trough), which marks a tectonic divide immediately to the north of East Timor, controls the passage of nuclear-capable, deep-water submarines between the Indian and Pacific Oceans, with all the implications this has for threats to five of the world's seven acknowledged nuclear armed states. This is not to mention the oil-producing capacity of the archipelagic states, the fact that the regional population is around 600 million or that, in the middle, Indonesia is the world's most populous Muslim country and the 'lynchpin of regional security' (Feinstein 1998). For these and many other reasons, the security and stability of SEA is of global strategic importance.

This chapter is intended to consider issues that have influenced strategic policy considerations in the SEA region. In particular, it will focus on the role of nationalist movements, communist insurgency and revolution and the relatively recent preoccupation with terrorism.

Despite the apparent stasis of the states of SEA, the competing historical claims that produced these states continue to be worried about by historians and, by extension, by contemporary political actors. It seems that anyone who writes about an SEA state, is in some way, trying to legitimise current state formation, champion nationalist causes or, more subtly, rationalise irredentist claims.

Each state in the region has sought to base the legitimacy of its borders (or border claims) on putative assertions of sovereignty over territory within that greatest area occupied during some real or imagined period of imperial glory. At different stages of the region's history, different states, including some that no longer exist, rose to regional prominence and many occupied or claimed suzerainty over areas vastly greater than currently exist. In this historical memory, the concept of the mandala comes into play, in which states, based on an exemplary centre, expand when strong and contract—or disappear—when weak. The general structure of such a political, as opposed to metaphysical, mandala was that outlying regions were not so much directly ruled by the centre as they were semi-autonomous and owed allegiance or were suzerain to it. The greater the distance from the centre, the greater the autonomy of the peripheral localities.

Invariably written by court sycophants or travellers unfamiliar with the reality of such claims, texts abound on the validity of each of the states, how the others have behaved in a perfidious or grasping fashion and, often, how the territorial and cultural claim of each state should, in a better world, extend beyond its present horizons. As survivors, or imaginative recreations of former states, these states are able to make such claims or at least justify their continued existence. But almost identical types of texts could have been written about, for example, the state of Lan Na, except that, due to the vagaries of history, it failed to survive as a state and is now a part of Thailand. The difference between it and, for example, what became Laos was more luck based on geographic proximity to a particular colonial power at a particular time than any intrinsic quality. Still, to write of Lan Na as one might now write of Laos would be to invite allegations of treason to the state of Thailand. There but for the grace of history went Laos.

Similarly, the once important state of Brunei is now but a shadow of its former territorial self and would now be a part of Malaysia, but for a royal decision one way rather than the other. Champa, once in what is now Vietnam, has long since ceased to exist, although Islamic Chams are still found in Vietnam and Cambodia, while the southern Lao province of

Champassak continues to reflect its former influence along what the Cambodians call the Bassak River (better known as the Mekong). Cambodia still lays an historical claim to Kampuchea Krom, in what is now southern Vietnam, while the early T'ai states of Sipsong Chu Tai and Sipsong Panna, among others, have completely disappeared, even though their people have not. Not surprisingly, as people continue where states disappear, an historical memory also exists, to a greater or lesser degree. The sack of Vieng Chan (Vientiane) by a Thai army in 1828 is a date that is still bitterly remembered in Laos, in particular in that city. When French explorers came to the site that was once the city of Vieng Chan some forty years after the event, all that was left was a handful of Buddhist ruins. The Thais had been successful in obliterating this rebellious vassal state, while managing to transport tens of thousands of its surviving citizens to populate an otherwise underpopulated region under its authority. Prior to the colonial era, people were more of a commodity to a regional state than was land, and captives of war were a conventional benefit of military success.

The predecessor state to Laos, Lan Xang, was, for a time, the greatest state of the Mekong region. Its decline and disintegration into three competing states allowed it to be vulnerable to incorporation into the growing Thai state. Yet that state was itself vulnerable, especially to the resurgent Burmese. Resentment and suspicion lingers between the Lao and the Thai and the Thai and the Burmese. Formal relations might be cordial— or might not—but historical memory cannot be completely erased. With the complete destruction of Ayudhya by the Burmese in the eighteenth century, the Thai state centred on this city dissolved, freeing the periphery. However, under the remarkable leadership of Taksin, the Thai state was quickly restored, with the capital being removed to Thonburi (now part of Bangkok). In reassembling the state, Taksin reasserted authority over the Lao states. The states of Vieng Chan and Luang Prabang had an established history of conflict, often one siding with an invading power against the other, for example Vieng Chan with the Burmese against Luang Prabang in 1765, and then, Luang Prabang with the Thai against Vieng Chan in 1779. This aided their disunity and made them more vulnerable to control by the resurgent Thai state. To the south, the vassal state of Pattani at different times attempted to dispel Thai authority, now referred to by the Thais as 'sometimes rebellious'. Similarly, the Karen state of Burma has never accepted its incorporation, while various other Burmese states have a long history of resisting the central Bhamese state.

Similarly, conflict between the Thais and Vietnamese reflected competing imperial agendas. When one looked at Thailand's close support for the Khmer Rouge of Cambodia, for example, what one saw was not some ideological agreement, but a continuation of an historical battle against the expansionist Vietnamese. Looking at it like this, there is no moral right or wrong, only survival and alliances that helped secure survival. In this sense, Cambodia has been allowed to exist as a buffer state, in much the same way that the states of Laos secured their pre-French existence. As imperial powers the United Kingdom and France did not wish to come into conflict over a border dispute in SEA, hence maintaining Thailand between their territories; so too have Thailand and Vietnam come to an understanding that good buffer states make good neighbours, even if Thailand has now dropped this long-standing policy in relation to buffer insurgencies along its border with Burma.

In the archipelago, the Javanese retain, or have reinvented, the glories of the Majapahit Empire of the fourteenth century as a means of providing a link between Indonesia's present and its somewhat mythologised past, even if via the intermediary of Dutch colonialism. The unity of the state is, according to most observers, desirable, at least for the purposes of regional stability, regardless, it seems, of how that is achieved. But desire does not always match outcomes and, for each territorial desire, there is usually a competing desire: only one can claim success. In a contemporary sense, there is still considerable support for the idea of being Indonesian, but there is far less support for the idea of being a Javanese colony. With the meaning of 'Indonesia' contested in places such as Aceh and West Papua, and formally rejected in East Timor, it is not surprising that its various groups have asserted their distinct visions against one they feel is imposed from outside.

Similarly, in the Philippines, the construction of the state is not accepted by a relatively small but nonetheless militant Islamic minority in the south, nor has it ever been. No one should be surprised that separatism continues to afflict Mindanao and Aceh in northern Sumatra, when it has done so since the first attempts to incorporate these territories into greater states. Similarly, the only glue holding Malaysia's eastern states together with the peninsula is economic prosperity. The vast majority of the population of these states, both indigenous and Chinese, is otherwise disinclined to be dominated by the peninsular Malays. In Burma, where no such economic prosperity exists, there is no tangible reason for the non-Bhamese population to remain as a part of what continues to be an extension of an older Bhamese empire.

The shape of the political world we now look at is vastly different to that which existed in the past and is not necessarily the same as that we will always look at. Historical memory runs deep and, as continues to be demonstrated, some grievances and aspirations, both ancient and contemporary, remain to be settled.

IDEOLOGICAL CONFLICT

In more recent history, ideology has come to play a significant role in SEA, especially as a means of nation-building. The first Indochina war, from 1946 until 1954, was clearly a war of national liberation on the part of the

Vietnamese. It was also participated in by Cambodia and Laos insofar as both had indigenous nationalist movements and, perhaps as importantly, their communist groups were influenced by or agreed with the central claim to independence put by Vietnamese communists. Perhaps another nationalist model might also have worked in Indochina, but communism had a number of points in its favour. It had a clear organisational structure, offered a rational analysis of colonial exploitation, supported the poor and, most significantly, could neither be bought off by nor would compromise with colonial capitalism. It was this implacability and consequent success that led to a further attempt to quash it.

The division of Vietnam at the 17th parallel in 1954, which marked the end of the first Indochina war, was intended purely as a device to allow the separation of combatants before elections were held. However, with the Cold War well underway by this stage and with a communist victory highly likely, if not inevitable, France and the USA were unwilling to allow the strategically important state of Vietnam to fall into the communist camp. Having secured a stalemate on the Korean peninsula in 1952, and with Germany and the rest of Europe having been partitioned along communist and non-communist lines from 1945, the USA in particular believed that it was possible to stall the communist advance in SEA. Indeed, if it did not, the states of the region could, as the later theory outlined it, fall one by one like a set of dominoes (McNamara 1995: 31, 32).

The USA was in some small measure reassured by the minor cultural distinction between the north and the south of Vietnam, by the fact that it had spent a part of its history divided and that it comprised three separate states when occupied by France in the late nineteenth century. The fact that the USA easily found willing accomplices for its anti-communist crusade among the local elite further bolstered its contention that an independent South Vietnam was not only viable but also legitimate.

The Second Indochina War is now formally recognised by the USA, for its own purposes, as having begun in October 1956, with the declaration of the state of the Republic of Vietnam. For others, especially in the south, there was no break between the conflicts. The USA was initially reluctant to involve itself in a major military commitment, believing that high levels of economic and military aid, coupled with the provision of so-called advisers to train South Vietnamese troops, could be enough to hold the line. It was not; the escalation of the conflict into the 1960s was for many—perhaps most—Vietnamese a continuation of their already long struggle for self-determination.

The success of communism in Laos and Cambodia can be seen as a spillover effect from the conflict in Vietnam. While both these countries had their own domestic causes for conflict and their own local communist insurgencies, they were undoubtedly pushed along by forces competing in Vietnam. A further spillover also affected Thailand, albeit in a more limited manner. As well, a general strategy of communist insurgency, then promoted by China, was also active in British Malaya, North Borneo and, later, in the Philippines.

Interestingly, the biggest communist party in the region until 1965, the Indonesian Communist Party (*Partai Komunis Indonesia*, or PKI), had not, since the creation of the state of Indonesia in 1949, ever attempted to overthrow its government (the 1948 Madiun Rebellion could not be seen in that light). In that respect, the Suharto-ist New Order rhetoric about the PKI's attempted coup of 1965 is, logically, absurd. Certainly, communism was gaining ground in the most populous country in the region and that might have been cause for concern for opponents of communism. But the events of 1965 and 1966 reflected more a desire by pro-USA generals to seize control of Indonesian politics than they did the likelihood of a communist takeover, as the events of 30 September 1965 reflected an internal army struggle. In that President Sukarno was implicated, it was as a supporter of the 'coup', not a victim of it.

NATIONALISM

Also problematic for Indonesia was the *Permesta*–PRRI rebellion of 1958, which threatened to re-order and perhaps dismantle the state, raising issues of ideology and conceptions of nationalism. PRRI was *Pemerintah Revolusioner Republik Indonesia*, or Revolutionary Government of the Republic of Indonesia, and–*Permesta* was *Perdjuangan Semesta*, or Overall Struggle. Many of the tensions that led to the *Permesta*–PRRI rebellion— poor economic distribution, excessive centralisation of government and corruption—were those that fed into events tearing at the fabric of the state in the late 1990s and into the early twenty-first century.

As one of the claims that challenged the idea of the state and, consequently, the nationalist ideology of the Unitary State of the Republic of Indonesia (*Negara Kesatuan Republic Indonesia*), Indonesia's claim to securing West Papua resulted from that territory being a part of the Dutch East Indies and the claim that the basis of the Indonesian state should be defined by the totality of the Dutch territories. That a number of early nationalist leaders had been imprisoned at Bovun Digul near the Papua-New Guinea border, further added to a sense that the territory had a legitimate, some claimed special, reason to be included in the new republican state. The Dutch, however, did not view West Papua in the same light as did Indonesian nationalist irredentists. Indeed, the Dutch administrative concept of the East Indies was that it comprised a collection of separately administered colonies that were coordinated from Jakarta. West Papua in particular did not fall into any greater concept of an overarching or single colonial territory, nor were its indigenous people, being Melanesian, related to the Malays, who comprised the vast majority of the rest of the population. As a consequence, the agreement of 1949 that secured Indonesian independence specifically excluded West Papua, to be negotiated at a later date. It also established a series of separate states to be joined with the republic in a federation, although this was scrapped by the government in Jakarta within a year.

The Dutch were strongly supported in their position by Australia, which directly administered Papua, the southeast quarter of the island and, under a League of Nations and then UN mandate, the northeast quarter of the island, New Guinea. During WWII, imperial Japanese forces had advanced as far as the southern coast of Papua-New Guinea before being halted by Australian troops on the ground and American ships and aircraft in and over the Coral Sea. It was clear to Australia's strategic planners that any future threat to Australia's security would probably come through the island of Papua-New Guinea. Australia was, therefore, concerned to either maintain a friendly Dutch presence in the western half of the island or to bring that part of the island under Australian administration (Osborne 1985: 18–28). The Dutch had been allies during the war, after all, while the Indonesian government was, at least in part, a creation of retreating Japanese and, moreover, increasingly seen to be influenced by communism. However, the USA, concerned to shore up relations with the government of the strategically important archipelago and with a tendency towards supporting the movement towards decolonisation, pressured the Dutch into surrendering the territory in 1962, to take effect in 1963. In 1968, a vote of 1025 specially selected village chiefs confirmed the incorporation of West Papua into the republic of Indonesia (Osborne 1985: 30–9), to be known thereafter as Irian Barat (West Irian), then, Irian Jaya (Victorious Irian) and finally, in 2000, Papua (the name 'West Papua' is used by the indigenous supporters of self-determination, but is not accepted by the Indonesian government).

The *Organisasi Papua Merdeka* (Free Papua Organisation, or OPM) was established in 1964 as a result of Indonesia's occupation of West Papua; the obviously rigged and unrepresentative 1968 vote pushed many West Papuans into rebellion against the government in Jakarta. Although militarily never a threat to the Indonesian government or its forces, OPM has continued with a low-level guerrilla campaign aimed at harassing Indonesian troops and settlers and continuing representation of anti-Indonesian sentiment. The displacement of indigenous peoples as a consequence of government-sponsored resettlement of other Indonesians in West Papua, and the often disruptive and exploitative practices of mining companies in the province, further exacerbated tensions between colonisers and colonised.

The two main strategic issues that have arisen as a result of this rebellion include the potential for the break-up of the state or at least the separation of a resource-rich component and the conflict spilling over into neighbouring states. In the first instance, the conflict in Irian Jaya stands with that which existed in East Timor and Aceh as those that had the greatest potential to bring undone the idea of Indonesia as a unitary state comprising more than 300 separate ethnic groups across some 13 000 inhabited islands. Beyond this, there are some fears, strongest in Jakarta and among the Indonesian military that, if one region were successful in pulling away from the state, this would give impetus to others, destroying the state of Indonesia as a cohesive entity. This concern also exercises the minds of more distantly placed strategic analysts, who regard the idea of the archipelago comprised of several independent, potentially non-viable and possibly confrontational states as a major problem. In this respect, though, West Papua was situated a long way behind East Timor in the possibility for success of its bid for meaningful independence.

The second major issue concerning West Papua was that, in their enthusiasm to pursue OPM guerrillas, Indonesian soldiers have crossed over the Papua-New Guinea border in hot pursuit, raising the spectre of a confrontation between Indonesian troops and PNG troops. Further, with Australian soldiers still patrolling the border region as a part of Australia's assistance to PNG, there was thought to be the possibility of clashes between Indonesian and Australian troops. Given the historical unease felt by Australian defence planners towards Indonesia (regardless of public statements to the contrary), this then raised the issue of such a confrontation becoming the trigger for a full-scale conflict between the two neighbouring states. Although such a fear was strongest in the early 1960s, when Indonesia's left-leaning government under Sukarno was regarded in Australia with considerable hostility, the hot pursuits that aroused the most controversy occurred in the mid 1980s, when diplomatic relations between Australia and Indonesia were again at a low ebb and were again delicately poised during Indonesia's fallout with Australia over the Australian-led military intervention in East Timor following the vote for independence there in 1999.

The point at which Indonesia and Australia, along with Malaysia, the United Kingdom and New Zealand, did come into more direct conflict was over the creation of the new state of Malaysia in 1963. Indonesia's President Sukarno viewed the creation of the state of Malaysia, comprising the former British Straits territories and a number of local sultanates, as artificially dividing the Malay world and creating what he saw as a neocolonial state that could be used to destabilise Indonesia. Sukarno's vision was for all Malay peoples, including those in the Philippines, to be united in a Greater Indonesia, which accorded with the Indonesia Raya plan developed by some Indonesian nationalists, including Sukarno, in 1945. The Confrontation with Malaysia was not well supported by Indonesia's army, which conducted secret negotiations to end the conflict throughout its duration. While Indonesian volunteers were active in Sarawak and Sabah[1] and there were forays into the Malaysian peninsula, it never presented a major military threat to Malaysia. The Confrontation was primarily a diplomatic battle, although Australian, New Zealand and British troops did engage Indonesian troops and irregulars on a number of occasions. The Australian government felt so concerned about the potential for a full-scale conflict with Indonesia that it ordered, off the drawing board, the F111 strike aircraft. The F111 had the capacity to bomb as far distant as Jakarta and to carry nuclear weapons (which Australia has never had). The F111 was not built or delivered to Australia until after this perceived threat had disappeared, although it was still in service in Australia in upgraded form in the early years of the twenty-first century.

In a military sense, the Confrontation was dissipating when Sukarno was deposed as president, which deposition ended the conflict. A military coup against Sukarno appeared increasingly likely, especially as his health was beginning to fail and the Indonesian Armed Forces (then *Angkatan Bersenjata Republik Indonesia*, or ABRI) desperately wanted to forestall the accession to power of the PKI. Some junior officers, intent on protecting Suharto, moved against the senior ABRI officers on the night of 30 September 1966, killing six of the most senior generals. In the counterattack the following day, Brigadier-General Suharto began the first part of his campaign to defeat the 30 September Movement and moved on to eliminate the PKI as a force within Indonesia. The Confrontation, already dwindling to a war more of words than of bullets, was quietly cancelled.

EAST TIMOR

The greater danger between Australia and Indonesia emerged at the end of the twentieth century over East Timor. Following the East Timor referendum on autonomy or independence, which overwhelmingly supported independence (78.5 per cent), and the subsequent Indonesian military-backed anti-independence violence, Australia led an international peace-enforcement team to East Timor under the mandate of the UN. The very direct response of many Indonesians was that Australia was interfering in Indonesia's domestic affairs. The Australian embassy in Jakarta was attacked, as was an Australian school, and many Australian businesses in Indonesia found their customer base disappearing due to quasi-official sanctions. There were threats to break off international relations between Indonesia and Australia and threats that hot pursuits would be regarded as invasions and met with force. Pro-integration militias were given safe haven near the East Timor border in West Timor and, for a few months from that position, harassed the international force, but, more importantly, continued to cross the border into East Timor, primarily to engage in smuggling, but also to intimidate the East Timorese population.

With the UN scheduled to completely withdraw from East Timor in May 2005, there were concerns that existing low-level, cross-border infiltration by militia members would escalate, as would increasing internal destabilisation. This destabilisation was conducted, in particular, by the misleadingly named Committee for the Popular Defence of the Democratic

Republic of East Timor (CPD-RDTL), which drew its membership from former militia and militia supporters, a few disenfranchised former Falintil fighters and unemployed youths. There was evidence that the CPD-RDTL was linked to and supported by Indonesian military intelligence, reflecting both a sense of Indonesian irredentism as well as a desire to ensure that the breakaway territory did not prosper in independence.

A desire to ensure East Timor's failure reflected a widespread concern in Indonesia with its potential to show that separation was viable, which could then encourage the breakup of the state. At the time that East Timor achieved effective separation from Indonesia—September 1999—Aceh had become its most violent and dangerous since perhaps the late 1950s, a situation that escalated over the following years and led to the imposition of martial law in May 2003. Thousands of people had also been killed in communal warfare in Ambon; parts of Maluku and West Kalimantan were beset by ethnic conflict. Throughout Indonesia there seemed to be considerable tension over the idea of what 'Indonesia' actually meant. Pro-Indonesianists formed into a strongly nationalist camp, while those with other ideas split along factional and regional lines. It increasingly seemed that Indonesia, as a unitary state, was not a given and that its longer-term future was uncertain. Many analysts suggested that the breakup of the state could present a strategic nightmare for other countries in the region. But others pointed to the erratic and problematic nature of the state as it had already existed, suggesting that separate smaller states might be more accommodating to their neighbours. Within Indonesia itself, such discussion was effectively forbidden.

BURMA

Burma has long been considered a major strategic crossroad in Asia, sitting as it does astride the only readily passable route between the world's two largest and often antagonistic nations, India and China. In recent history, the only external threat to Burma has come from Japan, which occupied it in 1941 as a part of its push towards India. While the target of that attack was never achieved, Burma was, until 1945, a battleground across which raged some of the Asian conflict's bloodiest and most destructive fighting.

Burma has always been influenced by its two giant neighbours, but, perhaps more importantly, it has been more dominated by its internal geography and ethnic makeup. Historically dominated by the Bhamese, who are said to comprise around 60 per cent of the population, Burma has a history of aggression towards its neighbours and towards its internal minorities. While internal conflicts and the demands of coming to terms with a rapidly changing external world have focused the attention of Burma's military dictatorship, there have also been signs that conflict could spill over into neighbouring Thailand, Burma's traditional enemy.

Since the late 1980s, Burma's army (*Tatmadaw*) has more than doubled in size, from fewer than 200 000 troops to more than 400 000. Given that Burma faces no credible external threat, this rise in troop numbers can only be attributable to the role of the army in domestic oppression, both towards the country's ethnic insurgents as well as towards its pro-democracy activists. In building up the strength of its army, Burma has established increasingly strong ties to China, which, at the beginning of the twenty-first century, was the country's biggest arms supplier. Reliable figures are unavailable, but a number of estimates put Burma's acquisition of Chinese arms, ranging from automatic rifles to jet fighters, at around US$1 billion a year.

The second biggest arms supplier to Burma was Singapore. In February 1988, in conjunction with Israeli consultants, Singapore had shipped to Burma's Directorate of Defence Industries a prefabricated factory designed and built by Chartered Industries of Singapore[2] to produce small arms and weapons up to 37 mm calibre. The first item thought to have been produced in the new factory is the EMERK-1, a locally designed assault rifle that could also be used as a light machine gun. Singapore previously supplied the Burmese government with weapons at critical times and has also built, in Rangoon, a cyberwar centre with telephone, fax and satellite communications capabilities. Chartered Industries of Singapore had previously supplied the Burmese government with tonnes of ammunition, mortars and other war materials at the time of the pro-democracy protests in 1988 (*Irrawaddy* 1998a: 13).

Further concerns have been raised over Burma allowing China, in a contra deal in which Burma receives cheap military goods in return, access to the Indian Ocean. Although little more than a gesture and a base from which China can gather intelligence, Chinese access to the Indian Ocean has the potential to alter the strategic balance of power within the region, which provided further fuel for tension between India and China (see Malik, in Pedersen, Rudland & May 2000: 249, 251, 253–4).

In large part, ASEAN's invitation to Burma to join the organisation was aimed at this increasing Chinese influence. The partial aim of ASEAN was to reduce Burma's reliance on China, which was widely perceived throughout ASEAN as the region's most significant long-term threat. In this respect, the addition of Burma to ASEAN and, hence, the strategically oriented ASEAN Regional Forum completed the cup that encapsulates the southern flanks of China. This, then, establishes a strategic bloc that is the only realistic way in which the smaller and more diffuse countries of SEA could contain a potentially expansionist or belligerent China. The lesson here is an old one: when China has been weak at the centre, it has withdrawn its focus to matters close to home; when China has been strong, it has tended to exert or extend its influence well into the SEA region.

As China's economy moves to become the world's largest, which it will within the next few decades, China, with the world's largest population, is again being perceived as growing in strength. Regional leaders look not so much towards what the present Chinese government has done or is doing, but to the actions of Chinese leaders dating back to the rise of the Han Dynasty some two thousand years before. Finally, it is widely hoped within SEA that, while China could well become a threat, it might also become an economic friend. To this end, Burma's increasingly close links with China offered the ASEAN states an opportunity to engage more closely with China in business, especially in the much vaunted, but underdeveloped, Yunnan–Burma–Laos–Thailand region.

Stuart-Fox has identified the relationship between the SEA states and China as one of small brother–big brother, where the regional states act in such a way as to recognise China's interests and concerns. In this, China is seen to prefer not to act, but to have its wishes anticipated. This relationship is seen to reflect a sense of traditional Confucian hierarchy—acknowledging one's proper place in the world, which allows for non-intervention (*wu wei*: inaction) (Stuart-Fox 1998b). Stuart-Fox also noted that China's regional significance has developed considerably as the USA has diminished its presence in the region, first by withdrawing from mainland SEA by 1975 and, later, from the Philippines, and by the withdrawal of the Soviet Union from its base at Vietnam's Cam Ranh Bay.

While the *Tatmadaw* has been preoccupied with quelling internal dissent, it has also followed, in hot pursuit, ethnic refugees who have spilled across the border to Thailand. There have also been the occasional exchanges of mortar fire, all of which has raised tensions between Thailand and Burma, most noticeably in the Tachilek–Mae Sai area at Thailand's northernmost tip, where, in February 2001, there was a three-way battle between the *Tatmadaw*, the Thai army and Shan State Army guerrillas. This followed years of skirmishes and conflict, including battles with the Mong Thai Army, which was formerly associated with drug lord Khun Sa.

Tensions between Thailand and Burma have also existed along the border of Karen state. Thailand enjoyed a significant surplus in trade across the Thai–Burmese Friendship Bridge, built by the Thais and which crosses their border at Myawaddy–Mae Sot, northwest of Bangkok. The bridge, which was opened on 15 August 1997, but closed by Burmese authorities on 14 April 1998 after a bomb was planted in the town of Myawaddy, has been a barometer of border relations. The bomb was suspected as having been planted by members of the Karen National Union, which had launched sporadic attacks against Burmese troops in the area. The Burmese government was thought to be using the bridge's closure as a means of pressuring the Thai government into helping destroy Karen forces on the Thai side of the border (Saritdet & Nussara 1998). The area between the border crossings of Mae Sot and Mae Sai—virtually all of the northern Thai–Burma border—remains vulnerable to instability. Since the turn of the century, activities by Burmese separatists in Thailand have been met by considerable Thai force, an indication that Thailand did not want to become a party to Burma's internal problems.

LAOS

Territorial control over Laos has always been contested to some degree. Its border areas expanded and shrank according to the fortunes of the state, but within the state there have always been groups of people who only distantly, if at all, recognise its sovereign authority. This has particularly applied to the highland regions, which have traditionally had a relatively independent existence from the rest of Laos. Most recently, that assertion of independence has focused on the Hmong, or Meo, people, who began to immigrate from southern China into highland Laos from early in the nineteenth century.

The Hmong have relied, for their own use and for trade with the outside world, on the growing of opium poppies, which are well suited to the region's rugged terrain. When the production of opium was legal, it was the major source of revenue for the state, notably under the French. However, as opium production has become an industry of international pariah status, there has been increasing conflict between the opium-producing Hmong and the Lao government. Since the 1960s, this conflict has been exacerbated by an ideological conflict, fed by the USA, which recruited Hmong to form a private anti-communist army under General Vang Pao. The USA's interest was twofold: it wanted a private army that could harass the Pathet Lao, but it also wanted an unofficial military force located in Hmong territory, in particular in the middle of the strategically important Plain of Jars, which sits astride the major routes from northern Vietnam into northern Laos, including to Luang Prabang and Vieng Chan. The Central Intelligence Agency (CIA) has been claimed to have assisted with the export of opium in exchange for—and to help finance—Hmong military support.

When the USA abandoned its attempts to control events in Indochina from the early 1970s, it also abandoned its Hmong allies. However, the Hmong, deeply entrenched in opium production, continued with the lucrative trade and, to a lesser extent, also continued to battle with rival Hmong groups and Lao government forces. Over the last decade of the twentieth century, the Hmong were increasingly brought under the control of the Lao government, especially with the completion of a sealed road that runs from Luang Prabang to Vieng Chan through the western section of the Plain of Jars. A large number of Hmong were resettled near this road, allegedly to curtail their traditional slash and burn agricultural practices, but more accurately to make them subject to military control. Even so, sporadic attacks against the Lao military and civilians continued along the road in the area of Kasi and the area further to the east was disputed; there have also been bombings in Vieng Chan and a guerrilla attack from Thailand at Pakse in the south. After a series of clashes in 2003, between 600 and 700 mainly Hmong rebels surrendered to Lao government forces in March 2004, effectively bringing their rebellion to a close.

CAMBODIA

Since its decline as a regional power, Cambodia has long been a battlefield for competing regional forces, in particular, Vietnam and Thailand. It would be far too simple to suggest this was the situation between 1978 and the end of the 1980s, when both countries were actively involved in Cambodia, but there were some historical memories at play when Vietnamese forces pushed the Khmer Rouge up to the Thai border region, which, in turn, prompted Thailand to unofficially support the Khmer Rouge. Beyond these two neighbouring powers, Cambodia has, in recent times, also attracted the interest of China, the former Soviet Union and the USA, each backing different factions within the country. In part, this international involvement in Cambodia and the disaster that was the Khmer Rouge era and its aftermath, induced these countries and others to broker an agreement to settle the conflict.

While the relative success of the UN-arranged elections is now history, what has subsequently happened has been that, as in past times, Cambodia has, in part, become a collection of semi-independent warlord states, as it was under the Khmer Rouge and, it is debatable, before that. Military chiefs hold considerable power and a great deal of independence from the central government, although the structure of the Cambodian People's Party, which is deeply centralised, has limited some of their centrifugal tendencies. But, like the former mandalas of the region, Cambodia seems only to be able to hold together under a relatively strong and centralised authority.

In one sense, however, Cambodia was more important for what it symbolised to the international community, in particular the depredations that could be caused by total civil war and for the guilt inspired in so many external states for their contribution to that conflict. As a strategic site, however, Cambodia was a relatively safe place in which a number of states could battle each other by proxy, rarely risking their own wellbeing. In that respect, Cambodia was strategically important only in that it provided a site for the release of aggression that could not have been expressed elsewhere without causing a major international conflict. By 1998, the international community appeared to have felt that, beyond normal aid flows, its debt to Cambodia had been paid and that the country now had to work out its own problems.

THAILAND AND MALAYSIA

As the Malayan Emergency subsided from the 1950s, Malaysia's remaining communist insurgents increasingly withdrew to the mountainous and relatively isolated region along and across the Thai border. While low-level campaigns against them by the Malaysian government continued, their major saving grace was an effective refusal by the Thai government to act against them. Had the Thai government done so, the guerrillas of the Malayan Communist Party (MCP) would have been caught between the two forces. But it did not. It was not as if the Thai government was sympathetic to the MCP's cause, especially as during the 1970s it had its own communist insurgency to counter; rather, it was unsympathetic towards appeals by the Malaysian government because of the presence of Thai Islamic separatists just south of the Thai border.

The effective standoff over the issue of Thai and Malaysian insurgents on either side of the border was a result of the mixed history of the region and the imprecise nature of precolonial political control. The sultanates of the Malay Peninsula had, at various times, been vassal states to precursor Thai states, as well as at various times to other powers, such as Sri Vijaya and later Aceh in Sumatra, possibly Majapahit in Java; they even occasionally achieved relative independence. However, the northernmost sultanates were the most susceptible to Thai influence and control and there was a long history of mandalic expansion and contraction of Thai influence. In particular, the northern Malay states were most firmly brought under Thai suzerainty after 1782, under the resurgence of what was to become the Chakri dynasty.

It was only as a consequence of British pressure in 1909, that Siam ceded suzerainty of the four states of Perlis, Kedah, Kelantan and Trengganu, bringing them under British protection. This left a number of ethnic Malay Muslims in Thailand's southern states. Of Thailand's approximately two million Muslims, about 75 per cent live in the southern Thai provinces of Yala, Narathiwat, Satun and Pattani, all originally comprising the single sultanate of Pattani.

Since the early twentieth century, there has been strong Muslim opposition to incorporation within the Thai state, which has been manifested in separatist sentiment. Constituting only 3 per cent of the Thai population, the southern Muslim minority has never been a threat to the Thai Buddhist state. But ethnic, linguistic[3] and religious differences, compounded by occasional official repression, pushed some into rebellion (Hewison 1994). The Malaysian government, responding to populist appeals from its Muslim community, as well as reflecting elements of a Malay irredentist sentiment, had not persecuted Thai Muslims operating out of Malay territory; however, by the end of the twentieth century, it seemed that the exigencies of the modern state had started to supersede ethnic identity, so the prime ministers of Thailand and Malaysia agreed to work more closely to 'suppress terrorist groups operating along the Thai–Malaysian border' (*The Nation* 1998: A2). It appeared as though the sporadic violence in this region had subsided, but on 28 April 2004, more than one hundred, mostly young, Muslims, armed only with machetes and knives, attacked police and soldiers stationed in Pattani, killing six. Troops and police responded by killing more than one hundred of the young Muslims, including more than thirty who had taken refuge in Pattani's main mosque, where they were shot at with rocket-propelled grenades. Violence continued as members of the Pattani United Liberation Organisation (PULO) and security forces murdered each other on a daily basis. In October 2004, a protest march by Muslims in Pattani led to the deaths of around eighty protesters after they were crammed into a truck and allegedly suffocated or were crushed to death. While there had been a renewed claim by PULO to local independence, the upsurge in violence in this region appeared to be precipitated by the Thai government's 'get tough' policy.

Thailand's other security concerns in the 1970s revolved around communist insurgencies in the south, the northeast and the north near the Burmese border. However, after alienating much of the northern population with its heavy handedness, the Thai government's policy of amnesties and development, along with a high level of military pressure and the loss of sanctuaries in Laos and Cambodia, saw that insurgency collapse. Thai military clashes with Burmese troops across the Thai–Burma border were sporadic, mostly reflecting Burmese incursions to chase after separatist rebels. The biggest strategic change to that situation was a shift in Thai government policy from tacitly supporting insurgents by means of creating a buffer zone, to abandoning the buffer policy and, hence, taking a much tougher line on Burmese refugees, especially Burmese separatists.

PHILIPPINES

The Philippines is affected by issues of ideology and nationalism, though by neither in ways that had wider strategic implications. In particular, the southern island of Mindanao, which was beset by issues of economic distribution, was also deeply beset by insurgencies led by both communist and Islamic groups, reflecting the tenuous nature of the consolidation of the state. As communism has waned internationally, so too for a while did it diminish as a threat in the Philippines, even though the issues that engendered it were still largely in place, which probably explains why, after years of turmoil throughout the 1990s, communist armed resistance again rebuilt to become a credible military force.

Militant Islam, on the other hand, had in the past a lesser grip on the islands, but had more consistency in terms of its appeal. Islam has been a driving force in the southern Philippines since the Spanish first colonised the region more than 400 years ago. This Islamic separatism was supported by Islamic groups throughout the world and represented a long-term, if localised, challenge to state integrity. If there was a wider strategic issue to be considered in the Philippines, it was that the string of islands between Mindanao and the Malaysian state of Sabah were regarded as having considerable strategic value, being an historic transhipment route through the archipelago. As a consequence, whoever controlled Mindanao and, as a result, these islands, controlled one of the region's main links. In historic terms, the Sultanate of Sulu was a significant regional power because of its control not just over these islands, but also over much of modern Sabah. But with Sabah firmly within the Malaysian state, there seemed about as much prospect of this region reconsolidating under an Islamic banner as there did the state of the Malay Peninsula forming a federation with the Malayu states of Sumatra.

Related to Sulu's former ownership of Sabah, the Philippines had claimed the territory as the inheritor state of the Sulu sultanate. A state of dispute between the Philippines and the United Kingdom over Sabah was first lodged in 1962, transferring to Malaysia after Sabah was incorporated into that state in 1963. The claim led to a serious rupture of relations between Malaysia and the Philippines when, in 1968, endorsed by the Philippines Congress, President Marcos formally announced the Philippines' right to the territory. The claim was exacerbated by a report that the Philippines military had been training young Muslims as a force to invade Sabah, which appeared to be confirmed by the arrest of twenty-six armed Filipinos on an island off the coast of Sabah in March 1968. The Philippines continued with its claim to Sabah, although with less conviction after a visit by Malaysian Prime Minister Mahathir Mohamad in 1994.

SPRATLY ISLANDS

The Spratly Islands are a major test case in terms of state control and nationalist assertion in SEA, being a small group of islands claimed at once by China, Taiwan (as a claimant to Chinese legitimacy), Vietnam, Malaysia, Brunei and the Philippines. The Spratlys are an outcrop of some 400 rocks, reefs, shoals and sandbanks spread over roughly 800 kilometres north to south in the middle of one of the world's major trading routes. The main islands of the group are located a little more than 450 kilometres almost directly north of Brunei (and Sabah and Sarawak) and about 600 kilometres west-southwest of the Philippines island of Palawan. The next nearest landfall, some 750 kilometres away, is near Ho Chi Minh City in southern Vietnam, although Vietnam claims islands that are about 150 kilometres from the nearest of the Spratly group, while the main Spratly islands are 1300 kilometres south of China.

China's claim to the Spratlys derives from its Nationalist government's claim following Japan's use of the islands as a submarine base and its defeat in 1945, reaffirmed by the People's Republic of China in 1951. Chinese fishermen had previously used the islands, although no previous Chinese claim had ever been made to them. The Philippines lays its claims to the islands as a consequence of an expedition there in the 1950s and a presidential decree concerning sovereignty in 1978. Malaysia's claim dates from 1979, with the publication of a map of Malaysia that included those islands closest to the north Borneo coast. Vietnam (south) claimed the islands in 1955 as a consequence of a French claim in the late nineteenth century.

Since the 1980s, China and Vietnam have placed armed forces on various of the islands, while the Philippines has also sent armed forces. Conflict over the islands has included the displacement of one military force by another, including a brief naval battle between China and Vietnam in January 1988. In 1999, Vietnamese gunners fired on Philippines reconnaissance planes, while planes from the Philippines and Malaysia also engaged in a standoff (Tiglao 1999). Mostly, the claimants are concerned to secure fishing rights to the region, as well as the rights to explore for oil and natural gas. In 1992, China signed a lease with an American oil company to drill for oil on some of the islands that are within waters claimed by Vietnam as part of its continental shelf, while in the following year, Vietnam built a lighthouse on one of the islands. There is also concern that China in particular wants to claim the islands as a part of an extension of its authority further into the SEA region.

The Spratlys have been controversial because of the strength— sometimes vehemence—with which China, Vietnam and the Philippines have laid their claims to sovereignty. Indeed, the Spratlys are probably the biggest point of contention between the member countries of ASEAN (Tiglao 1999). However, the Spratlys, other than by constant externally supplied relief, are uninhabitable and were historically uninhabited as a consequence. Fishermen may have visited the rocks in the past, but the legitimacy of each of the claimants is fragile. As a consequence of the disputation over the islands, the ASEAN states agreed to try to seek a peaceful resolution to a problem that appears to be, effectively, intractable (ASEAN 1976, 1992).

ASEAN

The Association of South-East Asian Nations (ASEAN) was founded in 1967 as a gesture of reconciliation between what had been somewhat antagonistic neighbours in the SEA region. Indonesia had, from 1963 to 1966, been engaged in its *Konfrontasi* with Malaysia (including Singapore), the Philippines disputed Malaysia's territorial claims to the latter's eastern reaches and tensions had arisen between Malaysia and Singapore over the latter's expulsion from the federation. Thailand and Malaysia also faced difficulties over the presence of Malaysian communists operating out of southern Thailand and Thai Muslim separatists finding haven in northern Malaysia. Each of these states had also experienced, or was still experiencing, a communist challenge,[4] which encouraged their respective strategic association with the USA.

It was also believed that mutual economic development by these states would contribute to political stability and help reduce or resolve domestic political unrest. By shoring up their economic and political position, these states also believed they would reduce the potential for outside involvement or interference in their domestic affairs.

A continuing focus for concern by the SEA states is China. By 1967, China had established itself as a significant actor in regional dissent. It had promoted predominantly ethnic Chinese communist parties in Malaysia and Singapore, supported the Communist Party of the Philippines (CPP), had close links with the PKI and had supported communist forces in the conflict in Indochina,[5] with which the ASEAN states were deeply concerned. ASEAN was also increasingly concerned over the role of the former USSR in the region, in particular in Vietnam and, by extension, Laos, although it did not formally regard the regional influence of the USA as problematic.

ASEAN has made a number of agreements on security, including the Bangkok Declaration of 1967, the Zone of Peace, Freedom and Neutrality (ZOPFAN) in 1971 and a further Declaration of ASEAN Concord and the Treaty of Amity in 1976. While these agreements reflect a particularly regional view of security matters, they did not imply consensus on how to deal with intraregional security issues. There has been a long-standing view within ASEAN that internal matters are sovereign and should not invite the interference of others, including other member states (preamble to *ASEAN Declaration* 1967).

The establishment of the ASEAN Regional Forum (ARF) in 1994 was a significant step towards the creation of an informal security alliance in the region, although on the surface it was intended only as a dialogue group and included such dialogue partners as the USA, China, Japan, Russia and Australia (Lau 1997: 36). However, the agenda for ARF discussions, as well as chairing of the ARF, were dominated by the ASEAN partners. The key areas of interest for the ARF include confidence and security building, nuclear non-proliferation, peace-keeping cooperation, exchanges of non-classified military information, maritime security, preventative diplomacy and norms and principles regarding political and security cooperation (ARF 1994). The primary purpose of the ARF was to act as a preventative forum, rather than as a forum that could respond after the event (Ball & Acharya 1999: ch. 6).

This view was increasingly challenged towards the end of the twentieth century, manifesting itself in a number of intraregional disputes. There has been disagreement between Indonesia and the Philippines over views expressed in the Philippines about Indonesia's former occupation of East Timor and Thai criticism of more recent ASEAN member Burma, over hot pursuits into Thai territory. The Philippines has been critical of the treatment of Filipina workers in Singapore and criticisms have been traded between Singapore and Malaysia over various minor matters, many of which seem to stem from the bitterness that came from Singapore's separation from Malaysia in 1965. Beyond this, there was also widespread criticism from various sources in ASEAN states over the jailing of sacked Malaysian deputy prime minister, Anwar Ibrahim.

Further, there is no consensus within ASEAN about the role of external powers, in particular the USA and its declining military role, under the Guam Doctrine of 1969, in the Philippines and Thailand. To a lesser extent there was also lingering concern about the roles of the United Kingdom (which, was, in practice, reduced to zero after 1968), Australia and New Zealand under the Five Power Defence Agreement of 1971. This latter association reflected a lingering unease with the strategic dominance of by far the largest ASEAN state, Indonesia, and a reluctance of the ASEAN states to enter into a formal military alliance with it.

A Malaysian proposal to secure the region's neutrality, presented to the Non-Aligned Movement's (NAM) summit[6] in 1970, received a generally negative response from the USA, the Soviet Union and China. At that time, each state wished to play a more active role in the region although the USA and the Soviet Union subsequently reduced their active participation in the region. Indonesia also opposed the proposal on the grounds that it could imply a less negative corporate relationship with China which, at that time, the New Order government viewed with some hostility. However, with the USA moving to redress its own hostility towards China, especially with the announcement in 1971 of President Nixon's visit to Beijing and China's resumption of its seat at the UN soon after, relations began to normalise. The ZOPFAN agreement soon after was a compromise response to the Malaysian proposal.

Given the commitment of ASEAN's founder states to an implicitly anti-communist position, it is not surprising that the member states found themselves ill at ease with Vietnam after the reunification of the state in 1975. While the ASEAN states were also ill at ease with Laos and Cambodia after their successful communist revolutions in that same year, Laos was not perceived as presenting a threat, while Cambodia had closed itself off from all but the most limited external contact. At this time, ASEAN was tending to flounder, with no clear purpose and no unifying theme. This was to come at the end of 1978.

In December 1978, when Vietnam responded to Khmer Rouge provocation by invading Cambodia, installing the Heng Samrin puppet government, the ASEAN states leapt to the forefront of international condemnation. Thereafter, the ASEAN states were not only the most vociferous critics of Vietnam, but they also actively engaged in supporting the anti-Heng Samrin coalition, which referred to itself as the Coalition Government of Democratic Kampuchea (CGDK). The CGDK comprised a royalist party headed by ousted Prince Norodom Sihanouk and the Son Sann group, comprising Lon Nol's republican government. But, most importantly, it also comprised the Kampuchean Communist Party (the Khmer Rouge), which had just been shown to have murdered or otherwise been responsible for the deaths of up to two million Cambodians.

Regardless of the morality of ASEAN's support for the CGDK, this issue served to give the member states a diplomatic rallying point for the next decade.[7] Thailand in particular played an historical game of trying to offset Vietnamese influence in Cambodia, in this case by allowing CGDK units to operate from refugee camps along its border. During this time, Thai officials and businesspeople actively traded with CGDK officers who maintained bases in western and northwestern Cambodia. The CGDK, in particular the Khmer Rouge, sold teak logs and gems in exchange for cash that was used to help finance their war with the Phnom Penh government and its Vietnamese allies.

While during the period of Vietnamese occupation of Cambodia ASEAN appeared united, there was actually considerable discord, primarily between Thailand and Indonesia. Thailand, sharing a border with Cambodia, had the most to lose from any potential spillover of the conflict. Similarly, Thailand had an historical interest in influencing events in Cambodia. Indonesia did not view the Vietnamese invasion with quite the same concern and, having finally thrown off the effects of its colonial heritage, instilled some respect for Vietnam in Indonesia. Further, at this time Indonesia was still highly wary of China's role in SEA and was not happy with China's active support for the Khmer Rouge or the implications of its assault on Vietnam after the latter's Cambodian invasion. Tensions were, generally, kept below the surface, but when talks began to consider resolving the Cambodian situation, Indonesia played a far more active role than did Thailand, especially by hosting the Jakarta Informal Meetings.

By the time Vietnam's involvement in Cambodia had begun to de-escalate—from around 1988—the ASEAN states were mostly riding a wave of economic development. Increasingly, the ASEAN states assisted in brokering a settlement, which contributed to the 1993 UN mission to hold general elections in Cambodia. Their intention, particularly Thailand's, was to bring peace to the region and, hopefully, engage in business. That this coincided with the collapse of the Soviet Union meant that the logic of the Cold War no longer shaped regional thinking. This movement towards political settlement in Cambodia, the increasing marginalisation and alienation from its erstwhile allies of the recalcitrant Khmer Rouge and the liberalisation of the Vietnamese and Lao economies led ASEAN to the once unthinkable step of inviting Vietnam to join the organisation, which it did in 1995. Laos and Burma followed suit in 1997, although a bloody split between Cambodia's coalition partners, just days before Laos and Burma joined, precluded Cambodia's inclusion. The initial failure of elections in July 1998 to satisfy UN concerns over the legitimacy of Cambodia's government further delayed its inclusion into ASEAN, although this was granted the following year. Various proposals for the ARF to develop into a more explicitly military treaty, which were still being made as recently as 2004, have continued to founder on a range of incompatibilities and disagreement over the role of the group.

THE INFORMAL COALITION AGAINST CHINA

China looms large in the strategic thinking of SEA. It has always done so and, conceivably, always will. China has been less at the forefront of regional strategic thinking in the twentieth and early twenty-first centuries because of its own economic and military weakness, especially earlier in the twentieth century, and because most of the regional states have been dominated by other external powers. However, as the states of the region have asserted their independence and, consequently, lost external protection, they have become increasingly vulnerable to China's influence. It has even been suggested that China has used the overseas Chinese as an arm of its foreign policy, fomenting dissent and discord, if not revolution, in states it wished to influence.

China has also used its support for regional dissident movements to much the same effect (see, for example, Miller 1967; Roy 1998: 25–8). This can be most clearly seen in early revolutionary Vietnam, Indonesia pre-1966, Malaysia and perhaps Brunei, Thailand in the mid to late 1970s, Cambodia, especially under the governments of Democratic Kampuchea and the Coalition Government of Democratic Kampuchea, in Burma through the Communist Party of Burma and in the Philippines through the Communist Party of the Philippines/New People's Army. It was not until 1978 that China's leader, Deng Xiao Ping, said that China would not interfere in the affairs of SEA states and even then, in some cases, this was more rhetoric than reality. But as the 1980s progressed, Chinese support for SEA communist parties disappeared, in part leading to the acceptance of an amnesty for the Communist Party of Thailand in 1985 and the truce arrived at with the Communist Party of Malaya in 1989.

But the peoples and states of the region have long memories. As already mentioned, there is a continued recognition that, when China is weak, its influence is limited, but when China is economically strong, it asserts its authority more comprehensively throughout the region. China has been subjected to a number of stumbling blocks in its development, from regional economic woes to untenable environmental problems, the inflexibility of the centralised state and, not least, its burgeoning and increasingly less sustainable population. But, for the last decade of the twentieth century, China posted growth rates of around 9 per cent or more a year and was predicted to have the world's largest economy, in absolute terms, by the year

2050, along with its existing and growing population of more than 1.3 billion. This has not only positioned China as having the potential to threaten SEA, it has ensured that China will want to play a more active—indeed, more dominant—role in regional strategic affairs.

To counter this, the states of SEA, informally defined through the ASEAN grouping, have begun to see themselves as constituting a cohesive and substantial bloc as a foil to Chinese strategic ambitions. The extremely poor relations between the Indonesian and Chinese governments in the wake of the anti-communist massacres in Indonesia from 1965 to 1966, marked a turning point in the establishment of a regional anti-communist bloc. Similarly, China regarded ASEAN as a manifestation of American imperialism (Roy 1998: 14–16; see also, Schurmann & Schell 1968: 293, 358, 574–5, on China and the earlier, more strategic South East Asian Treaty Organisation). However, relations between individual SEA states and China have been normalising since 1974, with Indonesia finally reestablishing relations in 1990. The Indonesian government first recognised the communist government of China in 1950, but broke off diplomatic relations in 1967. Similarly, Singapore did not recognise the government in Beijing until 1990. In part, the slowness in formalising relations resulted from the Chinese government's insistence that the Communist Party of China should be able to maintain links with local communist parties, even after establishing diplomatic relations. The logic of this was that the party and the government were separate entities. Since diplomatic relations have been restored, the ASEAN states have come to the view that contentious international issues, such as China's relationship with Taiwan and its occupation of Tibet, are China's domestic concerns (Roy 1998: 175–6, 179–80).

Vietnam showed that it was capable of mounting a strong defence against Chinese aggression[8] when the latter launched a punitive invasion with more than 200 000 troops from 17 February 1979. The maritime states have the advantage of defence in depth, being, as they are, beyond the land-based states; their position also raises issues of supply lines. The other states, Laos, Thailand, Burma and, to some extent, Cambodia, were far more vulnerable to possible Chinese manoeuvres. To that end, while the countries of the region have formed a sort of informal defence club, they have also embarked on a policy of incorporation.

China's incorporation into SEA was primarily commercial and economic, although a diplomatic element was also present. Acting independently and with the encouragement of their ASEAN partners, Laos and Burma have embarked on a course of developing cordial relations with China. In the case of Laos, this policy follows a period of relative isolation from China after the falling out between China and Vietnam. However, since the late 1980s and into the 1990s, Laos attempted to restore relations with its northern neighbour through diplomacy and trade. The trading element of the relationship was especially important for Laos, being a country with no sea borders and, consequently, being more reliant than most on having as much access by land as possible. Road links between Laos and China date back to the period of WWII and the anti-French conflict. However, the quality of the roads did not make them suitable for commercial traffic. A land route from Laos to China still exists, but, like many roads in Laos, it was a dry-weather road only. During 2004, that road was still in the slow process of being upgraded.

China and the ASEAN states have also presented something of a united front to the rest of the world over issues of government style. There is considerable consistency between the Chinese government's form of progressively more free-market, one-party authoritarianism and opposition to liberalism and a number of regional governments. There is also considerable consistency between these states over issues of human rights, especially as identified by the UN and Western countries. China is also a member of ARF, which includes it in SEA security discussions.

BURMA AND CHINA

Burma's relationship with China is particularly interesting. As noted, Burma has traditionally existed as a buffer state between the two rival powers, China and India. Burma has had poor relations with both countries and, while it has not been invaded by either in recent times, it remains an ideal staging ground should open conflict between the two break out. In contemporary terms, India regards Burma as an international pariah, while China has actively defended Burma's interests in the UN (Roy 1998: 173).

After decades of regarding China as an ideological enemy and a significant threat, not least through its support of the Burmese Communist Party, Burma has, since the late 1980s, more actively pursued a policy of close diplomatic and economic cooperation with China. Indeed, sharing an extensive border, China is one of Burma's major trading partners and arms suppliers and each supports the other in diplomatic affairs, especially in relation to international criticism over human rights issues. In recent times, China has been supporting an economic corridor through Burma by constructing a road from Kunming in Yunnan to the Irrawaddy River port of Bhamo, which then provides access to the Bay of Bengal. China has also been upgrading its naval facilities on the Burmese coast, giving it access to the Bay of Bengal and the strategically important Straits of Malacca[9] (Roy 1998: 174; Ball 1998: 219–26, 260; Olsen & Winterford 1996: 120).

There are still tensions between Burma and China, however, with Chinese investment in Burma displacing local Burmese, and some Chinese businessmen taking a less than gentle approach to crosscultural relations. The Chinese government is also less than totally happy, especially with the flow of heroin and its associated problems into Yunnan as a point of dispersal (Roy 1998: 174)

TERRORISM

As noted at the outset of this chapter, there has been considerable international attention focused on the issue of terrorism since the destruction of the World Trade Center buildings in New York on 11 September 2001. Much of this attention has been given to non-state terrorist groups in South-East Asia, including their claimed links to al-Qaeda. However, this simple focus on al-Qaeda ignores the rich history of jihadist Islamism and its ideological orientation, as well as the multiplicities of Islam that see it divided into two great streams—Sunni and Shi'a—as well as minor sects, four main schools and varying interpretations, ranging from the most liberal and democratic to conservative, anti-democratic and even absolutist.

Perhaps the most stringent of Islamic schools of thought, the Hanbali school, based on the teachings of the legal scholar Ahmad ibn Hanbal (780–855), minimises the private aspect of religion, rejects personal opinion and emphasises a near-total dependence on the divine in the establishment of legal theory. Legal decisions are heavily reliant on a literal reading of the Qur'an and Hadith (narratives relating to the Prophet's life and sayings); modernist reinterpretations are treated with hostility. The most well-known aspect of Ibn Hanbal's life is the suffering he endured during an inquisition, known as *al-mithnah,* ordered by the caliph al-Mamun. The unflinching spirit shown by Ibn Hanbal in the face of floggings and imprisonment, as well as his intellectual work on the Hadith, ensured his stature as one of the most venerated fathers of Islam and as a staunch upholder of Muslim orthodoxy. It would appear that Riduan Isamuddin, the terrorist figure known as Hambali, identified with Ibn Hanbal's stoicism, militancy and uncompromising attitudes. Although the Hanbali school is the smallest of the four Sunni schools of law, its importance and that of Ibn Hanbal derive from their impact on the development of Islamic religious history. In the Middle Ages, the school acted as a spearhead of traditionalist orthodoxy in its struggle against rationalism. One of Ibn Hanbal's greatest followers, Ibn Taymiyah (1263–1328), was claimed by both the Wahhabiyah, a reform movement founded in the mid-eighteenth century, and the modern Salafiyah movement, which arose in Egypt and advocated the continued supremacy of Islamic law, but with fresh interpretations to meet the community's changing needs (Fakhry 1983: ch. 11).

The Wahhabi version of Islam originated from the teachings and actions of Muhammad ibn-Abd-al-Wahhab (1703–92), who preached an austere doctrine that rejected Arabian folk Islam as well as Sufi beliefs and practices (Fakhry 1983: ch 11, Robinson 1999: 43–4). Wahhabist Islam gained influence in Indonesia during the 1970s (van Bruinessen 2002a, 2002c) and a range of radical Indonesian organisations are inspired by it. This influence is reflected in the organisation *Majelis Mujahidin Indonesia* (MMI, or Indonesian Mujahidin Council) (*Suara Pembaruan* 2002a, b) and can also be seen in the *Rabitat-ul* (International). It should be noted that adherents of Wahhabism strongly disapprove of the term, preferring instead to call themselves *Muwahhidun* (Unitarians). Modern Wahhabism is said to be a revival of Salafiya puritanism (from *as-salaf as-salih*, 'pious forefathers', or the community of believers in the early Muslim state of Muhammad and his companions) (Robinson 1999: 48). The Wahhabist movement identifies with an ideal time in history and deliberately advocates atavistic practices in order to bring present-day Muslims up to the standards of an earlier ideal.

While Muslim revivalist programs are often labelled 'fundamentalist', as Ansari notes, the label is 'often applied inaccurately to anything Muslim which challenges what the West assumes to be progress'. 'Islamism' is, therefore, a more accurate term, highlighting the importance of activism in 'creating a new religio-political order while preserving orthodox religious observances. It therefore appeals for reinterpretation of the sources of doctrine rather than the reassertion of traditional values'. Islamism is a twentieth-century phenomenon that usually holds the view that government, with the enhanced power of the modernised state at its disposal, should exercise much greater responsibility for the people. This difference gives a distinctly modernist look to the relationship between Islam and the state (Ansari 1998: 112) and has been characterised as reflecting more a resemblance to the structure and goals of European fascist parties and Marxist–Leninist organisations than to Islam as it is inscribed in the Qur'an (Robinson 1999: 57). Such a perspective is exemplified by the *Ikhwan al-Muslimin* (Muslim Brotherhood),[10] the leading Islamist force in the Middle East, which was founded in Egypt in 1928 by Hassan al-Banna (1906–49) with the intention of liberating Egypt and the rest of the Muslim world from foreign control and establishing Islamic states (Robinson 1999: 50). The *Ikhwan al-Muslimin* was further radicalised after it was suppressed in 1954, with its leading ideologue, Sayyid Qutb (1906–66), being hanged after being implicated in a plot to kill Egypt's President Nasser. Qutb developed the doctrine that it was permissible to engage in *jihad* against the government, a view that still underpins anti-state Islamism in South-East Asia. It is, in effect, this Qutbist version of Wahhabist Islamism that characterises violent Islam in SEA, which, in part, derived from links to al-Qaeda and in part from local adoption of Qutbist ideology.

Prior to, and as a consequence of, the USA-led invasion of Afghanistan in 2002, a large number of al-Qaeda personnel were dispersed to Islamic countries in South-East Asia, from where up to 1000 recruits to their cause had earlier been drawn and to where they felt some ideological affinity (Brownfeld 2002). It was these returnees, linked with former members of earlier radical Islamic organisations and new recruits, who formed the core of Indonesia's post-Suharto era militant Islam. Other recruits also returned and influenced Islamic movements in Malaysia, Singapore and, especially, the Philippines, where there were preexisting Islamist movements, responding to both local conditions (southern Philippines) and the opportunities provided by a supportive environment (Malaysia, Singapore).

It has been common enough for observers of Islam to note that Islam has not undergone a reformation, as had the Christian church, and this is usually cited by way of explaining its backwardness or conservatism. Yet the current Islamist movement seems to be just that—a reformation—and appears to derive as much from modernism as it does from Salafism (the two often being found together). The Christian Reformation was originally intended to purify the church of the corrupt influences of Catholicism and the priesthood and to restore man's link with God. The Islamist movement, or movements, is (or are) somewhat different, but the parallels are worth noting, if only because they indicate that the West might not be the primary target of the revolution; it might be that the revolution is primarily about reordering Islam in predominantly Islamic states.

The principle driver for terrorism and, indeed, for all political claims, is economic or political scarcity—real or perceived. Such scarcity is a contributor to and manifestation of reduced security, which, if not adequately addressed, can and often does call forth a reaction. This implies a degree of rational choice in political violence; in many cases, this is an accurate portrayal, that is, that violence is a response to an inequitable environment. While there are examples of reactions based on more or less purely ideological grounds, even in such cases they tend to claim to represent the interests of people affected by scarcity, although, in some instances, the interests being represented are much more personal and reflect a complex of economic considerations, status and power. Political violence can also be inspired by an idea somewhat divorced from real or perceived scarcity, such as the need to purify the community, that is to say, terrorism or revolutionary activity is not driven by deterministic factors alone or sometimes not even primarily driven by such factors, but is available to a range of issues that influence its flow and ebb. Indonesia's Abu Bakar Ba'asyir or his followers, for example, might be fired by an idea or set of ideas more than a specific grievance, as too might other radical regional Islamist organisations. This could also apply to other explanatory and prescriptive ideologies, such as communism, even if the ideology is based on emancipatory principles, as is Islam. But the logic of violent political change—revolution, terrorism—is primarily informed by emancipatory principles based upon a real, preexisting problem. Each ideological movement develops in response to a real set of circumstances and, in this respect, Abu Bakar Ba'asyir is, allegedly, an ideological follower, not an originator, as were al-Banna and Qutb. That is, the followers might act on the ideology, but the ideology itself is not divorced from the reality it intends to address. People do not have to be poor or desperate to become terrorists, but they do require a putative identification with such oppression, unless, of course, they are simple criminals. Recruitment to such causes, relies on experience of a real, lived scarcity, which can be channelled into an ideological framework that at once explains the problem and at the same time offers a prescription for its cure. Experience or awareness of scarcity and acceptance of an ideological explanation logically implies a call for political redress. Violence has been, and remains, a widely accepted if politically unsophisticated method of achieving compliance to a particular ideological prescription; within the context of imbalances of capacity for violence, terrorism can act as a persuasive shortcut.

Despite broad acceptance of the idea of terrorism being intended to obtain compliance, there remains no finite definition of terrorism; nor are its actors limited by position. The term 'terror', within a political context, usually means to attempt to persuade others of one's own political position by the use of exemplary violence or the threat of violence, instilling in the audience a state of heightened or absolute fear—or terror. Terrorism can also be used to persuade others not to accept a particular political perspective, but simply to engage in action in accordance with that perspective, for example, the release of political prisoners or the establishment of a material good, or to encourage a response that, in turn, supports the goals of the terrorists, for example, increased generalised repression leading to broad-based anti-repressive sentiment.

The term 'terrorist' is usually applied to individual or collective non-state actors, but state or state-sponsored actors can—and often do—also conform to either the methods or the purposes of non-state terrorists. This has particularly been the case in Indonesia, most notably with the TNI and, at its exemplary edge, *Kopassus*, in part through their involvement in and support for extremist Islamic organisations, but can also be seen to apply to Burma, the Philippines, Thailand and similarly perhaps in Vietnam, Cambodia and Laos.

As can be seen from the Philippines' New People's Army (NPA) and the various regional Islamic separatists groups, ideological division, shifting agendas and, in many cases, confusion and a lack of coherence have reduced their efficacy. Tactics have varied from outright military offensive to conventional guerrilla struggle, urban warfare and activities that might more readily be characterised as organised crime, if at a low and local level. In part, this reflects the localised nature of much of the grievance or alienation that has led to such activities, in part to a more generalised sense of disconnectedness and, in part, to echoes of a traditional type of local control over local affairs, which fluctuates according to the circumstances. The exception to this was, for a few years, the highly organised and centralised structure of the NPA, which, eventually, fell foul of its own internal rigidities.

If this might seem to reflect a functional inability, the fact that various terrorist and insurgent organisations continue, at varying levels of efficacy, indicates that they have a regenerative capacity, that they continue to undermine the authority of the state and the circumstances that give rise to them have not been ameliorated. Similarly, the incapacity of the government to either address the underlying concerns that continue to give rise to such dissent or to militarily crush such movements, equally indicates a low level of organisation, commitment, perhaps coherence and, almost certainly, a lack of focus of purpose. Thus, the circumstances that give rise to insurgency and terrorist organisations in Indonesia, Southern Thailand, Malaysia, Singapore and the Philippines and to other violent non-state organisations, and which allow them to continue, do not only seem unresolvable in the foreseeable future, but may also be implicit in the structure of the types of states and polities that characterise the region.

Considering the strategic implications of the region, it is clear that there are numerous local issues that continue to tear at the fabric of peace and unity. Further, tensions both historic and contemporary continue to generate friction between the states of the region, none of which, it appears, will be easily resolved. Given that SEA sits astride one of the major land and water crossroads of the world, there has long been and continues to be considerable international interest in local affairs. The states of SEA were, perhaps, at the beginning of the twenty-first century, more able to determine their own futures than at any time since the eighteenth century. But in doing so, they needed to be cognisant of the fact that, unlike their world view of the precolonial era, in which petty kings thought themselves omnipotent and local emperors thought themselves gods, the states and their leaders are small players on the world stage. They were important in their own region, but their continued internal focus was being challenged by the reality that the world was becoming an increasingly integrated place. The twin pressures of local identity and globalisation presented new challenges to many of the states of the world. The states of SEA were at least as vulnerable as any to such challenges.

NOTES

1   While some Indonesian troops did land on the Malay Peninsula, most of the actual fighting, limited though it was, took place in northern Borneo. The southern parts of the island, known as Kalimantan, had passed from the Dutch to the Republic of Indonesia in 1949, but the states of Sabah, Sarawak and Brunei remained under British protection. That Brunei's sultan decided not to join the new federation of Malaysia did not alter the United Kingdom's commitment to defending the state against what it then regarded as external aggression, though which was probably more an expression of local political frustration.

2   Chartered Industries is linked to the Singapore government and is run by a member of the family of former Prime Minister Lee Kuan Yew.

3   The ethnic Malays of southern Thailand mostly speak Jawi, a Malay dialect.

4   In each case, this had comprised insurgencies, except for Indonesia, where the PKI was an open and legitimate party until its destruction by the incipient New Order government.

5   It should be noted that China's contribution to the Second Indochina War was much less than analysts at that time believed and that, during the 1960s, China and Vietnam were increasingly retreating to their historical positions of mutual suspicion and hostility towards each other.

6   The NAM had twenty-five member countries in 1961, rising to 113 (with three suspended) by 1995.
7   My experience of this derived from being present at a number of media conferences held by ASEAN at the UN in 1983, as well as regularly reporting on Vietnam and its position vis-à-vis ASEAN in the latter 1980s for Radio Australia.
8   As a consequence, China's People's Liberation Army overhauled its human wave methods of attack and moved to update its weaponry.
9   Ball notes that China's primary involvement in the Bay of Bengal is assisting Burma with intelligence gathering and in undertaking some intelligence gathering, particularly of shipping, of its own.
10   This organisation has a number of ideological parallels with the MMI.

The Mainland | 2

5 | Burma:[1]
The Garrison State

FOUNDATIONS OF THE STATE

The region now known as Burma has been continuously inhabited since at least 2500 BC, with settlers taking advantage of the rich alluvial plains fed by the Irrawaddy River system. From around the middle of the ninth century, the first group to consolidate control over the central part of the valley was the Pyu, based in and around Pagan (see Htin 1967: 5–21). The Pyu, who practised Hinduism blended with Mahayana and, later, Theravada Buddhism (Cady 1958: 4–9), were overthrown by invaders from what is now Yunnan in China in the tenth century AD, which left the northern and central region without any coherent political control. Pagan's decline as a political capital was completed by 1289, with its sacking by the Mongols of Kublai Khan, which ushered in 250 years of chaos.

In the southern region, the Mon[2] began settling in the area between the Irrawaddy and what is now western Cambodia from about the sixth century. After a series of skirmishes with the ascendant neighbouring T'ai,[3] the Mon established their capital at Pegu, about 70 kilometres north of Rangoon (Htin 1967: 21–8). Around the late eighth or early ninth century, the Bhamese, a group related to the Tibetans, descended into the upper valley from the eastern slopes of the Himalayas. There they quickly supplanted the vanquished Pyu and battled with neighbouring Shans and other groups for dominance within the upper valley. These events set up the framework for competing ethnic divisions that dominate Burmese politics to this day. By the end of the fifteenth century, the Bhamese had consolidated their dominance over the northern Irrawaddy Valley and, in the following decades, entered into conflict with the Mon for control of the whole valley. It was not until 1555 that this conflict, including their defeat of the neighbouring Thais in 1549, was settled in favour of the Bhamese. The high level of Mon–Bhamese antagonism from that time continues to exist. To ensure the protection of the capital from recalcitrant Mons, the Bhamese retained the capital at Ava, moving back to nearby Pegu and back again to

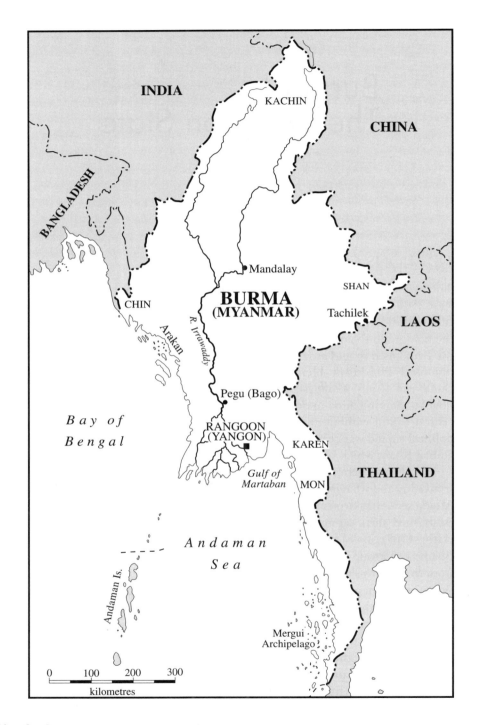

Map 2 Burma

Ava, depending on which king was in power and which site was regarded as most secure and auspicious. This general location of the capital had the effect of removing the political elite of the state from significant coastal contact and encouraged a sense of cultural and economic isolation; it also was a major contributing factor leading to conflict with the British.

The Burmese state went into decline after the death of King Baynnaung in 1581; by the mid 1600s, the authority of the state had retreated to its core. The hill tribes, including the Shan, began to raid the lowlands and, in the south, the Mon broke away, establishing a new kingdom at Pegu. In 1752 the Mon even succeeded in taking Ava, but that year, Alaungpaya, a new Bhamese king came to power in Shwebo, 80 kilometres north of Ava, and embarked on a period of reconquest, destroying all who stood before the rebirth of the new state. Such was the seeming invincibility of Alaungpaya that the Konbuang Dynasty he founded believed that it could not be successfully challenged. When a Bhamese general who had been installed on the throne of Chiang Mai in 1763 was overthrown soon after in a local rebellion, Alaungpaya's son Hsinbyushin commanded 30 000, mostly Shan, soldiers to invade the principality. The Bhamese-commanded army then moved on to Luang Prabang in what is now modern Laos, assisted by troops from Vieng Chan. Having reduced Luang Prabang, they then prepared for an assault on Ayudhya, near what is now Bangkok. The Thai capital was laid to waste, its inhabitants killed, dispersed or led away to slavery (Wyatt 1984: 134–7). It was to be the high imperial point of pre-United Kingdom Burma, to which contemporary Burmese leaders look for cues for the postcolonial Burmese state.

COLONIAL HISTORY

By the early 1800s, the British had consolidated their rule over Assam and the eastern Islamic states of the Indian subcontinent and established the Strait Settlements along the Malay peninsula. However, the British were concerned about growing French interest in the region—Thailand[4] and, later, Indochina—and so wished to extend their authority to the eastern part of the Bay of Bengal. The British and their new South Asian subjects came into contact with the Burmese in Chin and Arakan states (see Myint-U 2001: 12–20), especially over Burmese raids into British territory chasing disloyal Burmese subjects. This gave the British the excuse they needed to extend their control: they declared war in 1824 and, over the next two years, secured Arakan and the Tenasserim coast along the Thai border on the upper peninsula in the region of the Isthmus of Kra (Htin 1967: 210–32; Cady 1958: 68–74).

Still unaware of British power or intentions, the Burmese king at Mandalay neither improved defences nor engaged in constructive dialogue with them. In 1852, two British sea captains were held at Rangoon in lieu of paying a small fine for transgressing port rules, thereby providing the United Kingdom with a pretext to launch its second offensive, this time occupying the whole of southern Burma (Myint-U 2001: ch. 5). By this stage, the Burmese king realised the thrust of British intentions and attempted to establish good relations and engage in internal administrative reforms. However, the firm establishment of the French in Indochina by the 1870s and the growth of French interest in northern Burma in the early 1880s, which complicated British interest in access to China, coupled with declining royal Burmese authority (Myint-U 2001:135, 171-8), decided the British course of action. In 1885, two events sealed Burma's precolonial fate. The first was commercial difficulties between the expansionary Bombay Burmah Trading Company and the Burmese administration at Mandalay. The second was the bad international publicity accorded a traditional, though exceptionally bloody, massacre of kinsmen upon the succession to the throne of the new king, Thibaw. This latter event, in which a new king would have dozens—sometimes hundreds—of his relatives and acquaintances murdered to ensure no rivalry for the throne, horrified the newspaper-reading European public, leaving British public opinion in particular with little sympathy for the legitimising claims of the new king.[5] The British launched the Third Burma War by sending gunboats up the Irrawaddy River to Mandalay, formally annexing the remainder of the state the following year and administering it from India. Over the next two years, the British crushed resistance to their rule (Myint-U 2001:190-3). The indignity inflicted upon the state of Burma was reflected in the British establishing the capital of the colony at Rangoon, in the south, for better sea access, relegating the former capital of Mandalay to second-city status, from which it has never recovered (Fisher 1966: 149–56; Htin 1967: 233–65; Cady 1958: 125–54).

THE COLONIAL PERIOD

In Burma under the British, ethnic Indians moved into southern Burma to take up junior administrative positions and to work the newly cleared swamplands, which were turned into rice paddies, while the Bhamese were relegated to second-citizen status. By 1930, half the population of Rangoon was Indian. Commercial cropping turned the country into the world's rice basket, profits from which paid for increasing imports; and new systems of land tenure and money lending disrupted traditional social patterns. While the British administered Burma proper, as they called it, directly, they formally acknowledged the separation of the frontier states, allowing a relatively high degree of autonomy based on ethnicity in the Chin, Kachin, Karen, Shan and Kayah (Karreni) regions. It was from this recognition and consequent formalisation of national difference that the frontier states later sought to assert their independence from ethnic Bhamese domination.

While a Burmese sense of nationalism grew in the shadow of its Indian counterpart, in a practical sense it exceeded the nationalism of India. From as early as 1897, the British began to allow a degree of local autonomy, granting increasing degrees of self-rule and, in 1937, Burma had its own cabinet, based on a parliamentary system. It was noted soon after that, with the exception of the Philippines, no imperial colony had more political autonomy than did Burma and that, as a result, achieving independence was close at hand (Fisher 1966: 446).

Burma enjoyed four popularly elected governments until, in 1941, it was invaded by Japan as a part of that country's strategic plan for WWII. Prior to the Japanese invasion, though, there was considerable anti-British sentiment. For example, the student activist Aung San had opposed British colonialism and been arrested for his pro-independence activities. He and twenty-nine others, known thereafter as the Thirty Comrades, had fled to Japan in 1939 to receive military training, returning with the Japanese to lead the Japanese-backed Burma Independence (later National) Army (BIA). In a technical sense, by 1942, the BIA and the Japanese Imperial Army shared occupation of the state, however, as it became increasingly clear that Japan was losing the war, Aung San and the BIA switched sides and joined the British against Japan, thereby winning some legitimacy in the eyes of the British at the conclusion of the conflict (see Cady 1958: 427–84).

INDEPENDENCE

Aung San has been celebrated not only as the founding father of Burma, but also as a democrat (Silverstein 1993: 153–6), a mantle that his daughter wears to considerable political advantage. Aung San favoured elections through 'universal adult suffrage by secret ballot' (Aung San, Point 9: 'Fourteen Points', in Silverstein 1993: 69) and representation for ethnic minorities. But he was also a Burmese nationalist and was determined that the state remain united in what its ethnic minorities regarded, with considerable justification, as a unitarian rather than federal state under its ethnic Bhamese majority.

The Communist Party of Burma (CPB) also enjoyed considerable popular support at this time, but Aung San and his colleague U Nu systematically moved to have both its factions (White Flag and Red Flag) expelled from the umbrella party, the Anti-Fascist People's Freedom League (AFPFL)[6] in order to avoid the likely prospect of a coalition government. The more fanatical Red Flag group was outlawed in July 1946 and went underground in 1947, with the White Flag following suit and declaring war on the state the following year (Shwe 1989: 26–7). It was these two fields of division—ethnic identity and ideology—that led to the conflicts that beset the state from the end of 1948 and which came, in large part, to shape the state to the present time. In any case, whatever moderating influence might have been claimed for Aung San, which, in retrospect, accords him a more politically inclusive approach than his writings suggest, the rest of the Bhamese-dominated AFPFL was far less open to full political representation by Burma's communists and ethnic minorities[7] (Shwe 1989: 27–9).

In January 1947, Aung San reached agreement with the United Kingdom for full independence to be granted a year later. In February 1947, representatives of all of the states of the proposed federation met in the town of Pin-Lon in Shan State to formulate the process of union. This Pinlon Treaty was incorporated into the Constitution and allowed, under Chapter 10, 'The Right of Secession' (with the exception of Kachin State) after ten years, if the respective states so wished. With this agreement, Aung San formed a provisional government ahead of full independence.

But in July 1947, before independence was granted, Aung San and six cabinet colleagues were assassinated by two men with automatic weapons. The political leader U Saw, who led a movement in opposition to the AFPFL, was convicted of organising the murders and was duly hanged. Although the arms and vehicles used in the assassination were traced to the home of U Saw, where further stolen weapons were found, there remains a lingering doubt about his complicity or, if he was involved, whether he acted alone. There have been suggestions that the assassination was, in fact, organised by a rival of Aung San within the military wing of the AFPFL, although some claims that this person was General Ne Win, Burma's long-time military leader, plays rather too neatly into later political divisions.

THE MILITARY STATE

For many years after Ne Win officially retired, it was commonly assumed that he still provided a guiding hand for Burma's political direction and, even when he was not consulted, this was only because his successors were fairly certain they knew his preferences. Indeed, this was probably the case. Similarly, it was widely thought that when Ne Win finally died, Burma would begin to emerge from under his authoritarian shadow. However, on this most observers were quite incorrect. After Ne Win's death, Burma remained as authoritarian a state as it had been under his direct and indirect rule; by the end of 2004, Burma appeared to be lurching towards an even more conservative position. As usual, the on again, off again talk of the release of political prisoners was more intended to raise hopes—and quieten criticism—of prodemocracy activists and outsiders, which it did, than it was aimed to change in a system in which opposition meant jail, or worse. Optimism also surfaced from time to time about an eventual rapprochement between the ruling junta and the legitimately elected government of the National League for Democracy (NLD), but this was similarly disappointed. Burma was one country where cynicism about the motives and intentions of the ruling generals was all too easily rewarded.

The government of Burma has, since 1962, been a classic military dictatorship. The country has been ruled by the military and, as with all military dictatorships, despite its claims to do so on behalf of the Burmese people, it has ruled on its own behalf. As with many other countries in which the military has a prominent role in politics, Burma's military played a leading role in gaining the country independence from its colonial master, in this case the United Kingdom, thereby moving some way towards institutionalising itself in the process of government. However, the diverse ethnic nature of Burma or, more accurately, the incorporation of separate nations of peoples within a unitary Burmese state, has led to a constant conflict between these ethnic groups and the army, which has established for itself a role as guardian of the state. While the military government rules without the support of the great majority of Burmese people, it is able to maintain its internal cohesion as a consequence of four characteristics. The first is the army's caste-like sense of identity, especially among the officer corps. The second is a system of patronage by senior officers, which ensures loyalty and obedience, even when ordered to fire on unarmed demonstrators or other morally repugnant acts. Third, membership in the military is almost the only means of gaining upward social mobility (Pedersen, Rudland & May 2000: 5) and fourth, with such a large military, many families have a member who is in the armed forces. While Burma continues to be constructed of several separate nations under a constitution, as it is interpreted, which ensures ethnic Bhamese domination, the state will continue to be internally riven. This, in turn, means that the military will— or will want to—continue to play a prominent role in Burmese politics.

SEPARATISM AND ELECTIONS

Independence went ahead, being granted on 4 January 1948, with U Nu becoming prime minister. No sooner had independence been proclaimed, than Burma's ethnic minorities demanded independence and, upon refusal, rebelled against the Rangoon government, claiming, with considerable justification, that it had abandoned the inclusive form of government agreed to with the British and reasserted chauvinistic Bhamese authority. The main insurgent groups were primarily based on the Arakanese, Chin, Kachin, Mon, Shan and Karen ethnic groups, as well as the two communist parties, which had rebelled following a crackdown by the new government (Smith 1999: chs 7, 8; Lintner 1999: 1). From the late 1940s onwards, subfactions of these groups coalesced and divided.[8] By the end of 1949, the insurgent groups were so successful and the Rangoon government so disorganised that almost the whole of the country was in the hands of one rebel group or another, a situation further complicated by the defeat of the Chinese nationalist Kuomingtang (KMT) army by the Chinese communists in 1949. Between 1949 and 1952, the remnants of the KMT 8th Army and other

KMT forces crossed from Yunnan province into southern Shan State, from where they set up new bases. Not only were the KMT units well armed and located in remote regions, as well as being actively supported by Taiwan, they were also supported by the US government, which hoped these military units would continue to keep the new Chinese communist government off balance. Instead, the KMT troops aided Karen rebels and later turned to the lucrative opium-growing business, establishing themselves as an effectively independent state within the state (Lintner 1999:110-124, ch 4).

Over the following two years, the *Tatmadaw*, under the command of Ne Win, wrested control of much of the state back from the insurgents, which act was helped by the insurgents' general disorganisation, poor tactics, lack of unity among rebel groups and the two communist parties attacking the Karen National Union, the troops of which had at their most threatening members advance to within 16 kilometres of Rangoon. The communist groups attacked the Karen forces on the grounds that the Karens were splitting the state along ethnic lines, as claimed by U Nu and Ne Win, rather than along class lines, as the communists advocated. This triangulation of the conflict weakened the antigovernment groups, especially the Karen forces, which were exposed and spread out along the Irrawaddy plain among its ethnic Bhamese inhabitants. The Karen forces subsequently retreated to the Burmese–Thai border, giving the Rangoon government time to regroup. Meanwhile, the Arakanese rebels split between their nationalist and communist wings, further enhancing the position of the Rangoon government's forces (Lintner 1999: ch. 3; Shwe 1989: 30–1; see also, Trager 1966: ch. 6). A government amnesty also weakened the antigovernment forces, to the extent that, by 1951, the government was able to hold elections in some parts of the country. The AFPFL was returned to government with a comfortable majority. Elections were again held in 1956, returning the AFPFL in Bhamese-dominated areas and nationalist or ethnic representatives in non-Bhamese regions; in each case, the appointment of the head of each state required the approval of the prime minister.

The period from 1956 until 1962 has been termed one of 'parliamentary democracy' (Shwe 1989: 31), at least in the Bhamese heartland. In this period, the insurgencies were at a low ebb. However, non-Bhamese representatives in the parliament claimed that Burma was not a union of the eight states, as outlined in the Constitution, but rather, a unitary state; the regional states received, but did not determine, local policy.

The government of the Union of Burma used the term '*Burma Pyima*' to distinguish what the British had called the 'Burma Proper' region from what it had called the 'Frontier States'. However, the word '*pyima*' means 'a centre of ruling, administration, civilisation and benefactors'. Similarly, the non-Bhamese states were referred to as '*pyinay*', which denotes inferiority and subordination (Shwe 1989: 35). This placed the non-Bhamese states in a peripheral and subordinate relationship to the Bhamese, which they deeply resented. As a consequence of Bhamese rejection of a proposed Federation of Burma, in 1958, the Shan representatives chose to secede from the union, as was their constitutional right, determined by the incorporation into the Constitution of Chapter 10 of the Pinlon Treaty.

THE ARMY MOVES INTO POLITICS

While this further attempted secession of the Frontier States could have been a cause for Bhamese concern, it was, in fact, brought quickly under military control. At this time, the AFPFL was more preoccupied with internal divisions, which were based on personality clashes over the distribution of power within the government, in particular, between Prime Minister U Nu and Deputy Prime Minister U Kyaw Nyein (Shwe 1989: 37). As a result of the split, U Nu formed the Union Party, while U Kyaw Nyein's group retained the AFPFL name.

Unable to command a majority in parliament, U Nu handed political power to a caretaker government headed by General Ne Win, who would hold fresh elections in 1960. In the meantime, Ne Win had presided over the removal of the last vestiges of feudal rights of the Shan and Kaya lords, which included a guaranteed seat in the National Assembly. He also presided over the cession of territory to China, based on a Chinese claim that dated back to Kublai Khan's occupation of Pagan in 1279. This loss of territory especially affected the Wa National Area and Shan State which, in response, again attempted to secede as per Chapter X of the Constitution.

Despite acquiring a taste for political power (Cady 1958: 32), the army allowed Burma's third elections to be duly held in May 1960. U Nu's Union Party won 159 of 250 seats, the AFPFL won forty-two seats and forty-nine seats were distributed among state-based political parties. The army waited in the wings, 'prejudicing' the survival of constitutional government (Cady 1958: 34). While U Nu's government acceded to some regional demands by creating the new states of Arakan, Mon and Chin to add to the existing Kachin, Shan, Kaya and Karen states, their demands for a federated state continued unabated and the Bhamese majority continued to reject them. Added to this, the government making Buddhism the state religion caused protests and riots to break out, especially in Kachin State, where Christianity was the majority religion, and among Muslims. The Rangoon University Students Union and the All Burma Federation of Student Unions demonstrated against the bill, while opposition parties and the military also expressed their displeasure.

To compound this unrest, Burma's economy was stagnant while the population was increasing. From February 1962, leaders from the Kachin, Shan, Kaya, Mon, Arakan and Chin groups gathered in Rangoon to finalise their version of a proposed Constitution for a Federation of Burma. On 2 March, Ne Win took advantage of the situation by arresting these leaders and launching a coup against the government, replacing it with a revolutionary council of seventeen officers who ruled by decree. This set the stage for the subsequent institutionalised military domination of Burmese politics, with consequent domestic dissent, and the entrenchment of ethnic military opposition to the Rangoon government (M. Smith 1999b: 195–7; see also, Trager 1966: ch. 9).

ISOLATIONISM

In his first major act in government—accusing the previous government of putting the nation's integrity at risk and abandoning socialism—Ne Win formulated what was called the Burmese Road to Socialism, which claimed to mix socialist and Buddhist ideas with a policy of isolationist self-sufficiency. At this stage, it could be argued that the army was acting at least in part on principle, even if that principle was misguided. This move towards socialism reflected a high level of popular support for leftist ideas and disenchantment with parliamentary democracy, both for its corruption and for it being a legacy of imperialism. The Soviet Union, at this stage, looked to be a suitable alternative model for economic development, although there was considerable concern about Stalin's influence on the Soviet model and its general rejection of religion (Shwe 1989: 86–7).

To implement its program of Burmese-style socialism, the army formed the Burma Socialist Programme Party (BSPP), which, in 1964, became the only legal political party. Through the BSPP, a network of military-dominated councils administered the country, while the BSPP-controlled Peasants' and Workers' Council provided another avenue of political and social authority. Under the BSPP's program, some 15 000 private companies, including foreign-owned companies, were nationalised and international trade was severely limited. In response, the economy, which was already in poor shape, atrophied. Meanwhile, twenty-eight separate organisations formed to oppose the Rangoon government, most through military means (M. Smith 1999b: 219–27; Shwe 1989: 42–4). In July 1962, students at Rangoon University, protesting against strict new regulations, were met by around 2000 soldiers who, after a brief lull, fired on them, killing hundreds and arresting 3000 (Shwe, 1989: 47; Sesser 1993: 202–3). This event set the tone for BSPP rule for the next three and a half decades.

Between 1962 and 1987, as a result of instituting the Burmese Road to Socialism, Burma's economy had become a shambles. Production from the one-time ricebowl of Asia dropped from 2 000 000 tonnes to 200 000 tonnes, with consequent food shortages for the first time in memory. In 1987, the BSPP admitted its poor economic management and asked the United Nations for 'least developed country' status, making it eligible for additional foreign aid. As the per capita income was then about US$210 a year, this was granted. The formal acknowledgment that Burma had slid so far as to join the world's ten poorest countries came as a shock to the country's educated class and did much to undermine confidence in the military government. Burma's black market economy was, by this stage, already well developed.

In September 1987, the Rangoon government took a further economic initiative that was both inexplicable and deeply damaging. In a claimed bid to curb inflation and wipe out the black market, the government demonetised the three highest bank notes (kyats)—K75, K35 and K25, thereby making worthless around 56 per cent of the money in circulation in Burma at that time. Given that most people kept their savings in cash, including most of the military and the public service and, in particular, the farmer parents of most of the army's soldiers (due to the difficulty in accessing bank accounts), much of the savings of most Burmese was wiped out. The now-worthless banknotes were replaced with the equally oddly denominated notes of K45 and K90, reflecting Ne Win's obsession with variations on the number nine. (Ne Win was very superstitious, as are many Burmese, but he had the power to indulge his superstitions.) The move was intended to curb inflation, but the effect was the opposite. With no public faith in the future of cash, people spent it as quickly as possible, pushing up the price of goods and increasing inflation.

DISSENT

The central Irrawaddy Valley was, for the most part, relatively peaceful from 1962 until the late 1980s, indicating more the BSPP's firm grip on power and the effectiveness of its intelligence (Ball 1998: 61) and security apparatus than satisfaction with its rule. However, among a number of relatively minor disturbances, there were two serious incidents in Rangoon that indicated that all was not well within the Burmese heartland. The first incident, in 1967, was anti-Chinese riots in response to a perception that China was attempting to export its Cultural Revolution to Burma. In this incident, hundreds of ethnic Chinese Burmese citizens were killed by other Burmese, although the riots were almost certainly instigated by the Rangoon government, which, at that time, had poor relations with China. The next major incident, seven years later, revolved around the death and funeral arrangements for the Burmese former secretary-general of the United Nations (1962–71), U Thant.

U Thant died in New York in 1974, at which time his family brought his body back to Rangoon for burial. Tens of thousands of people lined the road to pay their respects, the gathering of which worried the government. Ne Win also harboured some animosity towards U Thant, because of the latter's close association with Ne Win's predecessor, U Nu. The government wanted a quick funeral at the Kyandaw Cemetery, but students and monks removed the coffin from the hearse at Kyaikasan Stadium, where it had been in state, and took it to Rangoon University, where it was draped with the banned student union's fighting peacock flag. Four days later, on 7

December, the army attacked the university, killing 135 students and arresting thousands more. The student union building, a symbol of Burmese nationalism since the 1930s, was dynamited at midnight that night. U Thant's body was exhumed from the university grounds and buried by the government in a rough mausoleum near the Shwedagon Pagoda in central Rangoon (Shwe 1989: 50–3; Sesser 1993: 203–4).

In 1976, there was a falling out between the then defence minister, General Tin Oo, and Ne Win, the former being sacked from his position and jailed for four years. Tin Oo was allegedly aware of a plan to assassinate Ne Win, but did not report it. Tin Oo later joined the National League for Democracy (NLD), becoming one of its leaders, along with another former Ne Win associate, Aung Gyi. Aung Gyi resigned from his powerful position in the army when Ne Win seized power and moved towards socialism. He was jailed for three years in 1965 and again, briefly, in 1988. Aung Gyi broke with the NLD in 1989, saying that he had always been close to Ne Win, despite having twice been jailed, and accused NLD leaders Tin Oo and the daughter of Aung San, Suu Kyi, of being associated with communists. It is possible that Aung Gyi reached an accommodation with Ne Win, probably in the mid to late 1980s, and was planted by him to discredit the opposition. Within the NLD, a distinction in political style began to emerge, which has subsequently evolved into a type of factionalism. Tin Oo led a more conservative and somewhat more accommodating group within the NLD to that of Suu Kyi and was seen as pressing this group's claims to a less confrontational style with the Rangoon government. The basic difference has been over tactics, with Tin Oo's group supporting accommodation with the government and Suu Kyi's group in favour of confrontation. The ethnic separatist groups, meanwhile, have tended to regard accommodation and unarmed confrontation as non-viable options, preferring instead to remain outside the formal Burmese political system.

THE ARMY AGAINST THE PEOPLE

After years of repression, the demonetisation of the three banknotes pushed many people into public protest. Clearly, a general mood of dissatisfaction was building. Then, in March 1988, a seemingly innocuous fight in a teashop over music selection sparked a major upheaval. The police came and arrested the participants in the fight, clubbing one to death in the process. Dozens more were left locked in police vans for hours in the midday heat, as a result of which forty-one people suffocated to death. A protagonist in the original brawl was released without charge; as it turned out, he was the son of a senior BSPP member. This sparked more protests, which quickly turned into riots. The death toll rose into the hundreds. Then, on 21 June, a student protest at Rangoon University was attacked by police. Hundreds more were killed. In a public response to these events, General Ne Win resigned as chairman of the

BSPP and as a member of the party; however, as with his retirement as president in 1981, he continued to hold power from behind the scenes.

Ne Win's replacement was General Sein Lwin, who had directed the dynamiting of the student union building at Rangoon University, the bloody assault on students after U Thant's death and the attacks on students in March 1988, for which he was known as 'The Butcher'; not surprisingly, he was an unpopular choice as public leader (Lintner 1990: ch. 1). Within weeks of Sein Lwin taking office, tens of thousands of Burmese were protesting in the streets of Rangoon and Mandalay; between 8 and 13 August, soldiers in formation firing on peaceful, unarmed protesters killed at least 2000 people (Lintner 1990: 94–105). On 19 August, Ne Win replaced Sein Lwin with the civilian Maung Maung, who had been attorney-general in Ne Win's cabinet and who was regarded as more conciliatory. Although still a Ne Win loyalist, Maung Maung announced there would be elections, to be held under the auspices of the military government. Opposition leaders rejected the proposal, saying that Maung Maung should resign and that a non-military interim government should oversee the election process.

With no movement from the government, protesters again spilled into the streets, now demanding immediate democratisation. Suu Kyi, daughter of assassinated Burmese leader Aung San, had recently returned from England to care for her ailing mother. Although she had no political background, as a symbol of Burma's initial aspirations for democracy she was immediately pushed into the forefront of the protest movement, being appointed general secretary of the NLD, a position that she took up with great enthusiasm. The protest movement had grown beyond students and monks and now included professionals, workers, even government officials.

A general strike was called, which received popular support. The protest movement was now a strong expression of widespread, popular opposition to the government. Government administration ground to a standstill and, after initially taking no action, soldiers began to uncoil barbed wire barricades in the streets of Rangoon. Burma's newspapers, long subject to strict censorship, began to publish articles critical of the government. By 19 August, the protesters controlled Burma's second city of Mandalay. It was two years after the so-called People's Power revolution in the Philippines, which ousted dictator Ferdinand Marcos. However, as so widely misunderstood elsewhere, those who took courage from the Philippines' movement, failed to acknowledge or understand that it was the military, in alliance with a disaffected elite, that eventually toppled Marcos, not the people. Without the army on side, even in similar circumstances, such an event could not be repeated.

THE ESTABLISHMENT OF THE SLORC

To destabilise this difficult situation, from 21 August Ne Win had Rangoon's prisons emptied. The resulting upsurge in crime included widespread looting, in which ordinary but desperate Burmese joined in. Vigilante committees were established, which themselves acted with violence against suspected criminals and government agents. On 18 September, the BSPP government was dissolved and replaced by the State Law and Order Restoration Council (SLORC), headed by close Ne Win associate, General Saw Maung, who had previously been defence minister and, since 1985, army chief-of-staff. The 1974 Constitution was suspended and martial law declared. The SLORC differed from the BSPP primarily in that it brought all government institutions—though not the party—under the direct control of the *Tatmadaw*, rather than them being controlled through the military's influence, and allowed for substantial increases in military spending. The *Tatmadaw* effectively doubled in size between 1990 and 2000 and its budget was estimated to consume up to half of total government spending (Callahan, in Pedersen, Rudland & May 2000: 23, note 1). All state bodies were abolished to be replaced by representatives of the SLORC (M. Smith 1999b: 365–73).

The SLORC ordered striking workers back to their jobs, outlawed demonstrations and banned gatherings of more than four people. The following day, the bloodbath began. That morning, 8 August 1988, as protesters moved into the streets, soldiers positioned on bridges and on the tops of buildings opened fire on the crowds. In what has been described as an 'ambush' (Sesser 1993: 220), thousands upon thousands of Burmese citizens were killed by their own army.

Perhaps believing their own propaganda, the military-dominated Rangoon government believed that it was sufficiently popular or had sufficiently rigged the prospective electoral system that it could now go ahead and actually hold general elections, which it believed would legitimise its rule. Even if the elections had produced a more even division of support for the contesting parties, the SLORC was of the view that it could at least broker a deal that would see the army as the only unifying factor in Burmese politics and, hence, ensure its continuation in power.

The elections were held in May 1990, but were hampered by restrictions placed on political activities and the arrest of NLD leaders Suu Kyi and Tin Oo, along with the head of the Liberal Democratic Party, U Nu. Contrary to the SLORC's clearly misguided expectations, the elections were overwhelmingly won by the National League for Democracy. Despite massive vote rigging and electoral fraud by the government, the NLD took 392 of the 485 seats. The BSPP, renamed the National Union Party (NUP), won only ten seats. Initially saying they would hand over power, the military refused to acknowledge the results of the elections. When protests ensued, soldiers shot dead hundreds of protestors, including some parliamentarians held in custody, and, in the following year, placed Suu Kyi and other NLD leaders under house arrest (M. Smith 1999b: 412–19).

In 1991, the NLD was barred from political activity. In April 1991, the SLORC formally announced that it would not transfer power to the civilian opposition. In October that year, Suu Kyi was awarded the Nobel Peace Prize, inspiring further protests, the closure of universities and the banning of more political parties. To illustrate the SLORC's alienation from the Burmese people, in Mandalay, in 1992, a protest by Buddhist monks over the government's failure to honour the election results was met with rifle fire; more than 600 protestors were shot dead. Buddhism is highly revered across all strata of Bhamese society, as are its monks. Attacking Buddhist monks was an extreme sign in Burmese society, even for the SLORC, that there was no longer even the faintest semblance of authenticity between its rule and notions of political legitimacy.

SUU KYI AND THE NLD

By this stage, there was a high level of international concern over events in Burma. The increasingly brave and highly quotable Suu Kyi was lauded by the international media as symbolising honourable opposition to an evil government. As well as being awarded the Nobel Peace Prize for what the committee described as 'one of the most extraordinary examples of civil courage in Asia in recent years', Suu Kyi was also awarded the European parliament's Sakharov Prize for freedom of thought and, in 1992, the Simon Bolivar prize for freedom.

Suu Kyi was released from house arrest in 1995, but remained under the very close eye of the government. In September 1997, the NLD was allowed to hold its ninth anniversary meeting, which was seen by some as a concession by the government to the NLD. However, later talks between government representatives and some NLD leaders were regarded as a government attempt to split the NLD. The talks were aimed at having some NLD members cooperate with the government in exchange for some possible political freedom. Suu Kyi did not agree to such cooperation, leading to a division between herself and Tin Oo.[9]

As with other members of the NLD, Suu Kyi's movements after her being released from house arrest, were, in theory, free, but in practice very limited. Apart from being watched at all times, her freedom of movement was restricted by the government's insistence that she be protected by armed guards and that she not be allowed to move around Burma without first notifying the government, which had the effect of inhibiting her movement on a number of occasions, perhaps the most celebrated of which was a standoff on a bridge in southern Burma in July 1998. Suu Kyi and her driver had attempted to visit some NLD members, but were stopped on a road about 64 kilometres south of Rangoon. Suu Kyi refused to leave her car and a stalemate ensued. Six days later, after much negative international publicity, government officers forced her driver from the car and drove her back to Rangoon. The government had broken the deadlock, but the incident had only served to focus further international attention on the repressive nature of the Rangoon government (Skehan 1998a).

A similar event took place in September 2000. While the overall approach of the Rangoon government appeared consistent, changes were occurring at the top levels. In April 1992, General Saw Maung had stepped down[10] as head of SLORC, to be succeeded by General Than Shwe, who also assumed the position of prime minister. However, the head of intelligence, General Khin Nyunt, was widely seen as a more powerful proxy figure, being a protégé of Ne Win. A major achievement of Khin Nyunt was to purge the National Convention of dissident voices, thereby enabling the armed forces, in January 1994, to push through acceptance of the idea of a draft constitution, which enshrined the leading political role of the armed forces (with 25 per cent of all seats in the legislature). It would have also removed the armed forces' financial allocation from the budgetary process. That Constitution was not yet ratified at the end of 2004. The proposed constitutional incorporation of the armed forces in the political process also corresponded to the former political and security dual function of Indonesia's armed forces. The accession of Than Shwe and Khin Nyunt also led to a change in political and military tactics on the part of the Rangoon government. In 1992, confident of its political control, the SLORC began to release political prisoners and lifted martial law restrictions (M. Smith 1999b: 425).

THE SLORC AND ETHNIC SEPARATISTS

With the NLD seemingly limited in its ability to oppose it, the SLORC turned its attention to the root of the political problems in Burma, the ethnic insurgencies. The SLORC's first act was to launch an all-out offensive against the Karen National Liberation Army, which was supported by the All Burma Students' Democratic Front. The government then focused its attention on other insurgencies, in particular that which gripped Shan State, large sections of which had fallen under warlord control. The most powerful of these was the Mong Tai Army, formerly led by opium baron Khun Sa. The Burmese Communist Party (BCP) also constituted a major insurgency problem, although its split in 1989 and subsequent abandonment by its Chinese sponsors as they improved relations with the Burmese government, led it to become ineffectual. Remnants of the BCP subsequently regrouped under four other ethnic organisations (M. Smith 1999b: 421).

The following year the SLORC made its first major breakthrough in its battle against separatists by signing a ceasefire agreement with Kachin Independence Army/Organisation (KIA/O), which was, at that time, regarded as the most significant antigovernment group. This had followed an earlier, but far less important, ceasefire agreement with the Shan State Progressive Party in 1989 and the Pa-O National Union and Palaung State Liberation Party in 1991. The Kayan New Land Party (KNLP) followed the KIA/O ceasefire in 1994, with the New Mon State Party signing a ceasefire in 1995 and the Myanmar National Democratic Alliance Army signing by

1998. These agreements freed up government troops to focus on Karen, Karenni, Naga and Shan rebels, who were increasingly driven from their bases to the border regions. The situation was further complicated by a split over religious differences within the Karen ranks, with the nominally progovernment Democratic Karen Buddhist Army attacking the predominantly Christian Karen National Union and the Karenni National Progressive Party. The combined strength of these two latter organisations had fallen to less than 10 000 by the late 1990s (Nussara 1997).

In 1996, the Rangoon government had another breakthrough, signing a peace agreement with Mong Tai Army (MTA) leader, Khun Sa. Apart from leading the Shan-based Mong Tai Army, Khun Sa was also the most notorious—and probably the second largest—opium and heroin producer in the world. After the peace agreement, Khun Sa quickly settled in Rangoon on the shore of Inya Lake near Lieutenant-General Khin Nyunt and on the same street as Ne Win. In Rangoon, Khun Sa established a large financial network including mining, transport and agriculture, and was believed to be, possibly, the largest single holder of wealth in the country. Khun Sa also maintained close relations with the chairman of the State Peace and Development Council (SPDC, successor to the SLORC) and commander-in-chief of the armed forces, Senior General Than Shwe, as well as with Khin Nyunt (Ball 1999).

Other deals were believed to have been struck with erstwhile separatist groups that allowed them to continue their production and trade of opium and heroin, with a proportion of profits being channelled back to government and military officials, and even to the government itself (Selth 2002: 139). The Rangoon government has constantly refused to extradite Khun Sa to the USA (*Irrawaddy*, 1998b), where he is wanted on drug smuggling charges.

But, despite the agreement reached between Khun Sa and the Rangoon government, most of the MTA decided that it had not reached any agreement that assisted the Shan people, and so, after a brief lull, the bulk of the Mong Tai Army reformed as the Shan United Revolutionary Army and later as the Shan State Army, resuming its battle against the Rangoon government. The Shan States National Army and the United Nationalities Shan States Army, smaller breakaway groups, were also said to have rejoined attacks on the Rangoon government's troops. From early 1999, there were reports in Bangkok that the Burmese army had launched a major offensive against Karen rebels, who were said to be attempting to sabotage the Yadana oil and gas pipeline from southern Burma to Thailand. According to the *Bangkok Post* (6 January 1999: 1), the Burmese army assault was financed by the main oil companies involved in the construction of the pipeline, the French company Total and the American company Unocal. The two companies denied supporting the military operations. However, two US Federal courts found that Unocal knowingly benefited from having forced labour on its Burma pipeline project (ILRF 2004, Los Angeles Superior Court 2004).

A total of seventeen armed ethnic groups had signed ceasefire agreements with the Rangoon government by the end of the 1990s, with four holding out. However, the ceasefires were military and did not offer political solutions to continuing problems (Pedersen, Rudland & May 2000: 10). A number of the ethnic military groups, including the United Wa State Party (Army), the New Mon State Party, KNLP and the KIA/O, subsequently broke with the Rangoon government and pursued an independent or oppositionist line. The main complaint by them, which led to the renewed hostilities, was that their ceasefire agreements had been abrogated by *Tatmadaw* troops, who continued to abuse the ethnic minorities. Common complaints against the army included the use of these people as slave labour, rape, looting and arbitrary executions (*Irrawaddy*, 1998b). In the middle of 1999, five ethnic groups had formed an alliance to fight the central government. They were the Karen National Union, the Shan State Army, the Arakan Liberation Party, the Karenni National Progressive Party and the Chin National Front (*Irrawaddy*, 2000a: 14).

OPIUM AND HEROIN

Apart from Burma's extremely poor human rights record—it is widely regarded as the worst of any existing government in the world—the other main issue that has marked it as an international pariah is its involvement in the illegal production of opium and heroin. Burma was the world's biggest producer of opium in the 1990s, accounting for more than 60 per cent of the world's production and, following Afghanistan's return to massive opium production (36 000 tonnes in 2004) after the defeat of the antidrug Taliban regime, still occupies number two position, producing around 20 per cent of the world's opium (800 tonnes in 2004). The views on who produces what vary widely, but it was known that most, if not all, of the independence groups or former independence groups engaged in the production and sale of opium to finance their battle against the Rangoon government. Further, many ethnic peasants in the hill areas also grew opium as a cash crop, as it is simple to grow and, unlike many other crops, well suited to the hill terrain.

There was significant international concern about the informal—and probably formal—involvement of the Rangoon government in the opium and heroin trade. At one diplomatic level, it was believed, or at least proposed, that non-commissioned officers were actively involved in the growing and distribution of opium. At another level, there was considerable belief that the government itself was involved in the opium business or received kickbacks from it (Selth 2002: 139, US Senate Burma Freedom and Democracy Act 2003), despite the fact that the government had, at least on the surface, begun a crackdown on opium production. In 1996, for example, the Rangoon government publicly burnt seized opium to show that it was serious about eradicating its growth; however, the amount—504 kilograms—was regarded as very small. Almost 23 tonnes of opium had been claimed as having been seized by the Rangoon government between 1988 and 1997, along with almost 4 tonnes of heroin (Embassy of the Union of Myanmar 1998b).

It was probable that the destruction of the opium crops or stores was primarily, if not solely, aimed at non-government or antigovernment groups, including opium production by ethnic rebels. Many of the people officiating at the 1996 opium burning were 'up to their necks in unofficially promoting production and trade' (*Thailand Times*, 2 May 1997). Burma's army commander, Major-General Maung Aye, for example, had a business arrangement with drug baron Kyaw Win and Thai timber tycoon Choon Tangkakarn, who ran logging operations out of Khun Sa's territory. Kyaw Win later established the May Flower Trading Company and the May Flower Bank, which, at that time, was the only bank to have a foreign exchange licence. The May Flower Bank was sold to the government-allied United Wa State Party in 2000 and went bankrupt in 2003. 'The Bank was so ostentatiously drug-linked that it had become an embarrassment even to the junta' (*Irrawaddy*, April 2004). From being near bankruptcy in 1995, business was booming by 1998. Kyaw Win also purchased the loss-making Yangon Airways and introduced new air routes, including to the drug towns of Lashio and Mergui, and the conduit town at the crossroads of the Golden Triangle,[11] Tachilek, on the Thai border. Yangon Airways was sold to the UWSP in 2000. The timing of these events was associated with Khun Sa's move to Rangoon (Davis & Hawke 1998). Lin Ming-xian, another major opium lord, being based in Rangoon, also enjoyed the protection of the Burmese government. Heroin purchasers had open access to northern Burma and military assistance with transhipment in exchange for 10 per cent of the purchase price of the drugs.[12]

Then secretary-general ('Number One') of the government party, the SPDC, Lieutenant-General Khin Nyunt, arranged most of the ceasefire agreements with the ethnic armies, through which they were allowed to continue or expand their opium and heroin production. It was Khin Nyunt who brokered agreements with the Kokang Chinese, allowing Lo Hsing-han to ship their heroin to Tachilek. He also brokered agreements with the Shan State Revolutionary Party, the Wa armies and the Kachin Independence Army. It was believed that Khin Nyunt had personally benefited from these arrangements. Further evidence to support the claim of government involvement in the international drug trade appeared strong. The renamed Kachin Defence Army, for example, delivered opium from the northeast of Burma to Manipur in India, securing their passage with government issued 'special permits' (Davis & Hawke 1998). Another main route for opium was through the Chinese town of Kunming, in Yunnan province, which had increasingly replaced smuggling routes through Thailand (*Irrawaddy*, 1998b; Selth 2002). Khun Sa's second son, Sam Heung, took over running Khun Sa's old operation near the Thai border, northwest of Chiang Mai (Davis & Hawke 1998), where he conducted his drug trade with the assistance of the army commander of Ho Mong, Brigadier-General Chit Maung.

Probably until his retirement, the world's biggest opium baron and warlord was Lo Hsing-han. Lo left the Kokang hills of Lashio, north of Mandalay, in 1973 for seven years in prison, which was followed by a pardon. After his release, Lo worked with the Rangoon government to establish a new antirebel militia (Lintner 1999: 365–6). He now has a gracious home in Rangoon, from where he ran 'one of Myanmar's largest business conglomerates—Asia World—with interests in real estate, manufacturing, export–import and construction that includes key infrastructure projects' (Davis & Hawke 1998). Lo himself had a 10 per cent share of Rangoon's five-star Trader's Hotel (Singaporean investors apportioned the remaining 90 per cent between them); his son, Steven Law, made regular business trips to Singapore, although he was banned from entering the USA due to his drug connections.

Since Khun Sa and Lo Hsing-han diversified into superficially legal businesses, Burma's biggest drug lord has been Lin Min-Shing, who operated out of Mong La opposite Yunan, on the Chinese border. In this, he and others were helped by, and shared in the drug business with, senior army officers. 'In addition to his heroin interests, Khin Nyunt... acquired shares in five amphetamine laboratories in areas controlled by Lin Min-shing near Mong La' (Ball 1999). The SPDC's second secretary and number four in the Rangoon government, Lieutenant-General Tin Tun, was part-owner of two heroin refineries at Murng Kerng and Kesi in central Shan State. Commander of the South-East Command (Moulmein) and previously tactical operations commander in the Mong Ton area of the Golden Triangle, Brigadier-General Myint Aung, was paid large bribes for his protection of heroin refineries. Numerous other regional military commanders and their battalions either conducted, protected or taxed heroin production of some of the largest refineries, which are located along the Indian and Thai borders (Ball 1999).

US Assistant Secretary of State Robert Gelbard stated that, when the army came to power in 1962, Burma was a minor opium producer, but that it agreed to allow opium growing in exchange for peace in the frontier areas. Further, he said, since SLORC was formed in 1988, Burma's production of opium had doubled. The US State Department estimated that heroin production in Burma had risen from a little more than 50 tonnes a year in the late 1980s to an average of more than 150 tonnes a year since 1989 (US Department of State 1996). Gelbard said that the government had become involved in the opium trade, through turning a blind eye to it as well as by allowing or encouraging money laundering from opium sales. Gelbard cited the example of the United Wa State Army (UWSA) as a major heroin producer. The UWSA and the Myanmar National Democratic Alliance

Army of Kokang, also a major heroin producer, comprised troops who had formerly served with the CPB, but had been allowed to trade freely in heroin since leaving the CPB (Lintner, in Pedersen, Rudland & May 2000: 168, 170). The UWSA in particular had wrested control of a significant part of the opium and heroin trade from remnants of the KMT troops based in Burma and other rebel ethnic groups, and then signed a ceasefire agreement with the Rangoon government. Gelbard called the UWSA 'East Asia's largest heroin trafficking organisation', saying it was allowed to buy property in Rangoon as a means of investing its illegally gained money (AFP 1996; Davis & Hawke 1998). As well as the production of opium and heroin, these drug-producing organisations were increasingly moving into the manufacture of amphetamines and hallucinogens, notably Ecstasy. By 2004, the UWSA was said to have around 20 000 troops armed with artillery and antitank weapons, making it the most heavily armed drug organisation in the world (*Asia Times*, 26 November 2004). The UWSA was also said to have replaced Cambodia as SEA's major supplier of small arms, predominantly shipped from China (*Irrawaddy*, 8 October 2004; Selth 2002: 167–70).

Beyond allowing former insurgent groups to produce and traffic in heroin and other drugs, the Rangoon government allowed profits from heroin sales to be laundered through the country's poorly regulated banking system. In 2003, Burma's banks were hit by a financial crisis after fourteen financial services groups failed to pay investors. This spurred a run on the banks, requiring the government to bail out twenty private banks to the tune of several billion kyat at the unofficial exchange rate of K860 to the US dollar. Three private banks operating at the time were reopened in early 2004.

The banks and other financial institutions had been offering returns on deposits of up to 60 per cent a year, which was six times higher than public institutions were offering (AFP, 2 January 2004; *Irrawaddy*, April 2004: 17–23), indicating potentially high income from irregular sources. This turning of a blind eye to heroin profits stemmed, at least in part, from the government's desperate need to bring hard currency into the country to prop up its ailing economy (Lintner, in Petersen, Rudland & May 2000). Under this blind-eye system, funds could be deposited in Burmese banks on payment of a 30 per cent tax, a figure that declines during periods of amnesty if certified by the government as investment for national development.

In response to international pressure, the Burmese government announced in 1999 that it had cleared 1386 hectares of opium poppy between September 1998 and February 1999, amounting to 15.25 tonnes . Burma's senior antidrugs officer, Colonel Kyaw Thein, also announced that 371 tonnes of opium had been destroyed over the preceding decade (probably from non-government linked areas). At the same time, the government announced a new fifteen-year program to end opium production in Burma, to begin in the year 2000. A number of other countries did not take the promise seriously and a European Union delegation refused to attend the meeting at which these claims were made (AFP 1999b). The director of Interpol's criminal intelligence unit, Paul Higdon, attended the meeting and later said that the Burmese government had to allow the drug trade to flourish in order to first bring under control its insurgency problem. 'Before the government could do anything with heroin, they had to do something with insurgencies,' he said. 'Sometimes you have to make a pact with the devil' (AFP 1999a). Higdon also endorsed the Burmese government's existing antidrugs campaign. Some observers wondered aloud about the reasoning behind Higdon's comments and, presumably, Interpol's position.

ECONOMY

It would seem rational for Burma's military to be primarily concerned about the continuing insurgencies in various parts of the country and the general sense of opprobrium felt towards it by both its own population and the international community. But the issue most preoccupying the minds of its leaders was the state of the economy. Even this would seem to make sense, especially given that much of the disaster that was the Burmese economy was a direct result of both Burma's relative international isolation and the structural inability of its citizens to engage in meaningful international trade, which was exacerbated by the downturn in East Asian economies in 1997–98, especially in South Korea, which was claimed by sources in Burma to have been a major supplier of fuel oil, which was bartered for manufactured goods and weapons.

However, the military's concern was not so much with the poor shape of the economy for state reasons, but with the fact that the economy had finally become so parlous that it had the potential to affect the operations of the military itself. The state is subservient to the needs of the army and, if the army could not organise the state to meet the army's needs, then it has failed in its primary objective. This led to divisions within the armed forces over economic policy and management and offered the greatest scope for some sort of rapprochement. The divisions were between older, hard-line isolationists and those eager to integrate into ASEAN and the international economy. At the end of the twentieth century, the isolationists had the upper hand being able to cite the downturn in the East Asian economies as proof of the unreliability of international economic engagement. However, a younger, more outwardly focused generation of officers saw the downturn as a temporary phenomenon in an otherwise broad tendency towards economic growth. There was also concern in Burma and abroad that there was considerable corruption at the higher levels of the military, with 5 per cent skimmed off most major international deals. The change of government from the SLORC to the SPDC in 1997 cleaned up some of the more corrupt officers, but had little real impact on corruption overall or, more importantly, on investor confidence. 'On the contrary, many investors are pulling out of Burma, partly as a result of the regional crisis but also because they have found it impossible to conduct business in the country' (Lintner 1998). In 2004, according to Transparency International, Burma was regarded as the fourth most corrupt country in the world.

As indicated at the outset, Burma's economy was, apart from heroin and other drug production, deeply disorganised and functioning extremely poorly. While it retained significant economic potential, nearly all of that potential has either been squandered or left unrealised by its military government. There was some economic liberalisation in the 1990s, but this was relatively superficial and had little impact on the lives of ordinary people. Into the new century, after an initial rise to around US$1200, the per capita income in 2002 had declined to around US$1000 on a PPP basis (UNDP *Human Development Report* 2004), while inflation continued at around 50 per cent a year and economic growth declined from being almost stagnant to around –0.5 per cent a year by 2004. Perhaps the most obvious sign of this freeing up of the economy has been the importation of new cars and trucks, supplementing the ancient road transport that had served the country since the 1950s. One of the main reasons why the liberalisation of Burma's economy did not have much impact on ordinary people was because most foreign investment, while it existed, was in joint ventures with the Union of Myanmar Economic Holdings Company (UMEHC) (Selth 2002: 146), which was run by the Defence Department's Directorate of Procurement. Other estimates suggest that close to half of Burma's gross domestic product, with the most obvious investments in real estate and with links to the government, was taken up by cashflows generated by the illegal opium and heroin trade.

Perhaps the most important aspect of Burma's economy, apart from its mismanagement, was the fact that the government spent around 40 per cent of its budget on the armed forces. The government deficit towards the end of the 1990s was, by comparison, at around 20 per cent of the budget. This is a figure that, in most countries, would be regarded as unsustainable. Because of its appalling economic management and its even worse human rights record, Burma has been banned from access to funding through the International Monetary Fund, the World Bank and from export credits and investment protection insurance. Needless to say, there is no open debate allowed about Burma's economic management or direction.

To complicate Burma's parlous economic state, the country had—and looked set to retain—a grossly inadequate infrastructure, with particular reference to electricity. There were regular power failures throughout Burma, including Rangoon, with power out in some areas all the time and, in a number of areas, such as Mandalay, about half the time. This appeared to be increasing, as the government was unable to afford diesel fuel to operate its power generators, while hydroelectricity was reduced due to low water volumes. The exploitation of natural gas in the Gulf of Martaban could go some way towards redressing the energy problem from the early years of the twenty-first century; however, most of the gas was to be shipped to Thailand and the profits were to go to the controlling companies, Unocal and Total, with Burma's share intended to help service debt repayments. As with Burma's other attempts to exploit existing resources, such as timber and fisheries, there was no environmental impact assessment made, so, as might be expected, the impact on these geographic areas has been, in most cases, devastating.

Further, government export figures were grossly inaccurate. Government bureaucracy was severely bloated, inefficient, labyrinthine and held no real power in terms of decision making. Government responses to requests were usually to say 'no', as it was too difficult to actually do anything. Further, there was always the risk that any active policy could step on the toes of another government service or a military person, which could have serious repercussions for the service or individual concerned.

Government employees, unable to live on their meagre salary, engaged in other businesses, usually to the detriment of government work. The economy was, in effect, the black market. In Rangoon, the black market competes openly with the legal market, though it probably has an advantage in terms of consumer goods and access to other, more modern, requirements such as medicine. Mandalay was, in effect, a black market town, being a hub for trade throughout northern, western and eastern Burma. An especially large amount of goods came in through Yunnan province in China, which had considerable ethnic crossover with Kachin and Shan States. Many goods were significantly cheaper than they are even in those countries in which they were manufactured, especially medicines and electrical goods, which seemed to imply that many of the goods for sale in Mandalay were not just smuggled into the country, but were also the end result of highly organised theft, piracy or, more probably, the crossborder drug trade. In Shan State, the black market was even more rampant, with the border town of Tachilek selling everything that it was possible to pay money for. The cured skins of leopards and elephant tusks vied for business with a huge range of consumer goods and, barely hidden below shop counters, all sorts of guns and vast quantities of opium and heroin. It was across the bridge from Tachilek into the boom town of Mae Sai in Thailand that most of the world's opium used to travel and over which drug battles had been fought. Although large quantities were still shipped across the river further upstream, Mae Sai was still an extraordinary clearing site for a significant array of the world's contraband. That the economies of Mae Sai and Tachilek were booming[13] was less a result of industry or the small trickle of tourists who came through there predominantly to see this infamous place, than because of the vast trade in contraband that washed through, leaving behind it a residue of loose cash.

If the Burmese economy needed any final push to ensure its failure, the government's appalling human rights record led to a series of trade and investment sanctions against it, most notably from 1997 by the USA and, later and less effectively, by the European Union. With an economy that was already largely disengaged from the West, the sanctions had a limited impact, although, in 2003, they were said to affect some US$356 million worth of exports (Radio Australia 29 August 2003). But the indirect impact of American pressure on its trading partners did act as a further brake on investment in this already parlous economic climate.

ELITE DIVISIONS

As well as divisions over economic policy, the military was also in disagreement over tactics to deal with the separatist movements; one view was that they should be crushed, the other that they should be accommodated or effectively left to their own devices. The crush option was made difficult by the economic problems the armed forces were facing, especially in relation to their operational capacity, as well as by the fact that, despite having some separatist groups make peace with the government, others continued to present a seemingly intractable challenge. Similarly, there was division within the military over an appropriate response to the NLD. One group suggested accommodating the NLD, the intention of which was, primarily, to appease international criticism, to end Burma's relative isolation and to open up Burma to more opportunities for aid and trade. The other faction was more hardline and oppositionist, asserting the capacity of the military to continue to function in a more constrained economic environment. It should be noted, however, that while there were disagreements about direction, the army remained essentially united and such differences of opinion did not debilitate the army's political activity.[14]

If these divisions within the military seemed to hold out some small hope for democratisation and greater political participation (or separation), the NLD itself was at least as divided as the military. The major division within the NLD appeared to be between Suu Kyi, who seemed to be under the influence of a younger NLD parliamentarian and the older 'uncles'— former Ne Win associates—who advocated a less confrontational, more engaged approach to political settlement. As noted by Selth, it was unlikely that the NLD could ever achieve office without at least the passive support of the *Tatmadaw* (Selth 1999: 20). In this sense, the political contest in Burma was not so much about the army versus the NLD, or even factions within either, but, following tradition, about intra-elite rivalry. Aung-Thwin notes that the postwar communist leader Than Tun was Aung San's brother-in-law, that the president of the government in exile is Suu Kyi's cousin, that Aung Gyi, former Ne Win confidant and briefly allied with Suu Kyi, was a student leader with Aung San and Ne Win, that seventeen of the twenty-one leaders of SLORC in 1988 had close or overlapping military training and that more than half of the nine individuals of Suu Kyi's inner circle were former military officers who were friends and followers of Aung San. Patron–client relations remained paramount in Burma's political arena, dominating military–civilian tensions and urban–rural dichotomies, as well as issues over support for market and command economies. 'In short, the contest is a personal, elitist struggle for power that has been shaped both by the continuity of traditional structures and the introduction of modern ideologies' (Aung-Thwin 1998: 94, 158–9).

In this respect, the intention of the Bhamese majority appeared to be to maintain Burma as a united, probably unitary, state (Smith 1999: 452). The NLD was not very far, in terms of policy, from the SPDC in how it saw the construction of a future Burma, although its fundamentally different approach to resolving differences of opinion and its willingness to talk with ethnic groups did stand as a radically different approach. However, if the NLD could achieve government, there remained some possibility that it would continue to confront and, perhaps, even battle separatist movements in the outlying regions. Suu Kyi's vision for the future of Burma under an NLD government was one in which ethnic minorities would be allowed to 'express their feelings' and through this reach an understanding with Burma's legitimate government (Clements & Suu Kyi 1997: 150–1; Suu Kyi 1991: 226–31). But, like her father (Cady 1958: 558), Suu Kyi did not countenance that expression of feeling to include formal separation.

While factionalism seemed rife within the government and the NLD, it also hampered the efforts of the ethnic rebels and their supporters. The All Burma Students' Democratic Front was riven by 'rampant factionalism', which was pushing some members of the group to give up their guerrilla struggle to seek refugee status in Bangkok (*Irrawaddy*, 2000a: 2). Meanwhile, the leader of the Karen National Union (KNU), General Bo Mya, was replaced by Saw Ba Thin Sein, following military setbacks, factional disputes and armed attacks against the Karen National Union by the breakaway Democratic Karen Buddhist Army (*Irrawaddy*, 2000b: 7–9).

THE SPDC

More in order to satisfy its external critics than appease internal dissent, the SLORC's successor, the SPDC, made some small rhetorical moves towards political legitimacy. The SPDC was established in November 1997, primarily as a means of rearranging some cabinet positions, especially those noted for excessive corruption (Callahan, in Pedersen, Rudland & May 2000: 39), and to bring some field officers more closely into line with the central government. The SPDC claimed to have held a constitutional convention, allegedly representing all groups, to draw up a new constitution for implementation in 2000, along with elections, but this tended to ring hollow, especially in light of the outcome of the 1990 elections.

After more than fifty years of independence and the same number of years battling separatists, the government was still only in control of about half a country in which most areas had an uncertain status or were strictly off limits to outsiders. While there was good reason for political change in Burma, it was unlikely that such change would take place while Ne Win was still alive. Indeed, in a reordering of Burma's senior political landscape in 1998, the old guard reasserted themselves. Under the newly proclaimed SPDC, the six most senior positions in the government were taken by top-level military officers, while twenty-three of the remaining thirty-five cabinet positions were also held by senior officers (Embassy of the Union of Myanmar 1998a). Ne Win himself was not much directly consulted by the SPDC ministers, who believed they understood his views so well that they could offer decisions that, if he were ever obliged to do so, he would endorse.

For there to be significant political change, there would probably have to be total economic collapse. The crunch would only really come if the economy deteriorated to the point that the army was unable to function relatively efficiently. It therefore seemed that, after Ne Win's eventual demise, there would be a power struggle within the government over whether it would loosen its grip on the body politic. Such a decision seemed far away, if at all possible, while the rationale for the military government in the first place—that of ethnic insurgency—remained an intractable problem.

ENDING ISOLATIONISM?

Since the attacks on unarmed protesters in the late 1980s, Burma has been an international outcast and is cut off from bilateral aid from a number of significant potential sources, including the USA. Finally deciding to abandon its policy of self-imposed isolation, Burma was, in 1999, attempting to reintegrate into the international economy, albeit slowly and very cautiously. However, its path was made difficult by its poor human rights record. By way of example, an offer by the World Bank for a loan of US$1 billion was refused by the SPDC because it had attached to it the condition of political concessions. 'The generals did not budge and claimed to be offended at the notion that they could be bought' (Mitton 2000b).

As an assertion of its independence, Burma, which had been one of the early members of the NAM, withdrew from this forum at NAM Havana summit in September 1979, allegedly over a lack of neutrality in Cuba's chairmanship. This marked the depths of Burma's international isolation. After criticism from Muslim states over its persecution of its Muslim Arakan minority, Burma sought and was granted readmission to NAM in 1992.

Burma then formally turned its attention towards China. After a long history of strident opposition to Chinese communism, the Rangoon government, by the late 1980s, began to reach an accommodation with China, with crossborder trade recommencing in 1988. To some extent, the development of trade and other links was, in part, China's response to the international opprobrium and isolation it had earned as a result of the Tiananmen Square massacre of student protestors in 1989. In this respect, Burma and China could view each other as mutual pariahs in the international community. From Burma's perspective, though, more important was gaining China's friendship as a means of having it withdraw support from the BCP, which it had previously backed. The BCP had been a major source of difficulty for the Rangoon government, being, arguably, the most organised and, potentially, the most powerful of the guerrilla groups arrayed against it.

China, as a source of trade with Burma, grew, especially in weapons,[15] which trade, by the end of the 1990s, was valued at somewhere towards US$1 billion a year. Smuggling, in such items as electrical goods, clothing and pharmaceutical drugs was estimated to be worth a similar amount, while legal trade also flourished. China also assisted in the development of Burma's communications network and a massive hydroelectric generator, although these proceeded far less quickly than did the arms trade (*Irrawaddy*, July 2004: 8–15). Part of the exchange was to allow China access to the Indian Ocean and an increased business presence in Burma's northern states.

BURMA AND ASEAN

By the early 1990s, Burma was also making overtures to ASEAN. For Burma, membership in ASEAN was intended to enhance its international trade and foreign investment, while for the ASEAN states, Burma represented a source of cheap labour, as well as being a source of oil, gas and timber within the structure of a stable political environment. Few of the ASEAN states have ever been concerned with the niceties of genuine political representation; their existing, though challenged, policy of non-interference in the affairs of member states suited Burma very well. With China's economic development starting to focus the attention of the SEA states, Burma's links there were also seen as very useful. On one hand, Burma acted as a bridge to and from China, while, on the other, it helped strengthen what could, in an emergency, be quite a powerful anti-Chinese alliance.

Singapore's prime minister, Goh Chock Tong, helped move Burma's regional acceptance along when he visited Rangoon in March 1994. Singapore thereafter became a major investor in Burma until the downturn in the SEA economies in 1997. In February 1997, Indonesia's President Suharto also visited Burma, signalling its increasing acceptance, even if by a regional politician who was soon to fall from grace. Among other things, the Rangoon government wanted to talk with Suharto about the 'dual [security and political] function' of Indonesia's armed forces, which they viewed as a potential model. Indicating his increasing distance from the realities of political events in his own country, Suharto did not point out that his relationship with Indonesia's armed forces was, even then, under strain. Burma was, in any case, formally admitted into ASEAN in 1997, along with Laos.

By early 1998, relations between Burma and Thailand had begun to deteriorate. While an oil and gas pipeline between the two states had been developed and a number of business deals for logging were underway, Burmese attacks against Karen National Union refugees along the Thai border soured relations. At the ASEAN meeting in Manila in August 1998, Thailand went so far as to call for ASEAN's cardinal rule of not commenting on the internal affairs of member states to be scrapped. This criticism of Burma's human rights record was in response to Burma's violation of sovereign Thai territory, when troops crossed into Thailand to attack Burmese refugee camps and to conduct armed intelligence gathering missions. The Philippines has joined Thailand in criticising Burma's poor human rights record. The SPDC responded by taking an increasingly isolationist, indeed, paranoid, position regarding external comments on the country's political development. The government newspaper, the *New Light of Myanmar* and other state-controlled media run regular vitriolic attacks on 'foreign conspirators' and 'neocolonialists who are colluding with traitors' (Lintner 1998).

In contrast to this deterioration of the Thailand–Burma relationship, in early 2000 Thai military forces killed ten members of the Burmese God's Army, a Karen rebel faction, who had taken over the Ratchaburi hospital near the Burmese border. The Karen rebels had occupied the hospital in response to Thai military bombardment of Karen rebel positions just inside Thai territory. It was claimed that Thai and Burmese forces had been coordinating their attacks on the rebels, following the peaceful settlement of the occupation of the Burmese embassy in Bangkok by members of the Burma Students' Democratic Front the previous October. It was believed that the coordinated action against the Karen rebels—and others—was part of a normalisation of relations between the governments of the two countries (*Irrawaddy*, 2000a: 6). Such normalisation continued to be troubled by border tensions. In early February 2000, six Burmese soldiers were arrested by Thai troops near Mai Hong Son in western Thailand. Burma responded to their arrest by sending more troops to the border area (*Irrawaddy*, 2000b: 2).

As if Burma was not beset with enough difficulties, its history of military domination and interethnic conflict mixed with its geography has led to the development of a type of regional warlordism, especially since 1990. A very high degree of regional autonomy was given over to local commanders to determine activities, necessities and relative freedoms (see

Callahan, in Pedersen, Rudland & May 2000: 36–9). This was one of the main sources of human rights abuse and support for the drug trade, given that such warlords were held little accountable to the central government—should it care to so hold them. There was also, according to reliable sources, a high degree of desertion from the army, with patrols going out but not returning. In those cases where they did meet ambush by ethnic separatists, the bodies were usually found.

INTERNAL TENSIONS

The key tensions that had characterised the internal politics of the SPDC, essentially around isolationism or engagement, began to be played out more forcefully in the early years of the twenty-first century. Reformists within the government wanted to engage more closely with Burma's ASEAN neighbours and even more widely; to do this they actively considered minor political reforms, including the release of prodemocracy leader Aung San Suu Kyi. That she continued to languish under house arrest was indicative of the caution being exercised by the reformist group and the power of the conservatives.

As these tensions were being played out, Burma's former leader for twenty-six years and for years after the power behind the government, Ne Win, died in December 2002 at the age of ninety-one. But Ne Win's death was less significant than the fact that he had been under house arrest since March that year, accused of planning to overthrow the military government. Along with the then ailing New Win's own house arrest, members of his family, including his daughter Sandar Win, her husband Aye Zaw Win and their three sons, Aye Ne Win, Kyaw Ne Win and Zwe Ne Win, were also arrested and charged with treason. It was alleged that the family had tried to recruit soldiers to kidnap three senior generals and proclaim a monarchy, with themselves as the royal family; they were also charged with corruption. Several military officials were also arrested in connection with the alleged plot against the government. The son-in-law and his three sons were convicted on the treason charges and sentenced to death, which, at the time of writing, was under appeal. The move against the family followed the death in a helicopter crash of the SPDC's second secretary, Tin Oo the previous month, which was said to have accelerated tensions.

The death of New Win, or the political demise of his family, did not signal any change of policy in the Rangoon government or resolve tensions within the leadership. Meanwhile, in 2004, the leadership of Burma's oldest secessionist organisation, the KNU, had begun peace talks with the Rangoon government, leading to what appeared to be a split within the KNU's senior ranks. The Karenni National Progressive Party also entered into peace talks with the government, further enhancing the SPDC's grip on the state, although the Kachin Independence Organisation purged its leadership following similar attempts at talks. Had the entire KNU arranged a ceasefire, it was expected that the remaining separatist organisations would follow suit.

In June 2003, in an act that was widely and strongly condemned by the international community, Suu Kyi was again arrested—'placed in protective custody'—for a year, after receiving head and arm injuries in an attack on her motorcade by out-of-uniform police, soldiers and others near the town of Dipeyin, about 700 kilometres north of Rangoon. In the attack, around seventy people were killed and 200 injured (AP 3 June 2003, 5 June 2003; *Washington Post*, 3 June 2003, 5 June 2003). Along with the jailing of the entire NLD senior leadership, universities were again closed, as were remaining NLD offices, to preempt possible protests, which was interpreted as indicative of a widening split in the military. The brief periods of freedom that Suu Kyi had were regarded by the hardliners, in particular General Than Shwe, then serving concurrently as prime minister, defence minister and chairman of the SPDC, as an end in themselves and were not indicative of the start of dialogue towards political reform.

The government's so-called pragmatic group focused on Lieutenant Khin Nyunt, who proposed a seven-step process to resolving Burma's political problems with the NLD, although the NLD noted that there was no step that proposed a democratic outcome. Even pragmatists in Burma were, by most standards, hardline. In September 2004, tensions between the more conservative isolationists and the pragmatists reached breaking point. There was a reshuffle of Cabinet positions, which saw the pragmatic group comprehensively defeated. The civilian foreign minister, Win Aung, was sacked, as was his deputy, Khin Maung, both being replaced by army officers, Major-General Nyan Win and Colonel Maung Myint. Other sackings included the ministers for Labour, Agriculture, Commerce, Cooperatives and Transport.

Then, on 19 October, just days before an ASEAN meeting, long-time intelligence chief and, from August 2003, Prime Minister[16] Khin Nyunt was also sacked. Several companies associated with Burma's intelligence community were shut down and dozens of officers associated with Khin Nyunt were taken into custody (*Irrawaddy*, October 2004: 8–16). Khin Nyunt was replaced by SPDC secretary and overall number three, Lieutenant-General Soe Win, who was close to the conservative general and Burma's overall leader, Than Shwe, and his supporter (and Khin Nyunt's main rival) Maung Aye. In a symbolic gesture, Burma's borders were again closed. A few days later, the Home and Labour ministers were also permitted to retire. In November 2004, at a time when the Burmese government was facing heavy international criticism for its appalling human rights record and dismay over its turn away from even Khin Nyunt's pragmatism, the government announced that Suu Kyi would remain imprisoned for another twelve months; since 1989, she already had spent nine years under house arrest. All of the signs were that Burma had retreated to as hardline a position as its military government had ever taken. Notions of pragmatism, much less reform, were completely removed from the Burmese agenda.

Beyond its elites, Burma was a place of fear for ordinary people. Long jail sentences for marginal crimes were common, people were afraid to speak openly for fear of being identified as antigovernment, phones and faxes were tapped and security checks and surveillance were constants of everyday life. Even slavery, in the service of the state, was common, especially for women, children, convicts and ethnic minorities. It would not be inaccurate to identify Burma as a totalitarian state, but, more accurately, it was a garrison state, in which the state continues to exist to serve the requirements of the military (see Selth 2002: 33, 37) and the military, in turn, had little compunction in exploiting whatever it could in any way it desired. This type of state has also been termed 'predatory' (Evans 1995: 45–7), a term that can only fill with horror those who understand the depredations of existence in such a political environment.

NOTES

1   The name 'Burma' is used here as it better reflects the name of the dominant ethnic group, the Bhamese, after whom the country was named. The alternative name, Myanmar, is also regarded as excluding the interests of the country's ethnic minorities. It is far from a settled question as to whether this name is acceptable to any but a government that, by its own admission, was voted out of power more than a decade ago and hence is illegitimate.

2   The Mon are related by language to the Khmer of Cambodia.

3   The T'ai of this period were the predecessors of the Thai of Thailand. However, at this stage they were not so clearly delineated from the T'ai of what is now Shan State, Chiang Mai, then the state of Lan Na, including parts of Yunnan, or Laos.

4   It was from this time that the Thais developed the term 'farang' to denote 'European'; it is a variation on the word 'France'.

5   The common method of killing royal Burmese was to tie the individual in a velvet sack and beat him or her to death, the intention being that no royal blood was thus spilled.

6   The AFPFL was formed out of the BIA to oppose the Japanese.

7   Interestingly, Aung San was close to or a member of the Burmese Communist Party in the 1930s, which was linked to his anticolonialist stance.

8   The official breakdown of Burma's ethnic composition is Bhamese 68 per cent, Shan 9 per cent, Karen 7 per cent, Rohingya 4 per cent, Mon 4 per cent, Chin 3 per cent and Indian 2 per cent, while the Akha, Danu, Kayan, Kokang, Lahu, Naga, Palaung, Pao, Rakhine, Tavoyan and Wa peoples comprise about 3 per cent between them. These figures could have been exaggerated to justify Bahmese domination.

9   According to two sources close to the NLD.

10 This change was seen by some observers as more of a 'palace coup'.

11 The term 'Golden Triangle' denotes the region covered by northern Thailand, northwest Laos and northeast Burma, which was said to be the world's second opium- and heroin-producing region. After a crackdown in Thailand, most opium and heroin was produced in northeast and northern Burma, with much smaller amounts produced in northern Laos. The Golden Triangle was primarily a conduit for the flow of opium and heroin to the outside world, although even this had shifted to include Assam in eastern India and Yunnan in southern China.

12   This was according to a person who claimed to have been earlier involved in the trade from northern Thailand.

13   The border crossing between Mae Sai and Tachilek was closed in late 1999 by the Burmese government in response to the Thais' handling of the Burmese rebel takeover of the Burmese embassy. The border was also closed for a year in 1995–96, following a gun battle over heroin shipments across the border.

14   It has been noted that, within the *Tatmadaw*, 'Splits along the lines of racial background, organisational origins and political affiliation have been resolved' (Maung Aung Myoe 1998). However, there appears to still be some competition over which officer will succeed Lieutenant-General Khin Nyunt, indicating a return to 1950s-style personality politics.

15   China came to dominate Burma's weapons procurement program in the late 1990s, although Burma sought to diversify its sources of weapons and to manufacture its own weapons (Maung Aung Myoe 1999: 20).

16   The position of prime minister in Burma is much more ceremonial than in most political systems, although Khin Nyunt was regarded as a powerful figure in the Burmese government.

6 | Thailand: The Survivor Mandala

Whatever failings might be ascribed to it, Thailand was widely regarded as the model state in SEA (Singapore being too atypical in size). After many years of military rule and coups, it appeared to have settled into a more or less democratic model of government. Further, after its devastating economic collapse of the late 1990s, Thailand had largely restabilised itself, again growing at over 5 per cent a year, reflecting a healthy mix of agriculture, manufacture and service industries in a more conventionally regulated economic environment.

The economic collapse from mid 1997 had seen the value of the baht fall by around half, numerous bankruptcies and the collapse of a number of banks and other financial institutions. But most importantly, the crisis also saw an increase in unemployment of huge numbers of workers who had no economic safety net. This followed a decade in which Thailand was the world's fastest growing economy, but in which an economic bubble grew. Although it burst, Thailand managed to retain hold of the political institutions it had been building, even if their control by the country's most successful entrepreneur as prime minister, Thaksin Shinawatra, and other surviving capitalists challenged the way in which a democracy should be managed or could be manipulated. 'A company is a country,' he famously opined in 1997. 'A country is a company. They're the same. The management is the same' (Phongpaichit & Baker 2004). For Thaksin, protecting his business investments and protecting the country amounted to much the same thing; the East Asian approach to state intervention in supporting leading businesses was preferred over the nominally free market model of the USA. That Thaksin was a direct beneficiary of this policy only confirmed, to him, the logic of such a system choosing its most successful candidates. That Thaksin intimidated and bought off some opposition; that some of the vibrancy of Thai democracy was cowed by this, did not bode well for conventional democratic ideas of political participation and equality before a

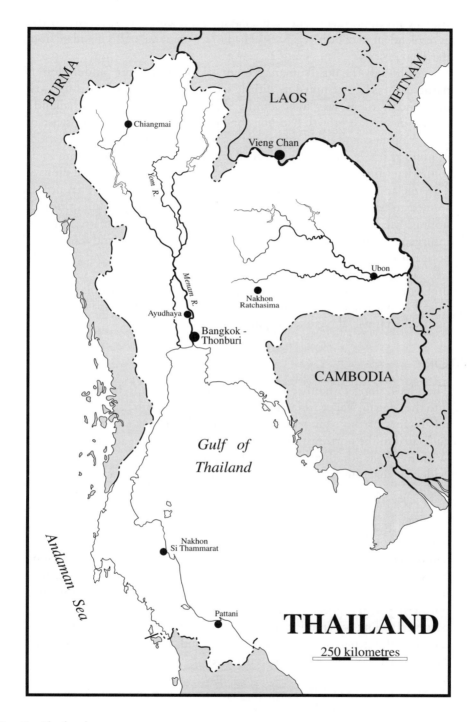

Map 3 Thailand

consistently applied law. But even Thaksin, represented on streetside posters as resplendent in courtly regalia, still had to seek renewal of his mandate from the Thai people.

Although Thaksin's management of politics came under doubt, particularly as he attempted to blithely sail across the increasingly rough seas of scandal, there was little doubt that the correction to Thailand's unsustainably fast growth had not done much to dampen a wider sense of industriousness and economic opportunism.[1] Similarly, after eight decades of military intervention in political affairs, Thailand had added depth to its somewhat fitful application of democratic principles to the political process. The role and scope of the military was being reduced and the Thai people seemed to have firmly embraced the idea of participatory politics. Indeed, noting that democracy in the Philippines continued to be marred by two insurgencies, the resurgence of crony capitalism, negligible land reform and pork-barrel politics, Thailand possessed the most democratic and politically free society in SEA. Like all places, it was less than perfect and some of its problems were greater than others, but, on balance, Thailand looked like the model of participatory and representative politics when compared with its politically tarnished regional neighbours.

HISTORY

The Thais, along with other T'ai–Kadai linguistic groups, began to descend into the Menam Valley from around the sixth to seventh century CE. Earlier inhabitants of the region date back as far as 8000 BCE, with rice being cultivated in the northeast of what is now Thailand from around 2000 BCE. Within Thailand, there is a belief, supported by some archaeological evidence, that the Ban Chiang culture, upon which this cultivation was based, was using bronze from before 3000 BCE, predating the Bronze Age of the Middle East by at least 200 years and China by 1000 years.

The most reliable accounts indicate that the T'ai originated in the region of southern China, in Yunnan and Guangxi provinces (both then comprising the state of Nan-Chao) and in the region known as Sipsong Panna (also as Xishuangbanna, which, translated, means '12 000 rice fields') in northern Laos and northwest Vietnam, which had long been a home to a northern T'ai group (see Cheah 1996). As with the Lao and the Shan, what is known about their immigration into the Menam Valley region is that they followed the geographic contours of the land from Nan-Chao into the Menam Valley. While T'ai peoples had been drifting south for centuries, the main wave of immigration was in response to the expansionary policies of the Sung Dynasty in China, which were carried out under the Mongols of Kublai Khan and which had followed centuries of conflict between Nan-Chao and its northern neighbour. As a result of this immigration, the T'ai spread from northwest Vietnam to Assam in eastern India and dispersed across what are today the seven contemporary states of Thailand, Laos, China, India, Burma, Vietnam and Cambodia. Laos can claim to be a predominantly T'ai state, as could Shan State of Burma. But dominant among the T'ai states is Thailand, a country that is largely and most successfully T'ai.

In particular, the T'ai of what was to become Thailand followed the Chao Phraya River towards the south. Others of the T'ai–Kadai linguistic group followed similar routes, the Shan following the Salween River valley, the T'ai of Assam following the Bramaputra, the Lao following the Mekong and the T'ai of northeast Vietnam following the Red River. The rivers and their flood plains assured the immigrating T'ai of suitable alluvial soil and a plentiful supply of water upon which to base their wet rice agriculture.

In pursuing this southward course, the T'ai came into contact with, and mostly assimilated, other peoples, largely other Austronesian groups, most notably, the Mon–Khmer, who spread across what is now southern Thailand between modern Cambodia and southern Burma. They also came into contact with the Tibeto–Burmans who were themselves moving south along the Irrawaddy and nearby valleys. In large part, the incorporation of the different ethnic groups the T'ai encountered was probably assisted by the fact that there were already significant numbers of T'ai living in the region. It was this cultural assimilation that led to the Siamese T'ai becoming distinct from their Shan and Lao counterparts. It is worth noting that the earlier inhabitants of the region northwest of the Gulf of Thailand were referred to by their neighbours as 'Syama' and their country as 'Syam' or Siam. This was in reference to the original people of the region, rather than to the T'ai, who had come to increasingly dominate the local populations (Manich 1979: 1–5). It was, however, a name that continued to be given by outsiders to the T'ai of the 'Siam' region.

The T'ai tended to establish local polities that could be described as districts or small principalities. As were those at the time in northeastern Laos and northwest Vietnam, they were called *meaung*, a name that continues to be used by the Thai in reference to Meaung Thai (that is, Thailand). In its original usage, a *meaung* was located by a river in a valley and usually demarcated by a mountain range and could include several nearby villages under the authority of a main central village or town (Gehan 1991: 163–70). As elsewhere, these *meaung* were usually ruled by an hereditary chief called a *jao* (or *chao*) *meaung*. Each *meaung* was based on a section of the river valley and usually extended to the peaks of nearby mountain ranges, with some *meaung* coming together under one powerful *meaung* or through alliances. Such arrangements were, however, short-lived. As noted in the chapter on Laos, one such powerful *meaung* was located at what is modern Dien Bien Phu in northwestern Vietnam, while another was located in southern China and later developed as the state of Nan-Chao.

While the T'ai were increasingly establishing themselves in the Menam River valley, by the first couple of centuries of the second millennium they were not yet politically organised. Insofar as there was any real political organisation in the region increasingly inhabited by the T'ai, it was in the Mon state of Dvaravati. While Dvaravati was a Buddhist state and, perhaps, a precursor to the T'ai state that followed, little is known about it and, in terms of ethnic dominance, it did not present a consistent genealogy with contemporary Thailand. Further, forestalling any such attempted political organisation by the T'ai, and eclipsing the state of Dvaravati, were two great regional empires. To the east was the Khmer empire, with its glorious capital at Angkor, to the west the Bhamese, with their almost equally glorious capital at Pagan. These two empires regarded the central region of the Mon and, later, the T'ai, situated along the mountain range of what is now Burma's Shan State and further south towards the Isthmus of Kra, as little more than a buffer state between them. During the eleventh and twelfth centuries, this buffer region and the fringes of the Khmer empire became more substantially T'ai. As the Angkorian empire underwent internal rifts, an outlying province centred on Lopburi attempted to assert its independence, even appealing to China for recognition, in 1001 and again in 1155 (Wyatt 1984: 20–8). It was from around this time that the first inscriptions mention 'Syam' and the 'Syama' people.

A PATCHWORK OF PROTO-THAI STATES

By the end of the twelfth century, the T'ai were beginning to organise new states in the Shan region of Burma, Nan-Chao and Sipsong Panna. Following the fall of the T'ai state of Nan-Chao to the armies of Kublai Khan in 1253, the T'ai of that area also began their immigration south. Within decades of the decline of the Angkorian empire, Lopburi had established itself as an independent state, which included the nearby centre of Ayudhya, founded in 1450 (Manich 1979: 8–10, 18–26; see also, SarDesai 1997: 52–6). Further to the north, the young state of Sukhothai had come to encompass the Menam River valley, a parcel west across to Martaban just south of Pegu, and a further larger parcel east to encompass Vieng Chan and its surrounding territory. To the north, Lan Na, centred on Chiang Mai, extended into southern Yunnan and west into Shan State. Between Lan Na and Sukhothai lay the smaller state of Pha Yao, in what is now the eastern portion of northern Thailand (Wyatt 1984: 38–60). In some respects, this rearrangement of the political landscape, splitting up larger regional empires and allowing the growth of new states, was an intentional product of China asserting regional military and political control (Coedes 1968: 250–1). In the face of a Mongol invasion at the beginning of the fourteenth century under the leadership of Mangrai, the king of Lan Na, his state, Sukhothai and Pha Yao combined forces to defeat the invaders and to conduct raids far into Chinese territory (Coedes 1968: 194–5). Although political stability was not yet a given, it was here that the seeds of the later Thai state were sown.

The T'ai state of Lan Na was one of a number of states that existed in the region between the eighth and sixteenth centuries; however, its central position meant that it was almost constantly buffeted by invading armies from Burma, Lan Xang or the southern T'ais of Ayudhya. Lan Na lost the last vestiges of its independence to the Burmese in 1564 and from that time on became a vassal state to one or other of the regional powers, eventually being subsumed into the expanding Thai (Siam) state (Wyatt 1984: 93).

BURMESE INTERVENTION

Being in close proximity to the states of Burma, the early T'ai states were regularly attacked and often occupied by Burmese forces. Although the historic memory of these events is not strong, there remains a lingering sense of Burmese aggression, although both states, in modern times, have attempted to maintain cordial formal relations. In a contemporary sense, Thailand has no formal aspiration to incorporate the T'ai Shan State into its territory, but there is a very clear feeling that the Shan and the Thai are at least ethnic cousins. The core region of what was to become Thailand evolved as a consequence of this protracted period of conflict with the Burmese state.

By the late fifteenth century, Toungoo had established itself as a prominent state and, in the early 1530s, took control of Pegu. In doing so, it marched on Chiang Krai in Moulmein district, then a tributary to Siam. The Siamese responded by driving the Burmese out in 1538. While internal squabbles over royal succession tore at the state in 1547, the Burmese crossed through the Three Pagodas Pass and attacked Siam. To further complicate Siam's position, the Khmers attacked the state's eastern region (Wyatt 1984: 90–1). After a break of some years and having settled renewed internal conflicts, Burma's new king, Bayinnaung, took advantage of the succession turmoil in Lan Na to march from a fresh conquest in Shan State to take Chiang Mai in 1558. The Burmese used Chiang Mai as a forward base for further attacks on Lan Xang and Ayudhya, as well as attacking from what is now Thailand's western town of Tak. The Siamese king, Chakkraphat, capitulated to the Burmese in 1564 and a Burmese vassal king was installed in Ayudhya five years later (Wyatt 1984: 90–6). Relations between the two states settled, remaining relatively quiet for almost 200 years, as Ayudhya drifted from Burmese control.

During a period of internal conflict, a new Bhamese leader, Alaunghpaya, arose. Settling the conflict in Burma, Alaunghpaya then turned his attention to Siam. Having established a successful military campaign, he simply followed the logic of expansion (Wyatt 1984: 133). It was left to Alaunghpaya's successor, Naungdawgyi, to capture Chiang Mai, which he did in 1763. In July 1765, a new Burmese army, boosted by troops from Lan Na and the Lao states, marched through central Siam, taking all the major cities, including Sukhothai and Phitsanulok. Meanwhile, another Burmese army landed at Mergui and marched down the Isthmus of Kra, taking Tenasserim and Chumpon on the Gulf of Thailand before marching north to take Phetburi. At Ratburi, it met a third Burmese army that had crossed at Three Pagodas Pass and together they took Ratburi and Suphanburi, meeting the northern army just outside Ayudhya in 1766. Siamese resistance was 'both belated and uncoordinated' (Wyatt 1984: 134).

The siege of Ayudhya ensued but, by early 1767, its fate was sealed. A fire broke out in the city, adding to the desolation and starvation already rampant as a consequence of the siege. Suriyamarin tried to negotiate a surrender based on his suzerainty to Ava, but the Burmese, from a position of absolute strength, rejected any proposition other than unconditional surrender. The ensuing slaughter and destruction was complete. Tens of thousands were led away as slaves. Those who survived were reduced to an animal-like existence, scavenging for food, often eating only leaves or grass (Wyatt 1984: 136–7).

SIAMESE RESURGENCE

According to legend, the governor of Tak province, Sin, had escaped the siege of Ayudhya and assembled an army that expelled the Burmese. Upon this victory, the renamed Taksin proclaimed himself king, removing the Siamese capital from the sacked Ayudhya downriver to Thonburi on the right bank of the Chao Phraya River. Taksin was successful in pulling together the fractured and fragmented state and expanded it into what is now Laos and Cambodia, but he quickly developed delusions of grandeur, in particular of being the next Buddha. Taksin was dethroned and, in front of his successor, executed in the traditional manner of being tied in a velvet sack and beaten to death.[2]

The current lineage of Thai kings and the founding of the modern state date from 1782, when the powerful general, Chao Praya Chakri, succeeded Taksin. Because Thonburi was exposed to Burmese attacks, Chakri moved the capital to the other side of the river, to Krung Thep (Bangkok), where it currently stands.

Conflict with the Burmese continued until the middle of the nineteenth century. The ruler of the Lu state of Chiang Hung, in what is now the northwest corner of Laos, had sent tribute to the court at Bangkok. However, the Burmese claimed suzerainty over the region through Kentung, in Shan State. At the request of the Chiang Hung ruler, King Mungkut sent expeditions against the Burmese between 1852 and 1853 and again in 1854. The timing of these expeditions followed close on the heels of the second Anglo–Burmese War of 1852 and reflected Burma's recent military weakness and an age-old desire for long-standing enemies to strike at times of greatest advantage. These Siamese forces were led by Mongkut's younger brother, Prince Wongsathirat, and manned largely by troops from Lan Na (Wyatt 1984: 182). The Burmese capitulated, as a result of which, Kentung was occupied by the Siamese troops. The attack on Kentung upset the regional court at Chiang Mai, which felt closer to Kentung as a brother T'ai state than it did to its master, Bangkok. But, from the Siamese perspective, the attack on Kentung was a preemptive strike aimed at securing the border regions of the state mandala (Ratanaporn 1988: 311–20).

A EUROPEAN PRESENCE

Thailand prides itself on being the only SEA state not to have been brought under European control during the colonial period, which reflects well on the diplomacy and far-sightedness of successive Thai rulers. Nonetheless, Thailand has a long history of European intervention and its boundaries were defined by colonial Europeans. The first European—from what today is Italy—to visit the coast of what was then a part of Thailand, the trading ports at Tenasserim, Mergui and Tavoy, was Nicolo di Conti, in 1430. In an early example of wars by proxy, the Portuguese supplied arms to the Thais and the Burmese in their various conflicts from as early as 1511 (Manich 1979: 9–10). Spaniards, in support of Cambodia, engaged Thai armies in 1594. Portuguese, Dutch, English, French and Japanese mercenaries also assisted the Thais in various conflicts. The English were especially interested in trade with Thailand, which came to more closely shape relations and Siam's responses to colonial intervention in the nineteenth century.

It was British representative John Cruwford's mission to Bangkok in 1822 that first proposed the dismantling of the Siamese king's monopoly of trade, which was, initially, not well received. The Siamese king was primarily interested in purchasing firearms from Britain, which it had already been buying from American and Portuguese traders. Britain initially refused the request, as its firearms were then needed for its campaigns in Burma (Ngaosyvathn & Ngaosyvathn 1998: 109–11); however, seeing the possibility of an economic opportunity wasted, Britain finally acceded to the Siamese request. In the early 1820s, Thailand bought firearms from Britain, some of which had been used in the final Napoleonic conflict, the Battle of Waterloo. While Thai use of these weapons was not yet up to European standards, they did give the Siamese army unparalleled military superiority over its near neighbours.[3] (Ngaosyvathn & Ngaosyvathn 1998: 117–20).

THE MANDALA EXPANDS

By 1828, Thailand reached what was probably the greatest extent of its territorial expansion and regional power, claiming or exercising control as far west as Shan State in Burma, all of the old empire of Lan Xang and most of the kingdom of Cambodia. At its far eastern reach, it exercised control of regions now occupied by northwest and southwest Vietnam and controlled as far south as Kedah, Perlis, Kelantan and Trengganu states in what is contemporary Malaysia (Corfield n.d.). In traditional mandalic fashion, the empire of the first Chakri, Rama I, exercised authority over these regions through the maintenance of minor kings or princes seated on suzerain thrones: 'In looking at Rama I's empire as a whole, one of its remarkable features is the large number of power centers that existed' (Wyatt 1984: 158). Wyatt also noted that, at the furthest reaches of the empire, local rulers were semi-independent and did little more than pay tribute. Among these were the later Malaysian states, Cambodia and Luang Prabang. States, usually principalities, closer to the centre included Vieng Chan, Champassak and Pattani. Closer still were quasi-independent provinces, including Songkhla, Nakhon Si Thammarat, Battambang-Siem Reap and, possibly, Nakhon Ratchasima (Wyatt 1984: 158–60). Similarly, the empire included the state of Lan Na, which retained its own ruler, but was otherwise beholden to Bangkok. Rama I regarded these suzerain states equally as a part of his empire and, but for the vagaries of history, the shape of contemporary Thailand might still have included Cambodia or the Lao states, but possibly not Lan Na, which is now northern Thailand. Siam's border regions had always varied according to its political and military fortunes, but were more or less fixed in their current alignment by the establishment, in the nineteenth century, of two new competing empires, those of Britain and France. France controlled Indochina, while Britain controlled Burma and the Malay peninsula. Both wished to retain a buffer state, so as to avoid conflict (Fisher 1966: 149–56).

By the middle of the nineteenth century, after a number of earlier attempts, France had occupied southern Vietnam and Cambodia, extending control of Cambodia to include the former Khmer heartland and the long-held Cambodian provinces of Battambang and Siem Reap. In 1860, upon the death of Cambodian King Duon, the successor to the throne, Norodom, faced a rebellion at home and fled to the court at Bangkok, where he sought protection. Being assured of his throne, with the blessing of his Siamese suzerain, he then faced pressure from the French, who now not only controlled Cambodia's access to the South China Sea through the Mekong, but also were clearly the strongest and most aggressive military force in what was to become Indochina. The French claimed they had inherited Vietnam's claim to dual suzerainty over Cambodia, a position that was never happily accepted by the Siamese court. In 1863, Norodom relented and accepted French protection, then set off for his coronation in Bangkok, where the royal regalia was held. No sooner had he left than the French raised the Tricolour over his palace at Udong, causing his abrupt return. The Siamese king, Mongkut, was unhappy about this change of political control, but there was little he could do to force a French withdrawal. In 1867, as a gesture towards placating the Siamese court to achieve a treaty, France returned to Siam the provinces of Siem Reap, Battambang and Sisophon.

Having secured Cambodia, as a part of its control over all Vietnam, France then sought to extend its control to other states that it claimed were suzerain to the court at Hue. Between 1866 and 1868, a French expedition explored the Mekong north of Cambodia through what was then Siamese territory. Having been slowed by the Franco–Prussian War of 1870, France renewed its efforts in the Lao territories under the pretext of Hue's suzerainty over Luang Prabang and Vieng Chan. Vietnam had briefly exercised suzerainty over these areas, but control had generally been retained by Bangkok, as was the case when the French confronted the Siamese in 1893. Auguste Pavie had been appointed vice-consul in Luang Prabang in 1886 and, in 1887, ingratiated himself with the king by saving him from attack by Ho bandits. In 1888, France occupied the T'ai *meaung* of the Black River valley and, in 1890, Pavie further spread French influence through the Lao region (Wyatt 1984: 202–3).

The Siamese responded by strengthening their military position at Nong Kai (opposite Vieng Chan), Ubon and Champassak. When two French commercial agents were expelled from the middle Mekong region and the French consul at Luang Prabang died (of natural causes), France sought reparations in the form of the lands on the left bank of the Mekong. In April 1893, Siamese forces resisted French troops sent to take control of the region, which led to the death of a French officer. The French response was to send gunboats up the Chao Phraya River, forcing the defences at Paknam in a short engagement. The French ultimatum, including a naval blockade of Siamese ports, could not be resisted. The court at Bangkok was caught off guard by this overt belligerence and by the United Kingdom's refusal to become embroiled in the affair.

Siamese relations with the United Kingdom were only slightly less troubled than those with France. The court at Bangkok quickly recognised British military power, but in testing it came close to suffering a similar fate to Burma. When the throne of the previously suzerain state of Trengganu fell vacant upon the death of the local sultan in 1862, Siamese warships landed their claimant to the sultanate. In response, a British warship shelled the local capital, Kuala Trengganu, encouraging the Siamese to abandon their involvement in Trengganu affairs.

The United Kingdom and France sealed an agreement on the borders of Siam in 1896 by marking the Mekong River as the boundary between British Burma and French Laos, jointly guaranteeing the independence of that territory claimed by Siam drained by the Menam River system. This left western Cambodia open to further French claims and states on the Malay peninsula to British claims. In 1897 Britain and Siam reached a secret understanding that Siam would not construct a canal across the Isthmus of Kra (Wyatt 1984: 205), which had the effect of limiting Siam's capacity to develop its economy independently of the colonial powers, thus forcing

French trade to go via the British colony in Singapore. In 1904 and 1907 France no longer felt it had to placate the Siamese court and, noting that these regions did not drain into the Chao Phraya River system, retook possession of the three western provinces of Cambodia (Manich 1979: 198–200). While these losses irked the Thais' well-developed sense of nationalism and imperial pride, it was their flexibility that helped to fend off possible war and preserve the state.

OPENING THE ECONOMY

Although Thailand has, since the beginning of the colonial period, remained politically independent, it was effectively economically colonised, especially by the British. This was the beginning of its bend-with-the-wind policy that ultimately ensured its survival. Britain and Siam both wished to avoid the sort of difficulties over trading relations that had led to the Second Anglo–Burmese War and, to this end, Mongkut, notably, personally entertained the newly appointed British governor of Hong Kong, Sir John Bowring. Bowring had arrived in Bangkok in 1855 with a considerable display of importance, the backing of significant military power and a thinly disguised threat to use force, if necessary, to protect British trading interests in Siam (Wyatt 1984: 183). Mongkut soon agreed to Bowring's request for the opening up of foreign trade. Import and export taxes were restricted to 3 and 5 per cent respectively, British subjects were allowed to reside and own land in Siam and government monopolies, the basis of government revenue, were abolished, except for opium (Wyatt 1984: 183). As a consequence of the treaty, state revenues initially dipped, but were soon restored by taxes on alcohol, gambling and a lottery, as well as by the continuing trade in opium, all of which fell outside the terms of the treaty.

At least as importantly, Mongkut also negotiated similar treaties with the USA, France and numerous other states. The importance of this lay in not being tied exclusively to the United Kingdom, as were India and Burma, or as Vietnam was to France. It was through playing off colonial powers against each other that Siam maintained its independence. Recognising these powers for what they were, Mongkut's strategy of acting as an equal—if a less powerful one—secured his state from the politically humbling circumstances that befell every other monarch of the region (Wyatt 1984: 184–5). It had the added advantage of bringing Siam directly, rather than indirectly, into contact with and to begin to become a part of the (then) modern world.

MODERNISATION

Recognising that it had to adapt in order to not be swallowed by the growth of European colonialism, Siam embarked on a conscious program of modernisation. These reforms were begun by Mongkut after he took the throne in 1851 and were continued by his son, King Chulalongkorn (Rama V), who succeeded his father in 1868. Apart from the European examples, Chulalongkorn also watched Japan's development as a rapidly modernising state. Although there were vast differences between the two, Japan's top-down modernisation stood as a model for the Siamese king and influenced his own attempts at modernisation from above, albeit deeply modified by Siamese norms and requirements.[4] Among his other achievements, Chula-longkorn abolished slavery and compulsory state labour, attempted to modernise Siam's legal and administrative structures and established a civil service (Terweil 1983: 162–215, 252–94).

To help strengthen Siamese identity in the face of so many challenges and to conform to a European standard, one of Chulalongkorn's last acts was to require all Thais to have a Thai family name as well as a given name, which had the added quality of forcing ethnic Chinese in Thailand to assimilate.

When King Chulalongkorn died in 1910, Thailand was a very different place to the Thailand that had existed when he had taken the throne forty-two years earlier. The country had assumed its present shape, with minor rearrangements made during and after WWII. The five tiers of gradually diminishing authority that characterised earlier royal rule were gone, replaced by a bureaucratic structure modelled, in principle, on that of the United Kingdom. The wasteful and inefficient rule of local elites was gradually being replaced by appointed officials, bringing the provinces more directly under the control of the centre. There had been resistance to these changes, resulting in rebellions in Pattani, the northeast and the north in 1902, but the old ruling families were eventually prised apart from the people who served as their generous source of income (Wyatt 1984: 212–14). A further legacy of Chulalongkorn was the enhanced role of the navy and, especially, the army in the affairs of the state.

THE ARMY AND THE END OF ABSOLUTE MONARCHY

King Vajiravudh (Rama VI) succeeded Chulalongkorn in 1910 and introduced, theoretically at least, compulsory education and other educational reforms. He also further Westernised the state by making the Thai calendar conform to the European. However, in 1912 a group of young military officers of mostly Sino–Thai ancestry attempted to overthrow the king in a coup. The inspiration for the coup attempt came from many factors: competition between the king's brothers for political power, the Chinese revolution of October 1911, the injustices of the existing political system and because of a perceived downgrading of the army in favour of the king's private Wild Tiger Corps (Wyatt 1984: 225–6, Terweil 1983: 291–9). The coup plot was foiled before it unfolded, but it was a sign that the army would play a very active role in Thai politics throughout the rest of the twentieth century.

The role of the Thai military was strengthened after the outbreak of the Great War (WWI) in 1914. The pro-Allies sentiments of the government were finally tipped into action when the USA entered the conflict in 1917; Thailand also chose to join the Allied cause. More than anything, though, Thailand did not want to be thought equivocal by the victorious Allies and thus have its sovereignty threatened (Wyatt 1984: 230). More than anything else, maintenance of state sovereignty in a rapidly changing world was the key aspiration of the Siamese government.

Vajiravudh was a controversial king because of social activities associated with his implied homosexuality, the distribution of power within the government and, in significant part, because of greatly inflated royal expenditure. After a long period of rapid social and economic change, including restructuring the system of government to more closely resemble the United Kingdom's bureaucratic model, Vajiravudh opposed further significant political change (Wyatt 1984: 231–3). Added to increasing economic instability caused by fluctuations in the price of Thailand's chief export, rice, not just the person but also the status of the office of the king was weakened.

Then, in 1925, Vajiravudh died suddenly at the age of forty-four, leaving as his heir his half-brother and the youngest son of Chulalongkorn, Prajadhipok. Prajadhipok's reign

> both began and ended under clouds of criticism and unrest, dogged almost constantly by economic problems. Yet its denouement was profoundly political, involving no less than the end of the absolute monarchy and the ascension to power of segments of the new elite that had been growing since Chulalongkorn attained control of his administration in the 1880s (Wyatt 1984: 234; see also, Terweil 1989: 84–5; Terweil 1983: ch. 8).

Prajadhipok inherited a high level of state debt within a disorganised economy, which, in turn, fuelled conflict between ministers over budgetary allocations, stalled the process of government and caused a general loss of faith in the political system. Being young and inexperienced, the new king was unable to control these problems. Having been educated in England and France, perhaps the one significant contribution that Prajadhipok did make was, in 1927, to raise discussion about a process of democratisation. At one level, his plans for introducing such a process were too far in advance of his countrymen's desires; at another, when events started to move out of his control, the king was too far behind those desires—they simply passed him by (Keyes 1987: 61–6, Wyatt 1984: 235–7). Between 1930 and 1932, when the Great Depression hit Thailand, the price of rice dropped by two-thirds and the value of land dropped to one-sixth of its previous value. Siam clung to the gold standard, which made the price of its rice more expensive than that of the competition on the international market, which further harmed its economy. Government spending was cut by one-third, while cash incomes fell by an average of two-thirds.

While popular discontent was at an all-time high, in the background hovered an old prophesy that purported that, after 150 years, on 6 April 1932, the Chakri Dynasty would end. Prajadhipok again raised the idea of representative government and was again rejected by his advisers, who proposed a Constitution that was quite similar to that which was eventually adopted. On 24 June 1932, while the king was vacationing by the sea, a small group of middle-level officers launched a swift coup. Bluffing or immobilising other military units around the capital, the Promoters, as they became known, forty-nine army and navy officers and sixty-five civilians, brought an end to absolute monarchy in Thailand (Wyatt 1984: 239–42; Steinberg 1971: 313–20; Kahin 1969: 15–21).

THE ARMY IN GOVERNMENT

The first constitutional governments of the 1930s were led by conservative, senior military officers. A provisional Constitution was established, a National Assembly of seventy members was appointed, from which a smaller Peoples' Committee was drawn to act as a type of cabinet. Many of the senior figures in this government had held high office in the government of the last king. Under the auspices of a People's Party, the Promoters sought popular support for their cause. Yet the civilian wing was relatively unsuccessful at attracting popular interest, while the military wing was busy consolidating itself in positions of power. It was this basic division, complicated by further internal factionalism, that led to a series of disruptions within the new government. A civilian proposal for a socialist-type state was rejected by the conservative military group, who branded the suggestion as being like communism; they even enlisted the support of the king to oppose it. The National Assembly, which was generally in favour of the plan, was prorogued; the architect of the plan, Pridi Phanomyong, went into temporary exile (Wyatt 1984: 247).

There was considerable discontent with the new government. In 1933, a grandson of Chulalongkorn and former Minister of War, Prince Boworadet, led a regional rebellion that marched on Bangkok. The response to the rebels was organised by Lieutenant-Colonel Phibun, who mounted a counterattack in the northern fringes of Bangkok between 13 and 16 October. After intense fighting, with heavy casualties on both sides, the rebel forces broke and retreated towards Nakhon Ratchasima. Realising his cause was lost, Boworadet fled to exile in France. A few months later, King Prajadhipok travelled to England, supposedly for medical treatment, from where he clarified the terms under which he would continue as monarch. When, in 1935, he was refused a role in the appointment of members of the already undemocratic National Assembly, he abdicated. In his place, the

National Assembly invited the ten-year-old son of Prince Mahidol, Prince Ananda Mahidol, then at school in Switzerland, to assume the throne, which he did (Wyatt 1984: 248–9).

The government had promised a fully elected National Assembly when educational levels rose and, between 1933 and 1934 and 1937 and 1938, expenditure on education rose fourfold, while total government spending only increased by one-third. This educational campaign raised literacy among both sexes to over 60 per cent; for males, the figure was over 80 per cent. Over the same period, the military budget also doubled, in part to defend Siam against perceived colonial threats and in part to defend itself against the greater war that appeared to be brewing in Europe and in Japan. Added to this was the favourable impact that Nazi Germany, Fascist Italy and, in particular, prewar Japan had on a large number of Siamese, especially in the military. From early 1932, younger army officers were in contact with their counterparts in Japan and militant nationalism was on the rise. At the same time, the economy began to improve, largely because the new government had taken power at the lowest ebb of the Great Depression (Wyatt 1984: 248–50).

In 1935, as Foreign Minister, Pridi Phanomyong, who had by then returned from exile, negotiated Siam's complete sovereignty. Following on from this wave of nationalism, Siam changed its name in 1939 to more accurately reflect what the Siamese called their state, Prathet Thai, rather than the name they were given by the outside world. The change of name had a further, double purpose: it cemented the ethnic Thais as the national group of the state and had the literal meaning of being 'free',[5] which was useful in terms of anticolonial and nationalist assertion during the last throes of European colonialism. Although Thailand changed its name back to Siam at the conclusion of WWII, it reasserted its own identity, again under Phibun, in 1948.

WORLD WAR II

The Second World War was less painful for Thailand than for its neighbours. Fearing that Japan, which was preparing to consolidate its hold over Indochina, would forestall Thai attempts to reclaim border territory lost to France, in November 1940 it invaded western Cambodia and disputed Lao territories. Japan intervened, forcing a settlement that gave Thailand the Thai side of the Mekong at Champassak in southern Laos, Sayabouri in northwestern Laos and Battambang and Siem Reap provinces in Cambodia (Terweil 1983: 344–6). The Japanese ambassador requested passage for Japanese troops through Thailand, but Phibun was touring the Cambodian provinces at the time and his Foreign Minister, Direk Jayanama, refused the request, to which Phibun would probably have agreed. The following day, 8 December 1941, coinciding with its attack on US installations in the Pacific,

Japanese forces crossed into Thailand at nine points. Phibun arrived back the next morning and ordered a Thai ceasefire. On 12 December, Phibun signed a military alliance with Japan, which allowed Japanese troops to be stationed on Thai territory, from which they launched attacks against Burma and Malaysia (Terweil 1983: 346).

There was no real choice in the agreement, although, as a result of their pre-war tendencies, many in government were comfortable with an alliance with Japan. In any case, this alliance reflected a continuation of the types of accommodationist policies that had allowed the country to negotiate its way through the colonial era. The ethic behind the decision was to bend with the wind, rather than breaking before it. Watching Japan's quick victories, Phibun expanded his alliance with Japan and, on 25 January 1942, declared war on the USA and the United Kingdom. In 1943, Thailand invaded the Shan region of Burma and, in August of that year, confirmed its incorporation into Thailand in a treaty with Japan. Japan also returned administration of Kelantan, Trengganu, Perlis and Kedah in northern Malaya to Thailand (Wyatt 1984: 257–8).

The Thai ambassador to Washington, Seni Pramoj, refused to deliver Phibun's declaration of war to the US government, regarding it as not reflecting the wishes of the Thai people, and set about organising a Free Thai movement. As the war began to go against Japan, the Thai government forced the resignation of Phibun as prime minister. The Free Thai movement, supported by the USA, operated out of Chongqing in southern China and from British bases in Sri Lanka and India. It had also infiltrated the Thai government and was, in effect, headquartered in the office of Pridi, who was acting as regent in the absence of the king[6] (Wyatt 1984: 258–9). With Japan's impending defeat, the National Assembly voted out Phibun and voted in Khuang Aphaiwong, who could deal with the Japanese, while Pridi, because of his ability to deal with the Allies, became sole regent. Thus began a period of quick diplomatic transition.

THE POSTWAR PERIOD

In the last days of the war, the United Kingdom, aggrieved at Thailand for allowing Japan to use its territory to launch attacks against Burma and Malaya, asked for reparations for its war costs. It also announced it would claim back the four Malay states and appeared ready to invade Thailand. The Free Thai movement worked more closely with the sympathetic USA, expressed a lack of Thai commitment to Phibun's declaration of war, noted that Thai troops had not actually engaged Allied troops in conflict and offered to field a force of 50 000 Free Thai soldiers against the Japanese. The USA acted as an advocate for Thailand against a less sympathetic British position. Upon the surrender of Japan, Pridi announced that Thailand's declaration of war was illegal and, hence, null and void, and repudiated all agreements made with Japan. Khuang Aphaiwong resigned as prime minister on the basis of his recent association with the Japanese and the National Assembly announced its intention to ask Seni Pramoj to become prime minister on his return from Washington. Ending the conflict with France proved more difficult, as Thai sentiment ran in favour of retaining the provinces of Laos and Cambodia occupied during the war. These provinces were only restored in January 1947, after the residents had already voted in Thailand's 1946 elections (Wyatt 1984: 260–2).

Despite Pridi's People's Party winning a majority of seats in January 1946, the assembly elected Khuang, from the Democratic Party, as prime minister. With the majority not holding power, this situation could not last and, in March, Khuang resigned. Pridi drew up a new Constitution, introducing an upper and a lower house, which came into effect in May 1946. Democratic prospects for the state began to look promising. But then, the highest Thai court refused to proceed with a war crimes trial against Phibun, who remained popular; along with the military, he was effectively exonerated for actions taken in difficult circumstances. Then, on 9 June 1946, the young King Ananda Mahidol was found dead in his bed, shot through the head. While the three chief material witnesses in the affair were quickly tried and executed, Pridi was popularly held responsible. In August, he resigned as prime minister and left the country. The government began to flounder. Although Pridi returned, his links with Indonesian, Laotian and Vietnamese nationalists had him labelled as a communist sympathiser. Rumours spread about the death of the king and an impending communist revolution. On 8 November 1947, soldiers seized the government, appointed Khuang as caretaker prime minister to forestall international condemnation and began a program of persecuting leftists, especially Pridi's supporters. In elections held in January 1948, Khuang's Democratic Party won a small majority in the National Assembly, but after three months Phibun and his Coup Group forced Khuang's resignation, installing Phibun as prime minister. Thai politics was fractured and shallowly rooted. Neither Pridi nor Phibun were much liked or trusted, but Phibun had recourse to real force through the army, whereas Pridi did not (Keyes 1987: 71–2, Wyatt 1984: 264–6; Wilson 1966: 24–6).

THE COLD WAR

Both Phibun and Thailand had to reinvent themselves politically in the postwar period, especially in order to regain the confidence of the international community. Seeking a new lead to follow, the postwar Phibun government modelled itself on the USA, which had three advantages as a new political model. The first was that it was the major power among the victorious Allies, the second, that it had shown itself to be a friend of Thailand, whereas the United Kingdom and France had been hostile, and the third, that it was emerging as the world's dominant anticommunist force and as the world's dominant economy. The move towards becoming closer to the USA was seen in some quarters as diminishing the nationalist aspirations that Thailand had built up in the 1930s and 1940s. As such, it engendered a nationalist backlash within some sections of the military.

In the Cold War climate of the late 1940s and early 1950s, Thailand faced insurgencies in the predominantly Lao northeast, but, more especially, in the south, where both Muslim separatists and communists were active. Closer to home were two attempted coups, the first in October 1948 and the second in February 1949. The first simply reflected dissatisfaction with Phibun within an anti-Coup Group section of the military. The second was a plot by sections of the marines and navy to restore Pridi to power, resulting in three days of heavy fighting in Bangkok. Phibun supporters defeated the dissident forces, stepped up oppression of his opponents and executed many officials and politicians (Elliott 1978: 86–8, Wilson 1966: 26). A façade of constitutional democracy was retained, but it was increasingly thin, with power transferred away from the National Assembly. On 29 June 1951, while on board a dredge ship being presented to Thailand by the USA, Phibun was taken prisoner by navy officers and held on the flagship, the *Sri Ayudhya*. Negotiations for a change in government broke down, there was heavy fighting in Bangkok, in which more than 1200 civilians were killed and then, the airforce attacked the *Sri Ayudhya*. As it sank, Phibun swam to safety. Following this coup attempt, the navy was cut to one-quarter of its previous strength and a further purge of perceived dissidents ensued. The suppression of this coup marked the rise in power of two chief rivals within the original Coup Group. One of them was Major-General Sarit Thanarat (Keyes 1987: 72–4, Wyatt 1984: 267–70).

The Thai economy improved throughout the 1950s, in part due to the demands for rice, rubber and tin stimulated by the Korean War, to which Thailand sent a contingent of troops. The growth of manufactured goods also increased. In 1954, confirming its position within the USA-led camp, Thailand joined the South-East Asian Treaty Organisation (SEATO). When compared to its neighbours, Thailand was viewed by the USA as powerful and stable and, when compared to the insurgency-wracked Burma, the defeat of France in Indochina in 1954 by communist nationalists, a communist insurgency in Malaya and the success of Chinese communism, Thailand was, indeed, safe and stable. At another level, however, US involvement in the Thai military, as an anticommunist bastion, led to an increase in official corruption. It also tied the Thai military elite very closely to US foreign policy, which continued to jar nationalist sentiment.

THE RISE OF SARIT

In 1955, Phibun returned from a trip to the USA and the United Kingdom espousing the cause of democracy, allowing the registration of political parties and the democratisation of local government. Phibun's group narrowly won the elections held in February 1957, but, despite his references to democratisation, 'only by blatant fraud, vote rigging, tampering, and coercion' did he secure his victory (Elliott 1978: 115–8, Wyatt 1984: 274). They were the 'dirtiest elections in Thai history' (Wyatt 1984: 274; see also, Keyes 1987: 76–7). In response to the public outcry over these elections, Phibun declared a state of national emergency and made Sarit, now a field marshal, responsible for public order. Phibun's government continued to reel under further crises, in particular, a drought in the northeast and a corruption scandal. Sarit publicly moved closer to the people, then, he and his deputies resigned from the cabinet. A group of appointed legislators also resigned and, as Sarit's popularity increased, he asked for the resignation of the government. Phibun attempted to have Sarit arrested, but Sarit was warned of the attempt and the next morning staged a quick and bloodless coup (Sulak 1991: 54; Wyatt 1984: 275). Thailand appeared to be incapable of escaping the domination of the army in the political process and, certainly, the army seemed to believe that it had a legitimate role in keeping a watching brief over and, when necessary, intervening in, the affairs of state. It was to be a self-perception a long time in changing.

As a political leader, Sarit was the archetypal military strongman. Although he claimed that he acted on behalf of the people, Sarit had little time for notions of democracy (Sulak 1991: 55). Under Sarit, in the face of a political deadlock and a critical media and labour strike on 20 October 1958, the Constitution was abandoned, martial law declared, the National Assembly elected in early 1957 dissolved and an interim cabinet appointed. Over the next five years, Sarit introduced a range of populist reforms, including on the law and order issues of prostitution, arson, opium and public hooliganism. He banned pedicabs, calling them archaic and uncivilised and he referred to virtually all of his critics as communists. Sarit's ideology was to turn the people's loyalty from the abstract notion of the state to the person of the king, whose executive officer was himself. In doing this, the king was 'restored to the apex of the moral, social and political order' (Wyatt 1984: 281). In a more positive, concrete sense, Sarit also embarked on a program of economic development, including bringing basic infrastructure, such as roads, to rural areas and boosting education. Sarit also encouraged foreign investment, which helped Thailand post growth rates of an average of 8.6 per cent a year from 1959 until 1969 (Wyatt 1984: 283).

In regional terms, Thailand accepted a high level of US military assistance in proportion to non-military assistance from the late 1950s until the late 1960s as a means of boosting Thailand's capacity to defend itself against revolutionary forces operating in Indochina. As a part of this program, the USA also used Thailand as its primary base for launching air attacks against communist positions in Indochina. When Sarit died in office in 1963, he left behind a personal fortune of almost US$150 million, land, houses, a second wife and more than fifty mistresses (Pongpaichit and Piriyarangsan 1994: 26).

THE 1960S

Sarit was succeeded by his deputy, General Thanom Kittikachorn, who had served as stand-in prime minister in 1958. Thanom was a milder military leader than Sarit; nevertheless, he continued Thai politics along military lines. Thanom's deputy was General Praphas Carusathian and their political relationship was made all the closer by the marriage of Thanom's son to Praphas' daughter. The Thanom–Praphas period was noted for Thailand's increasing involvement in the Indochina conflict, the continued modernisation of Thailand and, finally, for the development of wide-ranging political debate (Wyatt 1984: 286).

The Indochina conflict was of special concern to Thailand and, picking up where Sarit had left the relationship with the USA, Thanom and Praphas, during the 1960s, actively—if quietly—pushed Thai intervention in the conflict in Laos. American air bases were established in Nakhon Sawan province north of Bangkok, in Khorat in the northeast and in Nakhon Phanom. In the later 1960s, more than 40 000 US military personnel were stationed in Thailand along with almost 6000 aircraft. Direct Thai involvement in the Vietnam campaign began in 1964, with an airforce contingent going to South Vietnam, a naval contingent the year after and, between 1967 and 1969, up to 11 000 troops. Meanwhile, the American presence in Thailand increased the pace of Westernisation, at least in the most superficial sense of catering for American servicemen's interests (Wyatt 1984: 286–9). From around 1964, in response to its escalating involvement in the Indochina war, the Communist Party of Thailand, operating near and, later, from Laos and Cambodia and supported by North Vietnam, began a series of attacks in the northeast. By 1967 the insurgency had spread throughout much of the north as well, then into the south and, eventually, closer to the centre. 'By the early 1970s, the Thanom–Praphas regime faced a major security crisis' (Wyatt 1984: 290; see also, Battersby 1999). In response, Thanom decided to go to the polls.

DEMOCRATISATION

In 1969, Thanom allowed elections for the National Assembly, which gave the government a majority and at least the façade of civilian rule. In November 1971, in response to increasing political dissent, Thanom dissolved the parliament, banned political parties and restored the military to its earlier dominant position. By this stage, the military was increasingly factionalised and the government was no longer of the strong military type that had earlier dominated Thai politics. In 1973, expulsions from universities and arrests led to student demonstrations and mass protests involving between 200 000 and 500 000 people. Thanom ordered troops in against the protesters, but the army began to disobey him. King Bhumibol supported the protesters and, on 14 October 1973, Thanom and Praphas resigned and fled into exile (Elliott 1978: 133–7, Keyes 1987: 82–3).

While the army had been pushed from power in 1973, a bloody military coup on 6 October 1976 restored a right-wing military government. This military backlash was launched by a generation of Thai army officers known as the Young Turks, who had been blooded during the American war in Vietnam and who took a pro-active view of their role as guardians of the state (Keyes 1987: 86). It was this generation of army officers who came to dominate Thai politics—and military corruption—into the 1980s and 1990s and who, at the end of the 1990s, were only slowly being pushed from power by the government.

Corresponding to the rise of these Young Turks was the rise of Thai civil society; that is, those elements of Thai society that were increasingly inclined to engage in day to day politics, but who were not a part of the military or party structure. Thailand's increasing urbanisation and the greater education of its youth provided the context for the rise in civil society, but it was also, in large part, the failure of outright rebellion that encouraged many to seek alternative—but legal—paths towards changing the face of Thai political society.

REBELLION

In the poverty-stricken and generally neglected northeast, a communist rebellion that had been underway since the late 1960s (Wit 1968), was particularly well supported following the 1976 coup. By the early 1980s, however, this rebellion was effectively finished. The failure of the pro-Chinese Thai communists was primarily due to the cooling of relations between China and Vietnam and Laos, the latter of which had provided much sanctuary for the rebels. The rebellion was also hampered by the loss of support from the pro-Chinese Khmer Rouge after Vietnam ousted them from power in Cambodia in 1978. Government amnesties granted to communist rebels brought many in from the jungles and, by the mid 1980s, the rebellion was effectively finished. Many of those rebels who took advantage of the amnesty later became involved in non-government organisations that attempted to address local problems. Others became politically active in other ways and, although these former rebels were far from alone in promoting civil redress, they did contribute to its intellectual core. Along with idealistic students and businesspeople, who recognised that their interests would be better served by reducing the dead hand of the military in government and corruption (see Phongpaichit & Piriyangsan

1994 for a detailed account of the extent of corruption in Thailand), the idea of removing the military from politics and sustaining a representative form of government increasingly took hold. As the old party structures began to fragment, new actors moved onto the political stage.

Although Thailand is a unitary state, it has numerous ethnic minorities, including Muslims in the south, Lao in the northeast (Isan) region and numerous smaller hill tribes in the north and northeast. Many of these disenfranchised ethnic minorities supported the communist rebellion, particularly in the northwestern, northern and northeastern regions, with conflict into the 1990s and the first years of the twenty-first century usually blamed on Muslim separatists.

In 1986, the government, led by General Prem Tinsulanonda, dissolved the House of Representatives after it voted against a royal decree to amend the Land Transport Act. The Thai people and their political representatives were beginning to show impatience with the continuing military involvement in political affairs. In 1988, Prem again dissolved the House due to disunity between and within political parties. Majority votes from within a number of parties had been carried, but the parties themselves did not accept the votes, indicating that the undue influence the army continued to assert was no longer tenable. Although the army's position in politics had been under challenge since the early 1970s, this event marked the end of the autocratic style of military rule. Prem allowed, even encouraged, a gradual shift towards democracy, stepping down in 1988 in favour of a coalition government led by retired general, Chatchai Choonhavan.

Factionalism and rampant corruption (see Phongpaichit & Piriyangsan 1994: 26–57) led to another military coup in 1991. By this time, a significant middle class had become established, especially in Bangkok, and they and their student offspring were in no mood to continue supporting a non-reflexive military government. Spurred on by human rights and prodemocracy non-government organisations (Prudhisan & Maneerat 1997: 206), this dissatisfaction led to public protests in May 1992, to which the army responded by shooting unarmed demonstrators. It was at this time that the king stepped in to support the protests and, without that source of legitimation, the prime minister, General Suchinda Kraprayoon, resigned (SarDesai 1997: 262–4). With this effective defeat of the formal military in government, Thailand appeared to be on a course of liberal capitalist democracy. While retired military figures retained a high profile in Thai political life, they were too factionalised and spread across too many parties to present a united front for military interests (Wassana 1999b). This tendency was strengthened by the promulgation, on 9 December 1991, of a new liberal Constitution confirming Thailand as a constitutional monarchy. Thailand's fifteenth Constitution since 1932, this Constitution was amended again in 1997.

THE CONSTITUTIONAL STRUCTURE OF THE STATE

The Constitution established regular four-yearly elections for a 500-member House of Representatives, 400 of whom were from single-seat constituencies and 100 from party lists, and a 260-member Senate. The number of members of the Senate was reduced to 200 in March 2000, providing a ratio of one senator to each 300 000 citizens. Senators were also restricted to two six-year consecutive terms in office. The Thai prime minister is usually—but not necessarily—an elected member of the House of Representatives and, similar to the Westminster parliamentary system, leads the party or coalition of parties that enjoys the confidence of a majority of Lower House members. The prime minister's council of ministers, numbering thirteen, may also include non-elected members. The Lower House writes and approves legislation while the Upper House votes on Constitutional changes. Votes of no confidence can be taken by both Houses voting together, which means that the Senate only requires a further forty-six votes to topple the government.

THE MONARCHY

For a constitutional monarchy, Thailand has a relatively active king. In most constitutional monarchies, the monarch occupies the position of head of state, but has little real input into the affairs of state. Thailand's King Bhumibol has tended to stay aloof from day-to-day politics, but has intervened directly at critical moments and has taken an active interest not just in day-to-day affairs of state, but also in endorsing a strong role for himself. This intervention, for example, in supporting an end to military rule in 1991, went a considerable way towards strengthening and legitimising the role of the king in Thai political life. The underlying philosophy of the king (and the 1991 Constitution) was that the monarchy and the people are as one and that the people's interests are the king's interests (Hewison 1997: 61). This assumes that the king is familiar with the interests of the people and, logically, also assumes that the people's interest is served by the maintenance of the monarchy. The alignment between the king and the people is a relatively recent phenomenon. King Bhumibol Adulyadej, in an earlier period, was a supporter of 'stability and order, authority and tradition, developmentalism, unity and solidarity, national chauvinism, and national security and anti-communism' (Hewison 1997: 63). Bhumibol was an activist monarch, but he was conservative in his activism (Hewison 1997: 74).

Seen in this light, while King Bhumibol's intervention in state politics in 1991 was generally regarded as enlightened, it could also have been viewed as support for ascendant private capital. It seemed that the military parties had already lost the initiative, especially in the face of public protests reflecting a range of social groups. When the king stepped in, the public protests were legitimised, as a result of which, General Suchinda stepped down as prime minister. New elections were held, in which a prodemocracy coalition led by Democrat Party leader Chuan Leekpai was voted into government.

TRADITION AND AUTHORITY

Divisions exist in Thai society between what is known as 'big' and 'little' people, and between urban and rural dwellers, with Bangkok, in some respects, almost constituting a separate state to rural Thailand. Apart from the sheer fact of urbanisation, there are major wealth disparities between the people of the greater Bangkok region and the rest of Thailand, as well as disparities in government services. As noted at the time of the 2000 Senate elections, 'Thailand is still, no doubt, a tale of two democracies in which the middle and rural classes have conflicting expectations of politicians and government' (Crispin & Tasker 2000).

Much of Thai society remains distinctly Thai and quite traditional, despite the economic development, especially of the greater Bangkok region, since the 1970s. Notions of 'big person–little person' (*phuu yai–phuu nawy*) still prevail and dominate, not just in the formal aspects of political life, but also in power relations within the broader society. The notion of big person was later expanded to include simple social rank defined by age, wealth, status and personal and political power. In more contemporary terms, big people are much more widely dispersed among holders of real, practical power, including politicians and senior bureaucrats, army officers, wealthier businesspeople and so on. Small people, those without access to powerful positions, were usually deferential to big people for reasons real and imagined, including political threat or promise and the potential for loss or profit. Increasingly, as the Thais' sense of conspicuous consumption expanded in line with the country's economic development, money became the mark of a big person.

Another element of the idea of social hierarchy is reinforced by prescribed speech and manners. As such, in a formal sense, there are no equals at all,[7] although this assumption is perhaps more strongly asserted by those who perceive themselves higher in social ranking. The initial development of the big person syndrome was a consequence of royal privilege, such as royal appointment or related association. Royalty remains broadly held as sacrosanct, in part due to tradition and in part to the reconstruction of royalty in Thai political society following the coup of 1932 and under Sarit in the 1950s and early 1960s. As with other royal groups, when real power was diminished, symbolic power was enhanced, in many cases strengthening popular respect for monarchical figures and their families. The monarchy had become an important and, 'arguably, a central institution and political actor' in Thai politics (Hewison 1997: 58). Thailand remains one of the very few countries in the world to retain *lèse-majesté*, in which insulting or criticising the royal family is a criminal offence, punishable by up to seven years imprisonment. Despite the criminal nature of insulting the royal family, many Thais regularly gossip about the royal families and their affairs.

Along with royalty, religion is also held to be sacrosanct. Theravada Buddhism is the official state religion and around 95 per cent of all Thais are Theravada Buddhists. A small minority of Muslims living in the four southern provinces of Yala, Narathiwat, Satun and Pattani, all once part of the sultanate of Pattani, near the Malaysian border, fell outside this officially defined version of being Thai and, along with linguistic difference, often constituted themselves as unwillingly Thai, which led to what was a relatively low-level security threat in the region. This changed in 2002.

ISLAMIC SEPARATISM

A separate Islamic identity and claims to separatism have long troubled Thailand's southern provinces of Pattani, Yala, Narathiwat and, to a lesser extent, Songkhla and Satun; the actions of various organisations claiming to represent separatist movements has been characterised by the Thai government as terrorism. This terrorism has primarily been manifested as attacks on Thai officials working in rural Pattani, but also as attacks against symbols of the Thai state, such as the railway.

Pattani was established as a trading port by Muslim Malays, probably as early as the thirteen century, marking the narrowest point of the Isthmus of Kra and being a generally flat crossing just north of a difficult mountain range. This crossing point, which focused on a well-sheltered bay and wide river, was used by Arabic, Indian and Chinese traders who wished to avoid traversing the sometimes dangerous Malacca Strait and, especially, trading with Malacca after its fall to the Portuguese. The principality forged alliances with other regional Malay states, but succumbed to the Thais in the eighteenth century. Despite numerous rebellions, which led to the principality's dismemberment into a number of provinces, Pattani was not formally incorporated into the Thai state until 1902; it was recognised by the British in 1909. Since then, the 1.7 million Malay Muslims of the region have objected to the Thai policy of assimilation and have struggled in various ways to either become an independent state (*Negeri Patani Raya*)[8] or to assert a claim to incorporation with Malaysia (*Pattani Darussalam*),[9] towards which the Malaysian government has been quietly sympathetic but careful to never endorse. Notably, in 1948, more than 1000 Muslims in Narathiwat attacked police, leaving more than 400 Muslims and thirty police dead, in what was known as the Duson Nyor Revolt.

The primary separatist organisation in this region is the Pattani United Liberation Organisation (PULO), which has been claimed to act as an umbrella organisation for a number of smaller separatist groups. Despite occasional flare-ups of tension, PULO had been relatively quiet until 2002, when a change of policy towards the southern Malays under Thailand's new prime minister, Thaksin Shinawatra—notably, the closure of a government agency that dealt with regional issues, increased brutality on the part of police and the arrest of more outspoken Muslim clerics—alienated many local Muslims. In 2002, fifteen police were killed in separate attacks throughout the southern provinces. The Thai government's response was to crack down on separatism, which led to a more forceful backlash, culminating in an attack by Malay Muslim youths on military strongpoints. In June 2003, Thai police arrested three Thai Muslims and one from Singapore, some of whom were said by police to have later admitted that they were members of JI. Police later claimed that the Thai branch of *Jema'ah Islamiyah* (JI, or Islamic Community) was known as *Gerakan Mujahideen Islam Pattani* (GMIP, or Pattani Islamic Holy Struggle Movement) and alleged that it had links with both al'Qaeda and JI (Raman 2004). Thai police also claimed that PULO was linked to the Free Aceh Movement and had supplied arms to it, which the latter vehemently denied, saying they primarily bought their arms in Java. On 4 January 2004, around thirty men attacked a Thai military depot in Narathiwat, killing four soldiers and taking more than 100 weapons. Around eighteen schools were burnt in Narathiwat and Yala on the same day, while, on the following day, two policemen were killed while trying to defuse a bomb in Pattani province (Raman 2004). In response, the Thai government declared martial law in Pattani, Narathiwat and Yala provinces and, from this time forward, security matters worsened.

On 28 April 2004, more than 100 mostly machete-wielding Muslim youths, said to belong to *Sarigat*, a splinter group of the Islamic separatist *Barisan Revolusi Nasional* (National Revolutionary Front), were killed, along with two soldiers and three police officers when more than 150 Muslim youths attacked Thai army and police posts in southern Thailand (*Nation*, 28 April 2004). After being defeated, many of the youths fled to Pattani's Krue Se mosque, where soldiers killed thirty-two of the by-then unarmed youths with rocket-propelled grenades. Killings of civilians and alleged PULO members, as well as police, soldiers and Thai government officials, continued at a regular and gruesome pace in the following months, with much of the Pattani and surrounding areas becoming a region of active guerrilla warfare. Around eighty Muslim Malays were killed in October 2004 after police jammed them into overcrowded trucks following a riot in Pattani. Prime Minister Thaksin further inflamed local sentiment by claiming that the prisoners had died because they were already weakened by fasting during the holy month of Ramadan. While martial law had been declared in southern Thailand since the beginning of the year, rarely a day went by in 2004 in which people were not killed. Between the more aggressive policies of Thaksin's government and the regional rise of militant Islamism, Thailand appeared to have become embroiled in a local, but serious and long-term, security problem.

THAI MEDIA

Thailand's 1991 Constitution guaranteed freedom of the media, which was reflected in the country's generally unfettered and often high-quality news media. Thailand's newspapers were often the most informative and least restricted in SEA, while Thai television approximated Western television, including generally superficial news programming.[10] Similarly, Thai radio ran predominantly music-based programming formats, although there were some talk programs, which, like those elsewhere in the Western world, were often remarkably uninformed. The major exception was Thailand's national public broadcaster, Radio Thailand (*Sathaani Withayu Haeng Prathet Thai*), which ran quality local, national and international news, business, sport and news-related feature programming.

The Thai media often discussed critical or controversial issues, even though publishing permits could be suspended by the National Police Department for national security reasons. As elsewhere, there was an element of self-censorship on some issues in the Thai media. Thailand's royalty was treated with the utmost respect, an attitude that was enforced by the legal sanction of *lèse-majesté*. This was most clearly illustrated during the late democracy period by a ban on the movie *Anna and the King*, which was a 2000 Hollywood remake of the film *The King and I*. The ban was justified on the grounds that it was an historically inaccurate portrayal of Thai royal history, but was seen by many as a bid to rein in the country's increasingly unrestricted media.

Of the print media, the English-language press had, perhaps, the highest journalistic standards while the most popular Thai newspapers tended towards being tabloid and sensationalist. Better quality Thai-language journalism existed, but was less popular than these other two categories of print media. As Thitinam has noted, the Thai media have not always been so relatively free: under more oppressive governments, they have acted more as tools of the state, reflecting government views rather than independent news (Thitinam 1997). Along with the Philippines, this shows the media acting as a clear barometer of the political climate, rather than directly influencing that climate.

REINING IN THE MILITARY

By 1998, the government had begun to move to reduce the upper echelons of the armed forces by instituting a policy of replacing only 75 per cent of retiring senior officers (Wassana 1998). Nevertheless, Thai soldiers continued to enjoy special legal privileges not granted to ordinary citizens, in particular, the limited authority of police over soldiers, especially officers, who are suspected of committing crimes (Prakobpong 1998). This double standard was illustrated in a government crackdown on criminal activities within the army, which was officially described as the 'military mafia'. Four officers involved in such mafia activities were given a 'stern warning' by the Bangkok and regional military police chief, Major-General Boonyoung Bucha. A source said the four included two major-generals, a cavalry colonel and a sublieutenant. The report went on to note that efforts to 'clean up' the military mafia had caused 'unease' among some officers who derived most of their income from illegal activities (Wassana 1999a). At the risk of slipping into cynicism, it seemed that giving mafia types a stern warning, which caused them little more than unease, did not reflect a serious attempt to halt corrupt activity in the army or to treat all Thai citizens as legal equals. This was especially the case considering that an alleged motorcycle thief received somewhat more summary justice when he was shot dead by police (*Bangkok Post* 1999a).

Corresponding to this police 'crackdown', there was a series of bombings and bomb threats in Bangkok and elsewhere, which were linked to Thailand's army and some of which were directed against police in Bangkok. The primary link was that explosives found in one device, which was professionally constructed, were of the same type used by the Thai army (*Bangkok Post* reporters 1999d; *Nation* 1999b).

FROM MIRACLE TO CRISIS

While it had already been performing admirably since the 1970s, Thailand's economy grew rapidly from the late 1980s, averaging more than 10 per cent growth a year. Growth in the greater Bangkok region was phenomenal over this period, with light and heavy manufacturing pushing the country to the forefront of industrial development. Meanwhile, Thailand's traditional export base, agriculture, remained strong, even though its returns were far lower than those from manufacturing and led to what some observers referred to as a 'dual economy'. This economic growth, aligned with a lack of foreign support, effectively ended the prospect of a radical challenge to the government. Urban concerns focused more on democratisation and clean government, while rural concerns tended to focus more on adequate government support for infrastructure, including health and education, and the decentralisation of industrialisation.

Thailand was seen as possessing one of Asia's miracle economies. As perhaps the most important measure of growth, the number of people living in poverty in Thailand between the mid 1970s and the mid 1990s fell from around 30 per cent of the population to less than 15 per cent. The face of Bangkok changed to reflect this new-found wealth; skyscrapers dominated the skyline and more and more new cars clogged the already congested streets. New freeway systems and flyovers were built and wealth, long an indicator of social status, was conspicuously displayed. The World Bank, among others, attributed this 'miracle' to the 'sound fundamentals' of an aggressively export-oriented economy, openness to foreign investment, a high rate of savings and an increasingly highly educated workforce.

Yet, at what seemed the peak of this economic boom, in the middle of 1997, Thailand's economy collapsed, with the value of the baht falling by more than half on international money markets. After so many years of such strong growth, most people were taken by surprise. They should not have been, as the signs that the country's overheated and insufficiently regulated economy had boiled over were increasingly obvious. While many orthodox economists claimed that, as with Indonesia, the economic crash could not have been foreseen, others were more critical in their analysis. Rowley (1999) noted that the crash of the Thai economy was not especially unusual for a capitalist economy, given the cyclical boom and bust character of capitalism (Phongpaichit & Baker 1998: 320). Further, Rowley also noted that, in Thailand's case in particular, while its export industries had reached saturation point in their markets and that markets were, in fact, contracting, capital inflows had continued and credit had become almost dangerously easy to obtain. This easy and seemingly unstoppable flow of credit fuelled unproductive investment, especially in bidding up property prices, and was bled off into non-performing businesses or, indeed, into no businesses at all. As many businesses began to go bad, their earnings no longer covering debts, more capital was borrowed to cover the shortfall.

Corruption was behind much of this stage of the looming crisis, with good money being sent after bad through a series of payoffs and kickbacks that benefited the individuals concerned but, ultimately, not their institutions or the broader economy. Then, after defaulting on repayments, the banks themselves began to look seriously exposed (Phongpaichit & Baker 1998: 281–310). Financial analysts reassessed Thailand's miracle economy; funds went offshore while foreign banks halted lending. The net result was that 'the economy shrank at frightening speed' (Phongpaichit & Baker 1998: 318). In a bid to increase foreign capital inflows and to make export industries more competitive, the Thai government floated the value of the baht on the international money market. Rather than dropping the value of the baht slightly and boosting exports, this had the effect of taking the floor from underneath the value of the currency, which slumped (see Phongpaichit & Baker 1998, Rowley 1999). 'The bust was not simply the fault of careless lending by international finance. Nor was it simply caused by the pirate instincts of Thai businessmen. Rather it resulted from the explosive chemistry of mixing the two' (Phongpaichit & Baker 1998: 319).

The slump in the value of the baht exposed the seriousness of what had become a fully blown economic crisis, as most of the country's debts were denominated in foreign currencies, especially US dollars and Japanese yen. The slump in the value of the baht, in effect, increased this foreign denominated debt by the same proportion, making already unpayable debts more impossible to repay. Companies that had been able to meet their debt repayments under a steady baht suddenly found, in many cases, the size of their debt had doubled. More than half of Thailand's finance companies defaulted on their own debt schedules.

The Thai prime minister, Chavalit Yongchaiyudh, resigned in November 1997, to be replaced by Chuan Leekpai. Chuan began to push through economic reforms, but pressure by influential businessmen meant that these reforms were increasingly abandoned or soft-pedalled into 1998. Then, two of Chuan's ministers were forced to resign over corruption scandals, forcing Chuan into a new coalition government that reflected much of the old style Thai politics that had been largely responsible for the economic crash in the first place. Prime Minister Chuan Leekpai expanded his governing coalition to include new members from the Chart Pattana Party, but many of them were political veterans who were identified with the old money politics. While including the extra members in the coalition strengthened the government's position in terms of numbers, it also raised the spectre that, at a time when it needed to be clean and to be seen to be clean, it was not. The Chart Pattana Party, formerly a part of the Chart Thai Party, and the Social Action Party were also involved with military leader General Suchinda Kraprayoon, who, in May 1992 had ordered troops to fire on unarmed prodemocracy protestors. Chuan's reformist Democrats were, therefore, surrounded by politicians who were not averse to using money and power to shore up their political position, a style of politicking that Chuan had been keen to put behind Thailand (Tasker 1998). This situation was only slowly improving (see, for example, Crispin 2000), with the Senate elections of mid 2000 being noted for their corruption, in particular in the Isan area, where the ballot result was disqualified and the vote was conducted again.

As with all SEA states, corruption had been and remained a major issue in Thailand. By 2004 corruption was seen to have diminished and Thailand was ranked by Transparency International at sixty-fourth on a scale of 145 countries, whereas in 1997 it had been ranked thirty-ninth of fifty-two countries (that is, Thailand was approaching the top one-third of 'clean' countries, whereas it had previously been in the lowest quarter). Thailand's place on the Corruption Perception Index had improved slightly to 3.6 from 3.07. But corruption, though less evident than it once was, remained problematic. For example, buying jobs or promotion, a widespread tradition that had been relatively tolerated, continued in Thai society, especially within government service. Other corrupt activities involved members of Thailand's government, but were most widely practised at an institutional level, where the processing of applications, favours in the letting of contracts and involvement in illegal business practices was commonplace (see Phongpaichit & Piriyarangsan 1994). Even the Thai prime minister, Thaksin Shinawatra, had been found guilty of corruption prior to entering office ('hiding assets for dishonest purposes') by the National Counter Corruption Commission in 2001.

Although only just cleared of the corruption charge, Thaksin and his Thai Rak Thai Party achieved, for the first time, a majority of seats in the Thai parliament. With this unprecedented political mandate, Thaksin immediately promoted those close to him, including a cousin of a cousin, Chaisit Shinawatra, as chief of the army, with a former military precadet classmate promoted to head the Office of the Permanent Secretary and another to deputy chief of the First Army. Yet another former classmate became commander of Bangkok's main military force, the First Infantry Division, while another was promoted to major-general in charge of the Phetchaburi Army Circle. Other promotions of former classmates included to major-general in charge of the army's Directorate of Civil Affairs, commander of the Second Cavalry Division and deputy-director of Joint Operations of the Supreme Command. Thaksin's brother-in-law was also promoted to national police chief, along with a string of similar appointments in the military, police and other government posts. There was also the scandal involving the publication of 600 000 booklets promoting the use of mobile telephones; Thaksin's family company, Shin Corp, was Thailand's biggest mobile phone provider. Soon after, the managing director of Thailand's second biggest mobile phone provider and key government critic, Poosana Preemanoch, was arrested for fraud (*Age*, 5 September 2003). Even more disturbingly, during Thaksin's 2003 war on drugs, more than 2000 suspected criminals were arbitrarily killed by law enforcement officials employing a shoot-on-sight policy.

Thaksin was cleared of the preelection corruption charge on appeal by a decision of eight to seven, although he was later accused of lobbying the judges. In August 2004, an anti-graft investigator released information showing that, over the previous decade, politicians and state officials had taken some US$300 billion in bribes and kickbacks (*Asia Times*, 30 September 2004). Thaksin's government responded by launching an anti-corruption drive, first promised in 2001, although this was widely perceived as a method of attacking his political opponents ahead of coming elections.

Thaksin's premiership of Thailand was marked by crony capitalism along with a return to economic stability and growth, alongside a strict law and order campaign and an element of authoritarianism, as one might have expected from a former senior Thai police officer. But most Thais seemed to find his balance of pro-growth, Thai-centric economic development and order acceptable. Many agreed with Thaksin's view that running the state was like running a big business. It was this general agreement, leavened with vote buying, that gave Thaksin and his Thai Rak Thai party an historic second term in office, this being the first time a prime minister had been re-elected. Thaksin's party won 370 of the 500 available seats. Thaksin dismissed concerns over Thailand becoming a one-party state, saying the vote reflected people's wishes.

The January 2005 elections not only confirmed Thaksin as Thailand's political leader, they also dealt a body blow to the previously dominant

Democrat Party. As the results of the elections became clear, the Democrat's leader, Banyat Bantadtan, announced his resignation. The party itself was left in turmoil, further enhancing Thaksin's seemingly unshakeable political grip. But if the 2005 elections produced a less than ideal outcome, they were not marred by violence and were a reasonable reflection of popular political will. Like much else in Thailand, while far from perfect, it stood as something like a benchmark for good—or, at least increasingly stable—government, a strong economy and a generally peaceful and tolerant people in what was an otherwise less than perfect environment. Crossing the land borders into Thailand from Burma, Laos or Cambodia was regarded by many as a relief and the sense of relative security was palpable. If Thailand had begun to seem a little dull to some Westerners, it was only because the country had become increasingly successful at its own process of Westernisation or, more accurately, modernisation.

NOTES

1   This sense of Thailand's economic irrepressibility could have been superficial, but a couple of far more seasoned and critical observers of Thailand's economic development than I, to whom I mentioned this, tended to agree on this point.

2   This method of royal execution was in common with that of Burma.

3   The exception to this was, of course, the British presence in neighbouring Burma, which was then just beginning to make its colonial presence felt to Thailand, and in China.

4   This was the beginning of state-directed economic development, which has characterised the East Asian economies to the present time.

5   This connotation derived from when T'ai people moved into the Menam valley, enslaving the local people, who were not 'Thai'. To be 'Thai' thereafter came to be associated with not being enslaved, or being free.

6   King Ananda had been at school in Switzerland, but did not wish to return to Thailand during the period of hostilities.

7   A parallel has been drawn with the use of language to embed hierarchy in a similar manner to both Burma and Java. Yet in Burma and Java, not only have there been popular egalitarian (communist) movements, but the maintenance of social hierarchy through language is also often otherwise resisted at a common level (see Berman 1998).

8   During World War II, there were two separate independence movements, one fighting with the Japanese and wanting a republic, the other fighting with the British and wanting a sultanate.

9   After the 1948 Dusun Nyor Revolt, more than 250 000 Malay Thais signed a petition to the United Nations asking for the southern provinces to be incorporated into Malaysia.

10 Channel 9 was the national public television broadcaster, while Channel 5 was the military's broadcaster. Channel 7 was also owned by the military, but was privately leased, while Channel 11 was owned by the Ministry of Education and featured educational programming.

7 | Laos:
The Land in Between

For a country that lies within the tropical zone, the frequently mist-shrouded highlands of Laos can be cold. Mountains rise sharply out of the valley floors far below, their steep, inhospitable sides pushing up through the clouds. Among these mountains are the highland groups of Laos. In the region to the south of Luang Prabang towards Vieng Chan are many Hmong, a tribal group who arrived from southern China from around the end of the eighteenth century. The Hmong had no traditional links with the other Lao ethnic groups—sixty-eight in all (see Batson 1991)—and were disinclined to recognise the authority of the state, which led to conflict between the Hmong and the predominantly lowland Lao (Lao Loum) in the postcolonial state, a situation that was exacerbated by the USA using the Hmong as an independent military force against the communists in Laos and Vietnam in the 1960s and 1970s.

Until 1997, the road between Luang Prabang, the old royal capital, and its historical rival, Vieng Chan, was unsafe as a consequence of Hmong attacks. These attacks were specially troublesome during the opium cultivation season, but tended to represent a more fulsome political security problem than that represented by ordinary bandits, of which there were a few. But government control eventually extended over the mountainous regions in which the Hmong live. In 1997, government control was marked by the opening of a sealed road between the two former capitals, which meant that, not only did road transport become a regular, all-weather occurrence, but it also enabled regular access to the remote regions for government troops. Under the guise of attempting to limit the environmental damage caused by slash-and-burn agriculture, the Hmong were resettled into new villages along the side of the new, two-lane mountain highway. There, up in the clouds, with regular cold rain, without access to adequate clean water and traditional sources of food, sickness set in and the mortality rate began to rise. According to one well-informed source, in some of these new villages the death rate was as high as 50 per cent. After years of

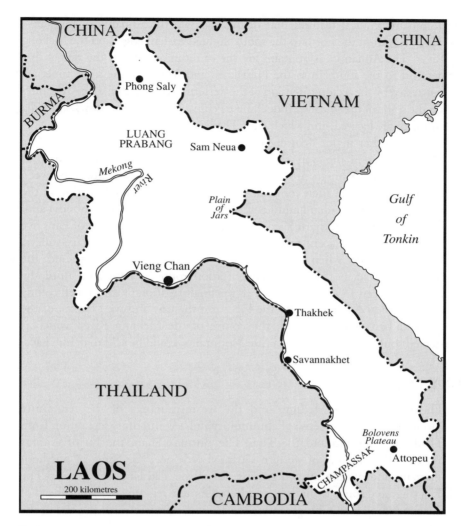

Map 4 Laos

battling the Hmong, government concern over their fate was cursory, to say the least. In 2004, following concerted military action, resistance to the Lao government, centred on the Hmong, was finally broken. An epilogue to the Indochina conflict and the last meaningful internal opposition to the central government had finally ended.

BETWEEN THE MOUNTAINS AND THE MEKONG

The country that is Laos or, more correctly, the Lao People's Democratic Republic, is based on a broad linguistic and geographic identity that at once separates it from and unites it to its imposing Thai neighbour. The two dominant physical features that define Laos are the Annamite Mountains, which run from the north to the south along its eastern edge, and the Mekong River. The Annamite Mountains are the easternmost arm of the ranges that descend to the south from the Himalayas and which, at the same time, are buttressed by the tectonic division of the western Pacific Ocean. The Annamites are the spine of the so-called Indochinese Peninsula, where Vietnam, Cambodia and Laos are located, and which cups Thailand to the west.

The other major defining feature of Laos is the Mekong River.[1] The Mekong rises in the watershed of the southeastern Himalayas and spills down through Yunnan province, marking the modern boundary between Burma and Laos. It then continues, demarcating the central portion of the border between Thailand and Laos, until entering northern Cambodia and, finally, exiting in southern Vietnam. The majority of the people of Laos live in the lowlands adjacent to the Mekong or in the nearby tributary valleys. Until the 1980s, when roads started to be more widely constructed, the Mekong served as the main transportation route in Laos and, until the period between 1893 and 1907, with the final partition of the French colony that became Laos, it was also the focus, on the east and west banks, of the lowland Lao people. Indeed, the course of the Mekong River, which is steered southward by the Annamite Mountains, could be said to define Laos.

EARLY LAOS

The focus on the Mekong and the western flanks of the Annamite Mountains leads to a sense of community in Laos and of its separation from Thailand. The Lao and the Thai, like Burma's Shan, the Lu of China's Yunnan, the Chuang of western Guangxi province, the Nung of northern Vietnam and other scattered groups, are of the T'ai language group.[2] The T'ai migrated south from these southern Chinese regions, probably ahead of the expanding Han Chinese influence, from the time towards the end of the pre-Christian period until the second half of the first millennium of the Common Era (Stuart-Fox 1997: 8). The first political communities established by these people were called *meaung*, a term that includes personal as well as spatial relations, or could also be a town or extend as widely as a network of villages or towns under a single *chao* (lord) (Wyatt 1984: 7). One of the earliest known *meaung* was Meaung Thaen, now known as Dien Bien Phu, just across the border from northern Laos in Vietnam. Such *meaung* developed to include wider areas of authority, being, in effect, principalities and comprising the first identifiable states in the region.

The T'ai, though, were not the only inhabitants of the region. As the T'ai moved south, they encountered existing Austronesian- and Austroasiatic-speaking peoples, who they displaced and drove into the relative security of the mountains. The major group in this region called themselves Lawa, or Lwa, which became Lao. According to Viravong, the name Lao was later applied by the T'ai outside the area of Laos to describe the T'ai inhabitants of that same region (Viravong 1964: 6–7). The original inhabitants of Laos, along with disparate groups that subsequently followed and settled in remote areas, are the people who have come to form many of the ethnic minorities of Laos.

The development of early Laos cannot be understood independently of the development of the proto-Thai state, as the two crossed over and were interlinked in a number of ways. In this respect, early state formation reflected the mandala principle, whereby states had varying degrees of control or autonomy that fluctuated and was poorly defined. What was to become the Thai state was comprised of competing states that were either subsumed into or divided by the whole. The early T'ai state of Lan Na typified this development. Lan Na—land of a million rice fields—was centred on Chiang Mai in northern Thailand, but extended into what is now northwestern Laos and northeastern Burma up to Yunnan and was typical of this mandala-type development. A number of other small mandala-type states are claimed to have existed in the region that approximates what was to become Laos, along with more northern regions inhabited by Lao people (Viravong 1964: 6–24). The dates of the establishment of these small states is suggested to be as far back as the last years before the beginning of the Common Era, although evidence for this, especially in the south (contemporary northern Laos), is slim.

The greatest threat to the development of such T'ai–Lao mandala-type states came from two sources, the first being the rise of strong states in the west of the region, now known as Burma, the most powerful of these being centred at Pagan, which conducted frequent raids into neighbouring territories. The second major threat came from the Khmer empire based at Angkor, in the northwest of modern Cambodia. Indeed, most of the Mekong valley in what is now Laos was under Khmer control by 1200 CE (Wyatt 1984: 26). However, by the middle of the thirteenth century, the Mongol armies of Kublai Khan were consolidating their control over the region; they had overrun and occupied the last independent states of Yunnan by 1253, then swept southwest to destroy Pagan. The Mongols, moving down the Mekong Valley, also asserted their authority over Angkor, although, by this stage, that once-great empire was already in decline. Under Mongol–Yuan suzerainty, three major T'ai mandalas became more formally established in the region. The first was the T'ai-Siam mandala of Sukhothai, from 1438, which incorporated the state of Ayudhya, the second, the northern state of Lan Na and the third, the state of Lan Xang, Land of a Million Elephants,[3] which was centred on Xiang Dong Xiang Thong, later known as Luang Prabang (Stuart-Fox 1997: 9).

A Lao *meaung* had existed on the site of Luang Prabang since the land was taken from earlier settlers by Lao invaders. It is probable that the site had been a settlement of some importance, located as it is on the confluence of the Mekong and the Nam Khan Rivers,[4] which provide fresh water and transport and protect it from three sides. The kingdom of Lan Xang was believed to have existed from 1271, under a ruler entitled a *phraya* (he who upholds). Other claims put Lao occupation of that site as far back as 757 CE (Viravong 1964: 25). Local claims to, and some evidence of, organised Mahayana Buddhist activity in the region in and around Luang Prabang appear to confirm this approximate date.

The development of the Lao *meaung* as a great kingdom is generally attributed to Fa Ngum, born in 1316 CE. A hereditary prince,[5] Fa Ngum is said to have been expelled from the capital, possibly for attempting to seize the throne (Stuart-Fox 1997: 9). It has been claimed that Fa Ngum grew up and was educated as a prince at Angkor in Cambodia (Viravong 1964: 27). He is generally regarded as having established his credentials with the Khmer court of the day and to have been equipped with an army with which to invade his former home. Between 1349 and 1357, Fa Ngum's armies conquered all of the region that was to be the empire of Lan Xang (Viravong 1964: 26–36). Fa Ngum was also credited with introducing Theravada Buddhism, then dominant in Cambodia, to the region under his control. The extent of the territory claimed by Lan Xang, at its height in the middle of the sixteenth century, extended to include modern Laos, the western periphery of modern northern and central Vietnam, northeastern Thailand and, through family rule in Lan Na, southernmost Yunnan and parts of what is now northeastern Burma (Wyatt 1984: 82–7). However, the greatness of Lan Xang was soon to be challenged.

THE DIVISION OF LAN XANG

As a typical mandala-type state, the strength of the Lao state was determined by the strength of its ruler and the ability of the state to withstand external threats. In 1479, Vietnam invaded the capital of Lan Xang and sacked Luang Prabang, while in 1558 Chiang Mai fell to the Burmese, under whose control it remained for the next two centuries. In 1560, the capital of Lan Xang was moved from Luang Prabang to Vieng Chan, while Lao settlers moved further down the Mekong Valley to Champassak and on to the Khorat Plateau of northeastern Thailand, shifting the geographic balance of power in the Lao world (Stuart-Fox 1997: 12). But all was not stable in the Lao world. In 1569, Burmese forces, which had already sacked Ayudhaya and who had, for the previous six years, been attacking Lan Xang, moved on Vieng Chan, but were forced to withdraw due to lack of supplies. Burmese attacks continued for the following six years. Lan Xang recovered and, under Xetthathirat, moved to invade Cambodia, where the Lan Xang army was soundly defeated. During its retreat, Xetthathirat disappeared, the consequence of which was a state being weakened through a series of succession disputes.

From 1637, under Surinyavongsa, Lan Xang entered a period of relative tranquillity and prosperity, which was remarked upon by European visitors at that time. When Surinyavongsa died in 1694 he left no heir, his only son having been executed for adultery. The state quickly fell into internal squabbling and, between 1707 and 1713, divided into three smaller states approximating the natural division of the rapids of the Mekong: Luang Prabang, Vieng Chan and Champassak. Over the next several decades, each of these came under the sway of the new and increasingly powerful Siamese state, which itself was subject to another Burmese expedition, with Chiang Mai falling in 1763, Luang Prabang in 1765 and Ayudhaya being sacked in 1767. When the Siamese state recovered and drove out the Burmese, it also asserted its control over the three Lao states.

Within the Siamese mandala state, the tributary states of Laos and Lan Na were independent in their day-to-day affairs, although this did not preclude the loss of authority of Vieng Chan over the Khorat Plateau, which recognised Siam as the dominant regional power. Within Vieng Chan, however, there was considerable resentment towards Bangkok and its offhand treatment of its suzerain states. In 1826, under Chou Anu, also referred to as Anuvong, Vieng Chan raised three armies and Champassak another, all of which crossed into the Khorat Plateau with the intention of reclaiming the region and, with Vietnamese support, uniting the Lao kingdoms and declaring Lao independence. Chou Anu believed that the Siamese would be too preoccupied with the British invasion of Burma to be able to respond, not knowing that the Thais had just concluded a treaty with the United Kingdom. The Siamese responded, defeating the Lao south of Vieng Chan, sacking the capital in mid May 1827 and forcibly resettling hundreds of thousands of its population on the Khorat Plateau. Even forty years later, Vieng Chan existed only as ruins (Ngaosyvathn & Ngaosyvathn 1998: 25).

Chou Anu returned the following year, but his efforts were no more successful. Fleeing to Vietnam, he and his family were handed back to the Siamese. The Vietnamese emperor, Minh Mang, though holding suzerainty over Vieng Chan, was at pains to maintain peace with Thailand due to internal difficulties at home (Ngaosyvathn & Ngaosyvathn 1998: 105–8). In 1829, Chou Anu died as a result of being tortured while in custody in Bangkok. The result was that, 'Not only was the Kingdom of Viang Chan erased from the map: so too was any remaining shadow of the mandala of Lan Xang' (Stuart-Fox 1997: 15; see also, Viravong 1964: 114–31; Ngaosyvathn & Ngaosyvathn 1998). Only Luang Prabang retained any semblance of autonomy, paying tribute not only to Bangkok, but also to the Vietnamese court at Hue and to Beijing. This was the state of affairs when France, under a doubtful assertion by the Vietnamese to suzerainty over Vieng Chan and the central region east of the Mekong, claimed a right of inheritance.

LAOS UNDER THE FRENCH

In a series of manoeuvres between 1886 and 1893, France moved administrators and troops to the east bank of the Mekong. Thai and British opposition, however, generally limited French claims to the west bank. After minor clashes between French and Siamese troops and a confrontation with French ships on the Chao Phraya River in Bangkok, the French issued an ultimatum that included formally ceding, by 1893, all territory east of the Mekong and all its islands and, in 1907, territory on the west bank in the north and south. In 1893, Siam agreed, creating the French protectorate of Laos from less than half the territory and as few as one-sixth of the population who could trace their descent from Lan Xang.

The northern demarcation of Laos from Burma was agreed upon in 1896 between the French and the British, the latter of whom had annexed Shan State as a part of Burma. This created a boundary along the deepest points of the upper reaches of the Mekong, while a reduced Thailand was left as a buffer state between the main forces of the two colonial powers. Other boundary changes were more administrative. Huaphan, Xieng Khuang and the Hmong-populated areas in the Plain of Jars[6] were returned from the French-administered Tonkin to Laos in parcels in 1893, 1895 and 1903. Stung Treng province was returned by Laos to French-administered Cambodia in 1904, while parts of the Central Highlands were returned to Vietnam in 1904 and 1905; a small area of land in Xainaburi was returned to Thailand in 1907 (Stuart-Fox 1997: 26–7).

France's original interest in Laos was to establish a route along the Mekong to trade with southern China. However, they discovered as early as the 1860s that the two sets of rapids and numerous other obstacles in the northern sections of the river made that an impractical goal. The French rationale for annexation then changed to one of rounding out their territories in Indochina and providing a potential base from which to launch the possible annexation of Siam. Yet the fear of conflict with the United Kingdom, which had a well-established economic presence in Siam, precluded the latter option. Having secured the territory, then, but having little practical use for it, the French administration tended to neglect Laos (Smith 1964b: 527–33), where infrastructure was almost non-existent, economic development continued at a very low level, education was underdeveloped and even the local people were rarely able to develop administrative skills because those positions were mostly taken by Vietnamese imported for the purpose. French policy was to use Vietnamese to work in Laos and to further populate it. This policy, which saw Vieng Chan and Thakhek with ethnic Vietnamese majorities, was kept intact until as late as 1945 (Stuart-Fox 1996: 32). Despite various French attempts otherwise, the only real growth area in the Lao economy was the sale of opium, which was a government monopoly[7] (McCoy 1970: 81–6).

RESISTANCE AND REBELLION

Lao resistance to French occupation was at a relatively low level, but fairly consistent throughout the colonial period. Upland revolts began in 1896, peaked between 1910 and 1916 and continued, in declining intensity, through to the 1930s. In the south, a revolt based on the Bolovens Plateau, started in 1901 and peaked in the following year when more than 7000 rebels attacked a French garrison at Kontum in Vietnam; about 150 rebels were killed. The French retaliated by building a series of block houses[8] around the edge of the plateau and burning most of the region's crops. While this broke most resistance, it was not until 1907 that the French launched a major campaign against the rebel leader, Ong Keo, forcing him to surrender and to swear loyalty to France. Other rebel leaders escaped and even Ong Keo's submission was only short-lived. Ong Keo was killed in 1910, when he went to negotiate with the French in Champassak. One of his comrades, Komadom, continued to lead a small resistance movement, which gained renewed momentum in the mid 1930s. Komadom's movement was effectively ended when, in 1936, he was killed during a 'massive pacification campaign'[9] (Stuart-Fox 1997: 33–41).

A number of other rebellions broke out in the north in the early 1900s; the most violent, from 1914 to 1916, actually removed French authority from a number of provinces in Laos and northern Vietnam. In Laos, about forty T'ai and forty Chinese attacked a French garrison at Sam Neua, slaughtering the colonial troops stationed there and ambushing and repulsing troops from a neighbouring French garrison sent to relieve them. The rebels retreated into Vietnam, where they fought two more battles, then returned to Phongsali province in northern Laos where, aided by local villagers, they captured nearly the whole province. After numerous inconsequential battles, the French finally organised more than 5000 troops from Hanoi who, after two months of fighting, drove the rebels into southern China. Three years later, the Hmong also revolted against the French. According to McCoy, these revolts ultimately failed because they were too splintered, failing to gain the support of other Lao minorities or, more importantly, the majority of Lao. As a small concession to protonationalist sentiment, the French allowed the establishment of an Indigenous Consultative Assembly from 1923, no more than a token gesture towards disgruntled Lao. It was not until the Japanese occupation interlude, which effectively began in 1940, that the Lao began to develop a cohesive sense of national identity (McCoy 1970: 87–92).

JAPANESE INVASION

Japan occupied Laos and the rest of French Indochina in 1941 as a part of its alliance with the pro-German Vichy government of France. The main effect of the Japanese occupation of the region was that it enhanced a sense of pan-Thai irredentism, which led to Thai attacks on French shipping. Japan, supporting its Thai allies, brokered an agreement that saw France cede all its territories in Laos on the west bank of the Mekong in Xianaburi and Champassak provinces. As a consequence, the Lao king, Sisavang Vong, threatened to resign, which would have further destabilised the French position in Laos and could have seen Thailand pressing for incorporation of the whole colony. The French responded by offering the king a number of concessions, including establishing the kingdom of Luang Prabang as a protectorate that would include the provinces of Nam Tha, Xieng Khouang and Vieng Chan, and the granting of some political autonomy.

The French governor-general, Admiral Decoux, believed that, if Lao nationalism was appropriately channelled, it could assist in gaining the return of the lost territories. To this end, he appointed a colonial official, Charles Rochet, to encourage the development of Lao nationalist sentiment, especially among the lowland Lao (Lao Loum). The movement with which Rochet was associated achieved, among other things, the construction of 7000 schools, expansion of the poor health system and the publication of the first Lao newspaper. While this new sense of national pride began to take hold among the Lao Loum, the highland Lao were moved by other activities, in particular, guerrilla warfare and the growth and sale of opium (McCoy 1970: 93–5). With the development of the conflict of World War II, Laos was cut off from much of its traditional sources of opium. Because of the social consequences for addicts and, more importantly, for government revenues, the French engineered the accelerated growth of opium by the Hmong, Yao and Tái tribes in northern Laos.

Competition for the lucrative opium trade engendered conflict between these tribes, which, in 1944–45, was exacerbated by the French arming tribal guerrilla bands against the Japanese. These conflicts produced 'permanent cleavages in Laotian society' (McCoy 1970: 97) which continued to plague the country into the twenty-first century. Probably the most significant cleavage was among the Hmong, one clan of which was at the centre of the French campaign against Japan, and later, the pro-independence Lao Issara (Free Lao), which was allied with another clan of Hmong. The military wing of the Lao Issara later transformed into the Pathet Lao. 'Pathet' translates from Lao as 'land' and the name Pathet Lao is held to mean 'Land of the Lao' (Stuart-Fox, personal communication). The former clan of the Hmong were armed by the CIA as a part of its covert war in Indochina. On 8 April, following a *coup de force* by Japan against the French in Indochina on 9 March 1945, at the behest of Japan,[10] King Sisavang Vong declared Laos independent. While France managed to return soon after, the idea of Lao nationalism had taken root, leading to an alliance of anti-French forces under the Lao Issara banner.

THE STRUGGLE FOR INDEPENDENCE

The situation among the small elite in the period leading up to and just after 1945 was complex, determined, in part, by ideology, but in large part also by strategic alliances. With Japan, France, Thailand, China and Vietnam all taking an active interest in Laos, the choice of available patrons based on who was perceived to be the best guarantor of power created multiple divisions, which were exacerbated by the shifting loyalties of some of the Lao elite (Adams 1970: 100, 105). When Japan surrendered in August 1945, its occupying forces fled south to escape the advancing Nationalist Chinese 93rd Division, hoping to surrender to the British. While the French assumed they would automatically resume control of Laos, premier, viceroy and soon to be head of a coalition independence committee,[11] Prince Phetsarath informed them they no longer had authority in Laos and that the independence that had been declared in April was still in force. On 15 September, Phetsarath took the further step of declaring the kingdoms of Luang Prabang and Champassak united.

No sooner had this declaration been made, than the king sent Phetsarath a telegram saying that he regarded the French protectorate as still in force. In response, a defence committee was established, which, on 12 October, voted in a provisional Constitution, formed a provisional people's assembly and nominated a Lao Issara government (Dommen 1965: 22). The pro-independence Prince Souphanouvong then made contact with leaders of the nationalist revolution of the newly proclaimed Vietnamese republic. The Vietnamese leader, Ho Chi Minh, offered Souphanouvong 'all possible assistance' and gave him a guard of fifty Viet Minh soldiers for his return to Laos via Lao Bao (between Hue and Savannakhet). The importance of this alliance was illustrated by the fact that Ho also allowed Souphanouvong's escort to take with them 100 of the Central Vietnam committee's 240 rifles. Ho foresaw that Laos—and the pro-Vietnamese Lao nationalists—would later play a strategic role in the Viet Minh's war with the French. The group marched to the Mekong and then north to Vieng Chan, recruiting soldiers along the way, where it joined the Lao Issara government, and Souphanouvong was appointed minister of defence (Dommen 1965: 23).

Recognising their weak position, the Lao Issara sent a delegation to Luang Prabang to seek the support of King Sisavang Vong. The king duly agreed to place himself under the authority of the provisional government and stated that, since the time of the Japanese surrender, he had no secret agreements with any representative of the French government. This was intended to be a means of preserving, or enhancing, his authority. On this basis, the Lao Issara asked Sisavang Vong to assume the throne of a unified Laos under a constitutional monarchy. The French, however, had other ideas and, after a brief diversion to quell an uprising in southern Vietnam, sent troops north from Champassak. The Lao Issara offered resistance, but, on 21 March 1946, the French occupied

Thakhek, north of Savannakhet on the Mekong, which led to the pass just beyond Na Pe, east of Vieng Chan, and the primary communications route to the Viet Minh-controlled areas of north-central Vietnam. The French thereafter moved to control the towns, including Vieng Chan, which they occupied on 24 April 1946, while the Lao Issara operated from the countryside or from the security of the Thai side of the Mekong, under the protection of the sympathetic government of Pridi Phanomyong (Dommen 1965: 25).

It was from around this time that the USA began to take an active interest in the region. Initially, agents from the Office of Strategic Services (OSS), forerunner to the Central Intelligence Agency (CIA),[12] formed links with the Viet Minh and opposed the French re-occupation of Laos. However, under the Wilsonian principle of self-determination, while the US government took a broadly anti-colonial position in the immediate postwar years, recognising Laos as an independent state in 1950, its position in the region began to harden along the same lines being drawn in the developing Cold War. What were essentially a series of wars of national independence in French Indochina were increasingly interpreted by the USA as communist aggression. Following the outbreak of the Korean conflict in 1950, the USA adopted the French position of communist containment.

A FRENCH UNION

While still in the immediate postwar period, the French secured an alliance with heir to the defunct throne of Champassak, Prince Boun Oum na Champassak, who was concerned about Vietnamese control of Laos. In exchange for being made inspector-general for life, Boun Oum renounced his sovereign rights over Champassak. In 1946, under a nominal concession to Lao aspirations for independence, the French allowed elections for a constituent assembly. The assembly was given the task of drawing up a new Constitution that would incorporate Laos as a part of the new French Union.[13] Meanwhile, Lao Issara attacks continued, increasingly assisted by the Viet Minh. The Republic of Vietnam was also incorporated into the French Union, but tension between the limited scope of the supposed independence it offered and the aspirations of the Viet Minh soon led to conflict. The Viet Minh withdrew to the mountains and the French position against them hardened to one of no negotiation. In 1947, the French further strengthened their position in Laos by having returned to Laos the territory ceded to Thailand during the period of Japanese occupation. But, following the Viet Minh experience, the Lao Issara increasingly recognised that little could be gained from negotiating with the French. The Viet Minh, especially, encouraged their ally, Souphanouvong, in this view.

The first constituent assembly sat in May 1947, but it was a feeble organisation with no real influence. In order to secure a quiet region at a time of their troubles with the Viet Minh, France granted Laos further concessions[14] in July 1949. Prince Souvanna Phouma and the king accepted the French proposal for the concessions, but Souphanouvong did not. In May 1949, with the support of the Viet Minh, Souphanouvong created a separate political front for his guerrillas, calling it the Progressive People's Organisation. In August the following year, the organisation's name was changed to Pathet Lao. Souphanouvong's split with the king was now irrevocable; he was removed from his ministerial positions in the Lao Issara government. In October that year, the Lao Issara formally disbanded, its more pro-French members returning to Vieng Chan (Dommen 1965: 30–4). Souvanna Phouma formed the first Royal Lao Government (RLG) in November 1951. Following French requests and its support for local governments, the USA agreed to give the RLG economic aid, which formed the basis of American economic involvement in Laos until the mid 1970s.

DEFEAT OF THE FRENCH

In 1953, in response to continuing internal pressure for genuine independence, the French government agreed to invite selected representatives to a new round of negotiations. At these talks, the French agreed to greater autonomy for Laos, but the growing war for Vietnam's independence continued to pull at its vulnerable neighbour. What had started out as a police action grew into a full-scale conflict, which the French neither understood nor, when they realised its scale and potential, wanted. Much of the conflict in Vietnam focused on the mountainous terrain in Vietnam's northwestern Lai Chau Province, with the Viet Minh spilling over into and, in effect, invading neighbouring Laos. By 1953, the Viet Minh were routing the French and were within striking distance of Luang Prabang, though the attack did not materialise because of the coming monsoon. After the monsoonal rains ended, another column of Viet Minh crossed the Annamite Mountains and captured Thakhek.

Planning to thwart further Viet Minh advances, in November 1953, French paratroops reoccupied the valley of Dien Bien Phu, just across the Lao border in Vietnam, through which numerous Viet Minh had crossed from their mountain bases into Laos. By January 1954, the French garrison at Dien Bien Phu was surrounded by Viet Minh. The Viet Minh commander, General Vo Nguyen Giap, sent a diversionary force towards Luang Prabang, which distracted French support while building strength around Dien Bien Phu. The French believed their entrenched and externally supported fortifications were the answer to Viet Minh attacks, but by August 1953, Dien Bien Phu was the only French base that had not been overrun by the Viet Minh. Inaccessible by ground and hundreds of kilometres from air support, the reinforced garrison was subject to severe bombardment from the surrounding hills by Viet Minh cannon and mortars. From the laying of the trap to its closure, there was never any doubt that the Viet Minh would claim the battle of Dien Bien Phu as its greatest victory (Dommen 1965: 40–3). That victory came to the Viet Minh on 7 May 1954, just days before a new round of negotiations with the French in Geneva, which ensured that the French position in Indochina was irretrievable.

Despite attempts by the Viet Minh to have the Lao guerrillas represented at the Geneva talks, the Chinese and Soviet representatives at the talks did not adequately support the official Lao representative, who was not given official status. The agreement reached saw Vietnam partitioned at the 17th parallel, with the Democratic Republic of Vietnam administering the north. But the agreement left Laos intact as a unitary, independent state under the Royal Lao Government in Vieng Chan, despite the presence of a substantial revolutionary organisation. Members of the forces of the Lao Resistance Government—the Pathet Lao—regrouped in the two northern provinces of Sam Neua and Phongsaly, prior to being integrated into the Lao army or demobilised. The practical effect of this and clashes between the RLG forces and the Pathet Lao was to permanently allocate the two provinces to the Pathet Lao. This assured them of continuing North Vietnamese support and influence in Pathet Lao affairs. It also provided a base from which the Pathet Lao leadership could recruit from the country's minority groups.

AMERICAN INVOLVEMENT AND POLITICAL CHAOS

In 1955, the American legation in Vieng Chan was raised to the status of embassy and US involvement in Lao affairs increased. One effect of this was to bring into the country funds that increasingly destabilised the domestic economic base. Through the embassy, a US Operations Mission opened in Vieng Chan; it provided a large proportion of the RLG's finances. This mission, which was staffed entirely by military personnel who engaged in training army officers and expanding the Lao police force, was a precursor to the later substantial CIA presence in the country (Stuart-Fox 1997: 89–93). Negotiations began in 1956 to bring the Pathet Lao within the RLG. Despite continuing armed clashes between RLG and Pathet Lao forces, this was achieved in November 1957. However, while this government of 'unity' was accepted by the 'neutralist' group[15] it was increasingly opposed by the conservatives, who were strongly encouraged by the USA, in particular from 1958 onwards (Stuart-Fox 1997: 99–134). What had heightened US concerns was that, in supplementary elections in May 1958, there had been gains made by leftist candidates. This encouraged the USA to back the creation of the right-wing Committee for the Defence of the National Interest the following month.

CIVIL WAR

The view from the USA was, according to US President Eisenhower, that Laos, along with South Vietnam, was 'the present key to the entire area of

South-East Asia' (McNamara 1995: 35, 36–8). McNamara has since admitted the USA simply misunderstood the primarily nationalist motivation for ideological conflict. The Viet Minh did not, and exploited that sentiment. The suspension of US economic aid to Laos forced the resignation of Souvanna Phouma in July 1958, which, in turn, led to the formation of a right-wing government in August. Stuart-Fox regards this event as marking a shift in power in Laos from the Lao National Assembly to the US Embassy, which irrevocably committed the country to conflict. 'The First Coalition Government was the last occasion when neutrality remained an option for Laos' (Stuart-Fox 1997: 104). In its bid to end what it correctly perceived to be a leftist threat to its control, the following government attempted to force the integration of Pathet Lao forces into the RLG army. The attempt was successfully resisted, so the government responded by arresting Pathet Lao leaders still in Vieng Chan, which precipitated a return to a more advanced state of civil war. By this stage, government authority existed only insofar as it could be enforced by military means, its legitimacy being effectively finished.

While the country's political situation was spinning out of control, King Sisavang Vong died; he was succeeded by his son, Savangvatthana, in October 1959. Within two months, real rather than symbolic politics reasserted itself in an attempted military coup. The coup failed due to mounting internal and external opposition, but it forced the resignation of the right-wing Phuy Xananikon government, which was replaced by a new government strongly influenced by the RLG army and police and by the US Embassy.

Laos in the 1960s was a strife-torn, divided place where elites, mostly aligned with a branch of the royal family, competed for authority. On 24 April 1960, blatantly rigged national elections, won by rightists with no Pathet Lao candidates returned, were followed, on 9 August, by a neutralist *coup d'état* led by Captain Konglae. A week later, on 16 August, the third Souvanna Phouma government was formed. But the rightists regrouped in Savannakhet to the south and marched north, attacking Vieng Chan from 13 to 16 December. Souvanna and the members of his government fled to Phnom Penh, while Konglae and his troops retreated towards the Plain of Jars, where they made common cause with the Pathet Lao. The combined forces jointly occupied the region (Stuart-Fox 1996: 43–4).

Faced with a situation in which neither side could achieve overall victory, and with international support from the USA and the USSR enforcing the stalemate, the Kennedy administration announced, on 23 March 1961, its support for the neutralisation of Laos, which led to the Geneva Conference on Laos opening seven weeks later. The defeat of rightist forces at the Battle of Namtha in May 1962 sealed the uneasy balance. The Second Coalition government, which included two Pathet Lao ministers, was formed at the conclusion of the Geneva Conference on 23 June. The peace was fragile: on 1 April 1963, the assassination of Kinim Phonsena, a

Pathet Lao leader, signalled the de facto collapse of the Second Coalition government, at which time, the two Pathet Lao ministers fled the capital. The outer shell of the government remained, despite several attempts to demolish it, because it suited all to maintain the pretence of neutrality in light of the escalating conflict in neighbouring Vietnam. The practical fragility of the political environment was highlighted by an attempted rightist military *coup d'état* on 19 April 1964, followed the next month by a split between the Pathet Lao and the neutralists, with the former driving the latter out of the Plain of Jars. It was at this time that the USA began its bombing of Pathet Lao targets. On 31 January 1965 there was another attempted rightist putsch, but this was foiled.

If ideological conflict was not sufficient to tear apart Laos, the effective growth of warlords acting independently of the central government and the unrestricted greed of some sections of the elite seemed to complete the task. In January 1965, a group of rightist army officers seized the radio station in Vieng Chan and demanded an end to corruption and politicking in the army and improved conditions for soldiers and public servants. This led to fighting between police loyal to rightist army leader General Phumi Nosavan and soldiers loyal to the government. Government troops held the day and Phumi escaped to Thailand, leaving his own illegal economic empire to be carved up by greedy officers. Some officers took over the opium and heroin trade, tapping into the market of American soldiers in South Vietnam, others smuggled timber to Thailand or set up protection rackets, while yet others sold military hardware to the Pathet Lao. In October 1966, a dispute over an opium shipment led the Lao airforce to bomb the army headquarters near Vieng Chan (Stuart-Fox 1997: 146–7).

Between the war and the outright corruption of officers, when Souvanna's government attempted to rein in the country's growing deficit in September 1966, the budget was angrily rejected. Souvanna called new elections, which were held the following January. Souvanna was returned as prime minister of a 'neutralist' government, changing nothing of the increasingly corrupt society. 'By the late 1960s, corruption permeated all levels of Lao society' (Stuart-Fox 1997: 148–9).

By January 1968 the war in Indochina was not going the way the USA had hoped. North Vietnam and the Pathet Lao, renamed the Lao People's National Liberation Army (LPNLA; its political wing was the Lao People's Revolutionary Party, or LPRP), took Nam Bak and Phu Pha Thi. The USA was keen to destabilise the LPNLA and to secure the strategically important Plain of Jars. To this end, in 1969, and exploiting the divisions and antipathies between the various Hmong groups, the CIA armed and trained a Hmong secret army. In September, this secret army took control of the Plain of Jars, but in February the following year, the combined Vietnam People's Army (VPA, also referred to as the North Vietnamese Army, or NVA) and LPNLA retook the region.

But the Hmong continued to constitute a difficulty for the LPNLA and the VPA. By this stage, Laos had been inextricably drawn into the conflict in Vietnam. Arms and equipment were constantly being shipped down the network of tracks that was the Ho Chi Minh Trail, inside Laos and into northern Cambodia and northwestern South Vietnam. In a bid to stem this flow, the Army of the Republic of Viet Nam (South Vietnamese Army, referred to as the ARVN) launched a major operation, Lam Son 719, in February 1971, in which 20 000 troops left Khe San along Route 9 heading towards Xepon in an attempt to cut the trail. Souvanna declared a state of emergency and, while Royal Lao Army troops mounted a diversionary tactic to the west, the real battle was fought by troops from the VPA. The ARVN assault was heavily defeated and enabled VPA and LPNLA forces to consolidate their control over the entire Boloven region (Stuart-Fox 1997: 144).

THE LPRP TAKES POWER

By 1972, the USA was well advanced in its process of what it called the Vietnamisation of the regional war and was about to abandon its rightist Lao and Hmong allies. Reduced external support to the RLG meant that the LPRP had become militarily dominant. With the rightists increasingly on the military defensive, elections were held for the National Assembly on 2 January 1972. The elections and negotiations for a ceasefire and a coalition government came into effect on 21 February 1973, with the Third Coalition Government being agreed to on 14 September 1973 and taking office on 5 April 1974. From this time on, events began to move quickly.

On 13 April 1975 the National Assembly was dissolved by royal decree, to the backdrop of the imminent fall of the republican government in Cambodia to the Khmer Rouge, which came just four days later. Saigon fell to the VPA two weeks and three days after the dissolution of the Lao Assembly. Public demonstrations orchestrated by the LPRP forced rightist leaders to flee Vieng Chan on 9 May. The Liberation of Vieng Chan was formally proclaimed on 23 August, along with a People's Revolutionary Administration and the abolition of the Royal Lao Army and the police, which were replaced by newly formed workers' militia units, but the coalition government under Souvanna was maintained for more than three more months. In November, the LPRP held local and provincial elections, around the same time clashing with the Thai army across the Mekong, which led to the closure of the border. With Thai support for resistance forces operating from across the Mekong and in a move to stabilise the political situation, the LPRP forced the abdication of King Savangvatthana on 1 December. The following day, the LPRP proclaimed the formation of the Lao People's Democratic Republic, formally establishing the power that had increasingly been theirs since the beginning of the year.

Once in power, one of the LPRP's first moves was to send approximately 10 000–15 000 people to reeducation camps, some of whom remained there for up to thirteen years. The following year, heady with victory, the LPRP embarked on the socialist phase of its revolution. Between the LPRP's victory over its rightist opponents and the move towards creating a socialist state, thousands of Lao fled across the Mekong. Meanwhile, Hmong members of the secret army who had been abandoned at the close of the war staged an uprising. Afraid that rightists would attempt to use the king as a symbol of opposition or even try to spirit him out of the country, on 12 March 1977 the LPRP arrested Savangvatthana, his wife and his son, Vong Savang, and sent them to Vieng Xai, near the Chinese border. Vong Savang was believed to have died there of fever a year or two later (Sagar 1991: 130; Kremmer 1997: 195, 210). Because of fears of a Chinese attempt to seize the king, Savangvatthana and his wife were moved from Vieng Xai to Sop Hao, where they are believed to have died in approximately 1980 (Kremmer 1997: 196, 211).

LAO SOCIALISM

An early and major move on the part of the LPRP government was to formalise its relations with the new Socialist Republic of Vietnam, which it did through a twenty-five year Treaty of Friendship. It was at this stage that many observers believed that Laos was being turned into a Vietnamese satellite state. In practical terms, when Vietnam invaded Cambodia in December 1978 and China responded by invading northern Vietnam, Laos sided with Vietnam against China, despite sharing its northern border with China. While relations between Laos and Vietnam have remained close, Laos has subsequently gained more autonomy from its influential neighbour, especially in regard to its relations with Thailand and China. In 1990, the Chinese premier, Li Peng, visited Laos, marking the formal warming of relations between the two countries.

The LPRP's moves towards socialism were put into practice with the program of agricultural cooperatives launched in May 1978. In the face of practical difficulties and popular opposition, the program of introducing cooperatives was suspended in July the following year. The LPRP also announced an interim three-year economic plan, although this did not produce any noticeable benefits. As a result the LPRP's Central Committee endorsed a new economic policy in December 1980 and announced that its first five-year plan was to run from 1981 to 1985. Although, by this stage, the government of Laos was committed to the path of LPRP domination, its one link with the neutralism of the past ended with the death of Souvanna Phouma, at the age of eighty-two, on 10 January 1984 in Vieng Chan. It is worth noting that the types of policies pursued by the neutralists were later adopted by the increasingly pragmatic LPRP government.

One of the most noticeable aspects of the LPRP government has been, despite its close links to Vietnam, its policy of asserting Lao autonomy. In June 1985 Laos engaged in a short border conflict with its far bigger neighbour Thailand over three disputed villages. Despite the potential cost to trade and the real problems Laos would have in sustaining a major conflict, during the period November 1987 to January 1988 it did not shy away from further conflict with Thailand over disputed territory in Phongsali province. The dispute was over the demarcation of the border between the two countries, based on tributary streams of the Mekong. In reality, local Thai generals had been engaged in lucrative but illegal logging in the area, which the Lao authorities disputed. With little official support from Bangkok, the relatively intense conflict was settled in favour of Laos and marked a significant assertion of a Lao sense of statehood.

In a different direction, one practical step in ascertaining exactly what—or who—comprised the state of the Lao PDR was the conducting of the first nationwide population census in March 1985. Given the ethnic diversity of Laos, the remoteness of many of its hill tribes and the lack of specific clarity about where the border actually lay in some parts of the country along its frontier with Vietnam, the census was a major feat. At last, the government of Laos had a formal idea of who its people were, where they were and what they did.

In line with political and economic developments in the Soviet Union, Vietnam withdrew its remaining troops from Laos in 1988. In part, this reflected a greater sense of Lao sovereignty and in part a desire to improve relations with Thailand, which had always been sensitive about a Vietnamese presence so close to its borders. After the still recent border conflict, this was an important gesture. But driving the decision was a shift by the Soviet Union away from effectively propping up its allies, which greatly increased the cost to Vietnam of maintaining its troops in Laos.

Confident of its position, and limiting candidates to those either in or allied to the party, the LPRP endorsed the holding of the first elections for the Supreme People's Assembly in 1989.

ECONOMIC LIBERALISATION

Following the conventional centrally planned model for economic development, the Lao government announced its second five-year plan in 1986. The economic reality at this time was that, starting from an already underdeveloped base, having suffered decades of war, having what little business capital that was available in the country leave after 1975 and the less than inspiring economic management of the LPRP from that time, Laos was one of the world's poorest countries[16] (see Evans 1991). As a consequence, no sooner had this second five-year plan been adopted than the LPRP began to move towards the idea of opening up the Lao economy. The acceptance of the New Economic Mechanism introduced, tentatively at first, the free market to Laos. In 1986, the LPRP also began to actively seek economic advice from the IMF, the World Bank and other donor agencies. Two years later, in 1988, the Lao government separated the central and commercial banking functions of the existing banking system. This complemented the development of a legal and institutional framework for economic and commercial activities, along with the institution of a range of taxes (amended the following year) to ensure a flow of revenue to the government (Zasloff 1991:33-8).

In 1991, in a move significant for the ascendancy of economic pragmatists, the leader of the LPRP (in its various guises) since 1955, Kaison Phomivan, was elected president of the LPRP and the state, while, at the same time, the Supreme People's Assembly endorsed the country's first Constitution. Despite being the long-standing party leader, the election of Kaison reflected a move towards accepting market domination of the economy, for which he and his faction had been pushing. A year and a half after his election, in November 1992, Kaison died.[17] He was replaced by Nuhak Phumsavan as state president and Khamtai Siphandon as prime minister and president of the party, both of whom were seen as opposed to Kaison's economic liberalism.

By this stage, though, the economic cat was already out of the ideological bag. The following month, December 1992, elections were held for the renamed National Assembly. While the elections were open to all adult citizens, the choice of candidates was effectively limited to either LPRP members or candidates approved by the LPRP. Between 1975 and 1991, prior to the adoption of the new Constitution, the LPRP ruled by governmental decree and party directives. Power was centred in the Politburo and exercised in the name of the Council of Ministers. As a consequence of the adoption of the new Constitution, in 1991 the party secretariat was abolished and policy making was handed to the ministries; party control of all state institutions was strengthened. This latter move was in response to the collapse of the Soviet Union, with which Laos was allied. Despite the adoption of a Constitution, law in Laos remained based on party dogma, with a significant input from Lao Loum tradition (having dispensed with colonial and royal law in 1975). There have also been some contributions to the legal code from the requirements of economic liberalisation. Laos had a total of forty laws, supplemented by further decrees and regulations.

By the early 1990s, the government had begun to move relatively quickly, at least when compared to its original pace of development. In 1993, further economic reforms were promulgated and, importantly, an environmental protection law passed. Impetus for environmental protection came from NGOs and the international community, but also reflected a local awareness that, with so many other problems, the high quality of the physical environment was one advantage the country retained. For a country that has, relative to many other countries, a high proportion of forested area and which faces pressure from logging and damming interests, such environmental protection was a major step in preserving the Lao environment. However, as with most laws that have the potential to impede business, restrictions on logging have often been honoured more in the breach than in the observance.

As a symbolic gesture, the opening in 1994 of the first bridge spanning the Mekong marked the beginning of relatively easy access to Laos from Thailand. The Friendship Bridge, as it is known, was touted as a means for Laos to integrate more closely into the rapidly developing Thai economy. While there has been closer integration between Thailand and Laos since the bridge was opened, it has been less to the economic advantage of Laos and more to the advantage of Thai businessmen selling goods across the border. However, it did provide a direct road route from Vieng Chan, via Nong Kai on the Thai side of the Mekong, to Bangkok, which facilitated cross-border trade. One interesting response to the greater Thai presence, especially in Vieng Chan, was a concerted move to reassert Lao political and cultural independence. In this, one could detect a faint echo of historical rivalries. Another significant move that marked the integration of Laos into the region was its acceptance as a full member of the Association of South-East Asian Nations in July 1997. It was becoming increasingly clear that, though landlocked, Laos wished to become a regional participant. After hundreds of years of isolation, Laos was becoming less mysterious and more accessible to the outside world.

LIMITED POLITICAL DEVELOPMENT

National Assembly elections were again held in December 1997, with committed LPRP cadres dominating the conservative, party-oriented body. Reflecting the long-standing role of the army in political affairs, generals still held six of the nine Politburo seats in 1997 (Kremmer 1997: 212). As was noted in Laos in early 1999, the army existed before the party, so this was a natural extension of the army's political role. Accompanying the elections was a minor ministerial reshuffle, especially in economic portfolios, which, in a practical sense, acknowledged high-level economic mismanagement. Responsibility for foreign investment was split between two high-ranking officials, which was claimed would produce greater efficiency, but was, in reality, intended to check corrupt tendencies of officials who were not answerable to others.

The changed economic policies in Laos began to produce results, with economic growth over 1991–96 at 7 per cent and real per capita growth increasing to 3.8 per cent. Growth dipped a little in 1997, being estimated at 6.5 per cent, but dropped to zero in 1998 as a consequence of the downturn in the Thai economy, a more general domestic malaise and, to some extent, infrastructure bottlenecks caused by an inability to keep pace with economic growth. Investment from Thailand and South Korea, which constituted more than 50 per cent of foreign direct investment, had effectively dried up over 1997–98 and was slow in returning thereafter.

In the first half of 1998, foreign investment slumped by around 60 per cent compared to the same time the previous year. By the end of 1998, the trade deficit had worsened, the value of the Lao currency, the kip, had slumped from 3900 to 4300 to the US dollar within the four weeks of December and inflation hit 100 per cent (Pike 1999: 10). The kip soon fell further—10 000 to the US dollar—before settling at around 7500 in early 2000. As a consequence of the devaluation of the kip, Laos' balance of trade deficit grew to US$226 million over 1998–99, with the country having to import approximately twice as much as it exported (*Indochina Chronology* 1999: 11–12). Inflation came back to around 10 per cent, after peaking at 167 per cent in March 1999 (Lintner 2000). Inflation fluctuated thereafter, but had reduced to around 12 per cent by 2004, while growth was at 5.5 per cent and the kip had stabilised at around 10 800 to the dollar (*Lao News Agency*, 6 December 2004). Reflecting its increasing openness, by 2004 tourism had become an important source of Laos' foreign income, although, given its continuing impoverishment—Laos remained one of the world's poorest states—at US$243 million (2001 estimate, CIA 2004), foreign aid was also a major source of income.

While foreign aid was vital to Laos' economic survival, the country was approximately self-sufficient in terms of rice production, producing about 400 kilograms per person in 1999. Not surprisingly, in 2004, agriculture accounted for more than half (53 per cent) of the economy and 80 per cent of all employment. Despite the liberalisation of the Lao economy to the point where it was, in practical terms, a free market capitalist state, if not an especially successful one, there was little sign of an organised civil opposition to the monopoly rule of the LPRP, while the overall influence of the party at the central level remained strong. While discontent among ordinary Lao people was growing, especially in the larger cities and towns, it was largely limited to the small and still vulnerable middle class. As a part of the population who might want to encourage reform, this group was not sufficiently widespread or organised to have a meaningful impact on government.

By way of illustration, in a daring move in October 1999, a small group of teachers and students, led by local lecturer Thongpaseuth Keuakhoune, held a protest in Vieng Chan against the government. The protest was quickly dispersed and Thongpaseuth and others were taken into custody (Lintner 2000), with ten people still being held six months later. A further forty-six Protestants were also being held without trial as a consequence of their work for the Lao Evangelical Church (*Indochina Chronology* 1999: 11–12). The protest was regarded as a sign of external and domestic pressure on the government to reform, however, the rigid control held by the government meant that it was deeply reluctant to offer change lest it lose its grip on power. All electoral candidates continued to be vetted by the party-controlled National Construction Front. In 1992, several proponents (no one knows exactly how many – perhaps a dozen) of a multiparty political system were jailed; one died in jail in early 1998.

Opposition to the government was difficult to organise as the country's intellectual elite remained small and transparent. Although politically dominant, the LPRP tended to work in the background, setting overall policy directions. There also continued to be some distrust by the older, conservative party members towards younger, often tertiary educated officials. Despite its grip on power, there were increasing concerns at the elite level that the LPRP had been weakened by economic change and by the passing of its revolutionary generation. At the local level, where most people actually live, there was a growing perception that party units were failing to provide a lead for grassroots development.

THE ARMY AND BUSINESS

For administrative purposes, Laos is divided into sixteen provinces, each of which falls into one of three broad military regions, which are formally based on geographic distinction, but in practice, now conform to business enterprises operated by the army. Given its history of preceding the LPRP, the army operates relatively independently of the government, although it strongly influences the government. Also, as with a number of armies that trace their origins to (self-sustaining) revolutionary activity, the Lao army subsidises itself through independent and joint venture business activities, meaning that it operates somewhat independently of government policy other than regional commanders contributing to that policy. Business ventures include logging, shipping (a port facility in Vietnam is owned and operated by the Lao military), shoe manufacturing and so on. This, in turn, exacerbated a slight sense of warlordism that pervaded Lao political life. Until early 1999, for example, there were immigration checks between each of its provinces, which not only kept note of where people were going (or where they had been), but also acted as a security measure against anti-government groups. This compartmentalisation of Laos quickly receded with the opening of the state to business and to foreigners.

In a variation on the enterprising business theme, official corruption was fairly widespread throughout Laos, with government and military leaders skimming off percentages of business takings and arranging cosy deals for family members and clients (that is, of patron–client relationships). Corruption also existed at lower levels of officialdom, with payments of bribes helping to ensure that what should be procedural matters were appropriately looked after.

Given Laos' official parlous economic position, many aid donors have insisted on institutional checks to clean up some aspects of profit skimming, which has, in turn, led to some steps towards doing away with the worst cases of corruption. Some ministers and their staffs were removed, although many still held positions of power and were not entirely excluded from possibilities of making money. Much government middle-level management is run by technocrats, who were, in some cases foreign-trained, mostly in the former USSR and, later, in Russia. However, their policy advice, which was basically sound, tended not to be heeded by the older, revolutionary generation. That is, government decisions on economic policy tend to be taken according to the concerns of the older leadership, rather than reflecting rational economic decision making. This was a particular source of frustration to aid agencies and foreign investors, the latter having shown a marked disinclination to continue business dealings in Laos.

ARMED OPPOSITION TO THE LPRP

In the period after the revolution, there was a threat of small-scale insurgency by Lao rightists and Thai mercenaries operating out of northeastern Thailand. However, as American interest in mainland SEA diminished, so too did this threat. In the northeast of Laos, those Hmong who supported Vang Po's secret army and who did not escape, launched a rebellion against the central government, the scale of which never threatened the LPRP, but it did continue to make unsafe a large area of northern Laos, including the area within 100 kilometres of Vieng Chan. In the first half of 2000, a series of bombings upset the usual calm of Vieng Chan and, although no one claimed responsibility for them, an attack on a government post at Pakse in Champassak province in July 2000, in which five guerrillas and one government soldier were killed, was publicly linked to a revitalised wing of Vang Pao's Hmong guerrilla group.

The government likened the rebellion to banditry and, to some extent, this was an accurate characterisation. However, the continued existence of two separate—and antithetical—Hmong military groups with overtly political agendas undoubtedly constituted more than just simple banditry. The provinces still under threat at the beginning of the twenty-first century included Luang Prabang, Xieng Khouang, Vieng Chan and Saysomboun special zones. Apart from the bombings in Vieng Chan and that attack at Pakse, Hmong military activity was increasingly restricted to Xieng Khouang. There has never been a close formal relationship with the non-Lao Loum groups and the upland Lao and many non-Lao Loum continue to regard the policies of the lowland government as little more than an interference in their affairs. While this was particularly the case with regards to the Hmong, it could also be said to apply to many of the other ethnic minorities who inhabit Laos. It is interesting to note that the assertion of local independence tended to occur around the same time as the opium harvest and transhipment from the northern regions.

ARMS AND OPIUM

A major issue of contention between the Lao government and the Hmong was, not surprisingly given its international opprobrium, the cultivation and sale of opium. Given that there was a certain level of official involvement in the opium and heroin trade, helping Laos maintain its position as the world's third largest—after Burma and Afghanistan—illegal opium producer, with production of 180 tonnes in 2004, it was not at all clear whether the government's stated opposition to opium cultivation was genuine. As in Burma, it was quite likely that local military officers involved in the drug trade were simply trying to put their competitors out of business. Another related issue was that of the transhipment of heroin from Burma through Laos to Cambodia and Vietnam. The nature of the linkages between Burma and Laos were not clear, but again, it seemed that there was a significant degree of official involvement. This was especially so in relation to the transhipment to Cambodia and Vietnam, where political and military links were close.

The government was engaged in a campaign of relocation of Hmong villages to areas on or close to major roads, the ostensible purpose of which was to introduce the Hmong to cash cropping in order to stop slash and burn agriculture. The Lao government does have an active policy of protecting— or attempting to protect—the natural environment and it was believed that the growing population had made the relatively destructive swidden agriculture ecologically unviable. Government policy on the environment was reflected in logging in areas that were in the process of being flooded for dams, rather than more general logging, so there appeared to be some consistency to this program. However, the relocation of the Hmong also brought them under closer government supervision and control. In March 2004, formal Hmong anti-government activity ended when around 700 Hmong fighters and their families surrendered to the government following an intensification of the government's campaign to end the Hmong insurgency, especially in the Xieng Khouang Special Zone, and to dispel the last vestiges of the secret army. About 300 people surrendered near Luang Prabang, and a further 400 surrendered in Xieng Khouang (Agence France Presse, 5 March 2004, Radio Free Asia, 3 March 2004).

LAO TOLERANCE

The government checks that had been especially noticeable in the more troubled parts of Laos were not especially oppressive of ordinary people. There was, almost as a matter of course, a certain brusqueness and arrogance that seems to be a near-universal feature of wearing a uniform, and the starchy, authoritarian bureaucracy of communist officialdom in particular. But there was no overt intimidation and the Lao I saw in the presence of army or police officers, as early as 1998 and 1999, unlike people in a number of other developing countries, did not appear to be in the least cowed. There was, it seemed, an unstated belief that most people, or at least most Lao Loum, would behave towards each other with a degree of tolerance and respect, which was said, by those few outsiders who had visited Laos in the intervening years, to have become more pronounced as numerous restrictions were eased after 1989 and 1990.

In part, this tendency appeared to stem from the predominant influence of Theravada Buddhism on everyday life (Evans 1998: 49–70), which was manifested in *sangha* (Buddhist clergy) involvement with and support for ordinary people and the government's explicit respect for Buddhism and the *sangha*. Having said that, Theravada Buddhism appears to have less of a benign influence on officialdom in Burma and Cambodia, so it alone does not stand as sufficient explanation. In part, too, there was considerable support for the government on the part of many ordinary Lao Loum, which did not necessarily imply that many Lao would not like to have a more direct say in the policies of their government, but it did indicate a degree of popular support for the Lao government, in terms of its nationalist credentials and its more general developmental policies. Perhaps more importantly, though, was that many Lao did not have a particularly well-developed sense of political consciousness, so, if the Lao government allowed most people to live without interfering too much in their daily lives, that seemed to be reasonably well accepted.

In large part, the Lao government's broad sense of acceptability also stemmed from the loosening of its formerly fairly strict, orthodox Leninist policies that derived directly from the Communist Party of Vietnam and, before that, from the Soviet Union. Since the Soviet Union has ceased to exist and Vietnam has, since 1987, moved towards opening up its economy, Laos too has moved towards a less centrally planned, more free-market economy, which was, in any case, still largely irrelevant to a society that was very significantly subsistence-oriented and in which illicit cross-border trade was a fact of economic life. However, Laos' return to economic growth, its increase in foreign currency reserves and the slow shift towards creating an industrial base were all signs that there were positive, if still modest, economic outcomes available to the Lao people.

The international community, too, had a very significant impact on Laos. Thailand was in the process of attempting to reassert its economic, if not political, hegemony over Laos and the international aid agencies had a very significant presence in Vieng Chan. Vieng Chan was beginning to take on some of the feel—and the money—of being a smaller sibling to the mighty, bustling Bangkok. But an official and unofficial sense of Lao propriety tended to curb the greater excesses of the Thai capital. Development outside Vieng Chan and a few other major towns appeared to be so limited that it was almost non-existent. Village life was hardly touched by development.

At a local level, political society was still organised at village level, with the village headman being the principal political representative and arbitrator between ordinary people and medium echelons of government. The village headman held his position as a consequence of bi-annual elections and, short of losing consensual support, could be expected to maintain that position until he was no longer able to fulfil its functions. However, there were examples of village chiefs losing their positions because they had attempted to enrich themselves and their families through their position, so there was a degree of accountability for ordinary Lao people. The village chief was virtually always a member of the LPRP, so there was a direct connection between the party and community life.

Family and village life were further organised by mutually reinforcing communal values, which tended to be typical of societies that were in transition from being agrarian-based and premodern to urbanised. Even in the larger urban centres, the fundamental administrative unit was still based on the village or local community, so the model pertained across the state, not just to villages as such. Transgression of village rules could result in expulsion from the village, although redemption and forgiveness were marked characteristics of such situations.

At the more overtly political level, the government intelligence network was extensive. With everyone knowing more or less what everyone else is doing, there was little scope for antisocial, much less anti-government, behaviour. Similarly, although the law is technically quite strict in a number of matters, in fact its application is fairly lax. It depends more on whether there is a belief that a person has acted outside the bounds of socially acceptable behaviour rather than whether any actual crime has been committed. Of course, this did allow considerable scope for abuse, especially with reference to relatively low-level corruption. But in general there tended to be pretty much a live and let live approach to formal social organisation.

In part, at least, the increasingly relaxed approach of the government was a reflection of the Lao people themselves, for whom authority was not to be taken too seriously (and so has difficulty in asserting its authority). In some senses, this typified political life in Laos. Authority was an historical necessity, but tended not to be too oppressive, at least since the paranoia associated with running a state for the first time faded in the later 1980s. The government relaxed, incrementally; once-closed borders were re-opened and ordinary Lao citizens were allowed to get on with their lives. Insofar as the LPRP maintained any Marxist credentials, it was more as a government in which public welfare—and some self-enrichment—was a priority and in which final political control was still maintained at the centre.

The ethical values of Theravada Buddhism—tolerance and respect— were pervasive and managed to knock off the harder ideological edges, but perhaps underlying all of this was the usually open, receptive and forgiving nature of most Lao people (see Evans 1998). In the final analysis, unless a government wishes to oppress its own people, it must ultimately come to reflect their values. This slowly but increasingly appeared to be the case with the government of Laos.

NOTES

1　This name is actually redundant, as 'mae' is the Thai word for river, while its actual name is the Khong, hence Maekhong.

2　The T'ai languages, which are, to some extent, mutually intelligible, are largely monosyllabic and tonal.

3　The million elephants referred less to the predominance of elephants in Laos as such than to the military prowess accorded to elephants in warfare.

4　Like the Thai word 'mae' (as in Mae Khong), the Lao word 'nam' (as in Nam Khan) means 'river', so the English use of the term in this context is formally redundant.

5　Viravong claims Fa Ngum to have been the twenty-third in a continuing line of royal descent.

6　The Hmong had begun to move into the Plain of Jars region between 1820 and 1840, continuing the southward drift from southern China over the next several decades.

7　While some opium was grown and sold in Laos, until 1939 most of the opium from which the government derived its income was imported from India (Stuart-Fox, personal communication 1999).

8　The French use of block houses—small fortifications—was retained until the early 1950s, when they proved ineffective against the highly organised Viet Minh.

9　Interestingly, Komadom's son, Si Thon, who was captured by the French during the pacification campaign, was, in 1970, vice-chairman of the Pathet Lao for the southern hill people.

10　Towards the end of WWII in the Pacific, Japanese forces encouraged declarations of independence by former European-occupied colonies, in large part as a means of slowing the Allied advance.

11　The coalition represented the Committee of the People, the Lao-Pen-Lao (Laos for the Lao) and the Committee for a Free Laos.

12　The Central Intelligence Agency was later very active against a successor to the more leftist, military wing of the Lao Issara, the Pathet Lao.

13　The Indochinese Union included Laos, Cambodia, Tonkin, Annam and Cochin-China, the last three states comprising Vietnam.

14　Towards creating greater internal control over day-to-day matters of government, while leaving the crucial areas of foreign affairs, defence, monetary policy and customs in the hands of the French.

15　The neutralist group, led by Prince Souvanna Phouma (half brother to Souvanna Vong), was ideologically positioned between the Pathet Lao and the conservatives, and opposed to involvement of both North Vietnam and the USA.

16　Laos is now 125 on a listing of 163 countries with a per capita GDP of US$400, which places it above Vietnam at 139, which is just ahead of Cambodia.

17　Evans (1998: 24–40) notes that Kaison's death resulted in a high degree of traditional ancestor worship, leading to the Cult of Kaison.

8 | Cambodia: Electoral Authoritarianism

In October 2004, Cambodia's long-serving head of state, King Norodom Sihanouk, abdicated, appointing his son, Norodom Sihamoni, as his successor. Sihanouk had served through most of Cambodia's postcolonial history, variously as king, prince and prime minister. His tenure had seen Cambodia gain independence, become embroiled in the Indochina War, see him ousted in a US-backed republican coup, the nightmare of the Khmer Rouge era, Vietnamese occupation, civil war and, finally, transition to an open voting system in which the country's real ruler only accepted election results on his own terms. Between his advancing years, his declining health and his ultimate inability to influence real political power, Sihanouk decided to stop. In his place, assuming the now purely ceremonial role of king, was his son Sihamoni, a former ballet dancer, ballet teacher and ambassador to UNESCO. With his older brother Ranariddh leading a political party—somewhat ineffectually—and five of his other siblings killed by the Khmer Rouge, Sihamoni was handed the throne by his father, rather than wait until he died and allow the seemingly permanent prime minister, Hun Sen, to choose or, worse still, end the monarchy.

In the first few years of the twenty-first century, Cambodia entered what was its most stable political environment in decades. The Cambodian People's Party (CPP) and the National United Front for a Neutral, Peaceful, Cooperative and Independent Cambodia (FUNCINPEC) had again entered into a reasonably steady, if somewhat forced, coalition government under the prime ministership of Hun Sen. Cambodia had conducted its third set of popular elections, which were again marked by violence and intimidation, but which managed to produce a reasonably representative result. As with previous elections, the CPP did not achieve the two-thirds majority it required to rule in its own right and was again forced into a coalition government, despite both parties clearly not wishing to share such an arrangement. This was both the advantage and the problem of the Cambodian constitution, a legacy of UN intervention in the early 1990s:

government could not be formed without a two-thirds majority, hence, it almost always required a coalition government, which resulted in an inbuilt moderating influence on the exercise of power. The coalitions were rarely happy, but they were generally stable enough and precluded the possibility of a quasidictatorial 50 per cent plus one form of elected government. If Hun Sen's CPP was the forceful if unhappy suitor, Prince Norodom Ranariddh's FUNCINPEC was very much the bride reluctant to consummate the relationship, even though it had done so on three occasions.

This increasingly familiar political environment followed the collapse of the Khmer Rouge, which came after the death of Pol Pot. The last of the Khmer Rouge leaders had either surrendered or been captured. Three of them lived under an amnesty in their western redoubt at Pailin, while their troops had joined the government army or returned to civilian life. Even the millions of landmines, which continued to plague Cambodia, were slowly being cleared. Cambodia's belated inclusion into ASEAN in May 1999 and its readmission to

Map 5 Cambodia

the UN in November 1999 appeared to confirm, at least on the surface, that the country was moving towards being on a steady political footing.

From another perspective, Cambodia continued to bear the legacy of decades of war. Due to war and landmines, it had the highest amputee rate in the world, very little industry outside subsistence rice cropping, very poor infrastructure and little money to improve it. Most worryingly, the level of official corruption was breathtaking in its scope and audacity, while the country's human rights record remained poor. Meanwhile, the average income of an ordinary Cambodian had improved very little.

As in 1998, ahead of the 2003 elections there appeared little doubt that the CPP government of Hun Sen was employing the fullest extent of its institutionalised power to swing popular support behind it. In simple terms, the CPP not only had the advantage of being in government, but it also had the full use of government resources for its party political purposes. Of the twenty-two opposition parties (down from thirty-eight in 1998), only FUNCINPEC and the Sam Rainsy Party stood any chance of securing a sizeable block of votes, replicating their positions from 1998. Technically, Cambodia was a liberal democracy under a constitutional monarchy, but in reality, Cambodia veered very close to being, if not a one-party state, then at least a state in which one party, the CPP, appeared to have a vice-like grip on power.

OLD CAMBODIA

The contemporary Cambodian nation is effectively the remnant of the once-powerful Khmer empire, which, at its peak during the twelfth and thirteenth centuries, ruled much of what is now Thailand, Laos and Vietnam. Cambodia's origins lie in the fertile Mekong basin as the state of Norkor Kuork Phlouk, or Norkor Phnom (King of the Mountain), referred to by contemporary Chinese as Funan,[1] which dated to about the first century BCE. Prior to that, a mixture of prehistoric peoples and Khmers are known to have lived in the region as far back as 4000 BCE (Rooney 1994: 21). This state was located primarily in the region of the Mekong River to the north of present day Phnom Penh and Tonle Sap (Great Lake). The establishment of Funan, from around 100 BCE, corresponded with the introduction of Indianised culture into the region, most probably from Java, and included the widespread adoption of Hinduism and, later, the use of written Sanskrit. Sanskrit acted to divide the elites from ordinary Khmer-speaking people. It was at about this time that patron–client social relations were established in the region (MacDonald 1987: 34–6; Chandler 1983: 11–18; Coedes 1966: 1–2). Funan, which may have been just one local state among many (Rooney 1994: 23), shifted from predominantly dry rice agriculture to wet rice agriculture as late as 500 CE. Chandler noted that while the state of Funan existed and was a precursor state to Cambodia, it was decentralised, being based on an 'aggregation of leaders' and a 'multiplicity of centers' (Chandler 1983: 19). Funan was a despotic state, but not an integrated despotic state (Chandler 1983: 25).

Khmer Funan suzerainty extended over most of present-day Cambodia, as well as parts of Thailand and the Mekong delta region of Vietnam. However, by the seventh and eighth centuries, its power had declined and was replaced by a conglomeration of small principalities known to the Chinese as Chenla, located in Cambodia and southern Laos. Chenla was divided into Water Chenla and Land Chenla, the former located near the Mekong delta, the latter along the Mekong south of modern Laos (MacDonald 1987: 37–40). The greatest Cambodian empire rose in the area near the northwestern tip of Tonle Sap, taking its name Angkor from the Sanskrit term *nagara* (city).[2]

From the late eighth century for about 100 years, Cambodia was ruled by the Sailendra Dynasty of Java. The end of Javanese suzerainty in the ninth century led to the unification of the Khmer people and the establishment of the Khmer empire under Jayavarman II, who had returned from Java to proclaim the unity and independence of the Khmer state (Coedes 1966: 2–3, 73–83; Rooney 1994: 25). This new empire was centred on Angkor Thom and, during its peak in the twelfth century, extended its borders in Laos to the north, to the South China Sea in the east and to the Bay of Bengal in the west. On the scale of regional empires, the Khmer empire established sophisticated administrative structures, built a network of roads and government outposts throughout its territory and established cities and towns reflecting its cultural and political domination across a vast area. Its masterwork was the building of its capital, just north of modern Siem Reap, in northwestern Cambodia. The complex of temples, walls, reservoirs, moats, bridges and other structures that remain at the Angkor site are equal to or exceed the most impressive ruins in the world, covering a vast area and reflecting exceptional levels of technology, artisanship and artistry. It is instructive that the ancient Khmers did not live in the stone structures that remain, which had a religious purpose, but in wooden buildings that have long since disappeared. The walled city of Angkor Thom contained hundreds of thousands of people and was a cosmopolitan centre, attracting visitors from India, China and the whole of SEA.

Upon the death of Jayavarman VII, the empire began to decline. It is believed Angkor's decline was a result of internal rebellions, disregard for economic maintenance and the introduction of Theravada Buddhism, which preached salvation of the individual through his or her own efforts, rather than the hierarchy of Hinduism or Mahayana Buddhism (which preceded Theravada Buddhism). The rise of the Thais to the west also wreaked havoc upon the state and the capital at Angkor Thom was too close to the new Thai power to ever really be safe again (Herz 1958: 15–16; Chandler 1983: 67–70). By the middle of the fourteenth century, the state was weak enough for the neighbouring Thais to invade and capture the city, first in 1353 and again in 1430–31. The following year, the city was abandoned (see MacDonald 1987: 34–63).

When Angkor was abandoned, what remained of the elite shifted southward into the safer lower Mekong basin and Cambodian social structure, perhaps responding to a smaller population, became less exigent and more diffuse. Theravada Buddhism, which became the state religion, enshrined an ideal of egalitarianism (for men, at least) in a society that retained its hierarchical trappings. Angkor itself was soon forgotten. By about 1650, Cambodia had become one of a number of small, self-sufficient, relatively isolated Buddhist kingdoms that dotted the landscape of SEA between western Burma and Vietnam.

Prior to its breakup, this seemingly idyllic situation darkened when two strong, expansionist and competitive kingdoms came into being on either side of Cambodia. Vietnam had increasingly expanded southwards at the expense of Champa, until the latter ceased to exist. Champa had sent pleas to the Cambodian court, seeking assistance against the Vietnamese in 1471, but Cambodia was, at this time, preoccupied with internal squabbling and the threat of Thailand to the west (Herz 1958: 42–4). The decline of Cambodia thereafter was not a foregone conclusion and there were still brief moments of glory that marked the period between Angkor and the arrival of the French, for example, when the Burmese invaded Siam in 1556, the Cambodian king, Barom Racha, took advantage of the situation to also invade Siam the following year and again in 1559 and 1562 (Herz 1958: 44–5), although, in 1587, the Siamese retaliated, storming the Cambodian capital at Lovek and razing it to the ground. To the southeast, in the 1620s the Nguyen Dynasty of southern Vietnam had established itself at Saigon, eventually consolidating control over the previously Khmer Mekong delta and effectively cutting off Cambodia from its access to the sea. Cambodia's regional decline was now guaranteed.

Until France established its protectorate in 1863, Cambodian kings and regional rulers tried to avoid being dominated by either Thailand or Vietnam, mostly by offering a degree of suzerainty to both. They sought the patronage of their enemy's enemy, alternating between Thailand, whose Buddhist—and patron–client—culture was familiar, and Chinese-influenced Vietnam, which had a markedly different social makeup based, to a large extent, on Confucian thinking, which in theory promoted a bureaucratic hierarchy based on merit. Rivals for the Cambodian throne would seek help from the enemy of the incumbent, which exacerbated factionalism among Cambodian royalty along pro-Thai or pro-Vietnamese lines. The stakes in such factionalism were high and the costs in Cambodian lives and territory enormous.

By the 1830s, most of the kingdom of Cambodia was a satellite of Vietnam, with the Vietnamese putting King Ang Chan on the throne in

1833. Meanwhile, two northwestern provinces, including the one containing the ruins of Angkor, had been ceded to Siam. Years of warfare between Thai and Vietnamese armies devastated Cambodia. In this period, anti-Vietnamese feelings began to be identified, in many Cambodians' minds, with half-formed notions of nationalism. Vietnam and Thailand, for their part, developed the idea that Cambodia was not a sovereign country, but a place inhabited by inferior people that could be exploited or protected at will. In the 1840s, between Vietnam and Thailand, the state almost disappeared, although a popular anti-Vietnamese rebellion did break out in 1842 (Herz 1958: 52–4; Chandler 1983: 99–116). Siam, meanwhile, attempted to reassert its authority over Cambodia: it offered sanctuary to the Cambodian king when a rebellion against him broke out and, in 1862, sent him back to Cambodia, accompanied by Siamese troops. In 1863, frightened of his neighbours and under direct pressure from the French governor in Saigon, who noted that he could claim suzerainty over Cambodia as heir to Vietnamese suzerainty, Cambodia's King Norodom asked for French protection, a rare example of voluntary colonisation (Herz 1958: 57–60; Chandler 1983: 117–36; Osborne 1973: 13–19). Not surprisingly, the French had been seeking this request. There were subsequent revolts against the French, in 1866–67 and 1885–87 while the boundaries of Cambodia were renegotiated. To placate the Siamese, Siem Reap, Battambang and Sisophon were handed to Siam, but later returned to Cambodia, in 1904 and 1907 (Tully 1996: 41–112). In 1884, King Norodom handed over internal administration of Cambodia to the French. While the period of French colonialism did little to enhance Cambodia's development as a state, if France had not intervened, Cambodia, divided between Thailand and Vietnam, would have ceased to exist.

THE FRENCH PROTECTORATE

The period between the establishment of a French protectorate in 1863 and 1941 was marked by encroaching French control over the king and his ministers. However, French rule also strengthened the king's symbolic position, by the ministers retaining a high estimation of the king and by the style of Norodom's successor, his half-brother Sisowath. Succeeding to the throne in 1904 as a French appointee, Sisowath did not clash with the French, as had Norodom. Indeed, Sisowath was later castigated by supporters of independence as having been too acquiescent to the French. As a consequence of Sisowath's close collaboration with the French—and their support of him—during a quiet and untroubled period of Cambodia's history, there was further opportunity for 'the king's symbolic prestige to be enhanced', though limiting his real power (Osborne 1973: 21). This set up a situation in which, should he wish, the king's symbolic prestige could be used to gain temporal political advantage. Sisowath's reign ended when he died in 1927; he was succeeded by his son, Monivong, who reigned from 1927 until 1941. The period from 1904 until 1941 has, not incorrectly, been identified as 'the years of colonial calm' (Osborne 1973: ch. 3). There was some anti-French dissent during this time, but it did not amount to a threat to the state.

During World War II when Japanese forces occupied all of Indochina, French administrators[3] stayed on in Cambodia, as they did in Vietnam and Laos. To counter claims for independence, the French chose a nineteen-year-old prince, Norodom Sihanouk, to be king when his grandfather, the reigning monarch, King Monivong, died in 1941. The French assumed that Sihanouk would be pliant, which was only briefly correct. Having occupied Cambodia in 1941, Japan handed the western border provinces back to its ally, Thailand, but gave Cambodia independence in 1945. Sihanouk assumed the role of prime minister as well as king and appointed his own, largely conservative, cabinet. However, a coup launched by the strongly nationalist foreign minister, Son Ngoc Thanh, led to the arrest of all pro-French ministers. Sihanouk resigned and Thanh made himself prime minister (Kiernan 1985: 48–9). In a tense political environment and without recourse to a parliament, one Cambodian faction called for occupation by the British forces then in Saigon. Following this intervention, French administration returned to Cambodia soon after (Smith 1964a: 607). Thanh was arrested, charged with treason and exiled to France.[4] But as a concession to mounting political claims, the French allowed political parties and the first of Cambodia's five constitutions was announced in 1947.

Between 1950 and 1954, Cambodia's move towards independence operated on two levels. On one level, there were aboveground political parties that agitated for independence, dominant among which were the Democrats, who favoured the French model of government and independence as soon as possible. There was also the more conservative Liberal Party, which advocated the education of the Cambodian people and, in the interim, a close relationship with France. A third party, the Progressive Democrats, was also conservative, but quickly faded from significance. The Democrats, the best organised of the parties, quickly asserted their dominance of the elected political system (Chandler 1983: 176–8; Osborne 1973: 43–4). The political primacy of the Democrats and their generally anti-royalist tendencies worried King Sihanouk.

At a more underground level, supporters of the exiled Son Ngoc Thanh took to arms to form the non-communist Khmer Issarak (Free Khmer), which, with support from the Thai government, launched attacks against the French administration in 1946–47. A change in government in Bangkok, conflict with the procommunist Vietnamese nationalist forces, the Viet Minh, and an amnesty offered by the government quickly halved these rebels' numbers. To the east, those Vietnamese engaged in opposition to French occupation also became involved in the resistance movement against

France in Cambodia, under the umbrella of the Indochinese Communist Party (Kiernan 1985: 117–68; Chandler 1985: 183; Smith 1964a: 616). By 1952, these guerrillas controlled as much as one-sixth of the Cambodian countryside (Chandler 1983: 183). However, there were tensions between the Vietnamese and the Cambodian guerrillas. From around this time, at the beginning of the 1950s, a group of young Cambodian students living in Paris were forming themselves into a Marxist circle, which was to become the nucleus of the Cambodian Communist Party when it rose to military and political prominence in the 1970s. The group included Saloth Sar, Ieng Sary and Son Sen (Kiernan 1985: 121–4).

In 1952, Son Ngoc Thanh, now back in Cambodia, fled to the northwest, from where the Khmer Issarak resumed its attacks on the government, occasionally cooperating with pro-Viet Minh guerrillas (Corfield 1994: 14–15). By 1952, about two-thirds of Cambodia was no longer in government hands. Sihanouk launched an attack against guerrillas in the northwest in September 1952 and, on the strength of its claimed success, dismissed the Democrat government in mid 1952 (Smith 1964a: 614), proclaiming martial law, assuming power as prime minister and appointing his own cabinet. In January 1953, the Democrats responded by refusing to pass his budget, which he answered with the dissolution of the Assembly and the arrest of several Democrat assemblymen. The next month, Sihanouk travelled to France to seek Cambodia's independence as a part of his Royal Crusade for Independence. It was not granted. Sihanouk complained to an international audience about France's intransigence, then went into self-imposed exile, first in Bangkok, then in Battambang, to highlight the French position.

At this time, in mid 1953, the war against the Vietnamese nationalist Viet Minh was going badly for France, whose government was increasingly worried about the declining security situation in Cambodia. In order to reach a settlement in Vietnam, the French began to look at cutting their ties to Cambodia (Kiernan 1985: 140–64). Then, unexpectedly, in October, France agreed to grant Sihanouk authority over Cambodia's armed forces, judiciary and foreign affairs, effectively granting the country independence (although it maintained most of its economic interests in Cambodia until the early 1970s).

Sihanouk made the overstated claim that he had won this independence single-handedly. His public tactics had pushed the French, but, more so, the French position was influenced by the Viet Minh. In any case, the achievement of independence was enough to briefly end Son Ngoc Thanh's opposition to Sihanouk and to curtail the Khmer Issarak as a threat to the state. Sihanouk then abdicated the throne and, claiming a mandate as a consequence of independence, started a national political movement, the Sangkum Reastr Niyum (People's Socialist Community), intended to smother Cambodia's political parties. Despite its name, there was little about Sihanouk's new party that reflected conventional socialist ideas. By 1955, the Democrats, unable to counter Sihanouk's continued claims of having single-handedly achieved independence for the state, had effectively ceased to exist. When elections were held on 11 September 1955, the Sangkum Reastr Niyum won every seat in the National Assembly, enabling Sihanouk to run Cambodia as a personal fiefdom and impose consensus on his 'children' while attempting to modernise the country.

CAMBODIA, THE USA AND VIETNAM

Unfortunately for Cambodia, and despite attempts to placate the USA (Caldwell & Tan 1973: 91–7), Sihanouk's nominally socialist program and his neutral foreign policy were not acceptable to either his pro-USA neighbours or to the USA itself. In the late 1950s, Son Ngoc Thanh and the Khmer Issarak were revived by the USA and its Thai ally to destabilise the neutralist Sihanouk (Caldwell & Tan 1973: 99). An attempted right-wing coup in 1959 was foiled, although South Vietnamese incursions into Stung Treng province came soon after, followed by allegedly CIA-backed attempts by South Vietnamese agents to assassinate Sihanouk. These latter moves had the effect of strengthening Sihanouk's distrust of the USA and its South Vietnamese ally (Kiernan 1985: 187). As fighting intensified in Vietnam, Sihanouk chose to enter into secret alliances with the Vietnamese communists, allowing them to use Cambodia's eastern provinces bordering Vietnam for supply routes from the north and to base themselves in (Osborne 1973: 110). Sihanouk believed that, by reaching such agreements, he would stop the Vietnamese communists from assisting in the escalation of the insurgency against his own government. He feared that such an escalation would invite intervention on the part of South Vietnam and the USA and its other allies. As well as making secret deals with the Vietnamese communists, Sihanouk also sought economic and diplomatic help from China and France, who were sympathetic, but not able to offer any real protection to his government from either the insurgency or the pressure from the USA and South Vietnam.

Cambodia's economy, once strong and self-sufficient in food, began to suffer as harvests were drawn onto the black market and then into South Vietnam (Osborne 1973: 7), thereby depriving the government of revenue from export taxes and beginning to cause hardship through food shortages and price rises. Government spending, meanwhile, continued to grow (Corfield 1994: 30–6). By the mid 1960s, the country was spinning out of control.

In large part, Cambodia's increasing involvement in the Vietnam conflict was, in a fundamental sense, the cause of the country's problems. But it also appeared that Sihanouk was less focused on the country's internal affairs, to the extent that he often appeared out of touch with the day-to-day realities of life in his country. By the late 1960s, the Cambodian communist movement, which had, until then, almost disappeared, regrouped under Vietnamese guidance; the movement was led by Saloth Sar, who, fearing persecution, had fled Phnom Penh for the jungle in 1963 (Chandler 1992: 64–7, 1994: 4). After 1976, Saloth Sar became better known by his *nom de guerre*, Pol Pot.

The mid 1960s had seen the leftist anti-government movement quieten, primarily in response to the Vietnamese communists' agreement not to destabilise Cambodia in exchange for access to Cambodian territory and Sihanouk's logistical support. But pressure from Cambodia's conservative element was mounting, making this policy increasingly difficult to sustain. In response to the US bombing campaign of North Vietnam, its landing of combat troops in South Vietnam on 8 March 1965 and, most importantly, continued air attacks within Cambodian territory, on 3 May 1965, Cambodia severed diplomatic relations with the USA. In an attempt to counter pressure from the right, Sihanouk decreed that, for the 1966 elections, the electoral process would only play a part in designating candidates for the Sangkum (Assembly) and that he would also participate in choosing candidates. After deciding that, while the Right was troublesome, his main threat came from the Left, Sihanouk moved to bolster the Right, increasing its numbers in the Sangkum. But, rather than placate the Right, their ascendancy in the Assembly only enhanced their already developing ambitions for political control.

Despite his friendly actions towards North Vietnam and covert material support for Vietnamese guerrillas operating from Cambodia, by 1967, Sihanouk was losing control of his government's operations against Vietnamese and Cambodian communists operating on Cambodian territory. As a result, conflict reemerged between the Cambodian communists, by now popularly known as the Khmer Rouge, and the government. From around this time, Sihanouk tried to mend relations with the USA, but it appears that the decision to reject Sihanouk and to widen the Vietnam conflict to include Cambodia had already been taken in Washington (Corfield 1994: 53–79; Caldwell & Tan 1973: 177–91; see also, Norodom Sihanouk 1973).

At this time there were also signs of reemerging hostility between groups of Cambodian communist rebels and Vietnamese belonging to both the Democratic Republic of Vietnam and the National Liberation Front (NLF) of the South (see Kiernan 1985: 73–6, 87). Disputes between the Cambodian and Vietnamese communists ranged over a number of issues, including the Vietnamese approach of first winning the conflict in Vietnam and then pursuing the struggle in Cambodia and of wishing to generally retain friendly relations with Sihanouk for strategic reasons. Each also perceived themselves to be at differing stages of political development[5] and having varying responses to and support from the Chinese Communist

Party (Kiernan 1985). But probably most important in the distinctions between the Cambodian and Vietnamese communist guerrillas was the age-old antipathy of the Cambodians towards the Vietnamese, which, frequently for alleged allies, spilled over into conflict between units of the two groups.

A COUP, A REPUBLIC AND AN ESCALATING WAR

After more than two years of crossborder incursions to attack guerrillas at their bases and in a bid to disrupt DRV military supply lines into South Vietnam (Kiernan 1985: 285–6, 306, 307), on 17 March 1969 the USA began the first of its many secret bombing raids along the Vietnam–Cambodia border. The bombing raids had three consequences: the first was to further destabilise Sihanouk, the second to push Cambodian and Vietnamese fighters further into Cambodian territory and the third, to bolster popular support for the Khmer Rouge. By this stage, with support from the USA, and given Sihanouk's inability to control events at home, real power in Cambodia had passed from Sihanouk to Defence Minister General Lon Nol and the conservative Prince Sirik Matak. Responding to the developing situation and formalising what was already in practice the case, in 1970 a bloodless, pro-American coup removed Sihanouk from power while he was in France for medical treatment. Sihanouk learned of the coup while on his way to Beijing, where he established his government-in-exile.

Sihanouk's successor was Lon Nol. Lon Nol's coup can be seen as being in support of US strategy in the region—it was widely believed to be strongly backed by the CIA and received immediate US support—but it was also an expression of a long-standing tussle between Sihanouk, being both royalist and neutralist, and the successors to the conservative, republican Son Ngoc Thanh. The name of the state was changed to the Khmer Republic and the monarchy was abolished. Yet the Lon Nol government was riven from within by factional disputes and lurched from crisis to political crisis (Corfield 1994: 52–183).

With Sihanouk no longer leading the government, Cambodia's neutralism was ended and the country's communists could step up their anti-government activities without worsening the DRV's strategic position. This escalation of anti-government activity was taken under the guise of a new alliance between the Khmer Rouge and Sihanouk in exile. This alliance was known as the National United Front of Kampuchea (NUFK), although, in practice, it was dominated by the Khmer Rouge. Indeed, it now suited the DRV to have the Cambodian guerrillas actively engaged against their pro-American government. In this, DRV troops and their counterparts from the NLF, the Viet Cong (VC), were also actively engaged in military operations against the Cambodian government. These forces operated with Khmer Rouge troops, especially in the eastern provinces, as well as independently.

Also, the DRV and VC troops launched numerous campaigns from Cambodian territory into South Vietnam (for a more detailed discussion of DRV–NLF–Khmer Rouge relations, see Kiernan 1985: ch. 8).

For the USA, the war in Vietnam was still the main game, while conflict in Cambodia became what was widely referred to as a sideshow. Conflict between the Lon Nol government and the Khmer Rouge quickly developed into a full-scale civil war. By 1972, the Khmer Rouge fielded a force of 200 000 fighters and controlled almost half of the country, with the Lon Nol army being only a little larger (Kiernan 1985: 345). In response to this and, in particular, to the use of Cambodian territory by DRV and VC troops, the USA intensified its bombing campaign, especially in eastern Cambodia, where it disrupted civil society and plunged much of the country into famine and primitive conditions (Kiernan 1985: 349–57). Once a country well able to feed itself, Cambodia's government descended into reliance on US aid. Having been aided by the Vietnamese communists, which they resented[6] (Chandler 1992: 147–50), and with widespread rural support, the Khmer Rouge entered Phnom Penh and toppled Lon Nol on 17 April 1975.[7] The state was reinvented as Democratic Kampuchea[8] (Corfield 1994: 184–233).

CAMBODIA UNDER THE KHMER ROUGE

Inspired by a more purely agrarian version of Mao Zedong's collectivised Cultural Revolution and a sense of utopianism, and being progenitors of a peasant-based revolution without recourse to a modern or sufficiently literate bureaucracy or technology, the Khmer Rouge cleared the cities and began a campaign of producing food and manufactured surpluses (see Chandler, Kiernan & Boua 1988). The Khmer Rouge cut itself off from foreign assistance (except from China). Allied to its work campaigns, the consequences were horrendous; hundreds of thousands died from starvation and illnesses, the latter exacerbated by there being no doctors or medicine. Arbitrary violence had already become a trademark of the Khmer Rouge, as it had with other Cambodian political and military groups, with disobedience being judged as treason punishable by death[9] (see, for example, Kiernan 1985: 375–80, 384–93; Chandler 1992: 128–39). Members of Cambodia's small educated class were either killed in the period 1975–78 or fled.

Eventually, the Khmer Rouge began to turn on itself, in particular, the central group in Phnom Penh began turning on its members in the eastern zone who were believed to have been excessively influenced by Vietnam (Vickery, in Chandler & Kiernan 1983: 128–30, 1985: 330–7; Kiernan 1993: 192). As the Khmer Rouge program of producing surpluses led to economic failure, tens of thousands more who questioned the policy direction were purged from the party ranks and murdered (Kiernan 1985: 392). As the purges began to take hold, Khmer Rouge soldiers and commanders in the east began to desert, fleeing across the border into Vietnam (Kiernan, in Chandler & Kiernan 1983: 136–211). Cambodia's total death toll between April 1975 and December 1978–January 1979—from disease, starvation and murder—is variously estimated at up to two million from a population of six million. It was, both proportionately and in absolute terms, one of the worst genocides in modern history (Kiernan 1996).

In 1978, for reasons that had to do with historical animosity, ideological conflict, probably to divert attention from internal problems (Kiernan 1985: 393) and possibly the sanity of its leadership, the Khmer Rouge launched a series of border attacks against the recently unified and battle-hardened Vietnam. The border disputes, begun in 1975, were over Vietnamese claims to islands in the Gulf of Thailand, which had been formalised by the French during the colonial period. These claims were not accepted by Cambodia and, under the Khmer Rouge, there were now moves to have the islands returned (Chanda 1986: 12–13). There was also the lingering animosity over that part of southeastern Cambodia that had been incorporated into Vietnam some 200–400 years before. So much a part of the Khmer nation was this region of Khmer Krom, that it was considered normal by the Khmer Rouge that Brother Number Two, Ieng Sary, was born not in Cambodia, but in this Vietnamese-occupied territory. Similarly, ethnic Vietnamese living in Cambodia were increasingly persecuted, with large numbers being killed from 1975 until the Khmer Rouge was effectively finished as a military force in much of the country in 1979.

VIETNAM'S OCCUPATION

In December 1978, fronted by members of the Khmer Rouge who had escaped across the eastern border, the Vietnamese army struck hard and fast, within days pushing the Khmer Rouge to the western edges of Cambodia and into Thailand (Chandler 1992: 150–68; see also, Evans & Rowley 1990: 85–126). Vietnam installed a former Khmer Rouge officer, Heng Samrin, as president and head of the Kampuchean People's Revolutionary Party, later renamed the Cambodian People's Party, while its army, supported by the Soviet Union, formally occupied the country until 1989. Cambodia was again renamed, this time as the People's Republic of Kampuchea.

Heng Samrin joined the revolutionary movement in 1959 in the southeastern province of Svay Rieng[10] and was engaged in anti-government activity from that time. Heng Samrin was no doubt close to his Vietnamese allies and was among those who the central Khmer Rouge had attempted to purge in the late 1970s. Heng Samrin's protégé was a young officer by the name of Hun Sen, who first engaged in revolutionary activity as a student, but who fled to the guerrilla movement during a crackdown in 1967. He returned to Cambodia with the Vietnamese forces and was appointed foreign minister in 1979, becoming prime minister in 1985. Heng Samrin and Hun Sen were graduates of Vietnamese military training and the fighters in their zone were regarded as the most successful within the Khmer Rouge (Kiernan 1985: 310–12).

The period of Vietnamese occupation was characterised by a coalition in opposition to Cambodia's new pro-Vietnamese government and the Vietnamese occupation forces. The dominant group in the coalition was the Khmer Rouge, who operated from the hills and border regions in the northwest and west of Cambodia. Another group, based on Lon Nol's republican government and under the leadership of Son Sann, also participated in the coalition, but explicitly identified themselves as non-communist. A third group, loyal to Sihanouk and later to form the basis of the royalist FUNCINPEC, also participated in the coalition against the Phnom Penh-based government. This coalition styled itself the Coalition Government of Democratic Kampuchea (CGDK) (see Kiernan 1985: 32–3). The CGDK received most of its support from China, but some also came from the USA and Thailand.

Throughout the 1980s, a pattern emerged of wet season CGDK attacks against the Vietnamese and the PRK government and dry season offensives by the Phnom Penh government's forces and the Vietnamese army. Although the government and Vietnamese forces tended to dominate, much of the west and northwest of the country was under the control of the CGDK; guerrilla activity made much of the rest of the country unsafe. Refugees streamed to the Thai border, paddies were left fallow and mines were planted so extensively that large sections of the country, especially in the west, were unable to be used for any purpose at all. In a move that was designed to pressure Vietnam into leaving Cambodia, the UN recognised the CGDK. Technically, Pol Pot resigned the leadership of the Khmer Rouge in 1979 and disbanded the Khmer Rouge as a communist party in 1981; however, the Khmer Rouge retained its organisational structure and Pol Pot remained as its actual leader until shortly before his death in early 1998.

In light of its own economic difficulties, Soviet support for Vietnam began to decrease from 1985–86 and Vietnam was tiring of supporting an army in Cambodia when it was more interested in its own national development. From the early 1980s and, more noticeably, towards the end of the 1980s, Vietnam began a staged withdrawal from Cambodia, with the intention of Cambodianising the ongoing civil war (Kiernan 1993: 192–4). Sensing the opportunity to press home the military advantage that Vietnam's withdrawal offered the CGDK, the attacks on the Phnom Penh government forces intensified after Vietnamese troops withdrew from Cambodia formally in September 1989 (Kiernan 1993: 209–19). To help relieve the Phnom Penh government's embattled army, special Vietnamese forces were employed in 1990 and 1991, but their presence was temporary and all Vietnamese forces and advisers were permanently withdrawn in 1991.

THE UN AND ELECTIONS

With the withdrawal of Vietnam, the way was clear for the UN to work towards a resolution of the Cambodian conflict. Until Vietnam had withdrawn, the UN was diplomatically restricted from working in Cambodia and in any case was unlikely to have been receptive to a request for such intervention.

Moving towards an internationally brokered settlement, in 1990 the four parties to the conflict formed the Supreme National Council (SNC). Sihanouk was invited to return as its head, although, as the SNC failed to exist in a real sense he did not do so at that time. Events moved towards a resolution and, on 23 October 1991, the parties to Cambodia's conflict signed the Paris Peace Accord to form an interim coalition government to rule, ahead of national elections. One important aspect of this agreement was that it ended external support for the various parties to conflict in Cambodia, forcing most of the combatants to seek a genuine settlement (Kiernan 1993: 220–31).

To ensure that elections went ahead as planned, the UN established the UN Transitional Authority in Cambodia (UNTAC), its largest ever peacekeeping operation. This authority oversaw the establishment of the interim coalition government and monitored the ceasefire, started to regroup armed units of the different parties and disarm them, repatriated 300 000 refugees from the Thai border and organised general elections (Berry 1997). While the Khmer Rouge was a signatory to the Paris Accord, it refused to comply with its conditions, including regrouping in specified areas and disarming. It later also refused to participate in the elections, although its attempts to cause disruption were unsuccessful (Kiernan 1993: 232–46; Chanda 1986: 386–9).

With twenty political parties registered, elections were held in May 1993. For a country that had never previously experienced genuinely free elections,[11] the UN-supervised elections were a remarkable achievement, with a voter turnout in excess of 90 per cent. Some irregularities were reported, but, on balance, they were so minor as to not bring into dispute the outcome of the elections.

FUNCINPEC gained enough votes to make it the single biggest party, but did not achieve the two-thirds of seats in the Constituent Assembly[12] as required under the Paris Peace Accord. Even though it held more seats than any other party, it failed to assert the political power that would ordinarily be assumed to be its due on the basis of the elections as a consequence of the CPP's continued entrenchment in the institutions of state. The failure of any party to secure a two-thirds majority of the assembly led to killings and threats by elements of the CPP, who failed to accept their reduced position. But with a political stalemate, Sihanouk, who, from 24 September 1993 again assumed the dual status of king and head of state, pressured FUNCINPEC into joining a coalition with the CPP. In September 1993, with little reference to the Constituent Assembly, a power-sharing coalition of FUNCINPEC and the CPP, embracing the principles of constitutional monarchy and, at least nominally, liberal democracy, was formed. Sihanouk had agreed to stay outside the fray of day-to-day politics, so his son, Prince Norodom Ranariddh, as head of the royalist FUNCINPEC, became First Prime Minister and Hun Sen was appointed to a theoretically junior role as Second Prime Minister. The cabinet contained sixty-seven posts that were distributed among sixty-five individuals, thirty-three of them CPP members, while Hun Sen was, in practice, the more powerful of the two prime ministers.

STATE STRUCTURES

On the face of it, Cambodia had a formal political process that should have ensured the relatively smooth running of the state. The state was now established as a constitutional monarchy with the king as head of state, but without the ability to exercise any executive authority. During the king's absence or incapacitation, the chairman of the National Assembly, which was then a unicameral parliament, the CPP's Chea Sim, acted as head of state. The National Assembly itself comprised 120 members elected from twenty-one provinces, with a Council of Ministers (cabinet) formed by the government. In a practical sense, the two-thirds of seats required for forming government under the new Constitution meant that virtually all elected governments would be coalitions.

At a provincial level, where most Cambodians lived, local governors preside over provincial governments. Provincial governors and chiefs of districts were appointed by the First Prime Minister using a quota system. Chiefs of communes and village headmen were directly elected by their constituency.

Cambodia's judicial system, formalised at that time, was based on three tiers: the regular court, the Appeals Court and a Supreme Court. Judges were to be appointed, promoted and dismissed by a Supreme Council of the magistracy, consisting of a representative of the minister of justice, the president of the Supreme Court, the president of the Appeals Court and three elected judges, each with a five-year mandate. The council was chaired by the king, but was widely seen as politically compromised. A Constitutional council was intended to interpret the Constitution and laws passed by the National Assembly; after it was formed in July 1998, it comprised of nine members who have a nine-year mandate. Three of the members were to be appointed by the king, three by the National Assembly and three by the Supreme Council of the Magistracy.

Despite the theoretical separation of powers between the executive and the judiciary, the 'courts are subject to influence by the executive, and there is widespread corruption among judges, virtually none of whom receive a living wage' (US Department of State 1999a; An 2002). The composition of the courts was also widely regarded as favourable to the CPP, while the courts also require ministry of justice and other relevant departmental permission to prosecute civil servants, including members of the police force. A culture of impunity was thus allowed to flourish in Cambodia, especially among government officials. Police and soldiers, for example, were implicated in a spate of kidnappings in 1999 and 2000, while Hun Sen's wife, Bun Rany, was alleged to have ordered the killing in 1999 of Hun Sen's lover, the dancer Piseth Pilika. Both Hun Sen and his wife rejected the allegations and charges against Bun Rany were not laid.

In 2000, Hun Sen acted against 'corrupt and incompetent' members of the judiciary, 'responding in part to critics who said that Cambodia was incapable of mounting a fair and credible trial of the surviving Khmer Rouge leadership without UN participation' (Faulder 2000).

THE POLITICAL SYSTEM IN ACTION

For the first two or three years after the 1993 establishment of the Coalition government, political processes in Cambodia ran relatively smoothly, but before too long, the potential for long-term political stability in Cambodia was upset. With two prime ministers from two parties, neither of which trusted the other, there were, in effect, two bureaucracies running the government, which was expensive and unwieldy and led to considerable administrative friction and, consequently, instability.

As a political exercise, this arrangement enabled the establishment of a coalition sufficiently divergent that most Cambodian people were formally represented, thereby ensuring the coalition's de facto political legitimacy, which in turn, allowed it to begin the arduous task of rebuilding Cambodia's shattered economy and civic infrastructure. The Khmer Rouge chose to remain outside the coalition, but would probably not have been accepted into its existing form by the CPP in any case, given its history of atrocities in the period 1975–78. The situation in which the Khmer Rouge stayed outside the government caused two problems, one internal, the other external. The internal problem was that the CPP's unwillingness to incorporate the Khmer Rouge into the new political process—a situation exacerbated by the Khmer Rouge's own intransigence—led to conflict between Hun Sen and the Khmer Rouge's erstwhile partner, Norodom Ranariddh. The problem that was external to the government, but that deeply concerned it, was that, after 1993, the Khmer Rouge, under Pol Pot and Ta Mok, launched a new insurrection against the government.

In reality, Hun Sen was never going to genuinely share power with Ranariddh, a former colleague of Pol Pot, which events came to prove. There were initial attempts at doing so, but Hun Sen harboured too much suspicion of Ranariddh to want to allow him to exercise real, independent power. Further, Ranariddh's capacity as a leader was in some doubt, a fact acknowledged even by senior members of his own party.[13]

Beyond this, with the state relatively secure and operating under a moderately stable government, with China and Thailand agreeing to no longer support the Khmer Rouge[14] and with offers of amnesties by the government, the guerrilla organisation began to disintegrate. The disintegration of the Khmer Rouge was not in itself a problem. What was problematic was how units of Khmer Rouge soldiers were courted by FUNCINPEC and the CPP. The timing of the disintegration of the Khmer Rouge approximated and, to a large extent, was a contributing factor in, the deterioration of relations between CPP and FUNCINPEC functionaries in the coalition government, as well as between Hun Sen and Ranariddh. With the CPP tainted by its association with the traditional enemy, Vietnam, and FUNCINPEC similarly afflicted by association with the Khmer Rouge, both sides continued to genuinely believe that the other had been a traitor to the nation's cause.

THE DEATH THROES OF THE KHMER ROUGE

The edges of the Khmer Rouge had been breaking away for some time, but the pace of disintegration accelerated in 1996 and into 1997. The most significant blow came in 1996, when the Khmer Rouge's second-in-command (and Pol Pot's brother-in-law), Ieng Sary, defected to the government with 10 000 troops. Ieng Sary already occupied Pailin in the west of Cambodia and troops under his command had clashed with troops under the command of Pol Pot and Ta Mok. In exchange for his defection, Ieng Sary was given effective warlord control over Pailin. The disintegration of the Khmer Rouge was compounded by its structure as an organisation of quasi-autonomous groups led by regional warlords. As the strategic situation of the remaining Khmer Rouge became more desperate, the various groups began to act more independently. It was only a matter of time before individual leaders began to make their own deals with the government (Thayer 1998a).

The disintegration of the Khmer Rouge was played out in the idiosyncratic style of that notorious organisation. In March 1997, upon learning that fighters had entered into negotiations with Ranariddh in order to defect, Pol Pot ordered one of their leaders executed—his long-time friend and defence minister, Son Sen and his wife, nine children, and three other family members (Schanberg 1997). By this stage, Pol Pot was clearly losing control of the organisation; in a bid to save themselves, the remaining senior leadership arrested Pol Pot. He was put through a show trial for the killings and sentenced to life imprisonment. This split at the most senior levels of the Khmer Rouge led to rebellion within the ranks, with the Khmer Rouge's senior military leader, Ta Mok, taking Pol Pot and several hundred loyal soldiers as his prisoners and marching them further into the jungles of Anlong Veng in Cambodia's northwest. By April 1998, Ta Mok suggested that he could hand over Pol Pot in exchange for his own freedom. But on 15 April 1998, Pol Pot, who had long been sick,[15] died (Thayer 1998b). No autopsy was carried out, so no one knows whether he died of heart failure, as claimed, whether he committed suicide before being handed over to government authorities or whether, the proposed exchange for freedom deal being rejected, Ta Mok decided that Pol Pot had outlived his usefulness and killed him.

The rest of the Khmer Rouge leadership followed the remaining members by taking up government offers of amnesty or, in rare cases where they did not surrender, being captured (or handed over). In December 1998, Nuon Chea and Khieu Samphan, former Kampuchean head of state from 1975 until 1979, returned to Cambodia from Thailand[16] and were, in the interim, granted an effective amnesty, despite widespread calls within and without Cambodia for a trial to account for their involvement in Cambodia's killings. People on the street were saying they wanted the former Khmer Rouge leaders to be tried, even if it meant re-opening the old conflict. 'I want peace,' said one young Cambodian who had been a small child when he and his family were sent to the fields in 1975. 'But I also want justice. Without justice there is no real peace.' Nuon Chea was later identified by Deuch, the former chief of the S-21 (Tuol Sleng) interrogation centre in Phnom Penh, as being primarily responsible for the vast numbers of killings conducted at the prison (Camnews 1999). To the Cambodian people, Hun Sen said that a trial could re-open the now ended conflict with the remaining Khmer Rouge. The pair and their families then left Phnom Penh for Ieng Sary's stronghold of Pailin.[17] Around 2000 troops loyal to Ta Mok formally joined the Royal Cambodian Army in February 1999; just a few days later, Ta Mok was arrested near the Thai border, his Thai hosts apparently having handed him over to Cambodian authorities. By 2004, the general prosecutor had begun proceedings so that the two, along with Ieng Sary, would eventually face charges in relation to killings during the Khmer Rouge era.

THE 1997 COUP

As the Khmer Rouge's regional groups began to surrender, FUNCINPEC and the CPP saw the opportunity to bolster their own forces with new, ex-Khmer Rouge recruits.[18] The scramble to secure these recruits created a sense of insecurity that led, in July 1997, to an armed showdown between CPP and FUNCINPEC forces in Phnom Penh. This brief conflict between the two groups saw both sides trying to settle old scores. With the CPP clearly having the upper hand, the outcome was dubbed by some observers as a coup on the basis that Ranariddh had been First Prime Minister. The death toll from the conflict exceeded 100; Ranariddh and his key supporters fled the capital, either for overseas or to the hills of the northwest. More than 60 000 other Cambodians also fled for the border areas near Thailand.

This event appeared to horrify the international community,[19] which had invested so much in the peace agreement of 1993, and consequently led to Cambodia losing its seat in the UN and being cut off from multilateral and some bilateral aid. This loss of income plunged the country into economic crisis (Boyce 1998) at about the same time as a differently inspired economic crisis was hitting the rest of SEA and challenged the viability of the now CPP-dominated government. To overcome Cambodia's international credibility problem and to help restore aid flows, Hun Sen, acknowledging that they were due in any case, announced that elections would be held in July 1998. Initially, FUNCINPEC and the Sam Rainsy Party[20] said they would not contest the elections, primarily because the lead time was too short for them to adequately organise. However, Hun Sen countered by saying that, if he postponed the elections, the international community would not believe that he seriously intended them to go ahead. The opposition groups eventually relented and thirty-nine parties contested the polls in an atmosphere of intimidation and occasional violence.

With control over the electoral system and its domination of political life at the village level where the vast majority of Cambodians live, the CPP won a little more than half of the total vote. FUNCINPEC won the next biggest percentage. The CPP-dominated police in the provinces were active in removing signs for FUNCINPEC and the Sam Rainsy Party, which caused considerable concern. The government claimed that it did not direct such action, but the other parties claimed this followed direct government policy to use its institutional force to hamper the political process. More positively, the former Khmer Rouge bases were included in the political process and the Khmer Rouge was finally, formally finished. More negatively, Khmer Rouge remnants retained their warlord status in the provinces and, while the electoral process took place in these areas, it did so under the watchful eye and doubtful impartiality of the Khmer Rouge forces newly integrated into the CPP.

THE 1998 GOVERNMENT

International observers announced that the 1998 elections were a 'valid reflection of popular will', without going so far as to say they were free and fair. In November 1998, FUNCINPEC agreed to form a coalition government with the CPP, after much complaint about the fairness of the electoral process and under pressure from Sihanouk to resolve their differences for the sake of the country. In this government, Hun Sen became prime minister, Ranariddh took the powerful position of speaker of the Assembly, and ministries were distributed between CPP and FUNCINPEC members, with the CPP holding a slight advantage. As a compromise and to placate political functionaries who had lost out in the election, there was also an agreement to establish a Senate, to be headed by Chea Sim. As an inducement to join the CPP in the coalition government, FUNCINPEC had the physical security of its members against CPP attack guaranteed. The coalition secured for Cambodia's government its seat in the UN and began to see a return of multilateral aid. The CPP's clear dominance of the new government and the formal absence of the Khmer Rouge provided a higher level of potential stability than did the 1993 coalition government.

POVERTY

Cambodia is a poor country. The potential for it to provide for its own basic material needs has been well established and is reflected in the fact that the agricultural sector still accounts for almost half of total economic output, about 85 per cent of employment and more than 90 per cent of exports. But the turmoil and destruction that has been a legacy of the three decades to the end of the twentieth century reduced most of the population to economic levels below that of their neighbours to the east and the west. Per capita income pre 2002 was just US$321 a year, with the vast majority of the population, 80 per cent of them living in the countryside, subsisting at a much lower level than this. Absolute poverty was estimated, in 2002, to be at around 36 per cent of the population, with 34 per cent living on less than US$1 a day and 78 per cent living on less than US$2 a day (UNDP HDR 2004). Until 1996, Cambodia's macroeconomic performance had started to improve, especially in relation to its pre-1993 levels,[21] however, the violence and looting associated with the ousting of Prince Norodom Ranariddh and his supporters from the coalition government by the CPP in July 1997 led to a rapid decline in Cambodia's economic fortunes. Growth was down to zero while inflation, projected to be 5 per cent, was over 15 per cent. More importantly, though, about US$100 million in foreign aid and IMF representation was suspended, along with Cambodia's seat at the UN. By 2004, inflation was back to a tolerable 7 per cent (Cambodia National Institute for Statistics 2004), while growth was just above 4 per cent (UNDP HDR 2004).

Beyond the domestic political impact on the economy, the loss of its Eastern Bloc trading partners, a gap that was not filled by Western investors, and the economic crisis in Thailand in 1997–98, further hampered Cambodia's trade and investment. Having noted that, the country's black economy operated probably more strongly than ever during this period, indicating a weakness of the state to control internal markets and foreign exports and the limitation of its ability to raise taxes for urgent infrastructure projects. The profitable gem mining and timber exporting fiefdom around the former Khmer Rouge stronghold of Pailin (Puy 1998) in western Battambang province near the Thai border was indicative of the central government's inability to adequately exercise control over the state.[22]

Yet, if Cambodia is materially poor, based on anecdotal evidence and voter registration figures in 1998, there seemed to be a level of political consciousness that was most unusual for a developing country. Certainly, the population was directly affected by overt political developments from the late 1960s onwards, but the 1990s brought to Cambodia a realisation that some sort of representative political process was achievable, in theory at least, and that all Cambodians could and should take an active role in the political process. This active political life has been manifested in the plethora of political parties that have sprung up since the 1993 UN-brokered elections. By the time of the 1998 elections, the arrangement of those parties might have changed, but there appeared to be at least as strong a commitment to the electoral process by the people, if not by the country's political leaders. This appeared to also be the case in 2003, even if potential new voter registration was down by about one-third on expectations.

HUN SEN AND THE CPP

The Cambodian People's Party, increasingly dominated by the person of Hun Sen, directly controlled not just the party of the government, but also the administration of government. In many cases, there was no distinction between the party of the government and the institutions of the state, which meant that an impartial political process was impossible. It also meant that the government could use the organs of state to facilitate the electoral process to its own advantage. Yet even with such a massive advantage in all forms of official life, the high rate of voter turnout in the 1993 elections and the seemingly high level of political awareness in 1998 and into the 2003 elections meant that Hun Sen and the CPP were far from the favourite choice for most voters.

Within the CPP, there was growing disillusionment with Hun Sen's personalisation of power—Hun Sen primary schools, the Hun Sen Park in Phnom Penh, even Hun Sen's initials, in Khmer, printed opposite the CPP logo on electioneering T-shirts. Hun Sen's wife, too, had increasingly taking on the role of public benefactor, appearing at official functions as a powerful person in her own right. Hun Sen derived much of his personal power from manipulating the CPP, disposing of his enemies—figuratively and sometimes literally—and promoting his supporters. Supporters were looked after through a patronage system, by which they were rewarded with positions of power and the potential for corruption. The party itself continued to be funded by Chinese-owned businesses, which arranged lucrative logging and other contracts, the proceeds from which were directed towards the party and individuals, rather than towards the state. There was also reported to be a high level of official or military support for the transhipment of heroin from Burma and Laos through Cambodia to its sea port at Kampong Som and to the islands close to the Thai border.

The lack of official accountability that accompanied this situation reflected what was probably close to a genuine perception that the state and the party were, in effect, one and the same, and that the party was exemplified by its leader. In this way, traditional streams of patronage and favour have come to replace even nominally accountable government. The Leninist structure of the CPP, inherited from Vietnam and, in turn, from the former Soviet Union, placed primary political responsibility in the hands of the party's vanguard. The logic of this process is that, as the pyramid of power narrows towards the top, power is concentrated in the hands of an individual leader. In other Leninist systems this has given rise to the cult of personality, such as of Lenin, Stalin, Mao Zedong, Ho Chi Minh, Fidel Castro and various lesser political lights. As it happens, this concentration of power fits neatly into traditional Cambodian conceptions of power, which is concentrated at the exemplary centre of the political mandala. In this sense, Hun Sen brought together the logic of the traditional with the modern and, in doing so, managed to largely sidestep popular accountability. The processes of democracy, for Hun Sen, remained superficial. By way of illustration, just after the 2003 elections, but well before he had managed to form a two-thirds majority government, Hun Sen told his detractors that he would remain in power regardless of not having sufficient support to form a government (AFP, 1 September 2003).

Dissent within the party was muted by the Vietnamese party's insistence that the CPP not divide,[23] that party loyalty is more important than the niceties of decision making by committee and by Hun Sen's personal military following. His personal bodyguard and officers loyal directly to him, as well as the troops they command, easily comprised the single most powerful force in the country, and most Cambodians recognised the efficacy, if not the legitimacy, of rule through the exercise of military power. Formal education may still be quite limited in Cambodia, but practical political education is well entrenched. There may be groups or individuals who also command some military loyalty, but this, at best, is only a defensive measure against the omnipresent Hun Sen military group.

THE PRINCE AND HIS PARTY

Prince Ranariddh, on the other hand, was an ineffectual political leader. He insisted on being solely responsible for decision making within FUNCINPEC, but was not capable of running such a political organisation single-handedly. Of numerous factions that comprised FUNCINPEC, few regarded Ranariddh as the best, even most desirable, political leader. However, Ranariddh was able to draw on his status as the son of the king. Beyond the urban areas where CPP control was more muted, in a countryside that still venerates the king as almost god-like, Ranariddh still attracted considerable popular support, despite a sometimes oppressive CPP presence.

FUNCINPEC factions, however, were comprised of individuals who, as associates of royalty, by and large preferred not to mix with the peasants at village level. This fundamentally compromised FUNCINPEC's ability to function outside the urban areas, themselves almost entirely comprised of people who, until 1978–79, had no urban experience; Phnom Penh is populated mostly by ex-country folk. Added to still appallingly low levels of education and a lack of professionalism at senior levels of government, Cambodia was caught in a situation where collapse and turmoil were just a step away. The international community, which had a high presence in, and impact on, Cambodia, remained, largely through historical guilt and a sense of needing to resolve a site of former conflict between superpowers and external interests—the USA, the USSR and China, together with Vietnam, Thailand and France.

THE 2003 ELECTIONS

In what was widely regarded by electoral observers as a flawed process, Cambodia went to the polls in July 2003 amid problems with voter registration, intimidation and violence. In particular, ten political activists had been murdered since the local (commune) elections of February 2002, which, amid allegations of violence and vote-buying, gave the CPP 61 per cent of the vote.

Ahead of the 2003 elections, opposition groups claimed that, as well as violence and intimidation, they were also restricted in their access to broadcast and print media. According to the International Republican Institute (2003), the elections were, however, conducted in a peaceful and orderly environment and were said to have been an improvement on the ballots in 1998 and 1993. The 2003 election results delivered the CPP a little less than two-thirds of parliamentary seats, although FUNCINPEC and the SRP both claimed that the results had again been rigged through the state electoral bureaucracy (*Asia Times*, 30 August 2003). Both parties refused to join Hun Sen in government, which meant that the government could not pass legislation or initiate any new programs. However, under the Constitution, the CPP could remain in a caretaker role indefinitely, which Hun Sen decided was better than giving in to opposition calls and resigning. A waiting game ensued until, in June 2004, FUNCINPEC gave in and agreed to join the CPP in government in exchange for the CPP's original offer of 40 per cent of ministerial positions, having previously demanded an equal share. The newly functioning government was quickly able to begin passing stalled legislation, including Acts under which the Khmer Rouge trials could take place, Cambodia could join the World Trade Organisation and domestic violence could be legislated against. Cambodian politics had again assumed a familiar, if still troubled, pattern, but one in which the idea of sharing power—a prime criterion for eventual democratisation (Peou

2000: 427)—was becoming increasingly normalised. It appeared that while Hun Sen remained alive and active, he would attempt to remain in power by almost any means necessary. As other regional leaders had discovered, it was possible to achieve such outcomes even through a political system that nominally allowed all citizens an equal vote.

While violence tended to remain a lingering problem in Cambodian society and, in particular, continued to mar the country's political process, there was a sense that the country was continuing to move further along a path towards stability. Cambodia had never enjoyed a particularly peaceful existence, even in its good times, and authority had always been wielded without much regard for popular sentiment or equity of application. Despite Hun Sen's repeated promises to crack down on corrupt officials, corruption remained a major problem and much of Cambodia's business continued to be conducted under the counter or across the border.

But a better than usual rice harvest in 2004 satisfied many of the basic requirements of Cambodia's still largely rural population; even if material conditions were only improving slowly, at least they were improving. Political accountability and transparency were thought of as distant goals for many Cambodians, if they thought about such matters at all. But a pattern of elections had become established, the two-thirds requirement meaning that compromise had become a feature of Cambodian political life and legislative programs could sometimes be seen to reflect a wider set of norms and values, as well as having an eye to greater international engagement.

Meanwhile, the monarchy—that symbol of state only slightly less powerful than the magnificent site at Angkor—had made one of its most potentially difficult transitions in a manner that was remarkable for being unremarkable. Cambodia struggled into the twenty-first century carrying a burden of serious problems common to many underdeveloped states and quite a few that were specifically its own, but the worst of Cambodia's problems appear to be increasingly behind it.

NOTES

1   Early Khmer has the sinicised Funan as '*bnam*', or contemporary '*phnom*' (hill or mountain) (SarDesai 1997: 23). The state of Funan was linked to Javanese rulers, the later Javanese name '*Sailendra*' also meaning 'king of the mountain' (see also, McCloud 1995: 91).

2   The word '*nagara*' also corresponds closely with the Malay word '*negara*', meaning 'state', and probably reflects not just the Sanskritisation of Cambodia, but also the influence of the Javanese Sailendra Dynasty in the early days of Angkor.

3   The Vichy government of France was allied with Nazi Germany and, by association, with Japan.

4   Rather than being executed, Son Ngoc Thanh was exiled to France as a measured response to his popularity within Cambodia.

5   The Cambodian party tagged itself as 'communist', indicating what it regarded as its more complete political development towards the goal of communism, while the

Vietnamese party tagged itself a 'workers' party', indicating that it was still in the process of developing towards a communist goal. Central figures in the Cambodian party took this as a literal distinction between the two political organisations, marking themselves out as politically more developed or superior.

6   By 1973 the Khmer Rouge was attempting to drive out the Vietnamese communists (Kiernan 1985: 357).

7   Ieng Sary noted that Khmer Rouge and Vietnamese communists had clashed as early as 1972 (Kiernan 1985: 275).

8   It is perhaps a small distinction, but the state of Democratic Kampuchea was technically a new state, given that none of the institutions of the former state survived. However, it did occupy preexisting state boundaries and citizenship of one was transferred to citizenship of the other.

9   The Khmer Rouge had always had a relatively harsh policy towards dissidents and other enemies, but from 1973 began to actively execute prisoners of war and others deemed to be untrustworthy.

10 Svay Rieng is also sometimes known as 'the Parrot's Beak' for the way it protrudes into Vietnam to the northwest of Ho Chi Minh City. It was an area much influenced by the Viet Minh.

11 The elections of 1947 and 1951 were moderately free, but effectively meaningless, as France retained political control of the country.

12 The National Assembly was formed in September.

13 This is based on conversations with FUNCINPEC officials.

14 Although the Thai government had long denied such support, Ta Mok was known to have a house and business interests in the Thai provincial city of Surin. The last of the Khmer Rouge leaders did not leave (or were not expelled from) their bases in Thailand until early 1999.

15 It was widely believed that Pol Pot had malaria and perhaps other illnesses. However, while he was clearly enfeebled at this time, there is no evidence of any formal diagnosis.

16 The Thai government denied they had been living in Thailand, but they arrived in a Thai-registered car and, while younger members of their families could speak little Khmer, they appeared to speak Thai fluently (Agencies 1999).

17 At the beginning of 2000, it seemed that the pair would eventually be put on trial.

18 Attempts by the opposition leader and former FUNCINPEC member, Sam Rainsy, to take the high moral ground in the 1998 elections were compromised by his party also accepting Khmer Rouge members, in his case Colonel Chhuk Rin, the regional leader who was responsible for the kidnapping of three Western tourists from a train in 1994. Chhuk handed the three over to his superior, Nou Paet, who later had the tourists executed.

19 At least one element of that horror was presented as a means of asserting a sort of moral political standard, not against the coup, but against the CPP's Marxist background.

20 Not surprisingly, based around the person of former FUNCINPEC member, Sam Rainsy.

21 Almost US$2.3 billion had been pledged by the international community to Cambodia for the period 1992–95, though much of this was related to the UN-sponsored elections.

22 The area around Pailin was controlled by Ieng Sary, the Khmer Rouge's former second-in-command, until his defection, with his troops, to the CPP in 1997. The arrangement that secured his defection was that he would continue to run the region as quasi-independent, including its lucrative gem and timber exports to Thailand.

23 The VCP retains the status of elder brother to the CPP and is influential in the latter party's strategic affairs.

9 | Vietnam: The Little Dragon

History and culture can never be regarded as an excuse for transgressing the rights and dignities that apply to the human condition, and that applies to Vietnam, just as it does anywhere else. But history and culture can help explain why things are as they might be. In Vietnam, history and culture weigh heavily, even if the official ideology of the state would claim otherwise. Generally benign, but nonetheless stern, paternalistic neo-Confucianism plays out in the state, with the party structure and government reflecting the rote learning of principle combined with an element of meritocracy, blended with the politics of personal power and leavened with corruption. The historical lesson, painful as its memory continues to be, is never to let one's guard down, tempered by the fact that it is impossible to work while also assuming a conservatively combative posture.

If Vietnam has not yet embraced plural politics, it is because the grip of its Leninist old guard remains strong and, frankly, because there is a genuine fear that to let go will be to invite the return of the chaos and destruction that has left such scars as those that continue to disfigure the countryside and the minds of many of its people. But, similarly, power serves well those who wield it and the tendency over the past decade or so has been for more rather than fewer people to join the ruling party and take a small share of that authority. This may indicate political nepotism, but there is an oddly democratic quality to the idea of sharing power and its spoils by sharing political participation. Where this process fails is that not everyone is, or wants to become, a party member. However open the party is to joining, subscribing to a particular political vision should not be the principal criterion for material benefit or social advantage.[1]

In Vietnam, the prevailing political vision is not gentle with its outcasts. There is no effective distinction between political dissidents and criminals and the application of authority towards both is uncharitable. Here, there are echoes of sinicised influences, but, similarly, there is the even louder echo of colonial justice, both of which only go towards reinforcing

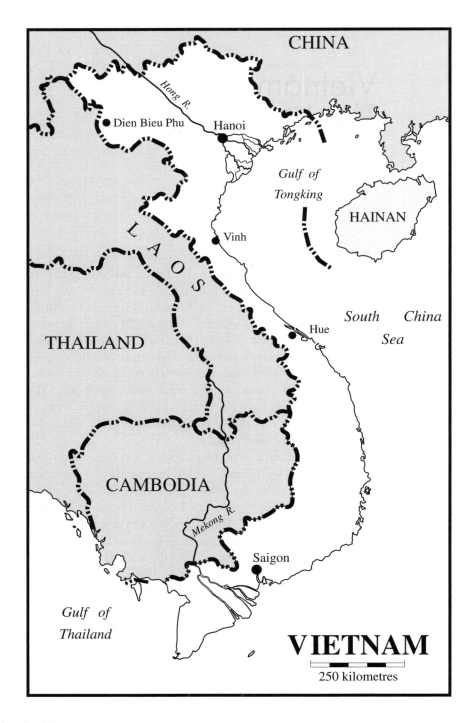

Map 6   Vietnam

patriotic duty, Leninist principles of authority and obedience and the all too human tendency to allow the exercise of power to be its own reward.

Seeing the Vietnamese border police in action, in what amounted to a minor border infraction, illustrated this point. The incident in question, which occurred not far from the border of Laos on Route 9, recalled those reinforcing messages that comprised the last major foreign intervention in Vietnamese domestic affairs. A small group of illegal border crossers—Vietnamese who had been illegally working in Thailand and who were travelling without the correct papers—were taken from a bus at the border to the old Lang Vei Special Forces Camp, which had once been one of a series of outposts established by the American military across the southern edge of the so-called demilitarised zone (DMZ). After the men were taken away, the bus they were on continued along Route 9 past some of the most infamous sites of the American war: Khe Sanh, Dakrong Bridge, the Rockpile, Ca Lu, Camp Carroll, Cam Lo, Con Thien, Dong Ha, Gio Linh and Cua Viet, just north of the Ashau Valley in which the first major engagement of the American war had taken place. All along here were extensive roadworks, part of an effort to provide a better link between Thailand and Laos and the port facility at Danang.[2]

The old imperial capital of Hue, by contrast, situated as it is alongside the Perfumed River and focused on the old citadel, which itself had been the scene of fierce fighting following the Tet Offensive of 1968, was a delight. Here there was a sense of the former colonial ambience in much of the architecture, while the streets were filled with bicycles and scooters, well-dressed people bustling to and fro—many women in the traditional *ao dai* (long dress),[3] a slit-sided dress worn over long, loose pants. Hue was perhaps not exactly indicative of life in Vietnam, as the road workers and many villagers elsewhere did not look so prosperous, but it had considerable charm and feel that had more to do with preserving local culture in the context of a developing economy than it did with a totalitarian, one-party state.

The army also features prominently in Vietnam, at least in roadworks and on television. The American War is now further away, but its legacy persists in many ways. The defoliated areas still struggle to regrow, unexploded ordnance still takes its toll on hapless people in the countryside and tourism, now a thriving industry, capitalises on tours of the major—and, in some cases, reinvented—sites of conflict. More importantly, the army has an honourable place in Vietnamese society. There is still quiet, though considerable, pride in the fact that the nation was able to defeat the might of the USA. With a longer-term view of history, there also remains a continuing sense that a viable defence force is necessary to protect the state against the dangers that could again threaten its existence, experience with Cambodia and China strengthening that view. Of course, having become so institutionalised, the bureaucracy that is the army no doubt wishes to perpetuate itself, but this does not take away from the fact that it has earned and continues to hold an important place in the life of the state.

ORIGINS OF THE STATE

Vietnam has the oldest continual history of any SEA state, being able to trace its lineage back more than 2000 years. Relics from the Neolithic period have been found, as have bronzes in the Red River delta region dating from the middle of the second millennium BCE (Nguyen 1993: 7–19). Legend has it that the first Vietnamese state of Van Lang, in the Red River delta region, existed from 2879 to 258 BCE, although reality rather than legend puts Van Lang, under the Hung Dynasty, as being established around 500 BCE. The overthrow of this kingdom by northerners and the merging of the states of Tay Au and Lac Viet, created the state of Au Lac in 258 BCE, which, although it only lasted fifty years, marked the beginning of a clearly defined Vietnamese history (Buttinger 1968: 19–20; Nguyen 1993: 16–18). The capital of Au Lac was about 20 kilometres from modern Hanoi.

It was from around this time, in the third century BCE, that the people of what is now northern Vietnam began overseas trade with China and parts of what was to become Indonesia. A regional Chinese official, Trieu Da, taking advantage of the collapse of the Ch'in Dynasty in 208 BCE, founded the state of Nam Viet, which included the Red River delta to almost the centre of the modern state and parts of southern China. The people of Nam Viet were Viets from the lower Yangtze valley, who increasingly mixed with the local Austronesian population, as reflected in the development of their language, which includes elements of monotonal Mon–Khmer and multitonal T'ai. The Chinese referred to these people as the Bach Viet (the Hundred Tribes), which consisted of a number of ethnic groups, including the Lac Viet, descendants of the Au Lac and Nam Viet groups. The state of Nam Viet lasted for almost 100 years, until the rise of the Han Dynasty in 111 BCE, which crushed the independent Nam Viet state and, apart from a few brief uprisings, ushered in more than 1000 years of Chinese rule. It was this period that left a lasting impression on Vietnamese culture and marked it as distinct from the cultures of its SEA neighbours.

It was from around or just before the Chinese occupation of the Red River delta region that a new, Malayo–Polynesian state began to develop near Hue in what is now central Vietnam, spreading to between approximately the 12th and 17th Parallels. This state was Lam Ap, a precursor to the Indianised state of Champa, which came to vie with Vietnam to the north for regional supremacy and remnants of which can still be found in this area of Vietnam, in central Cambodia and in southern Laos. The southern Lao state of Champassak[4] is the most obvious nominal reminder of the state of Champa, while a Cham community continues to live separately from their fellow countrymen in Cambodia.[5] The early Vietnamese state was expansionist and clashed repeatedly with its neighbours, especially Champa. But it also came into conflict with states further afield, including the T'ai state of Nan Chao in what is now Yunnan and with the Javanese and Malay states of the southern archipelago.

Following the Han invasion, distinctly Chinese characteristics inherited by the Vietnamese included the removal of the old, purely feudal system of social and economic relations and its replacement with a new bureaucratic and administrative structure based on education, a standardised written language and examinations. The ethos of Confucianism[6] became dominant and Chinese technical advances and agricultural methods were passed on to the Vietnamese. There were constant efforts on the part of the Chinese to sinicise the Vietnamese, who, indeed, readily adopted Chinese ideas. Early Vietnam had a political social system akin to China's, where it had 'the mandarinate; the examination system; and the moral precepts embodied in Confucianism. Absolute authority in principle emanated from the emperor, who held the mandate of heaven as the representative of divine power on earth, similar to the celestial sovereigns of China' (Jumper & Normand 1969: 377–8).

While Chinese organisational forms were being embedded, the Vietnamese also maintained—even strengthened—their own identity. In part, the reason for this was geographic: the coastal region of Vietnam was relatively separate from the mass of China. But it also seems that the Vietnamese had, even by the end of the Nam Viet state, more than 2000 years ago, established an assertive cultural identity that continues to the present day (Buttinger 1968: 26–9). It is claimed by at least some Vietnamese that they are a people adept at copying forms from other cultures and applying them even more rigorously than the original, but this same claim also posits that it is only the outward characteristics that are copied, while the driving force for adoption remains distinctly Vietnamese.

VIETNAM'S EARLY ASSERTION OF INDEPENDENCE

The first recorded revolt by the Vietnamese against China was in 39 CE. Although there had been progress of a type under Chinese rule, there was also widespread discontent among indigenous lords who saw their power disappearing, as well as among peasants over high levies imposed by resident Chinese bureaucrats. The occasion of the revolt was in response to the killing of a Vietnamese lord, intended as a warning by the Chinese to other Vietnamese lords. The lord's widow, Lady Trung Trac, and her sister led other lords and their vassals against Chinese forces guarding the governor's residence. The success of this attack led to the establishment of an independent state, but within two years the Chinese counterattacked and, rather than be captured, the two sisters committed suicide by drowning. The death of the two sisters marked the formal end of Vietnam's feudal system and the beginning of almost a millennium of Chinese political hegemony (Nguyen 1993: 25–6; Buttinger 1968: 30–2). Buttinger notes three characteristics of the new Chinese-created dominant class. As a consequence of acquiring land, it became semifeudal, it was semimandarinal, with officialdom being largely based on education, and it was culturally Chinese, despite a growing input from ethnic Vietnamese. 'Its culture was Chinese, and it kept on being replenished with Chinese appointees, many of them refugee intellectuals' (Buttinger 1968: 32).

The collapse of the Han Dynasty in 220 CE created a loosening of political control throughout the empire, including in the southernmost region. Vietnam, the state then being based on the Red River Valley, asserted its practical independence under its governor, Che Sie (187–226 CE). Che Sie paid tribute to China and, when the Han Dynasty formally dissolved, he paid tribute to the Wu, based in Nanjing in southern China. Upon Che Sie's death, his son attempted to assert his right of succession; however, the Wu decided against the succession, defeating Che Sie's son in battle, killing him and reasserting foreign control (Nguyen 1993: 25–9; Buttinger 1968: 32–3).

The next successful attempt at asserting independence came with Ly Bon, who, in 542 CE, briefly broke Chinese domination of Vietnam. Although a member of Vietnam's ethnic Chinese elite he, like others, had become Vietnamised. While the revolt he led was successful, it lasted little longer than that led by Trung Trac some half a millennium earlier. Clearly, political tension existed between Vietnam and China and Vietnam had a well-established national identity, but it was unable to assert its independence in any permanent way. One of the factors that militated against change was the wholesale adoption of Chinese agricultural techniques. With a Sino–Vietnamese elite and Chinese overlords benefiting from this system, social and political relations remained relatively static (Buttinger 1968: 35). It was to be more than 300 years before Vietnam's peasants felt sufficient disenchantment with this state of affairs to join with their local ruling class, in what was perceived as a shared cause, to again throw off Chinese political domination. In 939, after a series of bloody encounters, the Vietnamese finally pushed the Chinese armies out of the Red River Valley and secured the country's independence. With the exception of the period 1407–27, when China reasserted its authority, Vietnam remained an independent state until 1883.

The initial years of Vietnam's independence were less than secure and danger was omnipresent, yet, after an initial period of relative instability, Vietnam established an efficient system of government, united under a hereditary monarchy and administered by a central government. Between 1010 and 1400, Vietnam had only two dynasties, the Ly and the Tran, each lasting close to 200 years. Apart from continuing to ward off potential threats from the north and dealing with the corruption and decay to which hereditary rule is prone, Vietnam was also successful in fending off challenges from the south. The nearby Khmer empire for a time threatened to swallow the whole of mainland SEA. But, more immediately, the successor state of Lam Ap, Champa, jostled for control of the region; Vietnam relegated Champa to a tributary state in 1312. Within fourteen years, however, Champa had freed itself and, in 1371, invaded the Red River Valley, while ethnic T'ai insurrections, in particular in parts of what was to become Laos, further weakened the state. Yet, after having successfully resisted the Mongol armies of Kublai Khan, Vietnam succumbed in 1406–07 to attacks by a huge army under the Ming dynasty. This period under Ming rule was oppressive and exploitative in the extreme (Nguyen 1993: 30–63).

Led by Le Loi, a newly resurgent and more fully developed Vietnamese nationalism asserted itself during the ten-year struggle to end this Chinese interregnum, effectively completed by 1427, with the last Chinese garrison at Hanoi falling the following year. This victory over the Chinese cemented the notion of Vietnamese national unity. The Le dynasty, related to an earlier, brief, ruler, was thus founded, remaining in power for the next 350 years. It was under the Le that Vietnam expanded southwards, at the expense of Champa by 1471 and, eventually, also of parts of the decaying Khmer empire. Vietnam grew from an inverted geographic triangle centred on the Red River in the north to close to its current shape of 'two rice baskets on a pole'. In particular, the south grew quickly, providing land for the growing Vietnamese population and, by beginning to move into the Mekong Delta where swamps were replaced with rice paddies, supporting a new and growing primary economy.

The first 100 years of the Le dynasty was marked by generally strong government. But the following 250 years were marked by 'political ineptitude and moral debasement, feudal impertinence and usurpation of royal powers [often marked by political assassination], occasional vain efforts to secure economic stability by aiding the peasants, and bloody civil strife' (Buttinger 1968: 47). Civil war rent the country twice, once in the early 1500s and again from the late 1500s, ending in a 100-year truce between north and south. It was this period of separation between the two population centres and the minor cultural and linguistic differences that arose from this time that gave rise to some claimed legitimacy for the division of Vietnam from 1954 until 1975. Although the circumstances were entirely different, some sense of distinction between the two halves remained and was exacerbated by the later French influence. The civil conflict in the latter 1500s also saw, for the first time, European powers playing a role in regional affairs, first with the Portuguese siding with the ruling Nguyen in the south, from 1535.[7] In particular, Portuguese involvement in the south, which dominated Western trade with Vietnam, assisted with counterbalancing the competing northern and southern forces. From 1636, the Dutch sided with the Trinh in the north. The new and increasing source of strength to the south was its more complete expansion into the Mekong Delta, until then a part of Cambodia.[8] From 1680, another new European power had started to make itself known to Vietnam: France.

The Portuguese had initially attempted to convert the Vietnamese to Roman Catholicism, but, when their main protagonist, Frenchman Alexander of Rhodes, was barred from both the north and the south in 1630 after his Portuguese superiors failed to act decisively on the matter, he turned to France. Thus began the arrival of French priests in Vietnam, under the French-directed Society of Foreign Missions. Merchants followed soon after. What was usually low-level conflict between the Vietnamese administrators and priests continued and was later to provide a useful pretext for expanding French involvement. French interest in Vietnam was initially limited to religious proselytising with a little trade on the side, but the French soon had reason to expand their interests. The 1784 Treaty of Paris, which ended the American war of Independence, required France to cede most of its Indian territories. As a result, and still seeking bases en route to China, it developed a stronger interest in Vietnam, encouraged by the individual financial and colonial interests of soldiers and regional administrators (Buttinger 1968: ch. IV).

THE TAY SON REBELLION

From the late seventeenth to eighteenth centuries, the situation in the north remained chaotic. Rebellions were frequent and often only barely suppressed. Famines were common, exacerbating rural unrest, and populist leaders repeatedly challenged the authority of the Trinh rulers. The situation in the south was similar, but made even more parlous by near-constant warfare with the north and with Cambodia, into which the south was expanding. The effects of misrule in the south were, to some extent, alleviated by the opening up of the new lands in the Mekong Delta, but away from the delta, regional life was almost impossible (Nguyen 1993: 97). In 1771, in the village of Tay Son in the north of the southern part of Vietnam, three brothers launched an insurgency that quickly spread to other provinces.

The three brothers, Nguyen[9] Nhac, Nguyen Hue and Nguyen Lu, presented themselves as defenders of peasants, but soon gained the support of wealthier merchants. In 1775, with the Nguyen lords on the defensive, the Tay Son rebels—Nhac, Hue and Lu—joined with the Trinh rulers from the north to defeat the remainder of the Nguyen army. Victory in the south was completed in 1776, with only one Nguyen prince, sixteen-year-old Nguyen Anh, managing to escape to the western area of the Mekong Delta, where he proclaimed himself King of Cochin China and harassed the new Tay Son rulers. In 1778, Nguyen Nhac proclaimed himself king, establishing his capital at Do Ban in Binh Dinh province. Nguyen Anh attacked, but was eventually pushed back by Nguyen Hue. Nguyen Anh then called on the Thai monarch for assistance, who sent him 20 000 soldiers and 300 vessels.

In 1784, in support of Nguyen Anh, the Thai army invaded the western part of the Mekong Delta, but was ambushed on the My Tho River by Tay Son forces under Nguyen Hue. Nguyen Anh managed to escape the Thai defeat by being rescued by the Bishop of Adran, Pigneau de Behaine, whom he asked for assistance in restoring him to the throne. Events in France precluded immediate assistance, but French interest was aroused.

The Trinh rulers in the north had, by this time, decided to move against the Tay Son Nguyen. Riding high on success against Nguyen Anh and the Thais, the Tay Son turned against the Trinh. At this time, the Trinh court was in crisis, with factions competing for power. Under Nguyen Hue, the Tay Son forces quickly marched from Hue to Hanoi in a 'brief but brilliant campaign' (Buttinger 1968: 71).

Nguyen Hue placed a Le descendant, Le Chieu Thong, on the throne of Hanoi. But Chieu Thong schemed against the Tay Son, was found out, and called on assistance from China. In 1788, the Qing ruler, Kien-lung, sent a force of 200 000 to reconquer Vietnam. The Tay Son Nguyen brothers divided Vietnam into three: Cochin China in the south, Annam in the centre and Tonkin in the north, with Nguyen Hue proclaiming himself king in Hanoi under the name Quang Trung. He then arranged a campaign against the Qing troops, defeating them in a series of battles culminating in the occupation of the Qing stronghold of Thang Long. 'In six days, the Tay Son troops had advanced 80 kilometres and defeated a 200 000-strong army. This was the greatest victory in Vietnam's history' (Nguyen 1993: 104). China reconciled itself to recognising the Tay Son Nguyens.

No sooner had the Tay Son Nguyens secured Vietnam, than the Nguyen prince, Nguyen Anh, recaptured much of the south with unofficial French financial aid and mercenaries. In exchange, Nguyen Anh ceded to France the port of Tourane (Danang) and Poulo Condor (Con Dau Island), as well as the right to free trade in Vietnam to the exclusion of other European nations. While Nguyen Hue was a great military tactician and politician, his brothers were not as skilled. The death of Nguyen Hue in 1792 and his brother Nguyen Nhac in 1793 led to squabbling within the Tay Son camp, weakening it considerably. From 1790 Nguyen Anh's forces battled the Tay Son forces indecisively. But the final fall of the city of Quy Nhon in 1800 tipped the balance in favour of Nguyen Anh. Hue fell, then Hanoi. In 1802, Nguyen Anh, under the royal name of Gia Long, proclaimed himself emperor of a united Vietnam (Nguyen 1993: 106–8).

EXPANDING FRENCH INFLUENCE

Despite de Behaine's assistance to the new emperor, Gia Long, Vietnam turned against Europe generally and France in particular. Gia Long's successor, Minh Mang, became even more hostile, largely in response to European expansion in Asia, and, in 1825, issued an imperial edict charging that Roman Catholicism was a 'perverse religion' that had been 'corrupting the hearts of men' (Buttinger 1968: 73). Between 1833 and 1838, seven missionaries were executed for their work, reflecting France's more general failure in its attempts to gain a commercial and diplomatic foothold in Vietnam. After a period of European consolidation and considering English, Dutch, Spanish and Portuguese colonisation of the region, France again looked at Vietnam. Using the pretext of the sentence of death upon a French priest under Minh Mang's edict and the requirement for all of freedom of religious practice, two French warships attacked Tourane in 1847. The attack was not officially sanctioned by France, but was later supported by influential missionary leaders in Paris (Buttinger 1968: 77–9).

Along with priests working against the government within Vietnam and in France, Minh Mang's successor, Emperor Tu Duc, believed he had little choice but to fight the foreign missionaries and Vietnamese Roman Catholics. The actively pro-Roman Catholic France of Louis Napoleon and the increasingly interventionist position of diplomats, military men and priests led, in September 1856, to a further attack on Tourane. The attack was poorly coordinated and resulted in no change other than to further inflame the Vietnamese government's anger against the Roman Catholics.

The following year, France revised its policies on the region and decided to enter the colonial race. In September 1858, the French fleet in the Far East took Tourane; however, an attack on the imperial capital at Hue was thwarted through wet weather, a lack of appropriate craft and sickness among the French marines. The commander of the expedition decided instead to attack Saigon,[10] taking it in February the following year. The garrison left at Tourane was withdrawn in March 1859, meaning that the focus of the French presence in Vietnam would, from then on, be in Saigon and the south.

In response to English advances in Burma and China, France renewed its efforts in Vietnam, with the region between Saigon and Cambodia falling to fresh French troops in 1861 and the Mekong Delta falling the following year. After resisting as much as possible, Emperor Tu Duc sued for peace, giving France possession of the three provinces adjacent to Saigon and Poulo Condor and opening three further ports to trade. This agreement also allowed French warships up the Mekong to Cambodia, barred Vietnam from ceding any part of its territory to any power other than France, allowed missionaries freedom of movement and reimbursed France four million piastres for costs expended in the conflict. Tu Duc was playing for time, for the French to weaken and for his own position to strengthen, especially against rebellion in the north (Buttinger 1968: 84–9). However, after the French had become established in Cochin China, their policy of expansion throughout the rest of the region, including into Cambodia in 1867, was largely driven by the resident governor.

France's expansion throughout the rest of Vietnam was not without difficulty. After the establishment of the colony of Cochin China and a protectorate over Cambodia, France consolidated its position there before looking towards the north. Also, it was distracted by the Franco–Prussian War of 1870, through which Napoleon III lost his throne, France lost the territories of Alsace-Lorraine and, for a brief moment, the communards of Paris took the city. With the French government inwardly focused, the French in Indochina had to act independently, especially under Admiral Dupre, governor of Cochin China from 1871, who was abetted by the trader Jean Dupuis and by Francis Garnier, a bright and energetic young promoter of French imperialism. In 1873, Dupuis, who had been trading arms in China, sailed up the Red River to Yunnan with a new supply of arms and returned with a cargo of tin. He was barred from taking salt on a second journey as, not only was exporting salt illegal, but the local authorities were also trying, belatedly, to keep foreign shipping out of the Red River Delta. Dupuis responded by taking 150 heavily armed Asians and twenty-five Frenchmen to occupy a section of Hanoi, where they hoisted the French flag and, then, appealed to Saigon for help. In 1873, Dupre responded favourably to Dupuis' request by sending Garnier to Hanoi with full military and political powers. Garnier unilaterally opened the Red River to international trade, replaced customs tariffs with rates linked to Dupuis and others and, eventually, shelled and stormed the citadel, following up with attacks on all the important towns and fortifications between Hanoi and the sea. On 21 December 1873, Garnier was killed outside Hanoi. Paris informed Dupre not to pursue the occupation of Tonkin and later sacked him, while Dupuis lost his ships. The French gain was the consolidation of its conquests in the south and a new treaty signed in Hue on 15 March 1874. Just after the death of Emperor Tu Duc, the French in Vietnam renewed their assault on the north in 1883, this time with the full support of their government. After being shelled, Hue capitulated. The Treaty of Protectorate, which put an end to Vietnam's independence, was signed on 25 August 1883. The bloody pacification of the north was to take another twelve years (Buttinger 1968: 91–8).

THE COLONIAL PERIOD

The first years of full-scale colonialism were marked by a disintegration of the Vietnamese emperorship. Tu Duc had died without leaving an heir, so the palace factions divided. One group continued their resistance to the French, while another worked with them. Tu Duc's successor, Du Duc (1883), was himself quickly succeeded by Hiep Hoa (1883), who, in turn, was succeeded by Kien Phuc (1883–84). Palace coups, dead emperors and unsubtle French involvement gave the court at Hue a farcical aspect. A fourteen-old-boy, Ham Nghi, was the next emperor (1884–85), fleeing the court because he chose to oppose France and resisting the French from the mountains, from where he was betrayed, captured and exiled to Algeria. The next time, the French took fewer chances, appointing their own emperor, Dong Khanh (1885–89).

France used a top-down method of local administration by a governor-general, usually supported by colonial career officials, who facilitated the economic exploitation of the primarily agrarian Vietnam for direct metropolitan profit (Jumper & Normand 1969: 384–5). The French, as colonial administrators, undertook some public works in Vietnam, including construction of the Saigon-to-Hanoi rail line, port facilities, irrigation and drainage works and establishing branches of a government bureaucracy. However, to fund these activities, the colonial government heavily taxed peasants, thereby ruining the rural economy. France also controlled the monopoly on the sale of alcohol, salt and opium.

French investment in Vietnam was, initially, centred in the mining sector—anthracite coal, tin, tungsten and zinc—with plantations in tea, coffee and, later, rubber soon coming on stream. Conditions for Vietnamese workers in these mines and on these plantations were appalling; one Michelin rubber plantation recorded that, between 1917 and 1944, of its 45 000 indentured labourers, 12 000 died from disease and malnutrition. As rural Vietnamese became poorer, the ownership of land became more concentrated: 2.5 per cent of the population in Cochin China owned 45 per cent of the land. In contrast to most Vietnamese having traditionally owned land, by the 1930s more than two-thirds were landless.

THE GROWTH OF NATIONALISM

Against this background, it was not surprising that many Vietnamese people, steeped in a tradition of fending off external conquerors, began to organise into armed opposition. When Emperor Dong Khanh died, he was replaced by a ten-year-old boy, Thanh Thai (1889–1907). However, by the time Thanh was eighteen, he too was plotting against the French, which resulted in him being deported to the Indian Ocean island of Reunion, where he stayed until 1947. His son and successor, Duy Tan (1907–16), was also a teenager when, with poet Tran Cao Van, he plotted a general uprising against the French in Hue. The poet was beheaded and the young emperor was exiled, also to Reunion. Duy Tan was succeeded by the compliant Khai Dinh (1916–25), who was followed by his twelve-year-old son, Bao Dai, at that time studying in France, who gave up his studies to return to Vietnam to rule.

Vietnamese nationalism was alive and well, if frequently rooted out and broken down by the French. Many Vietnamese nationalists looked to China and Japan as their role models for resistance to a European power, especially after Japan's defeat of Russia in 1905 and the success of Sun Yat Sen's Nationalist revolution in 1911. In 1911, a poor young peasant named

Nguyen Sinh Cung and of strong nationalist inclinations (Salisbury 1971), who was from Nghe An Province near Vinh, joined a ship running between Haiphong and Marseilles. After seeing much of the French colonial world, he disembarked in 1917 in France, moving to Paris where, in 1921, he enrolled in the ninth cell of the French Communist Party. Nguyen Sinh Cung later went under a number of names, becoming famous in Vietnam as Nguyen Ai Quoc. Apart from joining the French Communist Party, he also joined the Russian Communist Party and was, for a time, probably also a member of the Chinese Communist Party. In 1925, as Nguyen Ai Quoc, he founded the Vietnam Revolutionary Youth League (VRYL), a precursor to the Communist Party of Vietnam (*Dang Cong San Viet Nam*), founded in 1930, and later, the Indochinese Communist Party (ICP), from which grew the communist parties of Laos, Cambodia and Vietnam.[11] As revolutionary organisations, the VRYL and the ICP, like their founder, were necessarily secretive. This founder of, and inspiration for, the communist movement in Indochina was later known to the rest of the world as Ho Chi Minh.

Apart from the communist movement, a largely middle-class nationalist party, modelled after Sun Yat Sen's nationalist Guomindang, was founded in 1927.[12] Named the *Viet Nam Quoc Dan Dang* (VNQDD), it infiltrated the French garrison manned by Vietnamese troops at Yen Bai in 1930 and attempted an uprising. The French responded with an air, then ground attack, killing many and capturing thirteen of the group's leaders, who were later guillotined. A few escaped to Yunnan Province. The Yen Bai uprising was clearly ill-planned and was not supported elsewhere in the country, although it made a great impact within Vietnam and France. The ICP responded by organising peasants into a hunger march, which ended at Vinh. Large estates were shared out during the march and people's councils, called *Xo-Viets* (a nationalist twist to the Russian soviets) were established. Already the Vietnamisation of communism had begun (Lacouture 1969: 56). There were strikes and uprisings, but the biggest, in 1940, was brutally crushed by the French, almost breaking the communist party. It was from this time that Ho Chi Minh decided on a new course of action.

THE FRENCH WAR

In 1939, when France fell to Germany during WWII, Vietnam's pro-Vichy administration was recognised by the Japanese, maintaining a tenuous balance—with Japan having military occupation—between the two colonial forces. It was in this environment, in 1941, that Ho Chi Minh launched the armed wing of the VCP, the *Viet Nam Doc Lap Dong Minh Hoi*, better known as the Viet Minh. The Viet Minh actively fought against Japanese occupation, receiving Chinese and American support for their efforts. Based on a claim to nationalist credentials, the Viet Minh was relatively successful against the Japanese and, at war's end in 1945, constituted a major military force in the north of Vietnam. Towards the end of the war, Japanese forces ousted the French and, as they had done elsewhere in an attempt to slow the advancing Allies, prompted Emperor Bao Dai to proclaim Vietnam's independence.

This independence was weak, so the Viet Minh began an insurrection and elected a National Liberation Committee headed by Ho Chi Minh, which was tantamount to a provisional government. 'The truth is,' Ho Chi Minh said, 'that we have wrested our independence from the Japanese, not from the French' (Ho Chi Minh 1994: 55). The Viet Minh moved into the power vacuum in the north and central regions, but had difficulty bringing a united front to the southern groups, which were dealt a final blow by the occupation of British troops as a consequence of the Potsdam Conference. The British armed French prisoners, who then staged a coup in Saigon. The French formally returned to the south in 1946. In the north, the Chinese had occupation and forced some modifications on the new National Assembly (Jumper & Normand 1969: 392–3).

In 1946, the Viet Minh signed an agreement with France that recognised the Democratic Republic of Vietnam (DRV, which, from the mid 1950s until the mid 1970s, became known by most of the world as North Vietnam) as belonging to the Indochinese Federation and to the French Union (see Buttinger 1967a: 344–51 on the inclusive nature of the DRV government). As French troops gradually withdrew, the three provinces of Vietnam were to unite. In turn, the DRV promised not to oppose the arrival of French troops sent to relieve the Chinese. However, in negotiations, there were two sticking points: the definition of a 'free state' within the French Union and the status of Cochin China (Buttinger 1967a: 379–83). The situation deteriorated; in November 1946, fighting that broke out in the port city of Haiphong quickly escalated into a full-scale war, 'accomplishing for the Viet Minh what it had been unable to achieve on its own—the rallying of Vietnamese of all political beliefs to the Viet Minh banner in the struggle against French colonial rule'. The anti-colonial conflict was marked by 'extreme violence and cruelty' on the part of the French and the Vietnamese. Fighting covered virtually the entire country for almost eight years, leading to significant and often severe suffering throughout the rural population (Jumper & Normand 1969: 395).

The point on which the war turned was the Viet Minh's adoption of a guerrilla strategy as outlined by Mao Zedong, while the French stuck to a fixed position military stategy (Giap 1962). France's deteriorating military situation led to negotiations on the one hand and, on the other, calls to the USA to conduct air strikes. By 1954, there was a military stalemate in the south. In the north, the French believed they could win a decisive victory over the Viet Minh. Using the establishment of block-house fortifications throughout the highland region, the French had been able to suppress local anti-French activity. However, the size and organisation of the Viet Minh was more than they had bargained for. Having established themselves in a series of connected fortifications around Dien Bien Phu, which was far removed from their lines of supply, the French engaged the Viet Minh in battle. The Viet Minh, however, surrounded the French positions and, from the hills, bombarded them with cannon and mortar carried in pieces through the mountains and assembled when the Viet Minh reached their battle positions. In the final attacks, the linked fortifications fell one by one. The French were completely defeated (see Giap 1962: 206–217).

The 1954 fall of the French garrison at Dien Bien Phu, upon which the conflict finally centred, forced the French to agree to a provisional division of Vietnam at the Ben Ha River, near the 17th parallel. The intention was to separate the hostile forces and hold elections in 1956 to unify the country. Over the next three years, more than 300 000 refugees fled to the south (Karnow 1991: 203–39; see also, Buttinger 1967b). Conditions later became so harsh in the north that Vietnamese even fled to China, which was no liberal or tolerant state.[13]

At one level 'The Vietminh leaders intended to accomplish in a few years that which in more advanced nations had taken decades' (Buttinger 1968: 418). The state rebuilt itself from virtually nothing to a level of industrial capacity capable of conducting further warfare. However, the price of this rapid industrialisation was severe. Personal liberties were deeply restricted, food was closely rationed and dissent was not tolerated (Karnow 1991: 240–2). In North Vietnam from 1954 until 1990 and, after reunification, throughout the country, the supply of rice was restricted through the use of coupons to 13 kilograms per person per month. Meat was restricted to 200 grams at the same ratio. Food was available on the black market but had to be secretly eaten, lest one be denounced to police. Agriculture was collectivised, which, in some provinces, led to mass starvation. In Hanoi, between 1954 and 1990, there was almost no physical change, apart from bomb damage. Those who had money hid it and what was deemed to constitute excessive property was confiscated—no one was supposed to be able to afford property, hence ownership of it must be illegal. Secret denunciations instilled fear into ordinary people and the jailing of alleged dissidents became the primary means of quelling dissent.

In part because of the concern over the seemingly repressive government of the Democratic Republic of Vietnam and, more importantly, because of French and American financial and military aid to the south, the south was encouraged to establish a countergovernment, that of the Republic of Vietnam. Emperor Bao Dai, effectively a deeply corrupt puppet of the French, appointed the staunchly anti-communist Ngo Dinh Diem as prime minister. With two governments—one communist and the other anti-communist—plans for the elections faded as the southern government backed away from its commitment. Under Diem, the government of the newly proclaimed Republic of Vietnam was intent only on building up its own political base and, it hoped, managing to keep at bay the far better organised communists. It was clear at the time that, if elections had been held, the communists and their sympathisers would have won an absolute majority throughout the country. In the south, the plan was to divide the country in two.

THE AMERICAN WAR

The USA became involved in Vietnam because it regarded the rise of communism there—as elsewhere—'not as nationalist movements—as they largely appear in hindsight—but as signs of a unified communist drive for hegemony in Asia' (McNamara 1995: 31, 106; see also, Hammer (1966) and Smith (1968) by way of illustrating the misconceptions of the time). In this respect, the involvement of the USA in Vietnam—as elsewhere—was a manifestation of the Cold War, in particular aimed at stopping the spread of communism in SEA. The southern government, led by Diem, quickly established a military foundation, initially allying itself with, and then, by 1959, eliminating local sect and warlord chiefs, while DRV sympathisers in the south stored their arms and laid low. France withdrew military aid from the republic's government because the USA was now fulfilling that role.

Diem's government was notoriously corrupt and oppressive, enriching itself while alienating the very peasants it would have had to rely on to combat communism. 'By 1960 it had become obvious that Diem was not using American aid to woo his people' (Buttinger 1968: 433). While the initial policy of the DRV government was to wage a political struggle against the government of the south, with Diem's repression of political opposition this goal was seen as being achievable. The policy of the north towards the south changed in 1960: it now moved to the new phase of armed struggle, no longer relying only on political struggle . The first manifestation of this was the establishment of the National Liberation Front in the south, created to launch a guerrilla campaign against Diem's government. From the perspective of the communist party, which had steered the anti-French struggle, its continuing campaign against the government in the south and its American supporters was not a separate campaign, but 'two phases of the same fight' (Chanoff & Doan 1996: 30; Karnow 1991: 264–85; Young 1991: 60–74).

Rebels in the south became more active, but, in 1962, were countered by the establishment of the US Military Assistance Command, Vietnam (MACV). It was becoming increasingly clear that Diem's leadership alone would be enough to drive most of the population of the south into the hands of the communists. In response to this potential, Diem was overthrown and killed in a 1963 US-sponsored military coup (McNamara 1995: 51–87; see also Karnow 1991: 293–327; Young 1991: 95–104). Rid of Diem, the civil war in the south escalated; it involved more and more US advisers,[14] and then, on 3 August 1964, the commitment of combat troops[15] with air and naval support and included US allies in the region. The north also committed North Vietnam Army (NVA) troops at around the same time. In 1965, there were 25 000 US troops in Vietnam. The north, targeted for air attack by the USA, openly engaged in the conflict. The government of South Vietnam, propped up by the United States, was notable for its repression and corruption.

By 1968, after having taken the option of escalation when facing 'a fork in the road' (McNamara 1995: 169–206), there were half a million American troops in Vietnam. American briefings and body counts, together with the public rhetoric of the time, acted to reassure those outside that the USA and the Army of the Republic of Viet Nam (ARVN), in their battle to contain communist expansionism, were winning the full-scale war that the conflict had become. In truth, it was not about communist expansionism and it was not being won.

When Ho Chi Minh died in 1969, the party leadership was taken over by Le Duan, who led a more ideologically strict faction of the Communist Party of Vietnam (CPV). 'Le Duan inherited power, but not Ho's wisdom and flexibility, the Vietnamese said ruefully' (Sheehan 1994: 15). Already an austere, authoritarian state, the Democratic Republic of Vietnam became more ideologically rigid and less concerned about addressing the practical requirements of its people. In large part, this retreat to conservatism was engendered by the deprivations of the war and, to a lesser extent, by a lack of vision. At one level, the effect was to strengthen the armed effort against the government of the south, at another, it set up a division between hardline conservatives and more reformist-oriented members of the CPV and its Central Committee. This division remained the primary political issue affecting Vietnam in the early years of the twenty-first century.

The turning point of the war is generally regarded as being the Tet[16] Offensive, starting on 31 January 1968, when attacks by the Viet Cong and the NVA penetrated a number of targets in over a hundred cities and towns, including the US Embassy in Saigon. It was the turning point not because it was a great military success—in many ways it was the opposite—but because it showed that, at a time when the American and ARVN forces were supposed to be so clearly in control, they were not. The public realisation of this effectively broke the will of the USA to continue with the war and, without this support, it ended any chance of the Republic of Vietnam surviving (Young 1991: ch. 11).

In one respect, the Tet Offensive was intended to be the final push to end the war, but, in reality, the cost to the NVA and the Viet Cong was so great that, after losing around 32 000 troops and virtually all the military objectives they had gained, they needed to regroup, take stock of their horrendous losses and consider alternative strategies. The American army lost around 1000 troops in the Tet Offensive and the ARVN around 2000. The battle for the hilltop fortification of Khe San just south of the 17th parallel, which started a few weeks earlier, cost a little less than a further 500 American lives and around 10 000 NVA troops.[17] It was clear that one sudden push would be insufficient to topple the ARVN and the government of the Republic of Vietnam. Notably, as with much of the rest of the American war in Vietnam, it was the civilian population who bore the brunt of the fighting. In the three weeks of the Tet Offensive, around 165+000 civilians were killed and a further 2 million made homeless (Maclear 1981: 202–23).

Public opinion in the USA was turning against the Vietnam War. Richard Nixon was elected president in 1969 on a promise to reduce American involvement in the conflict and to encourage Asian states to become more self-reliant for defence. This was a double-edged plan, though. While ground troops were gradually withdrawn, the USA escalated its bombing campaigns in the north and extended them into eastern Cambodia (Engelbert & Goscha 1995: 58–100). In 1971, secret information about how the US government had systematically lied to Congress and the American public about its involvement in Vietnam was made public. In the spring of 1972, the NVA launched a new offensive across the 17th parallel, bringing forth a further wave of bombing of the north. Peace talks that had been underway in Paris since 1968 finally reached a conclusion during this period; documents of the agreement were signed by the combatants on 27 January 1973. In recognition of American desire to extract itself from Vietnam, the Paris peace talks did not mention the approximately 200 000 NVA troops still south of the DMZ (Karnow 1991: 638–84).

In January 1975, the NVA launched a massive attack on the 17th parallel, contravening the terms of the peace agreement. The Army of the Republic of Vietnam made what it called at the time a 'tactical withdrawal', which soon turned into a rout due to disorganisation and widespread desertion. A massive offensive in the south toppled its government; the thirty-year-long war of independence finally ended on 30 April 1975 (Young 1991: chs 13, 14; Maclear 1981: 313–49).

The Socialist Republic of Vietnam was formally proclaimed in July 1976, setting in train a process of reunification. The cost of this war to the Vietnamese was devastating: a little less than a quarter of a million ARVN troops killed, NVA and Viet Cong deaths were around 1 million and civilian deaths approximately 4 million. More than 300 000 Vietnamese have never been accounted for. While these figures are horrific enough, according to Ha Van Lau, Vietnam's ambassador to the UN, as many as 15 million people were killed or injured in the conflict (Maclear 1981: 351). More than a quarter of a century after the war ended, there were still many reminders of its horror in the twisted and burned bodies of those the war touched but allowed to survive.

AFTER THE AMERICAN WAR

In the south, reeducation programs, the collectivisation of agriculture, severe economic difficulties, generalised political repression and extensive corruption in the years after the war engendered considerable local bitterness. The country was in physical ruin, with virtually all the infrastructure of the north destroyed in bombing raids; the south had also been bombed, mined and saturated with poisonous chemicals. Mutual suspicion and hatred ran deep. Foreign aid, which would have alleviated many of Vietnam's difficulties, was limited; Vietnam was also diplomatically isolated because the USA, humiliated by its defeat in Vietnam, attempted to punish the newly unified state by freezing it out of aid, trade and diplomatic links. Within Vietnam, pushing towards socialism at any cost, the party collectivised agriculture in the south in 1978, along the lines of that already achieved in the north, while free trading of any goods or services was effectively abolished. Following the old Soviet model, Vietnam attempted to push through heavy industrialisation, but succeeded in only producing highly subsidised, inferior-quality products that had no market. By the late 1970s, with no incentive to produce, rice production had plummeted. A string of natural disasters compounded the problems and the shortage of rice became so severe that starvation was a real problem in the Red River delta and the central provinces.

The limited foreign aid that Vietnam still received, mostly from the Eastern Bloc countries, was, in terms of value, largely in the form of military hardware. This was especially so when tensions between Vietnam and Cambodia began to mount over the persecution of ethnic Vietnamese in Cambodia and increasingly frequent attacks against Vietnamese villages across the border. In December 1978, in response to these attacks, the Vietnamese army, fronted by a small number of Khmer Rouge who had fled the terror of Pol Pot's Cambodia, invaded and occupied Cambodia. The invasion was a military success, with the Vietnamese forces occupying the eastern and central provinces within weeks. However, the invasion led to a formal break with China, which supported the Khmer Rouge, and the invasion of northern Vietnam by China in February 1979. The Chinese attack caused considerable damage and loss of life in the northern region of Vietnam, but the battle-hardened army of Vietnam repulsed the Chinese army, inflicting on it severe losses (Evans & Rowley 1990: ch. 5). The cost of the war in Cambodia, already high, was exacerbated by the conflict with China. More importantly, Vietnam's continuing presence in Cambodia led to the country's few Western donors, such as Japan, cutting off remaining aid. Vietnam's economy thus slid into ruin.

ANTI-ETHNIC CHINESE PURGES, 1978–79

With Vietnam's long history of intimate association with China, the country's Chinese community had managed to coexist in relative tranquillity. Many Chinese married Vietnamese and often the distinction between the two groups became blurred. But, as with the rest of SEA, many

Chinese, especially those who had arrived during the colonial period, maintained close-knit communities. This was no more so than in Cholon, the Chinese city adjacent to Saigon and now an integral part of greater Ho Chi Minh City. As elsewhere, while many Cholon Chinese were involved in the struggle for reunification, a very significant number did not get involved. Indeed, many continued to develop their businesses, as they had always done throughout the region.

At the time of reunification in 1976, Vietnam's ethnic Chinese presented the government with a particular problem. There was considerable reluctance on the part of the ethnic Chinese in the south to either close their businesses or to bring them under state control as a part of the government's anti-capitalist campaign of 1978. Further, in Cholon, what had been an area effectively independent of the rest of the city was brought strictly under Communist Party control. These two moves generated considerable resentment on the part of the Chinese, prompting protests and minor clashes with authorities.

Further, Vietnam's relations with China had gone from warm to cool to chilly throughout the period of the American war (Karnow 1991: 653–4), as China first attempted to assert some degree of control over the CPV. By 1978, China had moved closer to the USA and clearly remained hostile to the Soviet Union, Vietnam's main ally. The Chinese in Vietnam, although having been there for several generations, were perceived as potentially disloyal as a result of their continued identification as Chinese rather than Vietnamese and the Chinese tradition of regarding overseas Chinese as still being loyal to the Chinese homeland. This problem has also arisen in a number of other SEA states. The Vietnamese government responded by actively encouraging Chinese, through negative rather than positive incentives, to leave Vietnam for China. The situation with the Chinese became significantly worse as tensions between Vietnam and China rose, culminating in China's attack in 1979. The ethnic Chinese in Vietnam were increasingly perceived as a potential fifth column and were duly harassed.

Between the economic difficulties faced by Chinese businesspeople in the south and the harassment they received throughout the country from the government, many Chinese decided to leave. Along with a number of Vietnamese who had suffered under the change of government, the small but steady stream of refugees that had been coming out of Vietnam since before the reunification became a flood in 1978. Over a period of several years, especially from 1978 to 1980, around 545 000 ethnic Chinese and Vietnamese poured out of Vietnam. The main method of leaving was by fishing boats or small ferries, marginally seaworthy craft that were not built for the open seas, nor able to withstand the attacks of pirates who operated from the coast of Thailand through to the eastern parts of the Indonesian, Philippine and Malaysian archipelago. It has been variously estimated that half or more of those people who left Vietnam in such boats (referred to as 'boat people') never reached their destinations. In some cases, especially among the later departures, where they did reach their destinations, they were eventually repatriated.

HUMAN RIGHTS ISSUES

As a part of its hangover from following a rather older-styled Soviet model of political organisation overlaying a base of neo-Confucian moralism, Vietnam has a history of strictly enforced responses to dissent. In the period following reunification in 1975, 'reeducation' was a euphemism for punishing citizens who had been either too active in support of the government of the Republic of Vietnam or had opposed elements of the new political and economic style that accompanied reunification. Tens of thousands of people were held in special camps for months or years, often without trial, and usually forced to undertake hard labour. The property of many of those who were believed to have collaborated with the Republican government was confiscated. Many skilled workers from the south, when they were eventually released, found that they could no longer practise their profession. It was not uncommon to find cyclo (three-wheeled bicycle cabs) drivers in Ho Chi Minh City who had once been teachers, doctors or dentists, eking out a living through this most menial work. Others were denied residence permits, which limited access to official services, including employment, attending school or owning property.

Religious freedom, too, was constrained. Lay people and senior leaders of the Unified Buddhist Church of Vietnam (UBCV) were variously harassed and arrested, including some of those who assisted in bringing about the downfall of Ngo Dinh Diem in 1963. Their crime was not submitting the UBCV to the control of the CPV. In 1981 an official Buddhist church was formed by the government. To the end of the 1980s, protests by Buddhist monks over what they believed were inappropriate government policies led to numerous arrests and detention without trial for more than four years. Roman Catholic and sect leaders fared little better under a government that regarded religion as, at best, misguided, and certainly as an overt political threat (Nguyen 1994).

ECONOMIC RENOVATION

The economic styles of the north and the south have always been different. The north was industrialised around Hanoi and Haiphong, but was otherwise relatively impoverished. The policies initiated by the CPV after 1954 encouraged a Soviet-style economic development; the destruction of the subsequent war erased the region's infrastructure. The south had opened up two centuries before, drawing in immigrants to its new land, prospering and, eventually, supporting a larger population. It was also in the south that the French first made their deepest impact on Vietnamese society and it was through there that most French investment flowed. Between 1954 and 1975, first the Viet Cong and then the government of the Republic of Vietnam instituted a small-holder land ownership policy, the former as a means of redistribution, the latter to thwart the appeal of the communists among rural peasants. By 1975, small landholdings in the south were common. Many small landholders were relatively well off, especially compared to both their time under the French and, more importantly, compared to their counterparts in the north (Beresford 1988).

In 1982, during the depths of economic failure, Nguyen Van Linh was elected general secretary of the CPV. Nguyen was a northerner who had spent the French and American wars fighting in the south and who had earlier been voted out of the Politburo for taking a qualified position on the introduction of pure socialism. As general secretary, Nguyen pulled Vietnam back from its headlong rush into socialism and began to introduce what became known as *doi moi*, interpreted as '(economic) renovation', but literally translating as the 'new way' (Vu 1995: 17–30). The policy of *doi moi* marked a significant change in Vietnam, with only three of the thirteen members of the 1982 Politburo remaining. However, while Vietnam spent the mid 1980s moving towards liberalising its economy (see Leung 1999 for an account of this liberalisation and continuing problems of subsidising exports), it did not liberalise its political structures. Those who believed that political liberalism should accompany economic liberalism were purged from the party, while outspoken opposition was punished by jail or, in extreme cases, death. A conservative, Pham Hung, was elected prime minister in 1987; when he died a year later, he was succeeded by Do Muoi, who was also regarded as a conservative.

While Vietnam liked to boast later that it led the Soviet Union into economic liberalisation, *doi moi* was most effectively put into practice from 1988 to 1989, at about the same time the Soviet Union was undergoing massive economic and political upheavals. As the Soviet Union reassessed its own parlous economic state, it began to radically reduce aid to Vietnam, which, along with international economic isolation, led Vietnam to disengage from Cambodia. By the late 1980s, party general secretary Nguyen Van Linh had begun to show clear liberal tendencies, political as well as economic, although the primacy of the party has never been open to meaningful challenge. Insofar as political reform was on the agenda at all, it was to be based on the premise that the party would remain the leading political force (CPV 1991). At the same time it was conceded that there should be greater internal party democracy, that the party should operate within the framework of the law and that the government should be guided by it rather than subordinate to it (Nguyen 1993: 400–5).

Vo Van Kiet, a managerialist, succeeded Do Muoi as prime minister, who himself succeeded Nguyen Van Linh as party general secretary. Non-party candidates were allowed to stand in the 1992 National Assembly elections, but not before being first approved by the Vietnam Fatherland Front, a party organisation. Non-party candidates took 8 per cent of the vote. The 1992 Constitution removed some of the more revolutionary rhetoric from the 1980 Constitution, opening the way for Vietnam's new open door economic policy. The National Assembly, formerly a rubber stamp for the Council of Ministers, now had enhanced powers of legislation and oversaw government activity. Today, Vietnam's president has the power to recommend dismissal of the prime minister to the National Assembly and to act as commander-in-chief of the armed forces.

Despite fluctuations, a consequence of regional economic imbalances, economic development appears to have proceeded at a considerable pace in Vietnam. Inflation, for example, which was once the major scourge of the Vietnamese economy, was brought down to 17.5 per cent in 1992 and just 3.8 per cent by 1997. By 1999, however, it was up again to 9.1 per cent as a consequence of the regional economic downturn, while the inflationary effect was even greater in the area of food, at 21.3 per cent in 1998 (Ha 1999). By 2004, inflation had reduced to 7.7 per cent (Vietnam Agency 2004), while growth remained steady in 2002 at 5.9 per cent (UNDP HDR 2004).

Vietnam's economic growth was not reflected in job creation, which tended to fluctuate, and, between 1998 and 2002, growth had dropped a little in response to the regional economic downturn. Fforde also recognised an ideological reluctance to fully accept what was touted as free market mechanisms, which corresponded to other models of economic development in the region (Fforde 1999). Regarding state owned enterprises, Fforde noted that, over the decade of 1992–2002, even 'where rationalization and regulation went hand in hand … their activities were clearly subject to the wider political and social intentions of government and party' (Fforde 2004: 24).

In spite of the economic downturn around 1998, there remained a profusion of motor scooters and television sets. Indeed, during the 1998 football World Cup, it seemed that virtually every Vietnamese home was lit by the muted glow of a television screen at night, the electronic light reflected off the faces of rapt viewers. Even in the more remote districts, television sets and often video cassette recorders were standard fare. It was only in the poorest, most basic of thatched huts that such items were found less, although, even here, an occasional aerial could be seen rising from the dried palm fronds. Motor scooters outnumbered bicycles by about ten to one. Overall, the common level of material development was at least on a par with that of Indonesia, which had long been claimed as one of the region's economic success stories. For most people, according to a United Nations report on Vietnam, despite the downturn, the economy continued to improve (Tu 1999). This was confirmed by later figures showing that Vietnam had escaped the regional economic downturn relatively unscathed and that, while its development might have been hampered by state policies, it continued to post steady improvement (UNDP HDR 2004).

THE POST-UNIFICATION STATE

Although it existed in various historical guises, modern Vietnam can be said to date from the reunification of the country in July 1976. Vietnam is a centrally controlled state, although Ho Chi Minh City, of which Saigon is the heart, challenged Hanoi for preeminence, particularly in the economic sphere. Vietnam is a functionally one-party, nominally socialist state, governed by people's representatives who are elected at a local level. Although there were some limited pronationalist non-communist parties in post-1975 Vietnam, they have been outlawed or have otherwise effectively incorporated into the communist framework. The Communist Party of Vietnam remains, effectively, the party of state, with no distinction between party ideology and state ideology and all state institutions, including the military, are beholden to the party. Government policy is set by the Politburo, a thirteen-member executive elected by the party Central Committee at approximately five-yearly intervals; the party secretariat directs government policy on a day-to-day basis. Of the thirty-four-member cabinet, thirty members are also members of the Central Committee. Of the 395-seat National Assembly, 92 per cent were held by the CPV.

Shifting towards a new, capitalist economy, Vietnam introduced a value added tax (VAT) at the beginning of 1999, the introduction of which sent two signals, the first being that the government was moving away from a progressive taxation system to a flat tax system, in which the tax burden fell proportionately more heavily on the shoulders of the poor; the second was a recognition that conventional income tax was not working in Vietnam, as too many people worked outside the formal economy and generated invisible income—as farmers selling surplus, artisans selling services for cash or in the wider black economy.

From having been the austere capital of the DRV, change began to take place in Hanoi from around 1990, which has drawn mixed responses from its citizens. Most people were happy about the improved material conditions (if they could afford them), but there remained many misgivings about the loss of traditional culture and architecture.

In 1999, bud lighting illuminated Hanoi's main streets at night, lending the city an air of prosperity and gaiety, even if many of the lit symbols were the communist hammer and sickle. Billboards throughout the country warned of the evil of AIDS, rather than the evils of capitalism. After decades of somnambulance, while perhaps not as brash as Ho Chi Minh City, Hanoi was clearly booming. Even the Hilton chain had established a hotel in the city, giving an ironic twist to the prisoner-of-war camp named by its American inhabitants from the time of the American war as the 'Hanoi Hilton'. In Ho Chi Minh City, between 1975 and 1990, the pace of life and development was very slow and opportunities were few (Sheehan 1994). Since 1990, though, the city has streaked ahead in terms of economic development and population growth, which has attracted immigrants from around the country and contributed to the development of a substantial manufacturing base.

Vinh, a major port city south of Hanoi, was bombed to rubble during the American war for its role as the major point of transhipment to the Ho Chi Minh Trail. Vinh has since been completely rebuilt, even if mostly in Comecon[18] architectural style, which looks forty years out of date when new and deteriorates at a rate to give its architectural style further apparent authenticity. An uninspiring city in so many respects, Vinh has a dilapidated grace that comes directly from its people—slightly reserved and unaffected, but warm and courteous.

But perhaps what Vinh most represents is the huge personal and economic cost to the Vietnamese of the attempt to halt international communism in communism's supposed bid for world domination. A city such as Vinh begs the question: Would communism have more quickly come to show its human face had capitalist countries not so violently attacked it? The answer to such a question will never be known and fading old Cold War Warriors still argue that those times were different. Perhaps the contest for world domination really was the main agenda, but then again, it is also possible that, after initially confusing communism with Russian political culture, the ideological response of hegemonic vested interests in Vietnam lost sight of the fact that, if left alone, most people and governments just wanted to get on with looking after themselves.

Unlike some SEA states, Vietnam's government structure was, by 1999, notable by its general absence. In each town or village there would be one building that was clearly for government administrative purposes, but there were no more than in any other country that has a town hall or municipal office. Police, similarly, were not thick on the ground, although an occasional police patrol could be spotted in the inner city area of Ho Chi Minh City at three o'clock in the morning. As for the army, there were groups of young soldiers here and there near army bases, but their profile was not high and, for the most part, they seemed no more out of place than would young recruits in towns adjoined to military camps in the USA. In part, this relatively low profile and seemingly high level of acceptance of the Vietnamese army by ordinary Vietnamese stemmed from the fact that it was, quite genuinely, a defence force and an original part of the contemporary political process, rather than a paramilitary police, as in Indonesia.

The purpose of the army is to defend Vietnam (rather than curtail the aspirations of its people) and, to a lesser extent, to assist in the development of public works. The army maintained a central role in the life of the CPV as well as the government, a legacy of the army's original political as well as its military role. Because the army was very much a creation of the party and the army's leaders were, originally, also the party's political leaders, the army and the party remain effectively two parts of the same organisation. While this has meant an active role for the army in political affairs, it has also meant that there has been no significant army–party friction, as is the case in many other countries in which the army is a dominant feature of political life (Turley 1988: 197–202).

As well as continuing its influential role in civil affairs, the army also maintained a substantial grip on the economy, participating in at least fifty-six joint ventures and wholly operating at least 200 other businesses. In 1998, army businesses generated US$609 million, in part through its timber concessions, offshore oil services and helicopter transportation (Balfour 1999). Perhaps for those who attempt to challenge more directly the authority of the government, Vietnam remains an oppressive place, but the truth is that the presence of the government is not high and most people seemed fairly free to get on with their lives. The main distinction between Laos and Vietnam was one of national style and levels of economic development, rather than any fundamental distinction about the degree to which the government engaged directly in the lives of ordinary people.

POLITICAL RENOVATION?

On 3 January 1999, Vietnam's Communist Party chief, Le Kha Phieu, pledged openness among the country's leadership and said that tolerance of 'more acceptable bounds of criticism was on tap for the new year'. It was a short-lived resolution and outspoken General Tran Do was the first major figure to pay the price for this inconsistency with party policy. Do, a lauded revolutionary turned government critic, had claimed that the party was riddled with corruption and had lost touch with the masses. As an interesting comment on the gap between the masses and the CPV, membership of the party rose by 106 000—3.18 per cent—over the previous year, the biggest increase since economic reforms were introduced in 1986, lifting membership to a record 23 million. It was widely believed that the rise in party membership reflected the increased opportunities for employment and other forms of profit taking for party members, which were not open to non-party members of the public. Corruption was so widespread in Vietnam and of such concern that there were public protests against corruption in Thai Binh in 1997. There have been subsequent efforts to eradicate or limit corruption, with little success, although more than 150 people convicted on corruption charges were executed in 2003.

For his criticism, Do was expelled from the Communist Party, ironically, the day after Le's announcement on openness. Do's offence was to call for democracy, free elections and an end to corrupt, state-controlled economic planning. A reshuffle of the Central Committee soon after placed conservatives and the military back in the ascendancy over reformers (DPA 1999). Reflecting that shift, some members were disciplined for excessive liberalism. The CPV soon passed a new resolution to punish members who persisted in disseminating views or documents counter to the party line (Reuters 1999b). The split within the top ranks of the CPV between reformers and conservatives was such that, respected leaders, such as former Prime Minister Vo Van Kiet and Deputy Prime Minister Nguyen Manh Cam, were vilified in an unsigned letter circulated to party members as working for Washington. How this translated in practice was that, with the leadership of the CPV unable to agree on basic economic issues, it had IMF loans deferred for two years, while foreign investment dropped to around a quarter of its 1996 high of US$1.8 billion (Keenan 1999). In April 2001 there was a cautious move away from a more conservative approach with the appointment of the cautiously reformist Nong Duc Manh as general secretary of the Communist Party. More positively, in 2001, the National Assembly voted to open up trade with the USA, with tariffs on Vietnamese products being reduced from a high of 40 per cent to 4 per cent, in exchange for Vietnam opening its state-controlled markets to foreign competition. While the existing economic slump persisted through to 2002, by the following year there was a revival in foreign investment, leaping to just over US$3 billion (Vietnam Ministry of Planning and Investment 2004), which flowed into 2004, that year reaching US$4 billion (*Vietnam Business News*, 17 November 2004). As Thayer has argued, Vietnam's greater regional economic and diplomatic integration, and its greater exposure to influences further afield, had weakened central government control and would, inevitably, require the state to adopt more universal norms and political processes (Thayer 2004).

It may seem vacuous to say that, with each passing year, Vietnam puts the American war a year further behind it, but, given the profound impact that the war had on the environment, infrastructure and industry of Vietnam, on the psychology of its people and the thinking of its leaders, it would be difficult to overestimate the importance of this increasing distance. While the memories—and many reminders—persist, they are quickly losing ground with growing speed to the exigencies of a transforming economy in an again economically robust region. The state is no longer directly threatened, although China remains a disturbingly large and still recently belligerent neighbour. Vietnam's unification is now long past being an issue and the CPV retains an effective monopoly on political power. The challenges the state now faces are in terms of how it manages further regional integration and whether this will require a further alteration—even a softening—of the top-down party structure and the possible freedoms that might consequently allow.

It is suggested in holocaust literature that it takes three generations before a people can begin to move on from an historical trauma. Vietnam's leadership was of the war generation, but was becoming increasingly influenced by postwar political and economic thinking. Regardless of the extent to which the American war has left scars in the thinking of the Vietnamese political leadership, they all remain resolutely Vietnamese, that is to say, the deep Confucian values of authority and obedience within a paternalistic state structure remained largely intact. If the state was to change, it would be through its own deliberation and the promotion of leaders with ideas that did not overtly threaten the status quo. If this meant that Vietnam was likely to remain an essentially authoritarian state for the foreseeable future, it would be hardly out of keeping with, and largely accepted by, the region in which it exists.

NOTES

1   In saying this, the parallel quality of pro-free market capitalist systems is painfully obvious.

2   A later crossing at the mist-shrouded 734-metre-high border post of Cau Treo, approximately southwest of Vinh, was marked by a surly Vietnamese immigration official taking small (about US$0.50) but consistent bribes from Lao and Vietnamese citizens to validate passports for entry. Truck drivers paid appreciably more.

3   The *ao dai* was developed as an item of women's wear in the mid 1700s; it is, therefore, considered by many to be a relatively new element of Vietnamese costume.

4   The Chams of Pasak, or the Mekong River.

5   Chams are identified as separate from both the Cambodians and the Vietnamese by their language, which is related to Malay (specifically Acehnese), and their adoption of Islam, as opposed to Buddhism.

6   As outlined in the section on 'Asian Values'.

7   This was just twenty-four years after the Portuguese conquered the Islamic Malay trading city of Malacca.

8   This area is still known to the Khmers as Kampuchea Krom and many ethnic Khmers born there have played a role in postwar events in Cambodia. Many Khmers still hold grievances over the loss of this region to Vietnam.

9   Nguyen is a very common name in Vietnam.

10   Saigon, now Ho Chi Minh City, was originally a small Khmer town.

11   The Communist Party of Vietnam, the original communist party in the region, later expanded to become the ICP, which, in turn, devolved into three separate parties.

12   There was also a Constitutionalist Party in Cochin China founded by wealthy, French-influenced Vietnamese. While it was a pliable organisation it was successful, but when, after 1930, it began to assert a more independent line, it quickly declined as French support evaporated (see Cook 1977).

13   Since the early 1990s, the population flow has gone in the other direction, with people moving from southern China to the liberalised economic zones in Vietnam's north.

14   Lacouture (1969: 245) claims there were 50 000 USA military 'advisers' in Vietnam in 1964.

15   The troops began landing, first at Da Nang, from 8 March 1965.

16   Vietnamese New Year.

17   It is an insight into American thinking at the time that the battle of Khe San was regarded by American planners as being the NVA's attempt to restage the pivotal 1954 battle of Dien Bien Phu against the French. In response, the US military command poured a huge amount of materiel into the base to fend off the mounting attack. The US commander, General Westmoreland, even believed that the Tet Offensive was designed to distract attention from Khe San. In hindsight, it seems that Khe San was intended to distract attention from the buildup for the Tet Offensive.

18   Council for Mutual Economic Assistance, the former Soviet Bloc economic trade group.

The Archipelago | 3

10 | Malaysia: Inclusion and Exclusion

In October 2003, after twenty-two years in power, Malaysia's often irascible seventy-seven year old prime minister, Mahathir Mohamad, resigned from office. His resignation, flagged a year earlier, ended an era in Malaysian politics in which the country moved towards a more authoritarian political style, the judiciary was deeply compromised and meaningful opposition to Mahathir's rule was not tolerated. Also during Mahathir's period as prime minister, Malaysia grew as one of the world's more successful developing countries and weathered the Asian financial crisis of the late 1990s better than most of its neighbours.

Mahathir's hand-picked successor, Abdullah Badawi, gave little indication of what his capacity or style would be as Mahathir's deputy, which he became following the sacking and then jailing of former deputy Anwar Ibrahim. But upon assuming office, Badawi quickly moved to assert his own style of authority on the second top position, marking what many took to be a meaningful shift in Malaysian political life.

Among Badawi's first acts in office was to announce a crackdown on corruption, including against some of Mahathir's former colleagues, who had not even been mentioned under his predecessor's reign, while another was to rebuild regional relations so strained under Mahathir's combative leadership. Badawi, the son of an Arab[1] imam and graduate in Islamic studies, gave Malaysia's courts the freedom to release Anwar Ibrahim from jail and, in the 2004 general elections, trounced both the Ibrahim-ite *Partai Keadilan* (Justice Party) and the harder line Islamic *Partai Amanat se-Islam*. Badawi's stunning victory reconfirmed the *Barisan Nasional* (BN, or National Front coalition) as the overwhelming political force within the country and that the United Malay National Organisation (UMNO) was the overwhelming political force within the BN. If the dispelling of the challenge to Malaysia's governing group since independence continued to raise doubts about Malaysia's claim to being a democratic constitutional monarchy, at least Badawi's open, if low-key, personal style and his move

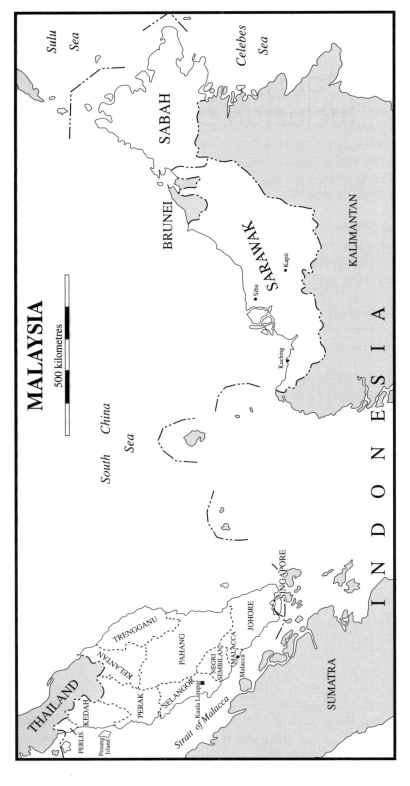

Map 7 Malaysia

away from Mahathir's authoritarianism marked Malaysia's return to a more benign political environment.

As a former British colony, Malaysia had shocked the world in November 1998 when the then recently sacked deputy prime minister and finance minister, Anwar Ibrahim, was photographed in police custody with a black eye. The charges against him at that time included sexual misconduct and attempts to corrupt the course of justice, the former of which was dropped during his initial trial. As it transpired, Anwar had been beaten up by the chief of police, who later resigned over the incident. A doctor's report, issued five days after the incident, said that Anwar was lucky not to have been killed by the beating. His appearance in public with the black eye occurred a week after the event, when his condition had started to improve.

Here was a picture of a repressive government using violence against one of its own who had fallen foul of his leader. The public protests against Anwar's treatment were seen by some observers as a prodemocracy movement, a reflection of the observers' wishful thinking rather than any political reality. What it did show was that Malaysia's aggressive prime minister, Dr Mahathir Mohamad, retained power through dubious means. Any notion of Malaysia as a democracy, which it had not functionally been for at least two decades, was irretrievably gone. Only with Mahathir's departure has Malaysia started to politically redeem itself.

PRECOLONIAL MALAYA

The state that was to become Malaysia has had a diverse historical existence, its limited unity being based on the spread of 'Malays' throughout the Malay Peninsula and, to a far lesser extent, along the coastal regions of the island of Borneo.

The Malay Peninsula was populated by Malayo–Polynesians at around the same time that they moved into the rest of the archipelago—the early years BCE—where they displaced the original aboriginal inhabitants. Most of this immigration to the peninsula came not from the north, but from Sumatra. It is from the Sumatran kingdom of Melayu that the peninsula and the state derive their names. More mountainous and less suitable to the wide-scale rice cultivation that developed, especially in Java, the original states of the Malay Peninsula developed along river banks and estuaries. They were small and largely cut off from one another, often existing as much from piracy as from trade or agriculture.

The Malays who currently live on the Malay Peninsula and on the north coast of Borneo supplanted the original inhabitants, who survive in small numbers in the upland areas of the peninsula and predominantly along and inland from the northern Borneo coast. While in some cases Malay immigration dates back more than a millennium, much of the migration to the west coast was over the last few centuries. The major sources of immigrants were Sulawesi to the east and, more importantly, various ethnic groups from Sumatra to the west, but included Javanese, Riau Malays, Acehnese, Arabs and Arab-Malays. The Bugis of Sulawesi and the Minankabau of Sumatra established states on the Malay Peninsula and its nearby islands; the political system, dominant religions (Hinduism, Buddhism and Islam), culture and language prior to the colonial period derive from Melayu–Jambi and, before that, from Sri Vijaya (Turnbull 1989: 1–98). Immigration from Sumatra to the Malay Peninsula continued until World War II, with a trickle following after that.[2] Sumatrans assimilated easily, having a common language and culture; the Javanese and Banjermasi had a little more difficulty (Turnbull 1989: 192).

The major contributing factor to Malaysia's political profile of this flow was in the traditional hierarchical forms the many immigrants brought to the peninsula. Perhaps less formal than in Java, there was nevertheless a greater sense of deference towards traditional leaders shown by them than by members of Malaysia's non-Malay communities.

Some larger states did develop in the region, although they were frequently indistinguishable from the larger regional empires of Java and Sumatra. Notable exceptions included the state of Johore and its trading city of Singapura (see the Singapore chapter) and the Islamic city–state of Malacca.[3] Malacca, as a free port, was exceptionally well placed to take advantage of shipping between India and China. At its peak during the fifteenth century, it was probably the world's busiest—possibly richest—trading port and the Sultan of Malacca commanded the loyalty of numerous minor sultans throughout the rest of the peninsula (Coedes 1968: 246).

The peak of Malacca's fortunes coincided with the development of European trade and adventurism. The first of Europe's explorers, the Portuguese, seized Malacca in 1511, leading to an exodus of the city–state's Muslim traders. Perhaps more than any other event, it was this dispersal of Islamic traders throughout the region that did most to spread and cement Islam as the dominant regional religion. However, the rise of Portuguese influence was soon challenged by the Dutch, who captured Malacca in 1641. The more restrictive trading practices of the Dutch, in which they demanded a monopoly on certain aspects of trade and heavily taxed others, sealed Malacca's fate as a great trading city.

BORNEO

A little later than Malacca's rise to prominence, another Islamic Malay state also grew in northern Borneo: the Sultanate of Brunei. By the sixteenth century, Brunei had established itself as a major coastal state, claiming control over an area extending from Borneo's western reaches across its north and down the eastern coast. So broad was its control that the island itself derived its name from this state.

However, the establishment of coastal towns and claims to political authority did not often match the reality of control. The inland tribes of proto-Malays, the earlier inhabitants of the island, only rarely acknowledged the authority of the Sultan of Brunei and, being out of reach of his limited and thinly spread forces, continued to exist more or less unmolested. As they moved down river in search of more productive lands on which to practise their traditional shifting agriculture, they increasingly came into conflict with the still small populations of coastal Malays. From time to time the inland tribes would cooperate with the coastal Malays (and visiting Chinese) for the purposes of trade and piracy, but there is little evidence to suggest that the inland tribes ever regarded this arrangement as anything more than a temporary convenience. Certainly, the inland tribes were frequently in revolt against the sultanate or its representatives and the history of the region, indicating that Malay control was limited to a few relatively small coastal pockets. This was the situation when the British adventurer Charles Brooke arrived in northern Borneo in 1839 (discussed in the section on Brunei).

While this situation of cooperation and conflict between the proto- and Deutero Malays dominated the northern coastal region to the west of what is modern Brunei, the northeast corner was a different situation again. While the various sultans of Brunei claimed that corner of the island, so too did the sultans of the Sulu Archipelago. For the majority of the inhabitants of the region, however, this was fairly meaningless, as they tended to live in small communities on the tops of the district's spectacular mountains and, apart from conflict, cut off from each other and from the coast. The village headmen might have nominal loyalty to the sultan, but they did not exist as part of a unified polity (Bedlington 1978: 44–6).

NORTH BORNEO

The first British contact with North Borneo was in 1761, when an agent for the East India Company concluded a treaty with the Sultan of Sulu to establish a trading station at Balambangan in return for protection from Spanish claims. However, due to chronic piracy by the Bajaus of the coastal and Sulu region[4] and mismanagement, the station was abandoned in 1775. In 1846, British attention later moved to the island of Labuan in Brunei Bay, to which they were given access in return for British protection and assistance in suppressing the still endemic piracy. Labuan was initially administered by the Brookes of Sarawak, but became a part of the Straits Settlements in 1907.

In 1865–66, Americans based in Hong Kong were granted a concession for small-scale cropping. But the major move came in 1877–78, when a mixed group of British and Americans (plus one Austrian) obtained grants for approximately 46 000 square kilometres of territory from the Sultans of

Brunei and Sulu. Aware of local competition and in an era of rapidly expanding colonialism, the British government granted the company a royal charter in 1881, thereby creating the British North Borneo Chartered Company. Over the next twenty years, the company expanded its holdings by annexing semi-independent territories of Brunei, sometimes by force. Conflict with indigenous inland peoples of the region was occasionally a problem, but much less so than in Sarawak.

North Borneo expanded its agricultural development and encouraged Chinese settlers, while regional Malays, especially those from Java, also moved to the region, both groups settling and intermarrying with local people. Sandakan on the east coast became the capital of North Borneo and the company was, in effect, the government. The model this colonial government followed was similar to that of Sarawak under the Brookes, although its resources were thinly stretched and most of the possession remained undeveloped and unexplored.

The discovery of oil in the region established North Borneo's economic fortunes, but it also acted as a magnet for the Japanese army at the onset of hostilities in WWII. To deprive the Japanese of facilities, the towns of North Borneo were bombed to rubble by the Allies during the conflict, necessitating extensive reconstruction in the postwar years. The territory was renamed Sabah upon its incorporation into the Federation of Malaysia in 1963.[5] Sabah and the other northern Borneo state of Sarawak were given one-quarter of all the seats in the new federal parliament, even though, between them, they only held 15 per cent of the federation's population.

THE BRITISH ON THE PENINSULA

The United Kingdom's first colony in what is now Malaysia was established at Penang, which was founded as a British post in 1786. The settlement of Penang followed a search by the British for a naval station from which to service its trade between India and China and from which to counter growing Dutch influence and later French expansion in the region. While other sites had been considered, Penang was chosen because of its strategic value, being near the head of the Malacca Straits, and because, in 1771, its then ruler, Sultan Muhammad Jiwa of Kedah, was prepared to cede the territory in exchange for defence support. The agreement between the United Kingdom and Kedah was formalised with Muhammad Jiwa's son, Sultan Abdullah Mukarram Shah. As a consequence of a dispute over payment for the island, the United Kingdom reduced the amount payable to Abdullah (Spanish $6000 a year, down from the requested S$10 000 a year). This was superseded in 1800 by a further Treaty of Peace, Friendship and Alliance, which included a further payment (S$10 000 a year) for the adjacent land on the peninsula, which became Province Wellesley. British defence support, though, was not given to Abdullah in his time of need.

Although the cosmopolitan population of Penang expanded quickly, the station was uneconomical and only retained as a base for the British navy as a consequence of its conflict with France, with two interludes, one of them that lasted from 1793 until 1815. Following French occupation of the Netherlands, the British occupied Dutch possessions in the region, taking Malacca in 1795, the Moluccas in 1796 and Java in 1811. Despite agreeing in 1814 to return the Dutch possessions, the United Kingdom began to develop commercial interests, primarily in tin, on the Malay Peninsula. In 1819, against Dutch wishes, Thomas Raffles reached an agreement with the chief of Singapore to establish a trading station there. Due to difficulties with succession to the local sultanate, the agreement remained intact until the 1824 Treaty of London. Under this treaty with the Dutch, in exchange for its possessions in Sumatra and all islands south of Singapore, the United Kingdom received Malacca and retained Penang and Singapore. It was this treaty that delineated the British sphere from the Dutch and which was to define modern Indonesia from Malaysia.

The present shape of Malaysia was settled in 1909, when the United Kingdom extended its protection to the four northern states of Kedah, Perlis, Kelantan and Trengganu, which had been suzerain to Thailand. Also in that year, the other Malay states—apart from Johore—were joined under a common federal legislative council. Although this council was suggested to the sultans as a means of lessening British control, the high commissioner, who presided over the council, assumed more authority, effectively relegating the sultans to advisers to the council.

ETHNIC COMPOSITION

Probably the single most important political issue in Malaysia is that of its ethnic composition. A little more than half of the country's population is ethnically Malay, approximately 35 per cent is ethnic Chinese and the remainder largely of South Asian (Indian, Pakistani and Sri Lankan) descent. This ethnic mix has proved at times to be explosive, with the ethnic Malays, self-styled as 'sons of the soil' (*bumiputra*), largely excluded from the process of economic growth in the state. This, in turn, has reflected the agricultural orientation of the Malays, which was encouraged by a land reservation scheme begun in 1913 and intended to protect them from the rapidly expanding, land-intensive rubber industry. The industrial focus of the Chinese, first in mining and, later, in commerce, followed their recruitment into largely Chinese-owned and operated tin mines and, later, into support services. Indians were recruited by the British primarily to work on rubber plantations.

One consequence of the British colonial policy of educating ethnic South Asians to work in the lower echelons of the bureaucracy, at the point at which they intermarried with Malays, was the growth of a small, locally born non-aristocratic intellectual elite. Able to claim a Malay heritage but with access to a British-based education, these Indian–Malays were among the first to consider alternatives to British rule and to provide intellectual guidance in terms of national development. Malaysia's long-serving prime minister, Dr Mahathir Mohamad, who is of mixed Malay and Indian descent, is a case in point.

Another small subgroup is the Portuguese–Malays, who continue to live in and around the area of Malacca. Although Malay in language and custom, they are not officially accepted as Malays by the state. A small number of original aboriginal inhabitants of the peninsula, the *Orang Asli* (Original People), live in small communities in the highland regions, effectively outside the Malaysian mainstream.

To a considerable degree, Malay resentment of the Chinese and, to a lesser extent of Indians, is based on two criteria. The first is the enhanced economic status of the Chinese relative to the Malays. The second is a consequence of the relatively recent arrival of the Chinese on the Malay Peninsula. What was perceived as relative indifference of Malays towards the Chinese changed early in the twentieth century, when it seemed that the Chinese would begin to outnumber Malays. Differences between the Malays and Chinese were centred on language and religion, the Chinese being predominantly Confucian or Buddhist and speaking one of the dialects of southern China as their first language, the Malays being largely Muslim and speaking a version of what was to become Bahasa Melayu.

In 1927 alone, 360 000 Chinese landed in Singapore; in 1931, for the first time, a census showed that non-Malays actually outnumbered Malays by 2.23 million to 1.93 million. From 1929, tensions were exacerbated by the impact of the Great Depression, which severely limited Malaya's exports of rubber and tin.

The Chinese received their first taste of official disapproval with the appointment in 1930 of Sir Cecil Clementi as governor. He quickly banned the Chinese nationalist party, the Guomindang (established in 1925) and fragmented the Chinese-dominated Malayan Communist Party (MCP, set up in 1927),[6] while also withdrawing government grants from Chinese schools, censoring the vernacular press and imposing the first restrictions on immigration (Turnbull 1989: 205–6). From the 1930s on, at the behest of the sultans, Malays were also actively promoted as the only suitable candidates for the civil service. Labour grievances among the Chinese fed the growth of the MCP throughout the 1930s. In 1937, in response to Japanese incursions into China, the MCP established the politically open Overseas Chinese Anti-Japanese National Salvation Association (OCAJNSA).

It was not until the 1920s that a modern nationalist movement began on the Malay Peninsula, influenced by the Reform Islam movement and culminating, in 1926, in the first Malay political organisation, the *Kesatuan Melayu Singapura* (Singapore Malay Union). This was followed, in 1937, by the formation of the *Kesatuan Melayu Muda* (Union of Malay Youth), which sought to achieve speedy independence from the United Kingdom. Both organisations appealed to the educated and rising Malay middle class, in particular those frustrated with colonial education policy and their employment prospects.

Based in Siam (Thailand), the Japanese occupation of the Malay Peninsula in 1942 was quick; Allied forces fell back ahead of the Japanese advance. Isolated, Singapore was surrendered to Japanese forces, dispelling forever any idea of British superiority. In their panic ahead of the Japanese advance, however, British forces accepted an offer from the MCP to organise an ethnic Chinese militia, especially from the OCAJNSA, which was named the Malayan People's Anti-Japanese Army (MPAJA).[7] Shortly before Singapore was surrendered, a number of the MPAJA were in position on the Malay Peninsula; some of them managed to escape capture (*A Short History of the Malayan Communist Party*[8] 1955: 15).

Survivors of the MPAJA fled to the jungle, from where they continued guerrilla operations against Japanese forces. By 1943, the United Kingdom was assisting the MPAJA by arming and helping to train them in preparation for the planned Allied invasion. By 1944, the MPAJA was attracting new recruits, including non-communists. However, the MPAJA leadership intended to use the final showdown after the defeat of the Japanese to establish a communist republic in Malaya (*A Short History of the Malayan Communist Party* 1955: 16–17; Turnbull 1989: 227–8).

THE EMERGENCY

Upon the surrender of Japanese forces, the MCP, which, at the time, enjoyed legal status, assumed authority until the return of the British. The open section of the MPAJA disarmed, but a secret group of about 4000, hid its arms. The MCP engaged in union activities until, after the murder of some plantation managers who had been involved in a violent industrial dispute, a state of emergency (the Emergency) was declared in June 1948. The MCP immediately went underground and its secret and much of its open sections embarked on an armed struggle marked by terrorism and a guerrilla campaign. This campaign was initially based on relatively indiscriminate violence, but, from 1951, it became much more selective. Perhaps the most effective outcome of this change in strategy was the assassination in October 1951 of the British High Commissioner of Malaya, Sir Henry Gurney.

The two long-term consequences of the Emergency were the delay in organising independence for Malaya and the introduction of the Internal Security Act (ISA), under which suspects could be held without charge or trial. The ISA and the related Sedition Act and Official Secrets Act were later used by the 'democratic' governments of both Malaysia and Singapore to silence and jail critics and members of opposition parties (Crouch 1996: 79–84). As a military venture, the communist rebellion failed, partly because of the inadequate arms, training and numbers of the MCP's armed wing (from 1949 called the Malayan Races Liberation Army, or MRLA). The British strategy of cutting off the MRLA[9] from access to Chinese communities also contributed to the failure of the rebellion. But the critical factor in the failure of the insurgency was the lack of support for the MCP from much of the Chinese and most of the Malay population.

By the late 1950s, the MCP's insurrection had tapered off to become a localised annoyance, restricted primarily to the area near the Thai border. The last MCP guerrillas did not formally end their struggle until 1989 and even then agreed only to a ceasefire, rather than surrender. At the beginning of the twenty-first century, a few ancient and fading comrades were still living in the remote and rugged jungle-covered mountains just over the Thai border. Despite the ceasefire, the border remained tightly sealed and Malaysian army units were conspicuous along the border area. The MCP continued to receive some support from the clearly delineated ethnic Chinese community that lived in southern Thailand.[10]

With the Emergency increasingly under control, the United Kingdom held elections in Malaya for a local parliament in June 1955. Of the ninety-eight members, fifty-two were elected and forty-six were appointed. The elections resulted in Tunku Abdul Rahman becoming chief minister and the counterinsurgency campaign being directed by the new Malayan government, rather than by the British government. Malaya was formally granted independence on 31 August 1957.

FORM OF GOVERNMENT

With its British parliamentary legacy,[11] the Federation of Malaysia began life in 1959 as a liberally oriented federated constitutional monarchy. Malaysia has a bicameral federal parliament, with sixty-eight members of the *Dewan Negara* (Senate), twenty-six of whom are elected from the state legislatures and forty-two of whom are appointed by the sultan and have a six-year term. The *Dewan Rakyat* (House of Representatives) has 180 directly elected members, each with a five-year term.

The monarchic aspect of Malaysia's Constitution is novel, in that the monarch (*Yang di-Pertuan Agong*) is elected every five years on a rotational basis by the State Sovereigns' Conference of Rulers. In practice, this means that the state sovereigns take turns in assuming monarchical duties, except where they decline the offer. The inspiration for this model was the Malay Minangkabau state of Negri Sembilan, whose four territory chiefs elected a *Yang di-Pertuan Agong*.[12] Negri Sembilan was originally a confederation of nine states (as its name implies) (Groves 1962: 271–3). The status and privileges of the state sovereigns were increasingly eroded in the last two decades of the twentieth century as more power became concentrated in the federal government. This has most obviously been so in the case of the prime minister, in this instance, Mahathir Mohamad. There are also thirteen state governments, nine of which have hereditary rulers as their head.

The three major communally based parties of Malaysia were founded in 1946. They are the United Malays National Organisation (UMNO), the Malaysian Chinese Association (MCA) and the Malaysian Indian Congress (MIC). Together, these parties continue to dominate the coalition of government, first known as the Alliance and, from 1974, as the *Barisan Nasional* (National Front), or BN. In its latter guise, the coalition further consolidated its grip over Malaysia's political system. Numerous smaller parties also exist, including the BN members *Gerakan Parti Pesaka Bumiputera* and Sarawak National Party. A number of parties also exist exclusively at state level. The smaller parties either tend to be coopted into the coalition in order to address their concerns and buy off their supporters (and sometimes dissolve thereafter), or are generally relegated to the political margins. Although a coalition, the BN works as a party in its own right, with internal elections, its own constitution and common policies for all the member parties.

One means by which UMNO and, later, the BN assured itself of retaining power was through the gerrymandering of the electoral boundaries, by which electorates favouring the government are smaller and therefore greater in number. The biggest electorate was approximately five times the size of the smallest, with the smallest electorates tending to be among the rural Malay areas (Rawana 1999). Another means of ensuring UMNO–BN dominance was through the exclusion of opposition candidates on minor technical grounds, as well as employing other means of control and intimidation (Crouch 1996: 58–64). One example was the failure of a potential candidate to write 'none' on an electoral registration form where it asked for 'aliases'. This has created what has been referred to as a 'hegemonic party system … in which opposition parties are legal but denied—through pervasive electoral malpractices and frequent state coercion—any real chance to compete for power' (Diamond, Linz & Lipset 1989: xvii, quoted in Crouch 1996: 6).

Through its support from the three major parties, its ability to coopt smaller parties and various means of manipulating the electoral process, the BN controlled the federal government with a two-thirds majority. This allowed it, if it so desired, to change the Constitution at will. The BN also controls most state governments, with the exception of Sabah in 1985–86 and 1990–95, and the Islamic states of Kelantan from 1990 and Terengganu from 1999–2004. These state governments were exceptions to the BN rule, primarily as a result of specifically local issues, including the political advantage or disfavour accorded to local political personalities.

In all, the electoral system in Malaysia gave a less than fair chance for genuine opposition to contest the government. The electoral system 'was so heavily loaded in favour of the government that it was hard to imagine that the ruling coalition, as long as it remained united, could be defeated in an election' (Crouch 1996: 75). In one analysis, the process of modernisation, or industrialisation, rather than leading towards greater liberalism, could, in fact, have the opposite effect because the mechanisms of state, which had to be employed to achieve the greatest potential growth, were, by nature of their application, authoritarian (O'Donnell 1973). It is also clear that, within a system that privileges one ethnic group over another and functions on the basis of patronage—cronyism—authoritarianism is also likely to be employed to retain those privileges.

THREATS TO THE STATE

The Federation of Malaysia came into being in 1963, bringing together the states of the Malay Peninsula, Singapore, Sarawak and Sabah. The new federation faced two immediate problems: the first was strident opposition to the creation of the federation by Indonesia and, to a lesser extent, by the Philippines; the second problem was the incorporation of the overwhelmingly ethnic Chinese city–state of Singapore. In short, Singapore's ethnic makeup made it an uncomfortable fit for a new state that was politically dominated by ethnic Malays (Crouch 1996: 17–20). The Singaporean Chinese also tipped the ethnic balance away from Malays towards Chinese and Indians, which was unacceptable to the traditional Malay elite, while the wealth of Singapore focused Malaysia's economy towards the Chinese city and away from the more evenly racial demography of the peninsula.

To exacerbate this problem, Singapore's leader, Lee Kuan Yew, insisted on retaining the title of 'prime minister' after federation, demanded aspects of autonomy from the rest of the federation and was considered too leftist by the conservative Alliance government. But what really annoyed the Malay leaders was when he launched his People's Action Party (PAP) on the mainland to contest the federal elections. The new party's call was for a Malaysian Malaysia, which was intended to signal to the Malay political elite that the ethnic Chinese wanted more of a say in federal affairs, effectively challenging their political preeminence. As a Chinese-based party, it opposed the Malaysian Chinese Association, which worked in coalition with UMNO as a part of the *Barisan Nasional*. The perception at the time was, not inaccurately, that the PAP was a vehicle for Lee Kuan Yew's wider political aspirations and that he hoped, through extending Singaporean political machinery to the peninsula, to challenge for Malaysia's prime ministership. His hopes were dashed when Singapore left the federation in August 1965 (see chapter 13). Following the split, the PAP on the peninsula was renamed the Democratic Action Party (DAP). The DAP remained Malaysia's primary opposition party, forming an alliance in 1999 with the *Partai Islam SeMalaysia* (PAS) (Pereira 1999).

Further afield, the growth of Filipino nationalism led that country to make a claim for the return of the state of Sabah and, upon federation, it voiced its objection to the existence of the new state of Malaysia on the grounds of Sabah's inclusion. The claim was based on the inclusion into the Philippines state of the Sultanate of Sulu and Sulu's former links with the territory of northeast Borneo (Tarling 1998: 115–16; McCloud 1995: 199–200, 292; Harrison 1966: 262). However, this claim was primarily diplomatic; the Philippines never actively threatened the existence of the new federated state.

The greatest threat to the Federation of Malaysia came from Indonesia, when its president, Sukarno, announced his active opposition to the new state. This *Konfrontasi* (confrontation) was primarily diplomatic, although, from 1963 until 1965, units of Indonesian troops, thinly disguised as volunteers, did land on the Malaysian Peninsula and attacked across the border from Kalimantan into Sarawak (Tarling 1998: 115; SarDesai 1997: 269–71). Units of the MCP began operating in Sarawak from 1963, receiving support from the communist-influenced Indonesian government. The communist insurgency in Sarawak operated somewhat distinctly from the MCP on the peninsula and had its origins among ethnic Chinese activists.[13] It was brought under control in two phases, in 1973–74 and 1989–90. Malaysia was able to fend off the threat of confrontation—and the MCP—with the assistance of British, Australian and New Zealand troops, who were active in Sarawak. However, the Indonesian threat did directly challenge the legitimate basis of the establishment of Malaysia as a separate and sovereign state.

A further challenge to the maintenance of the federation came from within Sarawak and Sabah. While local Islamic Malay populations were keen to join the federation, the Chinese and indigenous communities were less supportive (Sario 1999). Indeed, these groups refer to Peninsular Malaysians as *semananjung* (literally, 'peninsular', although with a pejorative connotation), which highlighted the difference and consequent political sensitivities for the Peninsular Malays. Most of the opposition to federation was, and still is, based on the allocation of income. Sabah and Sarawak contribute more to the federal government than they receive, which many in those states consider unfair. The terms 'fairness', 'justice' and 'equality' were commonly used, often by indigenous peoples, when talking about their grievances against the federal government.

Similarly, the ethnic Chinese of east Malaysia claimed theirs was a better region because of the greater proportion of Chinese to Malays.[14] While there are significant cultural gaps between the Chinese and indigenous peoples, they view each other with much greater equanimity than they do the Malays. Some of the bases of understanding between them revolve around their mutual antipathy towards the local Islamic Malays, as well as towards Peninsular Malaysia more generally. Politics in Sarawak has been more plural and fluid than in Peninsular Malaysia, with indigenous groups (combined, representing the largest potential voter block) represented by a number of organisations. As with the politics of Malaysia more widely, the Alliance and the *Barisan Nasional* after that have wielded considerable influence over which parties are included in the coalition and which are kept—or pushed—outside it (Cramb & Dixon 1988: 11). Further, also reflecting peninsula politics, a small elite allied to the government has tended to control the political process of the state and the 'land, timber and minerals' from which it draws its significant wealth (Cramb & Dixon 1988: 11–12).

DOMESTIC TENSIONS

Tensions between the ethnic Malay and Chinese populations, which culminated in race riots in May 1969, contributed to modifying Malaysia's earlier more liberal orientation (Crouch 1996: 24–7). The following year, internal factional battles within the UMNO led to the downfall of Tunku Abdul Rahman as prime minister; he was succeeded by the more nationalist pro-Malay Tun Abdul Razak. Following the 1969 riots, internal security laws were strengthened and, to redress Malay grievances about economic disparities, the government introduced its New Economic Policy (NEP) in 1971. Among other things, NEP legislation was intended to break down the Chinese commerce–Malay farmer/labourer dichotomy by shifting a greater proportion of corporate wealth into Malay hands (Crouch, 1996: 24–5; 37–8; Goldsworthy 1991: 53).

Until the mid 1980s, the *Barisan Nasional* coalition worked well; however, by 1986 there were tensions over the increasingly authoritarian style of both UMNO and Prime Minister Mahathir, as well as within the Malaysian Chinese Association (MCA). These tensions were exacerbated by a downturn in Malaysia's economy, which included higher unemployment and increased bankruptcies, the result of an international recession and a related rise in ethnic tensions.

Following the death of Tun Abdul Razak, Hussein bin Onn became prime minister in 1976. Onn's prime ministership was noted for its relative moderation and consolidation following the turmoil of 1969. However, while Onn's leadership was regarded as moderate, he still had to preside over a difficult period, including internal UMNO scandals caused by the beginning of the Malay elites' push towards entrepreneurial activity (Shamsul 1999: 5). Onn's deputy prime minister was Mahathir Mohamad, who had previously been education minister and had presided over putting down the student protests of 1974 which were led by Anwar Ibrahim.

In early 1981, Onn was hospitalised and underwent heart surgery, leaving the country in the hands of Mahathir Mohamad. Onn formally resigned on 16 July and Mahathir was elected UMNO party president and, hence, prime minister. While the election of Mahathir was fairly straightforward, there was a bitter factional struggle for the deputy prime ministership between the education minister, Satuk Musa Hitam, and the finance minister, Tungku Razaleigh Hamza. Razaleigh had challenged Mahathir for the deputy prime minister's position, so there was already an antithetical relationship between the two. Mahathir backed Musa, who won the party ballot. The poll was repeated in 1984, with Musa again winning, this time with a slightly increased majority (Case 1996: 152–60; Rinn-Sup 1984: 210–15).

The 1984 poll was complicated by the arrival of the former Muslim youth leader and perceived Islamic moderate, Anwar Ibrahim, who had been detained under the ISA for almost two years from 1974 for organising student demonstrations. However, Mahathir soon came to recognise Anwar's political usefulness and set up the youth organisation that Anwar headed. In 1982, Mahathir asked Anwar to stand for election. Anwar was immediately appointed deputy minister in the Prime Minister's Department and, in 1983, after being elected to head UMNO Youth (and automatically becoming a vice-president of UMNO), was made Minister for Youth, Sports and Culture. Anwar's rapid rise provoked tensions between Mahathir and Musa, which spilled into the open in 1986 and led to Musa's resignation as deputy prime minister. There were earlier signs of tensions between the two, in particular over Razaleigh's continued position in the cabinet, but the split between Musa and Mahathir was far less ideological than it was personal (Case 1996: 152–83).

As if this were not enough to destabilise Malaysia's political environment, a further major division within UMNO centred on the party's long-standing commitment not to emphasise ethnic issues. One faction of UMNO, self-styled champions of the Malay cause, challenged the more conservative faction, which also said it represented the Malay cause. In part, these tensions within UMNO reflected unease with the Chinese community, notably through its two main political representatives, the MCA and the DAP. Within the Chinese community, there were tensions over the DAP's strong performance in the 1986 elections, following deep concerns over senior MCA figures being implicated in business scandals involving the $1.5 billion collapse of Chinese-based deposit-taking cooperatives, which affected about 600 000 ethnic Chinese. Tensions between the MCA and UMNO were also heightened after an MCA convention declared that all of Malaysia's inhabitants were of immigrant stock and, consequently, none should claim themselves as natives and label others as immigrants. There was also concern over the potential to undermine the use of Chinese language in Chinese schools, which was played upon by the DAP with the support of the MCA (Crouch 1996: 106–8).

Then, while Mahathir was abroad, several UMNO leaders decided to stage a public rally as a demonstration of Malay unity. The rally was expected to bring together hundreds of thousands of Malays, which had the potential to spark an uncontrollable protest or riot. But Mahathir returned and called off the rally, giving approval under the terms of the ISA for police to arrest a total of 119 dissidents between late October and mid November 1997. Among those arrested were ten DAP members of parliament, five members of the Chinese education movement, eight members of the MCA and five members of *Gerakan*. Only three members of UMNO were arrested, one of whom was believed to have been detained for unconnected reasons. The three UMNO arrestees were supporters of Razaleigh, who was, at that time, fomenting a challenge to Mahathir's leadership of UMNO.

A number of others arrested were equally prominent in Malaysian society. Seven DAP members and five Chinese education movement detainees were among those jailed for two years. The UMNO, MCA and *Gerakan* members were quickly released (Crouch 1996: 106–13).

In order to attack Mahathir, Musa settled his differences with Razaleigh. Together, the pair challenged Mahathir and his new favourite, Ghafar Baba, for the leadership and deputy leadership of UMNO. Baba was a millionaire businessman who owed much of his wealth to government patronage. As with most states that have a history of one-party domination, there were numerous reports of high-level corruption—masked as patronage—in Malaysia, with lucrative government contracts going to UMNO associates. Baba was but one example of this system at work (Shameen 1998a; Crouch 1996: 35, 38–43, 54). Issues of nepotism, crony capitalism, non-transparency and corruption were raised at an UMNO Youth meeting in June 1998, to which Mahathir responded by warning party members not to make accusations about such issues (Hiebert 1998). Mahathir and Baba narrowly defeated Razaleigh and Musa in the party elections of 1987. In the wider elections, Mahathir's candidates for vice-presidential positions came first and third (the latter position being taken by Anwar), while a Musa supporter came second. Of the twenty-five positions on the party's Supreme Council, the Razaleigh–Musa faction won eight positions. Following his reelection as leader, Mahathir took the opportunity to purge cabinet of remaining Razaleih–Musa supporters.

As a consequence of the split between Razaleigh–Musa and Mahathir–Baba, about half the party was opposed to Mahathir, although, both factions remained deeply divided within themselves. In a bid to continue the struggle against Mahathir, Razaleigh's group launched a challenge against the legality of the elections, which resulted not in new elections, but in UMNO being declared a technically illegal organisation. Mahathir reorganised UMNO into UMNO *Baru* (New UMNO), while an opposition group set up UMNO Malaysia. The battle was for the loyalty of UMNO's 1.4 million members and the party's assets. It also marked a shift in party style and policy direction. While UMNO Baru increasingly won over the loyalty of old UMNO members, it was not until Mahathir enticed

Musa to defect that he truly won his battle. Razaleigh's response was to establish a new party, *Semangat '46* (Spirit of '46), a reference to UMNO's founding year (Crouch 1996: 114–21; Case 1996: 184–214).

HOBBLING THE JUDICIARY

Declaration of UMNO as an illegal organisation was a major setback for Mahathir and showed that, while he was increasingly master of his environment, there remained some important elements of the state outside his control. As a consequence, there was a series of overtly political moves that caused, perhaps, even more concern, in particular in international terms, than the UMNO split. In 1988, Mahathir sacked the judge responsible for organising the hearing of an appeal of the Razaleigh–Musa challenge, lord president of the Supreme Court, Tun Salleh Abas. The ostensible reason was gross misbehaviour, but the real reason appeared to be Abas' unwillingness to allow a backroom deal to be done on the appeal, which favoured Mahathir. A further five Supreme Court judges, who supported Abas in Mahathir's attack on him, were also suspended.

The Malaysian Bar Council was deeply disturbed by this overt attack on the independence of the judiciary and weighed in, supporting Abas and the five suspended judges. It also brought contempt proceedings against the acting lord president, who headed a tribunal hearing a case against Abas. The government retaliated by evicting the council from its offices in the High Court building. New and more sympathetic judges were appointed to the Supreme Court; they eventually ruled on the original UMNO case, providing the Mahathir group with the opportunity to reconstruct UMNO as a stronger, more cohesive and more Mahathir-loyal UMNO *Baru* (Case 1996: 201–14). 'We used to be a very democratic organisation,' said one former UMNO official. 'Now the members can't do anything without Kuala Lumpur telling them to go ahead' (Burger & Bogert 1988). In all, Mahathir's challenge to the courts seriously hobbled the independence of the judiciary and blurred the basic democratic tenet of the separation of executive and judicial power. It also brought the party and the state more directly under Mahathir's personal control.

FREEDOM OF SPEECH AND THE MEDIA

There were some human rights concerns over political opposition and indigenous peoples and the media was fairly tightly controlled, with UMNO controlling, although no longer directly owning, the country's two largest newspaper groups and one commercial television station, as well as the government television station. Free speech was generally tolerated and the political atmosphere, while limited, was not very repressive for most people.

In terms of the mass media, it has been subject to direct and indirect government control, through ownership, licensing and bans. Malaysia's most influential newspaper, the *New Straits Times*, was owned by UMNO until 1993, after which it was bought by four newspaper executives who were close to Anwar Ibrahim. The two newspapers of the *Utusan Melayu* group were also owned by a group of UMNO leaders, while the newspaper the *Sun* was started in 1994 by Tan Sri Vincent Tan, who has close links to UMNO and who, as a publisher, did not resile from suing for defamation of his own character. Another paper, the *Star*, was once owned by a former chief minister of Sabah, who was a close personal friend of then Prime Minister Tunku Abdul Rahman. In 1977, it was bought by Huaren Holdings, which is largely owned by the MCA. Because of its sometimes pro-Chinese views and a column by the former prime minister, Abdul Rahman, the *Star's* licence was suspended for several months in 1987. When it reappeared in March 1988, Abdul Rahman's column had been dropped.

Another means of control over the media was through criminal charges being laid over what was termed the 'malicious' publication of 'false news'. Under such an offence, the publisher, printer, editor and author (journalist) are all liable, as in a defamation case. The closure of papers has been used relatively sparingly, although, in 1987, during a period of considerable political unrest within UMNO over Mahathir's leadership style, three newspapers were temporarily closed, returning to print in a more subdued form.

More recently, two prominent newspaper editors, from *Utusan Malaysia* and *Berita Harian*, resigned after what was understood to be pressure to run anti-Anwar Ibrahim stories. There were also reports of pressure being brought to bear at the independent television station TV3. An UMNO leader from Johore said that both editors had been appointed with Mahathir's approval, but their independent line on Anwar led to their resignations (Sangwon 1998).

Malaysia was also considering introducing limits on the circulation of non-Malaysian media, along the lines of Singapore's foreign media restrictions, in an attempt to control negative reporting. This applied in particular to the trial of Anwar Ibrahim. Publications referred to for possible restriction included the *Far Eastern Economic Review* and *Asiaweek*.

THE FALL OF ANWAR IBRAHIM

Shamsul (1999: 4–9) has noted that the introduction of the NEP in 1971 eventually led to a realignment of traditional Malaysian politics away from a focus on security, exemplified by the ISA, the ethnic bargain, which retained Malays in power, and development planning, which included an economic bargain that complemented the ethnic bargain. The shift was towards entrepreneurialism by Malay elites, on the one hand, and a divergent focus on social justice on the other.

Upon becoming prime minister, Mahathir pushed the entrepreneurial aspect of Malaysian development with a passion, allocating the task of social justice to his deputy. Shamsul suggests that this led to the development of a grassroots-based new politics, of which then Deputy Prime Minister Anwar Ibrahim was increasingly seen as the head. Such new politics was suggested to include a range of non-communal, non-class-based social and environmental issues that had previously been left off the traditional or entrepreneurial agenda (Shamsul 1999: 9).

While an undercurrent of increasing authoritarianism has prevailed under Mahathir, the sacking and jailing of Anwar Ibrahim offered a stark reminder of how quickly benign authoritarianism was able to turn malignant. After entering politics in 1982, Anwar Ibrahim and his supporters swept into power in UMNO in 1983, when Anwar took the deputy prime ministership and his supporters took the Youth and Sport Ministry, Education and chief ministership of Selangor state.

Having started as Mahathir's favourite and, for a long time, considered to be the heir apparent, Anwar was sacked by Mahathir on 2 September 1998, a time when Malaysia's economy was convulsing as a consequence of the regional economic crisis. This situation had not been helped by intemperate remarks made by Mahathir about conspiracies to wreck the Malaysian economy by the international financial community generally, and by a Jewish money trader in particular. Then, Mahathir imposed controls on the repatriation of profits from Malaysia and the exchange of the Malaysian ringgit which, in the shorter term, further alarmed the international financial community, although, in the medium term, actually helped stabilise Malaysia's economy. These moves were seen, by some observers, to be in support of government cronies (Jomo 2003: 217).

Mahathir and Anwar disagreed publicly about policy direction, in particular over what Anwar increasingly identified as cronyism, nepotism and corruption (Jomo 2003: 721). The disagreements raged through Cabinet as well as in public, setting the two men on a collision course (Skehan 1998b; Fan 1999; Jomo 2003: ch. 28). An article by Anwar on the Filipino nationalist Jose Rizal in *Asiaweek* (21 June 1998), which mentioned 'dictatorship', 'graft, abuse of power, profligacy and the like', 'years of self-deception' and 'a new tyranny', was a major signal that something was seriously amiss between the two (Fan 1999: Introduction). It appeared that Anwar was beginning his push to replace Mahathir as prime minister. By August, it had become clear that there had been an irretrievable falling out between Mahathir and Anwar and there was speculation that he could be removed from office (Shameen 1998b: 2).

The sacking just a few days later immediately led to an upsurge in public support for Anwar, with demonstrations calling for Mahathir to resign. Following from the prodemocracy protests in Indonesia, protesters began calling for *reformasi* (Skehan 1998c). Anwar hinted that he might soon be charged in order to remove him as a focal point for opposition to Mahathir. One view of events was that a change in Malaysia's leadership was becoming increasingly inevitable and, indeed, Mahathir said in 1998 that he intended to retire soon and that Anwar would succeed him. He reiterated his comments about retiring during Anwar's trial, but changed his successor to the new deputy prime minister, Abdullah Badawi. While Anwar was seen to be patiently waiting for Mahathir to step down and, he hoped, hand leadership to him as his deputy, Anwar's supporters became impatient and began pushing the issue. It was the tension created by this push and growing impatience with Mahathir's allocation of economic favours—said by many to constitute corruption—that led to Mahathir first establishing grounds for sacking Anwar and then doing so, following up quickly with having him charged under criminal law. Mahathir said, during the period of the trial, that he could not condone having a deputy who had allegedly committed the crimes of sexual misconduct and corruption, which necessitated his removal from office. After Anwar was arrested, the protests became larger and more vocal, with tens of thousands of protesters calling for Anwar's release and Mahathir's resignation. On 24 October, the protests turned violent as police and demonstrators clashed in the streets of Kuala Lumpur. The sacking of Anwar was interpreted by non-Malay Malaysians as a 'family' dispute, meaning it was a matter to be sorted out within the Malay community. As a consequence, while non-Malay Malaysians looked on with considerable interest, it was not a dispute they wished to involve themselves in.

Although there had been considerable speculation about a leadership challenge and Mahathir had mentioned Anwar as his eventual successor, Anwar was not in the throes of mounting a direct leadership challenge when he was sacked. Anwar was, thereafter, unable to put together a viable opposition political organisation once he was charged with criminal offences, although his wife, Wan Azizah Wan Ismail, did organise the *Partai Rakyat Keadilan* (People's Justice Party) on his behalf. There remained considerable support for Anwar, particularly from urban middle-class Malays, who were the most active group within UMNO. UMNO did not openly fracture, but the Anwar issue deeply divided the party (Choong & Arjuna 1998).

ANWAR'S TRIAL

Anwar noted during his trial that the charges against him were a consequence of his 'major differences' with Mahathir, in particular over economic policy in response to Malaysia's economic crisis (*Daily Express* 1999a). This evidence was disallowed by the trial judge. Apart from the legal campaign, Mahathir also launched a two-pronged attack on Anwar that effectively found him guilty before he had been tried. In a conventional judicial system, these comments would be regarded as *sub judice*, that is, as interference in or having the ability to sway the independent affairs of the court. Mahathir told a news conference,

I interviewed the people he sodomised, the women he had sex with, the driver who brought the women to him ... They told me this in the absence of the police or anybody else ... They denied being forced and they told me they were telling the truth. Several of them even said this man was not fit to become leader (Baker 1998; Stewart & Alford 1998).

Such comments were not only subsequently denied by some of those Mahathir supposedly interviewed, they also prejudged the trial. Further, Malaysia's tightly controlled media also ran a series of stories on Anwar that recounted in full Mahathir's claims against him, as well as recounting details of the charges. Along with a booklet entitled *50 Reasons Why Anwar Can Not Be Prime Minister*, which was anonymously circulated at a party congress in June 1998, Anwar was clearly being set up as the victim of a well-orchestrated smear campaign. A number of witnesses later said that they had been forced to lie and that their allegations against Anwar were not true. The local media continued to disclose allegations against Anwar outside evidence presented in his court case. Mahathir also made several announcements that Anwar was clearly guilty of the charges, even though the court case was continuing and that the charges to which Mahathir referred were dropped.

Initial signs that the trial of Anwar would reflect Mahathir's wishes occurred when Anwar was refused bail. Given that the charges against him did not imply a threat to anyone else, the only reason he could have been refused bail was if his freedom during the trial could have drawn his supporters together. A further indication of how proceedings did not conform with conventional procedures was when the trial judge, Augustine Paul, disallowed what would have been the submission of conventional evidence in the defence. He also refused to allow the trial to be adjourned, even though Anwar was required to give evidence at a Royal Commission of Inquiry and could not attend his own trial. The Royal Commission was investigating the cause of Anwar's injuries while in police custody (*New Straits Times* 1999).

Anwar told the Royal Commission that, while he was blindfolded and handcuffed, he believed that he had been assaulted by the chief of police, Rahim Noor. He said he heard the distinctive sound of Noor clearing his throat. Anwar was hit seven times during the assault and was bleeding from the nose and mouth. He later lost consciousness (Wong 1999). Noor later said he assaulted Anwar because Anwar had insulted him. It was three days after the assault before Anwar was examined by doctors. Noor resigned from his position in December 1998 and was convicted of assaulting Anwar.

Anwar ended up facing four counts of corruption for allegedly using his former position to (unsuccessfully) order police to quash charges of sexual misconduct that had been levelled against him. There was also another count of corruption, although, the sexual misconduct charges were dropped during the trial, which itself was a highly unusual procedure. Judge Paul said the sexual misconduct charges need not be established to prove the corruption charges.

While in prison during the period of his trial, Anwar began communicating with another jailed DAP member of parliament, Lim Guan Eng, who 'sits in a dingy cell with only a ventilation hole in the ceiling. His crime: asking why a powerful government politician was not detained in a statutory rape case'. The reference was to Abdul Rahim Tamby Chik, a 'Mahathir loyalist' (*FEER Yearbook* 1997: 164) and former chief minister of Lim's home state of Malacca. Lim had previously been jailed for eighteen months when Mahathir 'cracked down' on the Opposition in 1987 (Roy 1999).

On 14 April 1999, Judge Paul sentenced Anwar to six years in jail for corruption and sodomy. Part of the significance of this sentence was that it was far in excess of any previous sentence for a similar offence (usually about two years) and that it did not take into account the nine months Anwar had already spent in prison, which was contrary to the British legal convention upon which Malaysia claims to base its own laws. More importantly, though, it showed that Mahathir would not hesitate to use whatever means he believed necessary to quell genuine opposition to his rule.

MAHATHIR'S FIRST POST-ANWAR TEST

The first political test for Mahathir in the wake of the start of the Anwar trial came with state elections in Sabah. Responding to reservations by the opposition *Partai Bersatu Sabah* (PBS, United Sabah Party) about Sabah's continuing links with the federation, Abdullah Ahmad Badawi, then deputy prime minister and home affairs minister, threatened the opposition. He said the government 'may have to act' as a consequence of what it called 'fanning anti-Federalist sentiments that arouse feelings of hatred towards Peninsular Malaysia and the Federal Government' (Sunar 1999). The PBS was in particular disfavour with the government as it had left the *Barisan Nasional* in 1990 and achieved state government in Sabah in 1994.

A second indication of the deeply patronising tone of Malaysian politicking was in a public statement by a sitting BN candidate to a challenger. 'As an older brother, I advise [Dayang] Maimuh not to challenge me,' said Kahar Mustapha, the *Barisan Nasional* member for Banggi. 'Maimuh is only wasting her time because the people in Banggi have already decided who to support in the coming state polls' (*Daily Express* 1999c). There was also a tendency for sitting government members to criticise ungrateful voters, who were expected to show loyalty to the government. Sabah's deputy chief minister, Joseph Karup, told local community leaders not to 'collaborate with the Opposition' or 'anti-federal elements'. Karup described people who did so as 'traitors ... as they forgot that the infrastructure and basic amenities they currently enjoyed were through the efforts and initiatives of the Barisan Nasional leaders' (*Daily Express* 1999b). Clearly, the use of such language, including the terms 'directive' and 'traitors', introduced a degree of partisanship that did not reflect the idea that governments carried out their time in office as a public duty, but did indicate a linkage between voting and rewards.

The *Barisan Nasional* took the elections very seriously, spending a lot of money on campaigning. Local people noted that there were more than the usual number of *Barisan Nasional* flags fluttering from many homes and other buildings throughout the state. The elections were contested by a large number of small parties, including ethnic-based parties, many of which were linked to the *Barisan Nasional*, as well as the *Barisan Nasional* and the PBS. While the *Barisan Nasional* won the Sabah state elections, it did so with a considerably reduced majority, indicating that the antics of Mahathir, in what was increasingly seen as the political persecution of Anwar, were having a detrimental effect on his legitimacy as leader.

THE 1999 ELECTIONS

While the Sabah elections were an initial post-Anwar test, the elections of November 1999 clearly delineated the fallout from the affair. The BN won 148 of the 193 available seats, giving it the election. But UMNO lost nineteen seats to PAS, reducing its total to seventy-four. PAS also captured the state of Trengganu while making further advances in the state of Kelantan, which it already held. In Mahathir's home state of Kedah, PAS had eight federal seats to UMNO's seven. Four UMNO ministers lost their seats as a consequence of the shift in UMNO's fortunes. Anwar's wife, Wan Azizah, won Anwar's seat in Penang representing the newly formed *Partai Keadilan Rakyat*. The DAP won ten seats, but appeared to be in long-term decline (Alford 1999: 7). The damage inflicted upon UMNO, notably in the northern Malay heartland seats reflected a high level of disapproval for Mahathir's leadership style and was worrying to UMNO strategists.

What was also of interest in the 1999 elections was that Malaysia's ethnic Chinese community fell more strongly behind the MCA and the BN, reflecting what was said to be a deep concern over the rise of a more fundamentalist Islamic political orientation. The formal alignment of the DAP with the PAS for the 1999 elections no doubt contributed to Chinese voter support for the MCA.

The mixed showing of the BN generally and of UMNO in particular confirmed Mahathir's decision to retire from the prime ministership. While Mahathir had publicly anointed Abdullah Badawi as his successor as UMNO president and prime minister, Razaleigh Hamza indicated that he would challenge for the succession. Who won this contest was less important than the divisions it demonstrated within UMNO. Razaleigh could probably have counted on less than one-third of the votes from UMNO members for himself, but angry Anwar supporters could have shifted a further one-third of the party behind him (Elegant 2000; Singh & Ranawana 2000). This meant that somewhere close to half of the members of UMNO, perhaps more, were not prepared to accept Mahathir's candidate and, consequently, were rejecting his style of rule.

One thing the election results did show was that, for there to be a credible alternative to Mahathir—and to UMNO—the opposition against him had to be united. To date, they have not been and this division has been a significant factor in the opposition's weakness. While UMNO remained united and could count on the loyalty of the MCA and the MIC, it was not likely to be removed from office, despite the varying positions of the minor parties. The variety of controls ranged against the opposition, from media restrictions to electoral rorts, also limited the real possibility of political change.

RADICAL ISLAM

In the period after, but not corresponding to, Malaysia's 1999 elections, there was a marked rise in the activities of Malaysia's radical Islamism. Malaysia's Malay community had always been more formally Islamic than many of their regional Malay siblings, and Islam is the required religion for all ethnic Malays, as is observance of *syariah* (Islamic law). In particular, in the northern states and among the Malay community of Singapore, Islam had a very strong hold, and it was in the north that PAS had its strongest support base. It was also here that radical Islamism, that is, ideological Islam, developed its deepest roots. With Malaysia's commitment to Islam for Malays, it was a natural home for Muslims from regional Islamic communities who had been persecuted for various Islam-related activities. Prominent among those were political refugees from Indonesia, notably key members of the organisation that came to be known as *Jema'ah Islamiyah* (Islamic Community).

KAMPULAN MILITAN MALAYSIA

The best known—and perhaps only—militant Islamic group in Malaysia is *Kampulan Militan Malaysia* (KMM, or Malaysian Militant Community), which is the name given to this group by the Malaysian government, rather than identifying it as *Jema'ah Islamiyah* (JI) (see Indonesia chapter) and which is a more organisationally correct nomenclature.[15] JI had established a business and commercial network in Malaysia in the 1990s in order to help fund its various projects and, at this time, also established a full administrative structure, fitting in with JI's wider if somewhat less formal regional structure. Among the early targets of KMM were selected Western embassies in Singapore, Changi Airport, Singaporean defence facilities, visiting US military personnel and Western warships in the Straits of Malacca (Apdal & Thayer 2003: 21; see also, RS 2003: 11, 14). In this, JI–KMM did not distinguish between Malaysia and Singapore, regarding both as being within the same (first) *mantiqi* (field of operations) along with southern Thailand and parts of Cambodia.

Although local contacts with notable JI figures such as Abu Bakar Ba'asyir dated back several years, JI Malaysia and JI Singapore were probably founded around 1994 or 1995 by Hambali and Abu Jibril, who focused their efforts on Indonesian immigrants and students and lecturers at the *Universiti Tecknologi Malaysia*, as well as among local Islamic schools. Ali Ghufron (Muklas) and Imam Samudra, who were central to the bombing of two nightclubs in Bali in October 2002, which killed 202 people, both came from one school in Johor Baru. KMM's local founding member was an Afghan war veteran, Zainon Ismail, who, in keeping with the JI caliphate model, promoted the violent overthrow of the Malaysian government and the creation of a pan-archipelagic Islamic state.

Under the tutelage of Hamabali, Abu Jibril and Zainon, militant young Malaysian and Singaporeans were sent for religious indoctrination in Pakistan, while about fifty others were sent to al–Qaeda training camps in Afghanistan, while yet others went to MILF camps in Mindanao (see Philippines chapter). Total membership of JI–KMM probably did not exceed seventy or eighty people at any one time. Around 1999–2000, JI groups in Malaysia and Singapore were converted into operational cells, with leadership of the KMM passing to Nik Adli Aziz. The Singapore branch, referred to by the Singaporean government as *Jema'ah Islamiyah* rather than KMM, dated to 1988–89, with the induction of Ibrahim Maidin by Abu Jibril. Maidin was subsequently appointed to JI's consultative council, although, while remaining as spiritual adviser, was replaced by Mas Selamat bin Kastari as JI Singapore leader in 1999 (RS 2003: 10).

The Malaysian and Singaporean JI network was damaged in 1999 after a series of arrests by Malaysian police (Jibril was arrested in June 2000) and Singapore's Internal Security Department. A further twenty-one suspects, nineteen of whom were identified as JI members, were arrested in Singapore in 2001 and 2002, thwarting a bombing campaign against Western embassies and ending JI operations in Singapore from that time. However, KMM members did carry out a number of attacks, including the murder of a Kedah politician in 2000, after which Malaysian police arrested a further sixty members.

KMM–JI had been able to operate in Malaysia and Singapore due to a high level of sympathy for anti-Western views, especially after the US-led attack on Afghanistan, protest against which was led by the religiously oriented but mainstream *Partai Islam se-Maaysia* (PAS, or Malaysian Islamic Party), which had called for jihad against the USA. Most of the sixteen detainees the Malaysian government had claimed were members of KMM were also affiliated with PAS, including PAS youth committee member, Mohamad Lotfi Ariffin, together with KMM leader Nik Adli Aziz, who was the son of PAS spiritual leader and senior minister of Malaysia's Kelantan state, Nik Aziz (HRW 2004). Nik Adli Aziz had been named as one of those present at a 1999 meeting of some twenty people called by Abu Bakar

Ba'asyir and Hambali, which discussed the establishment of a Mujahidin International (*Rabitatul Mujahidin*). The meeting included representatives from the MILF, the Burmese Rohingya Solidarity Organisation, the Arakanese Rohingya Nationalist Organisation, Thailand's Pattani United Liberation Organisation, Front Mujahidin and the *Republik Islam Acheh*[16] (Wong & Lourdes 2003). In late 2001, the Malaysian government arrested former Philippines Moro National Liberation Front leader and ex-governor of the Autonomous Region of Muslim Mindanao, Nur Misuari, for illegal entry into Malaysia, marking increased cooperation between regional countries in their mutual fight against Islamist terrorism.

MAHATHIR RESIGNS

In June 2002, at the UMNO general assembly, Mahathir announced that he would resign his posts in UMNO and in BN, meaning that he would also resign as prime minister. Although long expected, the announcement caused shock and a general sense of disbelief among Mahathir's followers. In response to the reaction, Mahathir agreed to stay on as prime minister for a further sixteen months to allow a smooth transition to his anointed successor, Deputy Prime Minister Abdullah Badawi. If his decision to retire marked the coming end of his political career, it was not because he had lost any of the rancor that seems to fire him. Indeed, just four months later, in a speech he made while hosting a summit of Islamic countries, Mahathir stunned and outraged most of the world by claiming that Jews ruled the world by proxy, getting other nations to fight their wars for them.

Mahathir's twenty-two years as prime minister thus ended as he had characterised them: combative, insular and combining his authoritarian tendencies with fantasist delusions. Yet those years also saw Malaysia's economy become one of Asia's tiger cubs, that is, a newly industrialising economy. His grand 2020 vision for Malaysia was manifested in 1996 in the erection of the world's tallest building, Kuala Lumpur's Petronas Towers, and in the technology corridor centred on the small new city of Cyberjaya. However, twenty years of subsidisation for a loss-making national car, the Proton (Jomo 2003: ch. 11), losses on the national steel company, Perwaja, and a range of other losses on ventures that attempted to copy the Japanese and Korean models of internally self-supporting conglomerates, also marked Mahathir's rule (Jomo 2003: ch. 20). In one sense, Malaysia appeared to prosper, almost despite some of Mahathir's economic policies. His support for ethnic Malays acquiring businesses and the privatisation of government industries did not meaningfully shift the economy towards non-Chinese ownership or control. What it did, however, was engender a sense of nepotism and corruption that became the prime focus of Mahathir's successor.

When Abdullah Badawi assumed the prime ministership in October 2003, few had much expectation that he would mark himself out as distinct from Mahathir. Most believed he would be, at best, a pale imitation. Yet the first year or so of Badawi's prime ministership were marked by a distinct and well-received style. His move against nepotism and corruption was well received, as were his clear Islamic credentials, especially among voters who had begun to turn to PAS and PAK, and he worked behind the scenes to have Anwar Ibrahim freed after almost six years in jail, in which Anwar's convictions were overturned. When the Mahathir-less UMNO was tested in the 2004 elections, the BN won 198 of the possible 219 parliamentary seats (*Star*, 5 April 2004) on 64 per cent of the vote, with UMNO securing 109 seats in its own right, an increase of thirty-two seats. There was no doubt, from this result, that Mahathir had outlived his political usefulness and, similarly, no doubt that Badawi was widely regarded as representing a return to a type of politics preferred by a large majority of Malaysians.

While UMNO did well in the elections, the main opposition party, PAS, did very poorly, losing twenty of its twenty-seven seats, including that of its leader, Abdul Hadi Awang. This result was widely interpreted outside Malaysia as a victory for moderate Islam and a blow to Islamic extremism. There was some accuracy in this analysis, at least in terms of it being a victory for moderate Islam, which Badawi represented; however, the view that it was also a defeat for radical Islamism reflected more the preoccupations of outside observers with Islamic terrorism than any fundamental shift in Malaysia's Islamic landscape. The radicals were still there, if increasingly in jail; it was just that most Malaysian Muslims saw their problems being better addressed by the new leader than by lodging what, in hindsight, looked like a protest vote.

Yet if anyone thought that Badawi intended to turn back the clock, especially in relation to Anwar Ibrahim, they were mistaken. Despite being material in obtaining Anwar's release, Badawi made it clear that, even though the charges against him had been dismissed by the Appeals Court as unsubstantiated, he was not welcomed back into UMNO. Badawi had achieved not just the prime ministership, but also a legitimacy that could not be obtained simply as Mahathir's successor. There was little prospect, having made the position his own, that he was prepared to share its authority.

NOTES

1   The name Badawi is Malay for 'Bedouin'.
2   Following in this tradition, there was a renewed flow of migration from Sumatra to the Malay Peninsula in the wake of Indonesia's economic crisis from mid 1997, and from Aceh from 1999.
3   Most of the inhabitants of Malacca had converted to Islam following the conversion of Raja Kasim (later known as Sultan Muzaffar Shah), who took the throne in 1446.
4   The Bajaus and the related Illanuns were 'by nature and education undisciplined robbers, searovers and freebooters' and, under the leadership of one Mat Saleh, 'gave the Directors many uneasy moments' (Evans 1922)

5   The background to Sarawak is included in the section on Brunei.

6   The Malayan Communist Party was originally established under a front organisation, the Nanyang General Labour Union, in 1926, and under the name Nanyang Communist Party the following year. Nanyang is the Chinese term for the 'South Seas'. The Malayan Communist Party was formally established in 1929.

7   This was in exchange for the release of political prisoners. Four MCP groups totalling 165 men were trained by the British before the fall of Singapore on 15 February 1952 (Comber 1995).

8   This was a 'confidential' government document, so its author (probably an MI6 intelligence agent) was not identified.

9   This 'systematic resettlement of Chinese squatters in New Villages' (*A Short History of the Malayan Communist Party* 1955: 23) was later adopted, with less success, by the USA in its strategic hamlets program in South Vietnam.

10   The Chinese community in Thailand has largely blended with the Thais. However, in the less clearly defined region of southern Thailand, there is a greater Islamic Malay population, which the Chinese remain quite separate from, hence their more clearly defined local identity.

11   It has also been suggested that universal suffrage and the elected position of the leaders of Negri Sembilan also acted as a model for the federation of Malaysia (Groves 1962: 270).

12   This is usually translated as 'supreme ruler', but literally recalls the regional title 'lord of the mountain (*agong*).'

13   This assertion is based on material publicly available at various historical sites in Kuching, Sarawak.

14   Based on private conversations in Kota Kinabalu, Kuching and Sibu.

15   The Malaysian government had previously called KMM *Kampulan Mujahidin Malaysia*, although this was thought to be too explicitly Islamic in orientation; hence the change.

16   The *Republik Islam Acheh* was originally formed in the early 1960s after the collapse of the Darul Islam revolt; that movement ended soon after. The version referred to here is regarded by the Free Aceh Movement (*Gerakan Aceh Merdeka*, or GAM, formally Acheh–Sumatra National Liberation Front) as a fake organisation fronting on behalf of the Indonesian intelligence community.

11 | Brunei: Floating on Oil

Brunei is an interesting anomaly in the makeup of SEA, being a tiny sultanate that could not afford to exist if not for its very considerable supplies of oil and natural gas. Because of this, Brunei chose to stay outside the Malaysian Federation, even though, apart from its sea border, it is entirely bounded by Malaysia. Brunei has a similar history to the other sultanates that came to comprise Malaysia and, because of its geography, history and ethnic composition, is considered adjacent to the section on Malaysia. While Brunei is a sultanate and, for more than 40 years, an absolute monarchy, it has recently begun to change, with the sultan introducing reforms intended to engage the citizens, in particular, through reactiviating the legislative council.

Formally known as Negara Brunei Darussalam, Brunei is located within the Malaysian state of Sarawak in the centre of the northern part of the island of Borneo.[1] Its earliest population is believed to have come to the island around 2000 BCE. These Proto-Malays lived predominantly inland, along the island's many significant rivers and, in some areas, in the mountains. Chinese traders are known to have visited the north coast of Borneo, in particular, from early in the CE, trading manufactured goods such as pottery and later metalwork for jungle produce such as plant extracts, animal skins, and feathers. Immigration to Borneo probably continued at a low level from the earliest times, as waves of people leaving the mainland and western archipelago drifted eastwards, many ultimately settling in the Philippines. Thus, the north coast of Borneo was an early trade and migration route.

Deutero-Malays began to make a noticeable impact on coastal Borneo from around the eighth and ninth centuries CE, as regional states began attempting to assert their trading and political hegemony over the region. The sea-based trading state of Sri Vijaya, located near modern Palembang in southern Sumatra, was the first regional power to lay claim to Borneo's coast and, therefore, to its interior. From this time until the rise of a domestic sultanate, coastal Borneo received increasing, although still relatively limited, numbers of Malay immigrants. It was upon this predominantly Malay population that the first local power was based, the remnant of which exists today as Brunei.

Brunei rose to prominence as a Malay state between the fourteenth and sixteenth centuries and exercised political control over much of coastal Borneo, the Sulu Islands and parts of the southern Philippines. During the fifteenth century, Brunei rivalled Malacca as the leading regional power, although the two states traded amicably. In 1511, Malacca fell to the Portuguese and from then onwards growing Portuguese, Spanish and, later,

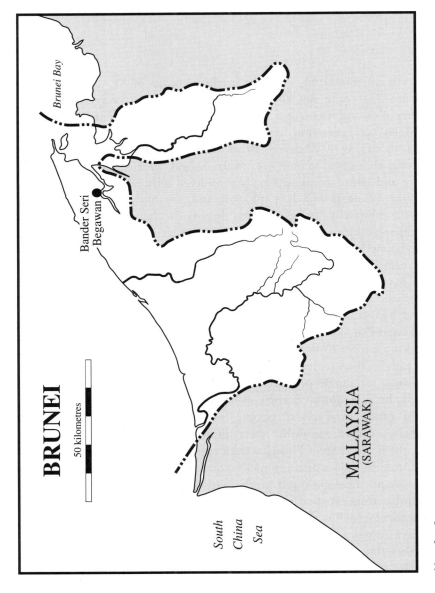

Map 8 Brunei

Dutch and English, influence in the region limited Brunei's influence to Borneo's northern coast. Mostly as a consequence of Dutch intervention in the regional spice trade and the growth of sea trade with China, local seamen took to piracy, which had long been considered a viable way of making a living. Success made these pirates 'bolder and more insolent' (Runciman 1960: 17–25). Between the power of the local sultan and the high level of piracy, European attempts at establishing bases in Borneo met with little success.[2] The British contented themselves with establishing a new base at Penang, while the Dutch abandoned Borneo in the face of greater economic difficulty and conflict with the United Kingdom over their involvement in the American War of Independence.

In 1811, Thomas Raffles led the British occupation of Java and, under the conditions of its occupation, the United Kingdom, through the East India Company, renewed its commercial and political interests in north Borneo. This interest was piqued when Raffles was informed that pirates from Serawa (Sarawak) had taken a British ship, in response to which, by 1813, Raffles had secured the entire coast of the island, except for the northwest tip. Under the new agreement, it was intended that British control be relinquished in 1816, at which time the Netherlands would resume its regional control; the north coast of Borneo fell outside the terms of this agreement[3] (Runciman 1960: 34–41).

When Raffles later wrote of the potential of Brunei, one of his readers was James Brooke. Brooke had been born in India in 1803 and, after being educated in England, returned as an officer to India, where he became noted for his bravery and initiative. He was wounded in battle, which saw the end of his military career. After a long recovery and one failed venture, but still with a well-developed sense of the potential of the Far East, Brooke took his own ship to Singapore in 1839 and, thence, to the Sarawak River in the western part of what was then Brunei (Runciman 1960: 45–55).

Brooke ingratiated himself with Brunei's sultan by helping to suppress revolts of inland Dayaks[4] (predominantly Iban), who were noted for 'a weakness for "lifting" human heads from their owner's shoulders—purely as a matter of sport and prowess, partly as a matter of religion' (Evans 1922). In 1841, as payment in return for suppressing the revolt, Brooke negotiated his first gift of land from the sultanate of Brunei. Despite being unable to control piracy in the region, the sultan ceded two further parcels of land, to adjoin Sarawak (Runciman 1960: chs II–VI), as continued payment to Brooke. A formal treaty with the United Kingdom, signed in 1847, provided for the development of commercial links and the suppression of piracy, which continued as a regional problem. Brooke thereafter set himself up as a rajah and, in this guise, administered Sarawak, which remained under the direct control of his family for three generations, until its occupation by Japanese forces in WWII.

As an erstwhile part of Brunei, Sarawak underwent slightly unusual colonial development under Brooke and his successors. James Brooke was unable to attract British interest in colonising the region; indeed, setting himself up as rajah was generally not well received in London. Brooke's entreaties to England to establish a company there, which would, in effect, administer the region and allow Brooke the opportunity to develop his private commercial interests without the burden of territorial administration, were also unsuccessful (Reece 1988: 22–5). James Brooke's nephew, Charles, took local administration more firmly in hand, building the physical and the administrative structures of state. It was this nephew who more fully developed the natural resources of the state and who encouraged fixed rather than shifting cultivation as a source of the state's economy. He also strongly encouraged Chinese settlement, through gestures as diverse as assisted passage and nominal leaseholds for plantations of cheap opium. He encouraged mining for antimony, coal, mercury and, later, oil (Reece 1988: 26–30). Between Charles Brooke's development and the Japanese invasion, Sarawak underwent little further development, although it had secured for itself a future that was, by now, irretrievably separate from that of the sultanate of Brunei.

ESTABLISHING THE MODERN STATE

Sabah, a portion of which had also been a part of Brunei's territory, was ceded to the British North Borneo Company, which was chartered in 1881. All three states—Brunei, Sabah and Sarawak—became British protectorates in 1888, with Brunei negotiating its own treaty. From 1906, under the protectorate, Brunei's sultan was advised by a British Resident on all matters except local custom and religion. When the state of Malaysia was granted independence in 1959, Sarawak and Sabah moved to join the federation, formalising the arrangement in 1963; Brunei chose to stay apart, achieving its full independence in three stages. Because of the piecemeal way in which northern Borneo was carved up during the colonial period, Brunei came to exist in two closely located but physically separate parts (Turnbull 1989: 155–70, 283–5; Bedlington 1978: 257–9).

The United Kingdom was pressured by the United Nations to grant Brunei's independence, but the sultan and his son argued against it, fearing the state would either be swallowed by Malaysia or succumb to internal dissent. In 1959, Brunei was given a larger measure of internal domestic rule, in 1971 full internal sovereignty and, in 1984, full political sovereignty, including responsibility for its own external affairs and defence.

Brunei did briefly flirt with a representative form of government, holding its first and, for over forty years, last elections in August 1962, in which the *Partai Ra'kyat* (Peoples' Party) won an overwhelming majority. The main platform of the *Partai Ra'kyat* was the incorporation of Sarawak and Sabah into Brunei as a united state (Parmer 1969: 308). However, the Sultan refused to allow the convening of the Legislative Council and, in response, on 8 December 1962, the party's armed wing, the North Borneo National Army, launched an armed uprising against the sultan, Sir Omar Ali Saifuddin.

The cause of this uprising has been variously interpreted. One view is that the uprising was a sideshow in Indonesia's looming *Konfrontasi* with Malaysia, with the anti-government rebels being supported by Sukarno's government in a bid to bring North Borneo into a Greater Indonesia (*Indonesia Raya*). The revolt was, in fact, used as a pretext for Indonesia's launching of the *Konfrontasi*. Another view is that the anti-government rebels were communist-inspired, being linked to the Malayan Communist Party (MCP), which had been engaged in the Malayan Emergency, a communist insurgency, throughout most of the 1950s. These two views have been suggested as having a common cause, with the Indonesian Communist Party (PKI) being sympathetic to the MCP. A third view is that Brunei's rebels were genuine democrats who were opposed to the 1959 proclamation of Brunei's Constitution, claiming it allowed too much power to remain in the hands of the sultan, who exercised that power by not allowing the convening of the Legislative Council. Under British advice, the sultan declared a state of emergency in 1962, at which time the Constitution was suspended, the *Partai Ra'kyat* was proscribed and, with the assistance of the British military, the revolt quelled. Brunei was governed under this state of emergency until 2004.

The revolt in Brunei and its implied loss of monarchical power was a major factor in the sultan deciding that Brunei would not join the Malaysian federation. Other factors that have kept Brunei apart from Malaysia included a claim by the sultan, made in 1970, that, on historical and religious grounds, he had sovereignty over the neighbouring Malaysian towns of Limbang, Lawas and Trusan. Anti-Malaysian sentiment deepened when fifty-nine *Partai Ra'kyat* members, who had been imprisoned without trial since 1962, escaped to Malaysia, where they were given asylum and allowed to establish a political office. In 1975, the Partai Rakyat issued a manifesto in which it called for the establishment of an elected government under a constitutional monarchy (Bedlington 1978: 265–8).

According to the official *Brunei Darussalam in Profile*: 'Brunei's political system rests on the twin pillars of the country's written Constitution and the tradition of Malay Islamic Monarchy. These two facts dominate both the formal political life of Brunei and its government ethos' (1988: 21). In this sense, Brunei is one of the world's very few remaining monarchical states, with its sultan being the twenty-ninth in one of the oldest continual monarchical lines in the world. While this would imply an autocratic style of rule, *Brunei Darussalam in Profile* also claims that a further characteristic of Brunei's political structure is its adherence to the rule of law, which system is primarily based on English common law, and the independence of the judiciary. However, as the Constitution is in a state of indefinite suspension, the sultan rules by decree. To help ensure that there is no further threat to the monarchy, the sultan maintains a well-equipped standing army and employs a battalion of retired Ghurkha soldiers for state and, presumably, personal, defence. Singapore also bases an infantry battalion in Brunei for these reasons (Leifer 1995: 4).

After experimenting with slightly differing systems during each stage of its move towards full independence, Brunei's sultan, Hassanal Bolkiah, assumed the position of head of state, supreme commander of the Royal Brunei Armed Forces, minister of defence and minister of finance; he also retains full executive authority. Since 1984, Brunei has had a cabinet style of government, whose eleven members are appointed by the sultan. One of the sultan's brothers, Prince Mohammed, was appointed as foreign minister, and another, Prince Jefri, was, until 1998, finance minister. The Brunei Solidarity National Party came into existence in 1985, but has only a few hundred members. Government employees—about half the workforce—are not allowed to belong to a political party (Mitton 1998: 32).

Prince Jefri was banished from Brunei by the sultan in mid 1998 after his private Amedeo Corporation, the largest in Brunei, was found to have significant debts. According to one account, the debts amounted to US$16 billion (Spillius 1998; AP 1998), although that figure had been reduced to a more manageable US$3.5 billion when the company was formally wound up in July 1999 (Mitton 2000b). In February 2000, Prince Jefri's assets in the United Kingdom were frozen and the prince was officially said to have made 'improper withdrawal and the use of substantial funds from the Brunei Investment Agency' (BIA) (Mitton 2000a). The BIA was said to have controlled more than US$30 billion when Jefri took over, but less than US$20 billion when he left in 1998.

Along with this profligacy, Brunei's attempts to diversify its economy away from an almost total dependence on oil were 'desultory' (Gunn 2001: 80). In particular, the development of financial and investment services, fisheries and ecotourism were all attempted, but each floundered. In 2000, the Brunei Economic Council even tried to value add on its oil exporting by developing downstream refining (Gunn 2001: 80). However, Brunei faced key shortages in its bid for diversification, including 'labor, capital, resources, and management skills' in a 'political and cultural system that is often highly rigid, conservative and traditionalist' (Cleary & Wong 1994: 123, quoted in Gunn 2001: 80).

Despite having scope for what was claimed as financial irresponsibility, seemingly as a consequence of a lack of representation or public accountability, Brunei's political system was still alleged to 'provide for a degree of reciprocity in the relationship between subjects and Monarch' (*Brunei Darussalam* 1988: 24–5). The pending trial and open manner in which Prince Jefri's affairs were handled was seen by many as a move towards greater accountability, whereas others viewed it as more of a family feud, noting that it was highly unlikely that Prince Jefri would see the inside of a jail.

Perhaps the main reason this otherwise constrained political system worked was because of the wealth the country derived from oil and natural gas. With a population of just 300 000 people, about two-thirds of whom are ethnic Deutero–Malay, Brunei enjoys a high, if officially unstated, per capita income, although this has fluctuated considerably with the international price of oil. PPP GDP was somewhat lower, due to the relatively high price of goods in Brunei, although this was, in turn, balanced by the free or subsidised provision of a number of services. Because of this income, Brunei, until the end of the twentieth century, had a unique social welfare system, with free education, full healthcare benefits and no taxation. However, a 40 per cent slump in the price of oil in 1998 put pressure on Brunei's government to put the rest of its economic house in order.

Brunei once had an active anti-corruption unit and a relatively good human rights record, however, according to Amnesty International, Brunei had seven prisoners of conscience who had been held without charge or trial, four of them for more than twenty-eight years and one for fourteen years. Brunei's penal code is relatively harsh and lashings were common for many offences (Amnesty International 1990: 51–2).

In September 2004, the sultan amended the constitution to allow the reintroduction of the appointed twenty-one member Legislative Council, which had been abandoned in 1984. The new council members include the sultan, his brother and the foreign minister, Prince Mohamed Bolkiah, government officials, prominent business executives and community leaders. In addressing the council, the sultan did not discuss the option of elections, but did say that any expansion of the council would depend on its performance. 'Its existence is not designed to spark chaos and apprehension among the community,' the Sultan said. 'Any mistake carries risk that takes time to ameliorate. As such, we begin this process with caution' (AFP 25 September 2004). It was a modest step towards a government that focused on more than just the sultan and his immediate circle, although it represented a limited expansion of that circle. It was still a long way from the democratic process that had, four decades earlier, indicated that most citizens of Brunei wanted something quite different.

NOTES

1   The word 'Borneo' is a European derivation of the name 'Brunei'.
2   Madras being on the sea route from India to China, Alexander Dalrymple, who was stationed there, was sent in 1759 to Borneo, where he made an agreement with the sultan of Sulu in 1761 to exchange trade for defence cooperation. A trading post was thereafter established on Balambangan Island off the northern tip of Borneo in 1773 (Turnbull 1989: 89).
3   The agreement gave Dutch all islands south of Singapore, but was ambiguous about that part of Borneo north of Singapore.
4   It should be noted that these Proto-Malay people do not call themselves Dayaks, rather, they use their tribal names (Iban, Penan, Kayan, Baram, Kenyah, etc.). As with so many other smaller ethnic groups, they were given that name by their primary oppressors, in this case Deutero-Malays.

12 | Philippines: Oligarchic Democracy

The Philippines, named after Philip of Spain, is a country that is at the crossroads of various political cultures, all of which are combined to produce an only semi-functional state. At the most superficial level, Philippines political society seemingly literally interprets many aspects of popular American culture, but its background is steeped in the traditions of Spanish colonialism. The Philippines' political process is also superficially modelled on that of the USA, although notions of authority, power, legitimacy and natural justice—or lack thereof—similarly derive from the colonial Spanish, which latter finds reflection in the maintenance of large land holdings associated with politically powerful families, the construction of a politically and economically underdeveloped *campesino* peasant culture and the entrenched Roman Catholicism. Between them is the role of what is, at least nominally, a democratic society.

The Philippines has long been troubled by insurgencies, in turn mirroring its similarly long domination by a relatively small clique of wealthy families that control the country's businesses and political process (the so-called 400 families), who come from a political tradition in which the non-elite exists primarily to serve their interests, which has engendered a culture of exploitation. In this mutually reinforcing oligarchy, the sharing of favours—corruption—is deeply embedded. So, too, as a means of survival for the millions of poor, and taking a cue from the elite, corruption is also entrenched across other levels of Philippine society.

These factors are intimately linked. The ruling families include the Cojuangcos, who dominate Tarlac province north of Manila, the Osmenas, who control central Cebu province, the Macapagals, who dominate Pampanga, the second-largest province of vote-rich Central Luzon, the Bagatsings, whose land holdings underpin their authority in Manila, and the Lopezes, who dominate in central Iloilo province and nearby Guimaras island. These families, and their supporters have retained their influence and

Map 9 Philippines

wealth despite the reforms enacted—or not—since the overthrow of former President Marcos. While reformists have gradually gained some influence, changes have been slow and few and political violence has remained. The presidency of the Philippines has changed, in the post-Marcos era, with democratic regularity, but, as with much of public life in the Philippines, the changes have been relatively superficial.

BEFORE THE SPANISH

The history of the islands now known as the Philippines is, to a large extent, unclear prior to the arrival of Islam. No records were kept and archeological remains are few. The Philippines were populated through a series of waves of migration, first by Negritos, and then, after the loss of land bridges, by Nesiot peoples, whose descendants now occupy the inland regions and still practise shifting cultivation, predominantly of maize rather than rice. The last wave of immigrants were the Malay peoples, who began to arrive in the region from the last few centuries BCE and whose immigration probably continued, as an extension of their spread throughout the region, to colonial times. Contrary to some claims, it is highly unlikely that the Sri Vijaya or Majapahit empires, of Sumatra and Java respectively, ever extended more than occasional trade to this region (Fisher 1966: 698–9). Chinese traders, however, had been resident in the Philippines from around 1000 CE (Nelson 1968: 22–6).

The overwhelming religious influence of the region was animist, rather than the Indianised religions that became dominant further to the west. This was, in large part, due to the more western SEA states adopting these religious structures to better suit the hierarchical administrative requirements of the larger, more sophisticated political societies of the Indonesian–Malay archipelago. From a more cultural perspective, two prevailing influences were an 'obligation to avenge harm or insult to a member of one's family' and patron–client relations. This latter aspect neatly dovetailed with Spanish feudal traditions (Wurfel 1988: 2–3, 25, 34).

From around the fourteenth century, following its spread throughout the Malay world, Islam came to the coastal areas of southern Luzon, Mindanao and, in particular the Visayas via northern Borneo, Palawan and the Sulu Archipelago. With Islam came some attempts to set up forms of government such as under a *datu* (chief or lord) and the more Indianised rajahs (kings). But without a suitable political base upon which these more elaborate structures could build, even the arrival of Islam did not fundamentally alter the simple, local style of political organisation, as there was no preexisting state upon which it could found these institutional structures. And, despite following some of the political styles originating elsewhere in the Malay world, the impact of Islam was, in most cases, superficial, which enabled the succeeding Spanish to imprint their own colonial culture so effectively (Fisher 1966:

699–70). Had Islam had more time to implant itself, the Philippines might have become an Islamic society, as had its cousins to the west, but proselytisation was interrupted by the arrival of the Spanish and their at least equally aggressive proselytising Christian missionaries.

In the interim, political life in the Philippines continued as it had done since time immemorial, with only a local form of government, the *barangay*, which was a kinship group approximating a village. The political structure of a *barangay* comprised a *datu*, who presided over a community of free men, serfs and slaves. Sometimes such *barangay* would come together in a federation, but these alliances were brief and localised (Wurfel 1964: 680). With *barangay* unable to form lasting coalitions, there was no centralised governmental structure ruling over any large area. As a consequence, there was also no political elite of note or a court culture from which Filipinos might have drawn a political tradition. Without such a unifying tradition or a commonly accepted set of political values, there was no sense of a greater identity or national cohesion. This lack of national cohesion was reflected in the more than eighty distinct linguistic groups, eight of which comprise 90 per cent of all Filipinos (Wurfel 1988: 27) that make up the population of the contemporary state.

This lack of a broader history upon which nationalism might have been built had two, interrelated consequences. The first was that the Philippines has had a strong external focus, which made it highly susceptible to foreign influence, the result of its links with Chinese traders, Malays and Arab Muslims, the Spanish and, later, Americans. The second consequence was that the sense of nationalism that did develop in the Philippines was largely derivative, reflecting a feeling of cultural insecurity, taking as it did, ideological and cultural cues from its colonial masters (Steinberg 1982: 33–5). This latter aspect has negatively impacted on ordinary Filipinos, whose everyday indigenous reality, as opposed to and outside the country's foreign-influenced elite, has relegated them to the margins of public influence.

THE SPANISH ARRIVE

The archipelago was claimed for Spain by Ferdinand Magellan when, in 1521, having crossed the Atlantic Ocean, sailed south of Tierra del Fuego and crossed the Pacific, he and three of his original five ships landed at Cebu in search of spice. After stopping at Guam, they sailed on to the Philippines, arriving on 28 March. After befriending a *barangay datu*, Magellan became involved in a local conflict and was killed in battle on the small island of Lapu-Lapu, opposite Cebu, on 27 April 1521. One of his ships was burnt and, with depleted crew, the other two headed back to Spain, in opposite directions. Only one ship, the *Victoria*, managed to return, via the Cape of Good Hope, with just eighteen of the original 270 crew, making it the first vessel to circumnavigate the globe.

Magellan's voyage was an early expedition of exploration to the region; despite other attempts, it took another fifty years for Spain to extend its control to the Philippines.

Even the Philippine islands themselves were originally not recognised by the Spanish for what they were, rather, they were recognised for what they might lead to, such as trade and religious conversion in China and the Spice Islands (contemporary Maluku), ideas that were discounted as impractical at about the same time as Spain's colonial greatness began to wither. The Philippines was an extension of Spain's South American colonial expansion and its last outpost to the west (rather than the usual sense of European colonialism that posited Asia as the East). Its trade and administration were largely via Mexico and its early administration, particularly at junior levels, was often by those of mixed Spanish descent—Creoles—who were born in the Spanish colonies of the Americas. It was these Creoles, who often stayed on and married locally, who came to constitute the developing dominant economic class of the Philippines.

COLONIAL SETTLEMENT

In 1565, Legaspi established Cebu as the first permanent Spanish settlement in the Philippines, being attracted to that area because it lay across the main Pacific trade route with China and because it was the focal point of the islands of the Visayan Sea. However, in 1569, prompted by Portuguese activities in the Moluccas, Legaspi shifted to Panay, and then, quickly, to the small Muslim stronghold of Manila in 1570. Manila's chief advantage was its fine harbour, which was well sheltered from typhoons, and the large and rich area of low-lying land nearby. Within two years Legaspi had made Manila the centre of administration for the whole archipelago. Not only did Manila soon overtake Cebu as the main Spanish settlement, but it also, primarily because of Chinese trading contacts, quickly, if briefly, became the main trading port in eastern Asia. It was from Manila that Spain set out to consolidate control of the coastal regions, while Augustinian friars began to convert local inhabitants to the Roman Catholic faith. According to Wurfel, this proselytisation was particularly zealous to make up for the disappointment of not finding spices or gold (1988: 4). Due to the superficiality of Islam in the north, these friars met with considerable success, but in the south—Palawan, Sulu and Mindanao—Islam was too deeply entrenched. Spanish responses to Islam were predicated on their bitterness over the holy wars against the Islamic Moors of Spain (Wurfel 1988: 4). An attempt to establish a settlement near Zamboanga in Mindanao in 1596 was thwarted three years later when the settlers were driven out by local Muslims. These Muslims, referred to by the Spanish as 'Moros',[1] retained their independence until midway between the nineteenth century, when steamships shifted the advantage in favour of the Spanish, and the early twentieth century, more than a decade after American troops first arrived (Fisher 1966: 700; Wurfel 1964: 681).

Economic development was late coming to the Philippines. Its early economy relied on Manila as a transhipment port for the silk trade with China, however, cut off from direct contact with Spain due to an old agreement with Portugal not to sail via the Cape of Good Hope, the emerging group of Filipino merchants was unable to influence Madrid to look favourably on the colony's economic development. Instead, in order to secure their domestic business interests, Spanish silk merchants forced the Spanish government to impose limits on the Philippines' galleon trade. Assuming no galleons were lost, the trade left to them was just enough for the Spanish community of Manila to survive (Steinberg 1982: 35). This limited galleon trade also precluded opening up trading relations with other SEA ports, thereby restricting Manila's ability to grow as a regional trading centre. It further acted to distract the resident community from other forms of internal economic development. 'The ease with which the colony could survive created a kind of torpor and, for better or worse, kept the foreigners [Creoles]—except for the priests—isolated and uninvolved' (Steinberg 1982: 35). These strict limits to trade were often demonstrated more in the breach than the observance, which led to the development of a culture of corruption, exacerbated by a more general lack of distinction between public welfare and officials' private benefit, 'a confusion that survives today' (Wurfel 1988:i).

From the early nineteenth century, the Philippines' primary export economy came to rely on plantation crops such as sugar, coconut and tobacco. This agricultural development was managed under the *hacienda* style of economic progress, which was directly borrowed from Spain's American colonies and which reflected the still feudal state of social and economic relations persisting in Spain itself. Under this system, labourers lived and worked on a large, family-owned estate, invariably in highly exploitative circumstances. The inequities of distribution of land ownership exaggerated the already marked divide between the Creole landowning and administrative elites and indigenous Filipinos. This, in turn, has had repercussions for Philippine politics up to the twenty-first century, with a marked division existing between those who are descended from or married into landowning families and those who are landless peasants and, increasingly, urban workers. It also, according to Hutchcroft, gave rise to what was to become a powerful political elite whose interests lay outside concern for the state (1998: 25–6).

With the successful revolt of Spain's American colonies, starting in 1808, and with transhipment thereafter having to be undertaken directly from Spain via the Atlantic and the Pacific Oceans, the Philippines was even more cut off from its colonial master (De Comyn 1969). After 1813, with the ending of the papal decree on the division of the world between Spain and Portugal, the galleons traded directly with Spain via the Cape of Good Hope, a move that matched a gradual relaxation of trading restrictions on the colony. In terms of dominance of trade, however, by 1879 the Philippines was being referred to, in economic terms, as an 'Anglo–Chinese colony flying the Spanish flag' (Hutchcroft 1998: 24). A wave of liberalism in Spain introduced the education decree of 1863, which saw primary education introduced for children from seven to twelve years of age. Many similar decrees were either not implemented or were withdrawn as Spanish politics fluctuated between liberalism and reaction. Between 1810 and 1813, 1820 and 1823 and 1834 and 1835, the Philippines was represented in the Spanish parliament, but was, at other times, excluded, thus heightening the sense of injustice that was beginning to prevail among the Philippines' elite.

The opening of the Suez Canal in 1876 further facilitated contact between Europe and the Philippines, with greater trade between the two. But, politically more importantly, Philippine-born students were beginning to arrive to study at Spanish and other European universities. It was from these students, chafing under an increasing sense of injustice, that the nucleus of the first nationalist movement, known as the Propagandists, was formed. These Propagandists did not want revolution or independence; what they wanted was formal incorporation as a province of Spain (Wurfel 1964: 684).

AMERICAN COLONIALISM

The Propagandists movement was misunderstood by the colonial Spanish and, as a result, its leaders were imprisoned and their property confiscated. As such, the movement failed. A popular rebellion broke out around Manila in 1896, eight decades after almost all of Latin America had cast off the remnants of Spanish power. After months of fighting, the now revolutionary army retreated to the hills (Benitez 1954: 274–82). While initially not successful, this rebellion coincided with a similar revolt in Cuba, in which the USA intervened in 1898, bringing the USA and Spain to war. A US naval squadron destroyed the Spanish fleet in Manila Bay, thereby ending Spanish colonial rule (Benitez 1954: 286–90).

The USA brought back to the Philippines rebel leader Emilio Aguinaldo, who proclaimed Philippine independence in June 1898. However, through collusion between US armed forces and the departing Spanish colonial authorities, Manila was surrendered to the USA, not the Filipinos, with the Philippines being ceded by Spain to the USA for US$20 million. When the USA did not grant independence to the new republic, fighting broke out between the US occupying forces and the Philippine army. Although Aguinaldo was captured in 1901 and swore allegiance to the USA, a sporadic guerrilla campaign against the USA continued for the next ten years. This movement for independence was not successful, having succeeded only in transferring sovereignty from one colonial master to another, but it was, notably, the first significant revolt of an Asian people against their colonial masters.

Under US colonial rule, democratic institutions were introduced and Filipinos increasingly took over political and bureaucratic positions. English-language education was also extended throughout the country. However, the social and economic structure was little changed. Spanish civil law was retained, which did not include a jury system, although the American influence added the writs of habeas corpus and civil marriage. In 1899, the existing judicial structure was also capped by a US-style Supreme Court, the first chief justice of which was a Filipino. 'By 1912 half of the judges of the first instance were Filipinos; in 1926 only two out of fifty-five judges were American' (Wurfel 1964: 687).

In 1907, the Philippines elected its first government, the first country in SEA to do so. The electoral franchise was restricted, however, by property ownership (Wurfel 1988: 10) and the ability to speak either English or Spanish. The preexisting, American-dominated, eight-person commission that operated as the legislature and as the cabinet of the governor-general was reconstituted as the Upper House of a bicameral legislature. The lower house, the Assembly, comprised eighty members elected from single-member districts. For a bill to be enacted as law, it had to be passed by both houses. In 1916, the Jones Act abolished the commission and allowed for a twenty-four-person Senate, twenty-two members of which were elected from eleven districts and two of whom were appointed to represent non-Christian areas. The electoral franchise was broadened to include all literate males. Throughout this period, the US-appointed governor-general retained the right of veto over legislation, which thereafter required the ratification of the US president. Further, all laws concerning public land, currency, immigration and tariffs required the US president's signature, while the US Congress retained the right to annul any Philippine law.

LOCAL POLITICIANS

From its foundation in 1907, the Philippines' dominant political party was the elite-based *Nacionalistas*, which controlled both houses of the legislature until the Philippines was made a self-governing commonwealth in 1935. Full independence was planned for 1946, however, the American focus on self-government involved a somewhat contradictory policy. In the first instance, political power was to be gradually handed over to those capable of administering it and, in the second, the USA helped to build an economic base upon which a democracy could rest. Self-government meant rule by those Filipinos who were sufficiently educated to govern and that meant the elected were almost exclusively from the landed elite (see Wurfel 1988:

10–11). That elite was unwilling to give up its economic privilege, a position that had been enhanced by the Payne–Aldrich tariff of 1909, which hampered industrial development, but stimulated agricultural exports (Hutchcroft 1998: 27; Wurfel 1988: 9). Agrarian reform was, even from the early 1900s, not a program that would be undertaken with any meaningful success. Indeed, the number of tenant farmers doubled between 1900 and 1935 and, in response to this growing iniquity, there were three small rebellions in central Luzon during the 1920s and 1930s (Sturtevant 1976: 141–255); thus, elite domination of politics also ensured the retention of a quasifeudal economic system, which hampered economic growth and, eventually, engendered considerable political backlash. With the goal of preserving the economic status quo (Hutchcroft 1998: 65–70), the focus of the *Nacionalistas* was less on the legislative than on the more broadly defined, less obviously threatening and more patriotic goal of independence. The legislative program was thus dominated by the executive, which placed direct political power in the hands of a small group (Constantino 1975: ch. XVII; see also Lande 1968: 92–129; Friend 1969: ch. 4).

Despite the outward democratic appearance of the Philippines' political life, the country's *mestizo* (creole) elite cemented its control over the electoral process. The independence initiative, although cheered on by the elite, actually came from the USA. There were some moves towards agrarian reform, expanded education and infrastructure development under Manuel Quezon's presidency in the late 1930s, however, Japanese occupation of the Philippines in 1941 and the Japanese declaration of independence for the Philippines two years later interrupted this plan. The Japanese were not widely welcomed in the Philippines, not even initially, as they often were in other Asian colonial states, because the achievement of independence was not guaranteed by the Japanese, but forestalled.

The elite remained largely intact during the war and a good many members of its administration worked under the Japanese, including two-fifths of the Congress and most of the Senate. An associate justice of the Supreme Court, Jose Laurel, was appointed president in October 1943, a position that came with the power of absolute veto over the Congress and the ability to enter into unilateral agreements with foreign powers. Laurel was, in practical terms, a Japanese puppet. Quezon, who was president of the government in exile, died in the USA in August 1944, to be succeeded by vice-president Sergio Osmena (Stanley 1974: ch. 2).

THE REPUBLIC OF THE PHILIPPINES

The Philippines' political system is based on the US model, in which the president holds executive power and works with—or against—a bicameral legislature. As with the USA, at least in principle, the judiciary is independent of the executive arm of government. The Philippines also enjoys a free and unfettered media, which is, in principle, a cornerstone of a democratic society. With the exception of during the later Marcos period, this system has been in place since the Philippines achieved full independence in 1946.

Although collaboration with the Japanese became the major postwar political issue, the commander of the US forces in East Asia, General Douglas MacArthur, freed his friend, a collaborator with the Japanese, Manuel Roxas, who had served as a minister in the Laurel administration. This act confused the issue of collaboration and helped launch Roxas on his postwar political career. With independence looming, Roxas was elected leader of the Liberal wing of the Nacionalista Party in early 1946, ahead of the April elections to form a new government for the Republic of the Philippines. Roxas and what had become the Liberal Party (Wurfel 1988: 97) won by a slim majority after a big spending campaign. In July 1946, the Philippines was proclaimed a republic. In 1948, as president, Roxas granted amnesty to all those indicted for treason as a consequence of their collaboration, though not for people also found guilty of murder, rape or theft. After a minor change to the Constitution and a public vote, the Philippines ratified an agreement to allow free trade between the Philippines and the USA for eight years from the date of independence. The Philippines maintained close trade relations with the USA until 1974. In exchange, the USA agreed to pay war damages to the Philippines, which provided the Roxas administration with much needed funds to fight an escalating insurgency.

A DEEPENING DIVIDE

In 1942, a peasant group that had been demanding land reform since the 1930s reconstituted itself as the *Hukbo ng Bayan Laban sa Hapon* (Anti-Japanese Peoples' Army), abbreviated in Tagalog (the common language of Luzon) as *Hukbalahap*. The Huks, as they came to be named, were active in the guerrilla war against the Japanese. Although initially regarded as allies by the USA, leaders of the communist-influenced Huks were imprisoned by the Americans in 1945, while US military police assisted private landlord armies in restricting leftist political activity, most notably for land reform. Clashes between Huks and police became more frequent; in 1946 an attempted ceasefire between them failed. The Huks formally, although not actually, disbanded in 1946 in order to contest the forthcoming elections. Under the name of the Democratic Alliance, six Huks were elected to the Philippines Congress. However, Roxas barred them from assuming their seats (Wurfel 1988: 101) and two of them were killed by assassination squads (Monk 1990: 8). Meanwhile, approximately US$2 billion worth of economic aid from the USA was largely siphoned off by Roxas and the rest of the political elite, prefiguring the type of corruption that would become better known from the mid 1960s until the mid 1980s (Seagrave 1988: 126). Although the Huks did not present an electoral threat, Roxas declared the organisation illegal in March 1948 and refused them participation in the elections of the following year. Roxas died the month after the declaration.

Roxas' successor, Quirino, offered the Huks an amnesty in 1948, but the effort failed on both sides and quickly led to all-out conflict. Terror was used as an instrument of state policy during this period, which lasted until 1954. Paramilitary militias were recruited for the purpose of political thuggery and the imposition of ideological conformity. In the 1950s, the civilian guards system was re-instituted in order to serve large landlords and local government officials. The guards were an important part of the counterinsurgency structure. The US army and the Philippines military learnt valuable lessons in counterinsurgency as a result of these terror tactics, which continue to be cited in US army psychological warfare training materials. The Department of the Army's 1976 psychological warfare publication, *DA Pamphlet 525-7-1*, refers to some of the classic counterterror techniques and accounts of the practical application of terror. These include the capture and murder of suspected guerrillas in a manner suggesting it was done by legendary vampires (*asuang*) and a prototypical eye of God technique, in which a stylised eye would be painted opposite the house of a suspect (Lansdale 1976: 770).

The three-sided elections of 1948 were noted for their use of guns and money and a high level of fraud and intimidation, which secured a 52 per cent majority for Quirino. 'The way in which the Liberal regime achieved power substantially affected the way it exercised power, that is, corruption bred more corruption' (Wurfel 1964: 700). Foreign exchange reserves and treasury funds declined markedly, government employee salaries went into arrears, public projects were stopped and, not surprisingly, the public lost faith in the government. In February 1950, the Huks changed their name to the *Hukbong Mapagpalaya ng Bayan* (People's Liberation Army) and called for the overthrow of the government. The USA stepped in to assist the Philippines government sort out its economic problems, in large part with a grant of US$250 million. The Philippines government responded by failing to adopt a land reform program that had been drawn up by American adviser Robert Hardie (Monk 1990: chs I, II, III). Ramon Magsaysay was appointed secretary of national defence and rebuilt the Philippines armed forces. Magsaysay's army ensured that the 1951 elections were relatively honestly administered, thereby boosting his popularity. In 1953, at the instigation of the USA, Magsaysay resigned his position, joined the Nacionalista Party and, in the elections of that year, was elected president with a two-thirds majority. Despite being regarded as a great nationalist leader, Magsaysay had only come to power with the direct support of the USA (Smith 1958: chs 4, 5).

Despite its claimed aspirations, the Magsaysay government did not achieve all its goals. The Agricultural Tenancy Act, for example, was mangled, which meant that those who worked the land continued to have little or no ownership of or control over it (Wurfel 1988: 15, 167). But the

Magsaysay government did inaugurate the beginning of a relatively unfettered trade union movement, cleaned up customs and foreign exchange dealings and reduced corruption. Most importantly, between holding out the promise of reform to disaffected land labourers and embarking on an active military campaign with the help of the USA, Magsaysay managed to end the Huk rebellion in 1954 (Smith 1958: chs 6, 7). The USA continued its high level of military interest in the Philippines after independence and maintained its close association until 1991. In 1991, an increasingly well-developed sense of Philippine nationalism manifested itself in the high rents charged to the USA for the sites where its military bases were located, in particular the Clarke Air Force Base and the Subic Bay Naval Base. Along with an increasing tendency for the USA to put into effect its Guam Doctrine, that is, of withdrawing forces west of that island, it finally decided to end its long, direct, military involvement in the Philippines.

Magsaysay's personal popularity was still high when he was killed in a plane crash in 1957; the route of his funeral procession was lined by hundreds of thousands of mourners. His death led to a four-cornered presidential election, which was won by the vice-president, Carlos Garcia. While Garcia's victory appeared, in one sense, to promise a continuation of Magsaysay's trajectory, it actually put power back into the hands of the party's old guard because of divisions within the Nacionalista Party, which saw younger members break away to form the Progressive Party, which in turn, led to a high level of spending on the elections and flowed on into the Garcia administration with unprecedented levels of corruption. Garcia also refused to liberalise import controls, which supported new local manufacturers. As a result of his support for local capital, Garcia's administration 'may have marked the zenith of the national bourgeoisie's influence within the political elite' (Wurfel 1988: 16). Garcia's presidency was blessed with a divided opposition, at least until the elections of 1961 in which the Progressives merged with the Liberal Party. In that campaign, corruption was the major political issue. Wurfel notes that, in the eight years between the election of Magsaysay and Macagapal's victory in 1961, spending on presidential campaigns rose tenfold and senatorial campaigns nearly as quickly, although congressional campaigns only sixfold (1988: 100).

From the American occupation until the late 1960s, the Philippines had witnessed sporadic uprisings and rebellions. None, apart from the Huk rebellion, was ever likely to directly challenge the government, but they did indicate a deep-seated sense of untenable oppression among the country's rural poor, even among its urban poor (Sturtevant 1969). The outcome of conservative agrarian legislation and a structural failure to implement land reform programs, was the 'proliferation throughout the archipelago in the 1960s of all those pernicious institutional practices which had triggered the Huk rebellion in the 1940s' (Monk 1990: 84). This laid the groundwork for further radical rebellion in the late 1960s.

MARCOS

Ferdinand Marcos was born in 1917 in Ilocos Norte, the illegitimate son of Ferdinand Chua, who was from the wealthiest family in the region: 'Of the top ten Chinese clans in this inner group of forty billionaire families, Ferdinand's clan ranked number six' (Seagrave 1988: 14; see also, 22–3). While Chua never openly acknowledged Marcos as his son, he did financially assist him, including with his education; in 1939, Marcos graduated with a law degree. At the same time, he was charged with murdering Julio Nalundasan, who had defeated Marcos' nominal father, Mariano Marcos, in his bid to be elected to the Congress for Ilocos Norte. The conviction was overturned in 1940 with the assistance of President Jose Laurel, to whom Marcos became indebted as one of his clients.

Marcos was in officer school for the Philippine army when war broke out in the Pacific in early 1942. Although there were many stories from the war period of Marcos' heroism, these were almost entirely invented. Marcos was captured by the Japanese in August 1942 and released soon after. After the war, in 1949, he was elected to Congress for Ilocos Norte, the same seat occupied by the person he was alleged to have killed. Elected to the Senate in 1959, he became Senate president in 1962. Marcos stood against Diosdado Macagapal, the incumbent, in the 1965 elections, winning with money and nationalist slogans.

Marcos had promised to end rice shortages and importation, to reduce graft and corruption and punish those who had enriched themselves in office and to implement faster land reforms. As with his predecessor, in office Marcos fulfilled none of these promises (Monk 1990: 84). Under Macapagal, but more so under Marcos during the 1960s, the Philippines had begun to shift its economic foundation from import substitution, in which local industry was protected from external competition, to an export-oriented economy, which exposed local businesses to greater external competition. The purpose of this change was to drive down the value of the peso and to enhance the profitability of primary commodity exporters, who were almost entirely dominated by the traditional landed elite, but which also included major multinational corporations (Hawes 1987: ch. 1; Bello, Kinley & Elinson 1982: ch. 5). This led to a division within the Philippines elite group, and 'opened the floodgates of popular political participation by peasants, workers, students and intellectuals' (Hawes 1987: 37).

At around the time the floodgates were opening, a different set of floodgates opened—those through which flowed the US$50 million that was paid for Marcos' 1969 election campaign. In line with this unprecedented pork barrelling, the corruption and maladministration of his government only worsened (Monk 1990: 87), while protest against a perceived loss of legitimacy grew (Wurfel 1988: 38). As demonstrated by his campaigning technique, Marcos had been a keen political operator and used every facet under his control to continue his tenure in office (Infante 1980: 10–11). Pressure had been building for land reform (Wurfel 1988: 17), but even Marcos' 'espousal of land reform in 1971–72 must be interpreted in terms of his determination to outbid and outmanoeuvre all possible rivals for political supremacy and not in terms of a sober and responsible philosophy of statesmanship' (Monk 1990: 90). By the beginning of the 1970s, Marcos' grip on power appeared to be slipping, but, in the end, the continuation of the Philippines' exploitative agrarian policies and continuing Islamic unrest in Mindanao gave him the excuse he needed to continue his rule unimpeded (Infante 1980: 11–12).

Under the Marcos administration, the guards system was updated to become the Barrio [Neighborhood] Self-Defence Forces (later designated the Civilian Home Defence Forces). These paramilitary forces were more organisationally sophisticated than the guards system, with local detachments formally integrated into the armed forces command structure through local constabulary forces. Marcos' first term saw an increase in government expenditure, which was financed by foreign loans. By the end of the 1960s, the principal and interest payments fell due, these debt servicing requirements, as well as rising imports and massive election spending, threatening a balance-of-payments crisis. In addition, there was a rising tide of nationalism, fuelled by hostility to the Vietnam War and by resentment at continued US economic dominance. There was increased student activism and an increasing challenge to central authority from the Moro National Liberation Front (MNLF).

In 1968, reflecting Sino–Soviet tensions, the *Partido Kommunista ng Pilipinas* (PKP, or Communist Party of the Philippines) split when Jose Maria Sison led a Maoist breakaway group to form the Communist Party of the Philippines (CPP), whose military wing, the New People's Army (NPA), which was formed in 1969, frequently clashed with government military forces. The NPA focused its efforts in central Luzon, first around the key agrarian centre of Tarlac, and then, around Isabella; later, its area of operations spread to other rural areas. A commander in the early years was Victor Corpus, an army officer who seized the military academy's arsenal in Manila in 1970 and defected to the NPA with the weapons. In the early years, China was a source of weapons and expertise, although that support ended after 1977 as a result of the changing political climate.

As the corruption and repression of the Marcos regime continued, many Filipinos came to view the CPP-NPA as the only viable force for overthrowing the dictator. In the mid 1980s, the NPA was believed to have 25 000 fighters and it operated in sixty-three of the country's seventy-three provinces. A well-organised political coalition operated alongside the NPA; there was an alliance of underground groups under the umbrella organisation, the National Democratic Front (NDF), and a range of legal organisations, including peasant groups, labour unions, other sectoral organisations, political parties and development groups.

MUSLIM SEPARATISTS

Secessionism in the southern Philippines dates to the establishment of the state and focuses on the Islamic identity of many of the region's inhabitants. In more recent times, separatist conflict has been dominated by the Moro National Liberation Front, the Moro Islamic Liberation Front, the smaller but more extreme Islamic *Abu Sayyaf Group* (ASG) and those with links to external terrorists, including al-Qaeda and *Jema'ah Islamiyah* (JI). The contemporary secessionist movement followed years of neglect, semi-official persecution and the alienation of the indigenous Islamic population under the weight of increasing numbers of Christian settlers in Mindanao. In response, a small group of students and intellectuals formed the Moro National Liberation Front in the late 1960s, becoming the largest grouping of armed separatists fighting a war with the Armed Forces of the Philippines (AFP) that ended in a stalemate in the mid 1970s. In December 1976, under the auspices of the Organisation of Islamic Conference, the Marcos administration conducted negotiations with the insurgents, reaching a settlement that was sponsored by Colonel Muammar al-Qaddafi of Libya and known as the Tripoli Agreement. According to this agreement, both sides would stop fighting and an autonomous Muslim region in the southern Philippines, consisting of fourteen provinces, would be established, although this agreement was not honoured by the Marcos government.

The Mindanao Christian population strongly opposed the settlement, especially its endorsement of a legal Islamic framework. Fighting broke out again at the end of 1977, although it was less intense than earlier conflicts. It was at this time that the separatist movement began to fragment. Hashim Salamat broke away from the MNLF in 1977 over a leadership dispute and ideological differences with MNLF chairman, Nur Misuari. Salamat established the Moro Islamic Liberation Front (MILF) in 1977, attracting many supporters from Mindanao. Misuari remained in control of the MNLF, whose membership was dominated by partisans from Misuari's Tausung tribe and other Sulu-based ethnic groups. Further factionalism followed. Another breakaway group, the Bangsamoro Liberation Organisation (BLO), initially compounded the MNLF's decline. Having faltered under pressure of leadership disputes, the BLO later emerged as the MNLF-Reformist Movement, which, by the late 1980s, was better known as the Moro Islamist Reformist Group (MIRG). While the MNLF and its offshoots were products of local conditions, they were increasingly contacted and influenced by external groups wishing to harness their role in Islamic revolution; the first contacts with al-Qaeda dated back to 1988, the year before al-Qaeda was formally founded (Apdel & Thayer 2003: 17).

DICTATORSHIP

Taking into account the corrupt practices used to win office, including the election of Marcos to the presidency, the Philippines political elite had alternated in power in a relatively stable fashion. But in 1972, near the end of his second term, Marcos knew that, under the eight-year (two-term) limit on the presidency, he was about to leave office for good. So, citing the threat of subversive forces—a reference to the Islamic and communist rebellions— he imposed martial law. In doing so, Marcos did not just impose a more strict control over those areas in which the rebels were believed to be operating, but he also closed the Philippines Congress, subordinated the judiciary to the executive and engineered the ratification, by a show of hands, of a new Constitution that gave him permanent tenure in office (Hawes 1987: 13; Infante 1980: 12–16).

> In retrospect the proclamation of martial law appears to have been produced by a convergence of three growing conflicts: between power-holding elites and increasingly discontented masses, between foreign investors and economic nationalists ... and within the power elite, between Marcos and his two most potent competitors, Benigno Aquino and 'sugar baron' Euginio Lopez (Wurfel 1988: 21).

Marcos' control was complete. For the next thirteen years,[2] the Philippines effectively underwent one-person rule, supported by violence and exercised in an arbitrary manner. It was, in a practical sense, a dictatorship. With no recourse to an electoral contest, the Philippines suffered looting of tens of billions of dollars by Marcos and his cronies, a hitherto unprecedented scale. By the early 1980s, even the elites who had supported Marcos and who had profited so richly from his patronage, had begun to reconsider their position (Wurfel 1988: 235–40). What had started out as yet another example of elite rule on behalf of their own economic interests, soon became plunder of the economy from the centre, with presidential clients (cronies) being secondary beneficiaries of the economic rape of a state no longer even protected by its own self-serving elite (see, for example, Hutchcroft 1998: 111–15, 136).

By the end of 1985, the Philippines had the lowest per capita income of any of the ASEAN states, contracting rapidly between 1982 and 1985 in particular. In the 1950s, it had been the highest. External debt was almost equivalent to the gross national product and was three times the value of exports. The country was in the grip of economic crisis (Jayasuriya 1987: 80), in part, a result of a fall in world commodity prices, but also as a reflection of poor economic planning and wildly excessive corruption.

The economic elite, as well as suffering as a result of Marcos' unrestrained greed, also feared—not unreasonably—the flow-on effect of the sort of radical, even popular, backlash that Marcos' rule was beginning to engender.

In 1983, the usually conservative Roman Catholic Bishops' Conference vigorously and unanimously criticised Marcos for the excesses of his government and for his use of political violence (Wurfel 1988: 279). From 1972, as Archbishop of Lubrense, Jaime Sin had been a critic of Marcos, albeit a mild one. Sin was made Archbishop of Manila in 1974 and, while agreeing to tone down his criticisms of Marcos, 'continued to visit jails, detention camps and asylums, to which many political prisoners had been sent'. Among those Sin stayed in regular contact with was Senator Benigno Aquino, including later by correspondence in the USA when Aquino went into exile there in 1980 (Lyons & Wilson 1987: 33–4). In 1984, Sin publicly embarrassed Marcos by calling on him to release all political prisoners. Sin had claimed that Marcos was deliberately attempting to silence the church from speaking out on matters of Roman Catholic morality. The following year, a number of churches were raided by the military and some priests were charged with having links to the NPA. In 1986, Sin was a prime activist in bringing tens of thousands of people onto Manila's streets to call for the resignation of Marcos.

OPPOSITION

Long averse to being brought into the Philippine nation and chafing under the relocation of Christian immigrants to traditionally Islamic lands, in the 1960s Islamic separatism in Mindanao developed a militant character (Wurfel 1988: 28–31, 154–60). The armed wing of these Islamic separatists, the MNLF, was becoming increasingly aggressive, while the armed wing of the CPP, the NPA, had become a military force to be reckoned with. For its support, the CPP–NPA drew on disaffected peasants, urban poor and radical students, but could trace its lineage back to the same support base as the Hukbalahap rebellion. The primary difference was that, while the Huks were communist-inspired, the CPP–NPA was directly influenced by the radical version of communism outlined by Mao Zedong during the period of China's Cultural Revolution (Weekly 1996: 35).

The Philippines' elite was also increasingly horrified at Marcos' unrestrained abuse of power, offending even their easily assuaged sense of propriety. The Philippine economy was beset by the linked problems of an inefficient local industry, unsustainable levels of government foreign borrowing for often highly dubious projects and myriad forms and levels of official corruption. The political mechanism over which Marcos presided was, along with the economy, rapidly crumbling. Even Marcos' political guarantor, the USA, had become heartily sick of his unrestrained excesses.

It was against this backdrop that Marcos' foe and former Philippine senator, Benigno Aquino, who had been living in exiile in the USA since

1980, returned to the Philippines. Aquino was from a provincial dynasty in Tarlac, north of Manila (Seagrave 1988: 14) and, as a son of a former cabinet member, was a member of the Philippines' economic elite (Wurfel 1988: 205). Despite his post mortem sanctification, Aquino was not a liberal reformer and, like many of his class, favoured authoritarian political methods. Aquino was elected to the Senate in 1967 and, by 1972, even he had told journalists that if he ever became president he would declare martial law, as Marcos was later to do (Wurfel 1988: 18). If Aquino was, like Marcos, a conventional representative of the elite, he was no less seen by Marcos as an enemy, in the traditional manner of politics being about elite competition rather than policies. It was in this context that there was an attempt on Aquino's life and those of his Liberal Party colleagues, in a bombing at a rally at the Miranda Plaza in 1971.

With the backing of the country's wealthiest family, the Lopez clan, it had been expected that Aquino would win the 1973 presidential elections (Wurfel 1988: 18), but, unfortunately for Aquino, when Marcos declared martial law in 1972—a move that was, in principle, favoured by Aquino—he was one of the first picked up and was charged with subversion and murder the following year (Wurfel 1988: 206–7). In 1977, Aquino was sentenced to death, a sentence that was probably not intended to be carried out, given the disquiet it would have caused among the Philippine elite. In 1980, Aquino was beset by a serious heart complaint and sent to the USA for heart surgery because Marcos feared he would be blamed if Aquino died in the Philippines. Aquino recovered from a triple bypass operation and remained in the USA until 1983.

THE END OF MARCOS

Aquino's return to the Philippines on 21 August 1983 was a direct challenge to Marcos' increasingly shaky grip on Philippine politics, as, by this stage, Aquino was openly supported by the USA. Upon alighting from his plane after landing at Manila airport, Aquino was shot dead on the tarmac. The alleged assassin was gunned down on the spot in an attempt to cover up the source of the order for the assassination. But the attempt to infer responsibility for Aquino's death on the lone gunman was feeble; it was subsequently attributed to General Fabian Ver, Marcos' long-time confidant and, from 1981, military chief-of-staff. Ver had previously been a policeman, head of Marcos' personal security and director of the National Intelligence and Security Authority. His relationship with Marcos had extended to assisting Marcos in having an affair with an actor, bombing the Liberal Party headquarters in 1981 and arranging the killing of one of the doctors involved in Marcos' failed kidney transplant in 1982. After Aquino was killed, Ver was tried for the crime but acquitted. The Supreme Court ordered a retrial, but before the retrial could take place, Philippine politics turned critical (Corfield 1998).

Aquino's death galvanised the non-violent opposition, particularly among the middle and business classes, with the USA distancing itself from Marcos and aligning itself with Aquino's widow, Corazon. In the face of mounting criticism over Ver's putative involvement in Aquino's assassination, Marcos called for presidential elections to be held in February 1986, assuming that he would prevail. With the aid of widespread voting irregularities, including the discovery of ballot boxes full of marked papers before the election and hacking into computer records to alter the voting tables, Marcos did win the election, but the vote was seen as a sham by the opposition, the USA and, finally, a large section of the armed forces led by the Defence Minister Juan Ponce Enrile and Deputy Chief-of-Staff General Fidel Ramos. As pro-Marcos troops attempted to locate and destroy pro-opposition radio stations, the troops' communications were scrambled by the American forces that had initially set them up. Although Ver ordered a commando helicopter-borne assault against the rebel soldiers based at Camp Crame, once inside the camp the commandos defected. Hundreds of thousands of protestors packed the streets around the camp and troops sent against them joined them instead. In response to this overwhelming show of antipathy, accompanied by Ver, Marcos fled to Hawaii, where he remained until his death in 1989 (Lyons & Wilson 1987).

Corazon Aquino's legitimacy as the succeeding president was not challenged. Although she moved to restore civil liberties and put into place a new Constitution with controls on the power of the president, the Philippines social and economic structure was left basically intact. A promised land reform program, not surprisingly, failed to materialise in any significant sense. Similarly, the Civilian Home Defence Forces system was modified to include the reinforcement of an elaborate command and control structure and the mobilisation and deployment of greater forces as vigilantes.

One of the most important immediate effects of the accession of Corazon Aquino to the presidency was the lifting of controls over the news media. Under Marcos, the news media were repressed and had become, in effect, public relations tools for his government. Under Aquino, a sense of exuberance burst forth. In a similar manner to reflecting other aspects of American culture, the media almost immediately took upon themselves the role of outspoken critics of all that was wrong and unjust. Newspapers flourished and restraint and taste were cast aside in a headlong rush towards freedom of speech.

One of the lasting benefits of this change is that a culture of free expression appears to have deeply and, perhaps, permanently permeated Filipino society. The few serious commentators writing for the Filipino press were as acute in their observations, as trenchant in their criticisms and as sharply analytical in their commentaries as any in the world. But they are few, they are generally little read and even less regarded. Most newspapers quickly reflected a lack of constraint in garish headlines, graphic images and salacious stories that more paralleled gossip than news. This appeal to a lowest common denominator is the price paid for a relatively unfettered news media around the world, but in the Philippines, with only a limited understanding of the role of the media in an open and plural society, the lowest common denominator was quickly reached and fully exploited. Serious news and commentary, while existing, was relegated to the margins.

DISSENT WITHIN

After Marcos fled, Enrile was not accorded the senior position he coveted and so set himself up in opposition to Aquino, while Marcos used his financial reserves and the remnants of personal loyalty to urge the armed forces to overthrow her, which resulted in a series of attempted coups in 1986, 1987 (which came close to success), 1988 and 1989. The attempted coups generally, and the 1987 attempt in particular, made worse by mounting NPA activity, shook public confidence in Aquino's government (SarDesai 1997: 224–5). The 1989 coup attempt, which appeared to be otherwise succeeding, was quashed with the aid of US war planes from the Clarke Field air base. The main group behind the coup attempts was the Reform the Armed Forces Movement (RAM), which later became known as the Revolutionary Alliance Movement (RAM).

As with many other aspects of the cultural life of the Philippines, the armed forces adopted a variation of the American sense of collegial loyalty, which was reflected in the RAM. This sense of duty to each other did not sit well with the armed forces' sense of duty to the state. One of the leading figures of the RAM, Colonel Gregorio 'Gringo' Honasan, was a Scarlet Pimpernel type of figure, who, after orchestrating the 1987 attempted coup, was on the run but thumbed his nose at the government, often through statements to the media. Honasan was later pardoned and stood for and was elected to the Philippines Senate. At the end of the 1990s, Honasan was still antagonistic towards the government, threatening the state with dire consequences should thirteen RAM members charged with killing a union leader be convicted.

REVOLUTIONARY DISSENT

In the south, the island of Mindanao, being a hotbed of communist and Islamic rebellion, continued to be a deeply troubling area for the Philippines government. By the end of 1992, Corazon Aquino had moved politically to the Right, to assuage opposition complaints that she was too liberal and, with little real reform (including land reform) having taken place, she lost much of her initial popularity. Probably the most important aspect of Aquino's presidency was that, at the end of her term, when Fidel Ramos was elected president in 1992, power was transferred peacefully, indicating a sustained return to democracy. Ramos succeeded in forming a progovernment coalition in congress, appealing to the country's economic creditors and achieving a cessation of hostilities with the MNLF and, briefly, the NPA.

The MNLF reached its ceasefire agreement with the Manila government in 1996. As a consequence, Nur Misuari became the provincial governor in southern Mindanao. Having reached an accommodation with the government, the MNLF's place on the battlefield was taken by the MILF led by Salamat Hashim. The main difference between the two groups was that the MNLF accepted a degree of regional autonomy along with the promise of extra funds for local infrastructure projects, which, four years later, were still only partially forthcoming. Misuari said that billions of dollars promised by the Philippines government for a new airport, an irrigation project, reafforestation and other smaller projects had instead materialised as millions of dollars. In contrast, the MILF demanded total independence. 'The only way to solve the problem permanently is to give the Bangsa Moro people independence,' Hashim said. 'They believe that the homeland of the Bangsa Moro people was annexed illegally and immorally' (Hashim 2000).

The MILF claimed 120 000 fighters, although more sober estimates put the real figure as low as 12 000 members under arms, with an active support base of perhaps another 50 000 (Davis 1998). The MILF admitted to receiving funds until 1997 to help them establish a *bangsamoro* (Islamic homeland) from international Islamic terrorist, dissident Saudi millionaire Osama bin Laden (*Philippines Star* 1999). Other global Islamic communities were also claimed to contribute to the MILF's coffers. It also claimed that 1000 of its fighters had battle experience in Afghanistan against the former Soviet Union.

The Ramos presidency was basically a period of consolidation. While some divisions within the elite of Filipino society remained, the sharp divisions that characterised the early part of Aquino's presidency were absent. In large part, this was achieved by restoring many of the privileges to the Marcos era cronies and treading softly on their prosecution. While Ramos quelled a significant part of the rebellion in the Philippines, his successor, Joseph Estrada, was not nearly as adept at diplomacy or, it seemed, economic management.

Under Estrada, the Philippines government began in early 1999 to indicate it would try to reach a settlement of the rebellion, perhaps including a type of regional autonomy for Mindanao. However, Estrada soon wrecked that discussion by grandstanding with a policy of no negotiation. The MILF, on the other hand, demanded full autonomy for a region that remains within the island of Mindanao, upon which the majority of the population is not Muslim (being around 4 million of a total of 21 million). The MILF's military chief, Al Haj Murad, said that, as a consequence of the failed negotiations, the conflict would be spread beyond Mindanao. However, the MILF's ability to carry out attacks beyond the island were limited to terrorist rather than full-scale military activities (*Borneo Post* 1999), which were, arguably, manifested in *Jema'ah Islamiyah*-linked attacks that killed twenty-two people in Manila in December 2000 (*Manila Times*, 19 July 2003), as was a money trail to pay for bombings that led to Khalid Sheikh Mohammad, a senior al-Qaeda figure, being arrested in Pakistan in 2003 (*Manila Times*, 8 May 2004). Just ahead of a visit to Mindanao by Estrada in February 2000, MILF guerrillas blew up two buses on board a passenger ferry at Ozamiz City, killing forty-five people; they conducted a number of other similar attacks (Lopez 2000a). In response, Estrada ordered the further escalation of attacks against the MILF.

In the late 1990s and into the next decade, *Abu Sayyaf* also stepped up its campaign. In early 2000, the group was responsible for numerous kidnappings, including twenty tourists from a Malaysian resort island off the east coast of Sabah; eventually, *Abu Sayyaf* retreated to the island of Basilan, off the coast of Mindanao. This indicated, if nothing else, that the traditionally dangerous waters between the Philippines and Malaysia had not yet come fully under state control. A Filipino author noted that 'Islamic Mindanao [was] the lynchpin of border security in the ASEAN region', indicating, at least in part, why the government in Manila felt it could not let go of the province (Mastura 1999).

THE NPA

Following the collapse of international communism and the purges within the NPA, in which numerous comrades and supporters were executed, the guerrilla army's numbers shrank and it broke into several effectively independent factions, for example, the Revolutionary Proletarian Party. Operating at a peak strength of around 26 000 armed guerrillas in 1987, the combined strength of the remaining forces was around 6000 in 1999.

The reasons for the decline in the strength of the NPA included the return of more mainstream members to civilian life following the fall of Marcos, the offer of a government amnesty, separation between the overseas-based leadership and the harder-line membership at home and ideological and personality divisions between the often very autonomous NPA units. But what capped this decline was the 1985 purge, conducted while the leaders of the Mindanao branch of the NPA[3] were in Manila to help decide the next phase of the revolution. Informed that there were spies operating within the NPA, local commanders took the process into their own hands, arresting and killing almost a thousand, mostly loyal, NPA members. Although this process was halted as soon as the horrified leaders returned from Manila, the effect of the purge was to leave the Mindanao branch shattered, its strength declining from 9000 to 3000 within nine months. The CPP also lost over 50 per cent of its mass base. In response, the 'ferocious' criticism of the Mindanao purges by the CPP's leader, Jose Maria Sison, further weakened and dispirited the party (Abinales 1996).

Most of the communist-based groups' continuing military activity appeared to be on the islands of Negros and Mindanao. 'Sparrow Forces' of urban guerrillas conducted a sporadic terror campaign, including political assassinations, in Manila up until the early 1990s. Attempts at negotiating a peace accord between the government and the NDF, the umbrella organisation for the former CPP–NPA, floundered again under Estrada's tough-guy intransigence.

SECESSIONIST VIOLENCE

Similar to the NPA following the fall of Marcos, a greatly weakened MNLF agreed to a ceasefire when Marcos was ousted from power. Following a 1989 plebiscite, an Autonomous Region in Muslim Mindanao (ARMM) was established. It was based in Cotabato, which consisted of the four regions of Tawi-Tawi, Sulu, Maguindanao and Lanao del Sur. In 2001, this province was expanded to include the island of Basilan and Marawai City in central Mindanao. Many of the ex-MNLF leaders joined the political institutions of this body, but the MILF rejected the ARMM, believing it to be riddled with corruption and unable to promote complete Muslim independence.

Nur Misuari led the MNLF into peace negotiations with the Manila government in 1996 and, as a result, was installed as governor of the ARMM on 30 September 1997. The armed wing of the MNLF, the Bangsamoro Army, was disarmed and gradually integrated into the national armed forces and security services. In the years since the 1996 accord, the MNLF's record of running the ARMM failed to satisfy even its supporters. Erratic and authoritarian, Misuari himself performed consistently badly as an administrator and was finally shunted aside as MNLF chairman in April 2001. He was replaced by a committee of fifteen and his position as ARMM governor was later taken by Parouk Hussin, a member of that committee. Angered by this dismissal, Misuari and his loyalists launched an armed revolt in November 2001 on his home island of Jolo that was swiftly put down. He later fled to Malaysia's Sabah state, where he was arrested and repatriated to the Philippines at the behest of Malaysian Prime Minister Mahathir Mohammed. Misuari remains in custody, while on Jolo his hardcore supporters have joined the ASG.

MORO ISLAMIC LIBERATION FRONT (MILF)

With its leaders drawn from a group of Muslims educated in religious academies in the Middle East, primarily Egypt, the MILF has a stronger religious component than does the MNLF. Despite their reputation, MILF leaders typically follow a brand of Islam that is more moderate than that of the Islamic fundamentalists of the Middle East. They refuse to publicly criticise the USA and remain officially committed to negotiations with the Philippine government.

The MILF had an estimated strength of between 10 000–11 000, according to the Philippines government, and 40 000, according to various Western estimates. It has been held responsible for highly visible terrorist bombings in Manila in 2000 and 2001 and Davao City in 2003. In contrast to the ASG, the MILF is a political movement with an Islamist ideology and secessionist ambitions that fields a substantial guerrilla army. The MILF maintains contacts with international jihadist groups, including JI, which used MILF-based methods at its own training camps, in particular Camp Abubakar on Mindanao. Activists from JI have been implicated in a number of attacks in the Philippines. In 2002, senior Indonesian JI member and link to MILF (US State Department 2002: 21), Fathur Rahman Al-Ghozi, was arrested, although he managed to escape from custody in July 2003, probably with inside assistance. Al-Ghozi was killed the following October in a shootout with police and soldiers in North Cotabato, Mindanao.

The MILF distinguishes itself from other revolutionary organisations in the Philippines by supporting development efforts in its area of operation and by refusing to describe the USA as an enemy. The MILF supported meetings between USAID and the Bangsa Moro Development Agency, an NGO supported by the MILF. It vowed not to launch sympathy attacks during the Iraq war and has not taken a public stance on joint US–Philippines exercises in Sulu. Sporadic negotiations between the government and the MILF have taken place and a ceasefire put in place. In May 2003, talks broke off after three months of fighting between government and MILF forces.

In June 2003 both sides focused anew on the politics of the conflict with the MILF declaring a temporary cessation of offensive operations and the government countering with an informal offer of a permanent ceasefire. Both sides expressed scepticism about the other's offer and some fighting continued. In June 2003, the US continued to express public support for peace negotiations between the Philippines and the MILF. The MILF has consistently rejected the ARMM as a vehicle for addressing grassroots Muslim grievances.

ABU SAYYAF GROUP (ASG)

Abu Sayyaf, Arabic for 'bearer of the sword', was originally known as the Mujahideen Commando Freedom Fighters (MCFF), which was founded in the mid 1980s; it was also referred to as *Al Harakat-ul Al Islamiyya* (the Islamic Movement), and formally renamed *Abu Sayyaf Group* in 1991. The founders were Abdurazak Abubakar Janjalani, who studied Islamic law and fought in Afghanistan during the 1980s, Wahab Akbar, who studied in Iran and Syria, Amilhussin Jumaani and ten other former members of the Moro National Liberation Front. Janjalani drew his two younger brothers, Hector and Qaddafi, into the group. Later, the two underwent explosives training in Pakistan. Hector was arrested and is currently held by the Philippines government, but Qaddafi went on to become amir, or spiritual leader, of ASG after Janjalani's death during a clash with Philippines police on 18 December 1998. ASG has had active links with al-Qaeda since 1992 and is claimed as one of al-Qaeda's training and development success stories in the region.

ASG fighters operate in small units under a single commander and those with experience gained in Afghanistan are accredited with greater seniority and respect. Recruits come from the southern Philippines, in particular Patikul, Sulu, Lebak, Sultan Kudarat, Malapatan, Sarangani and Zamboanga City. Members use the Tausung dialect for communication within the group, all volunteers are given instructions on explosives and jungle guerrilla warfare tactics at camps run by *Abu Sayyaf* in remote jungle locations and some are trained for sabotage, kidnapping and urban guerrilla activities. The most valued recruits were singled out for training in Pakistan and Afghanistan.

ASG's first recorded action was the 1991 attack on a military checkpoint in Sumagadang near Isabela. Wahab, the ASG leader who commanded the attack, fled to Malaysia, only to return a few years later to campaign for governor. After the 1991 action, wider bomb attacks followed in 1992. These attacks targeted locations in Zamboanga and Davao and resulted in an increasing public awareness of ASG. Also in 1992, ASG member Edwin Angeles abducted a businesswoman in Davao and hid her at a residence in Basilan. She was released after paying a ransom. In April 1993, in Basilan, Angeles abducted a bus company owner and his five-year-old grandson. The grandfather was released three days later, but the grandson remained in custody. In a press conference soon after the grandfather's release, ASG member Ashmad announced that the group would continue to hold the grandson until its demands were met. The demands included the removal of all Catholic symbols in Muslim communities, the imposition of a ban on all foreign fishing vessels in the Sulu and Basilan Seas and the involvement of Muslim leadership in the negotiations. Later in 1993, ASG abducted an American language scholar, Charles Walton, from his home on Pangutaran Island. Following the intercession of the Libyan ambassador, Walton was released a few weeks later without a ransom being paid.

In 1994, Ramzi Yousef visited the Philippines and is alleged to have made contact with ASG members to discuss plans for an assassination attempt on the Pope, who was scheduled to visit Manila. In April 1995, ASG, along with guerrillas from the Moro Islamic Liberation Front (MILF), attacked the town of Ipil on Mindanao. The attack resulted in fifty-four deaths and hundreds of wounded. A dozen Christian villagers were taken hostage and later killed. Following the attack on Ipil, the ASG clashed with Philippines security forces throughout 1996 and 1997. Between 1991 and 1997, ASG conducted a total of sixty-seven terrorist attacks (Apdal & Thayer 2003:19). In August 1998, ASG announced its intentions to target foreigners as well as Philippines security forces personnel. In July 2000, ASG abducted three French journalists, who were released after ransoms were paid. Later that month, ASG abducted twenty-one people from a dive resort on Pandanan Island; a ransom of several million dollars was paid in exchange for the prisoners' release.

In August 2000, ASG abducted Jeffrey Schilling, a US citizen. Schilling met with a senior guerrilla leader, who had accused Schilling of being a member of the CIA. A US$2 million ransom was demanded for his release. Schilling was later freed by security forces without the ransom being paid. This was followed in May 2001 by ASG abducting seventeen tourists. When Philippines government forces attempted to pursue the kidnappers, 200 more hostages were seized from a nearby church and hospital. All but five were later rescued by security forces.

In January 2002, in the name of the USA's war on terror, some 1200 US troops arrived in the Philippines to support the government's operations against ASG, many of them Special Forces personnel who were sent to train Philippines forces. In June 2002, a group of US-trained Philippines troops stormed an *Abu Sayyaf* jungle camp in an effort to rescue two Americans and a Filipino nurse being held hostage. During the rescue attempt, the nurse and one of the Americans were killed, but the third hostage, US missionary Gracia Burnham, was freed, suffering only minor injuries. In July 2002, many US special forces personnel departed, while several hundred support personnel remained on the island of Basilan to carry out infrastructure projects and medical assistance.

In August 2002, ASG abducted a further six hostages, later beheading two of them. In December 2002, Philippines soldiers captured an ASG member believed to have been involved in the executions. Also in December 2002, approximately 150 US Special Forces troops were deployed to the Philippines in order to train government forces in counterterrorism and anti-terrorism operations. After heavy fighting on Basilan Island, ASG members were reported to be fleeing to Malaysia by means of fast watercraft. In January 2003, Merang Abante, reportedly a senior member of ASG, was captured. His capture was followed by the capture of Maid Sampang, another ASG member. Also in January 2003, an additional 200 US soldiers were reported to have arrived in the Philippines to support the government's military operations. As a result of the intense fighting in Basilan, ASG forces were reported to be regrouping on the island of Sulu, an area commanded by Abu Jumdail (Dr Abu), Galib Andang and Mujid Susukan.

The group has become increasingly factionalised. The Basilan group was greatly influenced by Janjalani and was more religiously motivated, while the Sulu group has been criticised by the Basilan faction for concentrating on criminal activity at the expense of strategic goals.

THE FALL OF ESTRADA

Joseph Estrada was a B-grade actor turned B-grade politician, first as a regional mayor during the Marcos regime, and then, as vice-president

(*Asiaweek* 1998a). Estrada's early popularity, which was briefly at an historical high for a Philippine president, did not reflect his policies or lack thereof. The lack of policy debate ahead of his election was 'extraordinary' and the election itself was described as 'probably the worst in the country's history' (Easton 1998). Estrada reverted to the time-honoured tradition of pork barrelling, guaranteeing favours for his supporters and himself being beholden to his own patrons. But the Philippine voting public's fascination with and admiration for empty rhetoric, delivered in what was perceived as authentic Hollywood style, won Estrada the day.

A self-confessed economic illiterate, despite being supported by his Harvard-trained economist vice-president, Gloria Arroyo, Estrada seemed to have few concrete plans for developing the Philippines' economy. 'Estrada's critics say he shows several weaknesses: lack of direction on the economy, inertia in pushing through economic reform bills, a tendency to coddle cronies and an erratic governing style' (Tiglao & Vatikiotis 1999). His public pronouncements on finally sorting out the legacy of the Marcos era seemed even more doubtful. Officially, work on the Marcos legacy was going ahead and, after thirteen years, the Presidential Commission on Good Government (PCGG) appeared to be moving towards preparing for the final confrontation with the Marcos family. This followed the failure of the government to reach an acceptable agreement with the former president's family over their ill-gotten wealth. The PCGG had already tracked down some of this money—about US$520 million—in two Swiss bank accounts under six pseudonyms. Billions more were still to be accounted for. There was never any doubt that Marcos was an enormously corrupt political leader, but, eventually, his widow, Imelda, in effect, confirmed it. She was quoted in a local Philippines newspaper as saying that her husband had bought large parcels of shares in major Philippine companies. Investigating these share holdings, the Philippines senate was told by Mrs Marcos that her family could be worth as much as US$13 billion.

Estrada said that his government was nearing the end of talks with the Marcos family regarding this fortune. A significant proportion of the funds was expected, after negotiations with the government, to be left in the family's hands (Reuters 1999a). Marcos' son, Ferdinand Marcos Jr, was elected governor of Ilocos Norte, the Marcos family's home province, in 1998, indicating that they were far from defeated. It may have helped that the Marcos family supported Estrada's campaign and was regarded as his friend (Tiglao 1998b).

While this rhetoric of the PCGG and Estrada, with his professed concerns for the Philippines poor, assuaged some, the reality was that many of Marcos' cronies were 'likely to escape virtually unscathed from charges of ill-gotten wealth, as long-running cases against them flounder in the courts' (Tiglao 1998a). Indeed, not only were the cronies continuing with their business interests, they were also establishing new and close relations with

Estrada, indicating that some things in Philippine politics do not change. The most notorious Marcos crony, for example, billionaire Edouardo Cojuangco, headed up Estrada's political party, *Laban ng Masang Pilipino* (Fight of the Filipino Masses). Other cronies had also escaped prosecution, including Jose Yao Campos, who owned the largest pharmaceutical company, United Laboratories and real estate. Roberto Benedicto, who, under Marcos, had the sugar monopoly, under Estrada owned a major hotel and bank, Traders Hotel and Traders Royal Bank. Enrique Razon, who was considered to be the boss of Manila's port, retained the International Container Service and also owned the newspaper, the *Manila Standard*. Lucio Tan had retained his Fortune Tobacco company and Allied Bank. These were just some of those who benefited under Marcos' corrupt rule and who maintained much of their fortune after his political demise (Lopez 1998; Tiglao 1998a).

On 19 January 2000, the head of the Philippine Stock Exchange, Perfecto Yasay, claimed that Estrada had told him by phone to exonerate Dante Tan, a friend of Estrada's (Saludo & Lopez 2000) who was being investigated for stock manipulation. A nun who was famous for her work with the poor in the Philippines, Sister Christine Tan (no relation), claimed that US$10.5 million intended for the poor went to projects headed by Estrada, his wife Maria Louisa and their son, Jinggoy Estrada, mayor of suburban San Juan, along with other officials. This left just US$1.6 million for the charity's intended beneficiaries (Lopez 2000b). Even in the Philippines, Estrada's emptiness could not be hidden forever and, by late 1999, the popularity rating of the Philippines' most popular president ever had slumped (Crowell & Lopez 1999).

Upon assuming the presidency he appeared to allow the Philippines to slide back into a Marcos-type cronyist method of doing business. Groups and individuals who had been at the forefront of the fight to topple Marcos became increasingly vocal about Estrada's own corruption, despite his avowed intention to fight poverty. In particular, criticism focused on his return to doing business with a number of Marcos cronies, as well as on Estrada's own patronage of and payoffs from gambling (US$11 million in one case and more than US$70 million in total) and other illegal businesses (*Asia Times*, 29 February 2000; ABC, *Foreign Correspondent*, 14 November 2000).

In response to the mounting criticism of Estrada and the apparent evidence to justify such criticism, the Philippines Congress moved to impeach him, which process formally began in November 2000. As with Marcos, even big business turned against the president, meaning that the House of Representatives faced few hurdles in removing Estrada from office: within days, the impeachment had been confirmed. Estrada responded by flying to Ilocos Norte to appear on a stage at a public rally with Imelda Marcos and two of her sons. Estrada's impeachment was then considered by the Senate, where, in January 2001, Estrada supporters blocked the opening of his bank accounts to inspection. The impeachment process thus collapsed.

This move was greeted by massive protests and the withdrawal of support by his ministers and senior military officers. In the face of his collapsing support and his failure to call snap elections, Estrada resigned as president. He was succeeded by Gloria Arroyo Macapagal, daughter of the president who had preceded Marcos. In April, Estrada was jailed and, the following July, indicted on the capital charge of economic plunder.

ARROYO AS PRESIDENT

As vice-president, Gloria Arroyo automatically succeeded Estrada and was duly sworn in as president, on which occasion she promised to 'lead by example'. Estrada questioned the legality of Arroyo's succession, but, as well as the legal argument for his removal, there was overwhelming public support for replacing him as president. Arroyo assumed the presidency as a fill-in president, but quickly moved to make the presidency her own, in public charting a cautious, reactive and slightly austere course, relying on the strong support of government officials who had abandoned Estrada and hoped to rebuild their own political careers.

While the Philippines' economy had, for many years, been very weak, it did not assist Arroyo that she inherited a bankrupt treasury, an economic slowdown, falling investor confidence and a still-corruption-ridden bureaucracy. Her promise to end poverty within a decade was hollow; her promise to increase government transparency was well received, if not implemented. More positively, she did restart peace talks with the MILF and the NDF.

Within months of assuming the presidency, Arroyo became yet another Philippines president to face a fractious military. In July 2003, almost 300 soldiers attempted a coup against her government, ostensibly in support of Estrada and again linked to Gregorio Honasan. The soldiers' attempted coup fell flat when the coup plotters having taken a hotel building in the Makati business district of Manila, were abandoned by their colleagues. They were eventually allowed to return to barracks without loss of life, although they were later court-martialled. The incident reconfirmed the extent to which at least some of the Philippines military still considered itself to be a law unto itself. The defence minister, Angelo Reyes, resigned after the incident.

Despite a Senate investigation into her husband for money laundering, her marginal popularity and her announcement in December 2002 that she would not contest the presidency, Arroyo changed her mind and did contest the May 2004 presidential election, campaigning on an anti-corruption ticket and marginal improvements in the economy. Her primary opponent was a semi-educated, half-American movie actor, Fernando Poe, who was supported by some pro-Estrada groups, but who quickly showed himself to be out of his depth on policy issues, particularly economics. Arroyo and vice-presidential candidate and former national television news host, Senator

Noli De Castro, narrowly defeated Poe, 40 per cent to 36.5 per cent, with the remainder of the votes being taken by minor candidates and Arroyo supporters winning a majority of contested seats in the House of Representatives and in the Senate.

Almost half of all Filipinos live on US$2 a day or less, the economy was growing at around 3.5 per cent in 2004—less than most of its neighbours—official corruption remained problematic and the military, although more trusted, was not entirely believed to have lost its interest in politics. The NPA had rebuilt itself and again fielded around 10 000 guerrillas, while the MILF and the *Abu Sayyaf Group* also presented a major insurgency problem on Mindanao and close by islands and were increasingly identified as being linked to al-Qaeda and related regional organisations, such as *Jema'ah Islamiyah*. On 26 July 2004, in her state of the nation address, President Arroyo offered a frank observation: 'The next six years we hope is when we finally get things right', implying that, in the Philippines to that time, they had not been 'got right'. She concluded her speech by saying, 'The time for change is well past due.' On this she was correct. The Philippines had, for too long, been dominated by corrupt and self-serving elites who displayed all the ethics of robber barons and by a fulsome appreciation of superficiality, particularly that which aped the USA, which crippled recognition of a need to address substance. Arroyo appeared to be, at least in part, aware of that.

Yet the Philippines continued to seem like a country unaware of itself, other than as a mangled reflection of images of the USA. If the country of such dire poverty was burdened by separatist and revolutionary movements and an appallingly high crime rate, it is hardly surprising that alienation was their cause. The biggest long-term threat to Philippine political stability was—and remains—economic; the roots of the NPA and the MILF will remain strong while income and land distribution remain so uneven.

The elites remained entrenched, the rich remained rich, although with some small redistribution of wealth, the Philippines remained a poor country and ordinary Filipinos reflected that condition in the poverty of their lives. The deep institutionalisation of what is basically feudalistic–hacienda power appeared to be the greatest legacy of the Philippines history of being a Spanish and an American colony.[4] When Filipinos, as a nation, were required to deal with complex issues, when aping the surface aspects of another culture were found to be inadequate, where others might draw on a deep local cultural reserve, they found virtually nothing. The *tabula rasa* that the Spanish created left the Philippines hollowed out, lost for political values and without a past of its own to refer to. Perhaps there was a growing awareness of this and a genuine, popular desire to be rid of corrupt, self-serving politicians.

Arroyo was a conservative reflection of this desire, but her tenuous grip on the presidency combined with what appeared to be a deeply ingrained weakness for appearance over substance, threatened to limit her efficacy in office, and did not mean that, upon her leaving office, she would not be replaced with another actor, news reader, ex-general or some other form of shyster fronting for the landed and business elites.

NOTES

1   That is, Moors, after the Islamic invaders of Spain from Morocco.
2   Marcos was reelected as president in 1981, against what was, in effect, a non-existent opposition.
3   The Mindanao branch of the CPP–NPA arose largely in response to the depredations caused by the influx of the Philippines armed forces in response to MNLF rebellion.
4   Again, this can be seen in Central America, where US influence has been pervasive.

13 | Singapore: The Corporate State

When Goh Chock Tong resigned as Singapore's prime minister and Lee Hsien Loong, son of former prime minister Lee Kwan Yew, stepped up to take that position, it looked nothing so much as like a prince assuming his place as rightful heir to the throne. It had always appeared that the younger Lee was being groomed to assume the leadership of the city–state of Singapore, yet those who believed that Goh was just a temporary seat-warmer could not have counted on the fourteen years he spent as the country's most senior politician. It was a strong apprenticeship in which Lee Junior established that he had the potential capacity to run the city–state.

Lee Junior had been appointed as deputy prime minister in 1990 and as finance minister in 2001. His whole career smacked of nepotism, basking, as he did, in the advantage subtly conferred upon him by his father, Singapore's founding prime minister and, after retirement, senior minister Lee Kuan Yew. With Lee Junior's ascendancy, Lee Senior was appointed as minister mentor, while Goh assumed the position of senior minister. Political office looked most like a business run by family and friends.

Lee Junior graduated with honours in mathematics from Cambridge University and successfully completed postgraduate studies in public administration at Harvard, which, even with tutoring, required at least some capacity. Lee's rapid elevation through the ranks of the Singapore armed forces between joining in 1971 and retiring as brigadier-general (Singapore's youngest ever) at the age of 32 in 1984, raised eyebrows. Yet despite his easy entry into politics and rapid rise through the ruling People's Action Party, of which, within four years—in 1988—he was appointed to the ruling Central Executive Committee, Lee's battle with cancer (lymphoma) from 1992 was very much his own. The cancer was, no doubt, also what slowed his move to occupy Singapore's most powerful position.

As a minister, Lee impressed as being organised and decisive. Lee Senior had said that had his rise been a result of nepotism, he would have elevated him more quickly; he also said that his son was the best person for the job. What Lee Senior did not acknowledge was that the grooming took time, that Lee Junior's political rise had been interrupted by illness and that, for such nepotism to work in a state that still paid lip service to parliamentary principles, the pace of its procession needed to be seemly.

Perhaps, too, this was a case of the son having the capacity and the upbringing to fulfil his father's ambitions. But the younger Lee did enjoy advantages in his public life that directed and enhanced his rise. At the very least, he was a good Chinese son, his father was proud of him and Singapore's future was retained within hands that its founders and shapers regarded as secure.

Another of Singapore's sons had a less easy political path. Secretary-general of the Singapore Democratic Party, Chee Soon Juan, had an even

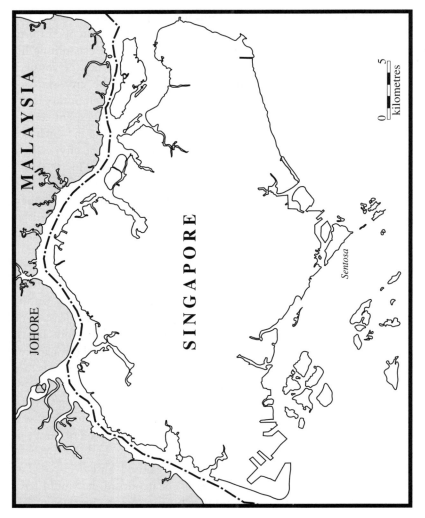

Map 10 Singapore

more distinguished academic career. He enjoyed none of the benefits that accrue to an autocratic prime minister's son, yet he achieved a PhD in neuropsychology. Chee was thrown out of his university job for what amounted to challenging the monolithic People's Action Party, was sued and all but financially ruined for making comments that, at worst, amounted to a public defence of his own position and which, in a democracy, would be regarded as fair comment and therefore part of the game. His speaking in public without an entertainment permit earned Chee fines and jail sentences, ironically, even when he spoke in public about the right, under Singapore's constitution, to free speech. Chee was also vilified by the government and in Singapore's tightly controlled media in ways that, should the position have been reversed, would have resulted in defamation suits. His was no easy ride; it reflected no official grooming and indicated limited prospects for a successful future. Lee the younger held power, but of the two of them, it was Chee who represented democratic aspiration.

The circumstances of Chee Soon Juan perhaps best reflect the state of contemporary politics in Singapore. Here is a state that is clearly successful at the economic level, having lifted its citizens out of developing country status within three decades. Yet the price of the material advance has been the institutionalisation of a political organisation that is more efficient and precise in its suppression of dissent than any other in SEA. According to Chee Soon Juan, although Singapore derives its political institutions from the United Kingdom, it offers 'not the rule of law, but rule by law'.[1] Having said that, most Singaporeans appear to be well satisfied with their lot, perhaps a reflection of the effect of a successful process of hegemony and because all they want is a materially prosperous life. For those less satisfied, however, Singapore is a daunting place.

EARLY HISTORY

Singapore's pre-British history is not clearly recorded, although it is known that the island was, at different times, home to at least a couple of Malay polities. Chinese records referring to the island, known by them as P'u Luo Chung, date back as far as 231 CE, although that information is incomplete and suggests a lack of direct knowledge. In the eleventh century, the then flourishing empire of Sri Vijaya based in southeast Sumatra established an outpost on the strategically placed island referred to by its inhabitants as called Tumasik. One version of lore has it that, during a visit by a prince of Sri Vijaya, Sri Tri Buana, he sighted an animal he confused with what was to Malays a mythical lion. Suitably impressed, Sri Tri Buana decided to settle there and found a kingdom, naming the island Singapura (Lion City). A substantial city was located in the area of colonial Singapore, which was noted by the Portuguese explorer Alfonso de Albuquerque. It was, he said, 'a big town with a large population'. However, by the time de Albuquerque reached Singapore, he could only base his assessment on the remaining ruins (Flower 1984: 5–6). Singapore had become a home to sea gypsies and a place of execution for the victims of pirates (Flower 1984: 7).

The status of Singapore remained more or less unchanged until the arrival of Raffles, who is credited as the founder of the modern city–state. The island was a possession of the sultan of Johore when Raffles first identified it as the location for a British outpost. Raffles was then in his prime, having risen quickly in the service of the East India Company, helping establish the colony at Penang and having been given the governorship of the Dutch East Indies during the Napoleonic Wars. He was knighted as Sir (Thomas) Stamford Raffles and, before returning to SEA, wrote a paper emphasising the United Kingdom's longer-term interests in trade with China. This included the necessity of occupying one of the two strategically placed islands at the mouth of the main trade route of the Malacca Straits, Riau or Singapura. The Dutch quickly claimed Riau, narrowing the choices. Raffles then headed for Singapura, landing there on 29 January 1819.

THE BRITISH PERIOD

Acting outside official British policy, Raffles entered into an agreement whereby he would pay a rent of Sp$3000 (Spanish dollars) a year to the local sultan, Had Wa Hakim. However, real authority over the island lay with the sultan of Johore, who owed nominal allegiance to the Dutch. Raffles knew that the sultan of Johore had seized the sultanate in dubious circumstances, so he had the legitimate heir, Tunku Long, returned to Johore and restored him to the throne, encouraging his acceptance of the position with a payment of Sp$5000 a year. Raffles then sealed a treaty with the new sultan and left his second-in-command, Colonel William Farquar, as Resident and Commandant of Singapore. Raffles also designated Singapore a free port, a decision that was to have profound long-term implications.

The Dutch were, of course, furious with Raffles' move, claiming that Singapore was a part of Johore, which was, in turn, a dependency of the Dutch territory of Malacca. However, the Dutch were unable to enforce their bluster, as Holland was then in a weakened military state vis-à-vis the United Kingdom. The United Kingdom was unable to negotiate the situation, as news of the occupation only reached there in September, by which time Chinese, Malay and Bugis traders were swarming into the new colony, seeking respite from Dutch limitations on trade. It was a classic *fait accompli*. When Raffles' superiors found out about the move they were disturbed, but traders were delighted. Official opinion quickly moved in behind commercial opinion.

By the 1830s Singapore 'acted as a magnet for the region's trade', primarily as a result of its free trade policy (Turnbull 1989: 100), which contrasted favourably with the restricted Dutch trade. Already attracting local shipping, it increasingly attracted shipping from Europe, India and China, in the latter case mainly after the East India Company's monopoly was abolished. In the following decade, further trading links were initiated with southern Vietnam, Siam and northern Borneo. Between 1824 and 1868, Singapore's trade increased by more than 400 per cent and was valued at £59 million. As a trading state, its economy progressed in bursts, but the development of the steamship and the opening of the Suez Canal in 1869 established Singapore's central role in international trade. As the United Kingdom's main base in the Far East, Singapore was also vital to British imperial interests.

SINGAPORE AS CHINESE

Singapore was initially ruled from Bengal as a part of the British empire in the East, but the Indian mutiny proved the inappropriateness of this distant link. The Straits Settlements, including Singapore, Penang and parcels of land on the Malay Peninsula, were ruled as an independent entity from 1857. From around the 1860s, Singapore was the central point for the organisation of ethnic Chinese business interests throughout SEA—what has been referred to as the Nanyang[2] diaspora—and by the 1880s, the island had firmly established itself as the prime trading city in the region. It had become the headquarters for a number of shipping companies, businesses and trading agencies, and was central to financing and servicing the mining and agricultural industries in the Malay states (Turnbull 1989: 180). The sentiment in Singapore by this stage was that the city's success was 'self-engendering [and] that they were riding on a wave of destiny which could only lead them on to fulfilment. It was a moment of great excitement and self-esteem' (Flower 1984: 145). In a number of important senses, this sentiment has been reinvented in contemporary Singapore. Singapore's government and, through its tight and pervasive control of information processes, its people, are adept practitioners of the politics of self-congratulation.

As Nanyang, Singapore retained close links with China and its ethnic Chinese population continued to consider themselves Chinese rather than Singaporean. Although there were domestic issues to unite or divide the local population, the issues that commanded the high ground of ethnic Chinese attention in Singapore were those that prevailed in China. The rise of the republican movement in China spurred parallel interests among Singaporean Chinese, with a Chinese revolutionary group being established in Singapore as early as 1906 (Bedlington 1978: 58). The establishment of the republican Guomindang (or Kuomintang, KMT) government in China in 1912 saw the founding of KMT branches in Singapore soon after. When the KMT, under Chiang Kai-shek, finally managed to impose government on all of China in 1927, the first of Sun Yat Sen's Three Principles of the

People, the indivisibility of Chinese people (and rejection of foreign control), gave impetus to a Singaporean Chinese protonationalism.

Although there was considerable anti-imperialist and nationalist activity in India, Indians in Singapore did not form themselves into political parties at this time. In part, they were quietened by the failed mutiny of an Indian regiment stationed in Singapore in early 1915 (Turnbull 1977: 128–30). Similarly, ethnic Malays did not form themselves into formal political organisations in Singapore, not least because of the outsiders' overwhelming numerical majority. While politics—and trade—developed, so too did Chinese language education, which stressed Chinese culture and ignored indigenous culture. Although this was to have been expected, it began to shape Singapore as an overwhelmingly and somewhat formal Chinese city (Turnbull 1977: 133–4).

The purge by the KMT of the Chinese Communist Party (CCP) in China caused a similar split in Singapore. In 1929, the International Committee of the Communist Party, the Comintern, recognised the founding of the Nanyang Communist Party (NCP). The NCP and its related branch on the northern peninsula, the Malayan Communist Party, were based in the trade unions and among teachers and leftist intellectuals. The KMT appealed to more conservative and affluent Singaporean Chinese. Both parties received considerable impetus from Japan's attack on China in 1937. This rise in Chinese nationalism, reflected in the political activism of KMT and NCP and MCP branches, caused the British colonial government to suppress these organisations (Turnbull 1977: 134–7).

THE JAPANESE INTERLUDE

Launching from Thailand in December 1941, Japan's imperial forces struck down the Malay Peninsula in a manner that the British forces there could not comprehend. Singapore had been established as a major military base, but the view had always been that any threat to it would come from the sea. Singapore was, the British presumed, safe from attack through the Malay Peninsula. Yet in less than three months after launching the beginning of their attack on Malaya, Singapore was surrendered to the besieging Japanese army. This event was significant for a number of reasons, but mostly because it marked the beginning of the end of imperial power in SEA and, consequently, the first step towards the dismantling of colonialism more generally (Turnbull 1977: 173–88).

The response of the Japanese towards Singapore's population was, overall, brutal. After their experiences in China, the occupying force did not trust the ethnic Chinese and rooted out suspected opposition with great ruthlessness. Malays, on the other hand, were initially treated significantly better and were increasingly moved to occupy administrative posts, while some Indians also saw an anti-British advantage in cooperation with the occupying force. However, the use of Indians and Malays, as well as Chinese and prisoners of war, in slave-labour conditions shattered whatever bond might have been established between the great majority of Chinese and non-Chinese Singaporean residents and the Japanese. Despite this treatment of local people, what was perceived to be collaboration between many Malays and the Japanese on the peninsula sparked anti-Malay violence in the immediate postwar period, which influenced ethnic Chinese thinking in Singapore. The split between the Malays and the Chinese, long submerged under a colonial policy of political representation for the Malays and economic development for the Chinese, broke through the surface. Singapore was not as affected as the peninsula, but, as a predominantly Chinese city, it was regarded thereafter by politically organised Malays on the peninsula with suspicion and some hostility (Turnbull 1977: ch. VI).

POSTWAR SINGAPORE

Following the war, the United Kingdom moved relatively quickly towards establishing Singapore as an independent state. However, from the beginning there was perceived to be problems. Singapore, apart from the mainland states, was not regarded as materially viable, yet because of its overwhelming Chinese makeup, it was regarded as being difficult to integrate. The former view came close to holding true, while the latter most certainly did. In order not to upset the ethnic balance within Malaya, Singapore was initially created as a separate Crown Colony, in April 1946. In this, the governor was supreme administrator and was supported by an appointed executive council and legislative council (Bedlington 1978: 199).

To ensure that the United Kingdom did not dawdle on the issue of independence, the Malayan Democratic Union was formed by a group of middle-class intellectuals while interred by the Japanese during WWII, officially launching itself on 21 December 1945. Its program was to end British colonial rule and to join Singapore and Malaya in a united state (Shee 1985: 3). Until the Malayan Communist Party (MCP) launched its armed revolt in 1948, the Malayan Democratic Union (MDU) and the MCP worked together. Lee claimed that the MDU was, in fact, just a political front for the MCP (Lee 1998a: 88–9). Meanwhile, other areas of political development proceeded apace. The Progressive Party was launched on 25 August 1947 (Josey 1970: 2–3), the United Kingdom had announced that it would encourage self-government in Singapore after the war was concluded and, by 1948, had begun to prepare for a fully elected legislature. The first elections, in that same year, were restricted to the island's 22 000 British subjects, thereby disenfranchising most of Singapore's population.

Then, in 1951, the colonial government moved towards establishing local government in an effort to popularise self-government at the grass-roots level. In 1953 a review of the constitutional status of the colony was set up, marking another step towards the joint aim of granting independence and ensuring that Singapore remained non-communist in orientation, to which end the United Kingdom looked for a suitable anti-communist leader. According to Lee Kuan Yew, that person was a young, independence-minded, British-trained lawyer and former black marketeer: himself[3] (Lee 1998b: 50; Lee 1998a: 72, 89–90). In 1954, with the support of union activists Lim Yew Hock and Fong Swee Suan, they formed the People's Action Party (PAP). The PAP was the first non-communist political party to capture the imagination and interest of a large number of Singaporeans. In 1955, as a consequence of the earlier constitutional review, Singapore's first Legislative Assembly was established, consisting of thirty-two members, of whom twenty-five were popularly elected. Ultimate power, in the areas of foreign policy, defence and internal security, remained with the colonial government (Shee 1985: 4).

The 1955 election was won by the Labour Front under the leadership of David Saul Marshall, whose priority was to gain full self-rule. The PAP won three seats in the assembly, as a result of which they became the opposition. Marshall gained the expansion of the Legislative Assembly to fifty-one seats, but, having failed to secure independence through negotiation in 1956, he resigned to lead the opposition Workers' Party. Lim Yew Hock, who was more compliant to the United Kingdom's wishes, replaced Marshall as chief minister. A more inspiring potential leader was the PAP's Lim Chin Siong who, during a time of strikes and riots against British rule, rallied support among ordinary Singaporeans. However, because of his leftist sympathies, he was repeatedly jailed by the British.

A SPLIT IN THE PAP

A delegation led by Lim Yew Hock and including Lee Kuan Yew succeeded in gaining the United Kingdom's agreement in 1957 for a fully elected and more fully self-governing legislative assembly in 1959. The head of state under this system was to be the *Yang di-Pertuan Negara* the equivalent of the governor-general in other Westminster-styled parliamentary democracies. The *Yang di-Pertuan Negara*, appointed on the recommendation of the prime minister, called upon that person who appeared most likely to command a majority in the Legislative Assembly to form a government and assume the position of prime minister. The prime minister in turn appointed the cabinet, which was responsible to the Legislative Assembly. In all, it was a conventional Westminster parliamentary model. The primary exceptions to complete self-rule under this agreement were that foreign affairs would continue to stay with the United Kingdom, while internal security would be maintained by an Internal Security Council, consisting of three representatives each from the Singapore and British governments.

It was at the time of a heated debate with Lee about the ideological future of the PAP that Lim Chin Siong was arrested under the Internal

Security Act (ISA). With Lim in jail, this left the party in Lee's hands. In 1957, the left wing of the PAP rallied against Lee, but a continued British crackdown on alleged communists, including those within the PAP, ensured Lee's long-term control. Lee continued to rely on the support of this party's jailed members in the lead-up to the 1959 elections, which would provide the island with its first government under independence. He even promised to have his left-wing factional allies freed from jail before taking office. But, just before the elections were held, Lee asked voters for an absolute majority for his right-wing faction of the PAP. The result was an overwhelming victory, with the Lee-dominated faction of the PAP taking forty-three of the fifty-one seats (Chee 1998: 249–53; Shee 1985: 5–7; Turnbull 1977: 264–70). Lee subsequently left Lim in jail.

There were numerous early debates about Singapore's status and its relationship with the United Kingdom. In 1960, as a consequence of these debates and the factionalism that inspired them, the Minister for National Development, Ong Eng Guan, was sacked from the cabinet and the party, precipitating a by-election the following year, which Ong overwhelmingly won. Three months later, the death of a local PAP member of the Assembly led to another by-election, which was won by the leader of the Workers' Party, David Marshall. Among other things, Marshall demanded the abolition of the Internal Security Council, the dismantling of British naval facilities in Singapore and complete independence. A final blow to the PAP came when, soon after, eight PAP members of the Assembly openly supported demands by six trade unionists for full self-government and resigned from the government.

In 1961, Lee formally split with Lim—by now released from jail—over their ideological differences, with Lim and the resigned MPs forming the *Barisan Socialis* (BS, or Socialist Front). The PAP members of the BS believed that they could not achieve power from within the party, but would be able to do so from outside. They also believed that the United Kingdom would not hinder their plans so long as British interests were not threatened.

SINGAPORE AND MALAYSIA

In 1961, the PAP strengthened its appeals to the British government to have Singapore included in, or otherwise associated with, the new Federation of Malaysia. Inclusion within Malaysia was, the PAP believed, the only realistic means of halting the increasingly popular BS from achieving government. Apart from diluting the political presence of the BS within a larger political framework, the PAP knew that federation with Malaya under a right-wing Alliance government would bring with it tighter internal security rules that would hamper the BS. However, within this framework there was a continuing desire by the PAP to maintain self-government in the areas of education and labour. The BS labelled the planned association a 'phoney merger'. Further, being aware that a conventional democratic process might not continue in the PAP's favour, by 1962, Lee was already talking about a specifically 'Asian' form of democracy[4] (Chee 1998: 254–5; Shee 1985: 6–7; Bellows 1970: 41–5).

In 1963, Singapore voted to join the Federation of Malaysia in what Chee has identified as a rigged ballot. On 22 September 1963, five days after the merger with Malaya went through, the PAP called elections. With just nine days allowed for campaigning, thirty-seven seats went to the PAP and thirteen to the less well prepared *Barisan Socialis*. The year 1963 marked the beginning of the end of a viable political opposition in Singapore.

The incorporation of Singapore into Malaysia had been opposed by both Indonesia and the Philippines, as well as by Singapore's own BS. Lee campaigned, in part, on a platform that said that 'A vote for the Barisan was a vote for Sukarno'[5] (Lee 1998b: 53). However, after the elections there were serious tensions in the relationship between Singapore and the rest of Malaysia. Lee continued to insist on using the title 'Prime Minister', which irked non-Singaporean Malaysians, and he spearheaded PAP aspirations to achieve government in Kuala Lumpur, which was the beginning of what was Malaysia's primary opposition party, the Singapore-linked Democratic Action Party (DAP). The Malaysian Chinese Association, a party in the Malaysian government's alliance with UMNO, had earlier sent organisers to Singapore to oppose Lee, which also created tension.

There were also ideological differences, with concern over what Lee acknowledged as Singapore's pursuit of perceived socialist-oriented policies (Lee 1998b: 51), and there was real concern over Lee's refusal to allow Singapore to become financially or politically subservient to Kuala Lumpur. Most importantly, there was long-standing concern among ethnic Malays that the inclusion of Singapore into the Federation would help to establish an ethnic Chinese majority in Malaysia. It could not, as only 42 per cent of Malaysians at that time were ethnic Chinese, but combined with ethnic Indians, the balance would have been enough to tip the ethnic scales away from Malay domination.

Conversely, Lee Kuan Yew claimed that, rather than aim to establish a multiracial society, UMNO was intent on establishing a society politically dominated by Malays. After the Malaysian general election of 1964 resulted in the defeat of PAP candidates on the Malay Peninsula, the five ministerial members of parliament representing Singapore were moved to the Opposition benches 'to join seven others already there' (Lee 1998b: 54).

In July 1964, events began to come to a head, with Chinese-Malay riots in Singapore. Over the course of three days, at least twenty-three people were killed and 454 injured. Lee later blamed UMNO for being behind the riots to gather Malay support in Singapore and to consolidate support for UMNO on the peninsula. There were further clashes in August. In December, Malaysian Prime Minister Tunku Abdul Rahman told Lee that the constitutional arrangement, which included Singapore in the Federation, should be changed. Trade was to be independent but defence would remain Kuala Lumpur's responsibility, to which Singapore would contribute. Lee countered with the idea that the Malaysian and Singaporean governments should operate independently within their respective spheres of influence. 'Not surprisingly, we made no progress with the "rearrangements" … What was suitable for Singapore was not suitable for Malaysia and vice versa. Merger had been a mistake' (Lee 1998b: 56–7). After ordering financial arrangements for its central bank, Lee Kuan Yew announced in an emotional speech on 9 August 1965, that Singapore had separated itself from Malaysia. At the same time, a similar, irrevocable, announcement was made in Kuala Lumpur.

POLITICAL LIMITATIONS IN SINGAPORE

From 1965, the PAP increased its use of the intelligence apparatus to watch the Opposition. The following year, when Chia Thye Poh was elected as a candidate for the *Barisan Socialis*, he accused the ruling PAP of harassing BS leaders. In response, Chia was arrested and jailed under the ISA until 1989. Even after his release, he was held under house arrest on Sentosa Island for a further two years and was, thereafter, banned from writing or publishing, travelling overseas without government permission or belonging to any organisation (Chee 1998: 241–7). Following the arrest and detention of Chia, the BS withdrew from the parliamentary process, citing the impossibility of participating in the political environment while the PAP exercised regressive measures against duly elected members.

The by-elections of 1967, caused by BS resignations from the Assembly, gave the PAP forty-nine of the fifty-one available seats; the remaining two seats were held by independents. In 1968 all fifty-one PAP candidates were returned unopposed. Five independents and two Workers' Party candidates challenged seven PAP candidates; the PAP candidates won all contested seats. Singapore had started with thirteen political parties contesting the 1959 elections and, by 1970, a dozen parties were still registered, although only one, the PAP, was viable. From then on, the PAP overwhelmingly dominated the political landscape.

One factor that did tend to aid the consolidation of power by the PAP was the siege mentality engendered by the government in response to Singapore's economic development and, to some extent, to its changed security environment. Despite the United Kingdom's catastrophic defence of Singapore in 1942, after the war it was rebuilt as a major British naval base. But it became increasingly obvious that the United Kingdom's time as a world and colonial leader was fast coming to an end. The United Kingdom maintained international military links as long as it felt able to do so, but World War II had ended its period as a great power, in both an economic and military sense. As it shed its colonial empire, the United Kingdom also moved to reduce its overseas military commitment. By the late 1960s, it had decided on a policy of withdrawing all forces east of the Suez, including withdrawing from Singapore in 1971. While the United Kingdom's material withdrawal was replaced by the Five Power Defence Agreement,[6] Singapore, as a small and physically vulnerable state surrounded by potentially hostile states, had its sense of insecurity aroused by their leaving.

Although economic development during the 1960s was satisfactory, the withdrawal of British forces from Singapore precipitated a rise in unemployment to approximately double what it had been, that is, up to around 100 000 in a workforce of a little over 500 000 (Bellows 1970: 113–14). Singapore's already challenged political pluralism was 'regressing before the exigencies of economic survival'. Bellows pointed out that, by the late 1960s, Singapore was already choosing to go down an essentially non-democratic path. He noted in 1970 that a 'tightly organised society which demands order, discipline, involvement, and commitment on the part of each individual as the sine qua non for basic survival bodes ill for the continuance or renaissance of a competitive party system' (Bellows 1970: 114).

As early as 1960, Lee Kuan Yew had indicated that he did not think that democracy, in the conventional sense of one-person, one vote, was suitable for developing countries, within which he included Singapore. He said he believed that, for a government to at least give the impression it was effective, it must be seen as enduring. In this sense, an effective government, according to Lee, could not be subject to the vagaries of the electoral process. 'If I were in authority in Singapore indefinitely without having to ask those who are governed whether they like what is being done, then I have not the slightest doubt that I could govern much more effectively in their interests' (Josey 1970: 8–10). These words, uttered in a radio interview in 1960, turned out to be prophetic.

While it is open to debate whether the PAP under Lee had governed in the interests of all Singaporeans, it is true that Singapore did achieve remarkable economic development under his rule. The primary policy used to achieve this was a high level of government investment in and support for private industry, based on a high level of (enforced) savings (Low & Quan 1992: 15–27).

It is also true that, in practice, Lee and the PAP did not have to ask Singapore's people whether they liked what was being done. When some announced that they did not, in fact, like what was being done, they tended to be persecuted by the state through a variety of non-democratic means. According to Vasil, the PAP's leaders did not believe that a conventional representative democracy was workable in an economically developing society. 'The open and competitive system also had proved to be a source of special problems of political management in multi-racial societies. Furthermore, it was obvious that it acted as a barrier to rapid and substantial social and economic change and progress' (Vasil 1984: 115). And, further,

'... the PAP leaders were clear in their minds that they could not afford to allow any independent centres of power' (Vasil 1984: 117). Despite Singapore's undoubted economic development, this guiding philosophy has not altered since that time.

Lee went on to develop his views on autocratic government, citing what he called 'Asian values'. He later modified this rather vague term to 'Confucian values', which he regarded as more culturally authentic and more closely fitting with Singapore's predominantly ethnic Chinese population. Within this idea, Lee identified loyalty to and the dominance of the group, respect for authority and a paternalistic decision-making process. Lee's understanding of Confucianism reflected the reinterpretation of Confucius under the Sung Dynasty, which wished to re-impose authoritarian rule in China. It was a very particular interpretation of Confucius and certainly not the only one that was available. Lee adopted his version of Confucianism to suit his political style, employing it as legitimising rhetoric. Insofar as Lee was criticised for this position, he defended himself and his political style by denigrating the circumstances and values of Western states, very often to the point of caricature.

Singapore unicameral parliamentary democracy has a maximum life of five years, although elections have generally been more frequent, maintaining the façade of democracy. A chiefly ceremonial president heads the state, while real power resides in the hands of the majority party of parliament. The PAP has always held the majority of seats, but from 1968 to 1981 held all seats and has since then always held no fewer than seventy-seven of a total of seventy-nine available seats.

In 1990, Lee handed the prime ministership to Goh Chock Tong, but retained the number two position under the title of Senior Minister Without Portfolio and, as chairman of the PAP, was seen to still control events in Singapore. Goh was regarded as a capable administrator, but, in reality, was just filling in while Lee's son, Lee Hsien Loong, was being groomed for the prime ministership.

Then, in late 1992, Lee Jnr was diagnosed with lymphoma, throwing the future leadership of the PAP into some doubt. Upon Lee Jnr's remission, he assumed more political responsibility and again was seen to be on the path to eventual prime ministership.

BEING IN OPPOSITION

Based on a proportion of overall votes, electoral support for the opposition parties—the Singapore Democratic Party (SDP) and the Workers' Party—was at 24 per cent in 2001, down from 35 per cent in the previous elections. However, this was still a fairly remarkable achievement, given the restrictions placed on the SDP by the government through its control of the media, its use of legal action against SDP members, its control of the grassroots Residents'

Committees and its frequent recourse to changing electoral rules prior to elections. That the SDP survived in such a climate of harassment and official surveillance was in itself remarkable, although party membership was limited to about 200 by the significant personal costs borne by not just membership, but by association. 'With control of various organs of government in the hands of the dominant party or family, individuals participating in opposition politics are vulnerable to various methods that undermine their pursuit of public office.' These include public vilification, lack of recourse to action against attacks, defamation suits against critics of government members, contempt of court charges for criticism of the legal process, vigorous tax audits, and police surveillance, among many others (Lingle 1996: 22).

MAINTENANCE OF POWER

Methods of maintaining PAP political control were various, but three key points stood out as gross breaches of conventional democratic parliamentary behaviour. The first was the gerrymandering of electoral boundaries. In this process, electoral boundaries of unsafe or challenged seats were reconfigured to isolate polling booths that returned a strong anti-government vote. The effect of this was to incorporate those anti-government areas into more strongly pro-government electorates, hence diluting the anti-government ratio of the vote, or fragmenting the growth of anti-government sentiment within a particular area. For example, the government altered the boundaries for electoral districts in October 1996, just three months before the 1997 elections. In 2001, the government again dramatically altered the boundaries of election districts, just seventeen days before the elections. Some constituencies were abolished, while many other constituencies' borders were changed.

The second key method for the government to maintain political control through the electoral process was to change the electoral rules just prior to elections and, sometimes, after election campaigns had already commenced, for example, Singapore began as a one-person per-seat parliamentary system, but later introduced Group Representational Constituencies (GRCs), a multiperson, per-seat system in which the successful team takes all seats. This system required a particular ethnic mix of candidates for certain seats, the ostensible intention being to guarantee proportional ethnic representation in the parliament. However, the short notice with which this requirement was introduced and the organisational difficulties associated with standing a predetermined number of ethnically specific people in a particular seat presented major hurdles for opposition candidates to overcome. Under a conventional parliamentary system, if an individual candidate drops out, the candidate only invalidates his or her own candidature. Under the Singaporean system, if an individual candidate drops out of a multicandidate team, the whole team is invalidated. Since 1988, the government has changed all but nine single-seat constituencies into GRCs.

The third main method of maintaining political control was by instilling a degree of fear into the electorate. Residents' Committees (RCs) were used as a means of surveillance of disgruntled citizens and as a conduit for threats of loss of access to government services. An extension of this was that constituencies that vote away from the government were warned that their vote could earn them en masse a loss of government services. The RCs and the more recent government-organised and funded Community Development Councils acted, in effect, like the grassroots or local branches of the PAP.

These RCs were formed in the numerous tower blocks that dominate much of Singapore's architectural landscape, which themselves lend a brave new world feel to the physical infrastructure of the city. Although not formally founded as a part of the PAP, the chairman of each committee is usually a PAP member or is otherwise linked to the network of patronage within the PAP.

RCs are used for various purposes, including fundraising and as a means of vote buying at election time. In this sense, there was a parallel between the RCs and village or neighbourhood committees in communist states or under the New Order government of Indonesia. Participation in RCs was encouraged by inducements, such as enhanced ease of access to municipal services (for example, educational facilities) and through localised public works (for example, footbridges, street beautification, local infrastructure maintenance, etc.). A negative inducement for staying away from RC meetings was increased difficulty of access to municipal services or, on a wider scale, a loss or relocation of public works.

As with most states that fail to distinguish between the party and the state, active participation in RCs or membership in the PAP by individuals in the civil service had a tendency to smooth career paths. Alternatively, non-participation in RCs or the PAP or, worse, opposition to them, quickly led to the discovery of a glass ceiling to professional development. Loss of employment was not uncommon for government opponents. An employee so affected could not, in most cases, appeal to their union because there were few independent trade unions. Of the eighty-two unions that exist in Singapore, seventy-two were affiliated with the National Trade Union Congress (NTUC), which was closely linked to the government. Most unions were poorly patronised, comprising just 15 per cent of the working population of 2 million.

EMPLOYMENT

The relationship between the PAP and the NTUC was in any case so close that it was described by both as 'symbiotic' (Wong 1992: 145). Indeed, the NTUC's general secretary, Lim Boong Heng, was also minister without portfolio (previously minister for trade and industry) in the PAP government and, in 2004, was appointed chairman of the PAP. His predecessor, Singapore's President Ong Teng Cheong, was NTUC secretary-general and deputy prime minister simultaneously. As a consequence of the nominal nature of the trade union movement, there were no mechanisms for redressing worker grievances. To illustrate this point, if a worker or group of workers were sacked or retrenched, this occurred without notice and was done in such a way that the workers were individually removed from the workplace, meaning they could not share their grievances with other workers. Further, while not all employees were directly subject to the whims of the government, the government was the single largest employer in Singapore, with a majority of all employment made up between the government and government-linked corporations or government-friendly multinational corporations.

Despite a growing income gap between rich and poor Singaporeans, very little strike action has been taken by Singapore's workers in support of claims, the last such strike being in 1986. In part, this reflected a relatively high degree of worker mobility, almost full employment and overall real wage growth. But it also reflected in part a controlled dispute-management system, conducted through the Ministry of Manpower, the Industrial Arbitration Court and the unwillingness of most unions to confront the government.

Because of a long-standing labour shortage, Singapore had about 400 000 legal 'guest workers' and a significant number of illegal immigrant workers, constituting around one-quarter of the total workforce. A great majority of these workers were unskilled labourers and many lived at or near their places of employment, often in substandard conditions. Of this group, there were about 100 000 maids in Singapore, about 80 per cent of them from the Philippines, with the rest coming from Thailand, Indonesia and Sri Lanka. Most maids worked from early in the morning to late at night and were allowed between one day off a week and one day off a month. Not including room and board, maids were paid around S$250 (Singapore dollars) a month, which, after deductions, is as little as 25 Singapore cents an hour, although for the first few months of employment this was paid to a placement agent. The cost of living in Singapore was at a level in which S$250 would be considered about half or less of a low weekly income. Most low-paid guest workers were not covered by the Employment Act and did not qualify for the free legal assistance that is available to citizens; free medical services are not available to guest workers or to citizens.

POLITICAL LIMITATIONS

While the position of president of the state in Singapore was not powerful—that was left to the special ministership and the prime ministership—the candidacy for becoming president was even more tightly controlled than for ordinary parliamentary constituencies. Strict prerequisites were required for a person to become president, including having held one of several senior public offices, which meant being appointed by a government minister, which in turn required at least total loyalty to and usually membership of the PAP. One exception to this limiting requirement was the similarly limiting requirement that a prospective candidate be the chief executive of a company with a capital value in excess of S$60 million. All candidates had to be vetted by a three-person committee, of which two members were government appointees. Only around 400 Singaporean citizens could meet the first set of criteria for election as president, while applications by two opposition candidates were rejected by the three-person screening committee (Lingle 1996: 93).

Given these circumstances, while most Singaporeans were quiescent, there has been some political disquiet. Criticism of the Singaporean government and the PAP has centred on its authoritarian style and its questionable dealings with political opponents. The government has employed the ISA to arrest people allegedly involved in subversion conspiracies and, in one case, had a successful opposition candidate disqualified, in absentia, for income tax evasion, charges that were poorly supported in law. The ISA continues as a statute and may be employed against any person deemed by a PAP committee to have threatened the interests of the state, the interests of the state and the interests of the PAP usually being conflated.

The Singaporean government exercised relatively strict control over a number of elements of Singaporean life, including the media and, although perhaps less importantly, public behaviour. Singapore has been an economic success, in large part due to activist government policies.

> The PAP has maintained its political dominance in part by developing genuine voter support through honest, effective administration and its strong track record in bringing economic prosperity to the country and, in part, by manipulating the electoral framework, intimidating organised political opposition, and circumscribing the bounds of legitimate political discourse and action. (US Department of State 1999b: 11)

But most Singaporeans seemed happy with their government and did not appear to feel a strong need for political change, which is even acknowledged by opposition activists. Indeed, they say, the prime concern of most citizens is material development, with the maintenance of such being the first priority. Hence, if the government can deliver material development and challenging the government can remove it, there is considerable incentive for supporting the government, rather than opposing it. Combined with the government's tight control over the flow of information and its own active information campaign, there has developed in Singapore what has been described as a fairly clearly defined sense of hegemony. Where a hegemonic framework can be said to exist in any politically stable society, in Singapore the presentation of its construction is very clear.

FREEDOM OF SPEECH

Perhaps the best known means of controlling dissent in Singapore is the use of law. The most common method of silencing dissent was to sue dissenters for defamation. In Singapore, defamation was equivalent to expressing disapproval of a member of government, the implication being that such disapproval somehow lowers the public standing of the politician. Fines in defamation cases commonly run to the value of between S$200 and S$500 000. In 1995, the *International Herald Tribune* was sued for a record (for a publication) US$678 000 in a highly publicised and, outside Singapore, doubtful defamation case concerning the political rise of Lee Kuan Yew's son, Lee Hsien Loong. The use of defamation damages was often enough to cause bankruptcy, which disqualified one from standing for parliament. The use of defamation was also usually sufficient to otherwise financially ruin the person so sued, and acted as a considerable disincentive to criticism of the government.

Following the 1997 elections, Workers' Party candidate Tang Liang Hong was sued for defamation by Goh Chock Tong, Lee Kuan Yew and nine other current or former members of parliament. Tang was ordered to pay a record S$5.77 million, while tax authorities also charged Tang with tax evasion. Tang subsequently fled to Malaysia without paying the fine. Tang's WP colleague, J. B. Jeyaretnam, was also sued for defamation for telling a political rally that Tang had filed police reports against Goh Chock Tong and his people. In the first suit, Jeyaretnam was required to pay 10 per cent of Goh's damages claim and 60 per cent of his legal costs. Goh appealed and the figure was increased to half of his claimed damages and all of his legal costs, which were paid.

The most significant element of free speech is reflected in the mass media. In Singapore, the mass media was, and remains, tightly controlled and the government 'intimidates journalists into practicing self-censorship. The Government's authoritarian style has fostered an atmosphere inimical to fully free speech and the press' (US Department of State 1999b: 5; see also, US Department of State 2003). One means of influencing the mass media, in particular the print media, was through the government's close ties to Singapore Press Holdings, which owned all the official-language, mass-circulation newspapers in Singapore. The government also had right of veto over holders of management shares in the company, who, in turn, appointed all directors and staff.

Publications from Malaysia were banned in Singapore, but a wide range of other foreign newspapers and magazines were available. These publications had to post a bond of S$200 000 and have a legal nominee. Under the ISA and Undesirable Publications Act, the government could ban foreign publications and, under the Newspaper and Printing Presses Act, limit their circulation. Circulation of the *Asian Wall Street Journal*, the *Far Eastern Economic Review* and *Asiaweek* was limited, although approximated demand. The potential of being banned acted as a disincentive for publications to be critical of the Singaporean government, which also denied residency to a number of foreign correspondents, although it has, in the post-Lee Kwan Yew period, become increasingly more lenient in this regard.

The Singapore Broadcasting Authority regulated the broadcasting industry, including the internet, from which it filtered material (almost entirely pornography). The government-linked company, Singapore International Media, has a near monopoly on broadcasting, operating all four free-to-air television stations and ten of the fifteen radio stations. Of the other five radio stations, two were operated by the Armed Forces Reservists' Association, two by the government-controlled NTUC; only the British Broadcasting Corporation World Service is fully independent of the government. A government-controlled cable service was also available and, while Malaysian and Indonesian services can be received, satellite receiving dishes were almost entirely banned (see Gomez 2000: 41–54 for discussion of censorship in Singapore).

SPEAKING AS A POLITICAL ISSUE

Public speech was also tightly restricted, under legal provisions enacted by the colonial British government as a means of restricting communist dissent during the 1950s. Speaking in public required an entertainment permit, yet there was usually insurmountable difficulty in obtaining such a permit. Such difficulties vary from outright refusal to granting a permit at such late notice that it is practically impossible to organise the event to be addressed. In the free speech trials of the secretary-general of the Singapore Democratic Party, Chee Soon Juan, in January and February 1999, evidence was produced confirming that a refusal to grant entertainment permits or refusal to grant them in a timely manner for the purpose of political speeches was departmental (and, hence, government) policy. The ostensible reason for retaining this law was to guarantee public order.

The requirement for an entertainment permit seemed to contradict the Singaporean Constitution, which guaranteed freedom of speech; however, Singapore's courts ruled that there was no conflict between the permit requirement and the constitutional guarantee. It was an intentional irony that Chee Soon Juan's second public speech, for which he was tried, included that part of the Singaporean Constitution that guaranteed freedom of speech. Not surprisingly, government members are exempted from the requirements of this legislation and may speak in public at their whim, including speaking in what might be considered a defamatory manner against their political opponents. Chee was again arrested, along with Ghandi Ambalam, on 1 May 2002, again for speaking without a permit; he served a further five weeks in jail rather than pay the S$4500 fine.

THE LAW AND POWER

Beyond this, freedom of association was restricted by the government, which required regular meetings of groups of more than ten people to be registered under the Societies Act. While this can—and has been—applied to restrict the forming of illegal associations, such as criminal gangs, it also prohibited organised political activity other than by registered political parties.

The Singapore government retains the ISA, which allows the indefinite detention without trial of a person charged under it. The ISA was introduced in order to combat the communist insurgency in the 1950s, although it has been used against non-insurgent political opponents. Similarly, under related provisions, the government or its agents can and do undertake a wide range of surveillance procedures, including tapping telephones and otherwise monitoring private conversations, as well as monitoring internet usage. Numerous claims that the government routinely conducts surveillance of opposition figures was borne out in evidence presented in the second free speech trial of Chee Soon Juan, when the public prosecutor led evidence outlining detailed and precise movements of two SDP party members. One was an alleged 'offender' who assisted Chee Soon Juan in speaking without a permit, while the other was not charged with any offence. Beyond that, Chee Soon Juan was clearly under surveillance by a government agent in 1999 while he sold books.

The real question about such surveillance, apart from its obvious misuse of a state apparatus to thwart the democratic process, was whether it was made obvious in order to alert and, therefore, intimidate Chee or whether the agents were simply inept at being discreet about their activities.

SEPARATION OF POWERS

Although Singapore claims to derive its political processes from the United Kingdom, its practices were very far from those of a functioning democracy in which all people are regarded as equal before the law and the law is applied in an even-handed manner. The use of the law for political purposes would not be a tool available to the government under the conventions of the Westminster parliamentary system or under any system that accepted the necessity of maintaining a separation of the roles and influences of the political executive and the judiciary—the so-called separation of powers. However, under the Singaporean system, there was no effective separation of powers and, as a consequence, judges often handed down decisions based less on law than on political expediency.

Subordinate Court judges and magistrates, as with public prosecutors, had their area of operation determined by the Legal Service Commission. The Commission allocated judicial responsibilities and had the authority to transfer judges from the bench to non-judicial duties as a matter of bureaucratic decision making. The appointment of new Supreme Court judges required the recommendation of the prime minister in consultation with the chief justice. Subordinate court judges were appointed on the recommendation of the chief justice. According to the US State Department, 'Many judicial officials, especially Supreme Court judges, have close ties to the ruling party and its leaders' (US Department of State 1999b: 4; see also, US Department of State 2003). The Singaporean Constitution also allowed the prime minister or the chief justice to convene a tribunal for the purpose of removing a judge on the grounds of misbehaviour or inability, although this had not been used.

What this meant in a practical sense was that, for a legal worker to be appointed to a judgeship, that worker must be accepted as trustworthy by the PAP. Future promotion depended on continuing to satisfy political as well as legal requirements. One judge, who handed down a decision contrary to the interests of the government, was quickly transferred into a bureaucratic position, from which he soon resigned. The lesson to other judges was clear.

Beyond the threat and reward system of having judges hand down politically desirable decisions and the appointment of suitable candidates in the first place, was a type of legal hegemony. What this meant in practice was that there developed a kind of culture or world view that regarded the PAP as not only the legitimate government of Singapore, but also the natural government of Singapore, that is, there could not really be an alternative. As a consequence, opposition figures and other critics were not legitimate political participants, but troublemakers intent on accidentally or intentionally arousing antagonism and ill will. In a society that so highly valued order, critics of the government were implicitly culpable. In this sense, the letter—even the meaning—of the law was less important than the commonsense of the judge as understood from a peculiarly pro-PAP perspective.

While judicial appointments were usually made on the basis of suitable but otherwise anonymous candidates, it was not always so. In particular, there was the case where a long-time law school friend of Lee Kuan Yew was appointed to the High Court bench and, within a year, was elevated to the position of chief justice, the most important legal position in the country. Lai Kew Chai had not practised law for twenty years, spending much of that time in business in Malaysia, and his initial appointment, as well as his quick rise to power, shocked even Singapore's compromised legal fraternity. Not only was Lai a friend of Lee

Kuan Yew, but he had also formerly been employed as a lawyer with the Lee family legal firm, Lee and Lee. His appointment was a fairly blatant example of achieving pro-Lee–PAP political outcomes from ostensibly legally unbiased situations. The complicity of the courts has been noted by the US State Department and the human rights organisation, Asia Watch.

> Government leaders historically have utilised court proceedings, in particular defamation suits, against political opponents and critics. Both this practice and consistent awards in favour of government plaintiffs have raised questions about the relationship between the government and the judiciary and led to a perception that the judiciary reflects the views of the executive in politically sensitive cases. (US Department of State 1999: 4)

As one critic noted, 'The regime has a near perfect record in winning court cases against its opponents' (Lingle 1996: 92).

Interestingly, to say that the judiciary in Singapore is corrupt or unduly influenced by external powers is to beg being charged with contempt of court. In 1995, academic and author Dr Christopher Lingle and the *International Herald Tribune* were sued for contempt of court, as well as through a related defamation case, for suggesting that Singapore's courts were politically influenced.

CRONYISM AND CORRUPTION

It is a truism in politics that a government too long in power will become corrupt. The temptations associated with the power of office are great, while the lack of needing to genuinely face a test of political popularity in a free and fair election means that corrupt activities will not have to be accounted for. Given the Singaporean government's propensity towards suing any person who suggests such misdeeds, there could be no claim here that the Singaporean government or its members are corrupt or engage in illegal cronyist activities. It is also true to say that the public perception of corruption in Singapore, as measured by Transparency International, has it as one of a handful of least corrupt countries in the world (Transparency International 2003). Yet perceptions are not everything and there have been increasing complaints emanating from within Singapore about official corruption and nepotism from, for example, the underground group Singaporeans for Democracy, and concern over the effective censorship of media that might report such claims of corruption.

The family of Minister Mentor (former prime minister and senior minister) Lee Kuan Yew has done particularly well out of Singapore's economic development. It has been suggested that one of the reasons that the PAP is loath to even begin to allow a genuine opposition to become active in Singapore is because it could uncover activities that might not be regarded as strictly acceptable, most damagingly so if the PAP was no longer in power.

One such incident, in which Lee Kuan Yew's family did particularly well, revolved around the 1995 purchase of condominium properties called Nassim Jade. Shareholders of the public company, Hotel Properties Limited, were grumbling about what they perceived to be favours done for some people with political clout, such favours costing the company potential profits. Luxury condominiums, valued at millions of dollars per unit before the property value slump in 1998, were sold to the Lee family at a discount, while shareholders were obliged to pay full price for the same condominiums.

After an investigation, the Stock Exchange of Singapore publicly censured the company for not seeking shareholders' approval for the discounted sales. Dr Lee Suan Yew, younger brother of Lee Kuan Yew, was on the board of directors of the company, himself buying one of the properties at a discounted rate. Other purchasers of the properties included another Lee brother, Freddy Lee, and his wife Eleanor Ngo Puay Chin, and Lee Hsien Loong and Ho Ching, Lee's son and daughter-in-law. The chief justice of the High Court and close Lee friend, Lai Kew Chai, and his wife, Dorothy Yip, also purchased one of the condominiums, also at a discounted rate. The cost of the condominiums was between S\$3 342 800 and S\$4 734 600, representing a discount of between 7 and 12 per cent. Even at soft launches of property sales, a discount of 5 per cent was usually regarded as the maximum allowable. The total of the purchases amounted to more than S\$10 million, yet no mortgages or loans were taken out to secure the purchases.

Lee Kuan Yew and Lee Hsien Loong also purchased two properties at another HPL development, Scotts 28, for S\$2 791 500 and S\$2 776 400 respectively, each securing a discount of 5 per cent. In total, Lee senior received discounts totalling S\$416 252, while Lee junior received discounts totalling S\$643 185.

Other family members who were found to have made purchases in the Nassim Jade complex included Lee's daughter, Lee Wei Ling, her sister Lee Kim Mon and, as well as Freddy, another brother Lee Kim Yew (Dennis). Kwa Kim Li, a niece of Lee, and Lee's sister-in-law, Gloria Lee, also bought condominiums in the project at a discount.

Confronted by journalists with the evidence, Lee Kuan Yew openly admitted that he and his son, Lee Hsien Loong, were given preferential treatment in the purchase of the Nassim Jade properties. 'There is no way,' he said, 'and I say this with some sympathy for the young and aspiring professionals or young executives, for them to have the same value to a seller of a product as a well-known figure or sports star or a TV star' (*Business Times*, 22 May 1996). Lee's response came after two newspaper editors told Lee that 'the fuss was over equity, not legality. The common grouse was that ministers, senior civil servants and MPs on the "inside track" were invited to soft launches, while ordinary folk had to queue' (*Business Times*, 22 May 1996). 'It's a fact of life. There is no way of me having to join a queue to buy a house, or my wife,' said Lee. He also said that it was normal for a well-known or elite figure to receive preferential treatment in a variety of circumstances (*Business Times* 1996).

Despite the regional economic downturn, Singapore's major companies granted a number of board members big pay rises at that time. Kim Eng Holdings paid its board S$12.5 million, which was divided among eight board members. For her services, its chairman, Gloria Lee, would have received at least S$1.5 million. Similarly, Tat Lee Bank was given a banking licence in the mid 1970s, at a time when it was against government policy to grant private commercial banking licences. One of the directors of the bank was Lee Kim Yew.

Despite a S$39 million—35 per cent—loss, primarily due to unwise investments in Indonesia, directors were paid S$3 million. In December 1998, Tat Lee Bank was merged with the publicly owned bank, Keppel, but Tat Lee Bank's losses were not revealed until after the merger. Similarly, in December 1998, the brokerage firm of which Freddy Lee was chairman was bailed out by publicly owned Singapore Technologies. Singapore Technologies' head was (from 2004 prime minister) Lee Hsien Loong's wife, Ho Ching, who is, therefore, Lee Kuan Yew's daughter-in-law and Freddy's niece by marriage. A Singapore Technologies subsidiary company is Chartered Industries, which is a major weapons supplier to the government of Burma.

Even more notably, Lee's son, from 2004 Singapore's prime minister, Lee Hsien Loong, joined Singapore's peacetime army at the age of twenty-six and, within five years was promoted to the rank of brigadier-general. Six months later, he was elected to parliament, where he quickly rose through the party structure to become deputy prime minister. Lee Kuan Yew successfully sued the respected newspaper, the *International Herald Tribune*, for referring to the existence of dynastic politics in SEA, including in Singapore. Regardless of the competence—or otherwise—of a child of a political leader, their succession to leadership does reflect the creation of a dynasty.

In 2002, the new prime minister's wife, Ho Ching, was appointed executive director and chief executive officer of Singapore's state investment company, Temasek Holdings. To assume this position, Temasek's rules had to be changed so that Ho Ching did not report to her husband, then finance minister, but to the company's board. Temasek has a global portfolio worth around S$90 billion, including ownership of Singapore Technologies, which Ho Ching headed until assuming her new position. Temasek owns stakes in Singapore Airlines and Singapore Telecommunications, the largest telecommunications company in SEA and whose chief executive is none other than Mr Lee's brother, Lee Hsien Yang. In Indonesia, Temasek owns Bank Danamon and Bank Internasional Indonesia (BII). Both banks, among the biggest in Indonesia, had their operations taken over by the Indonesian Bank Restructuring Agency after they collapsed in 1998, controlling shares then being sold to Temasek. Both banks specialise in offshore banking, including in such places as the Cayman Islands, the Virgin Islands and Mauritius. Bank Internasional was previously owned by the Sinar Mas group, which had, in turn, been owned by Suharto crony Eka Tjipta Widjjya; BII had been owned by another crony, Usman Admadjaja.

CHANGE?

Following the retirement of Lee Kuan Yew, there was some hope that Singapore would begin to loosen some of its political constraints. Even if this was not to happen quickly, it was thought it would happen. Yet, while Goh Chock Tong was prime minister and with Lee Kuan Yew looking over his shoulder, there was no change. Indeed, at the 2001 elections, the PAP won eighty-two of the possible eighty-four seats, which meant that Singapore did not even have a three-member opposition, as required by the constitution. This was addressed, not surprisingly, by the government appointing a compliant opposition member.

The appointment of Lee Hsien Loong as prime minister in 2004 similarly failed to indicate that there would be any meaningful change to Singapore's political climate. Upon his assuming the prime ministership, many observers noted that Lee Junior had shown himself to be a competent technocrat and manager, with a sound understanding of finance. He was also widely regarded as a brusque autocrat who was occasionally short-tempered. In a bid to counter this perception, Lee talked up the death of his first wife and his battle with cancer. According even to Goh, 'Singaporeans would like Loong to be more approachable,' saying that Lee's 'public persona is that of a no-nonsense, uncompromising and tough minister', adding that these qualities sometimes make Singaporeans 'uncomfortable' (*Time*, 23 August 2004).

Lee Junior also appeared to be aware of claims of nepotism, when he said:

> I don't think it's a coincidence. We happen to have a family. I mean, everybody is competitive and has tried to do well. But are you there because of your family connection or are you there because you are best man for the job and the system has thrown you up? That's what people have to decide and I don't think anybody seriously believes that in Singapore, because of me or my wife or my brother, therefore, that nepotism prevails in Singapore. (*Age*, 12 August 2004)

Lee inherited a city–state in good financial condition, with the government announcing just before his succession that GDP growth for the first half of 2004 was booming at 10 per cent. Where Lee did look like introducing changes was to Singapore's financial sector, quickly pushing through reforms intended to free up industry to help it compete globally. This meant little for Singaporeans, who also wished to see Singapore being run less as an autocratic fiefdom and more as a participatory democracy.

Perhaps the most intriguing aspect of Singaporean politics was the question: Why, so long after Singapore has become established, its government continued to rule using such authoritarian methods? There are no simple answers to this. Some suggestions have revolved around the personality and continuing political grip of Lee Kuan Yew and that of his dutiful son, while others refer to the established style of the PAP, which remains dominated by the Lee family. Other responses include that Singapore's style of government genuinely reflected the wishes of the majority of its people. This may be correct, although it did raise the issue of the extent to which political thinking in Singapore—insofar as it exists at all—was shaped by four decades of one-party domination. A more subtle approach would talk of the creation of a hegemonic framework, in which economic reward, political pressure, the legal system and the provision of information all worked together to create a sense of the status quo being the only way. In late 1998 there were faint signals that Singapore was about to begin experimenting with liberalisation, but these signs soon disappeared and were quickly buried by the reemergence—and repression—of Chee Soon Juan and the SDP as a force to openly challenge the PAP. Those faint signs did not reemerge in the following years.

In the 1960s, and perhaps even into the 1970s, the PAP legitimised some of its action on the twin grounds of the threat of communism, however shallow that had become, and the need to develop Singapore's economy. As this book was being written, these arguments had long since faded into the distant past and the political style of the PAP as Singapore's government was becoming decidedly arthritic.

NOTES

1 Stated in evidence during his second freedom of speech trial, February 1999.

2 'Nanyang' was the term coined to denote the southern Chinese community. It literally means 'Southern Seas'. While Singapore was, and remains, the outstanding example, other major Nanyang centres included Penang, Kuala Lumpur and Kuching.

3 Lee not only regarded himself as a suitable leader, but also came to identify his views and Singapore's interests as one and the same. Indeed, his failure to distinguish between himself and the state was reflected in the title of his autobiography, *The Singapore Story*.

4 Lee noted in his autobiography that, as early as 1955, he had recognised 'the folly of adopting a democratic Constitution' (Lee 1998a: 271)

5 At this time, Sukarno was arguing that the creation of the federation of Malaysia was a product of neo-imperialism and proposed that Malaya be incorporated into a Greater Indonesia. The failure of this proposal led to the confrontation of 1963–66 between Indonesia and Malaysia.

6 The FPDA was a formal alliance of the United Kingdom, Australia, New Zealand, Singapore and Malaysia, intended to provide security for Singapore and Malaysia in the event of external aggression.

14 | Indonesia: Diversity in Unity

In September 2004, the people of Indonesia voted overwhelmingly and directly for a new president, former Lieutenant-General Susilo Bambang Yudhoyono. To many observers, the election of Yudhoyono, with 61 per cent of the vote, gave Indonesia fresh hope for its political future. This was especially so following the lacklustre presidency of Megawati Sukarnoputri, who had come to office on the back of the attenuated, chaotic presidency of Abdurrahman Wahid, himself following the widely disliked Habibie, who was the feared and corrupt President Suharto's chosen successor.

Yet even Yudhoyono, enjoying the greatest political legitimacy of perhaps any Indonesian president, appeared compromised almost before he had started in his new role. Being compromised appeared to be an integral part of Indonesian politics and, even as Yudhoyono talked publicly about eradicating corruption, it continued, even within his own presidential palace. Meanwhile, information began to circulate that the murder of anti-military human rights activist, Munir, just days before the final ballot, was linked not just to the siphoning off of funds from other ministries for use by the military's campaign in the war-torn province of Aceh, but also that some of those funds had been taken for the presidential campaign. In order to achieve office, Yudhoyono had surrounded himself with former military colleagues, his Cabinet reflected political favours granted as much as it did competence and a majority of the largely venal legislature, which had been elected months previously, announced its intention to closely scrutinise any legislation that the new president might propose. Indonesia, one of the most corrupt countries in the world and one in which the military appeared to have an increasingly free hand, appeared to be a country in which there was structural resistance to change.

Indonesia is a large and complex place, reflecting myriad cultures and societies, political and economic agendas and a geography that spreads itself across almost the entire width of southern SEA. Once constituted as a colonial empire, the postcolonial state reflects tensions recent and old, local

345

and global, immediately pressing and deeply underlying. Since the collapse of President Suharto's rule in May 1998, the state has ebbed and flowed along the shores of chaos. Regionalism, in particular, has come to the fore, with some provinces testing the possibilities of independence. This, in turn, has led to tensions between the original inhabitants of these islands and transmigrants and with the military. Religious difference, too, has developed; as orthodox Muslims cling more firmly to their faith, Islam has been used as

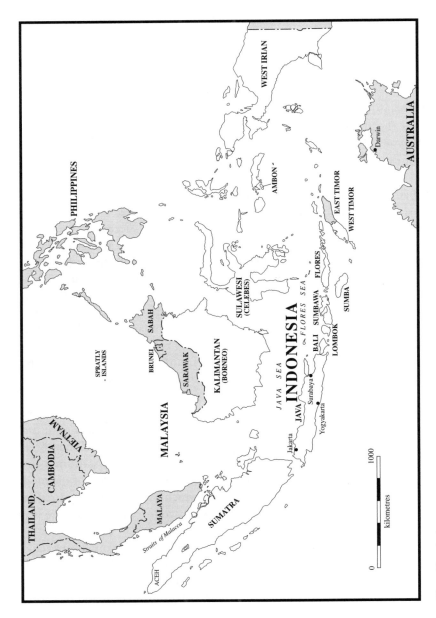

Map 11 Indonesia

a pretext for violence. Yet, for all of this and Indonesia's continuing economic problems, the structure of its post-Suharto democratic process has become increasingly strong. At one level, this situation showed that economic development was not a precondition for democratisation. At another level, however, it also tested the meaning of democratisation and its efficacy as an expression of public will.

PRECOLONIAL HISTORY

As such, Indonesia does not have a history before the period of colonialism, as the state known as the Republic of Indonesia is a postcolonial construction. Before the colonial period, there were two empires that held sway over some of the region now known as Indonesia, but both of these were relatively short-lived and neither could make a lasting claim to suzerainty over the archipelago.

Human occupation of Java, the most heavily populated of the Indonesian islands, dates back well into prehistory, but began to develop most noticeably after the immigration of ethnic Malays from the southeastern region of China in the last century before the Common Era (CE). These immigrants brought with them wet-rice agriculture, which was not only suited to the well-watered and fertile volcanic soils of the island, but which also encouraged a relatively high level of population growth. It has also been suggested that this wet-rice agricultural system, which required the investment of labour in preparation and thus did not encourage social movement, either led to or allowed the development of a relatively permanent military–political elite (Wittfogel 1957; Missen 1972: 51–2, 97–104). This gave rise to powerful and complex political structures, which, being both centralised and relatively stable, developed an autocratic political form. Court life became increasingly removed from village life other than through the payment of taxes or tribute and acknowledgment of loyalty.

From around the second century CE, along with the development of a centralised and sophisticated court structure, came the adoption of a formalised and hierarchical religion, Hinduism. This was most fully established by the tenth century and included a brief encounter with Buddhism, which, around the eighth and ninth century, was viewed as a type of Hinduism. However, traders from the Middle East, India and, increasingly, the Malay Peninsula, brought Islam to Java, which began to take hold from the fourteenth century (Caldwell & Utrecht 1979: 8–10; Grant 1996: 4–8; Geertz 1960: 121–5). The region of Central Java in the Yogyakarta–Surakarta–Kartasura area and to the near east, the most fertile and productive on the island, supported Java's most powerful rulers, the Sailendra, the early Mataram, the Majapahit and the late Mataram. What was most probably the first great sea power of the region, from the seventh to the thirteenth centuries, the Buddhist coastal state of Sri Vijaya on the

Palembang River in southern Sumatra, challenged the land-based Javanese states for the greatest regional hegemony. The Sri Vijayan empire joined the Sailendras (Coedes 1968: 144–7, 248), leaving as their legacy the mighty Borobudur monument in central Java. But being a maritime state, Sri Vijaya also had to contend with other sea powers, including the rise of Malacca; and its fortunes declined while those of the succeeding Javanese rulers continued.

The Sri Vijayan empire, at its height, probably claimed suzerainty over most of Sumatra and the Malay Peninsula and perhaps some outlying islands. The greatest empire, however, was that of Majapahit, founded in 1293. At its peak, it probably commanded loyalty from the whole of Java and Madura, much of Sumatra, the closer coastal areas of Kalimantan (Borneo), Bali, Lombok and other nearby islands. It also traded with and politically influenced the state of Champa on the Indochinese peninsula and was politically involved with the precursor states of Cambodia, as well as trading with the precursor states of Thailand and Vietnam, and was acknowledged by China as a regional power. By 1389, Majapahit was in serious decline, although it struggled on for a little more than another hundred years (Zainud'din 1980: 48–51). Despite this relatively brief and ancient flourishing of empire, it continues to be portrayed in Indonesian schools as the precursor state to Indonesia.

TRADITIONAL POLITICAL POWER

Throughout this period, a particular political style emerged that continues to be reflected in aspects of contemporary Indonesian politics. That style acknowledged that political power—or power alone—was more complex than the European concept and, at another level, more simple. In Javanese terms, the closest word to the English word 'power' is *kasekten*, which implies power, legitimacy and charisma; however, in contemporary terms, while this idea still has currency, it has also been modified by European political concepts as well as by the internally evolving state of Javanese (and Indonesian) thinking. The other significant aspect of *kasekten* was that it was without moral implications, that is, power was neither legitimate nor illegitimate; if it existed, it simply was (Anderson 1972: 1–8; see also, Moedjanto 1993; Proudfoot 1980; Zainud'din 1980: 97).

A related idea that continues to find reflection in contemporary Indonesian political thinking is that of the mandala. The Javanese concept of power dispersed towards the periphery and was 'fluid and unstable, always ready for dispersal and diffusion'. As a consequence, 'interstate aggression necessarily becomes a basic assumption about interstate relations' (Anderson 1972: 31). This 'doctrine emphasised the cult of expansion ... as the dynamic factor calculated to disturb the equilibrium of interstate relations. A state's belligerence is in the first place directed towards its closest neighbour(s) ...' (Moertono 1981: 71). If the *a priori* enemy of the state is its closest neighbour, Java is happier in a dominant rather than equal—or power sharing—role within the wider modern state. Implicit in this concept is the idea that Indonesia is, therefore, not a state in which all parts are equal, rather, it suggests that Indonesia is a reinterpretation of a Javanese empire.

ISLAM

The spread of Islam through the Indonesian archipelago varied in intensity and reach. Some regions, such as Aceh in northern Sumatra, were deeply influenced by Islam, as were parts of Java and Madura. However, inland Java and a number of other islands remained inured to Islam's reach or appeal. As such, a number of outlying islands or more remote regions retained their earlier religious practices, such as Hinduism in Bali and animism in a number of other areas. Where animism predominated, Christianity, following colonialism, tended to take root. Within Java and, to a lesser extent, Sumatra, Islam fell into two broad camps: formal (*santri*) Islam and informal, or nominal (*abangan*), Islam.

In part, the less formal *abangan* interpretation of Islam can be attributed to the mystical Sufi version, which made its way from India to the region. But perhaps the traditional resilience and syncretism of preexisting Javanese animist beliefs are more responsible for the distinction between those who profess a formal Islamic belief and those who are more nominal. In the provinces last to be colonised, animism remains a dominant religious form, although it is not formally accepted by the government, which requires people to profess Islam, one of two forms of Christianity (Protestantism or Roman Catholicism), Hinduism or Buddhism.

THE COLONIAL PERIOD

The influence of the Dutch on Indonesia's political development was important in two respects. In the first instance, through the colonial experience, the Dutch geographically defined what was to become Indonesia. The Dutch also restructured the ruling elites to serve their colonial interests, helping to reinvent and reimpose elite privileges beyond traditional limits, the influence of which remains.

The initial goals of the Dutch in what they termed the 'East Indies' was to seek spices and other tradeable goods, as well as to find routes to and from China through the Pacific. In 1602, the Dutch East India Company (*Verenigde Oost-Indische Compagnie*, or VOC) was established and initially based at Banten on the western edge of Java, although, in 1619 the Dutch seized Yacatra (Jakarta) on the northeast coast of the island and renamed it Batavia. From here they could trade with the other islands and further afield, as well as counter the strategic Portuguese stronghold in Malacca, which the Dutch captured in 1641.

Although the Dutch had some technological and military advantages over the Javanese, their primary method of political and military control was to play off royal Javanese households against each other or to exploit divisions within them (Ricklefs 1993a: 147, 1993b). Those royalty who sided with the Dutch or agreed to Dutch terms, remained intact and continued to exercise rule over vast tracts of the island; those who did not, were subjugated. Even though the royal houses of Java remained intact, the Dutch were the real power behind the various thrones. Due to corruption, mismanagement, piracy and changing patterns of trade, the economic fortunes of the VOC steadily declined. When the company's charter expired on the last day of 1799, it was not renewed (Caldwell & Utrecht 1979: 14–15; see also, Geertz 1963: ch. 4). The United Kingdom had, by this time, begun to move into the region and, following Holland's subjugation during the Napoleonic Wars, occupied and administered the East Indies from 1811 to 1816. The consequent Anglo–Dutch Treaty of 1824 reflected the growing Dutch hegemony in Java and Sumatra and the British control over the Malay Peninsula, formalising the situation and requiring the British to vacate the footholds it had gained on Sumatra, while the Dutch abandoned Malacca on the Malay Peninsula. The effect of these changes was to formally partition the Malay world along the Strait of Malacca and, from 1912, through northern Borneo, defining the borders of the postcolonial state.

Following economic and military catastrophes in Holland and the devastating Java War of 1825–30, in 1830, the Dutch raised the Royal Netherlands Indies Army (*Koninklijk Nedlandisch Indisch Leger*, or KNIL), which was largely manned by outer islanders and was used to quell uprisings in other parts of the archipelago. The KNIL later constituted a significant basis for outer island opposition to the government of what was then the new republic. Although earlier Dutch (and British) administrations had attempted to limit the power of the *priyayi*, or traditional aristocracy, under the *cultuurstelsel*, their rights were not only restored, but also reinforced, rewarding both Dutch and *priyayi* supervision of the system with a percentage of profits. It also introduced government more directly into the affairs of villages that had previously been left relatively untouched. This detached the *priyayi* from ordinary Javanese society and removed the restraints upon them that had been applied under *adat* (traditional law) (Ricklefs 1993a: 121–2).

While Dutch political hegemony was well established in Java and much of Sumatra by the nineteenth century, its control over the wider archipelago was not fully achieved until the early twentieth century. Aceh maintained its political integrity until, deprived of British protection in 1871, it was attacked by the Dutch in 1973, but it held out until 1908, with sporadic resistance continuing thereafter. Bali was occupied in 1906; eastern Nusa Tenggara, inland Kalimantan and Sulawesi were effectively ignored until being pacified between 1900 and 1910 (Grant 1964: 14). This completion of Dutch domination over the East Indies had a number of consequences, one of which was to transport indigenous troops from one area to assist in repressing the peoples of another, which, in turn, had the effect of spreading the old, simple Sumatra–Melayu-based trading language of market Malay. Increased trade between the islands also furthered the development of this language and, already the most common language between ethnic groups, it increasingly became the *lingua franca* of indigenous Dutch East Indians wishing to communicate with each other, thereby providing the disparate ethnic groups with their first sense of common identity.

In response to humanitarian indignation in Holland and a decline in the wellbeing of the local population, the colonial authorities also introduced what was called the 'Ethical Policy' early in the twentieth century. This policy had its most important impact in the field of education, which had the benefit of training indigenous peoples to assist in the rapidly growing primary sector of commercial cropping. One main consequence of this rise in educational levels of indigenous peoples was the growth and influence of Western educated local people, who began to question and rebel against the caste structure implemented by the Netherlands East Indies authorities. Thus was born the beginnings of Indonesia's independence movement.

TOWARDS INDEPENDENCE

Despite some changes in form, the pre-WWII Dutch administration in the East Indies retained a paternalistic ethos and continued to be both unitary and centralised in its political structure. The Japanese occupation of 1942–45 further entrenched this ethos; as a consequence, the political characteristics of paternalism, unitarism and centralism deeply influenced the new republican government, not only throughout the 1950s, especially after the proclamation of Guided Democracy in 1958, but also into and throughout the New Order government of Suharto after 1966.

One notable influence of the Japanese was that they founded organisations that were to play a key role in the establishment of the republic. For propaganda purposes, the Japanese brought together the major Islamic organisations, notably *Muhhamadiyah* and *Nahdlatul Ulama*, under the umbrella group *Masyumi* (Consultative Council of Indonesian Muslims), which later became a significant political player. The Japanese also trained Indonesian youths in Islamic and nationalist military units in order to police the colony and to assist in fending off expected Allied attacks. By 1943, there were over 35 000 men in the Javanese auxiliary army alone (Feith 1969: 198). This organisation, the Volunteer Army of Defenders of the Fatherland (*Tentara Sukarela Pembela Tanah Air*, or Peta) was to become the basis of the revolutionary army and, later, the foundation of the army (*Angkatan Bersenjata Republik Indonesia*, or ABRI; from 1999, *Tentara Nasional Indonesia*, or TNI).

Another impact of the Japanese military influence, which Indonesia academic Mangunwijaya described as 'fascist' in character, was to bring to Indonesia's incipient armed forces a notion that society could and should be controlled, and that the armed forces should be allied with government in closely directing and controlling Indonesian society (Mangunwijaya 1992: 6).

Under mounting pressure from nationalist leaders, but probably more as an attempt to forestall Allied military advances in the Pacific, Japan encouraged moves towards Indonesian independence. Two days after Japan surrendered, on 17 August 1945, Sukarno and Hatta proclaimed the Republic of Indonesia, of which Sukarno was to be president and Hatta vice-president, and which had an advisory Central National Committee of 135. The republic received almost immediate and widespread support in the former colony and, by the end of September, had obtained arms from surrendering Japanese soldiers with which to battle the Dutch and, possibly, the Allies in the period after the cessation of hostilities with Japan.

THE REPUBLIC

The Constitution of the republic, referred to as the 1945 Constitution, which was proclaimed at that time, was a short and, in many respects, ambiguous document, the intention being that it would allow considerable scope for decision making on the part of the president. The Constitution vested primary authority in the person of the president, who selected a cabinet and directed the affairs of state. The Constitution was changed in 1949 and again in 1950, to vest authority in the cabinet, with the prime minister being the senior office holder. This accorded with the parliamentary democracy period of 1949–57. However, following the move towards Guided Democracy from 1957, the 1945 Constitution was re-adopted in 1959 in the final act of abandoning the authority of parliament, the party system and democratic processes. It is the 1945 Constitution, slightly modified, that prevails still.

While Indonesia as a state has a clear association with the former colony of the Dutch East Indies, one influential school of thought, nominally led by Sukarno, in Indonesia's formative period took a larger view, incorporating not only the whole Dutch colony and Portuguese (East) Timor, but also the Malay Peninsula, northern Borneo and even the Philippines. There remains considerable local identity throughout Indonesia, but there is also a strong identification with the concept of the Indonesian state as it currently exists. This has, in large part, been brought about by the standardisation of a common, if synthetic, language, Bahasa Indonesia (Anderson 1990: 123–51), and the imposition of a 'national' culture (Atkinson 1987; Tsing 1987: 196–200). The efforts of the Sukarno and the Suharto-led governments further assisted in cementing the idea of Indonesia in the minds of ordinary Indonesians. This national culture, however, strongly reflects aspects, often reconstructed, of the political culture of Central and Eastern Java. That aspect of Indonesian culture that relates to a confluence of a Javanese understanding of power, received its modification under Dutch colonialism, with borrowings from the Western tradition of the nation state, and the exigencies of the survival of both the nation state and its elites. This political structure was then effectively imposed on the state as a national ideology.[1]

The 1945 Constitution, which was to have been temporary, was replaced, twice, although its replacements were themselves also short-term documents, looking forward to the creation of a more complete and representative document. However, because the 1945 Constitution places considerable power in the hands of the president and because it is both short and ambiguous, it is highly interpretable and has been claimed to mean many different things since it was reintroduced by Sukarno to help usher in the period of 'Guided Democracy'. Like his predecessor, Suharto also viewed the 1945 Constitution as a suitable vehicle for a strong presidential rule. And as with the *Pancasila*, strict adherence to the 1945 Constitution is required by all Indonesians.

THE REVOLUTIONARY PERIOD: 1945–49

While the Republic of Indonesia was proclaimed on 17 August 1945, the Netherlands government and others of the Allies initially regarded its establishment as an instrument of Japanese warfare. In the final months of the war, Allied, mostly Australian, troops had been involved in mopping up campaigns in the outer islands and, upon the cessation of hostilities, moved to take authority from the defeated Japanese. Within weeks, British troops had begun to land in Java; Dutch troops began returning soon after, assuming the role they had played before the war. At the same time, local units loyal to the republic had begun taking arms from surrendering Japanese. In this situation, in which authority was claimed by two armed groups, fighting inevitably broke out between the republicans and the British, particularly in Java and Sumatra.

Within the republic, political and administrative changes were implemented in order to make it more effective and, recognising the different sources of nationalist sentiment, there was a call for the establishment of political parties. Of the major groups, one was *Masyumi*, which was led by wartime Masyumi members as well as newer members. Another was the Indonesian Nationalist Party (PNI), established by Sukarno in 1927 and led by many of the older leaders who were active under the Japanese administration. Then, there was the Socialist Party (PSI), which had a strong youth wing and, finally, in August 1948, when the communist leader Musso returned from a twenty-year exile in the Soviet Union, he melded the fledgling republic's left-wing parties into an expanded and significantly more influential Communist Party of Indonesia (PKI), which he headed. Sjarifuddin's cabinet was replaced by a moderate Masyumi–PNI coalition. In response, in September, a group of second-tier leaders in the PKI at Madiun in Central Java announced a revolt against the Sukarno–Hatta government, believing the new government would move to disband local communist-led armed units (Hindley 1964: 21). The republic's army attacked the rebels and Musso and Sjarifuddin and a number of other senior leaders were killed in the following weeks, all of which constituted a severe blow to the PKI. The Madiun Affair, as it was called, was regarded by the republic's regular army as treachery during hostilities with the Netherlands and marked the beginning of a distrust between ABRI and the PKI that culminated in the events of 1965–66.

In December 1949, a second major attack by the Dutch resulted in increasing pressure from the UN and, in particular, from the USA through its postwar Marshall Plan, to resolve the dispute. In November 1949, the Netherlands agreed to a settlement in which fifteen outlying, Dutch-created, states would come together with Java and Sumatra in a federated Republic of the United States of Indonesia (RUSI). The creation of the outlying states reflected local conditions and loyalties, as well as the Netherlands' concept of its colony as comprising a number of smaller colonies rather than being one large, unified colony. But, if the state was to remain intact, it was an unworkable structure. The republic was also required to assume the Netherlands' East Indies debt of 4300 million guilders, of which 1291 million guilders (US\$339 million) was external debt repayable in foreign currency (Feith 1964: 203). From the very beginning, Indonesia's economic position was compromised, a situation that was exacerbated in the following decade by questionable economic decision making and management, and which pushed the state to the brink of self-destruction.

INDEPENDENT INDONESIA: 1949–65

On 27 December 1949, Sukarno was sworn in as president of RUSI; Hatta was chosen as prime minister. The cabinet reflected ministers from *Masyumi* and PNI, non-party ministers and five ministers from the federal states. But federalism was quickly abandoned. Sukarno's vision for the state, as manifested in government policies, was not universally accepted, particularly as it focused not only on power, but also on economic resources in Jakarta, and thence, Java, at the expense of the wider archipelago. Sukarno's nationalist aspirations for Indonesia were shared by many intellectuals and the newly emergent armed forces, but among the peoples of the former Dutch colony there was at least as much to separate as to bind. With the abandonment of the 1949 Constitution in 1950, former KNIL troops in South Sulawesi, and then, on Ambon in the Maluku group, raised themselves in revolt against the central government until defeated towards the end of the year.

More significantly, from 1950 there was a fundamentalist Islamic rebellion, known as the *Dar'ul Islam* revolt, in West Java, South Sulawesi and Aceh, the longest sustained rebellion in Indonesia. This rebellion was based on irregular Islamic military units that had been fighting since the Japanese occupation as well as later against the Dutch. These militant Islamic groups had always been outside the control of the central government and were unwilling to bow to central government directives. By December 1948, the Islamic guerrillas, under Soekarmadji Maridjan Kartosuwirjo, proclaimed the Negara Islam Indonesia (NII) (Indonesian Islamic State). Kartosuwirjo announced that the republic had ceased to exist and that the NII was the true embodiment of the revolution. After Indonesia gained practical independence in 1949, the so-called Dar'ul Islam (Islamic state) movement continued to defy the central government, at times extending its influence into Central Java and over Aceh and much of South Sulawesi. The Dar'ul Islam rebellion probably had most impact in the period from 1957 until 1961, largely as a reaction to the growing influence of the PKI in government. It also received a significant boost when rebels in South and Central Sulawesi joined the movement in 1952 and 1958 respectively, having been in their own state of rebellion since 1950. With the capture of Kartosuwirjo in 1962, the movement in West Java was militarily wiped out.

While the *Dar'ul Islam* revolt never threatened the cohesion of the state of Indonesia in the way that the *Permesta–PRRI* rebellion of 1957–58 did, in the late 1990s and into the early years of the new century, there was a revival of militant Islam, much of which could trace its origins to the *Dar'ul Islam* movement.

While the commitment to liberal democracy in the years from 1949 until the middle to late 1950s was less than total, there was a practical adherence to democratic forms. In 1952, the *Nahdlatul Ulama* (NU, or Awakening of Religious Scholars) left *Masyumi*, embarking as a political party in its own right. One consequence of the republic's commitment to democratic processes, combined with its multiparty system, was the regular rise and fall of coalition governments. This constant division, lack of political stability and tendency to compromise created an inability to engage in forward economic planning. As the sometimes chaotic events of the 1950s began to unfold, tensions grew between two broad groups within the political system, referred to by Feith as 'administrators' and 'solidarity makers' (Feith 1962).

In December 1956, matters worsened, highlighting the division between the centre and the periphery of the republic, between Javanese and non-Javanese Indonesians, between former revolutionary soldiers and former members of KNIL who were incorporated into the Indonesian army, and between the two main political groupings. Bloodless coups were enacted in the three provinces of Sumatra, in which newly established revolutionary councils, headed by indigenous (often former KNIL) army officers, claimed power, rejecting the central government and accusing it of excessive bureaucracy, overcentralisation, neglect, corruption and being too tolerant of the PKI. To effect their derecognition of the new government, the officers channelled exports directly to world markets which, along with extensive smuggling often sponsored by army units, deprived Jakarta of foreign exchange. In March 1957, a similar bloodless coup gave power to an army-led council in East Indonesia (Sulawesi, Maluku and Nusa Tenggara). The outer islands thus came to most strongly represent *Masyumi*–Socialist interests, while the centre was more strongly PNI–NU–PKI.

In 1957, ostensibly in response to a Dutch refusal to hand over West Papua to Indonesia, Dutch property was nationalised (formalised in 1958). The process of nationalisation of Dutch interests had the combined effect of halting foreign investment in the republic and cutting shipping within the multi-island state by the Dutch-owned shipping company, *Koninklijke Paketvaart Maatschappij* (KPM), which had provided about three-quarters of the transportation between the islands. The economy, saddled with debt from the outset, plagued by unstable government and almost no economic policy, slid further and further into ruin.

GUIDED DEMOCRACY

When the Ali cabinet, the seventeenth cabinet since 1945, resigned in March 1957, parliamentary democracy was finally abandoned and Sukarno's Guided Democracy was adopted in modified form. Along with Guided Democracy came martial law, on 14 March, strengthening the position of the army's central leadership under its chief-of-staff, Major-General Abdul Haris Nasution. Martial law provided legal grounds for army intervention in civil affairs and laid the groundwork for the military's dual function (*dwifungsi*) of both defending and helping to run the state. The Indonesian army had never confined itself to a purely military role, rather, had always run a parallel administrative structure to that of the state, from cabinet level to local administrative regions, even down to the village level.

Alienated both politically and economically from the central government, the 'revolutionary councils' of Sumatra and Sulawesi revolted, in what was called the PRRI–*Permesta* movement. The Sulawesi-based *Permesta* revolt was formally proclaimed on 2 March 1957. On 10 February 1958, rebellious officers in Padang, West Sumatra, demanded full autonomy and proclaimed the PRRI. With this proclamation, the leaders of the councils had demanded that the cabinet installed by Sukarno resign and be replaced by a new cabinet under either Hatta or the sultan of Jogjakarta and include attendant changes to financial arrangements with the outer islands. With no change in Jakarta, a revolutionary government was proclaimed on 15 February at Padang in West Sumatra. The PRRI invited other rebel groups outside Java to join it in opposing the Jakarta government and to accept its—PRRI's—authority. *Permesta* complied, but those areas already embroiled in the *Dar'ul Islam* revolt remained aloof from this conflict. Within two months, the army had crushed the PRRI rebellion and moved on the rebels in Sulawesi, defeating them three months later.

While the army formally included itself in government, the PKI also increased its standing as an independent political party and within the government. Along with his support of nationalism and religious practice, Sukarno coined the term *Nasakom*, incorporating and syncretising the ideals of *nasionalisme*, *agama* and *komunisme* (nationalism, religion and communism). It was, in practice, a grab-bag of political ideas. In such a confused framework, and based on low levels of economic development and little infrastructure within a rapidly declining economy, it is not surprising that Indonesia under Sukarno was politically unstable.

By 1965, the government under Sukarno had effectively lost control of the economy. In that year, the general rate of inflation reached 500 per cent and the price of rice rose by 900 per cent. The budget deficit had risen to 300 per cent of government revenues; if foreign debt repayments for 1966 were to be made on schedule, they would have taken up almost the total of the nation's export income (Crouch 1988: 204) Then, Sukarno's health appeared to begin to fail. With the process of succession left unresolved, the country's two biggest political players, ABRI and the PKI, viewed each other with increasing suspicion.

On 30 September 1965, at the height of this chaos, six senior generals were abducted and killed, precipitating a massacre of PKI members and suspected sympathisers and a change in the presidency. The abduction of the generals was organised by mid-ranking officers loyal to Sukarno, who believed that the six generals were planning a coup against the president for 5 October 1965, Armed Forces Day. In the abduction, the officers were probably assisted by— or at least informed by—senior PKI members. After the event, the leader of the affair, Lieutenant-Colonel Untung, announced the formation of a new revolutionary council under Sukarno.

By 1965, tensions between a majority faction of the army and the PKI had reached an almost hysterical pitch, with the PKI gaining more and more influence in Sukarno's government and the armed forces being required to compete with what it had previously considered an untrustworthy organisation. The army and the PKI were at odds over a host of fundamental issues and each viewed the other with great hostility (Hindley 1964: 286–97). What was later termed an 'attempted coup' by the PKI (not by the Untung-aligned officers) was put down by forces still loyal to the formal military hierarchy under the command of *Kostrad* leader, General Suharto. Over the next several months, having been caught unprepared and unarmed, the PKI was crushed by the army, with at least half a million party members, suspected sympathisers and victims of long-standing local feuds being killed. Some estimates put the figure of political deaths at up to 1.5 million over the period 1965–70 (Defence of Democracy Groups 1985: 4).

RISE OF THE NEW ORDER

In a letter dated 11 March 1966, Sukarno virtually gave Suharto *carte blanche* to restore order. The day after the letter was signed, Suharto formally banned the PKI. Four days later, after Sukarno refused to agree to an army demand to dismiss cabinet ministers distrusted by the army leadership, the army arrested the ministers. The signing of the letter by Sukarno marked the effective transition of power from the president to the general. In formal terms, the struggle for power between Sukarno and Suharto went on for another two years, but from 11 March 1966—indeed, it could even be dated from October 1965—power had been increasingly in Suharto's hands. In the political manoeuvring that went on between late 1965 and March 1967, Suharto and his supporters in the army not only purged the armed forces, but also cleared the civil service of pro-Sukarno elements. A part of the process of bringing the bureaucracy to heel was through the army's political organisation, *Golkar*, originally the Organisation of Functional Groups (*Golongon Karya*), which rapidly assumed the status of an institutionalised government party. The *Mejelis Permusyawaratan Rakyat* (MPR, or the People's Consultative Assembly), similarly purged of its old PKI and leftist members, formally stripped Sukarno of the presidency in March 1967, from which time Sukarno was placed under house arrest, where he remained until his death in 1970. Riding a wave of at least partly engineered anti-Sukarno sentiment and his own growing authority, Suharto was named acting president and formally endorsed by the MPR as president in 1968.

Under the provisions of the 11 March letter, Suharto used the establishment of the Operations Command to Restore Security and Order (*Kopkamtib*)[2] as his prime vehicle of control during this period. *Kopkamtib* not only had the authority to track down remaining PKI members and sympathisers, but also soon took responsibility for quelling other signs of dissent, including the issue and withdrawal of licences to publish. A parallel body was the Special Operations (*Operasi Khusus*, or *Opsus*), which was built up by General Ali Murtopo and used for covert operations, such as arranging the outcome of the act of free choice in Irian Jaya (West Papua) in 1969, organising key aspects of the first New Order elections in 1971 and the East Timor dispute, among many others (Lowry 1996: 71).

There was also a more clandestine body, the State Intelligence Coordinating Body (*Bakin*), established in 1967, which was a type of military-dominated secret police with responsibility for intelligence assessments and action aimed at the non-military population, such as political parties, dissidents and the Chinese community, and the possibility of a communist revival. After 1974, intelligence agencies were streamlined and concentrated under General L. B. (Benny) Murdani, then *Bakin's* nominal deputy head. From 1983, at which time Murdani was appointed commander-in-chief of ABRI, domestic and military intelligence organisations were further concentrated under Murdani through *Bakin*.

THE NEW ORDER POLITICAL SYSTEM

In 1973, Suharto abolished the plethora of small political parties and created two new parties, the United Development Party (PPP), comprised of former Islamic parties, and the Democratic Party of Indonesia (PDI), comprised of the two small Christian parties, the PNI and other nationalist parties. *Golkar*, which was, in effect, the party of government, was not formally considered a party for the purpose of this exercise. In the elections held between 1971 and 1997, *Golkar* won between 62 and 73 per cent of the vote. The PPP (or its predecessors in 1971) had achieved almost one-third of votes, but its political strength was severely diminished when the NU pulled out in 1987, at which time its vote plummeted to 16 per cent. The PDI (or its predecessors in 1971) achieved a low of 8 per cent in 1982; a high of 15 per cent in 1992 made it look to be gathering strength before it was split by government intervention in 1996, ahead of the 1997 election. During this period, there were numerous reports of vote rigging; there were also restrictions on political activity. *Golkar* could conduct its affairs as it liked, however, the PPP and PDI were restricted in when they could conduct meetings and could not campaign outside the election period. Further, the PPP and, perhaps even more so the PDI, were deeply influenced by government and ABRI agents, to the extent that the PDI prodemocracy push of the early to mid 1990s, reflected, in effect, the political aspirations of a significant faction of ABRI. The 1996 ousting of the PDI's leader, Megawati Sukarnoputri, by a government-supported rebel PDI congress, reflected more her gaining too much popular support and Suharto wishing to see a potential competitor deposed.

NEW ORDER POLITICAL STRUCTURE

In structural terms, Indonesia had a political system in which the executive was independent of what approximates the legislature. Until 1999, the legislature itself comprised half of the electoral assembly, which chose the president and vice-president on a five-yearly basis. Indonesia's legislative assembly, the *Dewan Perwakilan Rakyat* (DPR), had no effective legislative function until 1999, such a function being decided by presidential decree. The DPR has 500 members who divided into committees that oversee the work of government. From 1967 until 1999, one-fifth of the DPR was directly appointed by the president with a further thirty-eight positions (reduced from seventy-five and before that 100) being reserved for senior ABRI (later TNI) officers. To balance this, members of ABRI were not allowed to participate in the voting process.

Beyond the DPR, the political structure that formally supported Suharto and the New Order government relied for its legitimacy on the will of the People's Consultative Assembly, the MPR, which, until 1999, had 1000 members and is, in theory, Indonesia's highest sovereign body.

Members of the DPR have representation as members of the MPR. Until 1999, the president also directly appointed 100 members of the MPR (formerly one-third) to the assembly, while about half the assembly was comprised of members of the bureaucracy, ABRI and other social organisations. Only 40 per cent of the MPR was elected. Even then, given the provisions of the Indonesian electoral system in which *Golkar* was, until 1999, assured a majority of around two-thirds or more of the total vote, within the MPR the president commanded a very large and secure majority.

Despite Suharto's firm electoral grip on the presidency until just before his resignation, he did face challenges, notably from a growing faction within the military, over issues of corruption. Following one such dispute with Suharto in 1988, ABRI commander, General Benny Murdani, was sacked and given the less powerful position of defence minister, and his sacking occurred along with the gradual removal of senior ABRI officers from senior ministerial posts. In 1993, ABRI got its own back by having ABRI commander, Try Sutrisno, elected as vice-president against Suharto's wishes. In turn, Suharto moved to reduce ABRI's influence in *Golkar*. This series of events marked the formal rift between Suharto and the Red and White (nationalist–secular) group within ABRI, which was headed by General Wiranto. Recognising this rift, Suharto cultivated an Islamic support base through *Ikatan Cendekiawan Muslem se-Indonoesia* (ICMI, or Indonesian Association of Muslim Intellectuals) by supporting mosque-building funds, making the *hajj* and, most importantly, appointing more strongly Muslim officers to senior positions within ABRI.

THE ECONOMY

It is a common view that, within the space of a few months, Indonesia's economy in the 1990s went from being a showcase for economic development to a basket case. In early 1997, Indonesia's economy was still officially recording a growth rate that corresponded to 7 per cent or more a year. A little over a year later, that figure had plunged to an economic contraction of around 20 per cent a year (the government estimated 13 per cent), with consequent social and political upheaval. The official picture of Indonesia's economy had long been overly optimistic; at the same time, structural problems were largely ignored. The economic collapse, then, was not so much unexpected, as its looming issues related to its causes were not paid the attention they deserved. To start with, however, Indonesia's economy under the New Order government looked to be improving quickly.

Having attained power, Suharto's first steps were to placate what was to be his military support group and to get Indonesia's economy back onto a viable footing. The economy he inherited from Sukarno was even more of a shambles than it was in 1998, with rice production below consumption requirements and the state unable to meet its foreign debts. In his first move, Suharto established an economic environment that was attractive to foreign capital, which, in turn, helped resuscitate Indonesia's collapsed economy. Allied to this, Suharto ensured that his senior supporters were well looked after.

But it was the unplanned and unexpected oil boom, which resulted from the rapid rise in world oil prices in the early 1970s, that cemented Suharto's early years. While there were problems at home, the inflow of wealth from oil ensured that, by the time the boom ended, he would be firmly entrenched in power and the economy would be on a general growth trajectory.

The New Order government instituted a number of policies to attract foreign investors and to get domestic investors to rejoin the market. The first move, made in 1966, was to invite the International Monetary Fund (IMF), banned by Sukarno, back into the country and to bring in a World Bank mission soon after. In 1967, Suharto turned his attention directly towards private investors, sponsoring meetings and summits for investors and the media, in which representatives of the Indonesian government outlined new strategies to make Indonesia a more favourable place in which to invest.

Official corruption, which had been a significant feature of Indonesia's economic landscape since the first days of the republic, remained institutionalised. In keeping with this mode, Suharto and Sutowo had, in the late 1950s, been punished by the army for corrupt activities. When he became president, Suharto continued this culture; he topped up the officers' incomes through his access to revenue from the sale of oil, provided by General Ibnu Sutowo, head of the state-owned oil company *Pertamina*. From 1968, Suharto had received funding from Sutowo, in exchange for which Sutowo was given an almost entirely free reign over *Pertamina*, which was easily the country's largest source of foreign income and which operated in a manner effectively independent of official government policy.

Sutowo's primary method of raising funds was to borrow outside the existing government borrowing regime against the value of *Pertamina*. The effect of this process of unofficial fund raising was that Indonesia ended up running a two-track economic system (Winters 1996: 84). By 1972, the rogue economic policy of *Pertamina* was of such concern that, in support of IMF attempts to curtail the organisation's borrowings, the USA suspended eligibility for program loans (Winters 1996: 89). With long-term borrowing no longer available, *Pertamina*'s debt became unsustainable, the effects of which flowed into the conventional economy, with built-in crossover provisions meaning that, should the Indonesian government not guarantee *Pertamina*'s debts, the company would default on its own borrowings and all debts would have to be repaid in full. When *Pertamina* finally collapsed, it had over US$10 billion worth of debt (Mackie & MacIntyre 1994: 14; Hill 1994: 69).

The political fallout was significant, but, by then, the unexpected income from the first surge in world oil prices, soon to quadruple the price of oil, had begun to come in. Indonesia's overall economy became buoyant, providing Suharto with yet another method of ensuring development and increasing his system of patronage.

SUHARTO AND CORRUPTION

With the new revenues from oil, Suharto felt he could be less reliant on foreign investment and could afford to run a more nationalistic approach to economic development. Economic policies subsequently became more restrictive for international investors, opening the way for local businesspeople with close links to Suharto to expand their business interests. There was considerable resentment towards this policy, however, reflected in riots in Jakarta in 1974, which coincided with a visit by the Japanese prime minister, Kakuei Tanaka. The outward purpose of the riots was against perceived excessive Japanese investment and Chinese ownership, but they soon developed an anti-Chinese sentiment, reflecting a long-standing concern by ethnically indigenous Indonesians, referred to as *pribumi*, about what some Indonesians regarded as an excessively firm ethnic Chinese grip on the domestic economy. In particular, one small group of ethnic Chinese financiers and other intermediaries had provided funds and supplies to ABRI in return for political favours and corruption and profiteering were rampant.

As the government took tighter hold on the economy, Suharto began to build his own slush fund, as well as to reap rewards from private deals and allocate lucrative government contracts to his family and friends. By 1978, Indonesia's economy was dominated by a system of patronage and discretion, but, following the oil price collapse of 1982–83 and again in 1985–86, Indonesia's government began to rethink its economic policy direction and, along with it, the relationships that had developed between members of the country's political, military and economic elites.

In some senses, 1986 was a more difficult year than most for Suharto. With the price of oil having dropped to real pre-1973 prices, Indonesia's main source of income had all but dried up, its non-oil economy was a shambles and the funds for patronage, through which Suharto continued to derive support, were becoming increasingly difficult to come by.

As a consequence of the collapse in oil prices from 1983 until 1989, Indonesia's Berkeley Group of pro-free market economists was able to reassert its influence over economic policy. As a result, the New Order government implemented a number of initiatives aimed at restoring the country's economic health. Perhaps the most significant changes during this period concerned taxation. Income tax in Indonesia was, effectively, completely divorced from the limited earnings of ordinary people and, in particular, from farmers, which meant the government did not have access to this otherwise conventional source of revenue. This lack of access to tax-based funds was primarily addressed with the introduction of a value added tax on goods.

Despite the aftertaste of the *Pertamina* scandal, high and growing levels of corruption and an economic policy that zig-zagged between a type of free-market rationalism and crony-oriented profit taking, by the late 1980s foreign investors were considering Indonesia very closely. The New Order government looked to be securely in control; such political stability has always been regarded as desirable by foreign investors. Suharto and the New Order government were also considered to be friendly to the West, which further enhanced Indonesia's foreign financial appeal.

THE CRASH OF 1997

Despite fluctuations, until 1997 Indonesia managed to record average growth rates of around 7 per cent from 1990 onwards. Inflation decreased significantly and the broader social indicators showed that standards of living had increased from the low base of the late 1960s. The causes of the economic collapse from 1997 were various, but some key points included a greater potential to move capital in and out of the country, high-level government corruption, unsustainable non-productive investment, the country's unsustainably high level of foreign debt and, finally, with Suharto's grip on power becoming shaky in the face of increasingly loud calls for political change, most of the money that had been made in Indonesia during Suharto's rule began to flow offshore, the timing of which coincided with a currency collapse in Thailand, which encouraged money markets to reexamine Indonesia. When they did they panicked, and the rupiah plummeted, losing 80 per cent of its value in less than twelve months.

This collapse in the value of the rupiah wiped out any chance of Indonesian companies being able to repay their foreign debt, sending most of them into technical bankruptcy. The economy officially shrank by 13.6 per cent in 1998, unemployment leapt from around 20 per cent—the government's own conservative figure—to more than 50 per cent, with underemployment accounting for perhaps another 20–30 per cent. Starvation, which had effectively been wiped out, reappeared and malnutrition became widespread. Children were withdrawn from schools in vast numbers because parents were unable to meet educational costs and health problems escalated. Needless to say, the political tensions this engendered quickly broke to the surface, often exacerbated or exploited by factional interests.

THE PRODEMOCRACY MOVEMENT

In December 1993, despite Suharto's attempts to have her election thwarted, Megawati Sukarnoputri was elected to the chair of the PDI. Megawati had been supported by senior members of ABRI's Red and White group and her popularity reflected the relative economic egalitarianism of her father,

Sukarno, as opposed to the opulence surrounding Suharto's family and friends. In part, it was simply the name of the PDI that gave it its democratic credentials and, in part, it was that Megawati was increasingly perceived to provide a genuine political alternative to Suharto. That Megawati was the daughter of Indonesia's first president gave her a pedigree and some legitimacy. With the highly symbolic election of Megawati, the PDI appeared to grow in terms of popular support.

The media had been heavily censored and otherwise constrained during Suharto's period in office. Suharto took control of government amid a wave of press closures, with a second round of closures occurring in 1974 in response to the Malari riots. Radio and television news had to run official government news broadcasts; friends and family of Suharto owned or controlled very large sections of the media. Outside this direct control, individual journalists were harassed or not allowed to work and, although there were many brave attempts to work against government restrictions, Indonesia's public had to learn to read between the lines of what was openly reported. However, in the shifting climate of the 1990s, some media began to test the limits of government control. As a result, in May 1994, in response to articles that reflected tensions between ABRI and the government, the government closed three respected publications: *Tempo*, *Editor* and *De Tik*.

Despite this repression, the growth of democratic hope reflected the creation of a political space between the increasingly divided elite, especially within ABRI. In 1996, this space began to close; a number of senior ABRI figures, as well as Suharto, decided that Megawati's role of leader of the PDI had attracted too much attention. ABRI stage-managed an alternative PDI meeting at which Megawati was dumped and her predecessor, Suryadi, was elected to the chair. Megawati declared the meeting illegal and refused to resign; her supporters barricaded themselves in the PDI's headquarters in Jakarta.

By July 1996 the situation had come to a head. Anti-Megawati PDI members, liberally supported by soldiers wearing PDI T-shirts, stormed the PDI's headquarters. In the mêlée, several people were killed, dozens injured and several more disappeared. A riot broke out and Jakarta experienced its worst social upheaval since 1966.

SUHARTO'S DECLINE

The prodemocracy movement was in tatters, the effect of the raid on the PDI headquarters, which seemed to signal that a final confrontation over Suharto's leadership was looming. It was from this time that Indonesians with money began thinking about their security and started moving their money offshore. When, in mid to late 1997, the value of the rupiah began to fall, it seemed that the country—indeed, the region—was caught unawares. Most unprepared of all was Suharto who, in his January 1998 budget speech, outlined economic prospects that were wildly out of keeping with the reality fast befalling the country. This had the effect of further deepening the crisis, with the rupiah reflecting the loss of faith in Indonesia's economy and in its political system. From a high of R3500 to the American dollar in June 1997 it had, by 1998, plummeted to R17 000 to the dollar. Suharto's patent inability to deal with the crisis called into radical doubt his continuing suitability as president.

Spurred on by material desperation, protests that had been a scattered but relatively constant feature of Indonesia's landscape since 1996, became more frequent, larger and more violent. Ethnic Chinese were increasingly attacked by radical Muslim mobs, while students and others increasingly protested in and around universities. ABRI reacted with its traditional violence, which, in part, reflected the differing strategic interests of its key members. The Red and White faction had, by this time, decided that Suharto had to go, while the so-called Green (pro-Islamic) faction of the Indonesian military, promoted by Suharto and by now headed by his son-in-law, Prabowo Subianto, intended to support Suharto and crush public opposition.

Some of the rioting in the first part of 1998 appeared to reflect a degree of organisation not usually associated with a free-for-all. Some Islamic leaders were implicated, the belief being that they wished to strengthen the position of political Islam ahead of any political change. Similarly, troops from the Green group were believed to be acting as *agents provocateurs*. The students, by this stage, were leading the push for Suharto's resignation, daring to say out loud what only months previously would have been unimaginable (Van Klinken 1999b; Berfield & Loveard 1999). Increasingly, these students also found themselves supported by Indonesia's elite.

Then, in Jakarta, the direct security concern of Prabowo, while Suharto was attending a meeting in Egypt, students at the private Trisakti University campus joined the protest movement. With Suharto out of the country, the stakes over political leadership were critical and, on 12 May, Prabowo's men reacted with uncontrolled violence. As students began to run back to their campus, the troops opened fire. The final toll was four dead and many more wounded (Richburg 1999; Bourchier 1999). It was subsequently claimed that Prabowo had hoped to trigger a massive social breakdown, which could, in turn, be used to declare martial law in order to shore up Suharto's worsening political position.

There were more student protests, which, increasingly, Jakarta's poor and dispossessed began to join in. What had started as a naïve but politically motivated protest soon turned into an orgy of anti-government rioting and increasing attacks against ethnic Chinese. Looters were trapped in burning buildings and the death toll quickly rose to more than 1000, with the mayhem being quelled only by the army bringing armoured cars and tanks onto the streets. The public outcry for Suharto's resignation reached unprecedented levels, with former generals, academics and ordinary Indonesians calling for him to quit. Major-General Yudhoyono personally delivered a message from a group of retired generals addressed to ABRI commander-in-chief, General Wiranto, requesting that Suharto resign. A similar petition was presented to a special session of the MPR, of which, in an act of unprecedented defiance, half of the assembly called on Suharto to resign, its repeated calls headed by former Suharto loyalist, MPR chairman Harmoko (Schwartz 1999: 358).

THE FALL OF SUHARTO

On Tuesday, 19 May 1998, in a public speech televised live, President Suharto announced the formation of a reform committee and a new reform cabinet, but, more importantly, he also announced that there would be new presidential elections and that he would not stand as a candidate. No date was given for the election and many believed it could be more than a year away, which did not satisfy the protesters. With Harmoko threatening to have the MPR impeach Suharto, the MPR building swamped by protesters and all credible candidates refusing to join his reform committee, on 20 May 1998, Suharto began to waver. When Harmoko again spoke against Suharto and ABRI faction leader in the MPR, Syarwan Hamid, raised his fist in symbolic support, it appeared increasingly obvious that Suharto was alone. A visit to his home by three former vice-presidents—Try Sutrisno, Sudharmono and Umar Wirahadikusumah—that evening, further encouraged Suharto to resign. A visit later that night by Wiranto sealed the arrangement; it was agreed that Suharto and his family would be protected after his resignation. At around eleven that night, Suharto summoned Habibie and informed him that, on the following day, he would become Indonesia's third president (Schwartz 1999: 358–66).

THE HABIBIE PRESIDENCY

Habibie's appointment was supported by Wiranto, who was reappointed as commander-in-chief of ABRI and defence. The appointment in March of Habibie to the vice-presidency had been designed to allow Suharto to quietly step away from Indonesian politics during that five-year term of office. After a brief and somewhat ill-conceived show of power on the following day, 22 May, Prabowo was shuffled out of *Kostrad* to the staff and command college at Magelang and, soon after, sacked from ABRI. Meanwhile, in what was beginning to look like a purge, Prabowo's military allies were similarly being moved from influential positions to be replaced by Red and White loyalists. In particular, *Kopassus* commander Major-General Muchdi Purwopranjono was replaced by Major-General Sjahrir.

Despite Habibie's general unpopularity and through months of public protest, including widespread rioting in Jakarta in November 1998, with Wiranto's support he retained the presidency. An agreement was brokered over new elections for the DPR, with the presidency to be decided in October 1999.

In the days after Habibie took office, he made a number of moves towards establishing his reform credentials. Labour unions, previously banned under Suharto, were legalised, there was a start to delinking government and business and resolving other conflicts of interest and it was announced that all political parties could contest future elections. More than 140 political parties were formed during this period of openness, while the media attempted to reconstitute itself as a free entity. Economic constraints, however, tempered the media's capacity, while the ownership of some media organisations showed links to Habibie's government. Having said that, in October 1999, under Information Minister Mohamad Yunus, Indonesia formally lifted all political controls over its media (Anwar 2000).

As important was the political and ethnic violence that had been tearing at the fabric of Indonesian society since early 1998, much of the violence orchestrated by members of the political elite running competing agendas ahead of the elections. Such agendas included the assertion of Islamic nationalist identities of various types, scapegoating the Chinese for the country's economic problems, redressing local economic imbalances, the settling of ethnic rivalries, claims to separatism, the relative positions of various political parties and, not least, the role of, and factionalism within, the armed forces.

ECONOMIC REFORMS

The economic reforms that Indonesia was forced to undertake as a consequence of the collapse of the value of the rupiah and the associated economic decline were various and, in part, only haltingly implemented. Initially, Suharto agreed to economic reforms in late 1997, but failed to accomplish those agreements, either at all or in any meaningful way. His family and cronies appeared to be protected from the full thrust of the IMF's intentions.

After Suharto fell from power, Habibie realised that some significant reforms would need to be undertaken. His first moves were to delink some more notorious cronies from their monopolies and to end the monopoly system. Loss-making projects, such as Tommy Suharto's national car project, were scrapped, while investigations began into the collapsed banking industry. Between early 1998 and early 1999, more than fifty insolvent banks were closed by the government. One bank belonging to Suharto's middle son, Bambang Trihajmodo, was closed, re-opened under a different name and closed again, while another, belonging to Islamic leader

Abdurrahman Wahid, was also closed. The total cost of reforming the banking sector was estimated at between US$40 and US$50 billion, about three-quarters of the country's foreign debt, while recapitalisation was expected to cost more than US$33 billion. In March 1999, Indonesia's international economic rating, in the finance industry known as 'junk', was the lowest of any rated country except Pakistan (Hammond 1999). By mid 2000, the sense of growing stability, which had marked the economy and politics, by mid 1999 had begun to evaporate and political uncertainty fuelled continued selling down of the rupiah.

In January 1999, Habibie announced that East Timor, so long a trouble spot for Indonesia, would be given the choice of autonomy within Indonesia or independence. In response, Wiranto and other senior officers began creating and arming local militias. Ahead of the referendum, some thirteen pro-integration militias, comprising around 6000 members, had been created in East Timor, spreading fear and havoc and being responsible for up to 2000 East Timorese deaths. Even a growing UN presence in the province was not enough to quell the violence.

DEMOKRASI

On 28 January 1999, the DPR approved the legal foundation for a new political party system and the 1999 elections. Of the more than 140 political parties, forty-eight were regarded by the *Komisi Pemilihan Umum* (KPU, or National Electoral Commission) as satisfying electoral criteria, having executive boards in nine of the twenty-seven provinces and in half the towns and districts in each of those provinces. Candidates would be elected proportionally by province, but a party's winning candidates would be chosen on the basis of district results. New parties would also need at least ten seats in the national assembly to stand at the 2004 elections.

Election committees at various levels managed the campaign and elections. Half their membership was drawn from the political parties. For the first time, independent Indonesian and international observers were permitted to monitor the elections. The number of unelected TNI seats in the People's Consultative Assembly was reduced from seventy-five to thirty-eight. In provincial and local assemblies they were reduced to 10 per cent of the seats. The president would continue to be elected by the MPR, which was revised from 1000 to 700. Of these, 238 seats would be appointed (old MPR, 575), including thirty-eight military, 135 regional and sixty-five group representatives. Among the forty-eight represented parties, twenty-six were linked to the government party, *Golkar*, or Suharto's family. The electoral laws that do exist were also seen as biased in their direction.[3]

On 7 June 1999, the first post-Suharto general elections were held in Indonesia. The elections were remarkable for their transparency, lack of violence and the neutral role of the TNI, apart from in East Timor, Irian Jaya and Aceh. There were some minor irregularities and the count was slow, which confused many who were used to the results being known sometimes before the elections had been held. But, in all, it was a successful poll, with results that reflected a coalescing of political support around five main parties.

Partai Demokrasi Indonesia–Perjuangan, led by Megawati Sukarnoputri, was by far the most popular, with more than one-third of the votes, followed a distant second by *Golkar*, which used money, institutional power, the threat of the unknown and force of habit to secure a little over 20 per cent of the votes. The *Partai Kebangkitan Bangsa* (PKB, or National Awakening Party), led by Abdurrahman Wahid, came third, the PPP fourth and PAN a distant fifth. Along with the other seat holders, *Partai Bulan Bintang* and *Partai Keadilan*, Indonesian politics coalesced into two broad camps, or coalitions. Of the forty-eight parties that contested the elections, some twenty-six were seen as front parties for either Suharto or *Golkar*. None of these parties managed to secure a seat in the new DPR.

If PKB and PAN were considered within this camp, then, one of the main consequences of the elections was that nationalist–secular parties won the overwhelming majority of votes. There was also strong support for parties promoting the continued unity of the state, while political leaders, apart from Amien Rais, opposed federalism and supported retention of the 1945 Constitution.

The June 1999 general elections in Indonesia held out, for a while, great hope for the country's process of democratisation, but it soon became very clear that it was only the first step on a very long and difficult path. It seemed clear throughout 1999 that the TNI generally and General Wiranto in particular held real power in the country, although it was not entirely clear to what end they wished to use it (Kingsbury 1999). Continuing violence in Aceh between the *Gerakan Aceh Merdeka* (GAM, or Free Aceh Movement) and the TNI left hundreds, perhaps thousands, of people dead and identified Aceh as a region that radically challenged Indonesia's continuing ideological claim to unity in diversity. In Maluku, too, violence and carnage continued, most obviously in the main city of Ambon, which, over 1999–2000, left more than 3000 dead and brought into doubt the capacity of the president to rule. Here, tensions revolved around competition between the earlier Christian inhabitants and more recent Muslim arrivals. But behind this competition and, to some extent, events in Aceh, could be seen the hand of the TNI fomenting trouble, at least in part, to prove its own necessity.

And then came East Timor.

The TNI's support for East Timor's militias (see chapter 15, 'East Timor') was a very clear part of the military's attempt to impose its will, as well as to show what happened to recalcitrant provinces. In the final analysis, however, the TNI—and Indonesia—lost in East Timor. Not only was Indonesia's continuing presence there overwhelmingly rejected in the face of state-sponsored violence and intimidation, but events there came close to turning Indonesia into one of the world's pariah states. The USA , the UK and Australia all suspended defence links with Indonesia over events in East Timor. Indonesia's economy was also further destabilised as the international financial community wondered about unproductive military expenditure and punished Indonesia for its stand. This, in turn, led to a renewed collapse in the value of the rupiah, to more than R8000 to the US dollar. To deflect attention from these troubles, senior Indonesian authorities began to look for scapegoats for their problems, in particular focusing on near neighbour Australia for interfering in Indonesia's internal affairs.

GUS DUR AS PRESIDENT

The election of Abdurrahman Wahid—Gus Dur—as president on 20 October 1999 came as a shock to most people, not least the thousands of Megawati supporters in the streets outside the MPR building who immediately began rioting. A car bomb exploded, killing three people, while riot police fired tear gas into the angry crowd. The election of Gus Dur was a triumph of clever politicking over what appeared to be natural justice. While Gus Dur was clearly aiming for the top job, he had to work to achieve it. By contrast, Megawati, who could have secured it, failed to put in the work necessary to build a coalition of support. Instead, she remained aloof and indecisive, qualities that continued to dog her political career. Habibie had thought he could retain the presidency, but when he announced that Wiranto would be his vice-presidential running mate, Wiranto announced that he would not stand with Habibie. This humiliation and the rejection of Habibie's accountability speech to the MPR, at two o'clock. on the morning of 20 October 1999, ended his political hopes.

With just 10 per cent of the vote, Gus Dur's PKB did not look like presenting him as a strong contender for the top position. But *Golkar's* votes shifted in behind Gus Dur, rather than Megawati. In exchange, Gus Dur agreed that *Golkar* could have a number of cabinet posts. With Rais' support already secured, Gus Dur then cemented his alliances with the small Islamic parties (Wagstaff 1999).

Amien Rais was central to the election of Gus Dur to the presidency, in that he helped to swing behind him the votes without which he would certainly have not gained the presidency. Gus Dur, in turn, supported Rais' gaining of the chair of the DPR. In the end, Gus Dur won by seventy votes, a little more than his party held. In obtaining the presidency, Gus Dur made commitments to share power, which was later reflected in the appointment of cabinet ministers. Megawati was humiliated by her defeat for the position she believed was rightly hers. But, for Gus Dur, building an inclusive government, Megawati's involvement at the highest possible level would be critical. With Gus Dur's support, Megawati was voted in as vice-president.

The new administration drew representatives from the five major parties—PDI–P, *Golkar*, PKB, PPP, PAN—and the TNI. In the first few months of Gus Dur's presidency, he initiated a number of significant reforms, gradually asserting his authority as he did so. His biggest task was to reform the TNI, which process he started by sacking Wiranto as coordinating minister for politics and security in February 2000. Wiranto's appointment to the ministry by Gus Dur in October 1999 had not weakened Wiranto's grip on the TNI; he was increasingly seen to be exercising power outside Gus Dur's control. Gus Dur then moved to shake up the TNI, promoting officers he felt were more loyal to him or in favour of reform.

Gus Dur attempted to resolve the Aceh problem, with little success. His main move in Irian Jaya was to change its name back to West Papua. Problems continued, however, in Ambon and, to a lesser extent, in many of the other outer islands. Similarly, while the economy had begun to stabilise, fundamental reform was still slow in coming and the country's banks were still technically insolvent. Moves to call Suharto to account for his corruption were slow, hamstrung by legal problems and, later, a series of bombings, although moves were made to reduce corruption elsewhere and to make some former cronies accountable.

Gus Dur's reformist zeal, complicated by his personal idiosyncrasies—humour, contradiction, lack of concern—and, occasionally, poor judgment, resulted in moves against him by the elite, manifested in early 2000 as two political coalitions, the *Poros Tengah* (Central Axis) and the *Poros Indonesia* (Indonesia Axis). The *Poros Tengah* was established with the intention of asserting political Islam in the DPR and, ultimately, over the presidency. The *Poros Indonesia* was a coalition designed to oust Gus Dur as president, the biggest delay to its plan being the lack of a suitable alternative. This political instability again destabilised the rupiah, dropping it to 9500 to the US dollar. But, more importantly, it again raised the troubling question of whether it was possible to govern Indonesia under a democratic political system.

INDONESIAN TERRORISM

In part reflecting Indonesia's unstable political environment and in part expressing long-held frustrations on the part of some more conservative Muslims, under Gus Dur's presidency, Islamist inspired violence began to make its presence felt. The desire for an Islamic state that fed the *Dar'ul Islam* movement had remained alive. Dating from a rebirth in the mid 1970s of the movement that had manifested as *Dar'ul Islam* (Laksamana.Net 2002), a group dubbed *Komando Jihad* succeeded in bombing the Borobudur Buddhist temple in Central Java and, in 1981, hijacked a Garuda aircraft to Bangkok. Following a crackdown on members and sympathisers, it was from this group that the core of new radical

Islamic groups, including *Jema'ah Islamiyah* (JI, or Islamic Community),[4] were drawn.

In the late 1980s and early 1990s, President Suharto shifted his position to encourage political Islam as a counter to forces mounting against him. When he fell from power in 1998, the lid came off the political pressure cooker that was Indonesia and the spectrum of political Islam arrayed itself to take advantage of the new opportunities available in the post-New Order era. It was in this climate of releasing repressed anger and frustration, of changes in the style and nature of aspects of political Islam, of opportunities, long-standing agendas and newfound allies, that more radical groups within political Islam discovered the will and the opportunity to assert their views, which were manifested in a series of new groups, all of which had ideological links, degrees of organisational association and a close and sometimes common history.

JEMA'AH ISLAMIYAH (JI)

All senior members of JI had 'trained in Afghanistan in the late 1980s and early 1990s, before JI formally existed. It was in the camps of the Saudi-financed Afghan mujahidin leader Abdul Rasul Sayaf that they developed *jihadist* fervour, international contacts, and deadly skills' (ICG 2003: 1). The group was held together by ideology, training and an intricate network of marriages. (ICG 2003: 26–8; see also, Murphy 2003).

JI came to public prominence after the 12 October 2002 Bali bombing. Members of JI have also been identified as being involved in attacks in the Philippines, bombings in Jakarta (in particular on Christmas Eve 2000) and attempted attacks in Singapore. As investigations into JI progressed through late 2002 and into 2003, dozens of alleged operatives were arrested in Indonesia in connection with the Bali bombing and with a series of earlier bombing attacks, predominantly in Jakarta.

In 1967, a radical preacher named Abu Bakar Ba'asyir and former Indonesian Muslim Youth Movement (GPII) leader, Abdullah Sungkar, established an Islamic school near the central Javanese town of Solo, Pesantren al-Mu'min, which, in 1973, moved to the village of Ngruki and was thereafter widely referred to as Pondok Ngruki.[5] In 1977, Sungkar was arrested for urging his followers not to vote in the 1977 elections. The following year, Sungkar and Ba'asyir were arrested, accused of being involved with *Dar'ul Islam* and what was referred to in court as *Jema'ah Islamiyah* (ICG 2002: 12). Sugkar and Ba'asyir were jailed in 1978 for promoting an Islamic state and in 1982 sentenced to nine years in prison, reduced to three years on appeal, which meant they were released for time already served. While awaiting the outcome of a prosecution appeal, in 1985 Sungkar and Ba'asyir fled to Malaysia, only returning to Indonesia following the fall of Suharto in 1998.

Links between the Ngruki group[6] in Indonesia and the exiles in Malaysia remained strong, through family ties, political and religious sympathies and instructions emanating from Malaysia (ICG 2002: 5). The internationalisation of this network increased, with Sungkar and Ba'asyir travelling to Saudi Arabia to raise funds, the sending of volunteers to southern Thailand, Pakistan, Afghanistan and the southern Philippines for military training and the dispersal of other members to Germany, Spain, Holland and elsewhere. After Ba'asyir's return, he helped found the Indonesian Mujahidin Council (*Majelis Mujahidin Indonesia*, or MMI), which was formed in Yogyakarta in 2000 (van Bruinessen 2002b) as an umbrella group for those wishing to build 'an Islamic state and ... an Islamic leadership in the country as well as in Muslim communities throughout the world' (Sipress & Nakashima 2003). Ba'asyir was elected *amir*[7] of MMI's governing council, the *Ahlul Halli wal Aqdi* (AHWA). Along with the MMI's commitment to introducing Islamic law to Indonesia, the AHWA had the additional goal of establishing a new international caliphate, which arose in alleged JI intentions for maritime South-East Asia (for discussion about the origins and intentions of the caliphate movement, see Ba'asyir, 2000; Abdul Qadir Baraja 2000; see also, Khilafah Online).

In 2003, Indonesia's defence minister, Matori Abdul Djalil, alleged that Ba'asyir was the leader of JI and that Riduan Isamuddin, also known as Hambali, was Ba'asyir's deputy. Speaking at his trial, Ba'asyir acknowledged that 'he knew fellow Indonesian Hambali as "a good man" who was active in channelling funds to Ambon, the capital city of Maluku province, to help Muslims who were battling Christians there' (AFP 2003). Acting under guidance from Riduan Isamuddin, more than thirty people, alleged to be *Jema'ah Islamiyah* operatives, were convicted of responsibility for the October 2000 bombings of the two nightclubs in Bali and the later bombing of the Marriott Hotel in Jakarta on 5 August 2003.

The investigation into the Bali bombing led to the arrest of Said Sungkar, the youngest brother of the alleged founder of *Jema'ah Islamiyah* and co-founder of *Pondok Ngruki*, Abdullah Sungkar. Also arrested in connection with the Bali bombings was Ali Gufron, alias Mukhlas. Mukhlas is said to have organised the Bali bombings and to have succeeded Hambali as operations chief of JI. Following the arrest of Mukhlas, Hambali became the most wanted man in Asia. On 12 August 2003, Hambali was arrested in Ayuthyah, Thailand, where he was allegedly planning to bomb a forthcoming meeting of the Asia Pacific Economic Cooperation (APEC) group. Hambali had been held responsible for organising the bombings of churches on Christmas eve 2000, in which eighteen people were killed, the bombing of the Marriott Hotel in August 2003, helping fund the first *jihad* to Ambon and was linked to bombings in Manila in December 2000, in which twenty-two people were killed, as well as a foiled bid to blow up embassies in Singapore in December 2001.[8] Hambali was also under investigation for his role in the 2002 Bali bombing.

The International Crisis Group (ICG) has claimed that it was the intention of JI to establish a group of caliphates in South-East Asia under an overarching *Daulah Islamiyah* (Islamic state), based on what it refers to as *mantiqi*. These *mantiqi* have political and military applications, representing distinct administrative territories. Mantiqi 1 is said to focus on peninsular Malaysia, southern Thailand and Singapore, and was led by Hambali until 2002. Mantiqi 2 focuses on Java, Sumatra and Kalimantan, while Mantiqi 3 administers operations in the southern Philippines, Sabah, Sarawak (Malaysia), Brunei and Sulawesi (Indonesia). A Mantiqi 4 was said to focus on West Papua and Australia, with its primary purpose being fund-raising activities (Republic of Singapore 2003: 10; see also, ICG 2003: 11).

LASKAR JIHAD (LJ)

In marked contrast to the internationalist orientation of *Jema'ah Islamiyah*, *Laskar Jihad* (LJ, or Holy Struggle Troops), who had fought Christians in Ambon has an explicitly nationalist political agenda. In this, there is a close overlap between its goals and those of the Green faction. The convergence of Green military personnel and hardline Muslim organisations led to alliances that were the precursors to the launching of LJ. The development of LJ also benefited from President Suharto's promotion of explicitly Islamic army officers, some of whom assisted with *Laskar Jihad's* training, funding and logistics (Huang 2002). Fighting between Christians and Muslims in Ambon provided the pretext for a reassertion of conservative military influence.

The fighting had begun in December 1999, with reports of a massacre by Christian militia of approximately 500 Muslims in Halmahera, North Maluku. The Sunni Communication Forum (*Forum Kommunikasi Ahlus Sunna Wal Jamaah*, or FKAWJ), an organisation formed in 1998, became the vehicle for a movement that arose ostensibly in response to this violence.

The ideology of LJ is deeply conservative. It opposes democracy, is influenced by conspiracy theories about Zionism and Christianity, and views the notion of a female head of state as incompatible with Islam (Schulze 2002: 59; see also, van Bruinessen 2002c). When approximately 3000[9] LJ members travelled to Maluku to fight Christians, they were not obstructed by the military, even though Abdurrahman Wahid's government had pledged to prevent them from leaving Java. Maluku regional governor, Saleh Latuconsina, pointed out that LJ had powerful backers because they were not being prevented from travelling. The Washington-based Center for Defence Information (CDI) reported that, according to Western intelligence sources, over US$9 million was transferred from *Kostrad* to LJ and further funds were diverted from the business branch of *Kostrad*; both the group and the military denied the accusation (Huang 2002).

As well as fighting in Ambon and North Maluku, LJ was also active in Poso, Central Sulawesi, from July 2001, where it engaged in violence against Christian groups and published a daily newsletter calling for, among other things, jihad. LJ was also active in West Papua against pro-independence activists and attempted to become involved in the conflict in Aceh.

LJ formally ended around the time of the 2002 Bali bombing—it claims a few days before, but the announcement was made the day after the bombing—however, it continued to operate in West Papua at Fak-Fak, Sorong, and near the border with Papua-New Guinea, at the transmigration camps of Imunda, Amanat, Green River and Waris. The US State Department noted that *Laskar Jihad* had 'active organisations in at least half of the province's 14 districts' (US State Department 2002). Here, LJ members, including some indigenous Papuans, members of or recruited by the pro-integrationist militia *Satgas Merah-Putih* (Red and White Task Force), were said to be armed and trained by *Kopassus* (Martinkus 2002, 2003). In August 2003, external and locally recruited members of a group that appeared to be an offshoot or locally recruited version of LJ, *Laskar Tabligh* (Missionary Troops), clashed with pro-independence protesters at Wamena, West Papua, over government plans to divide the province into three, in contravention of the province's special autonomy status.

LASKAR MUJAHIDIN

Laskar Mujahidin (LM) was the military wing of the MMI. The first contingent of around fifty LM recruits arrived in Ambon in February 1999, soon after the first wave of sectarian violence there. Initially, these recruits called themselves *Laskar Jundullah* (not connected with the group referred to below); many of them had been active with the MILF in the southern Philippines. By July 1999, several hundred LM members had become active in Maluku in operations against Christian militias and civilians and later, briefly, in Poso. At its peak, LM had about 2000 active members, who were better armed and more highly trained than LJ troops, but even so, LM probably fielded no more than 500 fighters in Maluku (and, briefly, central Sulawesi) at any one time (ICG 2002b: 19).

According to independent observers in Ambon in early 2002, while LM was linked to LJ through the MMI, it maintained separate operations in and around Ambon (personal communication) and Poso and were known to clash; they also clashed with soldiers and the police, whose authority they did not recognise. In part, hostilities between LJ and LM reflected personal animosities between LM leader Haris Fadillah, also known as Abu Dzar, and LJ leader Jafar Umar Thalib, who were known to have clashed on three occasions, once in the Middle East, once in Afghanistan and once in Ambon. However, LM did operate with a local Islamic force known as *Laskar Hitu* (Hitu Troops) in joint attacks on the Christian villages of Hitu,

Mamala and Morela, as well as others in the area (ICG 2002b: 20). In late October 2002, uniformed LM members were deployed to guard the hospital where Abu Bakar Ba'asyir had been taken for treatment after being arrested in the wake of the 2002 Bali bombing.

Haris Fadillah was killed fighting Christians in Ambon on 23 October 2000. Fadillah was the father-in-law of Omar al-Faruq, a Kuwaiti who is claimed to have been 'al Qaeda's principal relationship manager in Southeast Asia' (Murphy 2003a), initially as a key conduit between al-Qaeda and Filipino Islamic militants and, since the fall of Suharto, Indonesian militants. Al-Faruq was initially trained at al-Qaeda's Camp Khalden in Afghanistan. He fought in Ambon and was being held in detention in the United States. A videotape featuring Fadillah, in which he encourages young Muslims to take up arms, was distributed throughout Indonesia, Malaysia and the southern Philippines and shown during informal religious classes by clerics with alleged ties to *Jema'ah Islamiyah*. This and other videos, which were said to have been financed by Agus Dwikarna, who first met al-Faruq in Makassar in 1999 through another Camp Khalden trainee, Syawai Yassin, were produced by Aris Munandar, who was also said to be the right-hand man to Abu Bakar Ba'asyir (Murphy 2003b). In 2000, Dwikarna founded *Laskar Jundullah*.

LASKAR JUNDULLAH

The aim of *Laskar Jundullah* (Army of God), which was founded in September 2000 and is based in Sulawesi, is the imposition of *syariah* (Islamic law) throughout Sulawesi. *Laskar Jundullah* first appeared in Poso in July 2000 in response to religious violence there in June 2000, in which 200 Muslims were killed.[10] Based on earlier, sporadic religious conflict in the Poso area dating to the 1980s and, more substantially, from around 1995, it is possible there may have been other ad hoc *Laskar Jundullah* groups before the establishment of the group that currently carries that name. *Laskar Jundullah* was believed to have drawn its members from three sources: descendants, relatives and supporters of the *Dar'ul Islam* rebellion, a faction of the Indonesian Islamic student organisation, *Himpunan Mahasiswa Islam* (Islamic Senior Students' Assembly) and from Muslims from the Poso area, in particular, from the *Komite Perjuangan Mulsim Poso* (Poso Committee for Islamic Struggle) (ICG 2002b: 20).

One of the co-founders of this more permanent *Laskar Jundullah*, Agus Dwikarna, was arrested in the Philippines in March 2002 and sentenced to prison for illegal possession of firearms and explosives. Dwikarna was said to have close links to the head of the Spanish branch of al-Qaeda, Imad Eddin Barakat Yarbas, who, in turn, was closely associated with Mohammad Atta, the alleged leader of the 11 September 2001 attacks against the World Trade

Center and the Pentagon. In June 2000, Dwikarna allegedly acted as a guide for al-Qaeda figures visiting Indonesia, including Osama bin Laden's former second-in-command, Ayman al-Zawahiri, and former al-Qaeda military chief, Mohammad Atef.

A series of bombings occurred in Makassar, South Sulawesi, in December 2002. Four *Laskar Jundullah* members were arrested on charges relating to these bombings, while two others, who had not been caught, were named as suspects. One of those charged, Muchtar Daeng Lau, was claimed to have earlier trained in Afghanistan and the southern Philippines.

Despite a common religio-ideological background and membership of the MMI, *Laskar Jundullah* had poor relations with *Laskar Jihad* in the Poso area, where it preceded the latter organisation; it also had poor relations with *Laskar Mujahidin*.

RECENT DEVELOPMENTS

Despite JI being seriously damaged by a large number of arrests of suspected members, it still claimed to be responsible for exploding a car bomb outside the Australian embassy in Jakarta in September 2004, in which eleven Indonesians were killed and almost 200 injured. The dissolution of *Laskar Jihad* immediately after the 12 October—or before, if one believes its claim—JI bombing in Bali, was in response to its need to reorganise following the reduction of tensions in Maluku and the poor publicity it was bringing Indonesia in the eyes of the international community. Its resurrection in a smaller, modified form also showed the usefulness of such militia to the TNI and reinforced the nexus between the state and unofficial violence in Indonesia that had been so pronounced during the Suharto era.

Laskar Jundullah appeared to have become inactive in 2002, but in October 2003 and into 2004 and 2005, there was a renewed spate of killings of Christians in the Poso area and attacks against Christian churches in the provincial capital of Palu. Following arrests, there were official reports that elements of *Laskar Jundullah* were still active and had coordinated its attacks with representatives of JI, the latter of who were said to have become resident in Central Sulawesi (*Tempo*, 27 October–2 November 2003: 26–30; *Jakarta Post*, 21 October 2003). These attacks were also linked to individuals connected to the TNI who had large and expanding economic interests in the region.

So, too, had LM reduced its public presence to—unarmed—displays of solidarity for Abu Bakar Ba'asyir. Despite sharing similar goals, a basic ideology and membership of the MMI, relations between *Laskar Jihad*, *Laskar Jundullah* and *Laskar Mujahidin* were poor and were not immune from degenerating into violence, primarily reflecting animosities between leaders and, to some extent, conflict over control of particular regions.

THE RISE OF MEGAWATI

With Indonesia being destabilised by Islamic militants, ethnic violence—notably, in Kalimantan—and the promotion of controversial policies on Aceh, West Papua and military reform, Gus Dur's presidency had become unsustainable. His first cabinet was dysfunctional and a cabinet reconstituted in August 2000 did little to stem the flow of criticism against him. Gus Dur limped on, while his political opponents began closing in and, in early 2001, began an impeachment process against him. The grounds for the impeachment—initially, alleged corruption, which was later disproved—was always much less important that the simple lack of faith in his leadership. It was not even that he was such a bad president, although he certainly had shortcomings. Rather, he had simply alienated too many of Jakarta's elite and the military and they decided that it was time for him to go. Perhaps what was most disturbing about Gus Dur's ouster was not so much that the MPR voted overwhelmingly against him—even some of his own party voted against him—but that, on the morning of 23 July 2001, when he was voted out of the presidency, the square in front of the presidential palace, Medan Merdeka, was littered with armoured vehicles, tanks and soldiers, their weapons pointed at the palace.

With much support and no little sense of relief, Megawati was elected Indonesia's fifth president. The military felt more comfortable with Megawati, her support for its nationalist—anti-separatist—agenda, especially in Aceh and the fact that she did not push the military reform agenda. Further, she was seen as an inside member of Jakarta's elite who would do little to disturb the status quo. After the tumultuous events since 1998, Megawati's presidency was seen as a return to stability and relative normality.

Yet if Megawati's presidency was initially viewed with some relief, that relief quickly turned to dismay as she demonstrated her credentials as a do-nothing president. By the time her presidency ended on 20 September 2004, it was variously understood as a return to order, business as usual or as a failure. One report, reflecting a widely held view, said that her presidency had been 'defined by underachievment' (*Jakarta Post*, 15 September 2004: 6). Megawati's presidency could also have been characterised as passive, in that whatever happened under Megawati as president appeared to reflect less her own decision-making or hands-on approaches to executive authority, than more allowing—or being required to allow—those around her to assume control. This passive style had characterised her political career until she assumed the presidency; it seemed evident from the time of her election that support for her reflected her continuing status as the daughter of Indonesia's charismatic, flawed first president, images of whom she continued to use in her election campaign, and acquiescence to a range of other powerful figures around her, including her husband, Taufiq Kiemas, senior members of the PDI–P, major business figures, key countries in the international community, for example, the USA and, not least, the military, to all of which groups, Megawati's presidency, after the idiosyncratic reformism of Abdurrahman Wahid, was seen as bland and compliant.

After the repression of the Suharto years, the interim presidency of Habibie and the chaos of Abdurrahman Wahid's abbreviated term in office, Megawati's presidency was also seen by many Indonesians, at least initially, as reassuring. As head of the most popular political party in 1999, albeit with only around one-third of the total votes, Megawati enjoyed greater legitimacy as president than would have been afforded her political competitors. And the ringing endorsement of her ascension by the MPR in mid 2001 and backing by the TNI, ensured that there would be no significant mainstream dissent until the 2004 electoral period came around.

Megawati also carried with her the charismatic legacy of her father's founding presidency, which, with little doubt, could be considered her single greatest political asset. In a political society still reflecting a generally widespread and somewhat traditional (or reified) respect for authority, Megawati's ancestry was viewed by many non-elite Indonesians as a positive attribute, to the extent that many who became deeply disenchanted with PDI–P still regarded her as a desirable president.

The sectarian and communal conflict and rise in separatist aspirations that marked the presidency of Abdurrahman Wahid, lessened under Megawati's presidency, with a significant reduction—although not complete disappearance—of violence in Maluku and Central Sulawesi, the ending of public conflict in Kalimantan and the eventual repatriation of nearly all East Timorese who wished to return to their homeland from West Timor. However, in that there were improvements, these could, in part, have been attributed to the TNI withdrawing its support for various militant organisations and actively discouraging others it had allowed to run their course. If the TNI had as a part of its agenda the removal of Abdurrahman Wahid as president and used regional instability to demonstrate his lack of political control, then, the TNI did exactly the opposite for Megawati, who they correctly saw at that time as best representing their political and economic interests and hence worth protecting from being seen to lack such political control. In this respect, separatist tensions that had increased in Papua and Aceh after 1999 were met with an assertion of state control, manifesting as an escalation of state violence, reclaiming its authority in the fields of security and state maintenance. This at least showed that, between 1999 and 2001, Indonesia was not in imminent danger of breaking up, as some observers had thought it might do.

Indonesia's economy stabilised during Megawati's presidency, satisfying most of the IMF's key macroeconomic requirements, notably around capping government spending and a reduction in official debt. There was also a return to sustained economic growth, if, by the end of 2004, at a still insufficient level to meet growing requirements. Inflation continued to improve, too, falling from a post-Suharto high of 58 per cent in 1998 to 5.3 per cent in 2004, while interest rates also fell, although they remained high against competitors' standards. After the massive devaluation of the rupiah in 1997–98, there was a relative stabilisation of its value on world currency markets, although it did fluctuate, remaining vulnerable to numerous political factors considered by money markets to be a high-risk investment.

Arguably the single greatest achievement of this period of Megawati's presidency was the July 2003 passing of law number 23/2003, which was introduced to the DPR in August 2002 and provided for the direct election of the president and vice-president. This removed from the politicking and vote-buying of the MPR the authority to choose the country's executive leader and instead placed this decision directly into the hands of the people. Separating the presidential electoral process from the legislative electoral process meant that there would need to be two separate electoral procedures. Due to their complexity and separation of functions, it was decided that they would be held on different dates. Assuming a plurality of candidates for the presidential election, the leading two candidates and their running mates would go through to a second run-off round. It is worth noting, however, that while this important piece of legislation was proposed and passed under Megawati's presidency, she did not support it and, indeed, questioned whether Indonesian voters were 'mature' enough to make such a decision (AP, 11 August 2002).

Yet the legislation was passed and, if this was of itself not an absolute affirmation of the notion of democracy, which, in Indonesia was still missing the generally considered essential component of the equal and consistent rule of law, it was the most important single step that could have been taken in that direction. If nothing else, this move broke the stranglehold the party structure had over the process of selecting a president. Overall, then, while Indonesia did show significant signs of improvement under Megawati—and there were some important gains—these were, in many respects, relatively easily achieved. It was on the less easily achieved improvements, in the economy and elsewhere, that Megawati's government more clearly stalled.

In that Megawati's presidency saw a return to what might be called business as usual, this could be taken as both a positive and negative observation. Business as usual was positive in that, while there remained a serious shortfall in foreign investment in Indonesia, local consumption and investment returned, if not to pre-1998 levels, then, at least to a level that appeared more or less sustainable. After the economic crash of 1997–98 and the restructuring of major elements of the Indonesian economy, many local businesspeople felt that conditions had settled to the extent that they could resume or restart business.

On the political front, the DPR appeared to function, if not at the cutting edge of efficiency or transparency, at least as a generally workable legislature which, given its circumscribed role under Suharto, was a significant achievement.

Perhaps less positively, business as usual also meant a continuation of widespread official corruption, including in the DPR, and an inept judiciary working under an increasingly creaky, contradictory—and contradicted—and often poorly conceived legal code. Business as usual also meant that there remained a significant gap between the elites and the little people and that politicians could largely disregard the direct needs of non-elite Indonesians, not least through an almost complete lack of policy development. It also meant a high level of inefficiency and ineptitude in the bureaucratic functioning of the state and, to a lesser although still often debilitating extent, in private enterprise.

In that Megawati's presidency could have been considered a failure, its shortcomings were numerous. Megawati's personal lack of leadership or vision for Indonesia's future (Gaffar 2002) meant that its policy program under her was essentially limited to implementing IMF economic reforms. Even the PDI–P's policies for the 2004 election were little more than saying it would fix those administrative problems it had neglected to tackle during her presidency, which could not be interpreted as anything other than an admission of failure. In this respect, while Megawati's government performed adequately on basic tasks, it did little that could have been considered as pro-active or reflecting any sense of initiative.

Indonesia's economy under Megawati improved, as indeed it almost would have had to, given how far it had plummeted in 1998 and in response to how much foreign assistance was provided. But while imports fell, due primarily to their increased cost in rupiah, Indonesia's exports also fell. At a time when a lower rupiah should have boosted export earnings, in particular from manufacturing, growth in manufactured exports actually declined between the beginning of 2000 and mid 2004, as did the critical production of oil, of which Indonesia became a net importer. Disputes between her two key and otherwise well-respected economic ministers, Kwik Kian Gie and Laksamana Sukardi, over how to deal with conglomerates, was emblematic of Indonesia's continuing economic problems and could have been resolved with decisive leadership. But Megawati distinctly lacked this sort of capacity.

While radical Islam may have been unleashed in Indonesia as a consequence of tensions built up under the repressive New Order era, the record of Megawati's government on this issue was at best ambiguous. It is correct to note that, at the time of the October 2002 Bali bombing, *Laskar Jihad* and the Islamic Defenders Front chose to close down, albeit temporarily, perhaps reflecting their declining usefulness to the TNI than for any underlying intentions. It was similarly correct to note that *Jema'ah Islamiyah* was seriously damaged, although far from destroyed, by official Indonesian efforts to prosecute those responsible for the Bali bombing, that of the Marriott Hotel and, to a lesser extent, a spate of other related attacks. Yet there was, initially, a high level of reluctance to acknowledge the existence of a problem with Islamic terrorism; indeed, it could be argued that it was foreign pressure and, to some extent, assistance that led to the relative success of the crackdown, in particular, on JI.

Notably, however, the government remained extremely sensitive, not just about the activities of radical Islamic organisations, but also about the freedom with which their associations and activities were discussed. As with earlier concerns with foreign journalism, it was the best and most accurate accounts—in this case, of Indonesia's radical Islam—that were the target of the government's wrath, which manifested itself in June 2004 when the ICG's Jakarta office was closed down and its director, Sidney Jones, and staff member Francesca Lawe-Davies were expelled from the country. Other limitations on freedom of expression became more common under Megawati, as powerful figures attempted to assert, often successfully, a capacity to silence their critics. In the defamation case brought by Tomy Winata against *Tempo* magazine, while the court's ruling found that the two journalists in question were not responsible for the proven defamation, the editor was. Against a backdrop of Winata's thugs milling outside the court and ignoring the overriding provisions of the Press Act, the court, under the provisions of the Criminal Code, sentenced *Tempo* editor Bambang Harymurti to a year in jail[11] (BBC *World Service*, 17 September 2004; *Kompas* 17 September 2004). In an editorial, the *Jakarta Post* described the ruling as 'persecution', which it regarded with 'contempt' (*Jakarta Post*, 17 September 2004).

The continuing failure and corruption of Indonesia's judicial and legal system also remained a major black spot on the record of Megawati's government, with only the most cursory of moves being put in place to provide the country with some semblance of consistent and equitable application of the law. There was some rewriting of the legal code— primarily around financial propriety, the imposition of Islamic law in Aceh and the introduction of laws against terrorism—and the establishment of a Constitutional Court. However, the law on terrorism and the Constitutional Court quickly assumed oppositional positions, reflecting less the validity of the new laws or the capacity of the court, but more what might have been understood as a (mis)reading of what constituted a major crime or crime against humanity.

While Indonesia's problems with corruption were well entrenched long before Megawati assumed office, they certainly worsened under her rule and her attempts to rein in corruption were, at best, half-hearted or token gestures. With so much of the political and institutional systems compromised by corruption and so much had it become a part of Indonesia's culture, that anything short of the most strenuous attempts to rid the state of this debilitating problem were always bound to fail.

In that there was dissatisfaction with Megawati's government, in some provinces, notably West Papua and Aceh, the sense of disaffection not just with her government, but also with the Indonesian state as a whole, was profound and had grown worse. This disaffection grew out of an extensive catalogue of grievances, yet there was virtually no effort made to address them and, in many cases, they were exacerbated. The introduction of Aceh's special provincial status as *Nanggroe Aceh Darusalam* appeared to garner little further support for the central government; the return to full-scale military operations in May 2003 showed only that any rhetorical overture by the government was, at best, hollow and, in Aceh, widely perceived as a betrayal. Similarly, in West Papua, the promise of special administrative status was undermined in reality by continuing military operations, not just against the OPM, but also against anyone who expressed concern about the exploitation of their homeland and their treatment as even less than second-class citizens by transmigrants, non-Papua officials and soldiers.

The promise of a modicum of autonomy was also undermined by the proposal to divide the province into three, and then, two. In what had, for a while, been touted as an era of reform, there were no moves to address the underlying problems that gave rise to grievances so strong that most people in these two provinces wanted to separate from the state. Indeed, the response of the state under Megawati was to return to those methods of repression that had given rise to separatist sentiments in the first place, thus ensuring a continual cycle of dissent and repression.

As a consequence, what was arguably the single biggest failure of Megawati's term in office was her disinclination to limit and, indeed, support the rising political authority of the TNI. She had been promoted as president by the TNI for exactly this reason, because she supported its nationalist agenda, because she looked to it for the imposition of stability, and because she recognised its power to undermine and effectively bring down any president who did not either subscribe to its increasingly conservative world view or at least allow it to put this into unimpeded practice.

The military solution to the Aceh problem was the primary illustration of this practice, although the TNI's reassertion of its territorial structure, its bid to return active officers to civil administrative positions, its impunity before the courts, its rebuilding and expansion of its business and criminal empire and its capacity to otherwise determine core state policy, regardless of civilian interests, all augured poorly for the substance rather than the form of Indonesia's otherwise much vaunted democratisation.

THE 2004 ELECTIONS

As early as six months or more before the first of 2004's three elections, it appeared as though Megawati's government was in political trouble. Even earlier reporting had shown that a sense of cynicism about or alienation from Indonesia's political processes was growing and that, while voters were not near any point of revolt, they were becoming disenchanted with their elected representatives (Meisburger 2003: 35–51; Emmerson 2004). As Megawati's popular standing declined, which began to occur from as early as the end of her first year in office (*Jakarta Post*, 24 July 2002; *Tempo*, 6–12 April, 2004), in typical fashion she responded by effectively doing nothing. In Java, where Megawati had also drawn a high level of support, an increasingly common view was that, not only was PDI–P inefficient, a reflection of party infighting, but also that local officials were more concerned with corruptly lining their pockets than looking after the interests of electors. From what should have been her strongest areas of support, the PDI–P, instead came a bad smell and, as a result, Megawati failed to retain much favourable perception of herself as a leader.

As the extent of the unpopularity of her party and, increasingly, of her, began to dawn, Megawati grew more concerned with the presidential ambitions of her coordinating politics and security minister, Susilo Bambang Yudhoyono, who, as Megawati floundered, the media increasingly referred to as an alternative president. Yudhoyono had never made any secret of his longer-term presidential ambitions, but when he was approached by Taufiq Kiemas to stand as Megawati's vice-presidential running mate, he refused. Taufiq responded by freezing Yudhoyono out of Cabinet, as a result of which, Yudhoyono resigned on 11 March 2004 and announced his intention to run for the presidency at the head of his tiny Democratic Party (*Partai Demokrat*, or PD).[12]

Golkar saw in PDI–P's decline—and in the public opinion polls (*Tempo*, 6–12 April 2004)—the seeds of its own revival, meaning the presidential nomination for *Golkar* became a strongly contested event. In what amounted to an election before an election, *Golkar*'s potential candidates began touring Indonesia, speaking to *Golkar* rallies in the last few months of 2003, hoping to achieve the minimum of support to contest *Golkar*'s presidential convention, from which the successful candidate would be chosen. In the end, the presidential convention chose Wiranto because *Golkar* president Akbar Tanjung's (overturned) conviction for corruption was seen as more of a political liability than was Wiranto's human rights record. Wiranto chose Abdurrahman Wahid's younger brother, Solahuddin Wahid as his running mate.

On 5 April, the elections were held for the new senate-like, 128 person Regional People's Representatives Council (*Dewan Perwakilan Rakyat Daerah*, or DPRD) and a Regional Representatives Council (*Dewan Perwaklian Daerah*, or DPD). The ballot was complex, in that it had to decide more than 400 district-level bodies and thirty-two provincial legislatures, as well as the state legislature, which comprised more than 1800 electoral contests across the country (Emmerson 2004), to be decided by Indonesia's estimated 147 million voters casting ballots on some 900 million ballot papers at 600 000 polling booths for almost half a million candidates contesting few more than 15 000 positions. The preelection campaign was replete with the usual street theatre and mass rallies that had marked the

1999 elections, yet, despite the size of its public rallies, the public opinion polls still showed that Megawati's PDI–P was still struggling. As with the 1999 elections, the 2004 DPR elections were largely bereft of policy debate or, indeed, any policies. Not surprisingly,· this lack of policy and the previously mentioned growing cynicism was reflected in a high proportion of voters—between 17 and 58 per cent, depending on the survey—who remained undecided about who they would vote for up until a few days before the elections.

In the event, the 5 April vote showed that *Golkar* had secured just over 23 per cent of the seats in the DPR, PDI–P just under 20 per cent, the PPP 10.5 per cent, the Democratic Party, Amien Rais' PAN and PKB 9.5 per cent, the PKS (the reinvented *Partai Keadilan*) just over 8 per cent and the PBB, PBR (Reform Star Party) and the PDS (Prosperous Peace Party) just over 2 per cent each, with six other minor parties securing less than 1 per cent of the seats each. PDI–P was dealt a serious blow; its presence in the DPR was reduced by around 40 per cent.

THE PRESIDENTIAL ELECTIONS

The first round of the presidential election on 5 July 2004 was the culmination of a campaign period that had stumbled along, in various guises, since late 2003. The final contenders for the presidency were the PDI–Ps Megawati and former NU head, Hasyim Muzardi, PD's Yudhoyono with his *Golkar* running mate, Jusuf Kalla, *Golkar's* Wiranto and former NU deputy leader Solahuddin Wahid, PAN's Amien Rais and former Suharto housing minister, Siswono Husodo, and PPP's Hamzah Haz with resigned Megawati transport minister, Lieutenant-General (retired) Agum Gumelar.

As the incumbent, Megawati, managed to personally retain a pool of public goodwill after initially failing to achieve the presidency in 1999. Megawati had been almost unanimously elected on the back of Abdurrahman Wahid, who was dumped by the legislature in July 2001. Yet, achieving office with such goodwill, she still managed to dissipate its opportunities. Megawati had one strength during her presidency, which was that, enjoying the overwhelming support of the Indonesian military, she was never seriously challenged until the presidential race started in earnest. Hasyim Muzadi was able to bring little popular appeal to the duo; he appeared solely as a bid to attract the NU vote, although he failed in this task. Megawati was also hampered by the increasingly negative profile of her husband, Taufiq Kiemas.

Wiranto was under a legal cloud at this time, having been indicted by a court in Dili on war crimes in East Timor in 1999. This was not so much a negative in Indonesia, where a strong sense of nationalism enabled Wiranto's candidature to be supported. However, being indicted meant that, even after the presidential elections, he could never leave Indonesia without risking being arrested. Wiranto's advantages included having *Golkar's* well-established political machine behind him, which was especially useful in the outer islands. On top of this, he was perceived as a strong (that is, quasi-authoritarian) leader and someone who had access to very significant funds, from his own extensive business investments and, it was widely believed, from sources close to Cendana (Jalan Cendana being the street on which Suharto lives in the leafy inner Jakarta suburb of Menteng) (*Tempo*, Presidential Election Edition, 2004: 16). The final—and, seemingly, most popular—candidate, according to the only semi-reliable polls, was Yudhoyono. Interestingly, for a TNI reformer, Yudhoyono was at pains to express his support for the TNI and its more conservative, arguably reactionary, turn in the post-Abdurrahman period. The other candidates were also rans, even before the first vote.

Generally speaking, the ballot was a peaceful affair, if one ignored West Papua and the continuing violence in Aceh. When the first round vote was in, it came as little surprise that Yudhoyono was returned as the most favoured candidate, even if his vote, at 33.58 per cent, was well below what the opinion polls had predicted. Wiranto proved, if nothing else, that a well-oiled (that is, well-funded) *Golkar* party machine could produce around 22 per cent of the vote, almost regardless of other circumstances, although this was not enough to secure him the coveted second position, which went to Megawati with 26 per cent. Even if Megawati's personal popularity, too, had slumped from her 1999 highs, in the final analysis, it was higher than that of her corrupt and faction-ridden party.

THE SECOND ROUND

In the period between the first and second rounds of the presidential elections, Megawati handed down a draft budget that she and her fellow drafters seemed to think would win public approval. Instead, the draft budget, which projected higher growth, lower spending and an increase in the fuel subsidy, was hailed as 'unrealistic' (*Jakarta Post*, 18 August 2004). Her sense of economic optimism was intended to appeal to voters, but, to some, started to look like Suharto's disastrous budget handed down at the beginning of 1998, which precipitated a further run on the rupiah and, soon after, his political demise.

The polls continued to show that Yudhoyono and Kalla were the preferred candidates, tracking between 56 and 66 per cent of the vote in the weeks before the ballot. Regardless of who was to take the presidency, with so many parties taking a share of the vote for the legislature (DPR), with none achieving even one-quarter of the legislative vote and with the increased power of the post-Suharto DPR relative to the presidency, any president would have to work with and reflect at least some of the various parties' interests.

MONEY POLITICS

In bidding for the presidency, the primary advantages that the PD and Yudhoyono enjoyed were that both were seen by the general public as untainted by corruption, they were viewed as the political underdog and thus gained the sympathy vote and that, after Megawati's failure, they represented a new hope for Indonesia's political future. Less positively, Yudhoyono had been a central figure in national politics over the preceding four years and he continued to work at retaining links with many of his former TNI colleagues. Reformist Lieutenant-General Agus Widjojo became his campaign manager and questions were increasingly asked, including in the media, about Yudhoyono's financial backing, not least from wealthy TNI-linked businessman and reputed gambling and vice godfather, Tomy Winata. Yudhoyono was linked to Winata through Major-General T. B. Silalahi, who was Yudhoyono's campaign team adviser as well as being president commissioner of Winata's Artha Graha Bank, in which the TNI had a 20 per cent shareholding.

Yudhoyono also received support from provincial military commanders where the DP had no local base. They were able to bring on side local business leaders, who also contributed funds, and organised criminal elements that often had links to the regional TNI and who worked in Tomy Winata's organisation. At the village level, the TNI and street-level *preman* (gangsters) helped mobilise votes. In elite support shifting to Yudhoyono, it could have been seen as self-interest, as elites jumping onto the bandwagon of the likely winner. Or, more disconcertingly, it could have been seen as Indonesia's traditional elites swamping whoever was likely to become president by way of seeing that their overwhelming weight of numbers would ensure that the president ended up reflecting their various and usually interlinked interests. In consolidating military support for his candidacy, Yudhoyono was also believed to have offered senior administrative positions to a number of generals.

THE TNI

Meanwhile, the military (TNI)—in particular the army—had reestablished itself as a major political force in Indonesian domestic affairs. The army effectively decided policy on a range of interrelated issues, such as security, the scope for changes to or reform of the constitution and on its own reform process, such as it has—or has not—been. As Abdurrahman Wahid discovered, the capacity for the TNI to undermine a president was—and remained—substantial. Fomenting disturbances in outer islands was easy to achieve in Indonesia's fragmented and still often fraught political environment and such disturbance was invariably held as reflecting the inability of a president to control the country. Knowing its own vulnerability,

Indonesia's political and economic elite had been quick to coalesce around the TNI, making it relatively easy for the military to construct a substantial opposition to political leaders it believed were trying to obstruct its self-selecting political agenda. If a president was able to come to power on the back of a block of party support in excess of 50 per cent of the vote, it might have been possible to act relatively independently of the TNI and other political parties, but with the new president coming to office with 50 per cent plus one of the direct vote (or, in the case of Yudhoyono, 50 per cent plus 11), this would not have secured majority compliance within the legislature of which no candidate enjoyed even one-quarter support.

Recognition of the TNI's renewed political strength, its institutional capacity and Yudhoyono's history as an army officer all contributed to Yudhoyono's political capacity and, increasingly, to his political style. Two weeks before the final, September ballot, even army chief-of-staff and notorious hawk, General Ryamizard Ryacudu, was persuaded by his father-in-law and former military commander, Try Sutrisno, to switch his allegiance to support Yudhoyono, in exchange for which he was promised the position of military commander. In this, Ryamizard eventually, if reluctantly, fell into line with his fellow generals. The arch-conservative Ryamizard had teamed up with the architect of the military's reformist new paradigm, Yudhoyono, less a case of strange bedfellows than more one of practical politics and some indication that perhaps Yudhoyono was not so far removed from the TNI's core values as had been supposed.

As an inflection on the preelection period or, perhaps, as symbolic of it, Indonesia's most prominent critic of the TNI, Munir, died suddenly on 8 September, twelve days before the poll. Munir had been a founding member of the Commission for Missing Persons and Victims of Violence (*Kontras*) and had co-founded Indonesia Human Rights Watch (*Imparsial*), both of which were highly critical of the TNI. Munir had been highly critical, not just of the TNI, but also of the TNI's return to political prominence and, in particular, was publicly concerned about the TNI's support for and links to Yudhoyono. Munir had been awarded a scholarship to undertake Master's research in Holland and was believed to be intending to use this opportunity to not only protect himself from further attacks, but also to expose the highest level corruption between government ministries and the military.

Munir, who had earlier been the target of a bombing attack and was widely seen as marked by the TNI, was later found to have been poisoned with arsenic.

A BOMB

Then, on 9 September, just eleven days before the presidential election, a large car bomb exploded at the gates of the Australian Embassy on busy Jalan Rasuna Said in the middle of the diplomatic and business districts. At least eleven people were killed and almost 200 injured in the blast, which was officially attributed to *Jema'ah Islamiyah*. While the attack may, indeed, have been organised by JI, it did seem odd that the car bomb was fragmentary (anti-personnel), rather than one intended to destroy a building, that there were two suicide bombers in the vehicle and that it was not actually driven at the gate of the embassy. Also, there was virtually no residue left from the explosion, indicating the use of just military-type explosives, unlike, for example, the Bali bombing, in which a combination of explosives, including a simple fertiliser and diesel mix, was used. In all, in the bombing outside the embassy, it appeared that the bomb used appeared to be expertly constructed, making it different to the non-fragmentary—although still very effective—bombs used in the Bali and Marriott attacks and militated against any sympathy JI might have hoped to claim from the event.[13]

In response to the embassy bombing, the government announced the formation of a new, predominantly anti-terror taskforce, comprising members of an existing anti-terror taskforce established after the Marriott bombing, together with police, army, navy and airforce special forces (*Destasemen* 88/*Gegana, Kopassus, Denjaka* and Bravo) under the auspices of the State Intelligence Agency, BIN. The taskforce was given powers to operate openly as well as covertly and otherwise subvert the legislated sole investigative role of the police.

Meanwhile, the election campaign, such as it was, rolled on. With only three days of formal campaigning allowed by the KPU and one week before the ballot, a publicly televised and closely scripted dialogue instead of a debate, there was little development beyond the positions that had been articulated—or not articulated, as most observers agreed. Even after having demanded an ostensibly controllable dialogue, Megawati stumbled over the most basic questions from the carefully selected panel and asked for some of the questions to be repeated, seeming to not understand questions and not having a ready supply of answers. By contrast, Yudhoyono appeared calm and confident, with a ready supply of pat answers to the generally unchallenging questions.

THE ELECTION RESULT

Throughout Indonesia, the day of Indonesia's first direct presidential election, 20 September 2004, was largely quiet, with the usually teeming bigger cities seeming almost deserted. People had voted early and, in most cases, gone home to await the outcome. There were a few reports of relatively minor irregularities at polling booths, but anticipated violence, an almost standard prediction, completely failed to materialise. Voters did not have to wait long for the result as, with only one pair of figures to add up, it became clear within hours of the polling booths closing that, with a strong showing of the vote, Susilo Bambang Yudhoyono would be elected president. It was to be a convincing, perhaps emphatic, win—60.8 per cent of the vote—while allowing Megawati enough of the vote for it also to be accepted as credible.

Golkar chairman and arch political realist, Akbar Tanjung, had earlier said that any move that Yudhoyono wished to make as president would be closely scrutinised by the DPR. Since April, it had seemed that, if Yudhoyono was successful, he would encounter potential difficulties with a hostile DPR, but with Akbar's statement, the president-elect had been formally placed on notice. And, as if to hammer home the point about *Golkar's* lack of tolerance for compromise, at three in the morning on the day of the presidential ballot, a special meeting of its central executive board voted to expel nine of *Golkar's* so-called reform faction members, which, under Law 31/2002 on political parties, meant that two of them would lose their seats in the DPR. In 2005, Akbar was replaced as chairman of *Golkar* by vice-president Jusuf Kolla, ensuring Yudhoyono an easier time as president.

As Indonesia's new president, it was hard not to believe that Yudhoyono represented some sort of change for the better. Yudhoyono again trotted out the rhetoric of *reformasi*, which had become deeply devalued and had, in a practical sense, ceased to exist. But the task ahead of Yudhoyono remained enormous and expectations were likely to be dashed against hard political reality.

The first step that Yudhoyono took was to launch a campaign against corruption, which quickly began to snare at least some higher profile public offenders, such as Aceh's governor Abdullah Puteh, but a thorough overhaul of the judiciary and the legal code, which was critical, remained off the immediate agenda, being too hard to push through without legislative support. Indonesia's problem with terrorism generally and Islamic terrorism in particular also presented a major issue for Yudhoyono, acting as it did as a brake on foreign investment as well as a source of internal political instability. In this, Yudhoyono owed much to the more formally Islamic, or *santri*, vote he had received. The question of terrorism linked to the relationship that Indonesia's intelligence services and the military maintained with militant Islamic groups. This, in turn, led to the issue of military reform, in essence the need to put the military under civilian authority and to remove its relationships with politics, business and crime, all of which were interlinked and mutually dependent. As a former military reformer, Yudhoyono had the best credentials as president for undertaking such a task, but the ascension and hegemony of a conservative and politically active ideology within the military, and Yudhoyono's links to it, stood as a real obstacle to meaningful change in this area. As all political aspirants in Indonesia knew, no one could afford to alienate the military and still expect to be able to govern without serious interference.

Finally, Yudhoyono's financial backers would at least expect to be allowed to run their businesses without interference and would probably have expected the benefit of government concessions or contracts. As businesspeople—and criminals—there was little altruism in their support for Yudhoyono, but much expectation of backing a winner and, hence, receiving a payoff.

As president, no matter which way Yudhoyono turned, he was facing obstacles, impediments, vested interests and a still fragmented society ruled by a still venal elite. He was faced with the choice of acceding to these pressures and doing little, if anything, but running a reformist agenda despite such obstacles and, perhaps, facing some of the problems that beset Abdurrahman Wahid as president, or plotting a middle course, pushing through the easier changes, leaving those more difficult and rewarding some supporters and alienating others. The appointment of his new Cabinet suggested that Yudhoyono would appoint some ministers on merit, reward his supporters and try to alienate as few people as possible. Yudhoyono's reformism was tempered by his personal history of acting cautiously, yet, if Yudhoyono achieved only 20 per cent of that which he had announced as his goals, he would still have made some progress in exceptionally difficult circumstances. The Indonesian people now had the opportunity of removing him from office in five years time if he failed to meet their expectations.

NOTES

1   Pemberton discusses Javanese tradition and culture and the construction of the Indonesian state from a particularly critical perspective in his *On the Subject of 'Java'*, Cornell University Press, Ithaca and London, 1994.

2   *Kopkamtib* was formally dismantled in September 1988 in response to international criticism and to lower the profile of the army in internal security. It was replaced by the Body for Coordinating National Stability and Security (Badan Koordinasi Bantuan Pemantapan Stabilitas Nasional), known as Bakorstanas. Bakorstanas worked under the same legislative provisions as Kopkamtib.

3   These details are based on notes taken as an official election monitor at KPU briefings.

4   While Jema'ah Islamiyah has its own origins, it has parallels with not only the Ikhwan al-Mulsimin, but also the similarly named Jamaat-I Islami founded in India in 1941. Like Jema'ah Islamiyah, both organisations understand Islam as a totalising religiopolitical system that is incompatible with secular ideologies (Robinson 1999: 51).

5   'Pondok' usually means 'hut', but is also colloquially used to denote an Islamic boarding school.

6   A number of graduates of Pondok Ngruki have been identified with various terrorists and terrorist acts, including the Bali bombing of 2002 and Fathur Rohman al-Ghozi, a bomb-making expert arrested in the Philippines (studied 1982–89).

7   Arabic for 'leader' or 'commander'.

8   Indonesian police claimed that Hambali was involved in thirty-nine separate bombing incidents (*Jakarta Post*, 22 August 2003).

9   LJ's strength reached up to 10–13 000 fighters by 2001, with up to 6000 deployed to Ambon and environs, although some estimates suggest that it had no more than 7000 fighters, with 1–2000 deployed to Maluku (Schulze 2002: 60).

10   Van Klinken notes that sectarian violence in Poso began as early as December 1998 (van Klinken 2003).

11   Harymurti remained free, pending an appeal against the sentence.

12   Yudhoyono had founded the Democratic Party in 1999, but had left it fallow as he pursued his political career, first with President Abdurrahman Wahid, and then, with President Megawati. The party was revived in early 2004 to contest the DPR elections and to be his personal presidential vehicle.

13   One theory of terrorism is that its initial target is much less important than the generalised repression it inspires, thus creating a popular backlash that plays to the terrorists' agenda.

15 | East Timor: The Difficult Birth of a New State[1]

In the period after East Timor achieved its independence in 2001, it had become clear that at least some of the doubts and fears about the small county's future had been realised. Poverty and unemployment were serious problems, with East Timor immediately becoming not only the poorest state in SEA, but also one of the poorest states in the world. Unemployment, which was running at about 40 per cent, directly reflected the gap where many jobs generated by Indonesia had been. Revenues expected from oil and gas deposits in the Timor Sea were also limited by Australia's refusal to negotiate new seabed boundaries based on international law. And even East Timor's new government, dominated by members of the government party Fretilin, who had spent most or all of the period of occupation abroad, at times appeared distant and aloof, not only from ordinary East Timorese, but also even those of the leadership who had stayed and fought for independence.

As a consequence of a high level of disaffection, crime quickly became a problem, not least against the remaining foreigners, UN and aid agency staff. As well, a quasipolitical organisation, opposed to the government and even the nature of the state, had emerged, threatening widespread destabilisation. Meanwhile, just across the border in West Timor, former members of East Timor's Indonesian-backed militias continued to cause trouble, mostly through intimidation, cross-border smuggling and, increasingly, rare raids. As the UN formally began to leave East Timor, the tiny state appeared vulnerable.

The first attempt at an independent state of East Timor had been swamped by Indonesia's invasion within days of its declaration. The second attempt, which was ultimately successful, was marked by widespread bloodshed and massive destruction, from which East Timor was still struggling to recover.[2] The wave of Indonesian-sponsored violence and destruction left more than a thousand butchered and had displaced most of the population of 850 000, with around 250 000 being forcibly removed to West Timor. This violence, conducted by so-called militias made up of thugs, hired often from West Timor and led by members of TNI, outraged world opinion. As a result, although somewhat belatedly, a number of countries under the banner of the UN organised a peace-enforcement mission to East Timor, which was the forerunner of a UN-organised interim

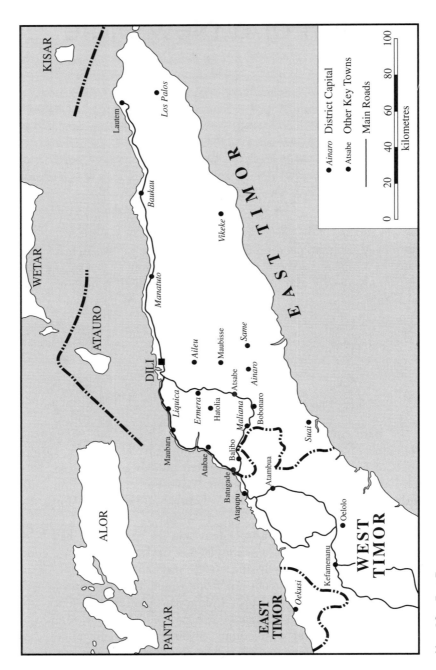

Map 12 East Timor

administration, the UN Transitional Authority in East Timor (UNTAET) ahead of full self-government. The task of this interim administration, and the government to follow it, was to build a state from the ground up and bring into focus the full range of political, economic, and sociocultural issues that creating a new state implied. In this it was only partly successful.

EARLY HISTORY

East Timor's history is more complicated than many, at least for such a small (19 000 square kilometres) and relatively obscure place. Prior to the Portuguese establishing a Dominican religious order and trading ports there in the mid sixteenth century,[3] Timor (*Timor Loroe Sa'e*, or Land of the Rising Sun) was a collection of small and competing states. The southern part of Timor was predominantly Polynesian in ethnic makeup, the north mostly Melanesian, the central regions largely aboriginal. Added to this ethnic mix, Chinese traders seeking sandalwood had been visiting the island for centuries before the Portuguese arrived, while traders from other nearby islands were regular visitors. As a result of the ethnic variety and the rugged, difficult terrain, sixteen separate linguistic groups along with around thirty-five additional dialects developed in that last area controlled by the Portuguese, corresponding to contemporary East Timor (De Matos 1974; Leitao 1956).

During the sixteenth and seventeenth centuries, the small states of Timor were frequently at war with each other, primarily in a bid to control the island's lucrative sandalwood trade. Their reception of the Portuguese was little different. Portugal only gradually extended its control over the island because it had to face several rebellions. By the time it had managed to subjugate most of the *liuri* (local kings), the Dutch had begun to expand their regional interests into this Portuguese territory. In two wars—1859 and 1913—Timor was partitioned along its present lines, leaving the enclave of Oecusse within the Dutch territory (Hiorth 1985: 6–7). This was the state of the island when Japanese forces occupied Dutch Timor in February 1942.

The Japanese left Portuguese Timor, as it was a colony of the fascist but otherwise neutral Portuguese government. However, on 17 December 1941, Australia, concerned about the potential for Timor to be used as a base for the launch of an invasion, violated Portugal's neutrality by sending 200 commandos to operate in the territory. In the ensuing conflict, the local people supported the Australian commandos in their work against the Japanese. The price for these people was that some 40 000 of them were killed by the Japanese in retribution, with more dying in later Allied bombing (Jardine 1995: 21–2). It was from this time that many Australians began to identify a special relationship with the people of East Timor, which both assisted and complicated East Timor's bid for independence in the last quarter of the twentieth century.

EXIT PORTUGAL

Portuguese Timor's postwar period was quiet, with the colony being perhaps the least developed of Portugal's overseas possessions. However, the cost of retaining its colonies burdened Portugal and, with the winds of political change sweeping the Iberian Peninsula, on 24 April 1974 the fascist dictatorship of Marcello Caetano was overthrown by a leftist military uprising. The intention was for Portugal to cast off its colonial dependencies quickly and, as a consequence, political parties began forming in the colony. Founded on 20 May 1974, the Timorese Social Democrats, soon renamed the *Frente Revolucionaria de Timor L'Este Independente* (Revolutionary Front for an Independent East Timor, known as Fretilin), was the biggest and most popular party. It was trailed by the *Uniao Democratica de Timor* (Timorese Democratic Union, or UDT), founded on 11 May 1974, which comprised small businesspeople, property owners and officials, and which, initially, supported continued integration with Portugal, then, quickly opted for independence, but later for integration with Indonesia. The *Associacao Popular Democratica de Timor* (Timorese Popular Democratic Association, or *Apodeti*) and *Kliban Oan Timor Aswain* (KOTA, or Sons of the Mountain Warriors) accounted for less than 10 per cent of popular support; each supported integration with Indonesia and were invented and supported by Indonesia's military intelligence (Dunn 1996: 65–6; Hiorth 1985: 21–3; Joliffe 1978: chs 2–5).

Fretilin and UDT initially came together in May 1975 in an alliance seeking independence. An election for a popular assembly to oversee decolonisation was planned for October 1976, but with Indonesian intelligence conspiring against the leftist Fretilin, the UDT was led to believe the leftist party would soon launch a coup. To forestall this possibility, UDT, supported by local police, made a preemptive strike on 11 August 1975 against Fretilin in what was called the Revolutionary Anti-Communist Movement of 11 August. However, Fretilin enjoyed the support of around 3000 Timorese soldiers who were members of the Portuguese army, as well as some thousands more of the local militia (Dunn 1996: 38). Fighting was fierce, but it was over within days, costing 2000–3000 lives. The remnants of the Portuguese administration fled to the nearby island of Atauro, and then, to Portugal. Never a great colonial master, the Portuguese left the colony in abject retreat, although Portugal continued its claim to East Timorese sovereignty, which it finally relinquished to the UN. UDT–*Apodeti–Kota* (pro-integration) remnants fled to West Timor from where, with the fulsome assistance of the Indonesian military, they began cross-border raids. In the post-civil war period, Fretilin reassembled the machinery of government and, apart from the security problem in the west, life resumed close to usual under an interim administration (Dunn 1996: chs 8, 9).

ENTER INDONESIA

The first Indonesian pro-integration raids were on the northern coastal border town of Batu Gade, which was abandoned by *Falintil* troops in the face of superior numbers and tanks. Skirmishes continued in the border area until October, when Indonesian troops and anti-Fretilin irregulars attacked the town of Balibo, about 20 kilometres southeast of Batu Gade. It was in this attack that five Australian journalists were killed by the invading force, which increased Australian interest in the territory, interest that was to have implications almost one-quarter of a century later. Despite these forays by Indonesian-backed forces across the border, *Falintil* (*Forcas Armada de Liberacao Nacional de Timor L'Este*, or Armed Forces for the National Liberation of East Timor, the armed wing of Fretilin, later under the CNRT) put up an unexpectedly stiff resistance, prompting Indonesian military planners to reconsider their approach to what was, by now, a clear desire to occupy the territory of Portuguese Timor. On 24 November 1975, Fretlin asked the UN to push for the withdrawal of Indonesian forces from its territory and, four days later, declared East Timor an independent republic. On 30 November, UDT and *Apodeti* announced their support for East Timor's integration into Indonesia. On 7 December 1975, Indonesia launched its formal invasion of East Timor, starting with a parachute landing on Dili ahead of more than 40 000 troops invading the territory. The wholesale slaughter of East Timorese people by Indonesian troops that immediately followed presaged a major campaign of violence and dislocation. It has been variously estimated that 60 000 people were killed in the first two months immediately following the invasion. In May 1976, hand-picked East Timorese delegates voted for East Timor's incorporation into Indonesia,[4] which was formally endorsed by Indonesia's President Suharto on 17 July. This decision was never accepted by the UN, which voted repeatedly for Indonesia to withdraw its forces from the territory.

Despite the overwhelming presence of Indonesian armed forces in East Timor, *Falintil* kept up an active military campaign throughout the later 1970s. Quickly abandoning conventional warfare, *Falintil* opted for guerrilla tactics, which were relatively successful in tying down more than 20 000 Indonesian troops. However, in the late 1970s and early 1980s, Indonesian forces instituted a policy of relocating villagers believed to be supporting *Falintil* to secured sites. Without adequate food, water or sanitation, these sites had, by the early 1980s, contributed in large measure to the deaths of more than 160 000 people, one-quarter of East Timor's population (Kiernan 2003; ACFOA 1991: 3).

UNDER INDONESIA

Under Indonesia, East Timor underwent a number of profound changes. Apart from the massive violence and social dislocation, which, on a per capita basis, matched the atrocities of the Khmer Rouge in Cambodia, Indonesia moved to put its stamp on the territory. The first move was for senior military figures to take over or set up businesses that traded directly with Singapore, bypassing Jakarta and, hence, the need for taxation or other forms of accountability. The military, for example, held a monopoly on East Timor's export of coffee, which, until the development of gas and oil, was by far its most lucrative trade. While this military-dominated economy proved to be a profitable source of income for many officers, it also had the effect of further impoverishing this already poor territory. Businesses and property once owned by Portuguese citizens were taken over by Indonesians. The military made considerable profits by selling established businesses to new Indonesian owners, even though the sellers did not legally hold title.

Under Indonesia, education was expanded and the number of secondary schools increased. In part, this policy of educational development was intended to inculcate in the East Timorese a sense of belonging to the greater Indonesian nation. The medium of education was Bahasa Indonesia, which did have the effect of standardising this language among virtually all East Timorese who went to school following the period of Indonesia's occupation.

Indonesia also built a number of health clinics, although most East Timorese received little benefit from them. Who the clinics and, increasingly, the schools did serve was the influx of transmigrants and economic migrants from around Indonesia. By 1998, it was widely estimated that more than 150 000 non-East Timorese lived in East Timor, up to two-thirds of them centred in the capital, Dili. Administrative jobs were created to run the territory, but these were often given to non-East Timorese. Those who were brought to East Timor on government business received a hardship allowance of 99 per cent of their salary, which boosted local inflation and artificially inflated the average income of people in the territory. The standard of living for some East Timorese did rise under the Indonesians, but for many it did not. Even the roads that Indonesia built in East Timor served, in large part, to transport troops and equipment from district to district, while many of the major bridges and water supply projects were built with foreign aid.

Throughout all of this, East Timorese people were regarded as less than human by their new Indonesian masters. Women were raped as a matter of course, opponents to Indonesian rule murdered and people regularly disappeared, although it was presumed that they had been killed. At no stage did the vast majority of the East Timorese people ever feel that they lived in other than an occupied territory. The Indonesian armed forces continued to act as if they were an insensitive occupying force, rather than as the guardians of the state and protectors of the peace.

Meanwhile, *Falintil* continued its guerrilla campaign from the mountains, reduced in the 1980s to a small and desperate force of a few hundred, then rebuilt from the late 1980s on a small but tough and highly disciplined military group, consisting of four semi-independent units totalling perhaps 2000.[5]

POLITICAL CONSOLIDATION

In 1981, after the Indonesian army's notorious 'fence of legs' campaign, in which East Timorese civilians were pushed in front of Indonesian troops advancing on *Falintil* positions, the political parties were more closely coordinated under the overall banner of national liberation, a policy that rejuvenated the independence movement. Briefly, in 1983, the Indonesian government agreed to enter into peace talks, however, General Benny Murdani, who became commander-in-chief of the Indonesian armed forces in that year, cancelled the peace talks and stepped up the military campaign against the resistance movement. As head of military intelligence, Murdani had been one of the two key proponents and architects of Indonesia's invasion of East Timor[6] and was regarded in Indonesian military circles as a hawk. If it were not to disappear entirely, the East Timorese resistance had little choice but to unite (Jardine 1995: 54–7; Singh 1995: 145–6).

As the senior ranks of *Falintil* thinned out as a consequence of Indonesia's continued attacks, particularly with the death of *Falintil* leader Nicolao Lobato in 1978, leadership was formally handed to regional guerrilla leader Jose 'Xanana' Gusmao in 1981. Gusmao was born on 20 June 1946 in Manatuto. As a young man, he trained at the Jesuit seminary near Dare, just south of Dili. As one of the territory's few well-educated young men, he quickly joined the then newly established political party, Fretilin. By August 1975, Gusmao was working for Fretilin's Department of Information and was elected to the party's central committee. However, following the Indonesian invasion in December that year, Gusmao fled to the east of the island, to a stronghold behind Mount Matebean, where he led the armed resistance movement in that area.

Gusmao's first major initiative as leader was, on 26 April 1986, to establish the Council of National Maubere Resistance (CNRM) as a clandestine coalition of all East Timorese groups, including Fretilin, UDT and the student group, *Restencia National dos Estudantes de Timor L'Este* (*Renetil*, or National Resistance of East Timorese Students). Maubere, which, in Tetun, means 'older brother', was used to describe the relationship between the active pro-independence fighters and ordinary East Timorese. This meant that *Falintil* worked more openly with East Timorese people and relied on them more closely to provide a support base for their activities, paving the way for the independence movement's next step.

The next major move in the political delineation within East Timorese politics occurred in 1987, with the formal separation of *Falintil* from Fretilin. This division did not reflect any ideological division between the political and armed groups, rather, it was a recognition of the need for the armed resistance movement to represent all anti-Indonesian political groupings. Despite being *Falintil's* commander, it was from this time that Gusmao steered the independence movement away from open armed conflict towards a policy of civil disobedience. The cost of the armed conflict, in terms of lives, and the slim chance that *Falintil* would ever be able to defeat Indonesia's military in the field, pushed Gusmao to look at attracting international attention to their cause, while still keeping up pressure on the Indonesian authorities within East Timor. The recruitment of young, urban East Timorese—in most cases, those born in the years since Indonesia's invasion—into the pro-independence ranks breathed new life into the independence campaign. It was from this time that independence started to look like a faint possibility. The adoption of this policy also stamped Gusmao's personal authority on the pro-independence movement, elevating him from the status of guerrilla leader to cult figure within the pro-independence community.

THE SANTA CRUZ MASSACRE

Despite the already long and bloody history of Indonesian atrocities in East Timor, perhaps the issue that most galvanised world opinion on East Timor was the killing of protestors at the Santa Cruz Cemetery in Dili on 12 November 1991. The protesters were attending the burial of a student who had been killed two days previously, although the event was also clearly an opportunity to protest against Indonesia's continued occupation of East Timor and active repression of its people. The attack against the protesters also corresponded to a planned—but abandoned—visit to Dili by a Portuguese delegation.

One version of events has it that the massacre was prompted by the former commander-in-chief of Indonesia's armed forces, Benny Murdani, as a means of embarrassing Suharto's son-in-law, (then) Lieutenant-Colonel Prabowo Subianto, who was at that time stationed in Dili. It was also a sign that the army would continue to take a tough line against protesters in East Timor. This incident backfired against this suggested plan, arousing even greater antipathy towards Indonesia among the people of East Timor. Prabowo was not held accountable for the incident and two key Murdani supporters lost their jobs.

A more conventional interpretation of events was that the army was trying to reassert its authority over dissident East Timorese, although this seems unlikely, given the public nature of the attack (Kingsbury 1998: 119–20).

Regardless of motives, almost without warning, soldiers opened fire on the protesters at close range. They later bayoneted wounded protesters and were alleged to have gone to a nearby hospital where they killed the wounded who had been taken there. Parts of the massacre were recorded on videotape and broadcast and rebroadcast throughout the world. It was a public relations disaster for Indonesia and aroused considerable international sympathy for the East Timorese cause. The Indonesian government exacerbated the situation by initially claiming that only nineteen had been killed and ninety-one wounded, later, after a formal inquiry, raising the number to fifty dead. However, other accounts put the final death toll from this encounter at 273 (Grant 1996: 40).

It was far from the most bloody of Indonesia's massacres of East Timorese, but it did come at a time when the issue of East Timor was widely thought to have been resolved. In fact, what it showed the international community was two things. The first was that Indonesia's army would not hesitate in using brutal force against unarmed civilians. The second was that popular opposition to Indonesian rule in East Timor continued to be widespread and growing. This, in turn, reflected the new policy on the part of *Falintil*, to shift the focus of its campaign against Indonesia from direct armed conflict towards bringing the conflict back to the towns of East Timor, through civil disobedience campaigns. It was a high price to pay, but the Santa Cruz massacre refocused world attention on East Timor in a way it had not been focused since—or perhaps even including—1975.

It was also from around the time of the Santa Cruz massacre that the Roman Catholic church, already converting East Timorese at a rapid rate, began to take on some of the traits of radical Latin America: liberation theology. Most ordinary East Timorese claim the church was slow to accept the independence struggle, but, as the ranks of its congregations swelled with pro-independence activists and it retained Tetum Praca as the language of instruction, it was transformed from the bottom up.

Although he had already begun speaking out about the possibility of a referendum on East Timor's future, by 1992 Bishop Carlos Belo was still very cautious about his role and the role of the church in pressing for independence.[7] However, within three years he had become an outspoken advocate of the human rights of East Timorese people and, by extension, an opponent of continued Indonesian occupation. In 1996, Belo and Fretilin's international spokesman, Jose Ramos Horta, were awarded the Nobel Peace Prize.

THE CAPTURE OF XANANA GUSMAO

As a part of the independence movement's policy to bring the struggle from the countryside to the towns, Gusmao moved to Dili in 1991. It was from there that he personally directed the civil disobedience campaign. Living in Dili was a high-risk strategy that was to come undone on 20 November 1992. Betrayed by an informer, Xanana was arrested. It was initially thought he would be charged with subversion, which, potentially, carried the death penalty in Indonesia, but the charges were later modified to those of rebellion, illegal possession of weapons and the advocation of separatism. Initially, he was sentenced to life imprisonment, but, following international pressure, in 1993 his sentence was commuted to twenty years in prison.

While Fretilin and UDT had worked closely together since the mid 1980s, there had been some reluctance on the part of their members to form a full coalition, which was based on the ideological differences of the two organisations, lingering animosities flowing from the August 1975 civil war and UDT's association, however forced, with the Indonesian army for some years thereafter. However, with UDT increasingly firmly in the pro-independence camp, it became clear to UDT and to Fretilin that, in order to secure international support, they needed to present a cohesive front. This was done through the establishment in 1997 of the *Conselho Nacional de Resistencia Timorense* (National Council for Timorese Resistance, or CNRT). CNRT became the primary vehicle through which aspirations for independence could be channelled. Leaders from both parties joined the CNRT, which became, in effect, a peak body; Fretilin and UDT continued to exist as separate political parties. *Falintil* shifted its political association to the CNRT, bringing some UDT members into its ranks in the process. The makeup of the CNRT included Fretilin and UDT members at its top level; Xanana Gusmao, leader of both *Falintil* and Fretilin while still in jail, was elected to the position of president of the CNRT while still retaining his title of supreme commander of *Falintil*.

INDONESIA RECONSIDERS

Following the resignation of Suharto as Indonesia's president in May 1998, his successor, Habibie, moved to assuage the international community's concerns over a range of issues, while also instituting some liberalising procedures. Apart from releasing some political prisoners, lifting many media restrictions and making moves towards cleaning up the most obvious cases of corruption and nepotism, Habibie began to look to further placating a restive international community. The cost of maintaining East Timor, in terms of military presence, the infrastructure required to support the military and the Indonesian bureaucracy and what the Indonesian government claimed was its investment in human infrastructure through education and health, was, at US$50 million a year, higher per head of population than for any other province. However, 'a lot poured out of it, into the pockets of corrupt military and civilian officials' (McBeth 1999c). Some estimates suggest as much as 30 per cent of spending was lost on corruption. In terms of revenues locally raised and expenditures, 7.6 per cent of local government expenditure was raised within East Timor, 92.4 per cent of it coming from Jakarta (Tesoro 1999). But this did not account for the redirection of a massive proportion of East Timor's economy, nor for the disparities in income distribution that were usually defined along ethnic lines.[8]

As a consequence, and because of the international concern expressed over Indonesia's continued involvement in East Timor, on 20 June 1998 President Habibie offered to free Xanana Gusmao, withdraw troops and create a state of special autonomy for East Timor if the world recognised it as a part of Indonesia. It was only the first step in a protracted negotiation and one that was quickly rejected by Gusmao as 'diplomatic blackmail'. Portugal, however, quickly jumped on the opportunity to re-open dialogue on East Timor, saying that, 'If Indonesia is aiming for democracy, it is their duty to guarantee the East Timorese people the right to choose how they want to live' (Spencer 1999). Discussion continued and, by November, it was becoming clear that Habibie was looking for a genuine resolution to the issue. On 27 January 1999, he announced that the people of East Timor could decide on their future. They would be given the chance to vote on whether they wished to remain a part of Indonesia, under what was claimed would be a wide-ranging autonomy, or to opt for independence.

While this offer was, at one level, widely appreciated, most commentators, including Xanana Gusmao, asked for a longer timeframe in which the process could be undertaken. The UN, which was to supervise the ballot, also asked for a longer timeframe. Habibie refused, locking the UN into conducting the ballot within seven months. In part, Habibie's refusal to allow a longer timeframe acknowledged that, at a later time, he would probably no longer be president and that his successor might have a very different policy on the status of East Timor. At that time, Habibie's most likely successor was Megawati Sukarnoputri, who had already made clear her opposition to East Timor becoming independent, a position she reiterated in East Timor just days before the ballot took place.

The agreement that formalised the arrangement, signed on 5 May 1999, precluded the UN from having an armed presence in East Timor (UN 1999a: pt 4). The Indonesian police would, the Indonesian government claimed, guarantee security. Yet, before the 5 May agreement had even been signed, the security situation in East Timor had begun to seriously deteriorate, reflecting a deep reluctance on the part of many senior TNI figures, including the commander-in-chief of the TNI, General Wiranto, to accept Habibie's decision on East Timor. It also reflected a deteriorating relationship between Wiranto and Habibie and what amounted to competing visions for Indonesia's future.

So far as Wiranto was concerned, East Timor was primarily a military issue and secondarily a political issue. Wiranto had spent most of his military career as a *Kostrad* officer, at least once taking part in anti-insurgency operations in East Timor during the bloody crackdown of 1981. Also at stake was the pride of the TNI, the fact that many hundreds of Indonesian soldiers were buried in East Timor (and up to 10 000 more elsewhere) and that the old bugbear of state unity was perceived to be threatened by one of the provinces achieving independence. It was from the time of Habibie's announcement that East Timor's TNI-backed pro-integration militias became active.

Wiranto was criticised for having failed to contain the activities of pro-integration militias in East Timor. The general belief is that Wiranto was well aware of what had been happening in East Timor (Tavares 1999) and that, by failing to act against it, despite Habibie's explicit wishes, he endorsed or even ordered the activities. Soon after Habibie's announcement on East Timor, a Crisis Team on East Timor was established to wage a 'dirty war' against pro-independence groups (Tapol 1999a). This team was headed by Major-General Zacky Anwar Makarim, who stepped down as head of military intelligence (*Baden Intelijen ABRI*, or BIA) to take up the new position; Zacky was head of intelligence in East Timor at the time of the Dili massacre in 1991. Extraordinarily, Zacky was also appointed as liaison officer between the TNI and the UN in East Timor, which was, at that time, his official public role.

With Zacky in charge, the crisis team set up the militias,[9] comprising around 6000 paid and press-ganged East Timorese, as well as large numbers of West Timorese and other islanders in thirteen organisations. The militias included the better known *Aitarak*, *Besi Merah Butih* and *Lahorus Merah Putih/Halilintar*, respectively in the districts of Dili, Liquisa and Bobonaro. *Naga Merah dan Darah Merah* was set up in Ermera, *Laksau Merah Putih* in Kova Lima, *Mahidin* was based in Ainaro, *Abelai* in Same, AHI in Aileu, *Mahadomi* in Manatuto, *Saka* in Baucau, *Sera* in Viqueque, *Tim Alfa* in Lauten and *Darah Merah* in Ambeno Oecusse. These militias were supported and largely armed by the regional Udayana IX Military Command and occasionally led in the field by (sometimes former) military intelligence officers associated with the *Satuan Tugas Intelijen* (Intelligence Duty Unit, or STI) and *Kopassus* (Tapol 1999b). Through what it called *Operasi Sapu Jagad* (Operation Global Clean-Sweep), these gangs were responsible for hundreds of deaths in East Timor between January and August 1999 and caused more than 60 000 people to flee their villages, creating a serious refugee problem. Officials from the CNRT were among the murdered and its offices in the western part of East Timor were closed (Tapol 1999a). At the same time, tens of thousands of non-East Timorese who had been living there began to stream out of the territory. It was clear that their time of relatively easy living in a relatively safe place was coming to an end. A further element of Operation Global Clean-Sweep was to disrupt the UN process in East Timor (Tapol 1999a). Requests by Habibie, the nominal supreme commander of TNI, for it to rein in the militias and to impose order in the province were contemptuously ignored.

Despite the efforts of the TNI-backed militias, it became clear well ahead of the ballot that the pro-independence vote would succeed. This was even noted in a letter from a senior Indonesian bureaucrat in Dili to

Indonesia's coordinating minister of politics and security (Garnadi 1999). Despite the atmosphere of violence and intimidation, UNAMET functioned with great precision, reaching into the most remote villages and registering the most distant residents. Even at the most basic level,[10] its public education campaign appeared to sink in; its registration of virtually all eligible voters—some 460 000 of the territory's 850 000 people—as well as those living in other parts of Indonesia and overseas, was an outstanding success.

THE BALLOT

The weeks leading up to the ballot were marked by a high level of violence and intimidation that escalated after UNAMET began its active presence in East Timor. The thirteen militias set up by Zacky, under the control of the *Apodeti* military leader Joao Tavares, operated under the banner of the *Pasukan Perjuangan Integrasi* (PPI, or Integration Struggle Troops) (Tavares 1999). Despite the legality of the CNRT as a party to contest the ballot, the pro-autonomy (pro-integration) groups kept up a campaign of violence against CNRT members and offices. The pro-autonomy groups divided into the *Forum Perdamaian, Demokrasi dan Keadilan* (FPDK, or Forum for Peace, Democracy and Justice), the *Barisan Rakyat Timor Timur* (BRTT, or People's Front of East Timor) and the militia-based PPI. Roadblocks were put up to stop the movement of pro-independence supporters and to stop humanitarian assistance getting to the refugee camps that had been established in remote areas. These roadblocks were manned by militia members armed with often crude homemade weapons. Their guns, in particular, were based on the firing mechanism of shotguns housed in homemade bodies. Throughout August, as they began to hand in their homemade weapons, the militias were increasingly armed with the TNI's own weapons, including M-16, G3, SS-1 and AK47 automatic rifles, 9 mm pistols and, in the period just before the ballot, hand grenades. By this stage, the distinction between the militias, the TNI and the police had become effectively non-existent.

In Maliana, the provincial capital of the district that was the site of some of the most obvious militia activity in the pre-ballot period, the local Halilintar militia openly operated out of the local TNI headquarters.[11] The police, mostly from the paramilitary *Brimob* (Mobile Brigade) group, actively assisted militia members with transport and were reported by eyewitnesses to have shot villagers when militia rampaged through the village of Memo, near Maliana, on 28 August. There were many such reports of close association between the TNI, police and militias. Militia openly occupied police posts between Batu Gade and the outskirts of Dili. TNI officers and non-commissioned officers were, in some cases, belatedly removed from their posts as a consequence of official and repeated UNAMET complaints about their involvement with the militias.[12]

'JUST KILL—KILL EVERYBODY'

Despite such superficial acknowledgment of the links between the TNI, the police and the militias, the violence continued almost unchecked. The two moments that it seemed to stop were, in early August, around the day of the visit to East Timor by Australia's foreign minister, Alexander Downer, and during the day of the ballot itself. Apart from that, it escalated in ferocity from July onwards. Killings and kidnappings became more frequent, more homes were burnt and more villages ransacked. When faced with the prospect that the pro-integration camp might not win the ballot, one of the key organisers of the FPDK, Filomeno Orai, was asked if he would guarantee a peaceful outcome. 'Peace?' he said. 'Why would we want peace? If the vote is for independence we'll just kill—kill everybody' (McBeth 1999c: 13). Even on the night of the ballot, the village of Ritabou, near Maliana, was put to the torch. It was from this time that UNAMET staff, in particular the polling staff, began to pull out of the provinces. This time also marked the beginning of the killing of East Timorese people employed by UNAMET, as well as of pro-independence supporters.

While the violence during the campaign period and in the days following the ballot had escalated, no one seemed prepared for the tidal wave of killing, burning and looting that took place starting within an hour of the announcement of the ballot outcome. Even if the ballot had been cancelled, there was a widespread belief among UNAMET security advisers and the CNRT that there would be an attempt to kill or scatter pro-independence supporters. As it turned out, the overwhelming vote for independence unleashed a wave of fury the scale of which neither the CNRT nor UNAMET seemed to expect. Despite all the intimidation and the fact that many people did not believe their vote was secret, an amazing 98.6 per cent of registered voters participated in the poll and, of them, 78.5 per cent voted in favour of independence.

THE REACTION

In many parts of East Timor, the killings were wholesale. The official death toll, based on a body count by UN staff, was less than 2000, however, local reports continued to refer to much larger numbers, such as between 2000 and 3000 people being killed in and around the town of Suai alone. No one was safe from the slaughter, except for the 250 000 or so forced at gunpoint to be shipped to refugee camps in West Timor (UNHCR 1999). Hundreds of others were herded onto boats, ostensibly to be sent to other islands, yet the boats began to return within hours, with no refugees on board. The refugees never made it to any islands and the belief was that the passengers had been killed and their bodies dumped at sea (see McDonald et al. 2002 for a detailed account of this violence). Despite claims by pro-integration groups, the violence was not in response to what they alleged was electoral fraud. The ballot was probably the most clean and transparent in Indonesia's history, despite the pre-ballot violence perpetrated by those people who later claimed the vote was somehow rigged.

At least some of the attacks on civilians were an attempt to intimidate them into accepting continued Indonesian rule. It was a blunt method, but one that had been used with some success elsewhere in the archipelago in earlier times. In East Timor, it only hardened resistance to the idea. Another reason was to try to provoke *Falintil* into retaliation, thereby enabling the pro-integration forces to claim a state of civil war and cancel the ballot or annul its result. Yet another reason was to use East Timor as a lesson to the other provinces of Indonesia considering breaking away: 'This is what happens if you try to leave', it seemed to be saying. The TNI also had problems with the idea that so many of their comrades had been killed in East Timor and now it seemed to be for nothing. The anger and the sense of betrayal, however misguided, was real for some. And then there was the question of the TNI trying to save face in what was a humiliating defeat, not by force of arms, but at the hands of an unarmed population. It was a rejection not just of Indonesia, but also of the idea of Indonesia. The unity of the state was challenged, the concept of nationalism slapped in the face, the guardians of the state made to look foolish and the people of East Timor were made to pay for it. There were also some elements of Jakarta's palace politics being played out in East Timor, where a contest of wills between Habibie and Wiranto, or between reformists and nationalists, determined policy on the ground.

Of all the pro-integration group's claims, one does stand up to some scrutiny. The group claimed that UNAMET employed mostly pro-independence workers for its local staff. Given the overwhelming support for independence among ordinary East Timorese, it would have been impossible for a representative grouping employed by UNAMET to be otherwise and, given the pro-integration groups' active opposition to the whole idea of a ballot, they were much less likely to actively work on a committee promoting independence.

All the other claims were spurious.

AN ARMED INTERVENTION

Responding belatedly to calls by observers and East Timorese support groups, members of the international community began to coalesce around the idea of sending an armed mission into East Timor. The USA was reluctant, but Australia, the population of which was outraged by events there, agreed to head such a mission (see Fernandes 2004 & Cotton 2004 on the Australian government's reluctance to become involved). By mid September, the UN had given approval to a peace-enforcement mission to East Timor, comprising military from Australia, New Zealand, Thailand, Portugal, the Philippines, South Korea, Cambodia, Britain, Ireland, the USA, Singapore and Malaysia (UN 1999b). Many empty threats were made against the force, in particular the Australian contingent, as Australia had been seen by many Indonesians as a driving force behind East Timor's push for independence.

Ahead of the first landing of International Forces to East Timor troops (INTERFET), 'high walled intelligence and interrogation centres were emptied and documents hastily dumped onto bonfires … Two decades of evidence went up in flames' (Murphy & McBeth 1999). By the time INTERFET troops landed on 20 September 1999, members of the TNI and the militias had already begun to move across the border into West Timor, taking huge quantities of looted goods with them.

THE AFTERMATH

Even before the ballot, Xanana Gusmao had said that the East Timorese needed to look to the future and forget about the past. Rather than blame those East Timorese members of the militias for the violence, Gusmao laid the blame at the feet of the TNI. 'We will do everything to avoid vengeance and hatred between people,' he said. 'Of course we have to focus on reconciliation between East Timorese' (Gusmao 1999). Gusmao also pointed to the enormous development issues that the fledgling state would face: 'We also have to eat,' he said. 'And I can say to you that we have been preparing our development policy since the beginning of April this year' (Gusmao 1999). However, the task of developing the half-island state was complicated by the TNI's scorched earth policy, carried out as it left East Timor. Infrastructure, including communications and water supply, was almost non-existent, most major buildings were destroyed or damaged and industry was non-existent.

In the years of the Indonesian occupation, most of the disparate peoples of East Timor had been bonded by a common enemy and by what was, increasingly, a common religion, Roman Catholicism. The language of Tetun Praca had increasingly become the standard non-Indonesian language of communication, in a similar manner to that of Tagalog in the Philippines. However, most people, in particular those under forty, also spoke Bahasa Indonesia, while some over forty often also spoke Portuguese. These were, in short, the identifiable characteristics of a nation, quite distinct from those of West Timor.

In the period after peace was restored to East Timor, the UN installed an interim administration, the UN Transitional Authority in East Timor (UNTAET), and gave it the task of rebuilding the basic infrastructure and institutions of state. Apart from the obvious infrastructure requirements, institutions such as a bureaucracy, the education system, including rebuilding the university, the health and legal services, including courts and police, would need to be established. In particular, the almost overwhelming health problem presented by malaria needed to be tackled as a matter of urgency, a fact recognised by CNRT. Similarly, a security or law enforcement and judicial apparatus was in the process of being established for internal policing and to secure East Timor's border with West Timor. There remained concerns that militia groups would continue to attempt to conduct cross-border raids against East Timor after the establishment of the independent state.

A NEW STATE

At one level, there were grounds for the establishment of the institutions of state among East Timor's diaspora that indicated, in large measure, people's desire to return. But it was clear that there would be external administrative support for East Timor while these institutions were rebuilt. In this respect, the administrative role of the UN was vital to East Timor securing a stable future. East Timor's economy was also a critical issue. As the second poorest province in Indonesia (average income in 1997–98 was US$138 a year, down from US$431 in 1996) and, as an impoverished Portuguese colony, East Timor never had a strong economy. However, it did have some scope for economic development, which could possibly provide the basis of a viable state. In the first instance, the Timor Gap gas and oil field reverted to East Timorese–Australian control and, through an arrangement that favoured Australia, began to provide a flow of state income. The gas revenues have not been insignificant and could contribute considerably to the fledgling state's coffers. East Timor also has a strong coffee production industry and, even though world coffee prices were not high, it was—and remains—another source of foreign income, at around US$40 million a year.

Despite the damage that has been done to it, East Timor is, in many senses, a physically beautiful place and, as such, slowly began to attract tourism. It has been said that, in 1974, East Timor enjoyed the same level of tourism development as did Bali. While Bali was perhaps not the best example of tourism development, tourism was certainly a major revenue generator there. The market for East Timorese sandalwood, once the reason for foreign interest, is now very small. Mineral deposits, mostly of marble, were also available for development, while East Timor's coastal region abounds with fish and has the potential to generate income from exports and from licensed fishing, although, were it to become too large, this could interfere with an important local food source.

THE END OF CONSENSUS

With the removal of the last Indonesian forces in October 1999 and the effective quelling of the immediate threat from pro-Indonesian militias, political organisations in East Timor began to look to the future and to their various visions for it. Not surprisingly, this led to divisions within the CNRT along Fretilin and UDT lines, between radicals and moderates in Fretilin and between younger and older members. Even the armed wing of the CNRT, *Falintil*, began to identify its interests somewhat separately from those of the politicians. Within Fretilin and CNRT, there were also divisions between those sections of the organisation that wanted to maintain a clandestine political organisation, so successfully built up under Indonesian occupation, and those who wanted CNRT and Fretilin to be fully public organisations. In part, this reflected a lack of a sense of security about the prospective political environment, but it also indicated where respective political power bases lay. The Timorese Democratic Party stood, in effect, as the reform faction of Fretilin.

At the left-wing end of the political spectrum was the small Timorese Socialist Party (PST) and the Revolutionary Front for the Independence of East Timor. The PST was largely based on a younger membership than that of Fretilin and was more radical in its views. Older, more subterranean, distinctions also existed between what might be broadly described as the more ethnically pure *kampones* (peasants), also known as *indijenas* (indigenes) or *rai-na'in*, and the more usually *mestisu* (Portuguese–Timorese mixed-blood) elites. Much of the older generation of Fretilin–CNRT leaders, who were more educated, tended to be of the traditionally more favoured (by the Portuguese) *mestisu* background.

Even language policy had become divisive, with the older members of the CNRT and, later, the government establishing Portuguese as the official language of state and education, with Tetum Praca also being an official language. Younger CNRT members strongly preferred Bahasa Indonesia and English as more practical alternatives.

At the right-wing end of the political spectrum, the Timorese Nationalist Party (PNT) appeared to be linked with other pro-integration organisations and had a senior membership who had a history of working with the Indonesian military and members of Jakarta's elite.

Apart from Fretilin and UDT, pro-integrationists revived themselves as a minor political force. The two main pro-integrationist organisations were the National Union Front for Political Affairs (NUFPA) and the Popular Timorese Party (PPT). PPT had expressed an interest in registering for the proposed 2001 elections in East Timor, doing so from Kupang in West Timor. While there was some concern for the safety of members of a pro-integration party, the move was also seen as a spoiling manoeuvre, indicating that the pro-integrationists would neither quickly fade away nor allow the territory to get on with establishing itself as an independent state. As another part of their spoiling campaign, these groups continued to challenge the validity of the UNAMET ballot process and denied its democratic credentials. The NUFPA also took the view that UNAMET had sided with the pro-independence group during the ballot. These pro-integration groups replaced the PPI and its militias, some of which continued to exist in West Timor, including the FPDK and the BRTT.

Finally, the Council for Popular Defence of the Democratic Republic of East Timor (CPD-RDTL) appeared as perhaps the greatest threat to the stability of the new state. Comprised of former militia members, unemployed youths and a few disaffected *Falintil* members who had not been selected to join the new military, CPD-RDTL staged flag-raisings and rallies and was involved in at least one serious riot in Dili, in which two people were shot and a number of buildings were burnt. Related to the CPD-RDTL, at least in terms of its disaffection over treatment of former *Falintil* guerrillas, was the *Sagrada Familia* (Sacred Family), led by the charismatic former guerrilla commander known as L-7 (Cornelio Gama). Based in the Baucau region, *Sagrada Familia* brought together their history as anti-Indonesian fighters, religion, folk magic and criminal activity. L-7 claimed that the government had a responsibility to look after the welfare of the former fighters, however, the cash-strapped government said that former guerrillas, who had not been taken in to the new military, would have to return to civilian life.

SELF-GOVERNMENT

In the period before full self-government, which was scheduled for 2001, East Timor was formally run by UNTAET, in collaboration with CNRT, as the de facto government of East Timor. This coalition, the National Consultative Council, functioned until the 30 August 2001 election of East Timor's first independent government. The elections were contested by the Timorese Social-Democratic Association (ASDT), the Christian Democratic Party of Timor (PDC), the Christian Democratic Union of Timor (UDC), the Democratic Party (PD), the Liberal Party (PL), the Maubere Democratic Party (PDM), the People's Party of Timor (PPT), the Revolutionary Front of Independent East Timor (Fretilin), the Social Democrat Party of East Timor (PSD), the Socialist Party of Timor (PST), Sons of the Mountain Warriors (*Kota*), the Timor Democratic Union (UDT), the Timor Labor Party (PTT), the Timorese Nationalist Party (PNT) and the Timorese Popular Democratic Association (*Apodeti*). As expected, there was again a high voter turnout—93 per cent—and also as expected, Fretilin won the elections with just under 60 per cent of the vote, giving it fifty-five of the eighty-eight seats of the new unicameral legislature. PD came second, with seven seats, ASDT followed with six, PDC, UDT, KOTA, PNT and PPT each with two seats and UDC/PDC, PST and PL each with one seat and one seat was allocated to an independent.

On 22 March 2002 East Timor's Constitution, which is based on the Portuguese model, was proclaimed. Elections conducted on 14 April 2002 for the largely ceremonial role of president were also unsurprising, with former resistance leader and head of the CNRT, Xanana Gusmao, winning with just under 85 per cent of the vote, his only opponent being a former *Fretilin* leader, Francis Xavier do Amaral.

As the new state settled down with the assistance of the now renamed UN Mission in Support of east Timor (UNMISET), it became clear that there were real weaknesses with the skills base of the country's judiciary and similar, although less critical, problems with its administration. The new policeforce, however, appeared to be relatively professional and well trained by overseas police; its new 1500 strong Falintil–East Timor Defence Force (F–FDTL), with its 1500 reservists, was located near the border with West Timor, although not so close as to be regarded as a provocation. A small policeforce border patrol unit had responsibility for ensuring the integrity of East Timor's unmarked and usually poorly defined border with West Timor and, hence, Indonesia, while Indonesia itself stationed a battalion of troops along its side of the border.

Poverty, always a problem in East Timor, even under Indonesia, remained worryingly high at 42 per cent of the population, which roughly matched unemployment and underemployment, which ran at around half of the potentially employable population. In 2001, purchasing parity power still only gave the average East Timorese an income of US$500 a year. More positively, growth in 2001 was at 18 per cent, even if it was off an almost non-existent base. In 2001, exports totalled around US$8 million, while imports were around US$240 million. The difference—and East Timor's administrative budget of US$97 million and its revenues of US$36 million—was made up by foreign aid.

East Timor did stand some chance of becoming more economically self-sufficient as revenues from oil and gas in the Timor Sea increasingly came on line. However, while Australia gave East Timor a 90 per cent share in the existing oil and gas deposits in the Timor Gap, it stalled talks on the vastly more lucrative oil and gas fields in Timor Sea territorial waters ceded to Australia by Indonesia, but which, under international law, were in East Timor's territorial zone. While this dispute dragged on, Australia took approximately US$1 million a day in profits from those fields and appeared to be set to renegotiate with East Timor only once the reserves had run out. Having assisted East Timor in its immediate post-Indonesia period, Australia had now become one of East Timor's biggest problems.

East Timor's relationship with Indonesia, too, remained problematic, with human rights abuse trials continuing in Dili, some of them occasionally convicting former militia members of various crimes. In Indonesia, nationalists still bitter about East Timor's departure, continued to criticise the fledgling state, keeping alive irredentist aspirations. Across the border, while many militia had given up the fight, about 2000 remained armed and active in West Timor. These 'clandestine' militia continued to operate with the backing of senior officers within the TNI, who supported them by arranging illegal activities, such as working in protection rackets in Jakarta and cross-border smuggling. These militia and the generals who supported them would remain a potential problem as long as the generals retained their positions within the TNI. This, in turn, was dependent on the territorial structure of the TNI and its involvement in business, both legal and illegal.

Resolution of these issues was on the Indonesian political agenda, but was far from being resolved. There were some moves to ease tensions, such as talks between Indonesia's President Susilo Bambang Yudhoyono and East Timor's President Xanana Gusmao in December 2004, which talks promoted truth and reconciliation over criminal trials. But the relationship remained ambiguous and East Timor's future appeared to still be very much dependent on the attitude of its large neighbour. It was not to be until after May 2005, when the UN finally left East Timor for good, that the real test of its future would begin.

NOTES

1   This chapter is accorded relatively more space than the similarly small state of Brunei. The reason for this is the more tumultuous history of East Timor, as well as the greater number and depth of the issues it raises.

2   The author was in East Timor, on this occasion, as the East Timor coordinator of the Australian NGO observer group, the Australia East Timor International Volunteer Project, from late July until early September 1999.

3   Portuguese explorer Duarte Barbosa was one of the first to visit the territory, in 1518.

4   This was a very similar process by which West Papua was, in 1969, formally incorporated into Indonesia.

5   This estimate is based on discussions held with Falintil members, aid workers in East Timor and, in 1999, with UNAMET political officers.

6   The other had been Murdani's mentor, General Ali Murtopo, who was head of Opsus (Special Operations), a secretive quasimilitary organisation.

7   Based on a conversation between the author and Bishop Belo in Melbourne, 1994.

8   Based on observation and discussions during a visit to East Timor in 1995.

9   Cotton says the militias were 'raised by the Interior Ministry but attached to territorial or combat military groups' (Cotton 1999: 15).

10   Based on personal observation during the campaign period and on reports by AETIVP members.

11   Based on personal observation.

12   For example, in late August the military head of Bobonaro district (around Maliana) and three NCOs were removed from their posts.

Conclusion

It can be taken as read that any work on South-East Asia presupposes the existence of such a region other than in a purely imaginary sense. Given the diversity within the region referred to, without some imaginative leap such a construction would not exist. Yet South-East Asia is a part of the world that can be, in some broad sense, defined, and is occasionally self-defining (for example, ASEAN, SEATO). South-East Asia is, in the contemporary sense, beyond the immediate orbit of both China and India, although it reflects the influences of both. The region is also almost entirely within the tropical belt and is, for the large part, mountainous, apart from river valleys and deltas and very occasional plains, lending an element of geographic uniformity. But, more importantly, while retaining distinct cultural elements, there has been considerable exchange throughout the region as well.

Coedes noted the 'Indianised' elements of Java and Sumatra, Cambodia, Burma, Thailand and Laos (1968), and further identified the early Javanese influence in Cambodia and Champa. Champa no longer exists as a state, although small Cham communities continue to exist in Vietnam and Cambodia, to where they fled ahead of the invading Vietnamese. The state may now be extinct, but the culture is not, and to watch contemporary Cham dance is to visit the stone relief of the Khmer Angkor Wat, to see the engraved *apsara* (heavenly nymphs) in human form. Contemporary Cambodian dance, on the other hand, reflects Thai influences rather than those of Angkor. The ebb and flow of armies, but, more importantly, peoples, has similarly spread cultural influences and muddied what some irredentist nationalists would like to claim as distinct identities. The neatness of states indicated by borders is contradicted by the untidiness of physical human drift, although the latter more accurately corresponds to the precolonial environment than does the former.

Archipelagic South-East Asia has its own shared, often confused, identity as well, with maritime and Islamic influences among its predominantly Malay community spread as wide as Sumatra in the west to the Philippines in the east. Where else but among a coastal trading community would identifiable ethnic groups find themselves not only scattered across a region, as are the Bugis, for example, but also often living side by side with communities that have also come from elsewhere?

The inland peoples of these regions were less influenced by such trade and cultural mobility and, in many places, developed cultures that were linked only to their nearest neighbours. But common communal patterns and forms of authority were, and often are still, found in the more remote places. The traditional local chief, the *datu*, is still to be found from as far apart as remote villages in Sumatra to the mountains of Sabah and the valleys of the Philippines.

It is interesting to speculate on what might have been had South-East Asia not been subjected to European colonialism. Assuming no internal catastrophe, Thailand would probably be a significantly larger state than it now is, encompassing Laos, half of Cambodia and the northern peninsular Malay states. On the other hand, Lan Na, centred on Chiang Mai, could have reasserted its independence and, perhaps, rejoined with Shan State in Burma. Vietnam, too, would probably be further extended at its southern and western reaches if it had maintained its on-again-off-again unity, while Cambodia, like Champa, would probably have ceased to exist, as it once almost did. Burma might exist in something corresponding to its contemporary form, although, given its expansionist tendencies in the past, it could also be greater at the expense of neighbouring Thailand. Alternatively, given its composite nature, it might also have fallen apart, as it has so many times in the past.

In the archipelago, it is possible that we could have witnessed the establishment of another Javanese-based empire. Indeed, some critics suggest that is precisely what did happen, after the Dutch left the region. The glory of Majapahit could have been revisited upon the numerous peoples of the nearby islands, although it is possible that they might not have seen—or see—such visitation in equally glorious terms. Equally as possible, the state structure of the region could indicate several independent sultanates or Islamic-based states, in Sulu and Mindanao in the southern Philippines, in Brunei and Sarawak, in Riau, Sumatra, Java, on the rump Malay Peninsula, West and East Kalimantan, north and south Sulawesi, Maluku and throughout the southeastern islands towards West Papua.

But history is, more or less, what it is, and the impact of European colonialism is difficult to ignore. One can argue over the costs or benefits of the colonial enterprise, but there is little doubt that colonialism effectively defined contemporary frontiers and, through borrowed or modified models, left a variety of forms of government. The precolonial versions of a state without defined borders, in particular, the centralised authority of the mandala model, are largely gone. Authority may be centralised, perhaps more effectively in some cases than in the past, but the traditional porousness of borders is anathema to the contemporary state, while authority within borders is only ever grudgingly incomplete.

Almost regardless of the political model adopted—or invented—in the region, some more traditional forms of authority continue. Most notably, variations on patron–client relations continue to dominate, running afoul of conventional statist notions of propriety and political party, not to mention law and human rights. No state in South-East Asia has shown itself immune to the continuation of this deeply entrenched system of social, economic and political relations, which has often been manifested in forms that have transgressed modern law, as with corrupt or nepotistic practices. Of course, such relationships are not exclusive to the region, but they are certainly well represented throughout it.

In a similar and related manner, notions of strong authority remain well entrenched throughout the region, in large part through their continued application. Rare and usually short-lived is the government that does not shore up its power base by methods other than direct electoral support, which has, in turn, had widespread implications for notions of political representation and participation and led to creative uses of the term 'democracy', some of which have ultimately included its rejection. Similarly, concepts of civil and political rights have usually received short shrift, mostly on the grounds that they do not conform to local patterns of authority and respect or because they constitute an inconvenience for wielders of power. It is accurate to identify numerous similar models that posit respect for authority as an admirable quality and that favour the collective good over that of the individual.

But the reification of these values, usually in a highly stylised and non-reflexive manner, speak more about the achievement and maintenance of political power than they do about the practical conventions of village-based, premodern society. Not surprisingly, for peoples who have been brought rapidly from institutionalised premodernism into the modern or, indeed, the postmodern world in a few short decades, it is not surprising that naturalised values do not quickly disappear or are recast in a bid to meet contemporary exigencies. What is of concern is that the reification of many of those values has led to rigid, even brittle, responses to situations that might benefit more from flexibility and adaptation. In particular, after the death or retirement of long-standing political leaders who have deeply personalised power poses problems, not just for transition processes, but also for attendant state stability. Singapore after Lee Kuan Yew dies is still an unknown quantity, as is Cambodia after Hun Sen or Burma after the generals. Malaysia after Mahathir is still in the process of change, while Indonesia has seen almost a revolving door on the presidency, although perhaps to stabilise a little under Susilo Bambang Yudhoyono. There may be people to rise to the occasion, but there may also be a fundamental shift in political processes, as seen after both Sukarno and Suharto in Indonesia, and after Marcos in the Philippines.

Despite such questions, in the early years of the twenty-first century, as something resembling democratisation appears to be taking root, there is a temptation to be hopeful, to see the uncharted future as pregnant with positive possibilities. It would be fair to say this of the future of the states and societies of South-East Asia, noting the achievements of each, often against the odds, in the postcolonial period. Yet the idea of a century, or a millennium, is, in a practical sense, arbitrary and its end or beginning is but one point on a continuum. Little of contemporary South-East Asia can be understood without at least a passing reference to its history, and very large parts of that history indicate that, while change and growth of one type or another is probably inevitable, much of it is unpredictable. There are certainly no guarantees that the future will correspond to most peoples' desires, much less any sort of democratic–capitalist end-of-history scenario as outlined by, for example, Francis Fukyama (1993). Interestingly, having seen that this idealised model has too many exceptions to remain useful, Fukyama has turned instead to addressing some of the structural issues in state building and state maintenance, although even here he continued to run shy of directly addressing the material conditions that give rise to political positions.

Notions of democracy might have a normative value for most readers of this text, but it would be a mistake to automatically assume that because they regard it as desirable it is not just a passing phase in a very long evolutionary political cycle. Many have, in the past, considered the divine right of kings, or the cult of the *devaraja*, to be normatively desirable too, yet that has not lasted. It might be that, in some future technocratic age (perhaps not so far away), political decisions will be seen to be too important to be left in the hands of the untrained or unskilled. Yet this itself raises questions about hegemony, and the representation of sectional interests. Alternatively, perhaps political decisions will devolve to those they most immediately affect, and that states will become mere middlemen in a benign relationship between global and local institutions.

Similarly, there are no imminent threats on the horizon either, although, with the benefit of an historical cast, it should be noted that events that correspond to decades or centuries can rarely be seen from the perspective of the present. We might know what is happening now, or think we do, but can we really know how what is happening fits into a bigger picture? Who was so aware of the mounting threat of Islamic terrorism before 11 September 2001, after which the first edition of this book was written, but when such a threat was clearly on its way? Who, too, knew of *Jema'ah Islamiyah*, apart from its participants and perhaps one outsider? Will political models that exist at the beginning of 2005 still be around in 100 years, or even twenty? Will state borders remain, or change, as they have done? Indeed, will states that we are so familiar with continue to exist in their present form into the indefinite future? Perhaps, but one need only look at contemporary Indonesia to understand the tensions that compete with the idea of the unity of the state are not to be underestimated. The idea of East Timor, as a late inclusion into Indonesia, was, for that state, seen as irrevocably included. Yet by the late twentieth century, that inclusion had been comprehensively revoked. What might this imply for Aceh, or West Papua, or any other part of the troubled archipelago? What of Malaysia? Singapore left the Malaysian Federation inside three years and perhaps Sarawak will one day find an independent place in the world, next to or part of Brunei, or vice versa. The Philippines, too, has serious internal tensions and comprises at least two nations, if still only one state. Burma, on the other hand, appears to be able only to maintain its unity through full-time repression, which has so fundamentally deformed the state that its founders had in mind. Or perhaps, as the world becomes more globalised, the idea of the state as such starts to recede in significance, the local unit of cultural and political expression perhaps becoming closer and more familiar.

At the beginning of this book we visited the fictional character Ni, who was taking a moment's break from his paddy field, contemplating just some of the manifestations of changing life in South-East Asia. There is much—probably most—of South-East Asia still, at the beginning of 2005, that is actually very close to Ni's experience. Some people of the region still live in societies little or not much touched by modernisation, while most are caressed so gently by it they are barely distracted from the concerns and aspirations that preoccupied their forefathers and mothers. Millions of others, though, have been caught up in the rising tide of modernisation and industrialisation, swept up and deposited in factories, schools and offices, living in often teeming cities with marginal infrastructure but limitless opportunity.

Or so it may seem, from the perspective of the paddy. How rich the variety and possibility of the occupants of shiny cars driving fast along new motorways, dashing from one interesting, almost unbelievable, site to another, if seen from the perspective of the uneducated worker standing knee-deep in brown water, shifting mud from one point to another? Perhaps the goal of the modernisation project is to take all the field workers from the paddies: the political leaders of the region are attempting to do that as best and as fast as they can. But perhaps, just perhaps, the logic of the process is self-generating and if there are winners, there must also be losers.

The distribution of material gain is a manifestation of the distribution of political power. The rhetoric of politics often espouses the ideal, but usually settles for the mundanely practical, or self-serving. The key to understanding the political dynamic of the various states and peoples of South-East Asia is, therefore, less related to political rhetoric, the espousal of worthy goals or claims to common good, than it is to actual outcomes. As with the rest of life, it is, therefore, not important what people say in politics; it is what they do.

EPILOGUE

On 26 December 2004, as this book was being completed, there was a massive earthquake in the Indian Ocean, about 250 kilometres west of the northwestern Indonesian province of Aceh. The waves generated by this earthquake—referred to as a *tsunami* (Japanese for 'giant wave')—reached as far as the African coast and caused major destruction and loss of life in Sri Lanka. But its main impact was on the nearby South-East Asian states. Much of coastal southern Thailand was devastated and it was believed that more than 5000 people died there. But the most significant impact of the tsunami was on Aceh, where it was estimated that over 280 000 people were killed and many more remained vulnerable to subsequent disease.

Most of Aceh's population lives along the fertile lowlands at the foot of the mountains that push Aceh up towards mainland Asia, alongside the Malaysian Peninsula. As a result, when the waves hit, whole towns and villages were inundated; many were completely swept away. It was a catastrophe of unimaginable proportions.

Within one day, after the Free Aceh Movement (*Gerakan Aceh Merdeka*, or GAM) declared a unilateral ceasefire in its long-running separatist battle with the Indonesian military (TNI), the TNI launched a major offensive against the rebels. Within two days, international aid began to arrive in Aceh, beginning what was the world's largest ever peace-time emergency aid program. While the TNI was initially reluctant to accept foreign aid workers into the country to assist, as the magnitude of the disaster overwhelmed it, it was ordered by the Indonesian government to allow in aid workers, journalists and, soon after, unarmed American, Australian and other military personnel to assist with the distribution of food, water and medical supplies and services.

In Thailand, meanwhile, the relief operation—much smaller in scale—quickly cleaned up much of the damage caused by the massive waves, identified and buried the dead and, as soon as possible, tried to move on. The scale of the disaster in Aceh, however, and the relative inefficiencies of the Indonesian government and military, meant the cleaning up process was much slower.

Among those Indonesians who went to Aceh to help were the Islamic Defenders Front and the *Laskar Mujahidin*, organisations connected to the Indonesian Mujahidin Council (*Majelis Mujahidin Indonesia*, or MMI), which was established and headed by alleged al-Qaeda-linked *Jema'ah Islamiyah* leader, Abu Bakar Ba'asyir. Such fundamentalist Islamic organisations had long wanted a foothold in Aceh, but had been bluntly rejected by GAM. Now, they came in under the guise of helpers, even though many Acehnese saw them as providing the basis of yet another group of militias to become involved in the separatist conflict there.

Meanwhile, the TNI used as an excuse its renewed attacks against GAM to limit the travel of aid workers and others and said it wanted foreigners to leave Aceh as soon as possible. At the time of writing, it appeared as though security would be used as a pretext to remove foreigners from Aceh, as the TNI had done in May 2003 and in East Timor in 1999. However, the international aid community appeared similarly determined to stay; both the UN and the USA called on the Indonesian government to find a solution to the conflict. Peace talks did begin between GAM and the Indonesian government following the disaster.

There were, too, mounting concerns about the TNI's control over and potential for syphoning off international aid and more general concerns over the corrupt use of the massive influx of aid. Having run out of money to prosecute the Aceh campaign, the hundreds of millions of dollars being poured into the province looked like a potential windfall for the TNI. The Indonesian government, meanwhile, vacillated, contradicted itself and the TNI and generally appeared incapable of getting fully in control of the situation.

While the post-tsunami situation in Thailand appeared, within weeks, to begin to approach normality, in Aceh it appeared as though it would continue to play out well beyond the publication of this book and, indeed, could have an impact that would last for years. As this book went to press, it was far from clear what all the consequences of the tsunami and its aftermath would be.

What did appear to be clear was that Thailand had responded to the—admittedly smaller—crisis with clarity of purpose and considerable efficiency. Indonesia, on the other hand, was much less sure and precise. As with the country itself, there were grounds for being—perhaps too hopefully—optimistic. As with Indonesia's more conventional politics, Indonesia had a future that, on the one hand, had some potential to improve.

On the other hand, the country's response to the disaster in Aceh was beginning to look like an intense microcosm of the Indonesian state. Its hopes and genuine efforts to come to grips with the disaster showed the best of many Indonesians. Unfortunately, it was not only the best that was on display.

BIBLIOGRAPHY

Abdul Qadir Baraja 2000, 'Kebangkitan dan Keruntuhan Khilafatul Muslimin', in *Risalah Kongre Mujahidin dan Penegakan Syariah Islam*, Yogyakarta, April.

Abinales, P. 1996, 'When a revolution devours its children before victory: Operasyon Kampanyang Ahos and the tragedy of Mindanao communism', in P. Abinales (ed.), *The Revolution Falters: The Left in Philippine politics after 1986*, Southeast Asia Program Publications, no. 15, Cornell University, Ithaca.

Adams, N. 1970, 'Patrons, clients, and revolutionaries: the Lao search for independence, 1945–1954', in N. Adams and A. McCoy, *Laos: war and revolution,* Harper & Row, New York.

Aditjondro, G. 2003, 'Muslim brotherhood, or pure business interests? The ASEAN-ization of the Suharto family business interests in the Philippines', quoted in 'The Suharto Islamic Network', Laksamana.Net, 9 September.

Agence France Presse (AFP) 1996, 'Burma admits drug problem, rejects US criticism', 3 December.

—— 1999a, 'Drug lords' presence a necessary evil—expert', *Bangkok Post*, 25 February, p. 4.

—— 1999b, 'Interpol endorses junta's drug proposals', *Bangkok Post*, 26 February, p. 5.

—— 2003, 'Ba'asyir says Hambali's arrest to boost President Bush's popularity', *Jakarta Post*, 20 August.

—— 2004, 'Three private Myanmar banks to reopen after last year's crisis: bank', 29 January.

Agencies 1999, 'Government denies hosting Khmer Rouge pair', *Sunday Nation*, Bangkok, p. 3.

—— *Jakarta Post*, 2003, 'Westerners trained in al-Qaeda camp in Indonesia, claims official', *Jakarta Post*, 18 January, reproduced in Ummahnews.com, 17 October.

Alford, P. 1999, 'Muslim surge sours Mahatir's triumph', *Australian*, 1 December, p. 7.

Amnesty International 1990, *1990 Report*, Amnesty International Publications, London.

An, S. 2002, Opening address, *Workshop on Doctrine of Precedents, Separation of Power, Checks and Balances*, Conference Hall, Ministry of Justice, Phnom Penh, 10–11 June.

Anderson, B. 1964, 'The idea of power in Javanese culture', in C. Holt, B. Anderson & J. Siegal (eds), *Culture and Politics in Indonesia*, Cornell University Press, Ithaca.

—— 1972, 'The idea of power in Javanese culture', in C. Holt, B. Anderson & J. Siegal (eds), *Culture and Politics in Indonesia*, Cornell University Press, Ithaca.

—— 1990, *Language and Power: exploring political cultures in Indonesia*, Cornell University Press, Ithaca.

—— 1991, *Imagined Communities*, 2nd edn, Verso, London.

Ansari, S. 1998, 'The Islamic world in the era of Western domination', in F. Robinson (ed.), *Cambridge Illustrated History of the Islamic World*, Cambridge University Press, Cambridge.

Anwar, D. F. 2000, 'Indonesia's transition to democracy: challenges and prospects', in A. Budiman & D. Kingsbury (eds), *Rethinking Indonesia*, Crawford House, Adelaide.

Associated Press (AP) 1998, 'Pomp and Bon Jovi herald a fresh heir', *Age*, 11 August, p. 7.

—— 2003, 'Myanmar says Suu Kyi safe in custody', 3 June.

—— 2003, 'Clash between followers of Myanmar opposition leader, pro-government supporters appears premeditated: U.S. official', 5 June.

Apdel, M. S. & Thayer, C. 2003, *Security, Political Terrorism and Militant Islam in Southeast Asia*, Trends in Southeast Asia series 7, ISEAS, Singapore.

ASEAN 1976, *Treaty of Amity and Cooperation*.

—— 1992, *Declaration on the South China Sea*, 22 July, Manila.

—— 1994, *Chairman's Statement*, ASEAN Regional Forum (ARF), 25 July, ARF, Bangkok.

Asian Development Bank (ADB) 1999, *Annual Report*, Asian Development Bank, Manila.

Asiaweek 1998a, 'Estrada's bumbling beginning', *Asiaweek*, 7 August, p. 19.

—— 1998b, 'The trigger', 26 December, p. 110.

Atkinson, J. 1987, 'Religions in dialogue: the construction of an Indonesia minority religion', in R. Kipp & S. Rogers (eds), *Indonesian Religions in Transition*, University of Arizona Press, Phoenix.

Aung-Thwin, M. 1998, *Myth and History in the Historiography of Early Burma*, Ohio University Center for International Studies, Monograph no. 102, Athens, Ohio.

Australian Council for Overseas Aid (ACFOA) 1987, *Life After Debt*, ACFOA, Canberra.

—— 1991, *East Timor: keeping the flame of freedom alive*, Development Dossier no. 29.

Australian International Development Assistance Bureau 1989, *Debt and the Developing World*, Australian Government Publishing Service, Canberra.

Bachrach, P. & Baratz, M. 1962, 'The two faces of power', *American Political Science Review*, no. 56.

Baker, M. 1998, 'Power without glory', *Age*, News Extra, 26 September, p. 3.

Bakker, J. & Ferrazzi, G. 1997, 'Weber's pure ideal type model of matrimonial prebendalism: testing the applicability of the model in Indonesia', unpublished paper presented to the 92nd annual meeting of the American Sociological Association, Toronto, 9–13 August.

Balfour, F. for Agence France Press 1999, 'Vietnam's communist party wants to walk a harder line', *Cambodia Daily*, 27 January, p. 10.

Ball, D. 1998, *Burma's Military Secrets: signals intelligence (SIGINT) from 1941 to cyber warfare*, White Lotus Press, Bangkok.

—— 1999, 'Burma and drugs: the regime's complicity in the global drug trade', *Asia–Pacific*, no. 14.

—— & Acharya, A. 1999, *The Next Stage: preventative diplomacy and security co-operation in the Asia–Pacific region*, Strategic and Defence Studies Centre, Research School of Pacific and Asian Studies, Australian National University, Canberra.

Bangkok Post 1999a, 'Motorcycle thief shot and killed', 13 January, p. 2.

—— 1999b, 'Sabotage on the waterfront', 13 January, p. 8.

—— 1999c, 'Opposition attack wins favor', 13 January, p. 3.

—— 1999d, 'Security tightened in Bangkok', 15 January, p. 1.

Baran, P. 1957, *The Political Economy of Growth*, Monthly Review Press, New York.

Batson, W. 1991. 'After the revolution: ethnic minorities and the new Lao state', in J. Zasloff & L. Unger (eds), *Laos: beyond the revolution*, Macmillan, Houndmills.

Battersby, P. 1990, 'Border politics and the broader politics of Thailand's international relations in the 1990s: from communism to capitalism', *Pacific Affairs*, vol. 71, no. 4, Winter, pp. 1998–9.

—— 1999, 'Border politics and the broader politics of Thailand's international relations in the 1990s: from communism to capitalism', *Pacific Affairs*, vol. 71, no. 4, Winter, pp. 1998–9.

Bedlington, S. 1978, *Malaysia and Singapore: the building of new states*, Cornell University Press, Ithaca.

Bello, W., Kinley, D. & Elinson, E. 1982, *Development Debacle: the World Bank in the Philippines*, Institute for Food and Development Policy, San Francisco.

Bellows, T. 1970, *The People's Action Party of Singapore: emergence of a dominant party system*, Monograph Series no. 14, Yale University, New Haven.

Benitez, C. 1954, *History of the Philippines*, Ginn, Manila.

Beresford, M. 1988, 'Issues in economic unification: overcoming the legacy of separation', in D. Marr & C. White (eds), *Postwar Vietnam: dilemmas in socialist development*, Cornell Southeast Asia Program, Ithaca.

Berfield, S. & Loveard, D. 1999, 'Ten days that shook Indonesia', in E. Aspinall, G. van Klinken & H. Feith (eds), *The Last Days of President Suharto*, Monash Asia Institute, Melbourne.

Berman, L. 1998, *Speaking Through the Silence: narratives, social conventions and power in Java*, Oxford University Press, New York.

Berry, K. 1997, *Cambodia from Red to Blue: Australia's initiative for peace*, Australian National University, Canberra, and Allen & Unwin, Sydney.

Bleaney, M. & Nishiyama, A. 2002, *Economic Growth and Income Inequality*, Centre for Research in Economic Development and International Trade, University of Nottingham.

Borneo Post 1999, 'Manila talks with rebels expected to fail', *Kota Kinabalu*, 15 February, p. 9.

Bourchier, B. 1999, 'Why Indonesia had to explode', in E. Aspinall, G. van Klinken & H. Feith (eds), *The Last Days of President Suharto*, Monash Asia Institute, Melbourne.

Bourchier, D. 1996, 'Lineages of organicist political thought in Indonesia', PhD thesis, Monash University, Melbourne.

—— 1998, 'More educated, more ruthless', *Inside Indonesia*, no. 53, January–March, pp. 14–15.

—— 1999, 'Skeletons, vigilantes and the armed forces fall from grace', in A. Budiman, B. Hatley & D. Kingsbury (eds), *Reformasi: crisis and change in Indonesia*, Monash Asia Institute, Melbourne.

Bowie, A. & Unger, D. 1997, *The Politics of Open Economies*, Cambridge University Press, Cambridge.

Boyce, D. 1998, 'Investment in Cambodia plunges this year', *Cambodia Daily*, Phnom Penh, 8 July.

Brandt, W. 1985, *Global Challenge*, Pan World Affairs, London.

—— (ed.) 1983, *Common Crisis*, Pan World Affairs, London.

Brewer, A. 1980, *Marxist Theories of Imperialism: a critical survey*, Routledge & Keegan Paul, London.

Brohman, J. 1996, *Popular Development*, Blackwell, Oxford.

Brown, M. 1974, *The Economics of Imperialism*, Penguin Modern Economic Texts, Harmondsworth.

Brownfeld, A. 2002, 'Al-Qaeda goes south east', *Jane's Defence Weekly*, 14 October.

Brunei Darussalam, Government of, 1988, *Brunei Darussalam in Profile*, Shandwick, London.

Budiardjo, C. & Liem. S. L. 1984, *The War Against East Timor*, Zed Books, London.

Bunbongkarn, S. 1997, *Thailand: state of the nation*, Institute of Southeast Asian Studies, Singapore.

Burger, W. & Bogert, C. 1988, 'Mahatir's heavy hand', *Newsweek*, 2 May.

Buttinger, J. 1967a, *Vietnam: a dragon embattled*, Vol. 1, Praeger, New York.

—— 1967b, *Vietnam: a dragon embattled*, Vol. 2, Praeger, New York.

—— 1968, *Vietnam: a political history*, Praeger, New York.

Cady, J. 1958, *A History of Modern Burma*, Cornell University Press, Ithaca.

Caldwell, M. & Tan, L. H. 1973, *Cambodia in the Southeast Asian War*, Monthly Review Press, New York.

Caldwell, M. & Utrecht, E. 1979, *Indonesia: an alternative history*, Alternative Publishing Cooperative, Sydney.

Cambodia National Institute for Statistics 2004, <http://www.nis.gov.kh>, accessed 10 October 2004.

Camilleri, J. & Falk, J. 1992, *The End of Sovereignty? The politics of a shrinking and fragmenting world*, Edward Elgar, London.

Camilleri, J. 1994, 'Reflections on the state in transition', *Arena*, Melbourne.

Cambodia News Digest (Camnews) 1999, 'KR jailer in protective custody', no. 389, May.

Campbell, T. 1983, *The Left and Rights*, Routledge & Keegan Paul, London.

Case, W. 1996, *Elites and Regimes in Malaysia*, Monash Asia Institute, Melbourne.

Castles, L. 2004, 'The strange saga of Indonesia's massive electoral malfunction', unpublished paper, 14 August.

Chalongphob, S. 1998, 'Thailand's debt crisis and economic outlook', *Trends*, Institute of Southeast Asian Studies/*Business Times*, no. 893, 1 January–1 February.

Chanda, N. 1986, *Brother Enemy: the war after the war*, Collier Books, New York.

Chandler, D. 1983, *A History of Cambodia*, 2nd edn, Westview Press, Boulder.

—— 1992, *Brother Number One: a political biography of Pol Pot*, Silkworm Books, Bangkok.

—— 1994, 'The roots of conflict in Cambodia', in D. Kingsbury & G. Barton (eds), *Difference and Tolerance: ethnicity, religion and human rights in South East Asia*, Deakin University Press, Geelong.

—— & Kiernan, B. (eds) 1983, *Revolution and its Aftermath in Kampuchea: eight essays*, Yale University Southeast Asia Studies Monograph Series, no. 25, Yale Center for International and Area Studies, New Haven.

Chandler, D., Kiernan, B. & Boua, C. 1988, *Pol Pot Plans the Future*, Yale University Southeast Asia Studies Monograph Series, no. 33, Yale Center for International and Area Studies, New Haven.

Chanoff, D. & Doan, V. T. 1996, *Vietnam: a portrait of its people at war*, I. B. Taurus, London.

Cheah, Y. 1996, 'More thoughts on the ancient culture of the Thai people', *Journal of the Siam Society*, vol. 84, part 1.

Chee, S. J. 1998, *To Be Free: stories from Asia's struggle against oppression*, Monash Asia Institute, Melbourne.

Choong, T. S. & Ranawana, A. 1998, 'A case of order and disorder', *Asiaweek*, 16 October, pp. 33–4.

Clegg, S. 1989, *Frameworks of Power*, Sage Publications, London.

Clements. A. & Suu Kyi, A. S. 1997, *The Voice of Hope*, Penguin, Harmondsworth.

Coedes, G. 1966, *Angkor*, Oxford University Press, Hong Kong.

—— 1968, *The Indianised States of Southeast Asia*, East–West Center Press, Honolulu.

Cohen, W. 1995, *The Cambridge History of American Foreign Relations: America in the age of Soviet power, 1945–1991*, Cambridge University Press, Cambridge.

Colmey, J. & Liebhold, D. 1999, 'The family firm', *Time*, 24 May, pp. 36–48.

Comber, L. 1995, 'The weather ... has been horrible': Malayan communist communications during "The Emergency" (1948–60)', *Asian Studies Review*, vol. 19, no. 2, November.

Communist Party of Vietnam (CPV) 1991, *Report of the Central Committee's 6th Term on the Documents of the 7th National Congress*, CPV, Hanoi.

Confucius 1995, *The Analects*, Soothill, W. E. (trans.), Dover Publications, New York.

—— 1997, *The Analects of Confucius*, Leys, S. (trans.), W. W. Norton, London.

Connor, W. 1994, *Ethnonationalism: the quest for understanding*, Princeton University Press, Princeton.

Constantino, R. 1975, *The Philippines: a past revisited*, Tala Publishing, Quezon City.

Cook, M. 1977, *The Constitutionalist Party of Cochinchina: the years of decline, 1930–1942*, Monash Papers on Southeast Asia, no. 6, Monash University, Melbourne.

Corfield, J. 1994, *Khmers Stand Up!*, Monash Asia Institute, Melbourne.

—— 1998, 'Detested confidant of Marcos', *Australian*, 25 November, p. 15.

—— (ed.) n.d., 'Selected chronicles from the reign of King Rama II: Thai–Malay relations during the early nineteenth century', unpublished manuscript, Skinner, C. (trans.).

Cotton, J. 2004, *East Timor, Australia and Regional Order*, RoutledgeCurzon, London.

—— (ed.) 1999, *East Timor and Australia*, Australian Defence Studies Centre, Australian Defence Force Academy, Canberra.

Cowen, M. & Shenton, R. 1996, *Doctrines of Development*, Routledge, London.

Cramb, R. & Dixon, G. 1988, 'Development in Sarawak: an overview', in R. Cramb & R. Reece (eds), *Development in Sarawak: historical and contemporary perspectives*, Monash Papers on Southeast Asia, no. 17, Centre of Southeast Asian Studies, Monash University, Melbourne.

Crispin, S. 2000, 'Tide of change', *Far Eastern Economic Review*, 13 April, p. 12.

—— & Tasker, R. 2000, 'First steps', *Far Eastern Economic Review*, 16 March, p. 16.

Crone, P. 1986, 'The tribe and the state', in J. Hall (ed.), *States in History*, Basil Blackwell, Oxford.

Crouch, H. 1988, *The Army and Politics in Indonesia*, Cornell University Press, Ithaca.

—— 1992, 'Authoritarian trends, the UMNO split and the limits to state power', in J. Khan & F. Loh Kok Wah (eds), *Fragmented Vision: culture and politics in contemporary Malaysia*, Allen & Unwin, Sydney.

—— 1996, *Government and Society in Malaysia*, Allen & Unwin, Sydney.

—— 1999, 'Wiranto and Habibie: military civilian relations since May 1998', in A. Budiman, B. Hatley & D. Kingsbury (eds), *Reformasi: crisis and change in Indonesia*, Monash Asia Institute, Melbourne.

Crowell, T. & Lopez, A. 1999, '"My ratings are down"', *Asiaweek*, 5 November, p. 29.

Dahl, R. 1971, *Who Governs?*, Yale University Press, New Haven.

Daily Express 1999a, 'Political conspiracy ruled irrelevant', *Kota Kinabalu*, 10 February, pp. 1, 2.

—— 1999b, 'Kurup hits out at the traitors', *Kota Kinabalu*, 10 February, p. 3.

—— 1999c, 'Fat hopes, Amir Kahar tells sis', *Kota Kinabalu*, 14 February, p. 3.

Davis, A. 1998, 'Rebels without a pause', *Asiaweek*, 3 April, pp. 30–5.

—— & Hawke, B. 1998, 'Business is blooming', *Asiaweek*, 23 January, pp. 46–52.

De Comyn, T. 1969, *State of the Philippines in 1810*, Filipiniana Book Guild, Manila.

Defence of Democracy Groups 1985, 'Suharto challenges the human conscience', *Inside Indonesia*, no. 6, December, pp. 3–5.

De Matos, A. 1974, *Timor Portugues 1515–1769*, Universidade de Lisboa, Lisbon.

Deutsche Presse-Agenteur (DPA) 1999, 'Ousting gives communist party jitters', *The Nation*, Bangkok, 9 January, p. A2.

De Waal, A. 1997, *Famine Crimes*, African Rights and the International African Institute, London.

Deyo, F. (ed.) 1987, *The Political Economy of the New Asian Industrialisation*, Cornell University Press, Ithaca.

Diaz, C. 1993, comment made during interview, *Lateline*, ABC-TV, 5 April.

Diokno, J. 1981, 'Untitled lecture, International Council of Amnesty International, Cambridge, 21 September 1978', in R. Alston (ed.), *Development, Human Rights and the Rule of Law*, Pergamon Press, London.

Dodd, C. 1972, *Political Development*, Macmillan, London.

Dommen, A. 1965, *Conflict in Laos: the politics of neutralization*, Praeger, New York.

Donnelly, S. 1984, 'Human rights and development: complimentary or competing concerns?', *World Politics*, vol. 36, no. 2, January.

Dunn, J. 1996, *Timor: a people betrayed*, ABC Books, Sydney.

Easton, A. 1998, 'The election follies roadshow wows the voters', *Age*, 25 April, p. 24.

Elegant, S. 2000, 'UMNO's dilemma', *Far Eastern Economic Review*, 2 March, pp. 19–29.

Elliott, D. 1978, *Thailand: origins of military rule*, Zed Press, London.

Embassy of the Union of Myanmar 1998a, 'The new cabinet', *Newsletter*, no. 1, 2 January.

—— 1998b, 'Achievements of the government in Narcotic Drug Control', *Newsletter*, no. 2, 20 January.

Emmerson, D. 2004, 'A year of voting dangerously', *Journal of Democracy*, vol. 15, no. 1, January.

Engelbert, T. & Goscha, C. 1995, *Falling Out of Touch*, Monash Asia Institute, Melbourne.

Erikson, J. 1998, 'Little room at the top', *Asiaweek*, 21 June, pp. 30–1.

Evans, G. 1998, *The Politics of Ritual and Remembrance: Laos since 1975*, Silkworm Books, Bangkok.

—— & Rowley, K. 1990, *Red Brotherhood At War*, 2nd edn, Verso, London.

Evans, I. 1922, 'Primitive people's of Borneo', *British North Borneo Herald*, reproduced in *Kota Kinabalu* (*Daily Express*), 14 February 1999, p. 5.

Evans, P. 1995, *Embedded Autonomy: states and industrial transformation*, Princeton University Press, Princeton.

Evans, G. 1991. 'Planning problems in peripheral socialiam: the case of Laos', in J. Zasloff, & L. Unger (eds), *Laos: beyond the revolution*, Macmillan, Houndmills.

Fakhry, M. 1983, *A History of Islamic Philosophy*, c2nd edn, Columbia University Press, New York.

Fan Yew Teng 1999, *Anwar Saga: Malaysia on trial*, Genting Raya Sdn Bhd, Seri Kembangan, Malaysia.

Far Eastern Economic Review 1981, no. 112, 29 May, p. 46.

—— *Yearbook* 1997, 'Malaysia', pp. 164–8.

Faulder, D. 2000, 'A state of injustice', *Asiaweek*, 3 March, p. 24.

Feinstein, D. 1998, text of speech to *Foreign Operations, Export Financing and Related Agencies Appropriation Act 1999* to US Senate, regarding political and economic reform in Indonesia, 1 September.

Feith, H. 1962, *Decline of Constitutional Democracy in Indonesia*, Cornell University Press, Ithaca.

—— 1969, 'Indonesia', in G. Kahin (ed.), *Governments and Politics in Southeast Asia*, 2nd edn, Cornell University Press, Ithaca.

—— & Castles, L. 1970, *Indonesian Political Thinking 1945–65*, Cornell University Press, Ithaca.

Feith, M. 1964, 'Indonesia', in G. Kalin (ed.), *Government and Politics in Southeast Asia*, Cornell University Press, Ithaca.

Fernandes, C. 2004, *Reluctant Saviour: Australia, Indonesia and the independence of East Timor*, Scribe, Melbourne.

Fforde, A. 1999, 'Current issues in Vietnamese socioeconomic development, in the wake of the regional crisis: Given the pattern of investment, does the standard development model apply?', seminar paper, Centre for Southeast Asian Studies, Monash University, Melbourne.

—— 2004, 'SOEs, law and a decade of market-oriented socialist development in Vietnam', paper presented to conference on *Law and Governance: Socialist Transforming Vietnam*, Asian Law Centre and the School of Law at Deakin University, at the Melbourne Law School, 12–13 June 2003; revised 19 April 2004.

Fisher, C. 1966, *Southeast Asia: a social, economic and political geography*, Methuen, London.

Fitzgerald, C. P. 1966, *A Concise History of East Asia*, Heinemann, Melbourne.

Flower, R. 1984, *Raffles: the story of Singapore*, Croom Helm, London.

Forrester, G. 1998, 'A Jakarta diary, May 1998', in G. Forrester & R. May (eds), *The Fall of Soeharto*, Crawford House, Bathurst.

Fowler, M. & Bunck, J. 1995, *Law, Power and the Sovereign State*, University of Pennsylvania Press, University Park.

Frank, G. 1981, *Reflections on the World Economic Crisis*, Hutchinson, London.

Friend, T. 1969, *Between Two Empires: the ordeal of the Philippines 1929–1946*, Solidaridad Publishing, Manila.

Friere, P. 1972, *Pedagogy of the Oppressed*, Penguin, Harmondsworth.

—— 1974, *Education: the practice of freedom*, Writers and Readers Publishing Cooperative, London.

Fukuyama, F. 1993, *The End of History and the Last Man*, Avon Books, New York.

—— 2004, *State Building: governance and world order in the twenty-first century*, Profile Books, London.

Gaffar, A. 2002, 'A question of leadership', *Van Zorge Report on Indonesia*, vol. IV, no. 20, 13 December.

Gamble, C. 1986, 'Hunter-gatherers and the origin of states', in J. Hall (ed.), *States in History*, Basil Blackwell, Oxford.

Garnadi, H. 1999, Memo number: M53/TM p4-OKTT/7/99 (*General Assessment if Option 1 fails*), 3 July, Office of the Minister of State for Co-ordinating Politics and Security, Republic of Indonesia, Dili Command Post.

Gearing, J. 2000, 'Thailand's new enforcer', *Asiaweek*, 24 March, p. 30.

Geertz, C. 1960, *The Religion of Java*, Free Press, New York.

—— 1963, *Agricultural Involution: The process of ecological change in Indonesia*, University of California Press, Berkeley.

Gehan Wijeyewardene 1991, 'The frontiers of Thailand', in C. Reynolds (ed.), *National Identity and Its Defenders: Thailand, 1939–89*, Monash Papers on Southeast Asia, no. 25, Monash University, Melbourne.

Gellner, E. 1983, *Nations and Nationalism*, Cornell University Press, Ithaca.

George, A. (ed.) 1991, *Western State Terrorism*, Routledge, New York.

Giap, V. N. 1962. *People's War, People's Army: the Viet Cong insurrection manual for underdeveloped countries*, Praeger, New York.

Giddens, A. 1987, *Social Theory and Modern Sociology*, Polity Press, Cambridge.

Goldsworthy, D. 1988, 'Thinking politically about development', *Development and Change*, vol. 19, no. 3, July.

—— (ed.) 1991, *Development and Social Change in Asia*, Radio Australia/Monash Development Studies Centre, Melbourne.

Gomez, J. 2000, *Self Censorship: Singapore's shame*, Think Centre, Singapore.

Goodin, R. 1979, 'The development–rights trade-off: some unwarranted economic and political assumptions', *Universal Human Rights*, vol. 1, no. 2, April–June.

Government of the Federation of Malaya 1955, *A Short History of the Malayan Communist Party*, Government of the Federation of Malaya.

Gramsci, A. 1971, *Selections from Prison Notebooks*, Q. Hoare & G. N. Smith (eds & trans.), Lawrence & Wishart, London.

Grant, B. 1996 (1964), *Indonesia*, 3rd edn, Melbourne University Press, Melbourne.

Groves, H. 1962, 'Notes on the Constitution of the Federation of Malaya', in K. Tregonning (ed.), *Papers on Malayan History*, Department of History, University of Malaya, Singapore.

Gunder Frank, A. 1967, *Capitalism and Underdevelopment in Latin America*, Monthly Review Press, New York.

Gunn, G. 2001, 'Brunei', in P. Heenan & M. Lamontagne (eds), *The Southeast Asia Handbook*, Fitzroy Dearborn Publishers, London and Chicago.

Gusmao, J. 1999, 'We will forget the past', answers to J. Tesoro, *Asiaweek*, 3 September.

Ha, T. 1999, 'Inflation hits vital foods by 21.3 pc', *Vietnam Investment Review*, 1–7 February, p. 4.

Hammer, E. 1966, *The Struggle for Indochina 1940–1955*, Stanford University Press, Stanford.

Hammond, A. 1999, 'Indonesia closes 38 banks', *Age*, 15 March, p. B1.

Handelman, H. 1996, *The Challenge of Third World Development*, Prentice Hall, New Jersey.

Harrison, B. 1966, *South-East Asia: a short history*, St Martin's Press, New York.

Hashim, S. 2000, 'Salamat Hashim speaks', *Asiaweek*, 31 March, p. 29.

Hawes, G. 1987, *The Philippine State and the Marcos Regime*, Cornell University Press, Ithaca.

Herman, E. & O'Sullivan, C. 1990, *The Terrorism Industry*, Pantheon, New York.

Herz, M. 1958, *A Short History of Cambodia: from the days of Angkor to the Present*, Atlantic Books, London.

Hettne, B. 1990, *Development Theory and the Three Worlds*, Longman, New York.

Hewison, K. 1994, 'Minorities and human rights in Thailand', in D. Kingsbury & G. Barton (eds), *Difference and Tolerance: human rights issues in Southeast Asia*, Deakin University Press, Geelong.

—— 1997, 'The monarchy and democratisation', in K. Hewison (ed.), *Political Change in Thailand: democracy and participation*, Routledge, London.

Hiebert, M. 1998, 'Tactical victory', *Far Eastern Economic Review*, 2 July, pp. 10–17.

Higgott, R. 1986, *Political Development Theory*, Croom Helm, London.

Hill, H. (ed.) 1994, *Indonesia's New Order*, Allen & Unwin, Sydney.

Hills, B. 1994, 'Darkness enfolds the little lord', *Age*, 25 January, p. 7.

Hindley, D. 1964, *The Communist Party of Indonesia*, University of California Press, Berkeley.

Hinsley, F. 1978, *Sovereignty*, 2nd edn, Cambridge University Press, Cambridge.

Hiorth, F. 1985, *Timor: past and present*, South-East Asia Monograph, no. 17, James Cook University, Townsville.

Ho Chi Minh 1994, *Selected Writings*, The Gioi Publishers, Hanoi.

Howard, R. 1983, 'The full bellies thesis', *Human Rights Quarterly*, vol. 5, no. 4, November.

Htin Aung 1967, *A History of Burma*, Columbia University Press, New York.

Huang, R. 2002, 'In the spotlight: LJ', Center for Defense Information, Washington DC, 8 March.

Human Rights Watch (HRW) 2004, *Malaysia: Security Act detainees launch hunger strike*, New York, 2 March.

Huntington, S. 1968, *Political Order in Changing Societies*, Yale University Press, New Haven and London.

Hutchcroft, P. 1998, *Booty Capitalism: the politics of banking in the Philippines*, Cornell University Press, Ithaca.

International Crisis Group (ICG) 2002a, *Al-Qaeda in Southeast Asia: the case of the Ngruki Network in Indonesia*, Jakarta and Brussels, 8 August.

—— 2002b, 'Indonesian Backgrounder: How the Jema'ah Islamiyah Terrorist Network operates in Paso and Maluku', *Asia Report* no. 43, 11 December.

—— 2003, *Jema'ah Islamiyah in South East Asia: damaged but still dangerous*, Jakarta and Brussels, 26 August.

International Development Program (IDP) 2002, *Philippines: GRP-CPP/NPA/NDF peace process (September 2002)*, Global IDP Database, Washington DC.

International Monetary Fund (IMF) 1999, *Articles of Agreement of the International Monetary Fund*, IMF, Washington DC.

—— 2000, *Enhanced Structural Adjustment Facility*, IMF, Washington DC.

—— 2004, *Review of the Key Features of Poverty Reduction and Growth Facility: staff analyses*, IMF, Washington DC.

International Labor Rights Fund (ILRF) 2004, Closing argument by ILRF executive director *Terry Collingsworth, on behalf of John Doe et al., plaintiffs, versus Unocal et al., defendants*, ILRF, 20 January.

Indochina Chronology 1999, 'Laos struggles through 1999', *Indochina Chronology*, vol. XVIII, no. 4, October.

Indonesia, Republic of, Department of Information 1989, *The 1945 Constitution of the Republic of Indonesia*, Department of Information, Jakarta.

Infante, J. 1980, *The Political, Economic and Labor Climate in the Philippines*, Industrial Research Unit, University of Pennsylvania, Philadelphia.

International Republican Institute 2003, *Cambodia Voter Registration Report*, 14 February 2003.

Irrawaddy 1998a, 'Burma making small arms', vol. 6, no. 4, 31 August.

—— 1998b, Mid-year Chronology.

—— 2000a, 'Bloody day at Ratchaburi Hospital', January, p. 6.

—— 2000b, 'Thai security net catches dissidents, intruders', February, p. 2.

Ja'far Umar Thalib 2002, 'Declaration of war', Radio SPMM, 1–3 May; also published in *Berdarah*, 8 May.

Jakarta Post.com 1999, 'Who's Who: Gen. Wiranto', *Jakarta Post*.com

Jardine, M. 1995, *East Timor: genocide in paradise*, Odonian, Tucson.

Jayasuriya, S. 1987, 'The politics of economic policy in the Philippines during the Marcos era', in R. Robison, K. Hewison & R. Higgott (eds), *South East Asia in the 1980s*, Allen & Unwin, Sydney.

Joliffe, J. 1978, *East Timor: nationalism and colonialism*, University of Queensland Press, St Lucia.

Jomo, K. 2003, *My Way: Mahatir's economic legacy*, Forum, Kuala Lumpur.

Josey, A. 1970, *Democracy in Singapore: the 1970 by-elections*, Asia Pacific Press, Singapore.

Jumper, R. & Normand, M. 1969, 'Vietnam', in G. Kahin (ed.), *Governments and Politics of Southeast Asia*, 2nd edn, Cornell University Press, Ithaca.

Kahin, G. (ed.) 1969, *Governments and Politics of Southeast Asia*, 2nd edn, Cornell University Press, Ithaca.

Karnow, S. 1991, *Vietnam: a history*, Penguin, London.

Kearney, A. 2001, 'Measuring globalisation', *Foreign Policy*, Washington DC, May–June.

Keenan, F. 1999, 'Comrades in conflict', *Far Eastern Economic Review*, 15 April, p. 28.

Keohane, R. 2002, *Power and Governance in a Partially Globalized World*, Routledge, London and New York.

Keynes, J. 1936, *The General Theory of Employment, Interest and Money*, Macmillan, London.

Keyes, C. 1987, *Thailand: Buddhist kingdom as modern nation–state,* Westview Press, Boulder.

Khilafah Online n.d., <http://www.hizb-ut-tahrir.org/english/books/state/State.htm.>, accessed May 2005.

Kiernan, B. 1985, *How Pol Pot Came to Power*, Verso, London.

—— 1996, *The Pol Pot Regime*, Yale University Press, New Haven.

—— 2003, 'The demography of genocide in Southeast Asia', *Critical Asian Studies*, vol. 4, no. 35.

—— (ed.) 1993, *Genocide and Democracy in Cambodia*, Yale Southeast Asia Studies Monograph Series, no. 41, Yale Center for International and Area Studies, New Haven.

Kingsbury, D. 1998, *The Politics of Indonesia*, Oxford University Press, Melbourne.

—— 1999, 'The political resurgence of the Tentara Nasional Indonesia', in S. Blackburn (ed.), *Pemilu: the 1999 Indonesian elections*, Annual Indonesia Lecture Series, no. 22, Monash Asia Institute, Melbourne.

—— 2004, 'Globalization and development', in D. Kingsbury, J. Remenyi, J. McKay & J. Hunt (eds), *Key Issues in Development*, Palgrave, London and New York.

—— 1998, 'Watch these five!', *Inside Indonesia*, no. 53, January–March, pp. 12–13.

Kissinger, H. 1969, *American Foreign Policy*, W. W. Norton, New York.

Korten, D. 1990, *Getting to the 21st Century*, Kumarian Press, Hartford.

Krader, L. 1976, *Dialectic of Civil Society*, Prometheus Books, New York.

Kremmer, C. 1997, *Stalking the Elephant Kings*, Allen & Unwin, Sydney.

Lacouture, J. 1969, *Ho Chi Minh*, Pelican, Harmondsworth.

Laksamana.Net 2002, 'Ambon: battlefield for Jakarta players', accessed 1 May.

—— 2002, 'Gufron arrest may lead to Suharto's dark forces', accessed 10 December.

Lande, C. 1968, 'Party politics in the Philippines', in G. Guthrie (ed.), *Six Perspectives on the Philippines*, Bookmark, Manila.

Landsdale, E. 1976, 'Practical jokes', in *U.S. Department of the Army Psychological Operations*, DA pamphlet, US Department of the Army, 525-7-1, April 1976.

Lane, J. & Ersson, S. 2003, *Democracy: a comparative approach*, Routledge, London and New York.

Laski, H. 1934, *The State in Theory and Practice*, George Allen & Unwin, London.

Lau, T. 1997, 'ASEAN Regional Forum as a model for North-East Asian security?', in T. Inoguchi & G. Stillman (eds), *North-East Asian Regional Security*, United Nations University Press, Tokyo.

Lee, K. Y. 1998a, *The Singapore Story*, Times Editions, Singapore.

—— 1998b, 'A statesman's write of passage' (excerpt from *The Singapore Story*), *Far Eastern Economic Review*, 25 September, pp. 50–9.

Leffler, M. & Foner, E. 1994, *The Spectre of Communism: the United States and the origins of the cold war, 1917–1953*, Hill & Wang, New York.

Leifer, M. 1995, *Dictionary of the Modern Politics of South-East Asia*, Routledge, London.

Leitao, H. 1956, *Vinte e oito ano de historia de Timor*, Agencia Geral do Ultramar, Lisbon.

Lembaga Survei Indonesia (LSI) 2004, Final LSI Survey, 16 September, 'Final LSI national survey predicts: victory for SBY in the presidential election, *Lembaga Survei Indonesia*, Jakarta, 17 September.

Leung, S. (ed.) 1999, *Vietnam and the East Asian Crisis*, Edward Elgar, Cheltenham.

Leys, S. 1997, *The Analects of Confucius by Confucius*, Norton, New York.

Liddle, W. 1996, *Leadership and Culture in Indonesian Politics*, Allen & Unwin, Sydney.

Lijphart, A. 1999, *Patterns of Democracy*, Yale University Press, New Haven and London.

Lingle, C. 1996, *Singapore's Authoritarian Capitalism: Asian values, free market illusions and political dependency*, Locke Institute, Fairfax.

Lintner, B. 1990, *Outrage*, White Lotus, Bangkok.

—— 1998, 'Final countdown', *Far Eastern Economic Review*, 10 September, p. 4.

—— 1999, *Burma in Revolt,* 2nd edn, Silkworm Books, Chiang Mai.

—— 2000, 'Frustrated reforms', *Far Eastern Economic Review*, 24 March, p. 26.

Lopez, A. 1998, 'The Marcos cronies come back', *Asiaweek*, 31 July, pp. 20–3.

—— 2000a, 'Meeting force with force', *Asiaweek*, 10 March, p. 23.

—— 2000b, 'The nun vs. the president', *Asiaweek*, 31 March, p. 28.

Los Angeles Superior Court 2004, '*John Doe I et al., plaintiffs, versus Unocal et al., defendants*; Ruling on Unocal Defendant's motion for judgment'.

Low, L. & Toh, M.H. (eds) 1992, *Public Policies in Singapore*, Times Academic Press, Singapore.

Low, L. & Quan, E. 1992, 'Introduction', in L. Low & M. H. Toh (eds), *Public Policies in Singapore*, Times Academic Press, Singapore.

Lowry, R. 1996, *The Armed Forces of Indonesia*, Allen & Unwin, Sydney.

Lukes, S. 1974, *Power: a radical view*, Macmillan, London.

Lyons, J. & Wilson, K. 1987, *Marcos and Beyond*, Kangaroo Press, Sydney.

Mabbett, I. 1968, *A Short History of India*, Cassell Australia, Sydney.

MacDonald, M. 1987, *Angkor and the Khmers*, Oxford University Press, Oxford.

Machiavelli, N. 1998, *The Prince*, Musa, M. (trans.), Oxford University Press, Oxford.

Mackie, J. 1998, 'What will the post-Soeharto regime be like?', in G. Forrester & R. May (eds), *The Fall of Soeharto*, Crawford House, Bathurst.

—— & MacIntyre, A. 1994, 'Politics', in H. Hill (ed.), *Indonesia's New Order*, Allen & Unwin, Sydney.

Maclear, M. 1981, *The Ten Thousand Day War—Vietnam: 1945–75*, St Martin's Press, New York.

Maha Sila Viravong 1964, *History of Laos*, Paragon Book Reprint Corp., New York.

Mangunwijaya, Y. 1992, 'Some notes about the Indonesia Raya dream of the Indonesian nationalists and its impact on the concept of democracy', in D. Bourchier & J. Legge (eds), *Democracy in Indonesia: 1950s and 1990s*, Monash Papers on Southeast Asia, no. 31, Centre for Southeast Asian Studies, Monash University, Melbourne.

—— 1994, 'The Indonesia Raya dream of the Indonesian nationalists and its impact on the concept of democracy', in D. Bourchier & J. Legge (eds), *Democracy in Indonesia: 1950s and 1990s*, Monash Papers on Southeast Asia, no. 31, Centre for Southeast Asian Studies, Monash University, Melbourne.

Manich Jumsai 1979, *History of Thailand and Cambodia*, Cahlermnit Press, Bangkok.

Maravall, J. & Przeworski, A. (eds) 2003, *Democracy and the Rule of Law*, Cambridge University Press, Cambridge.

Martinkus, J. 2002, 'An unwelcome mat in Papua', *Bulletin*, 30 October.

—— 2003, 'Jihad in Papua', *The Bulletin*, vol. 120, no. 27.

Mastura, M. 1999, 'A plot gone awry', *Manila Times*, 9 February, p. 6.

Maung Aung Myoe 1998, 'Building the Tatmadaw: the organisational development of the armed forces in Myanmar, 1948–98', working paper no. 327, Strategic and Defence Studies Centre, Australian National University, Canberra.

—— 1999, 'Military doctrine and strategy in Myanmar: a historical perspective', working paper no. 339, Strategic and Defence Studies Centre, Australian National University, Canberra.

McBeth, J. 1999a, 'Cameo role', *Far Eastern Economic Review*, 18 March, pp. 27–8.

—— 1999b, 'Military challenge', *Far Eastern Economic Review*, 2 September, p. 19.

—— 1999c, 'Bitter memories', *Far Eastern Economic Review*, 16 September, p. 12.

McClintock, M. 1992, *Instruments of Statecraft: U.S. Guerrilla Warfare, Counterinsurgency, and Counterterrorism, 1940–1990*, Pantheon, New York.

McCloud, D. 1995, *Southeast Asia: tradition and modernity in the contemporary world*, Westview Press, Boulder.

McCoy, A. 1970, 'French colonialism in Laos, 1893–1945', in N. Adams & A. McCoy (eds), *Laos: war and revolution*, Harper & Row, New York.

McDonald, H., Ball, D., Dunn, J., van Klinken, G., Bourchier, D., Kammen, D. and Tanter, R. 2002, *Masters of Terror: Indonesia's military and violence in East Timor in 1999*, Canberra Papers on Strategy and Defence, no. 145, Australian National University, Canberra.

McGillivray, M. 1991, 'The human development index: yet another redundant composite development indicator?', *World Development*, vol. 9, no. 10, pp. 1461–8.

McKay, J. 1990, 'The development model', *Development*, vol. 3, no. 4, pp. 55–60.

—— 1991, 'Economic and social change in the Asia-Pacific region', in D. Goldsworthy (ed.), *Development and Social Change in Asia*, Radio Australia, Melbourne.

McNamara, R. 1995, *In Retrospect*, Time Books, New York, and Random House, Toronto.

Meisburger, T. (ed.) 2003, *Democracy in Indonesia: a survey of the Indonesian electorate in 2003*, The Asia Foundation, Jakarta.

Mietzner, M. 1998, 'Between pesantren and palace: Nahdlatul Ulama and its role in the transition', in G. Forrester & R. May (eds), *The Fall of Soeharto*, Crawford House, Bathurst.

—— 1999a, 'Nationalism and Islamic politics: political Islam in the post-Suharto era', in A. Budiman, B. Hatley and D. Kingsbury (eds), *Reformasi: Crisis and Change in Indonesia*, Monash Asia Institute, Melbourne.

—— 1999b, 'From Soeharto to Habibie: the Indonesian armed forces and political Islam during the transition', in G. Forrester (ed.), *Post-Soeharto Indonesia: renewal or chaos?*, Research School of Pacific and Asian Studies, Australian National University, Canberra, with Crawford House, Bathurst.

Mill, J. 1961, *Utilitarianism and On Liberty*, Doubleday, New York.

Miller, J. 1967, 'Communist China's foreign policy', in J. Wilkes (ed.), *Communism in Asia: a threat to Australia?*, Angus & Robertson, Sydney.

Milne, R. & Mauzy, D. 1999, *Malaysian Politics under Mahatir*, Routledge, London and New York.

Missen, G. 1972, *Viewpoints on Indonesia*, Nelson, Melbourne.

—— 1991, 'Malaysia: a tiger or a mouse deer?', in D. Goldsworthy (ed.), *Development and Social Change in Asia*, Radio Australia, Melbourne.

Mitton, R. 1998, 'Troubled kingdom', *Asiaweek*, 16 October, pp. 26–31.

—— 2000a, 'Everyone was shocked', *Asiaweek*, 10 March, p. 25.

—— 2000b, 'Inside "secret" meetings', *Asiaweek*, 31 March, p. 30.

Moedjanto, G. 1993, *The Concept of Power in Javanese Culture*, Gadjah Mada University Press, Jogjakarta.

Moertono, S. 1981, *State and Statecraft in Old Java*, Modern Indonesia Project Monograph Series, no. 43, Cornell University, Ithaca.

Monk, P. 1990, *Truth and Power: Robert S. Hardie and land reform debates in the Philippines, 1950–87*, Monash Papers on Southeast Asia, no. 20, Monash University, Melbourne.

Moore, S. 2001, 'The Indonesian military's last years in East Timor: an analysis of its secret documents', *Indonesia 72*, October.

Morris, C. 1998, *An Essay on the Modern State*, Cambridge University Press, Cambridge.

Mortimer, R. 1971, 'Unresolved problems of the Indonesian coup', *Australian Outlook*, no. 25, April.

Murphy, D. & McBeth, J. 1999, 'Scorched earth', *Far Eastern Economic Review*, 16 September, p. 10.

Murphy, D. 2003a. 'How Al Qaeda lit the Bali fuse: part one', *Christian Science Monitor*, 17 June.

—— 2003b. 'How Al Qaeda lit the Bali fuse: Part two', *Christian Science Monitor*, 18 June.

Muslim Brotherhood homepage n.d., <http://www.ummah.org.uk/ikhwan/>, accessed 20 August 2003.

—— Frequently Asked Questions n.d.

<http://www.ummah.org.uk/ikhwan/questions.html>, accessed 20 August 2003.

Myint-U, T. 2001, *The Making of Modern Burma*, Cambridge University Press, Cambridge.

Nasution, B. 1993, 'Human rights have an Indonesian history', *Inside Indonesia*, no. 34. p. 1.

The Nation 1998, 'Thai–M'sia bid to suppress rebels', *The Nation*, Bangkok, 20 September, p. A2.

—— 1999a, 'Foreign press curbs likely', *The Nation*, Bangkok, 15 January, p. 1.

—— 1999b, 'PM reacts over series of bombings, threats', *The Nation*, Bangkok, 15 January, p. 3.

Nelson, R. 1968, *The Philippines*, Thames & Hudson, London.

New Straits Times 1999, 'Trial to proceed despite Anwar's absence', *New Straits Times*, Kuala Lumpur, 25 February, p. 4.

Ngaosyvathn, M. & Ngaosyvathn, P. 1998, *Paths to Conflagration: fifty years of diplomacy and warfare in Laos, Thailand and Vietnam, 1778–1828*, Cornell University Press, Ithaca.

Nguyen, K. V. 1993, *Vietnam: a long history*, revised edn, The Gioi Publishers, Hanoi.

Nguyen, N. P. 1994, 'Religious freedom in Vietnam', in D. Kingsbury & G. Barton (eds), *Difference and Tolerance: Human Rights Issues in Southeast Asia*, Deakin University Press, Melbourne.

Norodom Sihanouk 1973, *My War with the CIA*, Penguin Books, London.

Nurdin, A. 1999, 'Military faces dilemma at MPR general session', *Jakarta Post*.com, 30 June.

Nussara Sawatsawang 1997, 'Minorities determined to pursue autonomy', Democratic Alliance of Burma Statement, 12 February.

O'Donnell, G. 1973, 'Modernization and bureaucratic authoritarianism', *Studies in South American Politics*, Berkeley Institute of International Studies, University of California, Berkeley.

—— 1978, 'Reflections on patterns of change in the bureaucratic authoritarian state', *Latin American Research Review*, no. 13, pp. 3–38.

Olsen, E. & Winterford, D. 1996, 'The military role of Asian countries in the New Pacific community in the 1990s', in K. Young (ed.), *The New Pacific Community in the 1990s*, East Gate Books, London.

Ong, G. 2003, *Next Stop, Maritime Terrorism*, Institute of Southeast Asian Studies, Singapore.

Osborne, M. 1973, *Politics and Power in Cambodia*, Longman, Melbourne.

—— 1997, *Southeast Asia: an introductory history*, 7th edn, Silkworm Books, Chiang Mai.

Osborne, R. 1985, *Indonesia's Secret War: the guerilla struggle in Irian Jaya*, Allen & Unwin, Sydney.

Parmer, J. 1969, 'Malaysia', in G. Kahin (ed.), *Governments and Politics of Southeast Asia*, 2nd edn, Cornell University Press, Ithaca.

Paz, R. 2000, *Is There An Islamist Internationale?*, International Policy Institute for Counter-Terrorism, Herzlia, Israel.

Pedersen, M., Rudland, E. & May, R. (eds) 2000, *Burma Myanmar: strong regime, weak state*, Crawford House, Adelaide.

Peou, S. 2000, *Intervention and Change in Cambodia*, Silkworm Books, Chiang Mai, with Institute of Southeast Asian Studies, Singapore.

Pemberton, J. 1994, *On the Subject of 'Java'*, Cornell University Press, Ithaca.

Pereira, B. 1999, 'Malaysian opposition's unholy alliance', *Straits Times*, 24 February, p. 41.

Pettman, R. 1979, *State and Class: a sociology of international affairs*, Croom Helm, London.

Philippines Star 1999, 'MLF reveals Bin Laden connection', *Philippines Star*, Manila, 2 February, pp. 1, 5.

Phongpaichit, P. & Piriyarangsan, S. C. 1994, *Corruption and Democracy in Thailand*, Silkworm Books, Chiang Mai.

Phongpaichit, P. & Baker, C. 1998. *Thailand's Boom and Bust*, Silkworm Books, Chiang Mai.

—— 2004, *Thaksin: the business of politics in Thailand*, Silkworm Books, Bangkok.

Pike, D. (ed.) 1999, 'Laos: how to move the economy', *Indochina Chronology*, Texas Technical University, Lubbock.

Ping-chia Kuo 1965, *China*, Oxford University Press, London.

Pirenne, H. 1939, *A History of Europe*, George Allen & Unwin, London, 1939.

Plamenatz, J. 1968, *Consent, Freedom and Political Obligation*, 2nd edn, Oxford University Press, London.

Poulgrain, G. 1999, 'Who plotted the 1965 coup?', *Inside Indonesia*, no. 57, January–March, p. 24.

Prakobpong, P. 1998. 'PM urged not to amend military's "privilege" rule', *The Nation*, Bangkok, 21 September, p. A3.

Proudfoot, I. 1980, 'The early indianized states: religion and social control', in J. Fox et al. (eds), *Indonesia: Australian perspectives*, Research School of Pacific Studies, Australian National University, Canberra.

Prudhisan, J. & Maneerat, M. 1997, 'Non-government development organisations', in K. Hewison (ed.), *Political Change in Thailand: democracy and participation*, Routledge, London.

Putnam, R. 1993. *Making Democracy Work*, Princeton University Press, Princeton.

Puy Kea 1998, 'Former Khmer Rouge stronghold enjoys business boom', *Cambodia Daily*, Phnom Penh, 6 July.

Pye, L. 1985, *Asian Power and Politics*, Belknap Press, Cambridge, Mass.

Raman, B. 2004. 'Thailand and International Islamic Front', South Asia Analysis Group Paper, no. 890, 1 September.

Randall, V. & Theobald, R. 1998, *Political Change and Underdevelopment*, Palgrave, Houndmills and New York.

Rapley, J. 1997, *Understanding Development*, UCL Press, London.

Ratanaporn Sethakul 1988, 'Political relations between Chiang Mai and Kentung in the nineteenth century', in Prakai Nontawasee (ed.), *Changes in Northern Thailand and the Shan States 1886–1940*, Southeast Asian Studies Program, Institute of Southeast Asian Studies, Singapore.

Rawana, A. 1999, 'The maps to power', *Asiaweek*, 5 November, p. 30.

Rawls, J. 1991, *A Theory of Justice*, Oxford University Press, Oxford.

Reece, R. 1988, 'Economic development under the Brookes', in R. Cramb & R. Reece (eds), *Development in Sarawak: Historical and Contemporary Perspectives*, Monash Paper on Southeast Asia, no. 17, Centre of Southeast Asian Studies, Monash University.

Republic of Singapore (RS) 2003, 'The Jemaah Islamiyah arrests and the threat of terrorism', White Paper, Ministry of Home Affairs, Republic of Singapore, 7 January.

Reuters 1999a, 'Deal on Marcos funds soon, says Estrada', *The Nation*, Bangkok, 15 January, p. 3.

—— 1999b, 'Vietnam's communist party to clamp down on dissent', *The Nation*, Bangkok, 26 February, p. 6.

—— 1999c, 'TNI stance raises Megawati hopes', *Jakarta Post*, 17 June, p. 1.

Rhodes, R. 1970, *Imperialism and Underdevelopment: a reader*, Monthly Review Press, New York.

Richburg, K. 1999, 'Indonesia's unintentional martyrs: slaying of four students transformed a nation', in E. Aspinall, G. van Klinken & H. Feith (eds), *The Last Days of President Suharto*, Monash Asia Institute, Melbourne.

Ricklefs, M. 1993a, *History of Modern Indonesia Since c.1300*, 2nd edn, Macmillan, London.

—— 1993b, *War, Culture and Economy in Java 1677–1726*, Asian Studies Association of Australia, no. 24, Allen & Unwin, Sydney.

Rinn-Sup Shinn 1984, 'Government and politics', in F. Bunge (ed.), *Malaysia: a country study*, Foreign Area Studies, American University, Washington DC.

Robinson F. 1998, 'Knowledge, its transmission and the making of Muslim societies', in F. Robinson (ed), *Cambridge Illustrated History of the Islamic World*, Cambridge University Press, Cambridge.

Robinson, N. 1999, *Islam: a concise introduction*, RoutledgeCurzon, London.

Robison, R. 1985, 'Class, capital and the state in new order Indonesia', in R. Higgott & R. Robison, *The Political Economy of South-East Asia*, Oxford University Press, Melbourne.

Rooney, D. 1994, *Angkor: an introduction to the temples*, Asia Books, Bangkok.

Rostow, W. 1991, *The Stages of Economic Growth: a non-communist manifesto*, 3rd edn, Cambridge University Press, Cambridge.

Rowley, K. 1999, 'Boom, bust, and beyond: the Asian crisis in global perspective', unpublished paper, Swinburne University of Technology, Melbourne.

Roy, D. 1998, *China's Foreign Relations*, Macmillan, London.

Roy, R. 1999, 'Old rivals become pen pals', *Bangkok Post*, 26 February, p. 10.

Runciman, S. 1960, *The White Rajahs: a history of Sarawak from 1841 to 1946*, Cambridge University Press, London.

Sagar, D. 1991, *Indo-China 1945–90*, Facts on File, Oxford.

Said, E. 1991, *Orientalism: Western conceptions of the orient*, Penguin Books, London.

Sario, R. 1999, 'Vital votes of Sabah Muslims', *Star*, Kuala Lumpur, 26 February, p. 21.

Saritdet, M. & Nussara, S. 1998, 'Bridging the gap a second time', *Bangkok Post*, 17 September, p. 10.

Salisbury, H. 1971, 'Introduction', *The Prison Diary of Ho Chi Minh*, Bantam Books, New York.

Saludo, R. & Lopez, A. 2000, 'Accusing the president', *Asiaweek*, 4 February, p. 28.

Sangwon Suh 1998, 'The press under pressure', *Asiaweek*, 31 July, p. 26.

SarDesai, D. 1997, *Southeast Asia: past and present*, Westview Press, Boulder.

Scalapino, R. 1989, *The Politics of Development: perspectives on twentieth-century Asia*, Harvard University Press, Cambridge, Mass.

Schanberg, S. 1997, 'Return to the killing fields', *Vanity Fair*, October, pp. 110–21.

Schauer, F. 1982, *Free Speech: a philosophical inquiry*, Cambridge University Press, Cambridge.

Schulze, K. 2002, 'Laskar Jihad and the Conflict in Ambon', *Brown Journal of World Affairs*, Vol. IX, no. 1, Spring.

Schurmann, F. 1993, *Beyond the Impasse*, Zed Books, London.

Schurmann, F. & Schell, O. (eds) 1977, *Imperial China*, Penguin Books, Harmondsworth.

—— 1968, *Communist China*, Penguin Books, Harmondsworth.

Schwartz, A. 1999, *A Nation in Waiting*, 2nd edn, Allen & Unwin, Sydney.

Seagrave, S. 1988, *The Marcos Dynasty*, Fawcett Columbine, New York.

Segal, G. 1990, *Rethinking the Pacific*, Clarendon Press, Oxford.

Selth, A. 1999, 'The Burmese armed forces next century: continuity or change', working paper no. 338, Strategic and Defence Studies Centre, Australian National University, Canberra.

Selth, A. 2002, *Burma's Armed Forces*, EastBridge, Norwalk.

Sesser, S. 1993, *The Lands of Charm and Cruelty: travels in Southeast Asia*, Random House, New York.

Shameen, A. 1998a, 'The way of the cronies', *Asiaweek*, 28 August, p. 26.

—— 1998b, 'Who's next in line', *Asiaweek*, 28 August, p. 27.

Shamsul, A. 1999, 'The "New Politics" in Malaysia: a viewpoint', unpublished paper delivered to the Centre for Malaysian Studies, 14 April, Monash University, Melbourne.

Shee Poon Kim 1985, 'The evolution of the political system', in S. Jon, H. C. Chan & C.M. Seah (eds), *Government and Politics of Singapore*, Oxford University Press, Singapore.

Sipress, A. & Nakashima, E. 2003, 'Obscure cleric who dreamed of regional Islamic rule', *Sydney Morning Herald*, 3 September.

Sheehan, N. 1994, *Two Cities: Hanoi and Saigon*, Picador, London.

Shwe Lu Laung 1989, *Burma: nationalism and ideology*, University Press Limited, Dhaka, Bangladesh.

Silverstein, J. 1993, *The Political Legacy of Aung San*, Southeast Asia Program Series, no. 11, Cornell University, Ithaca.

Singapore Business Times 1996, 'Be realistic about level playing field: S. M. Lee', 22 May.

Singh, A. & Oorjitham, S. 1998, 'Speaking out for what he believes', *Asiaweek*, 26 December, p. 31.

Singh, A. & Ranawana, A. 2000, 'The wily prince', *Asiaweek*, 3 March, pp. 16–18.

Singh, B. 1995, *East Timor, Indonesia and the World: myths and realities*, Singapore Institute of International Affairs, Singapore.

Skehan, C. 1998a, 'Suu Kyi drives a bridge too far', *Age*, 1 August, p. 22.

—— 1998b, 'Malaysia takes tough stand on economy', *Age*, 2 September, p. 12.

—— 1998c, 'Mahatir defiant on sacking', *Age*, 5 September, p. 19.

Smith, A. 1986, 'State-making and nation-building', in J. Hall (ed.), *States in History*, Basil Blackwell, Oxford.

Smith, B. 2003, *Understanding Third World Politics*, Palgrave, Houndmills and New York.

Smith, M. 1999a, *Burma: insurgency and the politics of ethnicity*, White Lotus, Bangkok.

—— 1999b. *Burma: insurgency and the politics of ethnicity* , 2nd edn, Zed Books, London.

Smith, R. 1958, *Philippine Freedom 1946–58*, Columbia University Press, New York.

—— 1968, *Viet-Nam and the West*, Heinemann, London.

—— 1964a, 'Cambodia', in G. Kahin (ed.), *Governments and Politics of Southeast Asia*, Cornell University Press, Ithaca.

—— 1964b, 'Laos', in G. Kahin (ed.), *Governments and Politics of Southeast Asia*, Cornell University Press, Ithaca.

Smith, S. 1999, 'Hun Sen's ultimatum', *The Nation*, Bangkok, 18 January, p. 1.

Soeharto, 1989, *Soeharto: my thoughts, words and deeds: an autobiography*, PT Citra Lamtoro Gung Persado, Jakarta.

Spencer, G. 1999, 'Indonesia's leader's deal on East Timor rejected', *Seattle Times*, 21 June, p. 1.

Spillius, A. 1998, 'An era of extravagance ends for a rich kingdom', *Age*, 8 August, p. 11.

Spybey, T. 1996, *Social Change, Development and Dependency*, Polity Press, London.

Stanley, P. 1974, *A Nation in the Making: the Philippines and the United States 1899–1921*, Harvard University Press, Cambridge, Massachusetts.

Steadman, J. 1969, *The Myth of Asia*, Macmillan, London.

Steinberg, D. 1982, *The Philippines: a singular and a plural place*, Westview Press, Boulder.

—— (ed.) 1971, *In Search of Southeast Asia*, Praeger, New York.

Stewart, I. & Alford, P. 1998, 'Mahatir finds Anwar guilty', *Australian*, 23 September, p. 1.

Stiglitz, J. 2002, 'Participation and development: perspectives from the comprehensive development paradigm', *Review of Development Economics*, vol. 6, no. 2.

—— 2003, *Globalization and Its Discontents*, W. W. Norton, New York.

Stuart-Fox, M. 1996, *Buddhist Kingdom, Marxist State: the making of modern Laos*, White Lotus Press, Bangkok.

—— 1997, *A History of Laos*, Cambridge University Press, Cambridge.

—— 1998a, *The Lao Kingdom of Lan Xang: rise and decline*, White Lotus, Bangkok.

—— 1998b, 'China and mainland Southeast Asia: implications of strategic culture', paper presented to Asian Studies Association of Australian biennial conference, University of New South Wales, Sydney.

Sturtevant, 1969, *Agrarian Unrest in the Philippines: Guardia de honor—revitalization within the revolution, and rizalistas—contemporary revitalization movements in the Philippines*, Center for International Studies, Ohio University, Athens, Ohio.

—— 1976, *Popular Uprisings in the Philippines: 1840–1940*, Cornell University Press, Ithaca.

Suara Pemberuan 2002a, 10 October.

—— 2002b, 11 October.

Sulak, S. 1991, 'The crisis of Siamese identity', in C. Reynolds (ed.), *National Identity and Its Defenders: Thailand, 1939–89*, Monash Papers on Southeast Asia, no. 25, Monash University, Melbourne.

Sunar, T. 1999, 'Don't play with fire, PBS told', *Daily Express*, Kota Kinabalu, 10 February, p. 1.

Suu Kyi, A. S. 1991, *Freedom from Fear*, Viking, London.

Tambiah, S. 1976, *World Conqueror and World Renouncer*, Cambridge University Press, Cambridge.

Tapol 1999a, *The TNI's 'Dirty War' in East Timor*, Tapol, London.

—— 1999b, *The Dismissal and Indictment of TNI Officers for Human Rights Violations in East Timor*, Tapol, London.

Tarling, N. 1998, *Nations and States in Southeast Asia*, Cambridge University Press, Melbourne.

Tasker, R. 1998, 'Safety in numbers', *Far Eastern Economic Review*, 15 October, p. 21.

Tavares, J. 1999, Kesiapan dan Kesiagan Pasukan Pejuang Integrasi (Milisi) Dalam Menyikapi Perkembangan Situasi Dan Konisi Di Timor-Timur, 17 July, PPI, Balibo, East Timor.

Taylor, J. 1991, *Indonesia's Forgotten War*, Zed Books, London.

Terweil, B. 1983, *A History of Modern Thailand 1767–1942*, University of Queensland Press, St Lucia.

Terweil, B. 1989, *A Window on Thai History*, Editions Duang Kamol, Bangkok.

Tesoro, J. 1999, 'Voting for the future', *Asiaweek*, 10 September, pp. 24–5.

Tesor, J. & Loveard, D. 1999, 'The road to rejection', *Asiaweek*, 29 October.

Thailand Times 1997, 'Burma's military rulers live off opium', 2 May.

Thayer, N. 1998a, 'The resurrected', *Far Eastern Economic Review*, 16 April, pp. 23–4.

—— 1998b, 'Dying breath', *Far Eastern Economic Review*, 30 April, pp. 18–21.

Thayer, C. 2004, 'Vietnam's regional integration: the costs and benefits of multilateralism', paper presented to conference on *Vietnam's Integration into the World and State Sovereignty Issues*, Centre d'Etudes et de Recherches Internationales, Ecole des Haute Etudes en Sciences Sociales and Centre Asie–Europe de Universite Sciences Po Paris, 25 October.

Thitinam Pongsudhirak 1997, 'Thailand's media: whose watchdog?', in K. Hewison (ed.), *Political Change in Thailand: democracy and participation*, Routledge, London.

Tiglao, R. 1998a, 'Teflon friends', *Far Eastern Economic Review*, 16 July, p. 28.

—— 1998b, 'Her father's daughter', *Far Eastern Economic Review*, 27 August, p. 24.

—— 1999, 'A storm at sea', *Far Eastern Economic Review*, 9 December, pp. 24–5.

—— & Vatikiotis, M. 1999, 'Estrada in trouble', *Far Eastern Economic Review*, 23 December, p. 22.

Trager, F. 1966, *Burma: from kingdom to republic*, Pall Mall Press, London.

Transparency International 2003, *Corruption Perception Index*, Berlin.

Treaty of Amity and Cooperation in Southeast Asia 1976, 24 February, Jakarta.

Tsing, A. 1987, 'A rhetoric of centres in a religion of the periphery', in R. Kipp & S. Rogers (eds), *Indonesian Religions in Transition*, University of Arizona Press, Phoenix.

Tu, G. 1999, 'Doi Moi beating poverty', *Vietnam Investment Review*, 1–7 January, p. 8.

Tully, J. 1996, *Cambodia Under the Tricolor*, Monash Asia Institute, Melbourne.

Turley, W. 1988, 'The military construction of socialism', in D. Marr & C. White (eds), *Postwar Vietnam: dilemmas in socialist development*, Cornell Southeast Asia Program, Ithaca.

Turnbull, C. 1977, *A History of Singapore 1819–1975*, Oxford University Press, Oxford.

—— 1989, *A History of Malaysia, Singapore and Brunei*, Allen & Unwin, Sydney.

United Nations, 1999a, *Agreement Between Indonesia, Portugal and the Secretary-General of the United Nations*, 5 May, United Nations, New York.

—— 1999b, *Resolution 1264*, 15 September, United Nations, New York.

United Nations Development Program (UNDP) 2004, *Human Development Report*, UNDP, New York.

United Nations High Commission for Human Rights (UNHCHR) 1999, 'Economic rights', in *Papers of the High Commission for Human Rights*, no. 1, Office of the High Commission for Human Rights, New York.

United Nations High Commissioner for Refugees 1999, *Report of the High Commissioner for Human Rights on the Human Rights Situation in East Timor*, United Nations High Commissioner for Refugees, New York.

US Department of State 1996, *International Narcotics Control Strategy Report*, US Department of State, Washington DC.

—— 1999a, *Cambodia Country Report*, US Department of State, Washington DC, February.

—— 1999b, *Human Rights Practices for 1998 Report: Singapore country report*, US Department of State, Washington DC.

—— 2002a, *Indonesia: International Religious Freedom Report 2002*, Bureau of Democracy, Human Rights and Labor, US Department of State, Washington DC.

—— 2002b, *Pattern of Global Terrorism*, Washington DC.

—— 2003, *Singapore: country report on human rights practices 2002*, Bureau of Democracy, Human Rights, and Labor, US Department of State, Washington DC.

Van Bruinessen, M. 2002a, *The Violent Fringe of Indonesia's Radical Islam*, International Institute for the Study of Islam in the Modern World, Leiden.

—— 2002b, 'Wahhabi influences in Indonesia, real and imagined', paper presented to *Journee d'Etudes du CEIFR et MSH sur la Wahhabisme*, ecole des Hautes Etudes en Sciences Sociales/Maison des Sciences de l'Homme, Paris, 10 June 2002.

—— 2002c, 'Genealogies of Islamic Radicalism in post-Suharto Indonesia', *Southeast Asia Research*, vol. 10, no 2. pp. 117–54.

van Klinken G. 1999a, 'How a democratic deal might be struck', in A. Budiman, B. Hatley & D. Kingsbury (eds), *Reformasi: Crisis and Change in Indonesia*, Monash Asia Institute, Melbourne.

—— 1999b, 'The May riots', in E. Aspinall, G. van Klinken & H. Feith (eds), *The Last Days of President Suharto*, Monash Asia Institute, Melbourne.

—— 2003, 'New actors, new identities: Post-Suharto ethnic violence in Indonesia', paper to *International Conference on Conflict in Asia–Pacific: state of the field and the search for viable solutions*, Nikho Hotel, 22–23 October.

Vasil, R. K. 1984, *Governing Singapore*, Eastern Universities Press, Sdn Bhd, Singapore.

Vatikiotis, M. 1993, *Indonesian Politics Under Suharto*, Routledge, London.

—— 1998, 'Romancing the dual function', in G. Forrester & R. May (eds), *The Fall of Soeharto*, Crawford House, Bathurst.

Vervoorn, A. 1998, *Re Orient: change in Asian societies*, Oxford University Press, Melbourne.

Vidal, G. 1981, 'Verifying genocide', *The New York Review of Books*, vol. 28, no. 16, 22 October.

Vietnam Ministry of Planning and Investment 2004, <http://www.mpi.gov.vn/default.aspx?Lang=2>, accessed 14 October 2004.

Viravong, S. 1964, *History of Laos*, Paragon Books, New York.

Voltaire 1979, *Philosophical Dictionary*, Besterman, T. (trans.), Penguin Books, Harmondsworth.

Vu Tuan Anh 1995, 'Economic policy reforms', in I. Norlund, C. D. Vu & C. Gates (eds), *Vietnam in a Changing World*, Nordic Institute of Asian Studies, Curzon Press, Richmond, Surrey.

Wagstaff, J. 1999, 'Dark before dawn: how elite made a deal before Indonesia woke up', *Wall Street Journal*, 2 November.

Washington Post 2003, 'Burmese opposition leader may have been injured', *Washington Post*, 3 June, Washington DC.

—— 2003, 'Suu Kyi injured, diplomats confirm', 5 June, *Washington Post*, Washington DC.

Wassana Nanuam 1998, 'Number of generals in three armed forces drops', *Bangkok Post*, 22 July, p. 3.

—— 1999a, 'Mafia types told to shape up', *Bangkok Post*, 13 January, p. 1.

—— 1999b, 'Former brass vying for political positions', *Bangkok Post*, 21 May, p. 3.

Weber, M. 1958, *From Max Weber: essays in sociology*, H. Gerth & C. Wright Mills (trans and eds), Oxford University Press, New York.

—— 1964, *The Theory of Social and Economic Organization*, T. Parsons (ed.), Free Press, New York.

—— 1968 (1920), *Economy and Society*, G. Roth & C. Wittich (eds and trans), University of California Press, Berkeley.

Weber, C. & Bierstaker, T. (eds) 1996, *State Sovereignty as Social Construction*, Cambridge Studies in International Relations, Cambridge.

Weekly, K. 1996, 'From vanguard to rearguard: the theoretical roots of the crisis of the Communist Party of the Philippines', in P. Abinales (ed.), *The Revolution Falters: the Left in Philippine politics after 1986*, Southeast Asia Program Publications, no. 15, Cornell University, Ithaca.

Williams, M. 1969, *The Land in Between: the Cambodian dilemma*, Collins, Sydney.

Wilson, D. 1966, *Politics in Thailand*, Cornell University Press, Ithaca.

—— 1969, 'Thailand' in G. Kahin (ed.), *Government and Politics in South East Asia*, 2nd edn, Cornell University Press, Ithaca.

Winters, J. 1996, *Power in Motion: capital mobility and the Indonesian state*, Cornell University Press, Ithaca.

Wit, D. 1968, *Thailand: another Vietnam?*, Charles Scribner's Sons, New York.

Wittfogel, K. 1957, *Oriental Despotism*, Yale University Press, New Haven.

Wolters, O. 1999, *History, Culture and Region in Southeast Asian Perspectives*, Southeast Asia Program Publications, Cornell University, Ithaca.

Wong C. W. & Lourdes, C. 2003, 'Nik Aziz's son named in report', *The Star*, Kuala Lumpur, 2 January.

Wong, D. 1999, 'Anwar names ex-chief of police', *Straits Times*, Singapore, 24 February, p. 1.

Wong, E. 1992, 'Labour policies and industrial relations', in L. Low & M.H. Toh (eds), *Public Policies in Singapore*, Times Academic Press, Singapore.

World Conference on Human Rights 1993, World Conference on Human Rights, Bangkok.

Wright-Neville, D. 1993, 'Asian culture, Asian politics and Asian diplomacy: problems in theorising', Working Paper No. 3, Centre for International Relations, Politics Department, Monash University, Melbourne.

Wurfel, D. 1964, 'The Philippines', in G. Kahin (ed.), *Governments and Politics of Southeast Asia*, 2nd edn, Cornell University Press, Ithaca.

—— 1988, *Filipino Politics: development and decay*, Cornell University Press, Ithaca.

Wyatt, D. 1984, *Thailand: a short history*, Yale University Press, New Haven.

Young, K. 1998, 'The crisis: contexts and prospects', in G. Forrester & R. May (eds), *The Fall of Soeharto*, Crawford House, Bathurst.

Young, M. 1991, *The Vietnam Wars 1945–1990*, Harper Perennial, New York.

Zainud'din, A. 1980, *Indonesia*, 2nd edn, Cassell Australia, Sydney.

Zasloff, J. 1991, 'Political constraints on development in Laos', in J. Zasloff & L. Unger, (eds), *Laos: beyond the revolution*, Macmillan, Houndmills.

INDEX